Finland

Paul Harding
Jennifer Brewer

LONELY PLANET PUBLICATIONS
Melbourne • Oakland • London • Paris

FINLAND

INARI
A centre of Sami culture – take a morning trek to the Wilderness Church, an afternoon cruise on Lake Inarijärvi and then visit the Sami Museum in the evening

NAPAPIIRI (THE ARCTIC CIRCLE)
The official Arctic Circle marker is here, and so is the 'official' Santa Claus Village and Santapark

ROVANIEMI
Home to the Arktikum museum and a great base for exploring Lapland

OULANKA NATIONAL PARK
Excellent fell walking, well-maintained free wilderness huts and the best scenery in Finland

YLLÄS
One of Finland's most popular skiing centres, with a music festival in July, and mountain biking in summer

KEMI
Cruise the Gulf of Bothnia on the Sampo, an authentic Arctic icebreaker

OULU
A lively, fast-growing university town with an extraordinary number of outdoor bars, lots of festivals, and in June and July it never gets dark at night

ARCTIC OCEAN

RUSSIA

NORWAY

SWEDEN

White Sea

Barents Sea

ELEVATION

1000m
500m
200m
100m
60m
0

Arctic Circle

Murmansk
Kirkenes
Nikel'
Neiden
Näätämö
Nuorgam
Utsjoki
Inari
Inarijärvi
Kaamanen
Ivalo
Saariselkä
Raja-Jooseppi
Tankavaara
Tulppio
KOVDOR
Kandalaksha
Alakurtti
Oulanka National Park
Kuusamo
Salla
Suomussalmi
Kiantajärvi
Puolanka
Yli-Kitka
Posio
Kuusamo
KEMIJÄRVI
Kemijärvi
Pyöhtiovaara
Rauna
Pudasjärvi
ROVANIEMI
Napapiiri
Pyöhtiovaara
Oulasjoki
Sinetta
OULU
Hailuoto
Rauna
Pelkosenniemi
Savukoski
Tanhua
Lokan tekojärvi
SODANKYLÄ
Unari
Porttipahdan tekojärvi
Unari
Kongäs
Muonio
Hetta
Pallas-Ounastunturi National Park
Ylläs
Unari
Kolari
Lappea
Pajala
Pello
Mickojärvi
Tornionjoki
Övertorneå
Övertorneå
TORNIO
KEMI
Haparanda
Överkalix
Boden
LULEÅ
Kiruna

Lakselv
Alta
Karasjok
Karigasniemi
Kautokeino
Kaaresuvanto
Karesuando
Kilpisjärvi
Tromsø

NORWAY

SWEDEN

Kemijoki
Kemijoki
Ivalojoki
Muonionjoki
Könkämäeno
Kilpisjärvi
Tenojoki
Teno

Kem

N

0   30   50   100km
0   60m

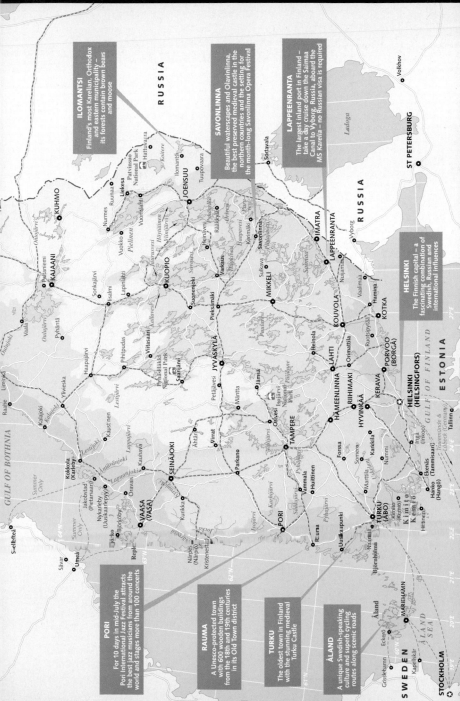

RUSSIA

ILOMANTSI
Finland's most Karelian, Orthodox and eastern municipality – its forests contain brown bears and moose

SAVONLINNA
Beautiful waterscapes and Olavinlinna, the best preserved medieval castle in the northern countries and the setting for the month-long Savonlinna Opera Festival

LAPPEENRANTA
The largest inland port in Finland – take a day cruise down the Saimaa Canal to Vyborg, Russia, aboard the MS Karelia – no Russian visa is required

HELSINKI
The Finnish capital – a fascinating combination of Swedish, Russian and international influences

GULF OF BOTHNIA

GULF OF FINLAND

PORI
For 10 days in mid-July the Pori International Jazz Festival attracts the best jazz musicians from around the world and stages more than 100 concerts

RAUMA
A Unesco-protected town with 600 wooden buildings from the 18th and 19th centuries in its Old Town district

TURKU
The oldest town in Finland with the stunning medieval Turku Castle

ÅLAND
A unique Swedish-speaking culture and superb cycling routes along scenic roads

ESTONIA

SWEDEN

ÅLAND SEA

STOCKHOLM

Finland
4th edition – April 2003
First published – January 1993

Published by
Lonely Planet Publications Pty Ltd ABN. 36 005 607 983
90 Maribyrnong St, Footscray, Victoria 3011, Australia

Lonely Planet Offices
Australia Locked Bag 1, Footscray, Victoria 3011
USA 150 Linden St, Oakland, CA 94607
UK 10a Spring Place, London NW5 3BH
France 1 rue du Dahomey, 75011 Paris

Photographs
Many of the images in this guide are available for licensing from
Lonely Planet Images.
w www.lonelyplanetimages.com

Front cover photograph
Lantern outside house in the snow, Magnusson, Photolibrary.com

ISBN 1 74059 076 7

text & maps © Lonely Planet Publications Pty Ltd 2003
photos © photographers as indicated 2003

Printed by The Bookmaker International Ltd
Printed in China

Contents – Text

THE AUTHORS   **6**

THIS BOOK   **7**

FOREWORD   **8**

INTRODUCTION   **9**

FACTS ABOUT FINLAND   **10**

History 10	Flora & Fauna 17	Arts 20
Geography 15	Government & Politics 18	Society & Conduct 26
Geology 15	Economy 19	Religion 27
Climate 16	Population & People 19	
Ecology & Environment 17	Education 20	

FACTS FOR THE VISITOR   **29**

Highlights 29	Photography & Video 40	Legal Matters 45
Suggested Itineraries 30	Time 40	Business Hours 45
Planning 30	Electricity 40	Public Holidays &
Tourist Offices 31	Weights & Measures 40	Special Events 45
Visas & Documents 32	Laundry 40	Language Courses 48
Embassies & Consulates 34	Toilets 40	Work 48
Customs 34	Health 40	Accommodation 48
Money 35	Women Travellers 43	Food 51
Post & Communications 37	Gay & Lesbian Travellers 44	Drinks 52
Digital Resources 38	Disabled Travellers 44	Entertainment 53
Books 39	Senior Travellers 44	Spectator Sports 54
Newspapers & Magazines ...39	Travel with Children 44	Shopping 54
Radio & TV 39	Dangers & Annoyances 45	
Video Systems 40	Emergencies 45	

ACTIVITIES   **56**

Trekking **56**	Where to Trek 58	**Water Sports** **61**
Right of Public Access 56	**Cycling** **59**	Rentals 61
Making Campfires 56	Bringing your Bicycle 59	Where to Row & Paddle 62
Gathering Berries &	Where to Cycle 59	**Other Activities** **63**
Mushrooms 56	**Winter Sports** **60**	Fishing 63
What to Bring 57	Downhill Skiing &	Bird-Watching 63
Accommodation 57	Snowboarding 60	Golf 63
Transport 58	Cross-Country Skiing 61	Tracing your Ancestors 64

GETTING THERE & AWAY   **65**

Air 65	Land 68	Sea 71

GETTING AROUND   **73**

Air 73	Car & Motorcycle 76	Boat 79
Bus 74	Bicycle 79	Local Transport 80
Train 75	Hitching 79	Organised Tours 80

HELSINKI   **81**

History 81	Information 82	Helsinki Zoo &
Orientation 82	Museums & Galleries 86	Maritime Museum 91

2   Contents – Text

Churches 91	Entertainment 99	Espoo 107
Parks & Gardens 91	Spectator Sports 101	Vantaa 107
Activities 92	Shopping 101	Järvenpää & Tuusulan
Organised Tours 92	Getting There & Away 102	Rantatie 107
Special Events 92	Getting Around 104	Porvoo 108
Places to Stay 94	**Around Helsinki** **105**	
Places to Eat 96	Suomenlinna 105	

SOUTH COAST   112

West of Helsinki **112**	Hanko 117	Ruotsinpyhtää 123
Inkoo 112	Around Hanko 121	Kotka ....123·
Ekenäs 113	**East of Helsinki** **121**	Around Kotka 126
Around Ekenäs 116	Loviisa 121	Hamina 126
Fiskars 117	Around Loviisa 122	

THE LAKELAND   130

Eastern Lakeland **130**	Valamo Orthodox	**Northern Lakeland** **149**
Savonlinna 130	Monastery 144	Kuopio 149
Around Savonlinna 136	Lintula Orthodox Convent 144	Lapinlahti 155
Mikkeli & Around 141	**Central Lakeland** **145**	Iisalmi 155
Varkaus 142	Jyväskylä 145	Around Iisalmi 156
Heinävesi & Around 143	Around Jyväskylä 148	

KARELIA   157

South Karelia **157**	Around Ilomantsi 170	Vuonislahti 176
Lappeenranta 157	Hattuvaara 170	Koli National Park 176
Around Lappeenranta 162	Around Hattuvaara 172	Juuka 177
Imatra 162	**Lake Pielinen Region** **172**	Paalasmaa Island 177
North Karelia **164**	Lieksa 172	Nurmes 178
Joensuu 164	Patvinsuo National Park 173	Around Nurmes 180
Joensuu to Ilomantsi 167	Ruunaa Recreation Area 174	
Ilomantsi 168	Nurmijärvi Area 175	

TAMPERE & HÄME REGION   181

Tampere **181**	**Häme Region** **192**	Around Lahti 201
North of Tampere **190**	Hämeenlinna 192	Heinola 202
Route 66 190	Hämeenlinna to Tampere ..196	Around Heinola 203
Keuruu 191	Häme Ox Road 196	
Mänttä 191	Lahti 198	

TURKU & THE SOUTHWEST   204

Turku **204**	Kustavi 217	Rauma 221
Around Turku **213**	**South of Turku** **217**	Around Rauma 224
Naantali 213	Turunmaa Archipelago 217	Puurijärvi-Isosuo
Rymättylä 217	Kemiö Island 218	National Park 225
Louhisaari Manor 217	**North of Turku** **219**	Pori 225
Nousiainen 217	Uusikaupunki 219	Around Pori 228

ÅLAND   229

Mariehamn **232**	Sund 237	Lemland 241
Mainland Åland	Saltvik 239	Lumparland 242
& Around **237**	Geta 239	Vårdö 242
Jomala 237	Hammarland 239	**Northern Archipelago** **242**
Finström 237	Eckerö 240	Kumlinge 242

Brändö 243
Southern Archipelago 243

Föglö 243
Sottunga 244

Kökar 244

POHJANMAA 246

Vaasa 246
Around Vaasa 250
South of Vaasa 251
Kristinestad 251
Kaskinen 252
Närpes 253

North of Vaasa 253
Nykarleby 253
Jakobstad 253
Around Jakobstad 255
Kokkola 256
Kalajoki 257

Around Kalajoki 257
Central Pohjanmaa 258
Seinäjoki 258
Around Seinäjoki 260
Kaustinen 260

OULU, KAINUU & KOILLISMAA 261

Oulu Province 261
Oulu 261
Around Oulu 268
Kemi 269
Tornio 270
Around Tornio 272
Kainuu Region 273

Kajaani 273
Around Kajaani 275
Kuhmo 275
Hossa 278
Koillismaa Region 279
Kuusamo 279
Ruka 281

Karhunkierros Trek &
Oulanka National Park 282
Paddling the Kitkajoki 285
Paddling the Oulankajoki ..285
Juuma 286
Iso-Syöte & Pikku-Syöte 286

LAPLAND & SAPMI 288

History 288
Rovaniemi 290
Around Rovaniemi 294
Napapiiri (The Arctic Circle)
& Santa Claus Village 294
Ranua Wildlife Park 295
Western Lapland 295
Ylläs 297
Kittilä 297

Sirkka & Levi 298
Muonio 299
Hetta (Enontekiö) 300
Pallas-Ounastunturi
National Park 301
Kilpisjärvi 302
Eastern Lapland 303
Kemijärvi 303
Sodankylä 305

Pyhä-Luosto Region 305
Saariselkä Region 306
Saariselkä Wilderness & Urho
Kekkonen National Park 308
Ivalo 310
Inari 311
Lemmenjoki National Park 313
Kevo Nature Reserve 316
Inari to Norway 317

LANGUAGE 319

Finnish 319

Swedish 322

GLOSSARY 326

THANKS 330

INDEX 331

MAP LEGEND back page

METRIC CONVERSION inside back cover

Contents – Maps

GETTING AROUND

Domestic Air Fares 73   Road Distances 78

HELSINKI

Helsinki............................84-5   Around Helsinki 105
Central Helsinki 93   Porvoo...............................109

SOUTH COAST

Ekenäs 113   Hanko 118   Hamina 127
South Coast 114-15   Kotka...............................124

THE LAKELAND

The Lakeland 131   Around Savonlinna............137   Kuopio..............................150
Savonlinna.........................132   Jyväskylä 145

KARELIA

Karelia 158   Imatra 163   Ilomantsi 168
Lappeenranta.....................159   Joensuu 165   Nurmes.............................178

TAMPERE & HÄME REGION

Tampere & Häme Region 182   Hämeenlinna 194
Tampere............................186   Lahti................................198-9

TURKU & THE SOUTHWEST

Turku & the Southwest 205   Naantali 214   Rauma 222
Turku 206   Uusikaupunki.....................220   Pori 226

ÅLAND

Åland................................230   Mariehamn 233

POHJANMAA

Pohjanmaa.........................247   Kristinestad 251   Seinäjoki 258
Vaasa................................248   Jakobstad..........................254

OULU, KAINUU & KOILLISMAA

Oulu, Kainuu & Koillismaa ..262   Kajaani.............................273   Karhunkierros Trek &
Oulu 264   Kuhmo..............................276   Oulanka National Park.......283
Tornio 270   Kuusamo 279

LAPLAND & SAPMI

Lapland & Sapmi 289   Western Lapland 296   Saariselkä Wilderness (Urho
Rovaniemi 290   Northeastern Sapmi 304   Kekkonen National Park) 309

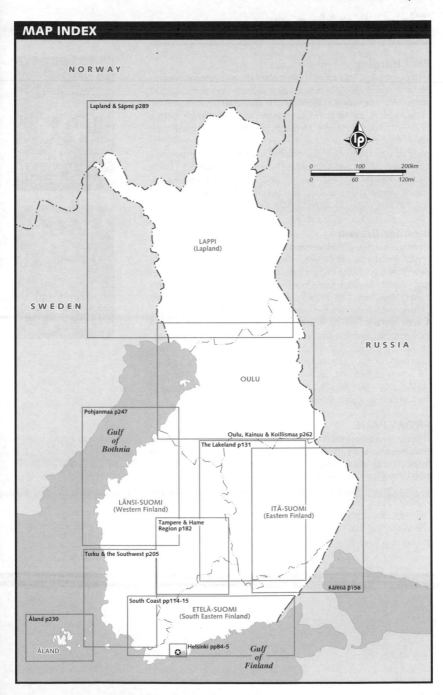

The Authors

Paul Harding

Melbourne born, Paul spent his formative years as a newspaper reporter in country Victoria before being sucked into the backpacker vortex. After travelling extensively in Europe and South-East Asia, he worked as an editor of a London travel magazine before landing at Lonely Planet's Melbourne home for wayward travellers. Realising he was on the wrong side of the desk, he eventually swapped his red pen for a blue one and now works as a full-time writer and researcher. Paul is the author of Lonely Planet's *Read This First: Europe* and *Istanbul to Kathmandu* guides, and has contributed to *Australia*, *New Zealand*, *New South Wales*, *India*, *South India*, *Middle East* and *South-East Asia*.

Jennifer Brewer

Jennifer is a native Californian and an honours graduate of the University of California at Berkeley. She worked for several years at a New York City–based fashion magazine before becoming a freelance travel journalist. Since then, she has covered the California desert, New York City, Belize, London and Hungary for Berkeley Guides, and has contributed articles on travel to various magazines. A year-long trip from London to Lhasa via the Middle East in 1996 led her to become involved in the Committee of 100 for Tibet organisation, for which she has served on the Board of Directors. Jennifer is currently earning herself a graduate writing degree from the School of Film and Television at the University of California at Los Angeles – but she still travels as often as possible. Home is in the Los Feliz neighbourhood of Los Angeles, California.

FROM PAUL

Thanks, as always, to the people at Lonely Planet who kindly enable me to keep travelling for a living. Everywhere I went in Finland I met many wonderful people from many walks of life. Thanks to James Luckhurst at the Finnish Tourist Board in London, Kaarina Pelkonen at the Finnish Tourist Board in Helsinki, staff at Helsinki Expert, and staff at many of the local tourist offices around Finland, particularly Turku, Tampere, Lappeenranta, Kuopio, Pori and Vaasa. Big thanks to Carolyn; to Markku, Jussi and everyone at Huvila in Savonlinna; and to Kaisa.

This Book

This 4th edition of *Finland* was updated by Paul Harding. The 1st edition was researched by Virpi Mäkelä. Markus Lehtipuu and Jennifer Brewer updated the 2nd and 3rd editions respectively.

From the Publisher

The 4th edition of *Finland* was steered through its production process in Lonely Planet's Melbourne office by coordinating editor Justin Flynn with help from Yvonne Byron, Susie Ashworth and Jocelyn Harewood. Csanád Csutoros handled the mapping side of things and was supported by Julie Sheridan and Tessa Rottiers. The Flying Dutchman Cris Gibcus whizzed through layout and took care of the colourwraps. Project manager Kieran Grogan made sure all the deadlines were met before jumping ship three weeks early to meet a deadline of her own – a baby! Celia Wood then took the reigns in Kieran's absence. Commissioning editor Amanda Canning did all the hard work when Paul's manuscript came in-house while Quentin Frayne cast his expert eye over the Language chapter. Thanks to Csanád for the climate charts and Margaret Jung for the cover.

THANKS
Many thanks to the travellers who used the last edition and wrote to us with helpful hints, advice and interesting anecdotes. Your names appear in the back of this book.

Foreword

ABOUT LONELY PLANET GUIDEBOOKS

The story begins with a classic travel adventure: Tony and Maureen Wheeler's 1972 journey across Europe and Asia to Australia. There was no useful information about the overland trail then, so Tony and Maureen published the first Lonely Planet guidebook to meet a growing need.

From a kitchen table, Lonely Planet has grown to become the largest independent travel publisher in the world, with offices in Melbourne (Australia), Oakland (USA), London (UK) and Paris (France).

Today Lonely Planet guidebooks cover the globe. There is an ever-growing list of books and information in a variety of media. Some things haven't changed. The main aim is still to make it possible for adventurous travellers to get out there – to explore and better understand the world.

At Lonely Planet we believe travellers can make a positive contribution to the countries they visit – if they respect their host communities and spend their money wisely. Since 1986 a percentage of the income from each book has been donated to aid projects and human rights campaigns, and, more recently, to wildlife conservation.

Although inclusion in a guidebook usually implies a recommendation we cannot list every good place. Exclusion does not necessarily imply criticism. In fact there are a number of reasons why we might exclude a place – sometimes it is simply inappropriate to encourage an influx of travellers.

UPDATES & READER FEEDBACK

Things change – prices go up, schedules change, good places go bad and bad places go bankrupt. Nothing stays the same. So, if you find things better or worse, recently opened or long-since closed, please tell us and help make the next edition even more accurate and useful.

Lonely Planet thoroughly updates each guidebook as often as possible – usually every two years, although for some destinations the gap can be longer. Between editions, up-to-date information is available in our free, monthly email bulletin *Comet* (**w** www.lonelyplanet.com/newsletters). You can also check out the *Thorn Tree* bulletin board and *Postcards* section of our website, which carry unverified, but fascinating, reports from travellers.

Tell us about it! We genuinely value your feedback. A well-travelled team at Lonely Planet reads and acknowledges every email and letter we receive and ensures that every morsel of information finds its way to the relevant authors, editors and cartographers.

Everyone who writes to us will find their name listed in the next edition of the appropriate guidebook. The very best contributions will be rewarded with a free guidebook.

We may edit, reproduce and incorporate your comments in Lonely Planet products such as guidebooks, websites and digital products, so let us know if you don't want your comments reproduced or your name acknowledged.

How to contact Lonely Planet:
Online: **e** talk2us@lonelyplanet.com.au, **w** www.lonelyplanet.com
Australia: Locked Bag 1, Footscray, Victoria 3011
UK: 10a Spring Place, London NW5 3BH
USA: 150 Linden St, Oakland, CA 94607

Introduction

Finland is not an easy country to pin a stereotype on. From a tourism point of view it has historically been regarded as the least prominent of the Nordic countries, a land of lakes, saunas and reindeer, but little else to stir the imagination.

With the rise of mobile communications and the Internet, though, Finland has suddenly become noticed. Companies such as Nokia are exploring areas of communications that were once imagined only in science fiction.

But what's in it for the traveller? In contrast to this hi-tech revolution, Finland is for the most part a land of quietness, where a ramshackle cottage by a lake and a properly stoked sauna is all that's required for happiness. Finland is a vast expanse of forests and lakes and more forests, punctuated by towns full of people who are genuinely surprised to find tourists visiting them. It's a country waiting to be 'discovered', which is an attraction in itself.

Sophisticated Helsinki is fast becoming one of Europe's hottest travel destinations (but is still far from overrun with tourists), and the historic towns of Turku and Savonlinna have plenty to attract travellers. Then there's wonderful Lapland, with its Sami reindeer herders, Santa Claus connections, northern lights and sheer, unadulterated wilderness. If you visit Finland in summer, there's always a feeling that something big is happening. Festivals explode into life everywhere and you could easily plan your entire trip around them.

Despite its size – at 338,000 sq km this is Europe's seventh-largest country – Finland has less than six million inhabitants, making it one of Europe's most sparsely populated countries. In place of sprawling cities are forests, lakes, rivers and, in the north, the flat featureless expanses of Arctic tundra.

What makes Finland different from its Scandinavian neighbours is the people. Finns are a tough, independent bunch – centuries of being sandwiched between Sweden and Russia have had such an effect. But they are also extremely curious and friendly to visitors: being invited to a summer cottage or to share in a sauna is an offer many travellers have received. Finns and Finland have a reputation for being quiet and mysterious, but if you have the time to look under the surface, you'll find some of the warmest people you'll ever meet.

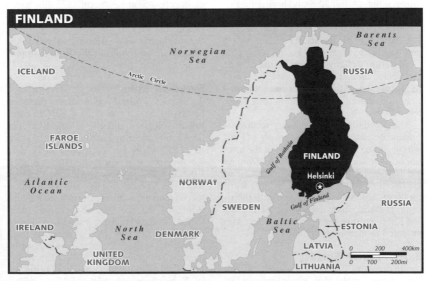

9

Facts about Finland

HISTORY

Finnish history tells the story of how a group of people emigrated from central Russia and strove for centuries to emancipate themselves from Swedish and Russian rule. The unfortunate thing about this history is that the earliest chronicles were written by Swedes, and much of ethnic Finnish culture and events before and well after the Swedish crusades has escaped written record altogether.

Prehistory

Little is known of human settlement in Finland before or during the Stone Age. However, the region was clearly inhabited at that time, as more than 60 Stone Age paintings have been discovered in Finland, predominantly around Lake Saimaa in the east. Sami emigrants arrived from the east approximately 6000 years ago. It's less clear when the Finns arrived in Finland, and there are a number of competing theories.

By language, Finno-Ugrians are a unique group, with more links to Asia than Europe. Most theories about the settlement of Finland by Finns hold that the Finns are descendants of nomadic tribes that arrived – some time after the Sami – from the land bordering Europe and Asia, near the Ural Mountains and the Volga River. It is likely that after migrating through north Russia, Finns, Estonians and Karelians (as they are known today) arrived during a relatively short period of time and settled along the Baltic coast and Karelia. It is believed that Estonia was inhabited first, and migration farther north took place thereafter.

The population of present-day southwest Finland became known as the people of Fennia (or Finns) and the inhabitants of the interior became known as Häme people, from an old Baltic word meaning 'an inhabitant of the interior', which is also the original word for Sami (or Sábme as Lapps call themselves). During their migration, Hämenites and Karelians displaced the Sami tribes, who migrated farther north to Lapland.

Early Finnish Society

Approximately 2000 years ago south Finland was sparsely inhabited by ethnic Finns and an untold number of other European peoples. The two Finnish tribes, Hämenites (Swedish: Tavastians) and Karelians, lived separately, in the west and the east respectively, but were constantly at war with each other.

There were trading contacts with Estonians and Swedish Vikings. The lands around the Kokemäki River and its tributary Vanajavesi in Häme (Swedish: Tavastland) were the most densely populated areas, with a chain of hill fortresses providing defence. In the east, there was a similar chain of defence fortresses in Savo, and along the shores of Lake Ladoga in Karelia (now an autonomous republic within Russia).

Furs were the main export item, and there were trading posts in present-day Hämeenlinna, Turku and Halikko. Many burial grounds and hill defences remain. It is probable that there was friendly contact between fortresses, despite each having its own social system. A common law and judicial system existed in each region.

The Åland Islands and coastal regions southeast of Turku were frequented by Viking sailors. One theory placed Birka, the main Viking centre during the 10th century, on Åland, although with the help of more elaborate scientific methods it has since been established that Birka was on Björkö Island in a lake to the west of Stockholm. Six hill fortresses on Åland date back to the Viking era and indicate the former importance of these islands.

Swedish Rule

To Swedes, Finland was a natural direction of expansion, on a promising eastern route towards Russia and the Black Sea. The Swedish chapter of Finland's history starts in 1155, when Bishop Henry arrived in Kalanti on a mission for the Catholic Church. Swedish crusaders manned Finnish fortresses to repel Russian attacks and protect its Christianisation efforts from Russian influence. As the Church became established, its headquarters moved to Nousiainen, and in 1229, by the order of Pope Gregorius, to today's Turku. Swedish settlement began in earnest in 1249 when Birger Jarl established fortifications in Tavastia and on the northern coast of the Gulf of Finland.

The upper layer of society in Finland was made up of newly arrived Catholic bishops and Swedish nobility, sent to govern the eastern province of the Catholic kingdom of Sweden. The Swedish nobility dates back to the 14th-century cavalry, consisting of the *frälset*, who enjoyed tax-free status.

It took more than 200 years to define the border between Sweden and Russia (Novgorod). In 1323, the first such border was drawn in a conference at Nöteborg (Finnish: Pähkinäsaari) on Lake Ladoga. Sweden gained control of southwest Finland, much of the northwest coast and, in the east, the strategic town of Vyborg (Finnish: Viipuri), with its magnificent castle. A suzerainty was established over Karelia by Novgorod and was controlled from a castle at Käkisalmi (Russian: Priodzorsk) that was founded in the 13th century. Novgorod spread the Russian Orthodox faith in the Karelia region, which became influenced by eastern Byzantine culture.

To attract Swedish settlers to the unknown land, a number of incentives were created, such as large estates of land and tax concessions. These privileges were given to many soldiers of the Royal Swedish Army.

In 1527, King Gustav Vasa of Sweden adopted the Lutheran faith and confiscated much of the property of the Catholic Church. Finland had its own supporters of the Reformation: Mikael Agricola, born in Pernå (Finnish: Pernaja) in 1510, studied literature and religion with Martin Luther in Germany for three years, and returned to Finland in 1539 to translate parts of the Bible into Finnish. More importantly, he was the first to properly record the traditions and animist religious rites of ethnic Finns. Agricola's work changed the religious tradition. Most of the colourful frescoes in medieval grey-stone churches, for example, were whitewashed with lime (only to be rediscovered some 400 years later in relatively good condition).

Sweden was not satisfied with its share of power in the east. In 1546 King Gustav Vasa founded Ekenäs (Finnish: Tammisaari) and in 1550, Helsinki. Using his Finnish subjects as agents of expansion, the Swedish king told Finns to 'sweat and suffer' as pioneers in Savo and Kainuu, well beyond the legitimate territory set down in treaties with the Russians. Russians grew alarmed and attempted to throw the intruders out. The bloody Kainuu War raged on and off between 1574 and 1584, with most new settlements destroyed by fire.

Golden Age of Sweden

The golden age of Sweden was the 17th century and during this period it controlled Finland, Estonia and parts of today's Latvia, Denmark, Germany and Russia.

Finally, after 65 years of Lutheranism, the Catholic Sigismund (grandson of Gustav Vasa) assumed the Swedish throne. Karl IX, Gustav Vasa's youngest son and Sigismund's uncle, was given control over Finland. Karl IX didn't give a hoot for the family business, however: he encouraged peasants in western Finland to mutiny in 1596, attacked the Turku Castle in 1597, and defeated his nephew Sigismund in 1598 to bring all of Finland under his reign.

While Gustav II Adolf (son of Karl IX and king from 1611 to 1632) was busily involved in the Thirty Years' War in Europe, political power in Finland was exercised by the General Governor, who resided at the Castle of Turku, capital of Finland. Count Per Brahe, a legendary figure of the local Swedish administration, travelled around the country at this time and founded many towns. You will see his statue in places like Turku, Raahe, Kajaani and Lieksa.

After Gustav II Adolf, Sweden was ruled from 1644 to 1654 by the eccentric Queen Kristina, namesake for such Finnish towns as Kristinestad and Ristiina. The queen's conversion to Catholicism and move to Rome marked the end of the Swedish Vasa dynasty.

The German royal family of Pfalz-Zweibrücken ruled Sweden (including Finland) after the Vasa family folded. During this period, Finland was considered an integral part of Sweden. The official language was Swedish, Stockholm was the de facto capital, and Finns were considered loyal subjects of the Swedish king (or queen).

By Swedish decree, Finland grew. A chain of castle defences was built to protect against Russian attack and new factory areas were founded. The *bruk* (early ironworks precinct) was often a self-contained society, which harnessed the power of water, built ironworks and transport systems for firewood. Social institutions such as schools and churches were also established.

Ethnic Finns didn't fare particularly well during this time. The burger class was dominated by Swedish settlers, as very few Finns engaged in industrial enterprises. Some of the successful industrialists were central Europeans who settled in Finland via Sweden. Furthermore, the Swedish 'caste system', the House of Four Estates, was firmly established in Finland. The Swedish and Finnish nobility maintained their status in the Swedish Riksdagen until 1866 and in the Finnish parliament until 1906. (The Finnish nobility still exists through a registered organisation.)

Although Finland never experienced feudal serfdom to the extent seen in Russia, ethnic Finns were largely peasant farmers who were forced to lease land from Swedish landlords. The last Finnish manor to release its serfs did so in 1858.

In 1697 Karl XII ascended the throne. Within three years he was drawn into the Great Northern War (1700–21), which marked the beginning of the end of the Swedish Empire.

The Turbulent 18th Century

While the Swedish King Karl XII was busy fighting for his empire elsewhere, the Russians under Peter the Great seized the moment. The Great Northern War resulted in Vyborg being defeated in 1710 and much of Finland conquered, including the Swedish-dominated west coast.

From 1714 to 1721 Russia occupied Finland, a bitter time still referred to as the Great Wrath. Russians destroyed practically everything they had access to, particularly in Åland and western Finland. The 1721 Treaty of Uusikaupunki (Swedish: Nystad) brought temporary peace at a cost – Sweden lost south Karelia, including Vyborg, to Russia. To regain its lost territories, Sweden attacked Russia in 1741–43, but with little success. Russia again occupied Finland, for a period called the Lesser Wrath, and the border was pushed farther north. The Treaty of Turku in 1743 ended the conflict by ceding parts of Savo to Russia.

Only after the 1740s did the Swedish government try to improve Finland's socioeconomic situation. Defences were strengthened by building fortresses off Helsinki's coast (Sveaborg, now Suomenlinna) and Loviisa, and new towns were founded. Sweden and

Russia were to clash once again, in the sea battles of Ruotsinsalmi off Kotka in 1788–89. This time it was King Gustav III who led the Swedish fight, which involved up to 500 vessels. Sweden won, but to no territorial advantage. The 'Gustavian Wars' continued along the eastern border of Finland until the king was murdered by a conspiracy of aristocrats in 1792. Gustav IV Adolf, who reigned from 1796, was drawn into the disastrous Napoleonic Wars and lost his crown in 1809.

Russian Rule

After the Treaty of Tilsit was signed by Russian tsar Alexander I and Napoleon, Russia attacked Finland in 1808. Following a bloody war, Sweden ceded Finland to Russia in 1809 as an autonomous grand duchy, with its own senate and the Diet of the Four Estates, but all major decisions had to be approved by the tsar. At first, Finland benefited from the annexation and was loyal to the tsar, who encouraged Finns to develop the country in many ways. The Finnish capital was transferred to Helsinki in 1812, as Russians felt that the former capital, Turku, was too close to Sweden.

Early in the 19th century, the first stirring of indigenous Finnish nationalism occurred. One of the first to encourage independence during the 1820s was AI Radisson, who uttered the much-quoted sentence: 'Swedes we are not, Russians we will not become, so let us be Finns'. His views were not widely supported and he was advised to move to Sweden in 1823.

As a Russian annexation, Finland was involved in the Crimean War (1853–56), where Russia fought Turkey and its allies, including Britain and France. British troops attacked Finland in many locations, and destroyed fortifications at Loviisa, Helsinki and Bomarsund. Following the Crimean War, the Finnish independence movement gained credibility. While still a part of Russia, Finland issued its first postage stamps in 1856 and its own currency, the markka, in 1860.

In 1905, a new unicameral parliament, the Eduskunta, was introduced in Finland with universal and equal suffrage (Finland was the first country in Europe to grant women full political rights). Despite these many advances, life under Russian rule continued to be harsh. Many artists, notably

Jean Sibelius, were inspired by this oppression, which made Finns emotionally ripe for independence.

Independence

The Communist revolution of October 1917 caused the downfall of the Tsar of Russia and enabled the Finnish senate to declare independence on 6 December 1917. Independent Finland was first recognised by the Soviets one month later, and a crafty Vladimir Lenin, looking for support for Russian troops devastated by WWI, followed by offering 10,000 guns to the Finnish Red cadres. Russian troops and the newly armed Finnish Reds attacked the Finnish civil guards in Vyborg during the following year, sparking the Finnish Civil War.

On 28 January 1918, the Civil War flared in two separate locations. The Reds attempted to foment revolution in Helsinki. The Whites (as the government troops were now called), led by CGE Mannerheim, clashed with Russian troops near Vaasa. During 108 days of fighting in two locations, approximately 30,000 Finns were killed by their fellow citizens. The Reds, comprising the rising working class, aspired to Russian-style socialist revolution while retaining independence. The nationalist Whites dreamed of monarchy and sought to emulate Germany.

The Whites eventually gained victory under Mannerheim, with Germany's help. The devastating war ended in May 1918. Prince of Hessen, Friedrich Karl, was elected king of Finland by the Eduskunta on 9 October 1918 – but the German monarchy collapsed one month later, following Germany's defeat in WWI. Finland now faced a dilemma: the Russian presence was a clear security risk, but Germany was a discredited political model because of its war loss.

Building a Nation

The defeat of imperial Germany made Finland choose a republican state model and the first president was KJ Ståhlberg. Relations with the Soviets were normalised by the Treaty of Tartu in 1920, which saw Finnish territory grow to its largest ever, including the 'left arm', the Petsamo region in the far northeast. But more trouble awaited.

Following WWI, bitter language wars between Finnish and Swedish speakers shook the administration, universities and cultural circles. Civil War skirmishes continued, mostly with illegal massacres of Reds by Whites. Indeed, the right wing became increasingly outspoken in Finland (as well as elsewhere in Europe). In 1930, 12,000 right-wing farmers marched from Lapua to demand laws banning communism. A mutiny in Mäntsälä in 1932 tried to prevent socialists from meeting and to make Marxism illegal in Finland.

Despite its internal troubles, Finland at this time gained fame internationally as a brave new nation, as the only country to pay its debts to the USA, and as a sporting nation. Paavo Nurmi, the most distinguished of Finnish long-distance runners, won seven gold medals in three Olympic Games and became an enduring national hero (see the boxed text 'Flying Finns' in the Turku & the Southwest chapter). With continuing Finnish success in athletics, Helsinki was chosen to host the 1940 Olympic Games (these were postponed until 1952 due to WWII).

WWII

During the 1930s, Finland developed close ties with Nazi Germany, partly in response to the security threat posed by the Soviet Union. On 23 August 1939, the Soviet and German foreign ministers, Molotov and Ribbentrop, stunned the world by signing a nonaggression pact. A secret protocol stated that any future rearrangement would divide Poland between them; Germany would have a free hand in Lithuania, the Soviet Union in Finland, Estonia, Latvia and Bessarabia. The Red Army was moving towards the earmarked territories less than three weeks later.

The Soviet Union pressed more territorial claims, arguing its security required a slice of southeastern Karelia. JK Paasikivi (later to become Finland's seventh president) visited Moscow for negotiations on the ceding of the Karelian Isthmus to the Soviet Union. The negotiations failed. On 30 November 1939, the 'Winter War' between Finland and the Soviet Union began.

This was a harsh winter, with temperatures reaching -40°C, and soldiers died in their thousands. After 100 days of courageous fighting Finnish forces were defeated. In the Treaty of Moscow, signed in March 1940, Finland ceded part of Karelia and some nearby islands. About 500,000 Karelian refugees flooded across the new border.

In the following months, the Soviet Union pressured Finland for more territory. Isolated from Western allies Finland turned to Germany for help, and although no formal agreement was signed, Finland allowed the transit of German troops. When hostilities broke out between Germany and the Soviets in June 1941, German troops were already on Finnish soil and the 'Continuation War' between Finland and the Red Army began. In the fighting that followed the Finns slowly began to resettle Karelia, including some areas that had been in Russian possession since the 18th century. When Soviet forces staged a huge comeback in the summer of 1944, President Risto Ryti resigned and Marshal Mannerheim took his place. Mannerheim negotiated an armistice with the Russians and ordered the evacuation of German troops. Finland pursued a bitter war to oust German forces from Lapland until the general peace in the spring of 1945. Finland remained independent, but at a price: it was forced to cede territory and pay heavy war reparations to the Soviet Union. The Porkkala Peninsula west of Helsinki was a Soviet military base and off-limits to Finns until 1956.

The Cold War

Finland's reparations to the Soviets were chiefly paid in machinery and ships. Thus reparations played a central role in laying the foundations of the heavy engineering industry that stabilised the Finnish economy following WWII. Finland had suffered greatly in the late 1940s, with almost everything rationed and poverty widespread. The vast majority of the population was still engaged in agriculture at that time.

Things changed quickly in the following decades, with domestic migration to southern Finland especially strong in the 1960s and 1970s. New suburbs appeared almost overnight in and around Helsinki. Large areas in the north and east lost most of their young people, often half their population.

Finland maintained an uneasy truce – bordering on friendship – with the Soviet Union during the Cold War. The Treaty of Paris in 1947 dictated that the Karelian Isthmus be ceded to the Soviet Union, as well as the eastern Salla and Kuusamo regions and the 'left arm' of Finland in the Kola Peninsula. Many Finns are bitter about the loss of these territories to the present day.

The Treaty of Friendship, Cooperation & Mutual Assistance (Finnish: YYA) with the Soviet Union was signed in 1948. This agreement bound the two countries into an awkward semi-military relationship, in spite of Finland's claim to neutrality. The agreement remained valid until 1992, when it was replaced by a loose agreement with Russia without reference to military cooperation.

Urho K Kekkonen, the Finnish president from 1956 to 1981, a master of diplomacy and one of the great leaders of his age, was responsible for steering Finland out of the Cold War and its difficult relationship with the Soviet Union. Often this meant bowing to the wishes of the Soviet Union. On 30 October 1961 the Soviets exploded a 58-megatonne nuclear bomb on Novaja Zemlja Island, not far from Finland. What shook Finland most was a message from Moscow: the Communist Party wanted changes in Finland's domestic politics. It got what it wanted. The Berlin Wall had just been erected and the Cold War was at its height.

Kekkonen gained fame abroad as an eccentric and witty president, and was also known for his role as host of the initial Conference on Security & Cooperation in Europe (CSCE) meeting, in Helsinki in 1975. However free-wheeling the Finnish president seemed to those abroad, at home he brought democracy to an all-time low in 1974, when a vast majority of delegates from all major parties decided to extend his term by four years. Political nominations were submitted to Moscow for approval within the framework of 'friendly coexistence'.

As recently as the late 1980s, the Soviet Communist Party exercised Cold War tactics by infiltrating Finnish politics, with the aim of reducing US influence in Finland and preventing Finnish membership of the European Community (today's European Union, or EU). Although continuous concerns about the Soviet Union overshadowed most of Finland's foreign policy decisions, relations with Scandinavia were also extremely important in the decades following WWII. Finland was a founding member of the Nordic Council (along with the Scandinavian countries), pursuing a similar social welfare programme to Scandinavia and enjoying the benefits of free movement of labour, passport-free travel, and even common research and educational programmes with its Western neighbours.

Modern Finland

In the 1990s Finland's overheated economy, like many in the Western world, went through a cooling off period. The bubble economy of the 1980s had burst, the Soviet Union disappeared with debts unpaid, the markka was devalued, unemployment jumped from 3% to 20% and the tax burden grew alarmingly.

Things began to change for the better after a national referendum on 16 October 1994, when 57% of voters gave the go-ahead to join the EU. Since January 1995, food has become cheaper and strict alcohol laws have been relaxed. In the ensuing years Finland has also received considerable assistance from the EU – assistance with rural development, tourism, infrastructure and agricultural diversification. Finland was one of 11 countries that qualified to begin using the new euro currency in 1999, and adopted it completely in 2001.

A 1998 United Nations survey rated Finland fifth in the world in terms of quality of life (the survey measured health, education, life expectancy and income) after Canada, France, the USA and Iceland. With a firm commitment to the European Union, a strong independent streak, a booming technology sector and a growing tourism industry, Finland appears well-placed for the new millennium.

GEOGRAPHY

Finland, with an area of 338,000 sq km, is the seventh largest country in Europe – behind Russia, Ukraine, France, Spain, Sweden and Germany.

The southernmost point, the town of Hanko, lies at the same latitude as Oslo in Norway, Anchorage in Alaska, and the southernmost tip of Greenland. The shape of Finland has been compared to that of a female, holding up her right arm (the 'left arm' was lost to the former Soviet Union after WWII).

Finland shares a 1269km border with Russia in the east; a 727km border with Norway in the far north; and a 586km border with Sweden in the west. The Gulf of Finland separates south Finland from Estonia.

Approximately 70% of Finland is covered by forest – the highest proportion in the world. There are no real mountains; rather, *eskers* (sandy ridges) and wooded hills (fells) dominate. The highest hills, or *tunturi*, are in Lapland, which borders the mountainous areas of northern Norway and Sweden. Finland's highest point, the Halti in the northwest corner of the country, rises only 1328m above sea level.

Much of the country is lakeland – there are 187,888 lakes in Finland. Together with marshes and bogs, inland water covers about 10% of the country. Finland is shaped by water: lakes and ponds, rivers and creeks, rapids and small waterfalls, islands and islets, bays, capes and straits, and the large archipelagos of Turku, Åland, Helsinki and Vaasa.

GEOLOGY

Most of present-day Finland was under water until recently. About 10,000 years ago, when vast expanses of ice were melting away, the powerful moving ice and water masses produced the characteristic Finnish

Midnight Sun & Winter Gloom

From mid-May to late July the town of Utsjoki, in the far north of Finland, experiences continuous daylight – this is the land of the midnight sun. Further south, Rovaniemi, on the Arctic Circle, enjoys the midnight sun from roughly 20 May to 20 July. In central and southern Finland, it isn't possible to see the midnight sun, but it never really grows dark during the summer months. Night is replaced by a kind of dusk in which it is possible to hike, cycle and play outdoor games at midnight. The Finns really take advantage of this short summer and many people are active well after midnight

The longest day of the year is Midsummer In late June and the weekend closest to Midsummer is a huge holiday event.

In winter the situation is reversed. In the far north, above the Arctic Circle, the sun never appears above the horizon between early December and early January. Day is replaced by a dark, bluish glow called *kaamos* (polar night). Elsewhere in Finland, days are short and the sun sits low on the horizon even at midday, creating a twilight effect. In Helsinki in December and January the sun rises at 9am and sets at about 3.30pm.

geography: sandy ridges, solid rock layers, deep stone-drilled wells and thousands of lakes, often flowing northwest to southeast. Vegetation slowly covered the barren landscape, with many (now rare) deciduous trees finding root: since then, trees have dropped their leaves every autumn, almost 10,000 times, thus creating a fertile black soil. After the thick ice layer had disappeared, lifting a huge weight off the bedrock, the Finnish land mass started to rise – this is happening even today, at the rate of 6mm per year.

CLIMATE

Finland enjoys four distinct seasons: from continuing darkness in Arctic winter (November to February) to a two-month-long 'day' in northern Lapland's summer (mid-June to mid-August). In between is spring (March to May), which is a fine time for winter sports in northern Finland; and autumn (August to October), when the lovely *ruska* (autumn) colours come out. Thanks to factors such as the Baltic Sea and the mild winds from the Gulf Stream along the Norwegian coast, Finland's climate is, on average, much warmer than in other places of similar latitude, such as Siberia, Greenland and Alaska.

Summer means hot spells and weeks of little rain, although temperatures can be as low as 10°C at any time in summer. Every now and then in summer, southern Finland is the warmest place in Europe! It is not unusual to have temperatures rise to 5°C in January or to get showered by a freak snowstorm in June, but yearly averages follow a logical curve: the shorter the nights, the warmer the days, and vice versa.

Of course, winters *are* cold, but the cold is dry. In most parts of the country snow first falls in October and vanishes by the end of March, but in Lapland snow can fall as early as September and linger until late May. In northernmost Lapland you might even find snow as late as June.

You can find everything about Finland's weather on the Finnish Meteorological Institute website (W www.fmi.fi).

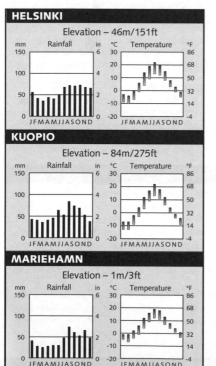

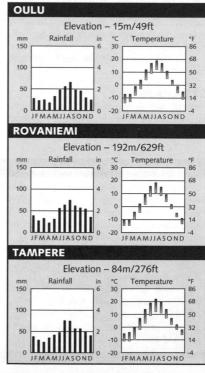

Street café, outside Hotel Kamp, Helsinki

Marsh and pine forest, northern Finland

Aurora borealis (northern lights)

Tuomiokirkko (Lutheran Cathedral), Helsinki

Country road, Laminka

Ice-hockey player

Pulp Fiction & Fact

Finland, a country that is incredibly green and covered with trees, appears at first glance to be quite ecologically conscious. Some 70% of Finland is forested, the highest percentage anywhere in the world. Indeed, according to the Finnish Forest Industries Federation (FFIF), Finland's forests are healthier than ever, with many thriving species of flora and fauna. Any logging that goes on, FFIF argues, merely imitates the effects of natural forest fires.

Environmental groups dispute the FFIF's upbeat claims. This is, after all, a country that depends heavily on logging – wood and paper products account for about one-third of all Finnish exports. Over the past 30 years or so, ancient woodlands have dwindled or disappeared in all parts of the country except sparsely populated northeastern Finland: the regions of North Karelia, Kainuu and Lapland. The World Wide Fund for Nature (WWF) and Finland's own environment ministry point out that only about 3% of Finland's native woodlands maintain the level of biodiversity of its ancient forests. Most forest areas are now planted only with trees of commercial value, chiefly pine and birch. .

The WWF and Greenpeace argue that short-sighted commercial practices have placed some 692 species of Finnish plants and animals at risk of extinction. These include flying squirrels, ospreys and white-backed woodpeckers, as well as fungi, mosses, lichens and invertebrates which need a variety of tree species of all ages, plus large quantities of dead or decaying wood, in order to survive.

Despite the impending environmental havoc, much of the paper produced from Finnish timber bears an ecofriendly label: 'This comes from sustainably managed Finnish forests'. The WWF argues the word 'sustainable' is used in the narrowest of senses – by concentrating on a couple of commercial species, the Finns have been able to maintain their timber yield but they certainly aren't sustaining the forest as a whole.

ECOLOGY & ENVIRONMENT

In Finland, forestry products are the main source of income and employment, the main cause of pollution and the main topic of environmental debate. Paper and pulp industries provide work for thousands but also cause environmental hazards, which are easily seen in areas surrounding factories. To put it bluntly, pulp factories stink, literally and figuratively.

Finland is the second largest exporter of paper products in the world and is dependent on paper manufacturing. Around 70% of the country is forest – the highest percentage in the world – and most of this land is managed forest that is harvested for cutting. If you look closely, you'll see that many thousands of acres of Finnish forest have only one, or at best two, species of tree – which creates a serious disturbance in the local ecosystem. Furthermore, pulp factories – and other heavy industries that have long been a staple of the Finnish economy – contribute to massive domestic water pollution.

Finland, the land of lake, river and ocean, may look idyllic and pristine – but this scene masks some harsh environmental truths. A 1997 survey ranked Finland's lake and ocean waters as some of the most polluted in the EU, failing to meet even minimum EU standards of cleanliness. Sweden was also at the bottom in terms of water quality.

Domestic conservation efforts are spearheaded by the Finnish Forest and Park Service, which oversees 120,000 sq km of publicly owned lands. This organisation also works to protect endangered species and promote biodiversity on forest lands that are used for commercial purposes. For more information about the National Park Service and protected wilderness areas, see National Parks in the following Flora & Fauna section.

FLORA & FAUNA
Flora

Finnish flora is at its best during the dynamic period between late May and September. The three main types of forest are pine, spruce and birch. Pine grows generally on dry ground and sand ridges, conditions which don't foster undergrowth. Spruce forests are dark and dense, while birch is the typical tree found in deciduous forests.

Fauna

There are quite a few mammals in Finnish forests. The largest (and one of the rarest) is the brown bear, which was once so feared that even mentioning its name *(karhu)* was taboo. Other mammals include elk (or moose), foxes, lynx, wolves and wolverines, and there are plenty of small animals such as lemmings, hedgehogs, muskrats, martens, beavers, otters and hares. *Hirvi* (elk) are solitary, shy animals – to see one is a real treat, unless it's crashing into your car windscreen. Despite the relative rarity, there are some 2000 road accidents a year involving elk. *Poro* (reindeer), on the other hand, abound in north Finland, with some 230,000 animals. These are all in semi-domesticated herds owned by the Sami; truly wild reindeer are rare. *Ilves* (lynx) used to be very rare but numbers are increasing. There are practically no home-grown wolves left in Finland, but plenty cross the border regularly from Russia. Hatred for, and fear of, the *susi* (wolf) is deep-rooted in eastern Finland, where they are hunted and killed.

There are more than 300 bird species in Finland (see the Bird-Watching section in the Activities chapter for more information). Large species include black grouse, capercaillies, whooper swans and birds of prey, such as the osprey. Chaffinches and willow warblers are the two most common forest species; sparrows are quite common in inhabited areas. Crested-tits, black woodpeckers, black-throated divers, ravens and many owls are common throughout the country. The Siberian jay is a common sight in Lapland because it follows people. Finns who watch migratory birds arrive from the south have a saying for how to determine when summer will come: it is one month from sighting a skylark, half a month from a chaffinch, just a little from a white wagtail and not a single day from a swift.

Less popular creatures include the viper, which is the most common poisonous snake.

National Parks

Much of Finland's forest covering is private, managed forest cultivated by forest-products companies. However, to keep everyone else happy, Metsähallitus, the Finnish Forest and Park Service, manages magnificent trekking and fishing areas totalling 120,000 sq km, with well-maintained hiking trails and a wide range of accommodation options available to all. Additionally, the independent Finnish Forest Research Institute manages a handful of superb nature preserves, including Koli

and Pallas-Ounastunturi. All together, national parks account for 7300 sq km of all publicly owned lands.

Metsähallitus publishes *Finland's National Parks*, a comprehensive booklet listing all of the national parks, with information on trails and accommodation as well as notes on flora and fauna. This is an extremely helpful resource if you are planning to visit several parks or are particularly interested in the Finnish wilderness. Alternatively, check out w www.metsa.fi where national parks are described in detail in English. Pamphlets describing individual parks are available at the national park tourist information offices in Helsinki and Rovaniemi, and are usually available at local tourist offices.

The largest and most pristine national parks are in northern Finland, particularly Lapland. Liminganlahti Bird Sanctuary, near Oulu in northern Finland, is arguably the best place in the country for bird-watching.

Linnansaari National Park, near Savonlinna, is probably the best park in the Lakeland area and is also home to the extremely endangered Saimaa ringed seal. To see larger mammals – such as the shy and elusive elk – it's best to visit one of the national parks in the northeast, such as Oulanka National Park, or further north in Lapland, such as Lemmenjoki, Pallas-Ounastunturi and Urho Kekkonen national parks. These parks are vast, and services and facilities are few; to make the most of a visit you should be prepared to spend several days trekking and camping. See the Activities chapter for trail recommendations and more information about trekking.

GOVERNMENT & POLITICS

Finland is a presidential republic. The president, in council with the prime minister and cabinet, forms the executive government. The president is elected to a six-year term by the people. The voting age is 18. Presidential duties include overseeing foreign policy and acting as the commander in chief of the Finnish army. The president has the right to veto a bill. Finland's first woman president, Tarja Halonen, was narrowly elected to office in 2000 and has proved to be a popular president.

The prime minister is elected every four years by the 200-member Eduskunta (parliament). Eduskunta members all get to serve four-year terms. The prime minister until 2003 is Paavo Lipponen, currently serving his second term as leader of the Social Democratic Party. The government holds 51 seats. Other important political parties and their representation as of 2002 are the Centre Party (48 seats), National Coalition Party (46 seats) and Left Alliance (20 seats). The Green League and Swedish Peoples Party have 11 seats each.

Members of parliament are elected from 14 national districts. There are six *lääni* (provinces): Lapland, Oulu, Western Finland, Eastern Finland, Åland and Southern Finland, and 452 *kunta* (municipalities). Åland has a small local parliament with a high degree of autonomy and sends one member of parliament to Helsinki.

Major political *puolue* (parties) in Finland include the Social Democratic Party, the agrarian Centre Party, the conservative National Coalition Party, the left-wing Alliance, the Greens, the Swedish People's Party and the Christian Union. Left-wing parties increased their share of the vote in the 1990s.

ECONOMY

The recent economic history of Finland is not very different from that of many other Western countries, but it may be more extreme. The transformation from a rural society to an urban industrialised country was a quick one. Economic growth was impressive. Post-WWII rationing was soon replaced by supermarkets with a wide variety of imported goods. When the regulated financial market was liberated in the mid-1980s, the result was an overheated economy, a well-known phenomenon in most Western economies at that time.

When the bubble inevitably burst, Finland went through one of the worst recessions any Western country experienced in the 1990s. For a time, Finland had been the most expensive country in the world; soon it was one of the cheapest in Western Europe. From almost full employment, 500,000 jobs disappeared in two years, saddling Finland with an embarrassing and costly 20% unemployment rate, the second highest in Europe. In order to reduce its budget deficit the government slashed spending by 20%. Two areas were spared these cuts: education was one, and grants for private research and development were actually increased. The gamble

paid off – in 1995 Finland was a net exporter of know-how and high-tech products.

The whole export sector boomed in the 1990s, and exports now account for about 40% of the GDP. Timber products, pulp and paper as well as metal products and mobile phones were shipped from Finland at a pace never seen before. The highly automated export industries, however, didn't much improve the unemployment situation.

Finland is the world's second largest exporter of paper and paperboard (Canada is the largest). Metal mining, technology and engineering contribute almost as large a share of export income; Finland's Nokia company is the world's second largest manufacturer of mobile phones. Services and construction are increasingly important to the Finnish economy.

Finland has made a remarkable recovery since the early 1990s. In 2001, unemployment was about 9% (a good average in Europe and down from 14.6% in 1996) and inflation was around 2.6%. Less than 10% of the population earned a living from agriculture, 32% from industry and 58% from services. The GDP in 2001 was €114 million.

Domestic tourism has been booming for some time, much of it centred on amusement and theme parks that appeal to Finnish families. Trade unions are a powerful force in the Finnish economy. They have a virtual monopoly on the workforce, with over two million members (or 83% of the working population). Wages are centrally determined, and there are strict rules governing working hours and holidays.

POPULATION & PEOPLE

The earliest Finno-Ugrians were nomadic tribespeople who inhabited much of north Russia, and there are still small Finnic groups living in the Ural Mountains. Karelians, Estonians and Hungarians are some other close relatives of the Finns. Over the centuries, however, a large Indo-European influence has affected Finland's population, to the extent that many Finns look very Scandinavian (blonde hair, blue eyes etc).

Finland's population is 5,194,901 (2001 census), with an annual growth rate of 0.4%. More than 50% of the population lives in the three southwestern provinces (around Helsinki, Turku and Tampere), which have 15% of the total land area.

The Greater Helsinki area, including Espoo, Vantaa and several municipalities, houses one million people, or 20% of the national total. The next biggest towns, in order of size, are Tampere, Turku, Oulu, Lahti and Kuopio.

The main minority groups in Finland are the 300,000 Swedish-speaking Finns (*Finlandssvensk*, or 'Finland's Swede') and the 6500 Sami people (4000 in Lapland). Only 2% of all Finnish residents are foreigners – the lowest percentage of any country in Europe – and the majority of these are Russians (almost 23,000), followed by Estonian, Swedish and Somalian. However, large numbers of Finns have emigrated to other countries: some 280,000 to the USA, 250,000 to Sweden, 20,000 to Canada and 10,000 to Australia. The average household size in Finland is 2.9 people, although 10 children in a family was not uncommon just 50 years ago.

EDUCATION

The literacy rate in Finland hovers around 99% and the number of newspapers and books printed per capita is among the highest in the world. Indeed, Finland's investment in education is higher than any other industrialised country: more than 7% of its GNP.

The nine-year *perus-koulu* (comprehensive school) is one of the most equitable systems in the world – tuition, books, meals and commuting to and from school are free. All Finns learn English and Swedish in school and many also study German or French. *Lukio* (secondary school) is three years in length and serves as a stepping stone to universities in Helsinki, Turku, Tampere, Oulu, Jyväskylä, Joensuu, Kuopio, Rovaniemi and Vaasa.

The first university in Finland was founded in Turku in 1640 and transferred in 1828 to Helsinki, where it now has some 26,000 students. These and other universities are state-owned and there are practically no fees. State grants, state-guaranteed low-interest loans, subsidised health care, meals and student hostels are available to most students. With these benefits, Finnish students stay an average of seven to eight years at university. In addition to higher education, Finns can choose from other kinds of educational institutes, from vocational schools to those specialising in an individual subject or just in 'how to live a happy life'.

ARTS

Dance

Dance is nurtured in Finland. The Finnish National Opera has its own ballet school, and there are a handful of small dance groups in Helsinki and other large towns. Attend the annual Kuopio Dance Festival to catch the latest trends.

Few traditional *kansan-tanssit* (folk dances) remain, but they can be seen on ceremonial occasions or at certain festivals. In summer you may come across a noisy dance stage in the middle of nowhere. Get ready to experience *lavatanssit*, where local singers and their bands play pop music, and people dance. If the participants are older, the music is *humppa* or *tango*, and instruments include the accordion and violin. Younger people demand a contemporary band, so the *lava* (stage) is almost like a disco. You could be interested in a *naistentanssi*, or 'women's dance', where women propose a dance. This arrangement is generally held once a week in many local dance restaurants. Don't confuse this with romantic interest.

Music

Music is a big part of Finnish culture, particularly in summer when music festivals are staged all over the country. As well as traditional dance bands, you'll find plenty of jazz, folk, classical and modern electronic music playing in a variety of venues.

Classical Music Composer Jean Sibelius' (see the boxed text 'Jean Sibelius' in the Tampere & Häme Region chapter) work dominates the musical identity of Finland. Born 8 December 1865 in Hämeenlinna, Sibelius wrote music for the glorification of his own people and in defiance of the oppressor, Russia. His most famous composition, *Finlandia*, became a strong expression of Finnish patriotism. Sibelius can be said to have composed the music for the *Kalevala* saga, while Gallen-Kallela painted it.

Sibelius' musical heritage can be heard in the work of a new generation of composers, conductors and musicians emerging onto the international stage. Many of these were pupils of the legendary Jorma Panula, professor of conducting at Sibelius Academy in Helsinki until 1994. Finland's national anthem, *Maamme* (Our Land; *Nårt Land* in Swedish), was composed by Fredrik Pacius.

Folk Music The Karelian region has its own folk music, typified by the stringed, harp-like instrument called the *kantele*.

Popular Music Finns are big fans of jazz, as can be seen by the huge jazz festivals at Pori, Espoo and Kajaani and the many jazz clubs in major cities. Notable Finnish jazz musicians include Raoul Björkenheim, and the late Edward Vesala, a visionary of the Finnish free jazz scene.

Finnish rock bands can be seen at pubs, clubs and festivals like Ruisrock in Turku and Provinssrock in Seinajoki. Some of the best-known Finnish rock bands are Hanoi Rocks, The Flaming Sideburns and The Hurriganes, the legendary rock 'n' roll trio.

Electronic music is also big business in Finland. Techno and trance artist Darude is huge in Europe and Bomfunk MC is big in the hip-hop scene. Other names to look for in the Finnish music business include Pan Sonic, known for abstract, minimalist and experimental electronica; Laika & the Cosmonauts, the world's most popular surf instrumentalists (believe it or not); and Jori Hulkkonen, a house producer and DJ.

Literature

Written Finnish was created by Mikael Agricola (1510–57), who wrote the first Finnish alphabet and covered traditional Finnish culture and religion in his writings. Because Finnish remained a spoken more

The *Kalevala*

Elias Lönnrot was an adventurous country doctor who trekked in eastern Finland on a scholarship during the first half of the 19th century in order to collect traditional poems, oral runes, folk stories and legends. Altogether, Lönnrot undertook 11 long tours, by foot or on reindeer, to complete his research. He put together the results with some of his own writing to form the *Kalevala*, which came to be regarded as the national epic of Finland.

Equally important was Lönnrot's work in creating a standard Finnish grammar and vocabulary by adopting words and expressions from various dialects. Finnish has remained very much the same ever since, at least in written form.

The first version of the *Kalevala* appeared in 1833, another version in 1835 and yet another, the final version, *Uusi-Kalevala* (New Kalevala), in 1849. Since then, the *Kalevala* has been translated into almost 40 languages.

Kalevala is an epic mythology that includes stories of creation and tales of the fight between good and evil. Although there are heroes and villains, there are also more nuanced characters that are not so simply described. The main storyline concentrates on the events in two imaginary countries, Kalevala (characterised as 'our country') and Pohjola ('the other place'). Some of the characters are:

Aino The bride of Väinämöinen and sister of Joukahainen.
Antero Vipunen A shaman. In one story, Väinämöinen is looking for the Right Words (which give omnipotence to the user) and ends up in Antero's belly. Eventually, Antero Vipunen has to let him go and give him the Words.
Ilmarinen One of the main characters, and the husband of the princess of Pohjola. He is a smith who makes the Sampo (a mysterious and powerful machine).
Joukahainen A youngster who is threatened with drowning in a swamp to the singing of the powerful Väinämöinen. In a vain attempt to be saved, he promises his sister Aino to Väinämöinen.
Kalervo The father of Kullervo.
Kullervo The main character of the Kullervo series of poems; he suffers under a terrible curse.
Lemminkäinen A hero whose character was created by Lönnrot based on oral tradition.
Louhi The matron of Pohjola, also called Pohjan Akka or Pohjolan emäntä, the leader of Pohjola.
Väinämöinen The main protagonist, a god-like, omnipotent figure. He was a bard and probably a shaman, a Santa Claus–type old man and a strong personality.

Places associated with Lönnrot and the *Kalevala* include Ilomantsi, Kuhmo and Kajaani. There is a *Kalevala* theme park in Kuhmo and a *Kalevala* exhibition at Parppeinvaara in Ilomantsi. The most notable *Kalevala*-inspired paintings are found in the Ateneum Art Museum and in the National Museum, both in Helsinki.

than written language (although it was emerging in schools), the earliest fiction was written in Swedish.

The most famous of all 19th-century writers was Elias Lönnrot, who collected poems, oral runes, folk legends and stories to pen the *Kalevala*, the national epic of Finland, which became the foundation of Finnish culture, literature and history (see the boxed text on the previous page). Other notable 19th-century writers include JL Runeberg *(Tales of the Ensign Ståhl)*, fairytale writer Zacharias Topelius, and Aleksis Kivi, who founded modern Finnish literature with *Seven Brothers*, a story of brothers who try to escape education and civilisation in favour of the forest.

In the 20th century, Mika Waltari gained fame through *The Egyptian*, and FE Sillanpää received the Nobel Prize for literature in 1939. The national bestseller in the postwar period was *The Unknown Soldier* by Väinö Linna. The seemingly endless series of autobiographical novels by Kalle Päätalo and the witty short stories by Veikko Huovinen are also very popular in Finland. Another internationally famous author is the late Tove Jansson, whose children's books on the

A Guide to Finnish Churches

The casual traveller will probably be happy to look at just two or three Finnish churches (which even at their best don't come close to Chartres), but any serious student of architecture will want to track them *all* down. Some of the churches mentioned here are described in more detail later in this book; for others, contact the local or regional tourist office, or simply jump aboard a bus with camera and sketchbook in hand. The following is a guide to the various styles common throughout Finland.

Medieval (1200s to 1520s)
Era: Swedish Catholic
Style: Gothic
Material: Stone, sometimes red brick in the facade
There are 70 medieval churches in Finland. The oldest ones are on Åland, in Hammarland, Finström, Lemland, Sund, Saltvik and Kumlinge. There are almost 30 medieval churches in the Turku area, including Nousiainen, Turku, Mynämäki, Korppoo, Parainen, Taivassalo, Rymättylä, Kalanti, Laitila, Sastamala and Rauma. Churches like those in Pyhtää, Hattula, Hollola and Isokyrö were once the religious headquarters for entire regions, and remain historically significant and worth visiting.

In addition to paintings and sculpture, note the unique facade and the ceiling in medieval churches.

Wooden (1600s to 1700s)
Era: Swedish Lutheran
Style: Varies locally
Material: Logs of locally obtained wood, painted red
Remote areas of Finland never enjoyed the privilege of having an imposing stone church. Instead, wood was used, as this was one material that was cheap and plentiful. Some of the oldest such churches were continuously renovated over the centuries and the original simplicity has been replaced by 19th-century style.

The best example of a Finnish wooden church is certainly the Petäjävesi Church in central Finland. Other good examples include the churches of Irjanne, Keuruu, Maakalla, Paltaniemi, Pihlajavesi, Pyhämaa, Sodankylä, Tervola and Tornio. There are also some colourful churches in Swedish-speaking western Finland, such as Vörå and Nykarleby.

In addition to fine paintings in many of the old wooden churches, look for detailed woodcarving.

Empire & European Gothic (1800s)
Era: Russian, Lutheran
Style: Imitations of central European styles, especially neoclassical and neo-Gothic
Material: Wood, painted various colours
The 20 largest churches in Finland were all built during the Russian era, between 1815 and 1907. They include imitations of central European Gothic cathedrals. Johannes Church in Helsinki and

Moomin family captured the hearts and imaginations of Finnish children, and adults. Tove Jansson's books are available in English, although most other works by Finnish authors are not.

Architecture

The high standard of modern Finnish architecture was established by the works of Alvar Aalto and Eliel Saarinen. People interested in architecture make pilgrimages to Finland to see superb examples of modern building. Unfortunately, much great Finnish architecture is overshadowed by supermarkets and other concrete blocks that dominate towns and villages.

The oldest architectural monuments include medieval castles and 75 stone churches, scattered around villages in Southern Finland. In these Catholic churches, Gothic ideals were emulated but with little success, and as a result, an original Finnish style emerged. Wood has long been the dominant building material in Finland. Some of the best early examples of wooden architecture are churches on Finland's west coast.

Eastern influences date back to 1809, when Finland became an autonomous grand

A Guide to Finnish Churches

churches in Pori, Kotka, Forssa and Nurmes are the most notable examples. Communities in the Lakeland and Western Finland are especially famous for their large wooden churches. Kerimäki Church in Savo is the largest wooden church in the world, dwarfing even the enormous churches of Mäntyharju, Merikarvia, Mikkeli and Heinävesi.

Many of these churches were built according to a style called Empire, which was influenced by Roman and French architecture. Carl Ludwig Engel, a German architect, was the leading designer of Finnish churches during this era.

National Romantic (late 1800s to early 1900s)
Era: Russian, Lutheran
Style: Art Nouveau, Karelian
Material: Cut granite, oak and other heavy wood, seldom painted
During the tsarist era, Josef Stenbäck designed the greatest number of granite churches, 30 in all – but others, such as Tampere Cathedral by Lars Sonck, are more famous. The rich ornamentation, often a reflection of Karelian heritage, is the main feature of these churches.

Orthodox (1700s to 1900s)
Era: Russian, Independence
Style: Byzantine, Karelian
Material: Red brick for the old ones; round logs for the more recent *tsasounas* (chapels)
Most Orthodox churches in Finland date from the Russian era, or time of independence. The style is Byzantine, with Russian flourishes, such as onion domes. Although there are fine examples of Orthodox architecture in eastern Finland, in towns such as Ilomantsi, Joensuu, Polvijärvi and Kotka, there are also chapels further west, most notably in Tampere and Helsinki.

The main feature of Orthodox churches, however, is the wall of icons, rather than the architecture. There is a fine collection of Orthodox art at the Orthodox Church Museum in Kuopio.

Modern (1900s)
Era: Independence, Lutheran
Style: Art Deco, modern
Materials: Various, but especially concrete painted white and light wood as interior decoration and/or furniture
The most famous modern churches in Finland are Alvar Aalto's churches in Seinäjoki, Lahti and Imatra, as well as more recent ones in Tampere (Kaleva Church by Pietilä), Myyrmäki (by Leiviskä) and Helsinki's Temppeliaukio Church (by Suomalainen).

Some of these churches do not look like churches at all, but more like a successful architectural adventure.

duchy under Russian rule, and to 1812 when Helsinki was made the new capital. The magnificent city centre was created by CL Engel, a German-born architect, who combined neoclassical and St Petersburg features in designing the cathedral, the university and other buildings around Senate Square. Engel also designed a large number of churches in Finland. All the largest churches in Finland were built during Russian rule. After the 1850s, National Romanticism emerged in response to pressure from the Russians.

The Art Nouveau period, which reached its climax at the turn of the 20th century, combined Karelian ideals with rich ornamentation. Materials were wood and grey granite. The best examples of this style are the National Museum (Eliel Saarinen) and the Cathedral of Tampere (Lars Sonck). After independence was achieved in 1917, rationalism and functionalism emerged, as exemplified by some of Alvar Aalto's work. The following list contains some of the most famous names in Finnish architecture.

Alvar Aalto (1898–1976) is the most famous Finnish architect. His earliest works can be seen at Alajärvi, and there is a museum dedicated to Aalto in Jyväskylä. There are individual churches in Lahti and Imatra, and public buildings in Rovaniemi. Several buildings can be seen in Helsinki, and at Otaniemi in Espoo, near Helsinki.

Eliel Saarinen (1873–1950) designed a great number of attractive townhouses in Helsinki, as well as working with two other architects, Herman Gesellius and Armas Lindgren, on projects like the National Museum and the Hvitträsk House, northwest of Helsinki. Town halls in Lahti and Joensuu are his own works, as well as the train station in Helsinki. Eliel's son Eero Saarinen worked primarily in the USA until he died in 1961.

Josef Stenbäck (1854–1929) designed more than 30 churches, most of them Art Nouveau.

Juha Leiviskä was awarded the international Carlsberg prize in 1995 for his works in Helsinki (Vallila Library and much more), Vantaa (Myyrmäki Church) and Kuopio (Männistö Church).

Lars Sonck (1870–1956) designed some notable stone edifices in National Romantic style, including Kultaranta in Naantali and churches in Tampere, Mariehamn and Helsinki (Kallio).

Raili and Reima Pietilä, a married couple, worked together and designed churches and other buildings in Tampere (Kaleva, Hervanta and the library in town centre) and Lieksa (the church).

Among the most famous postwar architects are Viljo Revell, Aarno Ervi, Heikki Siren, Toivo Korhonen, Timo Penttilä, Aarno Ruusuvuori, Erkki Kairamo, Kristian Gullichsen, and Timo and Tuomo Suomalainen (Rock Church in Helsinki).

Emerging regional schools of architecture include the Oulu School, featuring small towers, porticoes and combinations of various elements, most evident in the region around Oulu. Erkki Helasvuo, who died in 1995, did plenty of work in North Karelia, providing the province with several public buildings which hint at modern Karelianism.

Painting

Of the many prehistoric rock paintings across Finland, those at Hossa and Ristiina are the most famous. Medieval churches in Åland and in Southern Finland have frescoes, while interesting paintings by Mikael Toppelius and others feature in several 18th-century wooden churches, most notably in the village of Haukipudas, near Oulu. Modern art is alive and well in Finland; each large town exhibits paintings that provoke anything from astonishment to despair. Helsinki's Kiasma is a showcase for Finnish modern art.

Golden Age Although contemporary art enjoys a high profile in Finland, it is works by National Romantic painters that have been bestowed with Golden Age status. The main features of these artworks are virgin forests and pastoral landscapes. The following list includes museums that exhibit the best works. The most comprehensive collections are displayed by the Ateneum and National Museum in Helsinki, and the Turku Art Museum.

Akseli Gallen-Kallela (1865–1931), probably the most famous Finnish painter, had a distinguished career as creator of *Kalevala*-inspired paintings. His masterworks can be seen as frescoes in the National Museum in Helsinki, Ateneum, Turku Art Museum, Turku Ett Hem and at Jusélius Mausoleum in Pori.

Albert Edelfelt (1854–1905), one of the most appreciated of Finnish artists, was educated in Paris, and a number of his paintings date from this period. Many paintings are photo-like depictions of rural life. Most Edelfelt paintings are found at the Ateneum, but there are also a few at the Joensuu Art Museum and Turku Ett Hem.

Berndt Lindholm (1841–1914) is mostly known for his paintings of waves hitting a rocky shore.

He has also painted Finnish landscapes and rural life but unfortunately many of his works are in private collections. Some examples can be seen at the Ateneum, Turku Art Museum and Turku Ett Hem.

Brothers von Wright Magnus (1805–68), Wilhelm (1810–87) and Ferdinand (1822–1902). The brothers von Wright are considered the first Finnish painters of the Golden Age, most famous for their paintings of birds. They worked in their home near Kuopio and in Porvoo. The Ateneum in Helsinki has devoted a room to their work.

Eero Järnefelt (1863–1937) was a keen visitor to Koli, where he created more than 50 paintings of the 'national landscape'. His sister married Jean Sibelius, the composer. See his work at the Ateneum, as well as Mikkeli, Hämeenlinna, Turku and Kuopio art museums.

Ellen Thesleff (1869–1954) used strong colours in her landscape paintings. Visit the Ateneum for a good look at her works.

Fanny Churberg (1845–92), one of the most famous female painters in Finland, created landscapes, self-portraits and still lifes. Go to the Ateneum for a good look at her work.

Helene Schjerfbeck (1862–1946), probably the most famous female painter of her age, is known for her self-portraits, which reflect the situation of Finnish women 100 years ago; Helene didn't live a happy life. Go to Ateneum, Turku Art Museum and Turku Ett Hem.

Hjalmar Munsterhjelm (1840–1905), one of the most notable landscape painters in Finland, studied in Germany. There are paintings at the Ateneum, Turku Art Museum and Turku Ett Hem.

Hugo Simberg (1873–1917) is famous for his series of watercolours drawing on folk tales and employing a kind of rustic symbolism. His work can be seen at the Ateneum and Turku Art Museum.

Juho Rissanen (1873–1950) depicted life among ordinary Finns, and his much-loved paintings are displayed at the Ateneum and Turku Art Museum.

Magnus Enckell (1870–1925) is known for his paintings in Tampere Cathedral. His work can also be seen at the Ateneum, Joensuu Art Museum and Jyväskylä Alvar Aalto Museum.

Pekka Halonen (1865–1933) was a popular artist of the National Romantic era. His work, mostly devoted to typical winter scenery, is largely privately owned. Some of the best works are displayed in the Ateneum and Turku Art Museum.

Robert Wilhelm Ekman (1808–73), one of the founders of the Finnish school of art, worked in Turku and painted mostly altars for churches. See the Cygnaeus Gallery (Helsinki), National Museum and Ateneum.

Victor Westerholm (1860–1919), most famous for his large Åland landscapes, had his summer studio in Önningeby (see the Åland chapter for details) but there are landscapes from other locations too. The Ateneum, Turku Art Museum, Hämeenlinna Art Museum and Turku Ett Hem display some of his best works.

Werner Holmberg (1839–60) is an early Finnish artist whose classic painting is *The Ideal Landscape*. See the Ateneum.

Design

Finns have created their own design style through their craft tradition, the use of natural materials (wood, glass, ceramics, fabric and metal) and simple but pure forms. Stylistically they combined colourful, geometric, ornamental Karelian (originally Byzantine) design with a more Western European style.

Traditional textile art, such as *ryijy* (woven rugs) and *raanus* (national costumes) as well as wooden furniture and everyday utensils and implements, can be seen in various museums. This heritage is also clearly visible in the works of modern designers.

The products of some early designers, such as Louis Sparre, Gallen-Kallela and Eliel Saarinen, reflected the ideas of Karelianism, National Romanticism and Art Nouveau. In the 1930s architect Alvar Aalto invented wooden furniture made of bent and laminated plywood, as well as his famous Savoy vases. Aalto won a prize for his furniture in the Milan Triennale of 1933.

After WWII, the 'Golden Age of Applied Art' began, and in Milan in 1951 Finland received 25 prizes for various designer products. Tapio Wirkkala, Kaj Franck, Timo Sarpaneva, Eero Aarnio and Yrjö Kukkapuro were the most notable designers of the time. Iittala, Nuutajärvi and Arabia are some of the best brands of Finnish glassware and porcelain, and Pentik is a more recent brand. Aarikka is famous for wooden products, and Kalevala Koru for silver designs. Alvar Aalto, the famous architect, was also noted for his interior design work, particularly furniture. The *enfant terrible* (terrible child) of the current Finnish design scene is Stefan Lindfors, whose reptile and insect-inspired work has been described as a warped updating of Aalto's own influence from nature.

Helsinki's Museum of Art & Design is a good place to see the latest in Finnish design work.

Cinema

About a dozen movies are produced in Finland annually, and many of these films are sold to Norwegian state television. Mika and Aki Kaurismäki are currently the best known directors. Their success in *film noir* is based on their education in Leningrad (during the USSR era). Aki is probably best known for his 1989 road film *Leningrad Cowboys Go to America* (and the lesser known 1994 follow-up *Leningrad Cowboys Meet Moses*), and more recently for the downbeat 'grotty realism' of *Drifting Clouds* (1997). In 2002 he won the Grand Prix at the Cannes Film Festival for his film *The Man Without a Past*. The story centres on a man who is so badly beaten up he loses his memory and becomes homeless.

American director Jim Jarmusch is a personal friend of the Kaurismäki brothers, and has also presented his view of Finnish culture in some of his works. Another talented director, Markku Pölönen, has produced some very fine movies on Finnish rural life.

The most successful Finn in Hollywood, Renny Harlin (also known as the former husband of actor Geena Davis), directed the strongly anti-communist action movie *Born American* in the 1980s, portraying an imaginary Soviet prison camp. When the film was banned in Finland and Harlin accused of presenting a 'foreign nation in a hostile manner', the young director found himself directing box-office hits for Hollywood, including *Die Hard II* and *Cliffhanger*.

There are several annual film festivals in Finland, the Midnight Sun festival in Sodankylä being one of the most interesting.

SOCIETY & CONDUCT
Traditional Culture

Finns do not consider themselves Scandinavian, nor do they see themselves as part of Russia; nevertheless, Finnish tradition owes something to both cultures. For centuries Finns maintained a pragmatic independence from their Eastern and Western neighbours, preserved their own language (the language of the *Kalevala*) and developed their own distinctive culture. A famous quote goes: 'Swedes we are not. Russians we will never be. Therefore let us be Finns.'

The Finns' long struggle for emancipation, together with their ongoing struggle to survive in a harsh environment, has engendered an ordered society which solves its own problems in its own way. It has also engendered the Finnish trait of *sisu*, often translated as 'guts', or the resilience to survive prolonged hardship. Even if all looks lost, until the final defeat, a Finn with *sisu* will fight – or swim, or run, or work – valiantly.

Despite increased urbanisation, Finns remain a forest people at heart. The forests are crisscrossed with skiing tracks, some leading to the summer cottages (see the boxed text 'Summer Cottages' in the Facts for the Visitor chapter) where Finns get away from it all at any opportunity.

Other Cultures

Over the years, the very few Jews in Finland have kept a low profile because of the Nazis, the pro-Arab sentiments of Finnish leftists, and anti-Semitic voices from the Soviet Union and Russia. Some talented Jews have enriched Finnish cultural life, and there's a very beautiful synagogue in Helsinki.

Russians have also kept an extremely low profile, perhaps because in the past the Finnish authorities were notorious for expelling Russian defectors back to the Soviet Union. There is in Finland an ethnic Russian Orthodox Church different from the national Orthodox Church. Russian restaurants in Finland, particularly in Helsinki, are said to serve better Russian cuisine than those in Russia.

Sami Culture The unique Sami culture is almost exclusive to Lapland. See the boxed text 'The Sami of Finland' in the Lapland & Sapmi chapter.

Swedish Culture The Swedish-speaking minority in Finland is neither Swedish nor Finnish. Centuries of history divide them from the people of Sweden, and by their own definition they are ethnically distinct from the Finns.

Some Swedish-speaking people are children of ethnic German, Russian or Jewish families who adopted the Swedish language before learning enough Finnish to deal with daily life. Swedish-speakers are well represented in most cultural, economic and public fields. Although they are usually considered representatives of the 'old money' in Finland, the Swedish minority also has some well-known leftists, greens and other influential members in various 'alternative' groups.

Why Finland?

The Finns call their country *Suomi* (pronounced **swam**-ee′), so why is it generally known as Finland?

French may provide a clue. *Fin* means 'end', and *fin de lande* could easily be, if not 'the end of the world', the northern end of the European land mass.

The early Romans called this land Fennia. In English the word *fen* describes a swampy land, and is mostly used to refer to the watery land in eastern England. But Romans went to England too, and Finland is exactly such a swampy land, and swamp in Finnish is *suo*. A Finn in Finnish is *suomalainen*, whereas *suomaalainen* (with double a) means an inhabitant of a swampy land.

The resemblance of the word *suo* to Suomi is too close to be ignored, but the derivation of the name of the long-time inhabitants of Lapland, the Sami, offers another explanation. Finland is called *Somija* in Latvian, *Suomija* in Lithuanian and *Soome* in Estonian. The Lapps call themselves *Sábme*. The original word for Sami is *Häme*, which means 'an inhabitant of the interior'. The Häme are an ancient tribe that have given their name to part of the interior of Southern Finland.

Unimpressed by all these references to inferior interior swampy wetlands, many Finns would like their country to be called *Finlandia* or *Fennica* (in Latin) because that sounds more respectable.

Of course, Swedish-speaking Finns have always called Finland, Finland.

Swedish speakers are found mostly in coastal towns and communities, maintaining Swedish literature, newspapers, TV programs, and a number of cultural traditions different from Finns and even from Sweden. Their small towns and gardens are among the most attractive and well-kept in Finland. Sagalund, on the island of Kimito, and Stundars, near Vaasa, are two museums with plenty of cultural interest, and Åland province is culturally Swedish.

With a constant presence in the national government, the Swedish party makes sure that everything is fine with the 'most protected minority in the world', as some jealously put it.

Romany Culture The Finnish Romany (Gypsies) number about 4000. They are descendants of people who emigrated from India from around 500 AD and travelled throughout Europe. Romany people have their own language (with elements of Indian languages) and distinctive dress. For women this is usually a black lace dress with a hoop bodice. After 1584 when the first Romany people arrived in Finland, a law was passed that made it illegal *not* to kill a Gypsy. Today the term Romaani is preferred over the old racist term Mustalainet ('black people').

Social Graces

The Finns are naturally a reserved people, particularly towards foreigners. At first meeting they are likely to be quite formal – a handshake is appropriate, a hug is not. Likewise, extreme chattiness is viewed by many Finns with surprise or even suspicion – remember that silence is a virtue here.

The rules when visiting a Finnish family are quite simple: always remove your shoes when entering a home, and never refuse the offer of a sauna or cup of coffee.

You will come across many Swedish-speaking Finns along the west and south coasts of Finland. Don't mistake these people for Swedes, or assume that they are Swedophiles – that would be a faux pas not dissimilar to mistaking a Canadian for an American, or a New Zealander for an Australian.

A final tip: Finns, ever the stoic individuals, rarely drink in rounds. Buying a beer for a friend is fine, but when drinking in a group, it's wise to do as others do and pay for your own beer.

RELIGION

About 86% of Finns are Evangelical Lutherans, 1.1% are Orthodox and the remainder are unaffiliated. Minority churches, including the Roman Catholic Church, make up only a few per cent.

Early Beliefs

In the past, Finns lived in close harmony with nature and made a simple living by fishing, hunting and cultivating land. There were few gods; Finns generally preferred spirits that inhabited both *haltija* (forests) and *tonttu* (back yards). These spirits were offered gifts to keep them happy. Finns also believed that the dead wandered around, especially during festival seasons, and should be treated with great respect. The *kalmisto* (graveyard) was the place for offerings.

With the arrival of Catholicism, the animist religion was soon influenced by 'new gods' (Catholic saints), which were incorporated into the polytheistic society, although a handful of old shamans kept the old traditions alive for decades. The Church confiscated all traditional sacrifice sites around the 1230s but perpetuated their religious significance: churches were erected on traditional sacrifice sites or burial grounds.

Today's Finland still bears witness to the distant past. The Midsummer is a pagan holiday that is celebrated with bonfires, although it also commemorates St John the Baptist. Easter is a Finnish version of Halloween, with trick-or-treat-style traditions among children, who dress up for the holiday season as witches and trolls. Some of the old Finnish gods are: *Ahti* (god of waters and fish), *Ilmarinen* (god of winds and storms), *Tapio* (god of forests) and *Ukko* (god of growth, rain and thunderstorms).

Christianity

The Christian faith was brought to Finland by the Roman Catholic Bishop Henry from England, who arrived in mainland Finland from Sweden in about 1155. There were even earlier crusades to Åland, where the oldest churches in Finland are found. The Catholic Church was gradually displaced by the Reformation of Martin Luther, which reflected the rugged individualism typical of Finns.

Finland's own reformer, Mikael Agricola, also created the written Finnish language in the early 16th century. The first complete Bible in Finnish appeared in 1642. The Eastern (Greek or Russian) Orthodox Church is prominent in Eastern Finland, but there are also small *tsasounas* (chapels) in many western towns, as refugees from Soviet-annexed Karelia settled in these places after WWII. The Evangelical–Lutheran Church of Finland and the Orthodox Church are the 'official' churches and still collect taxes and register births, but about 10% of the population belong to the civil register. Some of these people opposed paying the church taxes, and many women left the Church in protest when the battle over women's priesthood was at its fiercest. There are now female priests in the Lutheran Church.

Facts for the Visitor

HIGHLIGHTS

Finland is an ideal country to visit if you enjoy outdoor pursuits. In summer the long hours of daylight provide opportunities for trekking, cycling, roller-blading, canoeing and boating, attending myriad summer festivals, or just joining the Finns enjoying the sunshine in parks and at outdoor cafés and bars. Winter brings short days but also the skiing, skating, dog-and-reindeer sledding, snowmobiling, ice fishing or catching an ice-hockey match. See the Highlights section at the beginning of each regional chapter for specific recommendations, and the Activities chapter for details on outdoor pursuits. The following offers a few ideas.

Cities & Towns

The national capital, **Helsinki**, is undoubtedly a highlight of any visit to Finland, and exploring its parks, museums, nightlife and nearby Suomenlinna Island is a must. **Tampere**, the industrial but electric 'Manchester of Finland' is perhaps the next most appealing of Finnish cities. Even outside the month-long Opera Festival, **Savonlinna** is a very pretty Lakeland town with an imposing castle, while **Lappeenranta** is an easy-going Karelian town with visa-free canal trips to Vyborg in Russia. **Kuopio** is worth a stop for its vibrant atmosphere, beautiful Lakeland scenery and king-size smoke sauna.

Further north, **Oulu** is a busy university town and home to some fast-paced techno companies. It has one of the best networks of cycling paths in the country. **Rovaniemi**, virtually at the Arctic Circle, is the capital of Lapland, home of Santa Claus and a jumping-off point for wilderness experiences in Arctic Finland.

Quite a number of towns in Finland qualify as 'medieval' – though due to rebuilding following the ravages of war and fire, few actually look their age. **Turku**, founded around 1200, is the oldest city in Finland but its oldest buildings date from the 18th century. **Porvoo** (founded 1346), World Heritage listed **Rauma** (1442), **Naantali** (1443) and **Ekenas** (1546) rank as the next oldest and all have picturesque Old Town quarters, while **Hanko** is a place to see (and stay in) late 19th-century Russian villas.

Museums & Galleries

Helsinki has several outstanding museums and galleries. **Kiasma** is the daring national museum of contemporary art, while the bulk of the national art collection is at **Ateneum**. The capital's **Mannerheim Museum**, preserving the home of Finland's great independence-era leader CGE Mannerheim, is intimate and intriguing. **Seurasaari**, near Helsinki, and **Luostarinmäki**, in Turku, are two of the best open-air, folk-history museums in the country (of which there are many).

The subterranean **Retretti** at Punkaharju, near Savonlinna, is an unusual art venue with offbeat exhibitions. For experiencing the northern culture, **Arktikum**, in Rovaniemi, and **Siida**, in Inari, are top class. **Carelicum**, in Joensuu, has the best display on the peoples and culture of Karelia, and Turku's **Forum Marinum** is the country's premier maritime museum.

Castles, Manor Houses & Churches

Olavinlinna, at Savonlinna, is the mightiest and best preserved of the northern medieval castles and is superbly set between two lakes. It's home to a world-class opera festival in July. Less imposing, but equally historic, are the castles of **Turku** and **Hämeenlinna**, each with extensive museums. Åland has the smaller **Kastelholm** castle. There are many manor houses in Finland – **Louhisaari** in Askainen is one of the most stunning.

There are churches around every corner, dominating every village in Finland. The largest wooden church is in **Kerimäki**, while the 18th-century peasant church at **Petäjävesi** is Unesco World Heritage listed. **Tampere Cathedral** is the most noteworthy example of National Romantic edifices, and imposing **Turku Cathedral** is Finland's Lutheran 'mother church'.

Winter Activities

Finland may not have the rugged mountains of Norway, but it does have some decent ski centres, particularly in Lapland. Better yet, these centres offer hundreds of kilometres of cross-country skiing trails, and some are illuminated for winter cruising. Other winter activities unique to Finland include ice-fishing, dog-sledding, reindeer-sleigh safaris, snow-mobile touring and snowshoeing.

Summer Activities

In summer, there's superb trekking in northern Finland, and many of the wilderness huts along trails are well maintained and free of charge. The Lakeland is the place to take an idyllic cruise on an old steamer ferry, or rent canoes and kayaks and explore the riverways on your own. Cycling is best in Åland, where distances are short and the scenery very pretty.

SUGGESTED ITINERARIES

Depending on the length of your stay you might like to see and do the following things:

Two Days

In Helsinki, visit Kiasma and/or Mannerheim Museum, and take a stroll down Pohjoises-planadi to the market square, then a boat trip to Suomenlinna Island. Have a drink at the famous Kappeli bar and join the locals for a night of bar-hopping. On the second day take a trip to historic Porvoo (by steamer ferry in summer).

One Week

After a day or two in Helsinki (with a possible day trip to Tallinn), either explore the eastern Lakeland towns of Savonlinna, Lappeenranta and Kuopio, or take an overnight train to Lapland (Rovaniemi) or Oulu for a couple of days. The Helsinki–Savonlinna–Kuopio–Rovaniemi–Helsinki route is a good option.

Two Weeks

Spend a few days in Helsinki, then visit Turku and Tampere, then move on to Savonlinna and the beautiful eastern Lakeland. After this either go up to Lapland, to Rovaniemi or perhaps as far as Inari. You could also incorporate a summer festival or two, a trip into North Karelia (Ilomantsi or Lake Pielinen) or perhaps a couple of days cycling on the Åland islands.

One Month

With a month to spare (and a healthy bank balance) you can cover practically all major regions, and include a bicycle tour in Åland, or a trek in Lapland or North Karelia. If you're travelling in summer, you should factor in some festivals – jazz in Pori, Kaustinen Folk Festival or opera in Savonlinna; see the boxed text 'Following the Festivals' later in this chapter for more information.

PLANNING
When to Go

The tourist season in southern Finland and the Lakeland is from early June to the end of August. This is when all attractions, hostels and camping grounds are open, steamboats and ferries ply the lakes and rivers, and festivals are in full swing. For Finns, the holiday season generally kicks off after Midsummer in late June. This is the time of long, light nights, when Finland doesn't seem to sleep.

The tourist season in northern Finland, including Lapland, is different. Mosquitoes can be unbearably annoying in July, but September is delightful with its *ruska* (autumn) colours. October and February/March are good times to visit Lapland to view the aurora borealis (northern lights) and enjoy winter activities such as skiing and dog-sledding. The Christmas holiday period is also prime time in Lapland – after all, this is the 'official' home of Santa Claus.

Helsinki is a year-round destination but it has a unique tourist season – in July locals desert the city for their summer cottages, and many businesses are closed. This is a great time for tourists to visit though. The weather is fine, the markets bustling, and cafés and bars set up their outdoor tables. Winter in Helsinki is less appealing – although the student nightlife is in full swing, the maritime climate creates slushy, grey snow underfoot, and some tourist sights are shut.

Maps

Almost all local tourist offices offer free city and regional maps that are adequate for finding your way around. Trekking, canoeing and road maps are available from **Karttakeskus** (☎ 020-445 5911, fax 445 5929; Unioninkatu 32, 00100 Helsinki). This company produces and sells the largest variety of Finnish maps, and will also ship maps abroad.

Karttakeskus' 1:800,000 AT road map *(Autoilijan Tiekartta)* of the entire country is sufficient for most basic road travel. There is also a series of 19 GT road maps at a scale of 1:200,000. These maps are very clear and show practically all the places that you might be interested in, including hostels and wilderness huts. For extensive driving you're best off with the GT road atlas (€42), updated annually.

Karttakeskus has produced approximately 40 titles for trekking areas, including walking-track presentations of town areas (in 1:25,000 to 1:50,000 scale) and national park maps (1:50,000 to 1:100,000). For the highest level of detail and accuracy, there are 1:20,000 maps available as well. Prices

Interpreting Maps

Here is a list of common Finnish words, some of which will appear as word endings on maps or street signs.

Finnish	English
asema	station
järvi, selkä	lake
joki	river
katu	street
kauppahalli	indoor market
kauppatori	market square
kirkko	church
koski	rapids
kylä	village
lahti	bay
linna	castle
lääni	province
maa	land, area
mäki	hill
museo	museum
niemi	cape
pankki	bank
puisto	park
ranta	shore
saari, salo	island
salmi	strait
suo	swamp, marshland
taival	rail, track
talo	house
tie	road
tori	market or square
tunturi	fell
vuori	mountain
yliopisto	university

are around €12. Maps for lakes and waterways are also available.

What to Bring

You can buy virtually anything you need in Finland, but bring what you can from home to avoid the relatively high retail prices of Finnish shops.

Sheets (or a sleeping sheet) and a pillowcase are essential if you plan to stay in hostels or cabins. Most hostels don't provide linen, so if you don't have your own you'll need to hire it at a cost of €3 to €5 a night, which really adds up. If you plan to camp or trek, bring a sleeping bag, a tent and the regular trekking kit.

Finns are very casual about clothing, so you'll rarely encounter strict dress codes at nightspots or restaurants. Even in summer you should pack warm clothes and a waterproof and windproof jacket, particularly if visiting Lapland. Layers work best.

If you travel in winter (which can last to the end of April), you'll need all of the above plus lined boots and mittens, a woollen cap and either an overcoat, quilted jacket, thermal suit or parka.

Many travellers find it difficult to sleep in summer when it's broad daylight outside, and Finnish hotel curtains and blinds aren't always the best. It's worth bringing an eye mask and ear plugs to get you through the night.

TOURIST OFFICES
Local Tourist Offices

All major Finnish towns have a tourist office with helpful, English-speaking staff, English-language brochures and excellent free maps. In summer, these offices are often staffed by enthusiastic university students on vacation. Most offices publish a miniguide to their town or region and all have a website (which is usually w www.nameoftown.fi). Additionally, many offices stockpile brochures, maps and advice for every single other town and region in Finland.

The main office of the national tourist information organisation, the **Finnish Tourist Board** (*Matkailun Edistämiskeskus or MEK;* ☎ 09-417 6911, fax 04176 9333; w *www.mek .fi*), is in Helsinki.

Tourist Offices Abroad

The Finnish Tourist Board maintains offices in numerous countries. These offices can assist you with tourist promotional material and inquiries, but are generally not offices where you can walk in for information:

Denmark (☎ 3313 1362, e findland.dk@mek.fi) Finlands Turistbureau, Nyhavn 43A, 1051 Copenhagen K
Estonia (☎ 06-997 010, e mek.tal@mek.fi) Soome Turismiarendamise, Uus 32, 10111 Tallinn
France (☎ 01 55 17 42 70, e finland@mek.fi) Office National du Tourisme de Finlande, BP 283, 75425 Paris Cedex 09
Germany (☎ 069-5007 0157, fax 724 1725, e finnland.info@mek.fi) Finnische Zentrale für Tourismus, Lessingstrasse 5, 60325 Frankfurt

Italy (☎ 02-6963 3578, |e| finlandia.info@mek.fi)
Ente Nazionale Finlandese per il Turismo,
Via Arco 4, 20121 Milan
Japan (☎ 03-3501 5207, fax 3580 9205,
|e| mek.tyo@mek.fi) Finnish Tourist Board,
Imperial Hotel, Room 505, 1-1-1 Uchisaiwai-
choi, Chiyoda-ku, Tokyo 100-0011
Netherlands (☎ 020-201 3489, |e| finland
.nl@mek.fi) Fins Nationaal Verkeersbureau
voor de Benelux, Johannes Vermeerplein 5,
1071 DV Amsterdam
Norway (☎ 2316 2430, |e| finland.no@mek.fi)
Finlands Turistkontor, Lille Grensen 7,
0159 Oslo 1
Russia (☎ 812-326 2522, |e| mek.pie@mek.fi)
Tsentr po razvitiju turizma Finljandii,
Europa House, 1 Artillerijskaya str,
191104 St Petersburg
Spain (☎ 91-749 7745, |e| finlandia@mek.fi)
Fernando el Santo, 27-5A, 28010 Madrid
Sweden (☎ 08-587 69121, |e| finland.se@mek.fi)
Finska Turistbyrån Snickarbacken 2,
111 39 Stockholm
UK (☎ 020-7365 2512, |e| finlandinfo.lon@mek.fi)
Finnish Tourist Board, PO Box 33213,
London W6 8JX
USA (☎ 212-885 9700) Finnish Tourist Board,
655 Third Ave, New York, NY 10017

VISAS & DOCUMENTS
Passport
For most foreign visitors, a valid passport is
all that's required to enter Finland. Citizens
of EU countries (except Greece) and of
Liechtenstein, San Marino and Switzerland
may use either a national identity card or a
passport. Citizens of Denmark, Iceland,
Sweden and Norway do not need a passport
to visit Finland.

Your passport is your most important
travel document, and should remain valid
until well after your trip. If it's about to ex-
pire, renew it before you go. Most embassies
have websites where you can get information on passport applications and sometimes
download application forms – see the following Embassies & Consulates section.

Visas & Residence Permits
Most Western nationals don't need a tourist
visa for stays of less than three months.
However, all foreigners (except citizens of
Denmark, Iceland, Norway and Sweden)
need a residence permit if they wish to stay
in Finland for three months or longer. Unless
you are a citizen of the EU you will need to
apply for a residence permit *before* arriving

in Finland, through the Finnish embassy or
consulate in your home country. You will
also need to apply for a residence permit if
you plan to work in Finland, even if the term
of employment is less than three months.
Typically, residence permits are valid for one
year and allow multiple entries into Finland.
Renewals are possible. For more information
contact the nearest Finnish embassy or consulate, or the **Finnish Directorate of Immi-
gration** *(☎ 09-4765 500;* |w| *www.uvi.fi;
Panimokatu 2A, 00580 Helsinki).*

Russian & Estonian Visas All foreigners
require a visa to travel into Russia from Finland. Russian visas take about eight working days to process in Helsinki (you must
leave your passport at the embassy) so you
may want to get one before leaving home.
Helsinki tour companies specialising in
travel to Russia can usually expedite a visa
much quicker, but for a fee.

European citizens and most Western nationals don't require a visa for a short stay
in Estonia, but citizens of Canada and South
Africa do (a valid visa for Latvia or Lithuania is sufficient). Check the Estonian For-
eign Ministry website (|w| www.vm.ee).

Travel Insurance
A travel-insurance policy to cover theft, loss
and medical problems is a good idea. Some
policies offer a range of medical-expense options; the higher ones are chiefly for countries such as the USA, which have extremely
high medical costs. There is a wide variety of
policies available, so check the small print.

Some policies specifically exclude 'dangerous activities', which can include skiing, motorcycling, even trekking. You may
prefer a policy that pays doctors or hospitals
directly rather than you having to pay on the
spot and claim later. If you have to claim
later make sure you keep all documentation. Some policies ask you to call back (re-
verse charges) to a centre in your home
country where an immediate assessment of
your problem is made.

Driving Licence & Permits
An international licence is not required to
drive in Finland. However, you'll need the
driving licence from your home country to
bring a car into Finland, or if you plan to
rent a car – your passport alone won't do. A

green card (insurance card) is recommended but not required for visitors from most countries that subscribe to this European insurance system. Those who are from countries who do belong to the green-card plan will need to arrange for insurance on arrival. Insurance is included with car rental.

The Finnish national motoring organisation, **Autoliitto** (☎ *09-774 761;* W *www.auto liitto.fi; Hämeentie 105A, 00550 Helsinki)*, can also answer questions.

Camping Card International

Check with your local automobile association to see if it issues the Camping Card International, which is basically a camping-ground ID. These cards are also available from your local camping federation and incorporate third-party insurance for damage you may cause. Many camping grounds offer a discount if you sign in with one.

In Finland, a camping card good for one year is available on the spot at most camping grounds; the cost is €4.

Hostelling Card

If you plan to stay in youth hostels in Finland, join the International Youth Hostels Association (IYHA), also called Hostelling International (HI). It's not mandatory to be a member in Finland, but having an HI card gives you a €2.50 discount (per person) every time you check in at an HI-affiliated hostel. (Prices quoted in this book are without the membership discount.) See Accommodation later in this chapter for details about becoming a member.

Hostelling cards may also bring discounts on some ferries, rental cars, museum admissions and train tickets. There are also 'Hostelling by Bike' and 'Hostelling by Rent-A-Car' discount packages.

Student & Youth Cards

The most useful of these is the International Student Identity Card (ISIC), a plastic ID-style card with your photograph, which provides discounts on many forms of transport (including airlines, ferries and local public transport), reduced or free admission to museums and sights, and cheap meals in student cafeterias – a worthwhile way of cutting costs in expensive Finland. Because of the proliferation of fake ISIC cards, carry your home student ID or a letter from your

university as a back-up. Some airlines won't give student discounts without it.

If you're aged under 26 but not a student, you can apply for a GO25 card issued by the Federation of International Youth Travel Organisations (Fiyto), or the Euro26 card, which goes under various names in different countries. All of these cards are available through student unions, hostelling organisations or youth-oriented travel agencies. They don't automatically entitle you to discounts, and some companies and institutions refuse to recognise them altogether, but you won't find out until you flash the card.

Seniors Cards

For a small fee, European nationals aged over 60 can get a Rail Europe Senior Card as an add-on to their national rail senior pass. It entitles the holder to reduced fares in some European countries, and percentage savings vary according to the route. There are also rail passes available for travel within Scandinavia for nationals of any country who are aged over 55; inquire at your local travel agency for information. Seniors with proof of age can also receive discounts at many museums and tourist attractions.

International Health Certificate

You'll need this yellow booklet only if you're coming to Scandinavia from certain parts of Asia, Africa and South America, where outbreaks of such diseases as yellow fever have been reported.

Copies

All important documents (passport data page and visa page, credit cards, travel insurance policy, air/bus/train tickets, driving licence etc) should be photocopied before you leave home. Leave one copy with someone at home and keep another with you, separate from the originals.

There is another option for storing details of your vital travel documents before you leave – Lonely Planet's online Travel Vault. Storing details of your important documents in the vault is safer than carrying photocopies. It's the best option if you travel in a country with easy Internet access. Your password-protected travel vault is accessible online at anytime. Go to W www.ekno.lone lyplanet.com to create your own travel vault for free.

EMBASSIES & CONSULATES
Finnish Embassies & Consulates

Visas and information can be obtained at Finnish diplomatic missions, including:

Australia (☎ 02-6273 3800, W www.finland .org.au) 10 Darwin Ave, Yarralumla, ACT 2600
Canada (☎ 613-236 2389, W www.finemb.com) 55 Metcalfe St, Suite 850, Ottawa K1P 6L5
Denmark (☎ 3313 4214, W www.finamb.dk) Sankt Annae Plads 24, 1250 Copenhagen K
Estonia (☎ 610 3200, W www.finemb.ee) Kohtu 4, EE-15180 Tallinn
France (☎ 01 44 18 19 20, e sanomat.par@ formin.fi) 1 Place de Finlande, 57007 Paris
Germany (☎ 030-505030, W www.finland.de) Rauchstrasse 1, 10787 Berlin
Ireland (☎ 01-478 1344, W www.finland.ie) Russell House, Stokes Pl, St Stephen's Green, Dublin 2
Japan (☎ 03-5447 6000, W www.finland.or.jp) 3-5-39 Minami-Azabu, Minato-ku, Tokyo 106
Latvia (☎ 371-707 8800, W www.finland.lv) Kalpaka bulvāris 1, LV-1605 Rīga
Netherlands (☎ 070-346 9754, e sanomat .haa@formin.fi) Groot Hertoginnelaan 16, 2517 EG The Hague
New Zealand Honorary Consulate General: (☎ 499 4599, e cab@sglaw.co.nz) 44–52 the Terrace, Wellington; or contact the embassy in Australia
Norway (☎ 2212 4900, W www.finland.no) Thomas Heftyes gate 1, 0244 Oslo
Russia (☎ 095-787 4174, W www.finemb -moscow.fi) Kropotkinskij Pereulok 15–17, 119034 Moscow G-34
Sweden (☎ 08-676 6700, W www.finland.se) Gärdesgatan 11, 11527 Stockholm
UK (☎ 020-7838 6200, W www.finemb.org.uk) 38 Chesham Place, London SW1X 8HW
USA (☎ 202-298 5800, W www.finland.org) 3301 Massachusetts Ave NW, Washington, DC 20008

Embassies & Consulates in Finland

The following is a list of foreign government representatives in Helsinki. Use the Helsinki area telephone code (☎ 09) if calling from elsewhere.

Australia Consulate: (☎ 447 233) Museokatu 25B, Vantaa; nearest embassy is in Stockholm
Austria (☎ 171 322) Keskuskatu 1A
Belgium (☎ 170 412) Kalliolinnantie 5
Canada (☎ 171 141) Pohjoisesplanadi 25B
Denmark (☎ 684 1050) Keskuskatu 1A
Estonia (☎ 622 0288) Itäinen Puistotie 10
France (☎ 618 780) Itäinen Puistotie 13

Germany (☎ 458 580) Krogiuksentie 4
Ireland (☎ 646 006) Erottajankatu 7
Italy (☎ 681 1280) Itäinen Puistotie 4
Japan (☎ 686 0200) Eteläranta 8
Latvia (☎ 4764 7244) Armfeltintie 10
Lithuania (☎ 608 210) Rauhankatu 13A
Netherlands (☎ 228 920) Eteläsplanadi 24A
New Zealand Contact the Australian consulate
Norway (☎ 686 0180) Rehbinderintie 17
Russia (☎ 661 876) Tehtaankatu 1B
Spain (☎ 170 505) Kalliolinnantie 6
Sweden (☎ 687 7660) Pohjoisesplanadi 7B
Switzerland (☎ 649 422) Uudenmaankatu 16A
UK (☎ 2286 5100) Itäinen Puistotie 17
USA (☎ 171 931) Itäinen Puistotie 14A

Your Own Embassy

It's important to realise what your own embassy – the embassy of the country of which you are a citizen – can and can't do to help you if you get into trouble. Generally speaking, it won't be much help in emergencies if the trouble you're in is remotely your own fault. Remember that you are bound by the laws of the country you are in. Your embassy will not be sympathetic if you end up in jail after committing a crime locally, even if such actions are legal in your own country.

In genuine emergencies you might get some assistance, but only if other channels have been exhausted. For example, if you need to get home urgently, a free ticket home is exceedingly unlikely – the embassy would expect you to have insurance. If you have all your money and documents stolen, it might assist with getting a new passport, but a loan for onward travel is out of the question.

CUSTOMS

Travellers should encounter few problems with Finnish customs. Travellers arriving from outside the EU can bring duty-free goods up to the value of €175 into Finland without declaration. You can also bring in up to 16L of beer, 2L of wine and 1L of spirits, 200 cigarettes or 250g of tobacco and 50g of perfume. If you're coming from another EU country, there is no restriction on the value of gifts or purchases for your own use, except for alcohol and tobacco products. Travellers can import duty-free up to 32L of beer and 5L of wine or 1L of spirits, 300 cigarettes or 400g of tobacco.

Although technically part of the EU, arriving on the Åland islands from anywhere (eg, Sweden) carries the same import restrictions as arriving from a non-EU country. Check the latest situation on the Finnish customs website w www.tulli.fi, at the border crossing or on an international ferry.

MONEY
Currency
The Finnish markka was officially replaced by the euro in 2001. Euro notes come in five, 10, 20, 100 and 500 denominations and coins in five, 10, 20, 50 cents and €1 and €2. The conversion has been complete, if a little unpopular at first – you won't find anything priced in markka anymore.

Swedish krona (including coins) are accepted on Åland and in western Lapland, and Norwegian krona can be used in areas near the Norwegian border in northern Lapland.

Exchange Rates
At the time of publication the following exchange rates prevailed:

country	unit		euro
Australia	A$1	=	€0.55
Canada	C$1	=	€0.65
Denmark	Dkr1	=	€0.13
Estonia	1EEK	=	€0.06
Norway	Nkr1	=	€0.13
Sweden	Skr1	=	€0.11
UK	UK£1	=	€1.56
USA	US$1	=	€1.02

Exchanging Money
The best way to carry and obtain local currency is by using an ATM or credit card, just as most Finns do. Another option is travellers cheques and cash, which can be exchanged at Finland's three main banks, Sampo, Osuuspankki and Nordea. In the big cities independent exchange facilities such as Forex usually offer better rates and charge smaller fees or commissions than banks. Finnish post offices also provide banking services and tend to keep longer hours than banks, particularly in remote villages. Airports and international ferries have exchange facilities.

Cash Nothing beats cash for convenience – or risk. If you lose it, it's gone forever and very few travel insurers will come to your rescue. Those that will, limit the amount paid out to about US$300.

Although carrying thousands of euros around in your pocket is clearly unwise, it makes sense to carry a daily amount of cash in local currency, for smaller purchases and for convenience. Some extra cash (say €100) hidden away in your luggage for an emergency is also a good idea. International ferries are good places to use up the last of your euros, as they generally accept the currency of both port cities.

Travellers Cheques The exchange rate for travellers cheques is slightly better than for cash, and travellers cheques offer greater protection from theft. American Express, Visa and Thomas Cook cheques are widely accepted and have efficient replacement policies for stolen and lost cheques. Most banks in Finland will exchange travellers cheques but charge commission fees of up to €7. Exchange offices, such as Forex and Tavex in Helsinki, Turku, Tampere and other big cities, exchange cheques quickly at good rates for a flat €2 fee. Overall, the fees you pay buying and exchanging travellers cheques are comparable to those you pay for using credit and debit cards. There are no American Express offices that change travellers cheques in Finland. Thomas Cook, represented by Travelex, has offices in Helsinki and Turku.

Keeping a record of the cheque numbers and those you have used is vital when it comes to replacing lost travellers cheques. You should keep this separate from the cheques themselves.

Cheques denominated in US dollars or pounds sterling are easily cashed but it makes sense to buy your cheques in euros so the currency doesn't have to be converted when you cash them in Finland.

ATMs & Credit Cards Finns are dedicated users of plastic. Credit cards are accepted and used virtually everywhere – purchasing a beer in a bar with a credit card is not out of the question and it's a common way to pay for accommodation and restaurant meals.

Finns conduct most of their banking transactions using ATMs ('Otto') and they can be found on seemingly every corner in cities, and even in small villages. Finnish ATMs accept foreign bank cards with Cirrus, EC, Eurocard, Visa, MasterCard and Plus symbols. Withdrawals using a foreign ATM incur a transaction fee (usually around US$2, but contact your home bank for details) so it makes good sense to withdraw a reasonable amount each time. However, the exchange rate is usually better than that offered for travellers cheques or cash exchanges.

Carrying a debit card (for use in ATMs) and a credit card will cover you for most situations and provide a backup if you lose one, or forget your PIN. Keep a copy of the international number to call if your cards are lost or stolen. Credit cards such as MasterCard and Visa are accepted at most hotels, hostels, restaurants, shops and department stores, and you'll need one if you want to hire a car.

International Transfers If you run out of money you can instruct your bank back home to send you a draft. Make sure you specify the city, the bank and the branch to which you want your money directed, or ask your home bank to tell you where a suitable one is, and ensure you get the details correct.

The whole procedure will be easier if you've authorised someone back home to access your account. Also, a transfer to a bank in a remote village in Lapland is obviously going to be more difficult than to the head office in Helsinki.

Money sent by telegraphic transfer (which typically costs from US$40) should reach you within a week; by mail, allow at least two weeks.

You can also transfer money quickly through Western Union, Moneygram (formerly American Express) or Thomas Cook.

Costs

Finland has a reputation for being an expensive country – a decade ago it was regarded as being the world's most expensive to visit – but times have changed. Travel in Finland is cheaper than Sweden or Norway and comparable to most of Western Europe. Your costs will depend on how you travel, and where to – if you stick to the cities like Helsinki and Tampere (and enjoy everything they have), costs will be higher than if you travel to small towns and the countryside. If you move around a lot, you will spend more than if you stay in one place.

At rock bottom budget travel, if you camp or stay in hostel dorms, prepare your own meals and stay away from alcohol, you might get by on less than €30 a day. If you stay in guesthouses (or private rooms in hostels) and eat at cheap restaurants, expect to pay about €60 a day if you're travelling alone or €50 a day if you have a travel partner.

To this you need to factor in museum admission fees, entertainment, transportation and incidentals. Trains are cheaper than buses (unlike in Sweden). Petrol is expensive (€1 to €1.20 for 1L of unleaded). A night on the town can wreck your budget, thanks to the high tax on alcohol, but alcohol bought at supermarkets or Alko stores (state network of stores selling alcohol) is relatively cheap. To travel comfortably in Finland, see a range of sights, get around by bus or train and enjoy a few nights out each week, a reasonable budget would be €80 to €100 a day.

Students with valid ID and seniors can receive substantial discounts on museum admission prices quoted in this book, as well as on transportation (including ferries) – if you fit the description, always ask.

Tipping & Bargaining

Tipping is not is an essential part of the culture and Finns generally don't do it, although in cities like Helsinki, Tampere and Turku, hospitality staff at decent restaurants will expect it. You will pay service charges in restaurants as percentages; these are generally included in the quoted menu price. You might tell the taxi driver to *'pidä loput'* ('keep the change'). Doormen at fancy clubs and restaurants may also expect a small tip, but this often comes as a mandatory payment in the form of a 'coat charge'.

Bargaining is not common in Finland, except at markets or when purchasing second-hand goods.

Taxes & Refunds

The value-added tax (VAT) of 22% is included in marked prices but may be deducted if you post goods from the point of sale. Alternatively, at stores showing the 'Tax Free for Tourists' sign, foreign visitors who are not EU citizens can get a 12% to 16% refund on items priced over €40. Present the tax-refund 'cheque' to the refund window at your departure point from the EU (eg, airport transit halls, aboard international ferries, at overland border crossings). For more information on VAT refunds contact **Europe Tax-Free Shopping Finland Oy** (☎ 09-6132 9600, fax 6132 9675; PO Box 460, 00101 Helsinki).

The 22% tax also applies to alcohol, whether it is bought at a pub or in a store.

POST & COMMUNICATIONS
Post

Stamps can be bought at bus or train stations and R-kiosk newsstands as well as at the *posti* (post office). Post offices sell packing material of various sizes.

Postcards and letters weighing up to 20g cost €0.60 to anywhere in the world (including within Finland) by *lentoposti* (air mail).

Letters posted before 5pm Monday to Friday will reach their destination the next working day. Letters to Scandinavia take a few days, to Australia less than a week, to North America almost two weeks.

Poste restante is located at main post offices in cities. Postcodes in Finland are five-digit numbers that follow this logic: the first two numbers indicate towns and areas, the next two identify the post office in the town or area, and the last number is always 0, except when you are sending mail to a post office box or poste restante, in which case the last number is 1. The main post office is always 10 in all large towns, so the postcode for the main post office in Helsinki is 00101, for Turku 20101, for Tampere 33101, for Savonlinna 57101, for Vaasa 65101 and for Rovaniemi 96101.

International parcel post is expensive in Finland (almost twice the price of sending from Sweden).

Telephone

Public telephones are reasonably common in Finland, although the high level of mobile phone usage is beginning to make them redundant. The vast majority accept plastic Telecards or credit cards, but a few older public phones accept coins. Phonecards come in denominations costing €5, €10 or €20 and can be purchased at post offices, shops and R-kioski newsstands. There are several different pay telephone networks in Finland, and in Turku some of the public telephones may only accept a local phonecard that is completely useless elsewhere in Finland. Sonera has the widest network of cardphones.

A short call to a local number will cost at least €0.50. International calls are expensive, but are cheapest between 10pm and 8am Monday to Friday and all day Saturday and Sunday. A three-minute call to the USA during peak time costs about €4. For national directory assistance dial ☎ 020 202, international ☎ 020 208.

Finland has 13 area codes, each starting with a zero. Include the zero when dialling from one area code to another within Finland, but omit it if you are calling from abroad. The country code for calling Finland from abroad is ☎ 358.

To make international calls from Finland you first need to dial an international access code (☎ 999, 990, 994 or 00), then the country code for the country you're calling followed by the telephone number. Access code ☎ 994 usually offers the lowest rates.

Ekno Communications Service Lonely Planet's ekno global communication service provides low-cost international calls – for local calls you're usually better off with a local phonecard. Ekno also offers free messaging services, email, travel information and an online travel vault, where you can securely store all your important documents. You can join online at ☒ www.ekno.lonelyplanet.com, where you will find the local-access numbers for the 24-hour customer-service centre. The toll-free access numbers for Finland are ☎ 0800 112 010 and ☎ 0800 114 009. Once you have joined, always check the ekno website for the latest access numbers for each country and updates on new features.

Mobile Phones Finland has one of the world's highest rates of mobile-phone usage, which is hardly surprising since Nokia is Finnish. Getting hooked up to the mobile phone network is easy with the prepaid system using either **Sonera** (☒ www.sonera.fi) or **Telia** (☒ www.telia.fi) – the two companies merged in 2002. You can bring your own phone and simply buy a starter kit from a phone shop or any R-kiosk. It costs €50 for a SIM card including €40 worth of call time, then you can buy recharge cards from the same outlets. Prepaid calls cost around €0.70 a minute. The main company offering connection to the GSM network in Finland is Radiolinja, but unless you're planning on a long-term stay, it's cheaper and easier to use the prepaid system – many Finns prefer to do so.

Fax Faxes can be sent from local telephone offices (usually adjacent to the post office in big cities). The going rate tends to be €2 for the first page and €1 for each additional page for domestic faxes, and €5/3 for international faxes – certainly not a cheap method of communication. Tourist offices, hotels and some hostels will also send and receive faxes for a fee.

Email & Internet Access

The good news is Internet access is free and widely available in Finland. Every public library in every town has at least one Internet terminal (big libraries have up to a dozen) that can be used free of charge. The downside is you may have to book a slot (up to an hour) in advance, although many libraries now have one or two terminals that allow 15 minutes' use on a first-come-first-served basis – just enough time to check and respond to email. You're also restricted by library opening hours, which vary but are typically Monday to Friday only.

Many tourist offices have an Internet terminal that you can use for free (usually 15 minutes), as do a handful of businesses such as cafés in larger cities. Coin-operated Internet terminals exist in some hostels and R-kiosks in Helsinki. Because of this free access, dedicated Internet cafés are not common in Finland, but you can find a few in Helsinki, Turku, Tampere and a few other towns. They charge €3 to €5 an hour. Check at W www.netcafeguide.com for a list.

If you have one of the free, Web-based email accounts such as those offered by **ekno** (W www.ekno.com), **Hotmail** (W www.hotmail.com) or **Yahoo!** (W www.yahoo.com) you will be able to send and receive email on the road without trouble.

Portable Computers Travelling with a portable computer is a great way to stay in touch with home, but unless you know what you're doing it's fraught with potential problems. If you plan to carry your notebook or palmtop computer with you, remember the power-supply voltage in the countries you visit may vary from that at home, risking damage to your equipment. The best investment is a universal AC adaptor for your appliance, which will enable you to plug it in anywhere without frying the innards. You'll need a plug adapter for each country you visit (often easiest to buy at home).

Also, your PC-card modem may or may not work once you leave your home country – and you won't know for sure until you try. The safest option is to buy a reputable 'global' modem before you leave home, or buy a local PC-card modem if you're spending an extended time in any one country. Keep in mind that the telephone socket in each country you visit will probably be different from that at home, so ensure that you have at least a US RJ-11 telephone adapter that works with your modem. You can almost always find an adapter that will convert from RJ-11 to the local variety.

Once you've dealt with the hardware, you'll need to worry about local dial-up numbers. Major Internet service providers such as **AOL** (W www.aol.com), **CompuServe** (W www.compuserve.com) and **IBM Net** (W www.ibm.com) have dial-in nodes throughout Europe; it's best to download a list of the dial-in numbers before you leave home. See the websites W www.teleadapt.com or W www.warrior.com for more information on travelling with a portable computer.

DIGITAL RESOURCES

The World Wide Web is a rich resource for travellers. You can research your trip, hunt down bargain air fares, book hotels, check on weather conditions or chat with locals and other travellers about the best places to visit (or avoid!).

There's no better place to start your Web explorations than W www.lonelyplanet.com. Here you'll find succinct summaries on travelling to most places on earth, postcards from other travellers and the Thorn Tree bulletin board, where you can ask questions before you go or dispense advice when you get back. You can also find travel news and updates to many of our most popular guidebooks, and the subwwway section links you to the most useful travel resources elsewhere on the Web.

As you'll soon come to realise, Finland has more websites per capita than any other country – virtually all of the city tourist offices have them, and so, it seems, does every other person, place and thing. In most cases, if you want to find destination information a simply type in 'www.nameoftown.fi' (eg, 'www.tampere.fi'). Most tourist-related sites have English and Swedish translations but they may not be complete.

A few good websites to start with include the **Finnish Tourist Board** (MEK; W www.mek.fi), **Finnish Youth Hostel Association**

(SRM; W www.srmnet.org), **Forest and Park Service** (Metsähallitus; W www.metsa.fi) and **Helsinki city tourist office** (W www.hel.fi). **Virtual Finland** (W virtual.finland.fi) is an excellent website maintained by the Finnish Ministry of Foreign Affairs. The 'international edition' website (W www.helsink-hs.net) of Helsinki Sanomat, Finland's leading daily newspaper, is a excellent resource for daily news stories in English and has good links

Finnish websites usually offer an English-language translation page or pages.

BOOKS

Most books are published in different editions by different publishers in different countries. As a result, a book might be a hardcover rarity in one country while it's readily available in paperback in another. Fortunately, bookshops and libraries search by title or author, so your local bookshop or library is best placed to advise you on the availability of the following recommendations.

Guidebooks

For a detailed treatment of languages in the region, see Lonely Planet's *Scandinavian Europe phrasebook*.

Facts about Finland (published by Otava, Helsinki) contains plenty of background information on the history, economy and society of Finland, written by Finns. This book is available in Helsinki in several languages.

History & Politics

Finnish history is constantly unfolding, especially with the opening of former president UK Kekkonen's archives, and of Russian archives from the Soviet Union era.

For a very readable history, see the paperback *A Short History of Finland* (1998) by Fred Singleton.

Finland in the New Europe (1998) is by Max Jakobson, a leading scholar of European history, a diplomat and a Finn. *Finland at Peace and War* by HM Tillotson and *Let Us Be Finns: Essays on History* by Matti Klinge are also of note.

Finland: Myth and Reality by Max Jakobson deals with postwar history. *Blood, Sweat and Bears* (1990) by Lasse Lehtinen is a parody of a war novel and deals with Soviet relations.

General

A good introduction to the Sami people and the Sapmi region is found in the EU's European Languages series (No 5), titled *The Sami: The Indigenous People of Northernmost Europe*.

The Kalevala – Poems of the Kaleva District compiled by Elias Lönnrot (1997) is the national folk epic and provides insight into the country and its people.

English-language translations of the works of notable Finnish authors – such as *The Egyptian* and *The Dark Angel* by Mika Waltari, and *The Unknown Soldier* by Väinö Linna – are produced by WSOY publishing company and are available within Finland.

NEWSPAPERS & MAGAZINES

The *Helsingin Sanomat*, the largest daily in Finland, doesn't have a word in English. Some local papers regularly publish an English-language summary of international and local news, but it may take a while to find these columns inside the paper.

English-language newspapers and magazines such as the *International Herald Tribune*, the *European* and the *Economist* are available at R-kioski newsstands and at train stations in big cities and major tourist hubs (eg, Helsinki, Turku, Tampere, Savonlinna, Oulu and Rovaniemi) but they are outrageously expensive – as much as €5. Public libraries and newspaper reading rooms in these cities may also keep some copies.

The weekly publications *Keltainen pörssi* and *Palsta* are the best sources for ads for used cars and bicycles.

RADIO & TV

There are four national (noncommercial) radio stations. A summary of world news is broadcast in English daily at 10.55pm on the national radio stations YLE 3 and YLE 4. In Helsinki, Capital FM (FM 103.7Mhz) broadcasts English programmes such as BBC World News, Voice of America and Radio Australia. Radio Mafia, the popular youth channel, plays pop music and a wide variety of 'world music'. Visit W www.yle.fi/rfinland for more information on Finnish radio stations offering programming in English.

The two national television networks, TV1 and TV2, broadcast British and US programmes in English with Finnish and Swedish subtitles. Hotels usually offer cable satellite channels such as the NBC Super Channel, MTV, CNN, BBC World and EuroSport.

VIDEO SYSTEMS

Finland uses the VHS-PAL 525 system. V-8 videos are not commonly available in Finland.

PHOTOGRAPHY & VIDEO

Finland's seasonal extremes – snow and very little sunlight in winter, followed by almost continuous daylight in summer – can pose some challenges for the inexperienced photographer. In particular, the risk of underexposure is great when photographing snowy landscapes – you should know how your camera works, and whether you'll need to correct for this.

Print and slide film is readily available in Finnish cities, and film processing is speedy, fairly cheap and of high quality. A roll of standard 36-exposure print film costs around €6.50 and 36-exposure slide film costs €10. Anttila department stores generally offer good prices on film.

TIME

Finnish time is two hours ahead of GMT/UTC in winter. When it's noon in Finland it's 2am in Los Angeles, 5am in New York, 10am in London, 8pm in Sydney and 11am in Sweden and Western Europe. Daylight Saving Time applies from late March or early April to the end of October, when clocks go forward one hour (summertime).

ELECTRICITY

The electric current is 220V AC, 50Hz, and plugs are of the standard northern European type with two round pins that require no switch.

WEIGHTS & MEASURES

Finland uses the metric system (see the conversion table at the back of this book). Decimals are indicated by commas.

LAUNDRY

Laundrettes are thin on the ground in Finland. Check the local telephone book – they are listed as *Pesuloita*. *Itsepalvelupesula* denotes self-service laundrettes.

The best options for travellers are the self-service laundry facilities at hostels and camping grounds. You might want to bring a universal sink plug, a length of clothesline and some soap powder so you can do your washing manually, in a pinch. Hotels typically offer laundry and dry-cleaning services, but you'll pay around €10 and probably won't see your clothes again for 24 hours.

TOILETS

Finnish bus and train stations have some of the most expensive toilets in the world, charging €1 or €2 for the privilege of using their potties. Other public facilities – such as the 'French toilet' kiosks in city centres – also charge a fee. Public toilets are always very clean.

By law, all restaurants and cafés must have a public toilet and it must be accessible to a person using a wheelchair. There are also free toilets in public libraries, department stores and hotels.

HEALTH

Health-wise, there's very little to worry about while travelling in Finland, unless you engage in endurance tests in the wilderness. Your main risks are likely to be viral infections in winter, sunburn and mosquito bites in summer, plus typical travellers complaints like foot blisters and an upset stomach at any time.

A healthy trip depends on your predeparture preparations and fitness, your day-to-day health care while travelling, and how you handle any medical problem or emergency that does develop.

Predeparture Planning

If you're reasonably fit, the only things you should organise before departure are a visit to your dentist to get your teeth in order, and travel insurance with good medical cover (see the Visas & Documents section earlier).

No special immunisations are required for entry into Finland. However, to put your mind at ease you might also ensure that your normal childhood vaccines (against measles, mumps, rubella, diphtheria, tetanus and polio) are up to date and/or you are still showing immunity, particularly if you're planning a lengthy trip.

If you wear glasses bring your prescription and a spare pair – new spectacles are not cheap in Finland.

Antibiotics are quite expensive in Finland and available only with a doctor's prescription. If you require a particular medication take an adequate supply as it may not be available locally. Bring the part of the packaging that shows the generic name, rather than the brand, as this will make getting replacements easier. To avoid any problems, carry a legible prescription or letter from your doctor to show that you legally use the medication.

Health Insurance Make sure that you have adequate health insurance. See Travel Insurance under Visas & Documents earlier in this chapter.

Medical Problems & Treatment

Apteekki (local pharmacies) – of which there are many in all Finnish cities and towns – and neighbourhood health care centres are good places to visit if you have a minor medical problem and can explain what it is. Visitors whose home countries have reciprocal medical-care agreements with Finland and who can produce a passport (or sickness insurance card or E111 form for those from EU countries) are charged the same as Finns for medical assistance: €8 to visit a doctor, €21 per day for hospitalisation. Those from other countries are charged the full cost of treatment. Tourist offices and hotels can put you in touch with a doctor or dentist; in Helsinki your embassy will probably know one who speaks your language.

Basic Rules

Water You can drink the tap water in all Finnish towns and villages, although it is not always as pure as a mountain spring.

Always be wary of drinking natural water; a recent survey ranked Finland's lakes and rivers among some of the most polluted in Europe. A burbling stream may look crystal clear and very inviting, but there may be pulp factories, people or sheep lurking upstream.

If you are planning extended hikes where you have to rely on natural water it may be useful to know about water purification. The simplest way to do this is to boil water thoroughly. Technically this means boiling for 10 minutes, something that happens very rarely. You can also use a water filter or treat the water chemically. Flavoured powder will disguise the taste of treated

water and is a good idea if you are travelling with children.

Many trekkers in the wilderness of eastern Lapland claim that springs there are safe to drink from without purifying – use your own best judgment as to whether you'd care to follow that advice.

Food If a place looks clean and well run, then the food is probably safe. In general, places that are packed with locals or travellers will be fine. Be careful with food that has been cooked and left to go cold – as is the case with some Finnish buffets.

Mushroom and berry-picking is a favourite pastime in this part of the world, but make sure you don't eat any that haven't been positively identified as safe.

Nutrition If your food is poor or limited in availability, if you're travelling hard and fast and therefore missing meals or if you simply lose your appetite, you can soon start to lose weight and place your health at risk. Make sure your diet is well balanced – and consider taking vitamin and iron pills if it isn't.

During treks and hot spells make sure you drink enough – don't rely on thirst to indicate when you should drink. Not needing to urinate or very dark yellow urine are danger signs. Always carry a water bottle with you on long treks.

Everyday Health Normal body temperature is up to 37°C (98.6°F); more than 2°C (4°F) higher indicates a high fever. The normal adult pulse rate is 60 to 100 per minute (children 80 to 100, babies 100 to 140). As a general rule the pulse rate increases about 20 beats per minute for each 1°C (2°F) rise in fever.

Respiration (breathing) rate is also an indicator of illness. Count the number of breaths per minute: between 12 and 20 is normal for adults and older children (up to 30 for younger children, 40 for babies). People with a high fever or serious respiratory illness breathe more quickly than normal. More than 40 shallow breaths a minute may indicate pneumonia.

Environmental Hazards

Hypothermia If you are trekking in Lapland or simply staying outdoors for long periods, particularly in winter, be prepared for the cold. In fact, if you are out walking or hitching, be prepared for cold, wet or windy conditions even in summer.

Hypothermia occurs when the body loses heat faster than it can produce it and the core temperature of the body falls. It is surprisingly easy to progress from very cold to dangerously cold due to a combination of wind, wet clothing, fatigue and hunger, even if the air temperature is above freezing. It is best to dress in layers; silk, wool and some of the new artificial fibres are all good insulating materials. A hat is important, as a lot of heat is lost through the head. A strong, waterproof outer layer (and a 'space' blanket for emergencies) is essential. Carry basic supplies, including food containing simple sugars to generate heat quickly and fluid to drink.

Symptoms of hypothermia are exhaustion, numb skin (particularly toes and fingers), shivering, slurred speech, irrational or violent behaviour, lethargy, stumbling, dizzy spells, muscle cramps and violent bursts of energy. Irrationality may take the form of sufferers claiming they are warm and trying to take off their clothes.

To treat mild hypothermia, first get the person out of the wind and/or rain, remove their clothing if it's wet and replace it with dry, warm clothing. Give them hot liquids – not alcohol – and some high-kilojoule, easily digestible food. Do not rub victims, but instead allow them to slowly warm themselves. This should be enough to treat the early stages of hypothermia. The early recognition and treatment of mild hypothermia is the only way to prevent severe hypothermia, which is a critical condition.

Sunburn You can get sunburnt surprisingly quickly, even through cloud. Use a sunscreen, hat and barrier cream for your nose and lips. Calamine lotion or Stingose are good for mild sunburn. Protect your eyes with good-quality sunglasses, particularly if you are going near water, sand or snow.

Fungal Infections Hot-weather fungal infections are most likely to occur on the scalp, between the toes or fingers (athlete's foot), in the groin (jock itch or crotch rot) and on the body (ringworm). You get ringworm (which is a fungal infection, not a worm) from infected animals or by walking in damp areas, like the shower floors in Finnish saunas.

To prevent fungal infections wear loose, comfortable clothes, avoid synthetic fibres, wash frequently and dry carefully. If you do get an infection, wash the infected area daily with a disinfectant or medicated soap and water, and rinse and dry well. Apply an antifungal powder like the widely available Tinaderm. Try to expose the infected area to air or sunlight as much as possible and wash all towels and underwear in hot water as well as changing them often.

Infectious Diseases

Diarrhoea Simple things like a change of water, food or climate can all cause a mild bout of diarrhoea, but a few rushed toilet trips with no other symptoms is not indicative of a major problem.

Dehydration is the main danger with any diarrhoea, particularly in children or the elderly as dehydration can occur quite quickly. Under all circumstances *fluid replacement* (at least equal to the volume being lost) is the most important thing to remember. Weak black tea with a little sugar, soda water, or soft drinks allowed to go flat and diluted 50% with clean water are all good.

Sexually Transmitted Diseases Gonorrhoea, herpes and syphilis are among these diseases; sores, blisters or rashes around the genitals, discharges or pain when urinating are common symptoms. In some STDs, such as wart virus or chlamydia, symptoms may be less marked or not observed at all, especially in women. Syphilis symptoms eventually disappear completely but the disease continues and can cause severe problems in later years. While abstinence from sexual contact is the only 100% effective prevention, using condoms is also effective. The treatment of gonorrhoea and syphilis is with antibiotics. The different STDs each require specific antibiotics. There is no cure for herpes or AIDS.

HIV & AIDS The Human Immunodeficiency Virus (HIV) develops into Acquired Immune Deficiency Syndrome (AIDS), which is a fatal disease. HIV is a major problem in many countries. Any exposure to blood, blood products or body fluids may put the individual at risk. The disease is often transmitted through sexual contact or dirty needles – vaccinations, acupuncture, tattooing and body piercing can be potentially as dangerous as intravenous drug use. HIV/AIDS can also be spread through infected blood transfusions; some developing countries cannot afford to screen blood used for transfusions.

If you do need an injection, ask to see the syringe unwrapped in front of you, or take a needle and syringe pack with you. Fear of HIV infection should never preclude treatment for serious medical conditions.

For assistance while in Finland contact the **AIDS Information & Support Centre** (☎ 09-665 081; Linnankatu 2B, 00160 Helsinki).

Cuts, Bites & Stings

Mosquitoes In Finland, the mosquito breeding season is very short (about six weeks in July/August), but the mosquitoes make good use of the time. They are a major nuisance in most parts of Finland, and those in Lapland are particularly large, fierce and persistent.

The best way to handle the mosquito problem is through prevention. From June to August, travellers are advised to wear light-coloured clothing, particularly long pants and long sleeved shirts, and avoid highly scented perfumes or aftershave. Use Ohvi (mosquito repellent) liberally; the 'Off' brand seems to be particularly effective. If you have a mosquito net, use this too. There are net hats available in sports shops; if you don't mind how absurd they look these are useful for treks and outdoor activities.

When all else fails, look for Etono, a concentrated antihistamine salve that is sold in stick form, for relief from mosquito bites. It is available at most pharmacies.

Other Insect Bites & Stings Bee and wasp stings are usually painful rather than dangerous. However in people who are allergic to them severe breathing difficulties may occur and require urgent medical care. Calamine lotion or Stingose spray will give relief and ice packs will reduce the pain and swelling.

Cuts & Scratches Wash well and treat any cut with an antiseptic such as povidone-iodine. Where possible avoid bandages and Band-Aids, which can keep wounds wet.

Ticks You should always check all over your body if you have been walking through a potentially tick-infested area – this would include rural areas of the Åland islands – as ticks can cause skin infections and other more serious diseases. If a tick is found attached, press down around the tick's head with tweezers, grab the head and gently pull upwards. Avoid pulling the rear of the body as this may squeeze the tick's gut contents through the attached mouth parts into the skin, increasing the risk of infection and disease. Smearing chemicals on the tick will not make it let go and is not recommended.

Snakes The only venomous snake in Finland is the common viper, and human deaths from viper bites are extremely rare. All snakes hibernate from autumn to spring. To minimise your chances of being bitten always wear boots, socks and long trousers when walking through undergrowth where snakes may be present. Don't put your hands into holes and crevices, and be careful when collecting firewood.

Women's Health

Sexually transmitted diseases are a major cause of vaginal problems. Symptoms include a smelly discharge, painful intercourse and sometimes a burning sensation when urinating. Male sexual partners must also be treated. Medical attention should be sought and, remember, in addition to these diseases HIV or hepatitis B may also be acquired during exposure. Besides abstinence, the best thing is to practise safe sex using condoms.

Antibiotic use, synthetic underwear, sweating and contraceptive pills can lead to fungal vaginal infections when travelling in hot climates. Maintaining good personal hygiene, and wearing loose-fitting clothes and cotton underwear will help to prevent these infections. Fungal infections, characterised by a rash, itch and discharge, can be treated with a vinegar or lemon-juice douche, or with yogurt. Nystatin, miconazole or clotrimazole pessaries or vaginal cream are the usual treatment.

WOMEN TRAVELLERS

Scandinavia is one of the safest places to travel in all of Europe. Women often travel alone or in pairs around the region, which should pose no problems, but women do tend to attract more unwanted attention than men, and common sense is the best guide to dealing with potentially dangerous situations like hitchhiking, walking alone at night etc.

Solo women are particularly vulnerable to harassment at Finnish pubs – that's a scene you might want to avoid, or at least gear yourself up for plenty of unwanted attention.

Unioni Naisasialiitto Suomessa *(☎ 09-643 158; Bulevardi 11A, 00120 Helsinki)* is the national feminist organisation.

GAY & LESBIAN TRAVELLERS

Though nowhere in Finland will you find the equivalent of Copenhagen's or Stockholm's large and active gay community, it is in most respects as tolerant as other Nordic countries, and Helsinki has a lively and developing gay scene. Current information is available from the Finnish organisation for gay and lesbian equality, **Seksuaalinen tasavertaisus** *(SETA; ☎ 09-681 2580; ⓦ www.seta.fi; Hietalahdenkatu 2B 16, Helsinki)*.

The *Spartacus International Gay Guide*, published by Bruno Gmünder Verlag (Berlin), is an international directory of gay entertainment venues, but it's best used in conjunction with more up-to-date information; as elsewhere, gay venues can change with the speed of summer lightning. *Places for Women* (Ferrari Publications) is the best international guide for lesbians.

DISABLED TRAVELLERS

By law, most public and private institutions must provide ramps, lifts and special toilets for disabled persons, making Finland one of the easiest countries for travellers in wheelchairs to negotiate. Trains and city buses are also accessible by wheelchair. Some national parks offer accessible nature trails. **Rullaten Ry** *(☎ 09-805 7393; ⓦ www.rullaten.fi; Pajutie 7, Espoo)* is the Finnish disabled travellers organisation. It specialises in advice on 'friendly' hotels. You can order a booklet detailing accommodation and travel for disabled persons through its website.

If you have a physical disability, get in touch with your national support organisation – preferably the 'travel officer' if there is one. These places often have complete libraries devoted to travel, and can put you in touch with travel agencies who specialise in tours for the disabled.

The British-based **Royal Association for Disability & Rehabilitation** *(Radar; ☎ 020-7250 3222; ⓦ www.radar.org.uk; 12 City Forum, 250 City Rd, London EC1V 8AF)* publishes a useful guide titled *European Holidays & Travel: A Guide for Disabled People*, which gives a good overview of facilities available to disabled travellers in Europe (in even-numbered years) and farther afield (in odd-numbered years).

SENIOR TRAVELLERS

Senior citizens are entitled to many discounts on public transport, museum admission fees etc, provided they can show proof of their age (such as a passport). The minimum qualifying age is generally 60 or 65.

In your home country, a lower age may already entitle you to all sorts of interesting travel packages and discounts (on car hire, for instance) through organisations and travel agencies that cater for senior travellers. Start hunting at your local senior citizens advice bureau.

TRAVEL WITH CHILDREN

People with children should have no qualms about visiting Finland: it's one of the most child-friendly countries around. Domestic tourism is largely dictated by children's needs: theme parks, water parks and so on, not to mention a real live Santa Claus waiting to greet children in Lapland, at the Arctic Circle. Most Finnish hostels have special 'family' rooms, supermarkets stock everything your children need and many trains and ferries have special children's play areas. If in doubt, ask around – special needs can usually be met.

Car-rental firms have children's safety seats for hire at a nominal cost, but it is essential that you book them in advance. The same goes for highchairs and cots (cribs); they're standard in many restaurants and hotels, but numbers may be limited.

Successful travel with young children requires planning and effort. Don't try to overdo things; even for adults, packing too much into the time available can cause problems. And make sure the activities include the kids as well – balance a day at museums with a trip to one of Finland's amusement parks. Include your children in the trip planning; if they've helped to work out where you will be going, they will be much more interested when they get there. Finland's best kid-friendly theme parks are Moominworld at Naantali, Särkänniemi in Tampere, and Wasalandia and Tropiclandia in Vaasa. Lonely Planet's *Travel with Children* by Cathy Lanigan is a good source of information.

DANGERS & ANNOYANCES

Finland is generally a very safe, nonthreatening country to travel in but there are some potential risks to consider. An ill-prepared traveller can easily get lost in rural Finland, including forests and national parks. There are few people around, and if you injure yourself and can't get away, the cold climate might even kill you.

Weather extremes in Lapland can cause unexpected danger at any time of the year. Extreme cold kills lone trekkers almost every winter in the wilderness, and cold rain can also be a problem in summer.

June and July are the worst months for mosquitoes in Lapland. Insect repellent or hat nets are essential.

In more remote places you may run across eccentric people, who you will have to accept as they are: sometimes extremely frustrated (even aggressive) and suspicious of outsiders. The gloom that winter brings may lead to unpredictable behaviour and alcohol abuse.

In urban areas, violence mostly occurs in association with intoxicated local males. Foreign men of dark complexion run the highest risk of street harassment.

Although theft isn't a major problem in Finland, you should use normal precautions, particularly when in busy markets, at crowded festivals or around the subway in Helsinki – pickpockets do their work here. Parked cars are prime targets for petty criminals in most cities, and cars with foreign number plates and/or rental-agency stickers are targeted. If possible, remove the stickers or cover them with something, leave a local newspaper on the seat and generally try to make it look like a local car. Don't ever leave valuables in the car. Likewise, don't leave valuables unsecured in hostels and hotels.

Whatever you do, don't leave friends and relatives back home worrying about how to get in touch with you in case of an emergency. Work out a list of places where they can contact you or, best of all, phone home now and then.

EMERGENCIES

Dial ☎ 112 from anywhere in Finland for emergencies and ☎ 10023 for 24-hour emergency medical advice.

LEGAL MATTERS

Traffic laws are strict, as are drug laws. Fines for minor offences (such as speeding) are based on the offender's income and assets. This system has led to some well-documented and slightly absurd situations where highly-flying Finns breaking the speed limit have been fined as much as €100,000! However, police usually treat bona fide tourists politely in less serious situations. Fishing without a permit is illegal.

BUSINESS HOURS

Banks are open 9.15am to 4.15pm Monday to Friday. Shops and post offices are generally open 9am to 5pm Monday to Friday, and to 1pm on Saturday. Alko stores (the state-owned network of liquor stores) are open 10am to 5pm Monday to Friday (sometimes until 8pm or 9pm on Thursday or Friday), and until 2pm Saturday. Many supermarkets and Helsinki department stores stay open until 9pm or 10pm Monday to Friday and open all day on Saturday and Sunday.

Town markets run from about 7am to 2pm Monday to Saturday. Generally, churches open on Sunday morning after 9am and close soon after the service, around 11.30am.

Public holidays are taken seriously – absolutely everything shuts at 6pm on holiday eve and reopens the morning after the holiday itself.

PUBLIC HOLIDAYS & SPECIAL EVENTS

Finland grinds to a halt twice a year: around Christmas (sometimes including the New Year) and during the Midsummer weekend at the end of June. Plan ahead and avoid travelling during those times.

The foremost special events are the Opera Festival in Savonlinna and the Jazz Festival in Pori, but there's also Provinssirock at Seinäjoki and the Folk Festival at Kaustinen, as well as Midsummer in any part of Finland. Every town and city in Finland puts on a barrage of festivals between mid-June and mid-August. A few smaller communities arrange some of the weirdest events imaginable (eg, the Wife-Carrying World Championships in

Following the Festivals

One of the great things about travelling in Finland in summer is the myriad festivals, concerts, competitions and events that take place around the country. On any given trip you're sure to stumble across a few full-scale festivals, but you could easily plan your trip around them, hopping from jazz to folk to dance to wife-carrying championships.

You could be in Pori for the week-long international Jazz Festival one day, in Kaustinen for the Folk Festival the next, in Turku for its medieval pageant, Tampere for Tammerfest, Savonlinna for the Opera Festival and up to Kuopio for the Dance Festival – all in the space of a fortnight. Even if you don't plan to buy tickets to particular events, the atmosphere generated by these festivals usually adds colour and excitement to otherwise staid country towns. The downside is that accommodation may be hard to find – plan ahead or carry a tent and be prepared to rough it occasionally. The biggest and best festivals are held between June and August, but there are events somewhere in Finland year-round. The following is a list of most of Finland's annual events – for more information see W www.festivals.fi or pick up the *Finland Festivals* booklet in any tourist office.

February
Runeberg Day 5 February, nationwide. People eat 'Runeberg cakes', available in all shops, to commemorate the national poet.

Laskiainen Seven weeks before Easter, nationwide. Festival of downhill skiing and winter sports. People eat *laskiaispulla*, a wheat bun with whipped cream and hot milk.

Jyväskylä Winter Festival Jyväskylä; concerts and dance

Northern Lights Festival Rovaniemi; sports and arts events

March
Pääsiäinen Easter. On Sunday people go to church or paint eggs and eat *mämmi* (pudding made of rye and malt).

Tampereen Elokuvajuhlat Tampere; festival of international short films

Oulu Music Festival Oulu; classical and chamber music

Finnish Ice-Fishing Championships Lake Lohjanjärvi, Lohja; ice-fishing

Lahti Ski Games Lahti; ski jumping

Tar Skiing Race Oulu; long-distance cross-country ski race

Marathon Ice-Fishing Oulu; world's longest nonstop ice-fishing contest

Ounasvaara Winter Games Rovaniemi; skiing and ski-jumping competitions

Maria's Day Festival Hetta village, Enontekiö; Sami festival of arts, sports contests

April
Tampere Biennale Tampere; new Finnish music. Held in even-numbered years only.

Hetan Musiikkipäivät Hetta village, Enontekiö; chamber music

April Jazz Espoo Espoo; jazz

Reindeer Champion Race Inari; reindeer-sleigh racing

May
Vappu May Day Traditionally a festival of students and workers, this also marks the beginning of summer, and is celebrated with plenty of alcohol and merrymaking. People drink *sima* mead and eat *tippaleipä* cookies.

Äitienpäivä Mothers' Day. Everyone takes their mother out for a buffet lunch.

Kemin Sarjakuvapäivät Kemi; international cartoon festival

Kainuun Jazzkevät Kajaani; international jazz, blues, rock acts

Vaasa Chorus Festival Vaasa; European choirs

June
Midsummer's Eve & Day Juhannus (Midsummer) is the most important annual event for Finns. Celebrated with bonfires and dancing. People leave cities and towns for summer cottages to celebrate the longest day of the year. It is also the day of the Finnish flag, as well as the day of John the Baptist.

Praasniekka These Orthodox celebrations are day-long religious and folk festivals held in North Karelia and other eastern provinces between May and September, most notably at the end of June.

Koljonvirta Wood-Sculpting Week Iisalmi and Koljonvirta; wood-sculpting done traditionally and with a chainsaw

Pispala Schottishce Tampere; international folk dance and music

Ilmajoen Music Festival Ilmajoki; classical and folk music, folk operas

Naantali Music Festival Naantali; chamber music

Jutajaiset Rovaniemi; folk music and dance, Lapp traditions

Midnight Sun Film Festival Sodankylä; international films

Down By The Laituri Turku; rock music

Riihimäen kesäkonsertit Riihimäki; classical music

Following the Festivals

Provinssirock Seinäjoki; rock music
Nummirock Kauhajoki; rock music
Åland Organ Festival Åland; organ music in medieval churches
Korsholm Music Festival Vaasa; chamber music
Puistoblues Järvenpää; blues, jazz
Avanti! Summer Sounds Porvoo; eclectic music from baroque to rock
International Kalottjazz and Blues Festival Tornio (Finland) and Haparanda (Sweden); jazz, blues
Kuopio Tanssii ja Soi Kuopio; international dance
Imatra Big Band Festival Imatra; big-band music
Ruisrock Turku; oldest and largest rock-music festival
Mikkeli Music Festival Mikkeli; classical music
Sata-Häme Soi Ikaalinen; accordion music
Midnight Sun Golf Tournament Tornio (Finland) and Haparanda (Sweden); golf competition
Postrodden Mail Boat Race Eckerö (Åland) and Grisslehamn (Sweden); rowing and sailing race
Jyväskylän Kesä Jyväskylä; music, visual arts
Helsinki Day Helsinki; celebrates the founding of Helsinki on 12 June.
Tar Burning Week Oulu; Midsummer festival

July

Rauma Lace Week Rauma; lace-making demonstrations, carnival
Festivo Rauma; chamber music
Isosaari Rock Joensuu; rock music
Savonlinna Opera Festival Savonlinna; one of Finland's most notable festivals
Tangomarkkinat Seinäjoki; tango music
International Pori Jazz Festival Pori; one of Finland's most notable festivals
Hamina Tatoo Hamina; military music
Kaustinen Folk Music Festival Kaustinen; folk music and dance
Kuhmon Kamarimusiikki Kuhmo; chamber music
Joensuu Gospel Festival Joensuu; gospel music
Lieksan Vaskiviikko Lieksa; brass music
Elojazz & Blues Oulu; jazz, blues
Kymenlaakson Folk Art & Music Festival Miehikkälä; folk music, traditions
Työväen Musiikkitapahtuma Valkeakoski; workers' music
Ioutsa Folk Festival Ioutsa; traditional Finnish summer festival
Wife-Carrying World Championships Sonkajärvi; unusual husband-and-wife team competition with international participants and big prizes
Bomba Festival Nurmes; Karelian folklore festival
Evakon Pruasniekka Iisalmi; traditional festival of the Orthodox church

Kotka Maritime Festival Kotka; music, sailing races, cruises
Sleepyhead Day Naantali; On 27 July the laziest person in the town is thrown into the sea.
Kihaus Folk Music Festival Rääkkylä; widely acclaimed festival of modern and experimental Finnish folk music and dancing
Pirkan Soutu Tampere; rowing competition

August

Taiteiden yö A night of art, held in Helsinki and other towns in late August. Street performances, fringe art, concerts – a good atmosphere and exciting.
Lappeenranta Music Festival Lappeenranta and Lemi; festival of international music
Tampere International Theatre Festival Tampere; international and Finnish theatre
Gipsy Music Festival Porvoo; concerts and carnival
Crusell-Viikko Uusikaupunki; chamber music, especially clarinet
Savonlinna Beer Festival Savonlinna; food and beer festival at Savonlinna castle
Lahden Urkuviikko Lahti; organ music
Turku Music Festival Turku; classical and contemporary music
Lahti Jazz Festival Lahti; jazz
Helsinki Festival Helsinki; all-arts festival
Helsinki City Marathon Helsinki; foot race

September

Ruksa Swing Kemijärvi; swing dancing and music
Savonlinna Theatre Festival Savonlinna; international theatre festival at Savonlinna castle

October

Oulaisten Musiikkiviikot Oulainen; eclectic music
Tampere Jazz Happening Tampere; jazz
Baltic Herring Market Helsinki; traditional outdoor herring market

November

All Souls' Day The first Saturday of November sees people visit the graves of deceased friends and relatives.
Etnosoi Helsinki; ethnic music
Oulu International Children's Film Festival Oulu; international children's films

December

Itsenäisyyspäivä Finland celebrates independence on 6 December with torchlight processions, fireworks and concerts.
Pikkujoulu 'Little Christmas'
Joulu Christmas is a family celebration.

Sonkajarvi or the Air Guitar Championships in Oulu). Anyone who has been in Finland on *vappu* (May Day) will know it's a big day for Finns, and that more alcohol is consumed in the 48 hours surrounding 1 May than over a similar period at any other time of year.

The following are public holidays celebrated throughout Finland:

New Year's Day	1 January
Epiphany	6 January
Good Friday	March/April
Easter	March/April
May Day Eve	30 April
May Day	1 May
Ascension Day	May
Whit Sunday	late May or early June
Midsummer's Eve & Day	third weekend in June
All Saints Day	1 November
Independence Day	6 December
Christmas Eve	24 December
Christmas Day	25 December
Boxing Day	26 December

LANGUAGE COURSES

The Council for Instruction of Finnish for Foreigners (UKAN) offers accelerated courses in Finnish each summer at the universities in Helsinki, Rauma, Savonlinna, Kuopio and Jyväskylä. Those who wish to participate must submit an application. For more information contact UKAN at the **Centre for International Mobility** *(CIMO; ☎ 09-7747 7067, fax 7747 7064; Hakanimenkatu 2, Helsinki)*.

Additionally, the following universities teach basic (or 'survival') courses in Finnish language and culture, with classes typically running a full term:

University of Helsinki Language Centre (☎ 09-1912 3234, fax 1912 2551, ⓦ www.helsinki.fi/kksc/language.services) Aleksanterinkatu 7, 00141 Helsinki – one-month classes €110.

University of Jyväskylä Language Centre & Department of Finnish (☎ 014-603 761, fax 603 751, ⓔ kalin@tukki.jyu.fi) PO Box 35, 40351 Jyväskylä

University of Oulu Language Centre (☎ 08-553 3200, fax 553 3203) PO Box 111, 90571 Oulu

University of Tampere Language Centre & Department of Finnish Language and General Linguistics, PO Box 607, 33101 Tampere

University of Turku Language Centre (☎ 02-333 5975) Horttokuja 2, 20014 Turku

WORK

There is very little work open to foreigners because of high local unemployment. It's possible to get a job teaching English at a Finnish company, but standards are very high so previous experience and good references are essential. Students can apply for limited summer employment, and au pair arrangements are possible for up to 18 months.

For any serious career-oriented work, a work permit is required for all foreigners other than EU citizens. Employment must be secured before applying for the work permit, and the work permit must be filed in advance of arrival in Finland, together with a letter from the intended employer and other proof of employment. Work permits can be obtained from the Finnish embassy in your home country. A residence permit may also be required (see the earlier Visas & Documents section). For more information contact the **Directorate of Immigration** *(☎ 09-476 5500, fax 4765 5858; ⓦ www.uvi.fi; PO Box 92, 00531 Helsinki)*.

ACCOMMODATION

Accommodation is always going to be a major budget consideration, but sleeping in Finland doesn't necessarily have to be expensive. Most of the wilderness huts along trekking routes are free. You can camp at well-equipped camping grounds for between €7 to €12 a night. A dorm bed in a hostel costs from €18, which is comparable to Western Europe. Several people travelling together can get bargains sharing cottages at camping grounds. Hotel rates are expensive but there are good discounts at weekends and in summer, when there are few business travellers around. The Finnish Tourist Board publishes an annual budget accommodation guide, available at tourist offices.

Camping

There are more than 200 official camping grounds in Finland. Although they tend to cater for caravans and motor homes, there are always an adequate number of grassy tent sites, so they suit the budget traveller carrying their own tents. Camping is clearly the cheapest way to the sleep in Finland. A tent site costs anything from €5 to €14 but is usually around €10. Some camping grounds have a rate for a single person, and another for a site, regardless of the number of people

Reindeer, Lapland

Cyclists, Helsinki

Protective headwear

European brown bear *(Ursos arctos)*, eastern Finland

European osprey *(Pandion haliaetus)*

Fly-fishing, Lake Savonlinna

Ecotourists crossing lake

in the tent. In addition, there are cabins that range from very basic two-person cabins at €25 to self-contained four- to six-person cottages with cooking facilities and sometimes even private sauna from €50 to €120.

Most camping grounds are in appealing locations – in a forest, by a lake, at the seaside, or close to popular trekking areas – but are rarely close to the centre of big towns of cities, so camping is inconvenient if you're in, say, Helsinki, Turku or Tampere. Note that the majority of camping grounds are open only in summer, say late May or mid-June to mid- or late August at the latest, and some only open during June and July. Typical camping-ground facilities include a kitchen area, laundry, sauna, children's play area, boat and bicycle rentals, and café or grilli.

The availability of pleasant cabins and bungalows makes Finnish camping grounds a good option even if you don't want to sleep in a tent. With a group of two to six, prices are comparable to or cheaper than hostels. Amenities vary, but a kitchen, toilet and shower are not uncommon. Some even have microwave ovens and TV sets.

In Finland the *jokamiehenoikeus* (right of public access) grants you legal permission to temporarily pitch your tent in a wide range of places. See the Trekking section in the Activities chapter for more information.

Hostels

If you're travelling alone, hostels generally offer the best-value roof over your head, and are also good value for two people staying in a twin room. However, many hostels in Finland are open during the summer only (June to August) and are often characterless, student-dormitory buildings. There are close to 150 hostels in Finland, and about half are open all year. Overall you might find Finnish hostels a little disappointing compared with others in Scandinavia or elsewhere in Europe, but there are a few gems, including converted manor houses and farmhouses, and you'll find them in the heart of cities and in isolated countryside locations.

Most Finnish hostels are run by the Finnish Youth Hostel Association (SRM) and are affiliated with Hostelling International (HI). The average cost is less than €15 per person per night. Most hostels offer private single/double rooms as well, at higher rates (around €25/40).

If you have an HI card you'll receive a €2.50 discount on the rates quoted in this book. You can join HI in your own country (check the website W www.iyhf.org for contact details of your home association) or you can join up in Finland at any HI-affiliated hostel, or at the head office in Helsinki *(Suomen Retkeilymajajärejesö or SRM;* ☎ *09-694 0377, fax 693 1349;* W *www.srmnet.org; Yrjönkatu 38B, 00100 Helsinki).* In Finland the cost is €17 for annual membership. Of course, you can stay at a hostel even without an HI card, and there are no age restrictions, despite the term 'youth' hostel.

You should also bring your own sheets (or sleeping sheet) and pillowcase, as linen rentals cost €2 to €5. Sleeping bags are usually not considered acceptable substitutes, although some summer hostels will accept them (or at least turn a blind eye). Breakfast is generally not included in the price of a dorm bed (but may be with a private room), but is available for around €4.

Generally, HI-affiliated youth hostels have a communal kitchen, although summer hotels (vacant student accommodation) often have private kitchenettes in rooms (apartment-style), but bear in mind that there may not be any utensils or cooking equipment. Farmhouses or rural locations may not have a kitchen at all. Saunas are common at hostels; often a morning sauna is included in the room rate but there may be a small surcharge to book or use them.

The free publication *Hostellit* gives a full listing of all HI-affiliated Finnish hostels.

Guesthouses

Guesthouses in Finland, called *matkakoti* or *matkustajakoti*, tend to be slightly run-down establishments meant for travelling salespeople and dubious types. They're usually in town centres near the train station, are cheap and offer rooms with shared bathroom facilities.

However, there are a few guesthouses out there – usually in smaller villages and tourist-oriented towns – that just don't fit the category. These places are exceptionally clean and offer pleasant, homey accommodation in old wooden houses. Ask to see a room before paying – that's the best way to know what you're getting. Naantali and Hanko on the southwestern coast are particularly good places for guesthouses.

Hotels

Most big hotels in Finland cater to business travellers and most belong to one of a handful of major chains, including **Sokos** (W *www*.sokoshotels.fi), **Scandic** (W *www.scandic-hotels.ee)*, **Cumulus** (W *www.cumulus.fi)* and **Finlandia** (W *www.finlandiahotels.fi)*. They are quite luxurious, although standard rooms are usually pretty compact and functional. Service tends to be good and the restaurants and nightclubs may be some of the most popular in town. Hotels are invariably spotlessly clean, efficiently run and always have a sauna, which can be booked for private use. Most hotels have suites with a private sauna.

Although full rack-rate prices are high, in contrast to much of the rest of the world, hotels in Finland offer lower rates in summer (from late June to mid- or end of August), and also at weekends (usually Friday, Saturday and Sunday nights). At that time you can usually get a double room in a reasonably fancy hotel from between €65 and €80. The discount for singles is marginal at weekends and in summer.

A bargain in practically all Finnish hotels is the buffet breakfast. It's invariably huge, delicious and included in the room price. Hotel guests will need no lunch.

Finncheques The Finncheque plan, available in most chain hotels throughout Finland, allows accommodation in 140 designated hotels at the discounted price of €34 per person in a double room. Each Finncheque is a 'coupon' good for one night's stay at a participating hotel (you purchase as many as you need), and any supplements are paid directly to the hotel. Finncheques are valid from mid-May to late September and can be purchased at a participating hotel or through a travel agency in your home country. If you're travelling during July and August, however, when hotels offer discounted summer prices, you may find Finncheques unnecessary and perhaps even overpriced.

Wilderness Huts

See the Activities chapter for details on huts, shelters and other options on trekking routes.

Holiday Cabins & Cottages

There are thousands of cabins and cottages for rent around Finland. They can be booked through tourist offices, generally from €200 a week or more for four people. Rarely are these available on a nightly basis, although weekend rentals are possible outside busy periods (eg, Midsummer).

Lakeside holiday cabins and cottages represent the classic Finnish vacation and are a terrific idea if you have a group (or family) and would like to settle down to enjoy a particular corner of the countryside. They are usually fully equipped with cooking utensils, sauna and a rowing boat, although the cheapest, most 'rustic' ones may not even have electricity and require that you fetch your own water at a well. However, this is considered a true holiday, Finnish style.

Prices are highest during Midsummer and the skiing holidays, when you'll need to book well in advance. Tax is not necessarily included in quoted prices. The following are a few companies that specialise in cottage rentals:

Ålandsresor (☎ 018-28040, fax 28380, W www.alandsresor.fi) PO Box 62, 22101 Mariehamn
Järvi-Savo (☎ 015-365 399, fax 365 080) Hallituskatu 2, 50100 Mikkeli
Lomarengas (☎ 09-3516 1321, fax 3516 1370, W www.lomarengas.fi) Malminkaari 23, 00700 Helsinki
Saimaatours (☎ 05-411 7722, fax 415 6609) Kirkkokatu 10, 53100 Lappeenranta

Farmstays

Many farmhouses around Finland offer B&B accommodation, a unique opportunity to meet local people and experience their way of life. They offer plenty of activities, too, from horse riding to helping with a harvest. Some farmstays are independent, family-run

---

Summer Cottages

About 25% of the population of Finland owns a *kesämökki* or summer cottage, and the majority of Finns at least have access to one. The *mökki* should ideally be on the shores of a lake and surrounded by forest. A genuine *mökki* has only basic amenities – some have no electricity or running water – but always come equipped with a sauna and rowing boat. These days you can rent a *mökki* with a fridge, TV and even a phone. Getting invited to a cottage is a great honour and an experience not to be missed.

affairs, while others are loosely gathered under an umbrella organisation. In general, prices are good – from around €25 per person per night, country breakfast included. The drawback is that farms are – by their very nature – off major roadways and bus routes, so you'll need your own transport (or enough money for taxi fare) to reach them. Also, your hosts may not speak much English, so it pays to at least arrange the booking through a local tourist office or one of the organisations listed below.

Lomarengas (☎ 09-3516 1321, fax 3516 1370, ⓦ www.lomarengas.fi) Malminkaari 23C, 00700 Helsinki
Suomen 4H-Liitto (☎ 09-645 133, fax 604 612) Bulevardi 28, 00120 Helsinki

FOOD
Finnish food has elements of both Swedish and Russian cuisines. Originally it was designed to nourish a peasant population who did outdoor manual work in cold weather. Consequently, Finnish food was heavy and fatty, made of fish, game, meat, milk and dairy products, oats, barley and dark rye in the form of porridges and bread, with few spices other than salt and pepper. Vegetables were rarely used in everyday meals, except in casseroles. Potato was the staple food, served with various fish or meat sauces.

So what's modern Finnish cuisine like? Well, little has changed, except that international cuisine has also made it to Finland. Soups such as pea, meat, cabbage and fish (the creamy salmon is delicious) are common. Hot and heavy dishes, including liver, Baltic herring, turnip and cabbage, and even carrot casseroles, are served as the main course or as part of it. Fish dishes – prepared from whitefish, Baltic herring, salmon and trout – are common everywhere.

Reindeer is commonly found on the menu in Lapland and in Finnish and Lappish restaurants elsewhere, but it's not cheap. The traditional dish is sauteed reindeer, perhaps served with lingonberry sauce, but at various places you'll find reindeer pizza, sausages and steaks.

Finns tend to eat their biggest meal of the day at lunchtime, so many restaurants put on an all-you-can-eat buffet lunch, usually between 11am and 3pm Monday to Friday. This costs approximately €6 to €8 and may include soups, salad, bread, cold fish dishes, hot meat dishes, coffee and possibly even dessert. Breakfast is another great time to fill up, as many hotels and hostels offer a cheap (or sometimes free) buffet breakfast, which includes bread, cheese, pastries, fruit, cereals, more fish, sausages, eggs and lots of coffee.

Like the baguette with camembert cheese and red wine in France, you can find some simple but tasty options in Finland. Take fresh, preferably still warm, brown rye bread, add medium-hard butter and plenty of cheese (say, Edam or Emmenthal), and enjoy with very cold milk or lager beer. Or try the Finnish version of sushi: salmon or herring slices on small new potatoes (available from July). Such fare is relatively cheap and delicious.

Cafés & Restaurants
Finns have well and truly adopted the European café culture, particularly in cities like Helsinki, Tampere, Turku and Oulu, but also in many smaller towns. In summer, chairs and tables appear outdoors. Most cafés in Finland serve snacks, light meals and desserts, as well as coffee – and lots of it. Finns drink more coffee per capita than any other people on earth and there's usually a self-service pot of coffee permanently sitting on a warmer near the counter. A *kahvila* is a simple café, a *kahvio* is a café inside a supermarket or petrol station, and a *baari* serves snacks, beer and soft drinks, and probably also coffee.

Restaurant meals can be expensive in Finland, particularly at dinner. Take advantage of the weekday lunchtime specials, where you can enjoy a buffet meal for under €10. Many cheaper restaurants in Finland close their kitchens (or shut entirely) around 5pm. Large towns have an increasing number of international or ethnic restaurants, and these may offer lunch specials as well. In places like Helsinki, Oulu, Turku and Tampere you don't have to look too hard to find Thai, Chinese, Indian, Italian and French restaurants, but in smaller towns the choice is much more limited. University eateries are terrific for budget travellers: a full set meal or buffet costs less than €5, and although you're technically supposed to be a student to eat in them, often you won't be asked.

Finns are quite partial to the familiarity of chain restaurants when it comes to eating out. As well as the usual fast-food places, in most towns you'll find a branch of Rosso (pizza, pasta, steaks, salads etc), Amarillo (Tex-Mex, steaks) and perhaps Fransimanni (French), among others.

Fast Food

The grilli is the venue for a takeaway meal of hamburgers or hot dogs for under €3.50. It's usually little more than a roadside stand, with or without a few seats. Hamburgers are usually a meat patty between two bits of flat bread and squashed to pancake dimension under a hot iron. Turkish kebab joints offer good value (around €5), and inexpensive pizzerias, where you can often buy by the slice, are ubiquitous. You'll see Golden Rax pizza outlets in just about every town. They offer an extremely good-value, all-you-can-eat buffet of pizza, pasta, chicken wings, salads, potatoes, soft drinks and even dessert for the fixed price of €7.90. The food is incredibly bland but you will certainly never go hungry. Koti Pizza is another popular chain and although the pizzas aren't particularly cheap (€5.50 to €7.50), they're quite good.

McDonald's has hit Finland in a big way (the world's northernmost McDonald's restaurant is in Rovaniemi), but local chain, Hesburger (originally from Turku) certainly holds its own. The burgers and menu are very similar to McDonald's but taste better and cost around the same – a full burger meal is around €5. The Finnish variation at Hesburger is the 'ruisburger', using typically Finnish dark rye bread.

Although you wouldn't immediately think to go to a petrol station or bus terminal for dinner, in Finland these are perfectly respectable places to get a quick, hot, nutritious and cheap meal, particularly between towns.

Vegetarian

Finnish cuisine isn't overly friendly to vegetarians, so you might find it easier to self-cater, or rely on ethnic restaurants – Chinese, Thai etc – that reliably serve vegetarian meals. However, Finnish buffets always include soups, salads, rye bread and potatoes, and are often cheaper if you don't want the meat or fish portion, so there's certainly scope for vegetarians there.

There are only a handful of true vegetarian restaurants in Finland, and most of them are in Helsinki. Whenever we've found them, we've included vegetarian restaurants in the Places to Eat sections of this book.

Another option if you are in a city with a university is to eat at the student cafeteria – these are required to carry at least one vegetarian dish at every meal.

Self-Catering

Every town has a *kauppatori* (market square) where you can buy smoked fish, fresh produce (in season), berries, pastries and the like. Most larger towns also have a *kauppahalli* (covered market) where stalls sell cheap hot meals, sandwiches, meats, cheese, produce etc.

The main supermarket chains include K-Kauppa, T-Market and S-Market. Discount stores include Alepa, Eurospar, Rabatti, Säästäri and Siwa.

Relatively cheap food for a simple meal includes fresh potatoes, yogurt, eggs, fresh or smoked fish and *hernekeitto* (canned pea soup) and, in late summer, any market vegetables. Salmon can be bought at reasonable prices if you shop around. Cheese, salami and meat are more expensive.

Shopping at discount stores, keeping your eyes open for discounts (*tarjous* means special price) and buying imported food, such as canned tuna, pineapple slices, sardines and bananas, are options to stretch the budget.

DRINKS
Nonalcoholic Drinks

Soft drinks and bottled water are expensive, around €3 for 1L of either. Local soft drinks include Jaffa, Aurinko, Frisco and Pommac. International brands are also widely available. You pay a deposit for all glass bottles of locally bottled soft drink and beer; when you return them to any store, your deposit is refunded, however, plastic bottles are starting to replace glass.

Alcoholic Drinks

Strong beers, wines and spirits are sold by the state network, beautifully named Alko (much more appealing than Sweden's Systembolaget!). There are Alko stores in every town and they're generally open 10am to 6pm Monday to Thursday, until 8pm on Friday and 2pm Saturday. Go to **w** www.alko.fi to survey its wares and prices online. Drinks containing more than 20% alcohol are not sold to those aged under 20; for beer and wine purchases the age limit is 18. Beer and cider under 4.7% alcohol are readily available in supermarkets and are surprisingly cheap at around €7 for a six-pack. Even imported wine is reasonably priced at Alko – you can get a drinkable bottle from €6 to €10.

What is served in Finland as *olut* (beer) is generally light-coloured, lager-type beer, although Guinness stout and other dark brews have gained in popularity in recent years (along with a proliferation of Irish pubs). Major brands of lager include Lapin Kulta, Olvi and Koff. There's also a growing number of microbreweries in Finland (called *panimo* or *panimonravintola*, which means brewery-restaurant), and these make excellent light and dark beers. Such places worthy of a visit include Huvila in Savonlinna, Plevna in Tampere, Koulu and Herman in Turku, and Beer Hunters in Pori.

The strongest beer is called IVA, or *nelos olut*, with more than 5% alcohol. More popular is III Beer (called *keskari* or *kolmonen*) and I Beer (called *mieto olut* or *pilsneri*), with less than 2% alcohol.

Drinking in bars and restaurants is costly. A pint of beer or cider (the latter is made from apple or pear) costs between €3.50 and €5.50. Alcohol is taxed by content, so the stronger it is, the more expensive.

Uniquely Finnish drinks to look out for include *salmiekkikoska*, a handmade spirit combining dissolved liquorice/peppermint flavoured sweets with the abrasive koskenkova vodka (an acquired taste!); *sahti*, a sweet, high-alcohol beer traditionally made at home by farmers' wives – you can find it in a couple of pubs in Lahti and Savonlinna; cloudberry or cranberry liqueurs; and vodka mixed with cranberry. Like the Russians, Finns are very fond of vodka – Finlandia is the Finnish brand.

ENTERTAINMENT

Finns of all ages love to drink and dance, so it's not hard to find some evening entertainment even in small towns. It may come in the form of a Finnish dance restaurant where live bands perform tango and traditional *humppa* tunes and couples crowd the dance floor. Karaoke is another popular form of entertainment – it's taken almost as seriously here as in Japan, usually with a mix of Western standards and melancholy love songs in Finnish or Swedish.

In summer, beer terraces – a clutter of tables and chairs set up outside bars and cafés – are the place to start an evening of drinking and socialising before moving on to other nightspots. Many young Finns get around the high cost of drinking in bars by visiting the local supermarket or Alko and finding a place in a park to get tanked.

Bars, Nightclubs & Discos

Finnish cities have a full range of bars, from Irish pubs to trendy bars to Finnish *ravintola* (restaurants that double as drinking spots). In the cities many pubs and bars have free live music, although to see a decent rock or blues band you can expect to pay a cover charge. Jazz clubs are also worth checking out in Helsinki, Turku, Pori and Tampere.

The majority of nightclubs in Finland, particularly outside the major cities, can be found in, or attached to, large business hotels such as Sokos, Scandic or Cumulus. In cities such as Helsinki, Tampere, Turku and Oulu there are plenty of independent nightclubs. A relative newcomer on the Finnish nightclub scene is the Giggling Marlin, a chain of 'Suomi pop' clubs with branches in Oulu, Kuopio, Vaasa, Porvoo and Jyväskylä.

Nightclubs usually charge €5 after 11pm (the usual age limit is 18 or 20 years, but sometimes 24), and are open until 4am. Note that in nightclubs and some bars, even when there's no cover charge, you'll have to pay a 'coat charge' of around €2, which usually goes to the doorman.

Little Weekend

Finns love the weekend, when they can get away to their summer cottages, play sport and party in the evening. But the working week is also broken up in the middle. On Wednesday nights the restaurants are busy, music is playing at all the nightspots, the bars are full – Finns are celebrating *pikku viikonloppu*, or 'little weekend'.

Classical Music, Opera & Theatre

Live music is the best option if you're seeking high culture, and good classical concerts can be heard in many towns, often in churches and often for free. Inquire locally to find out when and where you can see live performances. Major cities have opera halls, concert halls and a variety of theatres. Classical-music festivals – many with outdoor venues – are extremely popular in Finnish cities and towns during summer. The Savonlinna Opera Festival and Mikkeli Music Festival are two big events. Check the Web at W www.operafin.fi for information on the opera and ballet season in Helsinki.

Theatre performances are almost universally in Finnish and Swedish, and opera performances are subtitled in Finnish and Swedish. The exception is at the world-class Savonlinna Opera Festival. The season for theatre, opera and indoor concerts is generally September to March (ie, not in summer when outdoor festivals take over).

Cinemas

Nearly every town has a cinema and cities have several. Tickets cost around €8 but are cheaper on Tuesday. Films classified K are restricted to people over 16 or 18 years of age, films classified S are for general audiences. Foreign films are in their original language with subtitles in Finnish and Swedish. Almost half of the films screened each year are American. France is the second most popular source of imported movies, followed by the UK and Sweden. Finnish movies account for 15% to 25% of films shown.

SPECTATOR SPORTS

Ice hockey is Finland's number one national passion, but you'll have to visit in winter to see a game. The season is between late September and March. The best place to see a quality match in the national league is Tampere (home of the ice-hockey museum) or Helsinki, but Turku, Oulu and Rovaniemi also have major stadiums and teams in one of the national leagues. Ticket prices are reasonable (from about €15) and the atmosphere at big games can be electric. The best way to find out when and where games are on is to ask at the tourist office, at any bar or contact the national ticketing outlet **Lippu-palvelu** (W *www.ticketservicefinland.fi*).

Many indoor sports, including basketball and volleyball, also have their season in winter. Skiing events don't offer the same intensity as team sports, but national (and international) competitions provide a thrill worth experiencing. You can watch flying Finns at the ski-jumping centres in Lahti, Kuopio and Jyväskylä. Jyväskylä is the home town and former training ground of Olympic champion Matti Nykänen. Ski-jumping events are usually part of general ski tournaments, but even practice sessions can be fascinating and can be seen in summer on the dry slopes at Lahti.

In summer, football (soccer) has a national league, and is followed diligently, although nowhere near as obsessively as most European countries. Outside big cities, Finnish baseball, called *pesäpallo* or simply *pesis*, is the most popular team sport in summer.

Athletics (track and field) is very popular in Finland, as a result of the country's many successful long-distance runners and javelin-throwers. The national games are called Kalevan Kisat.

SHOPPING

On the whole, prices in Finland are lower than in other Scandinavian countries – which isn't to say that there are any real bargains here, particularly on those items for which Finland is famous: glassware, pottery, woollens and various handicrafts made from pine or birch.

If you're heading to the Baltic countries – particularly to Tallinn, Estonia, which can be visited on a day trip from Helsinki – you'll find that prices there are cheaper still, and for many of the same types of items of more or less the same quality.

Lappish, or Sami, handicrafts include jewellery, clothing, textiles and hunting knives, as well as other items made from local wood, reindeer bone and hide, metals and semiprecious stones. *Duodji* are authentic handicrafts produced according to Sami traditions. A genuine item, which can be expensive, will carry a special 'Duodji' token. Sami handicrafts can be found at markets and shops in Helsinki and throughout Lapland, but for the widest selections visit the Sami villages of Inari and Hetta (Enontekiö).

Trekkers will want to purchase a *kuksa* (cup) made in traditional Sami fashion from the burl of a birch tree. These are widely available throughout Finland, at markets and in handicraft or souvenir shops. Quality of workmanship varies, as does price, but the typical *kuksa* costs about €20.

Local markets are good places to purchase colourful *lapaset* (woollen mittens), *myssy* or *pipo* (hats) and *villapusero* (sweaters), necessary for surviving the cold Finnish winters, as well as *raanu* or *ryijy* (woven wall hangings). A good hand-knitted sweater sells for at least €300. Local folk – particularly in Åland – will often 'knit to order', taking your measurements and then posting the sweater to you in two or three months, once it's finished. It's possible to find cheaper, machine-knitted wool sweaters in Finnish markets, but check the labels – they probably were made in Norway.

If you don't care for other people's work, contact the nearest *Käsityöasema* (a centre that preserves cottage industries) and create your own handicrafts. There are hundreds of these in Finland, and many are especially geared towards visitors. You pay only for the material, plus a small fee for rental of the equipment.

For decades, Finland has been world famous for its indigenous glass production. The Savoy vase designed by Alvar Aalto is a good 'souvenir of Finland', although expensive. Department stores and finer shops carry it as well as other stylish vases by Iittala, Nuutajärvi and Humppila. Big roadside discount shops also stock Finnish glassware, plus designer pottery and cooking utensils; most of this is schlock.

You can find quite nice kitchen utensils of carved pine and attractive woven pine baskets at local markets. Every Finnish market also seems to have an old man who makes birdhouses – these, too, are uniquely Finnish souvenirs.

Hunting and carving knives made by the Marttiini company are well known internationally, as are fishing lures and flies made by Kuusamo.

It's possible – but unlikely – to find bargains on trekking goods such as jackets and down sleeping bags. Chains such as Partio-Aitta and Lassen Retkiaitta specialise in outdoor equipment, but many sports shops, such as Intersport or Kesport, also have good selections.

Activities

After a short time in Finland, you'll quickly realise that nature and the great outdoors is its biggest appeal. The land of lakes and forests offers plenty of scope for trekking, cycling, canoeing, boating, cross-country skiing and skating. Although some winter activities such as dog-sledding, downhill skiing and snowmobiling are real budget breakers, things like hiking and biking are surprisingly inexpensive or free. More importantly, these activities open up some of the most beautiful and fascinating corners of this northern country. Often, there is no 'next bus' waiting to take you to isolated national parks or small fishing villages. You will have to drive, pedal, paddle or walk to get there, and that's part of what makes Finland so appealing.

Trekking

Trekking, or fell-walking, is one of the most popular summer activities in Finland. The terrain is generally flat and easy-going, and pristine wilderness covers much of the country. National parks offer marked trails, and most wilderness areas are crisscrossed by locally-used walking paths. Nights are short or nonexistent in summer, so you can walk for as long as your heart desires (or at least until your feet start to complain) and even start a trek at midnight if you feel so inclined.

Water is plentiful everywhere, and you are allowed to camp practically anywhere – although it's important to always check for restrictions at national parks, where bird nesting sites and other fragile areas are protected.

The trekking season runs from late May to September in most parts of the country. In Lapland and the north the ground is not dry enough for hiking until late June, and mosquitoes are a serious irritation through to July.

Trekkers are strongly advised not to go hiking alone. For those who do insist on going solo, make sure you sign the trekkers' book as you depart. Write your name and next destination in the log at each hut you visit and don't forget to announce the completion of your trek.

RIGHT OF PUBLIC ACCESS

The *jokamiehenoikeus* (Swedish: *allemansrätt*), literally 'everyman's right', is a code that has been in effect in Finland for centuries. Basically, it gives travellers the right to go anywhere in Finland by land or water – as long as that person agrees to behave responsibly. A person may walk, ski or cycle anywhere in forests and other wilderness areas, and may even cross private land as long as they don't disturb the owners or destroy planted fields. Canoeing, rowing and kayaking on lakes and rivers is also unrestricted; travel by motorboat and jet ski, on the other hand, is severely limited. Likewise, restrictions apply to snowmobiles, which are allowed on established routes only.

You can rest and swim anywhere in the Finnish countryside, and pitch a tent for one night *almost* anywhere. To camp on private property you will need the owner's permission. Camping is not permitted in town parks or on beaches.

Fishing is not restricted if you are using only a hook and line, but you will need a permit if you plan to use a reel (see the Fishing section later in this chapter). Hunting is not allowed unless you have a licence.

Watch out for stricter regulations regarding access in nature reserves and national parks. In these places, camping may be forbidden and travel confined to marked paths.

MAKING CAMPFIRES

Under the right of public access, you may not make a campfire on private land unless you have the owner's permission. In national parks, look for designated campfire areas, called *nuotiopaikka* in Finnish, and watch for fire warning signs – *metsäpalovaroitus* means the fire risk is very high. When you do light fires, use extreme caution and choose a place near a river or lakefront if possible. Felling trees or cutting brush to make a campfire is forbidden; use fallen wood instead.

GATHERING BERRIES & MUSHROOMS

It's permissible to pick berries and mushrooms – but not other kinds of plants – under Finland's right of public access. Blueberries, which bring many walkers to a halt, come into season in late July. Red cranberries are common in late summer (and a good source of vitamin C) but are very sour. They taste best after the first night frost and can also be made palatable crushed and mixed with sugar.

Orange cloudberries are so appreciated by Finns that you probably won't have a chance to sample this slightly sour berry in the wild. In some parts of Lapland, cloudberries are protected – hands off!

Edible mushrooms are numerous in Finnish forests, as are poisonous ones. Unless you already know everything there is to know about mushrooms, you should avoid gathering them, or at least buy a *sieniopas* (mushroom guidebook) and learn such words as *myrkyllinen* (poisonous), *keitettävä* (has to be boiled first) and *syötävä* (edible).

WHAT TO BRING

You can purchase trekking equipment in most Finnish cities at sporting goods stores and supermarkets such as Spar or Citymarket, but gear is not cheap in Finland. Your best bet is to bring your own, and with things like boots, they should be sufficiently worn in. Kuusamo, a town near one of Finland's best trekking areas, has many shops selling trekkers' equipment and supplies, and prices are pretty good.

Food

You will have to carry all food when you walk in wilderness areas. Good packables that are commonly available in Finland includes oats, macaroni, *jälkiuunileipä* (rye bread), raisins, peanuts, chocolate, smoked fish, salami and soft cheese. Look for the Blå Band brand of trekking food packs in sports shops.

If you plan to walk from one wilderness hut to another, you won't need cooking equipment, but for unexpected situations it's good to have something to boil water in.

Fuel for Stoves

The most common fuels in Finland are *petroli* or *paloöljy* (kerosene), *spriitä* (methylated spirits) and *lamppuöljy* (paraffin). Camping Gaz and other butane cartridges are available from petrol stations and adventure sports stores.

An MSR stove is recommended as these can handle a variety of fuel types, including kerosene and *bensiini* or *kaasu* (regular gasoline). This type of stove can be tricky to use, however, so familiarise yourself with the parts and maintenance *before* hitting the trail. Petrol stations, camping stores and marine chandlers are the places to go to purchase fuel.

Insect Repellent

Mosquitoes are a big problem in Finland, particularly in summer, and particularly in Lapland, where they grow to be the size of elephants and are twice as dangerous. Skimp on protection at your own peril.

ACCOMMODATION

The Metsähallitus (Forest and Park Service) maintains most of Finland's wilderness huts. Finland has one of the world's most extensive networks of free, properly-maintained

---

Wilderness Huts

Wilderness huts in Finland have different names, according to their various forms and uses. If you find one with a name that isn't on this list, chances are it's private property – which means that it's off-limits unless you first obtain permission from the owner.

Autiotupa A general word for 'desolate hut', with unlocked doors, meagre facilities and hard bunks. You may cook inside.

Kammi A traditional Lappish hut (that is, made out of earth, wood and branches), usually in a very remote location. It will provide basic shelter for one or two people.

Kämppä This means simply 'a hut'. Kämpät are used by Sami reindeer keepers as a shelter, and are always open and uninhabited. They provide shelter for one to six people. In the south, kämpät are often private and locked.

Rajavartioston tupa A small hut built for border guards. Most of them have unlocked doors, and sheltering overnight is legal. Keep a low profile, however, as the primary users have a serious mission.

Tunturitupa A 'fell hut'. It has unlocked doors and basic sleeping and cooking facilities.

Varaustupa 'A hut to be reserved'. This kind of hut always has a locked door, although some may also have an 'open' side. The reserved side has better facilities, including mattresses.

Yksityiskämppä A private hut. It should not be used for any purpose other than as an emergency shelter when everything else fails.

wilderness huts. Some huts require advance booking, or they have a separate, lockable section that must be reserved in advance for a fee.

Huts typically have basic bunks, cooking facilities, a pile of dry firewood and even a wilderness telephone. You are required to leave the hut as it was – ie, replenish the firewood and carry away your rubbish. The Finns' 'wilderness rule' states that the last one to arrive will be given the best place to sleep.

The largest network of wilderness huts is in Lapland. Outside of Lapland, trekking routes generally have no free cabins, but you may be able to find a simple log shelter, called a *laavu* in Finnish. You can pitch your tent inside the laavu or just roll out your sleeping bag.

A 1:50,000 trekking map is recommended for finding wilderness huts and these cost €12 from tourist offices, national parks visitor centres or map shops.

TRANSPORT

Some trekking routes finish up in the middle of nowhere. Unless you have arranged for someone to meet you on arrival, you will have to walk to the nearest bus stop, which may be another long trek. In popular trekking areas such as Oulanka National Park and Saariselkä, transport to trailheads can often be arranged through local tour operators.

If there are private vehicles parked at the finishing point, you might want to leave a note under the windscreen wiper indicating that you have just finished a trek, and are walking down the road towards the bus stop. If you are lucky, a fellow trekker might offer you a lift. Remember that hitching is never perfectly safe under any set of circumstances.

WHERE TO TREK

You can trek anywhere in Finland, but national parks and reserves will have marked routes, designated campfire places, well-maintained wilderness huts and boardwalks over the boggy bits.

Lapland is the main trekking region, with huge national parks that have well-equipped wilderness huts and good trekking routes. These include Pallas-Ounastunturi, Lemmenjoki, Pyhä-tunturi and Urho Kekkonen National Parks. The Kevo Gorge Nature Reserve in the northeast corner of Lapland is also an excellent trekking area, although a tent is essential for travel there. There are other classic trekking areas at Oulanka National Park near Kuusamo, and in North Karelia.

Some recommended treks are described here. Excellent trekking maps are available in Finland for all of these routes.

Karhunkierros (Bear's Ring) This circular trail in northern Finland is the most famous of all Finnish trekking routes. It covers 75km of rugged cliffs, gorges and suspension bridges from Rukatunturi, 25km north of Kuusamo, through the Oulanka National Park. Huts provide shelter and free lodging en route, and there are good services and connections at several locations along the route. The nearest main town is Kuusamo, where you can organise guides, maps, transport and trekking equipment. See the Karhunkierros Trekking Route & Oulanka National Park section in the Oulu, Kainuu & Koillismaa Regions chapter for a description of the trek.

Karhunpolku (Bear's Path) This 133km marked hiking trail of medium difficulty leads north from Lieksa through a string of national parks and nature reserves along the Russian border to end in the town of Kuhmo. Some of the Lakeland's most stunning scenery is along this route. At the northern end of the trail there are connections to the UKK Route. The nearest town is Lieksa. See the boxed text 'Karelian Treks' in the Karelia chapter for a brief description of this trek.

Susitaival (Wolf's Trail) This 100km trail runs along the border with Russia, stretching from the marshlands of Patvinsuo National Park, north of Ilomantsi, to the forests of Petkeljärvi National Park. From there, it continues as the Bear's Path, or Karhunpolku. The nearest town is Ilomantsi. See the boxed text 'Karelian Treks' in the Karelia chapter for a brief description of this trek.

UKK Route This 240km route in northern Finland is the nation's longest trekking route. It was named after President Urho K Kekkonen, and has been in development for decades. The trail starts at the Koli Hill, continues along the western side of Lake Pielinen and ends at the Iso-Syöte Hill, going via Vuokatti, Hyrynsalmi and the Ukko-Halla Hill. Farther east, there are more sections of the UKK Route, including the Kuhmo to Lake Peurajärvi leg (connections from Nurmes) and the Kuhmo to Iso-Palonen leg. See the boxed text 'Trekking the UKK' in the Oulu, Kainuu & Kollismaa Regions chapter for a brief description of this trek.

Cycling

Riding a bike in Finland is one of the best ways to explore parts of the country in summer. Finns ride their bikes through the dark, snowy winters, but to do so voluntarily as a tourist you have to be a true masochist.

What sets Finland apart from both Sweden and Norway is the almost total lack of mountains. Main roads are in good condition and traffic is very light compared to elsewhere in Europe. Minor roads have very little traffic (other than farmers' tractors), especially in northern Finland. Bicycle tours are further facilitated by the liberal camping regulations and the long hours of daylight in June and July. All petrol stations have free toilets, and their cafés often serve perfectly edible home-cooked lunches until 4pm.

The drawback is this: distances in Finland are vast. From Helsinki to Rovaniemi is 837km, and from Turku to Savonlinna is 446km. And let's face it, a lot of the Finnish scenery (in Lapland and Pohjanmaa, for instance) is uniformly dull. If you've got three or more months to explore and buns of steel, get a bicycle and hit the road. Otherwise you'll want to look at planning shorter rides and explorations in particular corners of the country, combining cycling with bus and train trips – Finnish buses and trains are very bike-friendly. Even if your time is limited, don't skip a few quick jaunts in the countryside. There are very good networks of cycling paths in and around most major cities and holiday destinations (the networks around Oulu and Turku are very good).

Summers get pretty hot, especially in southern Finland, so carry plenty of water. Conversely, the weather can be unpredictable year-round, so pack rain gear. And don't forget to bring along a repair kit.

In most towns bicycles can be hired from sports shops, tourist offices, camping grounds or hostels for around €8 to €15 per day, or €45 to €60 a week. Another option is to buy a second-hand bicycle for around €100, then sell it once you have finished touring. Check local newspapers for listings; *polkupyörä* is Finnish for bicycle.

BRINGING YOUR BICYCLE
Most airlines will carry a bike free of charge, so long as the bike and panniers don't exceed

the weight allowance per passenger – usually 20kg (44lb). Hefty excess baggage charges may be incurred if you do, and this applies to both international and internal flights.

Inform the airline that you will be bringing your bike when you book your ticket. Arrive at the airport in good time to remove panniers and pedals, deflate tyres and turn handlebars around – the minimum dismantling usually required by airlines.

Bikes can be carried on long-distance buses for around €2 if there is space available (and there usually is). Sometimes they can go on for free. Just advise the driver prior to departure.

Bikes can accompany passengers on most normal train journeys, with a surcharge up to €7. Exceptions are Inter-City (IC) and Pendolino trains. Take your bike directly to the Konduktöörivaunu carriage, pay the conductor in cash and take the receipt. You must collect your bike from the cargo carriage when you reach your destination.

WHERE TO CYCLE
You can cycle on all public roads except motorways – these are either four-lane roads that carry a green road-and-bridge symbol, or two-lane roads marked by a green symbol of a car. Many public roads in southern Finland have a dedicated cycling track running alongside. The best place to cycle is Åland.

Åland
The Åland islands are the most bicycle-friendly region in Finland, and are (not surprisingly) the most popular region for bicycle tours. Bikes can be rented in Mariehamn and Eckerö, and come with a free island map. From either town there are clearly marked bike routes (with kilometre markers) to every corner of the island group, passing villages, medieval churches and quaint old farms every few kilometres. Bikes are transported free on car ferries between the islands, but three special bicycle-only ferries also operate in summer.

South Coast
Southern Finland has more traffic than other parts of the country, but with careful planning you can find quiet roads that offer pleasant scenery. King's Road, a historic route between Turku and Vyborg, passes old settlements, churches and manor houses. Even

quieter is the Ox Road that runs through rural areas from Turku to Hämeenlinna. There are also some good shorter rides around Turku.

The Lakeland

Two theme routes cover the entire eastern frontier area, from the south o Kuusamo in the north. *Runon ja rajan tie* (Road of the Poem and Frontier) consists of secondary sealed roads which pass several Karelian–theme houses where you can stuff yourself with Eastern food. The route ends in northern Lieksa. Some of the smallest, most remote villages along the easternmost roads have been lumped together to create the *Korpikylien tie* (Road of Wilderness Villages). This route starts at Saramo village in northern Nurmes and ends at Hossa, in northeast Suomussalmi. Some sections are unsealed.

The provincial tourist office has printed a leaflet, *Karjalan kirkkotie*, which guides riders along the 'Karelian church route' from the Heinävesi monasteries to the municipality of Ilomantsi in the far east.

A recommended loop takes you around Lake Pielinen, and may include a ferry trip across the lake.

Western Finland

This flat region, known as Pohjanmaa, is generally good for cycling, except that distances are long and scenery away from the coast is almost oppressively dull. Quiet roads along the rivers Kauhajoki, Kyrönjoki, Laihianjoki and Lapuanjoki are nice for touring. Further north, practically all towns and villages lie along rivers that run from southeast to northwest. Bring your bike by train to Seinäjoki or further north, and continue along the narrow roads. The 'Swedish Coast' around Vaasa and north to Kokkola, is probably the most scenic part of this region.

Winter Sports

Skiing seems to be nearly every Finn's favourite activity during winter, although the peak season is actually spring (February to May) in northern Finland. A short list of the best resorts – for downhill or cross-country skiing – includes Ylläs, Levi, Pyhä-Luosto and Ruka; although Pallas, Saariselkä, Iso-Syöte, Koli and Ounasvaara are also fairly good.

Finnish ski resorts offer more than just skiing: dog-sledding, snowmobile safaris, reindeer sleigh tours and ice fishing are usually also organised, provided you have the money to take part. As you might expect, ski resorts aren't really geared towards budget travellers. Virtually all resorts have their own website with current information – see the relevant section in this book or look up W www.finland-winter.com.

In the following list, roughly arranged from south to north, the nearest town is indicated in parentheses.

Iso-Syöte (Pudasjärvi) 21 downhill slopes, 11 lifts. Vertical drop 192m, longest run 1200m. Cross-country trails 110km.
Koli (Lieksa/Joensuu) 11 downhill slopes, 9 lifts. Vertical drop 240m, longest run 1500m. Cross-country trails 100km.
Levi (Kittilä) 45 downhill slopes, 19 lifts. Vertical drop 325m, longest run 2500m. Cross-country trails 230km.
Ounasvaara (Roveniemi) 6 downhill slopes, 4 lifts. Vertical drop 140m, longest run 600m. Cross-country trails 100km.
Pallas (Muonio) 9 downhill slopes, 2 lifts. Vertical drop 340m, longest run 2400m. Cross-country trails 160km.
Pyhä-Luosto (Sodankylä) 17 downhill slopes, 11 lifts. Vertical drop 280m, longest run 1800m. Cross-country trails 165km.
Ruka (Kuusamo) 28 downhill slopes, 18 lifts. Vertical drop 201m, longest run 1300m. Cross-country trails 250km.
Saariselkä (Inari) 12 downhill slopes, 6 lifts. Vertical drop 180m, longest run 1500m. Cross-country trails 217km.
Ylläs (Kolari) 37 downhill slopes, 17 lifts. Vertical drop 463km, longest run 3km. Cross-country trails 250km.

DOWNHILL SKIING & SNOWBOARDING

Finland has more than 120 downhill ski resorts – in fact, there are ski lifts in all major towns with a hill taller than the local apartment buildings. Most Finnish resorts also offer designated runs and halfpipes for snowboarders.

Finnish slopes are generally quite low and so are well-suited to beginners and families. The best resorts are in Lapland, where the vertical drop averages 250m over 3km. In central and southern Finland, ski runs are much shorter, averaging about 1km in length. For steeper, longer and more challenging slopes head across the border to Sweden or Norway.

The ski season in Finland runs from late November to early May, and slightly longer in Lapland and the north, where it's possible to ski from October through to Midsummer. Beware of the busy winter and spring (February to April) holiday periods, especially around Christmas and Easter – they can get too crowded to be appreciated, and accommodation prices are through the roof.

Accommodation at ski resorts is expensive in luxury cottages, hotels and apartments but there are hostels reasonably convenient to some ski areas, and basic cabin rentals (usually by the week or weekend in peak season) can be affordable if you're in a group. Prices naturally rise dramatically during holiday periods and bookings are advised at those times. In summer, ski resorts become ghost towns and accommodation (the few places that remain open) can be great value. Some resorts have started to offer programmes of hiking, river rafting and mountain biking to lure summer customers; inquire at a Finnish tourist office for more information on these resort packages.

You can rent all skiing or snowboarding equipment at major ski resorts for about €20/80 a day/week. A one-day lift pass costs around €26/120 a day/week (slightly less in the shoulder and off-peak seasons), although it is often possible to pay separately for each ride. Skiing lessons are also available from around €27 a day.

CROSS-COUNTRY SKIING

Cross-country skiing is one of the simplest and most pleasant things to do outdoors in winter in Finland. It's the ideal way to explore the beautiful, silent winter countryside of lakes, fells, fields and forests, and is widely used by Finns for fitness and as a means of transport.

Practically every town and village maintains ski tracks around the urban centre, and these are typically in use from the first snow fall in November through to early May – although die-hard skiers will grimly continue to ski across bare rock in spring if they feel that the season hasn't lasted long enough! In many cases, local tracks are *valaistu latu* (illuminated). Access is always free, and getting lost is impossible on municipal tracks as they are usually loops of only a few kilometres.

The one drawback to using local tracks is that you'll need to bring your own equipment (or purchase some in a sports shop), as rentals usually aren't possible.

Cross-country skiing at one of Finland's many ski resorts is another option. Once you venture to ski resorts, the tracks get much longer but also are better maintained. This means that tracks are in excellent condition soon after a snowfall. Ski resorts offer excellent instruction, and rent out equipment (skis, boots and poles) for about €15 to €18 per day or €60 to €75 per week. The best cross-country skiing is in Lapland, where resorts offer hundreds of kilometres of trails (a fraction of these are illuminated for night and winter skiing).

Keep in mind that there are only about five hours of daylight each day in northern Lapland during winter – if you're planning on a longer trek, spring is the best time. Cross-country skiing is best during January and February in southern Finland, and from December to April in the north.

Water Sports

Finland has no shortage of waterways and much of the country is best experienced from its bays, lakes, rivers and canals. You'll find it possible to make trips lasting anywhere from an hour or two to several weeks.

RENTALS

For independent travel on waterways, you will need to rent your own rowing boat, canoe or kayak. The typical Finnish rowing boat is available at camping grounds and some tourist offices, usually for less than €20 per day, and hourly rentals are possible. Hostels and rental cottages may have rowing boats that you'll be allowed to use for free. In a rowing boat, your back faces the bow of the boat and you'll have to turn your head to see where you're heading. Controlling a rowing boat is not as easy as canoeing, so rowing boats are never used on rivers with rapids. Use them on lakes, especially for visits to nearby islands.

Canoes and kayaks are suitable for trips that last several days or weeks. For longer trips you'll need a waterproof plastic barrel for your gear, a life-jacket and waterproof route maps. Route maps and guides may be purchased at the local or regional tourist office, at the **Karttakeskus Aleksi** map shop in Helsinki or through the **Karttakeskus mail-order service** (☎ *0204-455 911, fax 455 929*). Waterproof maps usually cost around €5 to €10; occasionally tourist offices and rental outfits will supply simple route maps at no cost. Canoe and kayak rentals range in price from €15 to €30 per day, and €80 to €200 per week. You'll pay more if you need overland transportation to the starting or ending point of your trip, if you wish to hire a guide or if you need to rent extra gear such as tents and sleeping bags.

Try to locate a rental company at both ends of the route, and compare rates (including transport). It would probably be more convenient to rent from the end point of your trip so that you will first be transported to the starting point, making your journey a bit more flexible. Contact local tourist offices for the names of rental outfitters.

WHERE TO ROW & PADDLE

The sheltered bays and islands around the Turku archipelago in southwest Finland are good for canoeing in summer. Ferries regularly shuttle between islands so it's easy to get from one safe spot to another. The Åland islands are also excellent for canoeing and equipment can be hired in Mariehamn.

Lakes provide the calmest waters for rowing or canoeing and boat is by far the best way to explore areas such as Linnansaari National Park (from Rantasalmi or Oravi) or Lake Saimaa, Europe's third-largest lake. Finland's system of rivers, canals and linking waterways means there are some extensive canoeing routes. The routes described in this section have been meticulously researched, and a route map and guide with detailed information – including the position of any and all rapids – is absolutely essential for a safe, fun trip. Most route maps and guides are available in English.

Rapids are classified according to a scale from I to VI. I is very simple, II will make your heart beat faster, III is dangerous for your canoe, IV may be fatal for the inexperienced. Rapids classified as VI are just short of Niagara Falls and will probably kill you. Unless you're an experienced paddler

you shouldn't negotiate anything above a class I rapid on your own.

Always be prepared to carry your canoe or kayak around an unsafe stretch of river (rapids, waterfalls, broken dams, hydroelectric power stations). This could save your life.

The Lakeland is, naturally, the most popular region for canoe and kayak travel. On established routes there are easy-to-follow route markers and designated camp sites along the way. North Karelia, particularly around Lieksa and Ruunaa, also offers good paddling. Rivers further north, in the Kuusamo area and in Lapland, are very steep and fast-flowing, with tricky rapids, making them suitable for experienced paddlers only.

If you're uncertain of your skills and just want to experience the thrill and beauty of the mighty northern rivers, contact one of the local tourist offices about joining a white-water rafting expedition. In summer, there are many operators that offer such tours. Also contact the **Finland Canoe Federation** (☎ *09-494 965; Olympiastadion, Helsinki*), which offers advice and has member organisations that arrange trips.

Ivalojoki Route The 70km route along the Ivalojoki in northeast Lapland starts at the village of Kuttura and finishes in Ivalo, crossing 30 rapids along the way.

Kyrönjoki Routes The Kyrönjoki in western Finland totals 205km, but you can do short trips down the river from Kauhajoki, Kurikka or Ilmajoki.

Lakeland Trail This 350km route travels through the heart of the lake district (Kangaslampi, Enonkoski, Savonranta, Kerimäki, Punkaharju, Savonlinna and Rantasalmi) and takes 14 to 18 days.

Naarajoki Trail This is an easy 100km route in the Mikkeli area, recommended for families.

Oravareitti (Squirrel Route) In the heart of the Lakeland, this is a 52km trip from Juva to Sulkava.

Savonselkä Circuit The circuit, near Lahti, has three trails that are 360km, 220km and 180km in length. There are many sections that can be done as day trips and that are suitable for novice paddlers.

Seal Trail From Kolovesi to Linnansaari, this is a 120km route that takes one to seven days.

Välivälylä Trail This Lakeland trail goes from Kouvola to either Lappeenranta (90km) or Luumäki (60km) and includes some class I to class III rapids.

Other Activities

FISHING

Finnish waters are teeming with fish – and with people trying to catch them. Finland has at least one million enthusiastic domestic anglers. Commonly caught fish include salmon (both river and landlocked), trout, grayling, perch, pike, whitefish, break and Arctic char.

With so many bodies of water – lakes, rivers, streams and the sea – there are no shortage of places to cast a line. In winter, when most water surfaces are frozen over, ice-fishing is all the craze. You simply cut a hole in the ice, drop in a line, and wait for a bite. Lapland probably has the greatest concentration of quality fishing spots, but the number of designated places in southern Finland is also increasing. Most fishing areas are privately owned. The exceptions are designated 'Government Fishing Areas' that are stocked by the Metsähallitus with tonnes of fish each year. Some of the most popular fishing areas are the Torniojoki and Muniojoki Rivers, the Kainuu region around Kajaani, Hossa, Ruunaa Recreation Area, Peurajärvi, Lake Saimaa around Mikkeli, Lake Inari, Kymijoki near Kotka, and Teno.

Local tourist offices can direct you to the best fishing spots in the area, and usually can provide some sort of regional fishing map. An annual guide to fishing the entire country is available from the **Metsähallitus** *(Forest and Park Service; ☎ 09-270 5221, fax 644 421; Tikankontti, Eteläesplanadi 20, Helsinki)*.

Permits

Several permits are required of foreigners (between the ages of 18 and 64) who wish to go fishing in Finland, and the system is strictly enforced by permit-checkers. First, you will need a national fishing permit, known as a 'fishing management fee'. A one-week permit is €5 and an annual permit €15; they're payable at any bank or via the Internet. Second, fishing with a rod or lure always requires a special permit, also available at banks and post offices. Finally, you will need to pick up a local permit which has time and catch limits (say, two salmon per day and an unrestricted amount of other species). The local permit can be purchased for one day, one week or even for just a few hours. Typically these cost around €8 per day or €30 per week and are available on the spot, from the location where you're planning to fish (from tourist offices, sports shops, camping grounds etc). Check local restrictions when buying the daily permit.

The waters in Åland are regulated separately and require a separate regional permit.

Equipment Rental

Many camping grounds and tourist offices rent out fishing gear in summer. To go ice-fishing in winter, however, you'll either need to buy your own gear or join an organised tour – nobody rents out ice-fishing tackle in Finland because every Finn has this!

BIRD-WATCHING

Bird-watching is extremely popular in Finland, in no small part because many bird species migrate to northern Finland in summer to take advantage of the almost continuous daylight for breeding and rearing their young. Look carefully when in Finnish forests and you'll see that bird-mad locals have filled the trees with birdhouses to encourage visits by their favourite species. The best months for watching birds are May to June or mid-July, and late August to September or early October.

Liminganlahti (Liminka Bay), near Oulu, is a wetlands bird sanctuary and probably the best bird-watching spot in Finland. Other good areas include Puurijärvi-Isosuo National Park in Western Finland, Oulanka National Park near Kuusamo, the Porvoo area east of Helsinki, the Kemïo Islands, and about a dozen other places. At any of these areas you can usually hire an ornithological guide. Otherwise, bring your own binoculars and a good bird book. An excellent guide is *Birds* by Peter Holden. The version available within the country is only in Finnish, so you will need to purchase an English-language version before you go.

GOLF

You need a green card (insurance card) to play on most Finnish golf courses, but many courses are open to the general public for €20 to €30 per round. At last count, there were around 100 uncrowded golf courses throughout Finland, typically open from late April to mid-October. The most unusual golf course in Finland is the Green Zone golf course in Tornio (see the boxed text 'Midnight at the Green Zone Golf Course' in the Oulu chapter) – it crosses the boundary between Finland and Sweden and thus a time zone. For information on Finnish golf courses, contact the **Finnish Golf Union** *(Suomen Golfliitto; ☎ 09-3481 2244, fax 147 145; Radiokatu 20, 00240 Helsinki)*.

TRACING YOUR ANCESTORS

Many visitors to Finland have Finnish ancestors. A trip provides a good chance to find out more about their lives, and you may even find relatives you never knew existed. Do some research in your local library, and some Internet research (see the relevant Finnish websites following) before you go.

Useful Organisations

The best place to visit first is **Suomen Sukututkimusseura** *(Finnish Genealogical Society; ☎ 09-278 1188, fax 278 1199; W www.genealogia.fi; Liisankatu 16A, 00170 Helsinki)*. There's an extensive library of published books of family surveys, and assistance is provided. You can join the society for €27 a year, which entitles you to receive various publications.

Kansallisarkisto *(National Archives; ☎ 09-228 521, fax 176 302; W www.narc.fi; Rauhankatu 17, 00170 Helsinki)* covers all of Finland. Other good contacts are **Siirtolaisinstituutii** *(The Institute of Migration; ☎ 02-284 0440, fax 233 3460; W www.utu.fi; Linnankatu 61, 20100 Turku)*, with archives and a library; and **Sukuseurojen Keskusliito** *(Central Association of Genealogical Societies; ☎/fax 09-694 9320; Työmiehenkatu 2, 00180 Helsinki)*.

Archives

The best information will come directly from archives, but you will have to pay a fee for the service. If you know for sure where your ancestors lived (and that they were members of the Lutheran church, which is very likely), go directly to the local Kirkkoherranvirasto (Parochial Archives), an office usually found near the local Lutheran church. The Kansallisarkisto (see Useful Organisations) is best if you are looking for ancestors from the 19th century, or earlier. If you have several ancestors from various places within a region, go to the Maakuntaarkisto (Regional Archives) in the nearest major town or city.

Getting There & Away

AIR

Direct flights to Finland are not the cheapest in Europe, since it's not currently served by any 'no-frills' discount airlines. Most flights to Helsinki or Turku are with Finnair or Scandinavian Airlines (SAS).

Holders of GO25 or the ISIC (International Student Identity Card) can find discounted flights to and from Finland at student travel agencies. In Finland, contact **Kilroy Travels** (W *www.kilroytravels.com*), the main student travel agency in Scandinavia. There are Kilroy offices in Helsinki, Turku, Tampere and Oulu. The student travel agency STA also has an office in Helsinki.

Airlines

There are good flight connections to Finland from all over the world. Finnair, the Finnish national carrier, and SAS have scheduled flights to Helsinki from most major cities in Europe, as well as from New York, San Francisco, Cairo, Bangkok, Singapore, Beijing, Sydney and Tokyo.

British Airways, Lufthansa, KLM-Royal Dutch Airlines, Air France, Austrian Airlines, Czech Airlines, Swiss, Icelandair and a handful of smaller airlines fly into the Helsinki-Vantaa international airport, including many flights daily between the Scandinavian and Baltic capitals. To Turku, Oulu and Tampere there are several nonstop flights daily from Stockholm.

From outside Europe, you will find that prices are similar to flights to any other European city. Within Europe, there is more variety in fares, depending on which city you want to fly from.

Buying Tickets

With a bit of research – ringing around travel agencies, checking Internet sites, perusing the travel ads in newspapers – you can often get yourself a good travel deal. Start early as some of the cheapest tickets need to be bought well in advance and popular flights can sell out.

Generally, there is nothing to be gained by buying a ticket direct from the airline. Discounted tickets are released to selected travel agencies and specialist discount agencies, and these are usually the cheapest

deals going. One exception to this rule is the expanding number of 'no-frills' carriers that sell direct to travellers – although at the time of research none was flying direct to Finland. The other exception is booking on the Internet. Many airlines offer some excellent fares to Web surfers.

Many travel agencies around the world have websites, which can make the Internet a quick and easy way to compare prices. There is also an increasing number of online agencies, such as W www.travelocity.co.uk, that operate only on the Internet. Online ticket sales work well if you are doing a simple one-way or return trip on specified dates. However, online, superfast fare generators are no substitute for a travel agent who knows all about special deals, has strategies for avoiding stopovers and can offer advice on everything from which airline has the best vegetarian food to the best travel insurance to bundle with your ticket.

You may find the cheapest flights are advertised by obscure agencies. Most of these businesses are honest and solvent, but there are some rogue fly-by-night outfits around. Paying by credit card generally offers protection, as most card issuers provide refunds if you can prove you didn't get what you paid for. Similar protection can be obtained by buying a ticket from a bonded agency, such

as one covered by the **Air Travel Organisers'
Licensing** *(ATOL;* w *www.atol.org.uk)* scheme
in the UK. Agencies only accepting cash
should hand over the tickets straight away
and not tell you to 'come back tomorrow'.
After you've made a booking or paid your
deposit, call the airline and confirm that the
booking was made.

Some online airfare agencies include:

Cheapest Flights (w www.cheapestflights.co.uk)
Cheap worldwide flights from the UK, although
you've got to get in early for the bargains
Cheap Flights (w www.cheapflights.co.uk) A
very informative site with specials, airline info
and flight searches from the UK
Expedia (w www.expedia.com) Microsoft's
travel site, this is for the USA but has links to
sites for Canada, the UK and Germany
Flights.com (w www.tiss.com) A truly international site for flight-only tickets; cheap fares
and easy-to-search database
Travelocity (w www.travelocity.com) This US site
allows you to search fares to/from practically
anywhere (in US dollars)

Round-the-World Tickets Round-the-
world (RTW) tickets are often real bargains.
They are usually put together by a combination of airlines and permit you to fly anywhere you want on their route systems so
long as you do not backtrack. There may be
restrictions on how many stops you are permitted and usually the tickets are valid for 90
days up to a year. An alternative type of RTW
ticket is one put together by a travel agency
using a combination of discounted tickets.

Finnair is part of the oneworld airline alliance scheme involving Qantas, British
Airways, Cathay Pacific, American Airlines, Iberia, Aer Lingus and LanChile.

Nordic Air Pass If you're in a hurry to see
Scandinavia and the Baltic states, the Nordic
Air Pass might be right for you. The pass is
good for limited travel in Finland, Denmark,
Norway, Sweden, Estonia, Latvia and
Lithuania from 1 May to 30 September.
(Residents of Scandinavia and Baltic countries may only use the Nordic Air Pass from
15 June and 17 August.) You can purchase
the pass – in reality a book of coupons, with
each coupon valid for a single one-way
flight segment – from a travel agency in
your home country. At least one coupon
must be used on an international flight. The

minimum purchase is four coupons per passenger, the maximum is 10. The cost is
US$360 for four coupons, US$90 for each
additional coupon. Taxes and service charges
are not included. It's possible to receive a refund for unused coupons – contact a travel
agency for details. Affiliated airlines are Air
Lithuania, Braathens SAFE, Estonian Air,
Finnair, Lithuanian Airlines, Maersk Air,
Skärgårdsflyg and Transwede.

Travellers with Special Needs

If they're warned early enough, airlines can
often make special arrangements for travellers, including wheelchair assistance at
airports or vegetarian meals on the flight.
Children under two years travel for 10% of
the standard fare (or free on some airlines)
as long as they don't occupy a seat. They
don't get a baggage allowance. 'Skycots',
baby food and nappies (diapers) should be
provided by the airline if requested in advance. Children aged between two and 12
can usually occupy a seat for half to two-
thirds of the full fare, and do get a baggage
allowance.

The disability-friendly website w www
.everybody.co.uk has an airline directory
that provides information on the facilities
offered by various airlines.

Departure Tax

In Finland, the quoted fares always include
VAT and an airport departure tax.

The USA

Discount travel agencies in the USA are
known as consolidators. San Francisco is the
ticket consolidator capital of America, although some good deals can be found in Los
Angeles, New York and other big cities.

Council Travel *(☎ 800 226 8624;* w *www
.ciee.org; head office: 205 E 42 St, New York,
NY 10017),* America's largest student travel
organisation, has around 60 offices in the
USA. **STA Travel** *(☎ 800 777 0112;* w *www
.statravel.com)* now has offices in Boston,
Chicago, Miami, New York, Philadelphia,
San Francisco and other major cities.

Finnair flies nonstop between Helsinki
and New York City, San Francisco and Los
Angeles. British Airways, SAS and United
Airlines also fly on this route, and there is a
wide range of connecting flights to and from
other cities in the USA. Advance-purchase

return fares from New York City start as low as US$400, and from Los Angeles or San Francisco from US$550.

Another option you might consider is looking for a discounted trans-Atlantic fare to, say, Frankfurt or London, coupled with a connecting flight to Helsinki, as fares between Helsinki and other major European cities can be quite low.

From Finland, you can fly from Helsinki to New York for as little as €250 one way, and to Los Angeles for €350 one way. Prices are for students and people under 26 years of age.

Finland is actually closer to the USA and Canada than some destinations in southern Europe, which makes flying time shorter.

Canada

Canadian air fares tend to be about 20% higher than those sold in the USA. **Travel CUTS** (☎ 800 667 2887; W www.travelcuts .com) is Canada's national student travel agency and has offices in all major cities.

Finnair flies from Toronto to Helsinki twice weekly, and you will find any number of North American and European airlines, including Lufthansa and Austrian Airlines, with connecting flights to Helsinki. Most airlines fly over Greenland on the way. A return fare from Toronto starts at around C$1360.

Australia

Flying from Australia is a two-stage journey (at least), with likely stopovers in either Singapore or Bangkok, or cities in Europe. It's also possible to go via Japan and/or Russia. Finnair flies to Sydney, in partnership with Qantas, Cathay Pacific or Thai Airways. British Airways, KLM, Lufthansa, Austrian Airlines and a few other European airlines fly to Helsinki from Australia via London, Amsterdam, Frankfurt, Vienna or other cities.

Return flights from Sydney to Helsinki cost A$1850 to A$2200. From Helsinki to Sydney, Kilroy Travels quotes a one-way fare of €540

Two well known agencies for cheap fares are STA Travel and Flight Centre. **STA Travel** (☎ 131 776; W www.statravel.com.au; main office: 224 Faraday St, Carlton, Melbourne) has offices in all major cities and on many university campuses. **Flight Centre** (☎ 131 600; W www.flightcentre.com.au; 82 Elizabeth St, Sydney) has dozens of branches throughout Australia.

Travel.Com (W www.travel.com.au) is a good Australian online site that allows you to look up fares and flights into and out of the country.

New Zealand

RTW and Circle Pacific fares for travel to or from New Zealand are usually the best value, often cheaper than a return ticket. Depending on which airline you choose, you may fly across Asia, with possible stopovers in India, Bangkok or Singapore, or across the USA, with possible stopovers in Honolulu, Australia or one of the Pacific islands.

Flight Centre (☎ 09-309 6171; W www .flightcentre.co.nz; National Bank Towers, Cnr Queen & Darby Sts, Auckland) has many branches throughout the country. **STA Travel** (☎ 09-309 0458; W www.statravel.co.nz; 10 High St, Auckland) has other offices in Auckland as well as in Hamilton, Palmerston North, Wellington, Christchurch and Dunedin. An excellent website for checking flights from New Zealand is **Travel Online** (W www.travelonline.co.nz).

The UK

Discount air travel is big business in London – this is the discount capital of Europe. Advertisements for many travel agencies appear in the travel pages of the weekend broadsheet newspapers, in *Time Out*, the *Evening Standard* and in the free magazine *TNT*. Shop around – many of the ultracheap fares you see advertised won't be available when you call, but something usually comes up. Popular travel agencies in the UK include: **STA Travel** (☎ 0870-160 6070; W www.statravel.co.uk), with branches across the country; **Trailfinders** (Europe line ☎ 020-7937 1234; W www.trailfinders.co.uk; 194 Kensington High St, London W8); **Flightbookers** (☎ 020-7757 2000; W www.ebookers.com; 177-178 Tottenham Court Rd, London W1); and **Flight Centre** (☎ 020-8543 9070; W www .flightcentre.com; 112-134 The Broadway, London SW19 1RL).

Finnair and SAS fly direct from London to Helsinki daily. One-way/return fares start as low as UK£100/160, although a fare this cheap carries plenty of restrictions. From Helsinki, Kilroy Travels offers student or youth one-way flights to London from €130.

Though none of the 'no-frills' airlines flies direct from the UK to Finland, a worthwhile consideration from London is to fly on the budget carrier **Ryan Air** *(w www.ryanair.com)* to Stockholm and take the ferry to Turku or Helsinki from there. One-way Internet fares can be picked up for as low as UK£5 (plus taxes), provided you book well ahead and are willing to fly midweek. Fares of around UK£45 are reasonably easy to find. The downside is that you must fly from Stansted airport in London to Nyköping in Sweden and put up with early-morning or late-night flights.

Continental Europe

Helsinki is well connected to most European capitals and major cities by a number of airlines. Particularly good are the connections with Scandinavian and Baltic capitals.

Some of the busiest European flight markets include Amsterdam, Athens, Berlin and Paris. In the Netherlands, **Holland International** *(☎ 070-307 6307; w www.holland international.nl)* is a recommended agency with offices in most cities. Recommended online sites include w www.budgettravel.com and w www.airfair.nl.

In Germany, **STA Travel** *(☎ 030-311 0950; Goethesttrasse 73, 10625 Berlin)* has branches in major cities across the country. The websites w www.justtravel.de and w www.last minute.de are also useful for checking fares.

In France try the student travel agency **OTU Voyages** *(☎ 01 44 41 38 50; w www.otu .fr; 39 ave Georges-Bernanos, 75005 Paris)*, with branches across the country; **Voyageurs du Monde** *(☎ 01 42 86 16 00; 55 rue Ste-Anne, 75002 Paris)*; and **Nouvelles Frontières** *(☎ 08 25 00 08 25 nationwide, 01 45 68 70 00 in Paris; w www.nouvelles-frontieres.fr; 87 blvd de Grenelle, 75015 Paris)*. Go to w www .anyway.fr or w www.lastminute.fr to check fares online.

Good travel agencies in Italy include: **CTS Viaggi** *(☎ 06-462 0431; 16 Via Genova, Rome)*; **Passagi** *(☎ 06-474 0923; Stazione Termini FS, Galleria Di Tesla, Rome)*; and **Viaggi Wasteels** *(☎ 06-446 6679; Via Milazzo 8/C, Rome)*.

The cheapest flights from Spain are out of Madrid or Barcelona. Agencies include: **Viajes** *(☎ 91-559 1819; Princesa 3, 28008 Madrid)* and **Nouvelles Frontières** *(☎ 91-547 4200; w www.nouvelles-frontieres.es; Plaza de Espana 18, 28008 Madrid)*, both with branches in major cities.

From Helsinki, Kilroy Travels quotes the following one-way fares for travellers aged under 26 and students under 33:

destination	cost (€)
Amsterdam	142
Athens	183
Berlin	140
Copenhagen	123
Paris	160
Moscow	173
Oslo	117
Reykjavík	241
Stockholm	80

Asia

Most Asian countries offer fairly competitive deals, with Bangkok, Singapore and Hong Kong the best places to shop around for discount tickets. Flights from Asia to Europe tend to be cheaper than flights in the other direction, so it's worth purchasing the return flight while in Asia. Most airlines sell a standard European fare, regardless of the distance flown from the first stop.

Finnair flies direct from Helsinki to all three major travel hubs, as well as to Tokyo and Beijing. Hong Kong is the discount capital but its travel market can be unpredictable. STA Travel has branches in Bangkok and Singapore. In Hong Kong, **Phoenix Services** *(☎ 2722 7378, fax 2369 8884; Room B, 6th floor, Milton Mansion, 96 Nathan Rd, Tsimshatsui)* is recommended.

From Helsinki, sample one-way fare include: Bangkok €350, Hong Kong €430, Singapore €400 and Tokyo €450.

LAND
Border Crossings

There are six crossings from northern Sweden to northern Finland across the Tornionjoki (Swedish: Torneälv) and Muonionjoki Rivers, and the main highway in both countries runs parallel to the border from Tornio/ Haparanda to Kaaresuvanto/Karesuando. There are no passport or customs formalities and if you're driving up along the border you can alternate between countries.

Between Norway and Finland, there are six border crossings along roads, plus a few legal crossings along wilderness tracks. The main Nordkapp route goes from Rovaniemi via Inari and Kaamanen to Karigasniemi. The western crossing at Kilpisjärvi is best if you're off to Tromsø or the Lofoten Islands.

Along the popular Helsinki–Vyborg–St Petersburg corridor there are two Finland–Russia road crossings: Nuijamaa (Russian side: Brusnichnoe) and Vaalimaa (Russian side: Torfyanovka).

Further north, it's possible to cross into Russia at the Finnish posts of Pelkola, near Imatra, and Niirala (Russian side: Vyartsilya), and continue 500km to Petrozavodsk.

From Salla, there is a road across the Russian border to Alakurtti, and from Ivalo, a road goes east to Murmansk via the Finnish border crossing of Raja-Jooseppi. Check current conditions with the Russian embassy in Helsinki.

Swedish and Norwegian border crossings are very relaxed, Russian ones less so. You must already have a visa to cross into Russia.

Bus

Sweden Buses from Stockholm drive along the Swedish east coast to Haparanda, and further north along the border. The only point where buses actually cross is Haparanda–Tornio, from where they continue on to Kemi (Skr45, 45 minutes), or just pick up a Finnish bus heading north or south. Regular buses link Boden and Luleå with Haparanda. **Tapanis Buss** (☎ 08-153 300 in Stockholm, 0922-12 955 in Haparanda; W www.tapanis .se) runs express coaches from Stockholm to Tornio via Haparanda twice a week via the E4 highway (Skr450, 15 hours).

Alternatively, pick a bus stop from where you can walk to Finland, although you can generally pick up a local bus to the station in the Finnish town or vice versa. North of Haparanda, Övertorneå and Karesuando are convenient crossings. Swedish trains travel as far north as Boden; from there take buses (train passes are valid) to Haparanda, and on to Tornio and Kemi. Inter-Rail passes cover bus travel all the way from Boden to Kemi.

Norway Finnish buses run frequently between Rovaniemi and the Norwegian border crossings, and some buses continue to the first Norwegian town, which is usually along Norwegian bus routes. Free timetables (ask bus drivers or at stations) usually list these connections.

Buses between Hammerfest and Kirkenes are very useful because they will drop you off at Karasjok, Levajok, Skipagurra and Neiden, with further connections to Finland available. There are several daily buses from Kirkenes to Neiden, but you may have to hitchhike onwards to Näätämö, stay there overnight, and catch a morning bus to Ivalo via Sevettijärvi. For Nuorgam, you can catch the nightly bus from Skipagurra via Polmak. There are also two daily departures from Polmak for Rovaniemi. From Lakselv, there are buses to Karigasniemi and Ivalo daily from mid-June to mid-August, and several buses from Karasjok to Ivalo, via Karigasniemi. For Kilpisjärvi, there are buses from Skibotn daily from mid-June to mid-August, with very early departures on weekdays. You can reach Skibotn daily from Tromsø, on the Norwegian coast. For Kivilompolo and Hetta (Enontekiö), catch the bus from Kautokeino; there are four buses per week. To get to Kautokeino from within Norway, you have a choice of buses from Alta or Karasjok.

Russia There are four daily express buses to Vyborg and St Petersburg from Helsinki, and one from Tampere and Lappeenranta. A visa is required to enter Russia. Check current timetables and book tickets at the city bus station or a travel agency. The one-way fare from Helsinki to Vyborg is €35 and to St Petersburg it's €48.

There are also buses from Joensuu to Sortavala and Petrozavodsk (Finnish: Petroskoi), and from Rovaniemi and Ivalo to Murmansk.

Train

There is no train service between Finland and Norway – but there are plenty of buses.

Sweden The typical route to Finland from any point in Europe goes via Denmark to the Swedish town of Helsingborg, from where there are regular trains to Stockholm. There are also direct long-distance trains to Stockholm from various major cities in Europe. Train passes give discounts on most ferry routes across to Finland. If you don't like the idea of a ferry ride, you can continue by train to the Swedish town of Boden or Luleå in the far north, then transfer to a bus to Haparanda and cross the border to Tornio or Kemi (the bus to Kemi is free for rail-pass holders). In summer the train goes all the way to the border.

Russia Finland uses broad-gauge tracks, similar to those in Russia, so there are regular trains to/from Russia. Tickets for these trains are sold at the international ticket counter at Helsinki train station. The rail crossing is at Vainikkala (Russian side, Luzhayka).

There are three daily trains from Helsinki to Russia, travelling via the Finnish stations of Lahti, Kouvola and Vainikkala. You must have a valid Russian visa but border formalities have been fast-tracked so that passport checks are now carried out on board the moving train.

The *Tolstoi* sleeper departs from Helsinki at 5.42pm daily, arriving in Moscow at 8.30am and one way costs €83/124 in 2nd/1st class. It departs from Moscow daily at 10.20pm. The fare includes a sleeper berth in both classes.

The *Sibelius* and *Repin* run daily between Helsinki and St Petersburg (5½ hours) via Vyborg (3¾ hours). The *Sibelius* (a Finnish train) departs from Helsinki at 7.42am (€44.10/77.90 2nd/1st class, seats only). The Russian *Repin* departs at 3.42pm and has 2nd-class seats (€49.10) or 1st-class sleeping berths (€86.10). Return fares are approximately double. Fares to Vyborg are €38.40/61.80 on *Sibelius* and €35.40/70.50 on *Repin*. From St Petersburg departures are at 4.48pm *(Sibelius)* and 7.48am *(Repin)*.

Asia To and from central and eastern Asia, a train can work out at about the same price as flying, depending on how much time and money you spend along the way, and it can be a lot more fun.

Helsinki is a good place to start your journey across Russia into Asia. Frequent trains run between Helsinki and Moscow (see the previous Russia section), and there are three routes to/from Moscow across Siberia with connections to China, Japan and Korea: the Trans-Siberian to/from Vladivostok, and the Trans-Mongolian and Trans-Manchurian, both to/from Beijing. There's a fourth route south from Moscow and across Kazakhstan, following part of the old Silk Road to Beijing. These trips take several days, often involve stopovers, and prices vary according to which direction you are travelling, where you buy your ticket and what is included.

For details on Trans-Siberian options see Lonely Planet's *Trans-Siberian Railway*.

Car & Motorcycle

Drivers of cars and riders of motorbikes will need the vehicle's registration papers, liability insurance and an international driving permit, in addition to their domestic licence. You may also need a *Carnet de passage en douane*, which is effectively a passport for the vehicle and acts as a temporary waiver of import duty. The *carnet* may also need to list any expensive spare parts that you're planning to carry with you, such as a gearbox. This is designed to prevent car-import rackets. Contact your local automobile association for details about all documentation.

Anyone who is planning to take their own vehicle with them on a long trip needs to check in advance the availability of spare parts and petrol. Unleaded petrol is not on sale worldwide, and neither is every little part for your car. See the Getting Around chapter for information about driving within Finland.

Russia If you plan to drive into Russia, you'll need an international licence and certificate of registration, passport and visa, and insurance. **Ingosstrakh** (☎ 09-694 0511, fax 693 3560; Salomonkatu 5C, 00100 Helsinki) is the only Russian insurer in Helsinki. It will cover you in Russia but not in other republics of the former Soviet Union. Roads on the Russian side are poor, some resembling potato fields.

Scandinavian car-rental companies do not allow their cars to be taken into Russia.

Bicycle

A cycling tour of Scandinavia or Europe that includes Finland will take quite a bit of planning and preparation, but cycling is a cheap, convenient, healthy, environmentally sound and, above all, fun way of travelling. Before you leave home, go over your bike with a fine-toothed comb and fill your repair kit with every imaginable spare part.

Bicycles can travel by air and ferry. You can take them to pieces and put them in a bike bag or box, but it's much easier simply to wheel your bike to the check-in desk, where it should be treated as a piece of baggage. You may have to remove the pedals and front wheel and turn the handlebars sideways so that it takes up less space in the aircraft's hold; check all this with the airline or ferry company well in advance, preferably before you pay for your ticket. On car ferries the bike can simply be wheeled into the hold.

See the Activities and Getting Around chapters for more information on cycling in Finland.

Hitching

Hitchhiking between Lapland and Sweden or Norway is only really recommended from June to August. Carry waterproof gear and expect long waits. Being positive also helps; getting stranded at an Arctic Sea fjord is a unique experience that you will probably never forget. There's the midnight sun, fresh winds and abundant birdlife to enjoy while you wait…and wait…and wait…

SEA

The Baltic ferries are some of the world's most impressive seagoing craft, especially considering they are passenger ferries rather than cruise ships. The big ferries are floating hotels-cum-shopping plazas, with duty-free shopping, restaurants, bars, karaoke, nightclubs and saunas. Many Scandinavians use them simply for boozy overnight cruises, so they can get pretty rowdy on Friday and Saturday nights, when you may need to book in advance. Services are year-round between major cities.

If you're travelling deck class (without a sleeping berth), the ferries are an inexpensive and interesting way to arrive or depart from Finland's main harbours at Helsinki and Turku. Many ferry lines offer 50% discounts for holders of Eurail, Scanrail and Inter-Rail passes. Some offer discounts for seniors and for ISIC and GO25 card-holders; inquire when purchasing your ticket.

Make ferry reservations well in advance when travelling in July, especially if you plan to bring a car. Fares are rather complicated and depend on the season, day of the week (Friday to Sunday is more expensive), whether it's day or overnight and, of course, the class of travel.

There are no departure taxes when leaving Finland by sea.

Sweden

Stockholm is the main gateway to Finland, due to the incredibly luxurious passenger ferries that ply regularly between Stockholm and Turku or Helsinki. There are two main competing operators, Silja Line (blue-and-white ferries) and Viking Line (red-and-white ferries), with smaller companies RG Lines, Seawind, Birka Lines and Eckerö operating on certain routes. Cabins are compulsory on **Silja Line** (W www.silja .com), but not on **Viking Line** (W www .vikingline.fi) – instead you can buy a passenger ticket and sleep in the salons or any spare patch of inside deck (or just not sleep at all, as many partying passengers do). There are luggage lockers on board. Silja gives some attractive discounts, so to get the best deal, compare before you buy. Viking Line is the cheapest, but note that Friday-night departures are more expensive than departures on other days of the week.

The major source of income for these two ferry companies is duty-free shopping. Because the ferries stop at Mariehamn in the Åland islands, tax-free shopping is possible on board, even though Sweden and Finland are both in the European Union. Thus Swedes and Finns can avoid the high sales taxes in both countries, especially for alcohol and cigarettes. Don't be fooled though – prices for alcohol on board are still much higher than those in the supermarkets of central Europe. Tax-free shopping between Finland and Sweden was technically wiped out when Finland joined the EU, but special exemptions for the Åland islands means ferries stopping over here can continue to offer duty-free goods. For the average traveller, this means ferry companies can afford to keep fares unusually low. Whether you choose to blow the rest of your cash on board on a megabuffet, disco dancing or a case of aquavit – well, that's up to you.

In summer, overnight crossings (passenger ticket only) from Stockholm start at €33 to Turku (11 to 12 hours) and €40 to Helsinki (16 hours).

Note that 'Åbo' is the Swedish word for Turku; many a confused traveller has left Stockholm for Åbo, only to find out the next morning that they have actually arrived in Turku! It is the same place.

All Viking and Silja ferries travelling between Stockholm and Turku call in at Mariehamn in Åland. Additionally, Birka Cruises travels between Mariehamn and Stockholm, and Viking Line offers service between Mariehamn and Kapellskär, Sweden, a small harbour in the northern part of Stockholm province.

Eckerö Line (W www.eckeroline.fi) sails from Grisslehamn north of Stockholm to Eckerö in Åland – at three hours and €5.50 (€8.90 in summer) it's the quickest and cheapest crossing from Sweden to Finland. From the main Åland island group it's possible to island-hop across the archipelago to mainland Finland (or vice versa) on free, ferries. See the Åland chapter for details.

RG Lines (W www.rgline.com) sails from Vaasa in Finland, to Umeå, Sweden (€41 or Skr360, three hours) one or two times daily in summer, less often in winter.

Estonia

Several ferry companies ply the Gulf of Finland between Helsinki and Tallinn in Estonia. Since most nationalities (except Canadians) don't require a visa and the trip is so quick and cheap, it's a very popular day trip from Helsinki. Competition between the companies keeps the price low and if you're heading to Estonia for onward travel it can be cheaper to get a same-day return ticket than a one-way ticket. Car ferries cross in 3½ hours, catamarans and hydrofoils in about 1½ hours. Service is heavy year-round, although in winter there are fewer departures, and the traffic is also slower because of ice. Cancellations occur if the sea is rough.

Ferries are cheapest: Eckerö Line has only one departure daily but is the cheapest with a return fare at just €12 from Tuesday to Thursday, except in July and August when it's €22. **Tallink** (W www.tallink.ee) and Silja Line have several daily departures. Catamarans and hydrofoils cost from €25 to €65 return depending on the company, time of year and the day of the week. **Linda Line** (W www.lindaline.fi) is the cheapest but also has the smallest boats. **Nordic Jet Line** (W www.njl.fi) is the priciest.

It is advisable to reserve a seat in advance during the summer, particularly if you wish to travel on a Saturday or Sunday.

Tickets can be booked at the ferry company offices in central Helsinki, from the ferry terminal, or from the Helsinki city tourist office (for a hefty €7 booking fee).

At the time of research, citizens of Australia, the UK, Japan, Korea, New Zealand, Singapore, USA and most of the countries of continental Europe need only a passport to visit Tallinn from Helsinki. Canadians and other nationals must obtain a visa (€40) from the Estonian embassy prior to travel. It takes three to five days and you need to show your ticket to Tallinn. Check the current situation at the Estonian consulate, Helsinki city tourist office or one of the ferry companies' offices before buying your ticket.

Germany

Finnlines (☎ 09-251 0200 in Helsinki; W www .finnlines.fi) has year-round service from Helsinki to Travemünde (€272 one way, 32 to 36 hours) with a connecting bus service to Hamburg. Silja Line also has a service from Helsinki to Rostock (via Tallinn) three times a week in summer, departing from Helsinki on Tuesday, Thursday and Saturday (24 hours).

Superfast Ferries (☎ 09-2535 0640, fax 2535 0601; W www.superfast.com; Melkonkatu 28, Helsinki) has a ferry between Rostock and Hanko on the south coast of Finland (22 hours), daily except Sunday. The ferries all depart in the evening and the minimum one-way fare is €138/69 per adult/child.

Russia

During the time of research there was no passenger-ferry service operating between Finland and Russia. **Kristina Cruises** (☎ 05-218 1011; W www.kristinacruises.com) offers cruises from Helsinki to St Petersburg in June and August, and **Karelia Lines** (☎ 05-453 0380) runs visa-free cruises from Lappeenranta to Vyborg. On both trips you must return with the same cruise.

Getting Around

There is plenty of free travel information available in English, but if you want just one book that contains accurate details of every train, bus, flight and ferry route in Finland, outlay €21 for *Suomen Kulkuneuvot*, published four times a year. The summer edition is generally referred to as *Kesäturisti*. It is in Finnish and Swedish, but there are summaries in English and a few other languages.

AIR

Finnair (W *www.finnair.fi*) is the principal domestic carrier, with services between major centres and to Lapland. SAS/Air Bothnia offers a limited service within Finland.

Although full-fare air travel within Finland isn't cheap (eg, Helsinki–Rovaniemi €223, Helsinki–Kuopio €167) flights make an attractive alternative to the train or bus on long flights. Advance-purchase return tickets give up to 50% discount, and summer and weekend deals are cheaper. If you're willing to fly stand-by you can save a lot of money.

Call ☎ 0203-140 160 from anywhere in Finland for 24-hour ticket sales (in English). Contact information for Finnair offices in some major Finnish cities follows:

Helsinki (☎ 09-818 800) Asema-aukio 1
Joensuu (☎ 013-611 7070) airport
Jyväskylä (☎ 014-445 5900)
Kajaani (☎ 08-689 7600) airport
Kemi (☎ 016-210 87777)
Kittilä (☎ 016-642 072) Valtatie 41
Kuopio (☎ 017-580 7400) airport
Kuusamo (☎ 08-851 8888) airport
Lappeenranta (☎ 05-541 8100)
Mariehamn (☎ 018-634 500) airport
Mikkeli (☎ 015-164 881)
Oulu (☎ 08-880 7950) airport
Rovaniemi (☎ 016-363 6700) airport
Savonlinna (☎ 015-523 206) airport
Tampere (☎ 03-383 5333) airport
Turku (☎ 02-415 4909) airport
Vaasa (☎ 06-212 6171)

Discounts & Passes

Children aged under 12 years and seniors receive a 70% discount. If you're between 17 and 24 the youth discount is 50%, but even better value is the youth stand-by fare. It's available to those aged between 17 and 24 and to you need to arrive at the airport one hour before the flight of your choice and wait to see if there are any seats. Under this plan, any one-way direct flight costs €50 or €64 depending on the flight – a huge saving on a flight from, say, Helsinki to Rovaniemi (cheaper than the train). If you don't get on your desired flight, your money is refunded

Special discounts are offered on selected routes in summer, and 'snow fares' give discounts of 50% to 70% on selected flights between Helsinki and Lapland during non-holiday periods from January to May.

For information on the Nordic Air Pass, a package of discount tickets that must include one international segment, see the Getting There & Away chapter.

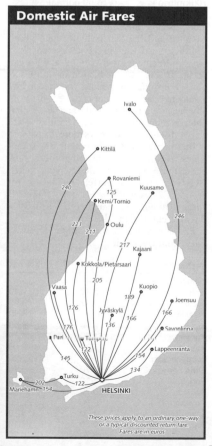

Domestic Air Fares

Ivalo

Kittilä

Rovaniemi
240
Kuusamo
125
Kemi/Tornio
246
223
Oulu
211
217
Kajaani
Kokkola/Pietarsaari
205
Vaasa
Kuopio
189
Joensuu
176
Jyväskylä
166
136
166
Savonlinna
Pori
Tampere
122
Lappeenranta
145
154
134
Turku
202
122
Mariehamn 154
HELSINKI

These prices apply to an ordinary one-way or a typical discounted return fare. Fares are in euros

Domestic Departure Tax

The VAT and a departure tax are always included in the listed fare.

BUS

Long-distance buses in Finland run efficiently and on schedule. They're comfortable, and service is comprehensive, covering 90% of Finland's roads. Compared with Finnish trains, buses are better for travelling from village to village, while trains are more convenient and cheaper for fast travel between the big centres. There are two kinds of intercity service: *vakiovuorot* (regular buses) stopping frequently at towns and villages, and *pikavuorot* (express buses) travelling swiftly between cities. Because there are few motorways in Finland, even express buses aren't that fast, covering 100km in less than two hours and 400km in about six hours.

Long-distance and express bus travel is handled by **Oy Matkahuolto Ab** (☎ 09-6136 8433; W www.matkahuolto.fi; Lauttasaarentie 8, 00200 Helsinki), while private companies handle regular bus services. In Lapland the main bus service is **Gold Line** (W www.gold line.fi). All share the same ticketing system.

Each town and municipal centre has a *linja-autoasema* (bus terminal), with local timetables displayed. National timetables are available at bus stations and tourist offices. Sometimes there's a separate Matkahuolto ticket office in the town centre where you can buy bus, train and ferry tickets. Bus schedules change often so *always* double-check – particularly in rural areas where there may be only one weekly bus on some routes. Though Matkahuolto and **ExpressBus** (W www.expressbus.com) have websites with timetables, neither have much information in English. National timetable info is available on ☎ 0200-4000 (premium-rate call).

Most buses run Monday to Friday, hourly between major towns. Restricted services operate on Saturday and public holidays. Few lines operate on Sunday, except between major centres. Some minor rural routes are served primarily by school buses, which don't run on weekends or during summer. Note that bus stations close at 6pm Monday to Saturday and at 4pm on Sunday.

Costs

A *bussilomalippu* (Coach Holiday Ticket), valid for two weeks and up to 1000km, costs €65. Used wisely it's cheaper than purchasing individual bus tickets – €65 would only get you about 650km in normal circumstances. The Coach Holiday Ticket is available from bus stations or travel agencies and is valid on all mainland buses (except local buses in the Helsinki, Tampere and Turku regions). There are no refunds. The ticket is valid for two weeks from the date of the first trip rather than the date of purchase. On some routes, buses may accept train passes.

Ticket prices are fixed and depend on the number of kilometres travelled; return tickets are 10% cheaper than two one-way fares, provided the trip is at least 80km in one direction. Express buses cost slightly more than regular buses. The minimum fare is €2.20 (up to 6km); the one-way fare for a 100km trip is €12.40/14.60 normal/express. Discounts are available for students and seniors, usually only if the ticket is booked in advance and the trip is more than 50km. Children aged four to 11 always pay half fare, children aged between 12 and 16 can get a 30% to 50% reduction on most services. For student discounts, you need to buy a student coach discount card (€5.40) from any bus station. Proper ID and a passport photo is required, and the card entitles you to a 50% discount on journeys more than 80km.

In summer special discounts are sometimes available on selected routes – ask about these before purchasing your ticket. Bicycles are transported on buses for around €2 – sometimes for free – if there is space available. The surcharge is usually at the discretion of the driver.

Following are some sample one-way fares from Helsinki:

destination	normal (€)	express (€)
Hämeenlinna	12.40	14.60
Ivalo	107.30	112.40
Joensuu	40.42	48.40
Jyväskylä	30.90	33.30
Kemi	67.10	69.80
Kuopio	41.50	44.20
Kuusamo	75.30	78.00
Lappeenranta	26.70	27.10
Oulu	52.70	65.40
Pori	27.10	29.10
Rauma	26.70	29.10
Rovaniemi	79.90	82.60
Savonlinna	33.00	35.40
Tampere	20.70	23.10
Turku	18.50	20.90

Reservations

Book domestic bus tickets at any bus-station ticket counter or through any travel agency, regardless of the starting and ending points. Tickets are valid for one month from date of purchase. A reserved seat is optional and carries a €2 surcharge. Reservations are advised on weekends and holidays (such as Midsummer and Christmas), but other times you should have no problems getting a seat. One-way bus tickets may be purchased on board the bus at departure if seats are available.

TRAIN

Trains of the State Railways of Finland (Valtion Rautatiet or VR) are clean, reliable and usually on schedule. They are fast, efficient and the best form of public transport for covering major routes such as Helsinki to Tampere, Kuopio, Oulu or Rovaniemi. On longer routes there are two- and three-bed sleepers and special car-carriers.

There are three main train lines: the Pohjanmaa (West) line runs between Helsinki and Oulu, and continues to Kemijärvi in Lapland; the Karelian route runs from Helsinki to Nurmes via Joensuu; and the Savonian route runs from Kouvola in the south to Kajaani, via Kuopio and Iisalmi.

One of the most popular routes for travellers in a hurry is the triangle between Turku, Helsinki and Tampere. Useful local routes can be found in the Helsinki area.

VR Ltd Finnish Railways (☎ *09-707 3519 in Helsinki;* ⓦ *www.vr.fi*) has its own travel bureau at main stations and can advise on all schedules and tickets. Prices, timetables and other information can be found on VR's website. Additionally, the Finnish Tourist Board office in Helsinki distributes a free booklet with English and German translations of the national train schedule. For individual routes, there are free pocket timetables available at local stations, and every station displays all departures and arrivals.

Train Passes

International train passes accepted for travel on trains in Finland include the Eurailpass, Eurail Flexipass and Inter-Rail Ticket, but these are only worth having if you're doing a lot of rail travel in Europe. Eurail passes (ⓦ www.eurail.com) can only be bought by residents of non-European countries and are supposed to be purchased before arriving in Europe. These are valid for unlimited travel on national railways and some private lines in Austria, Belgium, Denmark, Finland, France, Germany, Greece, Hungary, Ireland, Italy, Luxembourg, the Netherlands, Norway, Portugal, Spain, Sweden and Switzerland (including Liechtenstein), as well as Silja Line ferries between Sweden and Finland.

If you've lived in Europe for more than six months, you're eligible for an Inter-Rail pass (ⓦ www.interrailnet.com), which is a better buy. The Inter-Rail pass is split into eight zones, with zone B covering Sweden, Norway and Finland. The price for any one zone is UK£119/169 (up to/over 26) for 12 days and UK£139/209 for 22 days.

See your local travel agency for more information about these rail passes.

ScanRail Pass This is the best-value international rail pass to use when travelling in Finland (ⓦ www.scanrail.com). It's a flexible rail pass covering travel in the Scandinavian countries of Denmark, Norway, Sweden and Finland. The pass can be purchased in Scandinavia but there are restrictions on its use in the country of purchase. For instance, if you buy the pass in Finland, you can only use it to travel for three days in Finland. It's far better to buy the pass outside Scandinavia.

There are three versions. For travel on any five days within a two-month period, the pass costs €216/291 for 2nd-/1st-class travel (€218/161 for travellers under 26). For travel on any 10 days within a two-month period, the pass costs €288/388 (€214/290 for under 26). For unlimited travel over 21 consecutive days, the cost of the pass is €332/448 for 2nd/1st class (€249/336 for those under 26).

If you're aged 60 or over, then you're eligible for the ScanRail Senior pass, which will allow 2nd-/1st-class travel over five days in a two-month period for €190/258, 10 days in a two-month period for €256/345 and 21 consecutive days for €295/399.

Finnrail Pass A national rail pass, the Finnrail Pass, is available to travellers residing outside Finland and is the best-value pass if you're not planning on travelling elsewhere in Scandinavia. The pass is good for three, five or 10 days of travel within a one-month period. The Finnrail Pass may be purchased from the VR travel agency,

Matkapalvelu, at major train stations in Finland, or from your local travel agency before arrival in Finland. The cost for 2nd-/1st-class travel is €114/174 for three days; €154/232 for five days; €208/312 for 10 days. As with any pass, you need to plan your trips wisely to make it pay.

Classes & Reservations

VR has passenger trains in two classes – 1st and 2nd. Most carriages are open 2nd-class carriages with soft chairs. Many trains have just one 1st-class carriage, containing small compartments, each seating six passengers. On longer routes there are night trains with single, two- and three-bed sleeping berths.

Seat reservations are included in the ticket price on all trains except regional services. The main classes of trains are the high-speed Pendolino (the fastest and most expensive class), which currently operates on the Helsinki–Turku, Helsinki–Seinäjoki–Oulu, and Helsinki–Tampere–Jyväskylä–Kuopio routes; fast Intercity (IC); Express; and Regional trains. Advance reservations are mandatory on IC and the high-speed Pendolino trains, and are advised for travel on express trains during summer. Regional trains are the cheapest and slowest services. They have only 2nd-class carriages, do not require seat reservations and stop frequently.

Costs

Train tickets are cheaper in Finland than in Sweden or Norway. A one-way ticket for a 100km express train journey costs approximately €13/19 in 2nd/1st class. Different classes of trains are priced differently (Regional being the cheapest, Pendolino the most expensive) and a supplement is charged for travel on IC and Pendolino trains.

Children under 17 pay half fare and children aged under six travel free (but without a seat). There are discounts for families and seniors. Foreign students do not receive discounts on Finnish trains. Check at the train-station ticket counter for special summer fares.

If you purchase your ticket from the conductor after boarding from a station where the ticket office was open, a €2.40 'penalty' is charged (€5 on Pendolino). The 1st-class fare is 1½ times the price of a 2nd-class ticket, and a return fare is about 10% less than two one-way tickets. Single tickets are valid

for eight days from date of purchase, return tickets for one month. Sample one-way and return fares for 2nd-class, express-train travel from Helsinki are:

destination	cost (€)	duration (hrs)
Joensuu	41.80	5¼
Kuopio	44.60	5
Oulu	58.40	6½
Rovaniemi	67.40	10
Savonlinna	42.20	5
Tampere	23.20	2
Turku	21.40	2

Sleeping Berths These are available on overnight trains in one-/two-/three-bed cabins, and cost a flat rate of €42 for a single berth (with a 1st-class ticket), and €20.20/10 per person for double/triple berths, in addition to the cost of an ordinary ticket. These prices rise to €58.80/30.20/15 during the peak ski season (mid-February to late April). The main night train routes are Helsinki, Tampere or Turku to Oulu, Rovaniemi and Kolari.

Cargo & Bicycles Normal long-distance trains carry cargo; IC and Pendolino trains don't. Large train stations have a cargo office that takes luggage in advance. Sending a suitcase or backpack anywhere in Finland as cargo costs €5. The cost to transport a canoe is around €16.80.

Transporting a bicycle costs €8 if you wish to take the bike with you, or €16 if you wish to have it sent as cargo.

Car & Motorcycle Some trains transport cars from the south to Oulu, Rovaniemi and Kolari – which is handy if you've brought your own vehicle and are keen on exploring Lapland. From Helsinki to Rovaniemi, the high-season cost is €163 for car transport only, and €277.20 for a car and passenger ticket in a sleeping berth that accommodates one to three people. Motorcycles are charged at the same rate. Prices are highest on weekends in winter and spring and during holidays.

CAR & MOTORCYCLE

Driving around Finland is hassle-free, particularly in comparison to other Scandinavian countries where traffic is heavier, routes more complicated and drivers seemingly less polite. Finnish drivers are remarkably considerate and polite – rarely will you hear a horn blast in anger and 'road rage' is almost an unknown phenomenon. Finland's road network is excellent between centres – although there are only a few motorways around major cities – and well signposted. When approaching a town or city, look for signs saying *keskusta* (town centre) or *kauppatori* (market square), where you can usually find parking. Only in remote forests and rural areas will you find unsurfaced roads or dirt tracks. There are no road tolls.

Petrol is much more expensive than in the USA and generally above average compared with other European countries.

The national motoring organisation is **Autoliitto** *(Automobile and Touring Club of Finland; ☎ 09-774 761; Ⓦ www.autoliitto.fi; Hämeentie 105A, 00550 Helsinki)*.

Road Rules

Most Finnish roads are only two lanes wide, and traffic keeps to the right. Use extreme caution when passing on these narrow roads. The speed limit is 50km/h in built-up areas and from 80km/h to 100km/h on highways. Accidents must be reported promptly to the **Motor Insurers' Bureau** *(☎ 09-680 401; Bulevardi 28, 00120 Helsinki)*. All motor vehicles must use headlights at all times, and wearing seat belts is compulsory for all passengers. The blood alcohol limit is 0.05%.

Foreign cars must display a nationality sticker and foreign visitors must be fully insured – bring a green card (insurance card) if you have one (see Driving Licence & Permits in the Facts for the Visitor chapter). Foreign drivers should keep in mind that in Finland, cars entering an intersection from the right *always* have right of way, even when that car is on a minor road. Those who are used to driving in the USA and other countries where stop signs regulate every intersection will find that it takes some time to adjust to this system. Again, Finnish drivers are unexpectedly considerate and usually approach intersections with care.

When driving in rural areas beware of moose and reindeer, which do not respond to car horns. In Lapland, reindeer can make motoring somewhat slow and/or hazardous. Expect them to appear at any time. Police must be notified about accidents involving moose and reindeer. Report the accident; if you don't might there be legal trouble.

Winter Driving

Snow and ice on Finland's roads from September to April (and as late as June in Lapland) makes driving a very, very hazardous

Reindeer Roadblocks

For many travellers a highlight of a visit to Finland is the chance to glimpse some Finnish wildlife, such as bear or elk. If you are travelling in the far north you'll definitely see reindeer, and you won't have to go trekking in the wild to find them.

Reindeer – at least the kind of reindeer commonly found in Finland – are not wild animals. Reindeer herding has been an essential part of the Sami culture for centuries, and reindeer are semidomesticated but wander freely. With some 230,000 reindeer wandering around Lapland, it's inevitable that some will find their way onto the roads and they are unfortunately very blasé about traffic. Some 3000 to 4500 reindeer die annually on Finnish roads, and trains kill an additional 600.

The worst months for reindeer-related accidents are November and December, when hours of daylight are few and road visibility is extremely poor. Also bad are July and August, when the poor animals run amok trying to escape insects. The roads to take extra precautions on are in the far north, between major tourist centres (where most of the traffic is): Oulu to Kuusamo, Rovaniemi to Kemijärvi and Rovaniemi to Inari.

The best way to avoid an accident is to slow down immediately when you spot a reindeer, regardless of its location, direction or speed. Reindeer move slowly and do not respond to car horns. Nor do they seem to feel that vehicles deserve right of way.

Elk are not as common but are much larger animals and tend to dash onto the road if panicked by traffic. There are around 2000 accidents each year involving elk and generally neither the vehicle nor the animal come out of it looking too good.

Road Distances (km)

	Helsinki	Jyväskylä	Kuopio	Kuusamo	Lappeenranta	Oulu	Rovaniemi	Savonlinna	Tampere	Turku	Vaasa
Helsinki	---										
Jyväskylä	272	---									
Kuopio	383	144	---								
Kuusamo	804	553	419	---							
Lappeenranta	223	219	264	684	---						
Oulu	612	339	286	215	551	---					
Rovaniemi	837	563	511	191	776	224	---				
Savonlinna	338	206	160	579	155	446	671	---			
Tampere	174	148	293	702	275	491	712	355	---		
Turku	166	304	448	848	361	633	858	446	155	---	
Vaasa	419	282	377	533	501	318	543	488	241	348	---

activity without snow tyres. There are two types – regular snow tyres, and the far more serious 'studded' snow tyres that have tiny metal spikes. Studded tyres are allowed on Finnish roads from 1 November to the first Sunday after Easter and at other times when justified by road conditions. Snow tyres may be hired at **Isko Oy** (☎ 09-765 566; Mertakatu 6, Helsinki) from €140 for a set of four; installation and storage of your summer tyres are included. Cars hired in Finland will be properly equipped with snow tyres when required. It is illegal to drive with tyre chains in Finland.

Parking
In central Helsinki, every car park costs money, as much as €2 per hour. Some parking spaces in Helsinki and elsewhere require drivers to set a small cardboard parking clock (pysäköintikiekko, literally meaning 'parking puck') on the dashboard to indicate what time the car arrived, and signs will tell you how long you can park there. These can usually be picked up free at petrol stations, R-kiosks and some tourist offices. This works to some extent on an honesty system and there's nothing to stop you returning within the time limit and changing the clock.

In summer in some university towns, students are employed by local businesses to feed money into parking meters that have expired or almost expired. In return for possibly saving you a fine, they place an advertising leaflet on your windscreen. It's a good idea, but don't rely it. Fines start at €35.

In smaller towns and villages, parking is rarely a problem, and is generally free or much cheaper than in Helsinki.

Roadside Services
There are petrol stations throughout the country, although in Lapland and in other isolated regions you might want to get in the habit of filling up the tank before it's completely empty. Unleaded petrol (98E or 95E) ranges from around €1 to €1.15 a litre in southern Finland and even more in Lapland. Diesel costs around €0.75 a litre. A café or restaurant is very common at Finnish petrol stations, serving full meals, lunchtime buffets and snacks at surprisingly low prices and until late hours, especially as shops in Finnish towns close quite early. On Sunday and at night you can fill your tank by using Automaatti or Seteli/kortti automatic petrol pumps. These accept cash (euro notes) and credit cards, but most accept only Finnish-issued credit and debit cards, so are useless to foreign travellers without cash. Don't rely on them. If the instructions are in Finnish and Swedish only, you insert banknotes, press setelikuittaus after the last note, choose the pump, select the petrol type, and fill the tank.

Road Numbers

Each major road has a number (often referred to in this book). National highways are numbered with one- to two-digit numbers. Some of these highways – those between major cities – are also designated European Routes and bear an 'E' prefix. Three- and four-digit numbers are given to less important roads, often gravel ones. There are also plenty of roads with no number at all.

Rental

Car rental in Finland is more expensive than elsewhere in Europe, but between a group of three or four it can work out at a reasonable cost. From the major rental companies a small car such as a VW Polo or Renault Clio costs from €60 per day with 100km free, and €0.35 per kilometre thereafter, or €75 to €90 with unlimited kilometres. Weekly rentals with unlimited kilometres are from €350 to €420. For bigger cars, you're looking at more like €1000 a week for unlimited kilometres. Avoid renting at the Helsinki airport, if possible, as prices are highest there.

Car-rental companies with offices in many Finnish cities include **Budget** (☎ 686 6500; W www.budget.fi), **Hertz** (☎ 0800-112 233; W www.hertz.fi); **Europcar** (☎ 09-7515 5444 in Helsinki; W www.europcar.fi) and **Avis** (☎ 09-441 155 in Helsinki; W www.avis.fi). There are also local operators, especially in Helsinki (see that chapter). Check the Yellow Pages, under the heading *Autovuokraamoja*, for addresses and telephone numbers.

Purchase

Buying a car in Finland is not really practical unless you plan to stay for quite a while. Small 10-year-old sedans and old vans can cost less than €1500, but those costing less than €800 should have been recently *katsastettu* (inspected).

BICYCLE

Finland is flat and as bicycle-friendly as any country you'll find, with plenty of bike paths that cyclists share with inline skaters in summer. The only drawback to an extensive tour is distance, but bikes can be carried on most trains, buses and ferries. Daily/weekly hire at about €10/50 is possible in most cities, although hiring decent bikes in smaller towns is becoming difficult, as bike shops find it unprofitable – check with the local tourist office. Helmets are advisable but not compulsory. SRM (youth hostel association) offers a cycling and hostel package that takes in the flat south and lakes and costs €249/431 for seven/14 days, including bike rental and accommodation.

New bikes are expensive in Finland, starting at €250 for a hybrid, but good second-hand models may cost less than €100.

For more information about cycling in Finland see Cycling in the Activities chapter.

HITCHING

Hitching is never entirely safe in any country, and we don't recommend it. However, Finland would have to rank as one of Europe's 'safe' countries, although not the best for actually getting a ride. If you're determined to hitch in Finland you'll find that the going is fairly easy, especially if you try it outside the biggest cities and look 'respectable'. Relatively few Finns like picking up hitchhikers but the few friendly ones do it with enthusiasm. Drivers will ask 'Minne matka?' (Where are you going?), so you just tell them your destination.

Hitchhiking on motorways (freeways) is forbidden, but there are few motorways in Finland anyway. It's easy to hitch from Helsinki to Turku; more difficult is Helsinki to Tampere or Lahti, where there are complete sections of motorway. Some of the best areas to hitch are North Karelia and Lapland, although Lapland may be very frustrating as the interval between passing cars can be quite lengthy. Any secondary road, or a crossing at a middle-sized village, will be a potentially good spot for hitching. The best time to hitch is Monday to Friday, when traffic is heaviest, and weekends are the time when there are fewer bus services if you get stuck.

BOAT

Before the road network was constructed, lake steamers and 'church longboats' provided the main passenger transport in much of Finland. They disappeared until the 1970s, when quite a few were brought back into service. Many of the steamers now in use were built in the early 1900s and have plenty of character.

Lake & River Crossings

Lake and river ferries operate during summer. Departures tend to be sporadic from

May to mid-June and during August, but are very steady from mid-June to the end of July. These ferries are more than mere transport – a lake cruise, particularly from one town to another, is a bona fide Finnish experience.

Apart from two-hour cruises starting from Jyväskylä, Kuopio, Savonlinna, Tampere, Mikkeli and other towns, you can actually cover half of Finland on scheduled boat routes. The most popular routes are Tampere–Hämeenlinna, Savonlinna–Kuopio, Lahti–Jyväskylä and Joensuu–Koli–Nurmes. See Getting There & Away in the relevant town sections for details. From Lappeenranta there are visa-free day cruises down the historic Saimaa Canal to Vyborg, Russia. Most ferries take bicycles.

Sea Ferries

Several kinds of ferries operate between various islands and coastal towns. Most important to travellers on a budget are the free *lossi* ferries, part of the public road system. These run to a schedule, or just continuously, connecting important inhabited islands to the mainland. These simple ferries take vehicles, bicycles and pedestrians. Some ferries run between several islands to support the livelihood of small fishing villages, especially near Turku and in the province of Åland. These ferries also may be free to those who stay overnight on one of the islands, making it possible to island-hop from the mainland to Åland free of charge. See the chapters on Åland and Turku for specific information.

Several cruise companies run express boats to interesting islands off the coast, particularly along the south coast. From Helsinki the foremost tour is the short trip to Suomenlinna. Likewise, there are summer cruises aboard historic steamships to mainland towns that may be reached more routinely by car, bus or train. Popular sea routes are Turku–Naantali and Helsinki–Porvoo.

LOCAL TRANSPORT

The only tram and metro networks are in Helsinki. There is a bus service in all Finnish cities and towns, with departures every 10 to 15 minutes in Helsinki and other large towns, and every 30 minutes in smaller towns. Fares are less than €2. Train and bus stations are usually close together, within walking distance, and often close to the town centre.

Taxi

Hail taxis at bus and train stations or by phone; they are listed in the phone book under 'Taksi'. Like anywhere, taxis in Finland are expensive – typically the fare is €3.50 plus a per-kilometre charge. There's a surcharge for night or weekend service.

There is no shared taxi transport in Finland, the possible exceptions being airport taxis from Helsinki airport, from Turku train station, and local taxi-buses in some off-the-beaten-track places in Lapland and Karelia, sometimes replacing school bus services on weekends and summer. If you have a group of four and want to cover a lengthy distance 'in the middle of nowhere', you can negotiate with taxi drivers to get a good price.

ORGANISED TOURS

Many Finnish towns offer a great variety of tours – but in this lightly populated and under-touristed country there are not always enough people to go. Most reliable are those in Helsinki, Turku and Rovaniemi, where weekly tour programmes are offered in the summer and winter high seasons. In places like Lieksa and Kuusamo, tours can be the cheapest or the only way to visit isolated attractions. Adventure tours, such as rafting and trekking are the bread-and-butter in these regions. It's best to phone ahead for a confirmation to avoid the disappointment of showing up for a cancelled tour. Also, keep in mind that sometimes only two people are required for a 'group' tour. In addition to regular sightseeing tours, local tour operators take groups into the Finnish wilderness for trekking, white-water rafting, fly-fishing, dog-sledding and a range of other activities. Local tourist offices can provide information on how to contact these operators.

Helsinki

☎ 09 • pop 560,000

For many travellers, Helsinki (Swedish: Helsingfors) *is* Finland. But in truth, while Helsinki embodies much of the Finnish spirit and the progressive hi-tech push, it is unlike any other Finnish city, and this is due in part to the fascinating combination of Swedish, Russian and international influences. Helsinki is undoubtedly Finland's most cosmopolitan mix.

And while the nation as a whole still struggles a little to gain the attention of international tourists, Helsinki is fast becoming one of Europe's hottest destinations. Its nightlife is the envy of northern Europe and in summer its cafés, beer terraces and parks are humming with life. Although this is by far Finland's largest and most vibrant city, Helsinki is small and intimate compared to other Scandinavian capitals, and in summer walking or cycling is the best way to appreciate its sights, parks, markets and nearby islands.

Surprisingly, Helsinki bears little resemblance to other Scandinavian or Baltic cities. Rather than the ornate and grandiose buildings of Stockholm, it's a low-rise city of understated, functional architecture (its only 'skyscraper' is still just 12 storeys high). But in summer, the appeal is as much in the atmosphere and upbeat nature of the people as in any particularly sight. Strolling around the harbour area, picnicking on Suomenlinna island or joining the throngs sunning themselves in the many cafés and terraces is every bit as good as ticking off the museums or architectural highlights.

The huge Baltic ferries chug right into the heart of the city, and smaller boats regularly ply between the city and outlying islands. From here, roads and rail lines fan out across the country. It may not be completely representative of the country, but Helsinki is the perfect place to start and end your Finland travels.

HISTORY

Helsinki was founded in 1550 by King Gustav Vasa, making it only the sixth-oldest town in Finland. The king longed to create a rival to the Hansa trading town of Tallinn, the present-day capital of Estonia. An earlier trial at Ekenäs proved unsuccessful, so by royal decree traders from Ekenäs and a few other towns were bundled off to the newly founded Helsingfors.

For more than 200 years Helsinki remained a backwater market town on a windy, rocky peninsula. The Swedes built a fortress

Highlights

- Poking around the harbourside *kauppatori* (market square or fish market) in search of fresh salmon chowder, Finnish handicrafts and a splash of local colour

- Visiting some of Finland's best museums and galleries, including Kiasma and the Ateneum

- Strolling around the imposing 19th-century Senate Square, and taking in the scene from the steps of the blue-domed Lutheran Cathedral

- Taking the ferry to historic Suomenlinna island and spending the afternoon walking and picnicking among the ramparts

- Rollerblading or cycling in Kaivopuisto Park

- Listening to gospel and classical concerts at Temppeliaukio Church, an underground church hewn from solid rock

- Scoring tickets for a high-level winter ice-hockey match at Hartwall Arena

- Summertime bar-hopping around central Helsinki's many terraces, bars and clubs

named Sveaborg in 1748 to protect the eastern part of the empire against Russian attack. Following the war of 1808, however, the Russians succeeded in taking the fortress and a year later Russia annexed Finland as an autonomous grand duchy. A capital closer to St Petersburg was required, to keep a closer inspection on Finland's domestic politics. Helsinki was chosen – in large part because of the sea fortress (now called Suomenlinna) just outside the harbour – and so in 1812 classy Turku lost its long-standing status as Finland's capital and premier town. Its people continue to gripe about this demotion to the present day.

In the 19th and early 20th centuries, Helsinki grew rapidly in all directions. German architect CL Engel was called on to help design the city centre, which resulted in the stately, neoclassical Senaatintori (Senate Square). The city suffered heavy Russian bombing during WWII, but in the postwar period Helsinki recovered and went on to host the Olympic Games in 1952. It is still the smallest city ever to stage the summer games.

In the 1970s and 1980s, many new suburbs were built around Helsinki and residents celebrated their 'Helsinki Spirit', a term used for Cold War détente. Since then, Helsinki has served as an international conference point on numerous occasions – for everything from weighty economic summits to Sexhibition '98 – and it was a European Capital of Culture in 2000. It is the seat of national parliament and official home to the president.

ORIENTATION

Helsinki is built on a peninsula and there are links by bridge and ferry with nearby islands. Surrounding satellite cities include Espoo to the west and Vantaa, with the international airport, to the north – Finland's second and fourth most populous cities respectively.

The city centre is built around the main harbour, Eteläsatama. The *kauppatori* (market square) – also known as the fish market – is a central hub on the waterfront between the ferry terminals. From here the twin shopping avenues of Pohjoisesplanadi and Eteläesplanadi lead to Helsinki's main thoroughfare, Mannerheimintie. The bus and train stations are smack in the middle of the city on either side of Mannerheimintie.

Maps

The city tourist office can supply a good free map of Helsinki, as well as walking and cycling maps and a public transport route map. *See Helsinki On Foot* is the tourist office's free, step-by-step map and guide to the city centre.

INFORMATION
Tourist Offices

The busy **Helsinki City Tourist Office** (☎ 169 3757; W www.hel.fi/tourism; Pohjoisesplanadi 19; open 9am-7pm Mon-Fri, 9am-3pm Sat & Sun May-Sept, 9am-5pm Mon-Fri, 9am-3pm Sat Oct-Apr) will give you an updated city map and lists of events, restaurants, nightclubs and much more. Buy your Helsinki Card here (see the boxed text 'Helsinki Card' on the next page). Also here is the **Helsinki Tour Expert** desk where you can book hotel rooms and purchase tickets for train, bus and ferry travel around Finland and for travel to Tallinn and St Petersburg.

Just opposite, across Esplanade Park, is another useful office – the **Finnish Tourist Board** (☎ 4176 9300; W www.finland -tourism.com; Eteläesplanadi 4; open 9am-5pm Mon-Fri year-round, 10am-4pm Sat May-Sept), which stocks brochures and information for the entire country.

In summer you'll probably see uniformed 'Helsinki Helpers' wandering around – collar these useful multilingual volunteers for any tourist information or to ask directions.

Tikankontti (☎ 270 5221, 0203-44122; W www.metsa.fi; Eteläesplanadi 20; open 10am-6pm Mon-Fri, 10am-3pm Sat) is the Helsinki office of Metsähallitus, the Finnish Forest and Park Service. It has information and maps for national parks and protected hiking areas, and you can buy maps and fishing licences or rent wilderness cottages around the country.

The youth information and counselling centre **Kompassi** (☎ 3108 0080; W www .lasipalatsi.fi/kompassi; Mannerheimintie 22-24; open 11am-6pm Tues-Thur, 11am-4pm Fri, 11am-6pm Sun), part of the Lasipalatsi Multimedia Centre, sells youth cards and offers general advice and information on travelling in Finland.

Apart from the tourist office publications, free tourist magazine-style brochures such as *Helsinki This Week* (published monthly) and *The City in English* are available at

Helsinki Card

If you intend to do some serious sightseeing, or even have a few particular places picked out, the Helsinki Card can save you money. This pass entitles you to urban travel, entry to more than 50 attractions in and around Helsinki, and discounts on day tours to Porvoo and Tallinn. A card valid for 24/48/72 hours costs €24/33/39, and €9.50/12.50/15 for children. It's well worth the price if you plan to visit several museums, use the island ferries and organise your day wisely. If you buy one, take the discounted 1½-hour sightseeing bus tour first up. Buy the card (and a brochure outlining the discounts) at the city tourist office, or at hotels, R-kiosks and transport terminals.

tourist offices, bookshops and other points around the city.

The official Helsinki website at [w] www .hel.fi has many good links – including one that lists Helsinki public transportation routes and fares. At [w] www.helsinkiexpert.fi you can find up-to-date information on the Helsinki Card.

Money

Major banks (with international ATMs) are plentiful and easy to find throughout the city, but the best place to exchange cash or travellers cheques is at the official moneychangers. **Forex** offers the best rates, with a flat €2 fee on travellers cheques and no commission. There are offices at the train station, at Mannerheimintie 10, and at Pohjoisesplanadi, open 8am to 9pm daily in summer and 8am to 7pm Monday to Saturday the rest of the year. **Tavex** also offers good rates and there's a convenient office behind the Helsinki City Tourist office on Unioninkatu. Both Forex and Tavex give commission-free cash advances on foreign credit cards. The **Change Group**, which seems to have the largest advertising banners, charges higher fees and an outrageous 8% commission on credit card cash advances.

Thomas Cook (Travelex) is represented at Vantaa airport (open 5am-midnight daily) and at Aleksanterinkatu 19 (open 9am-6pm Mon-Fri, 10am-4pm Sat). Also at the airport there's an **exchange counter**, and a 24-hour exchange machine.

Western Union (Aleksanterinkatu 52; open 9am-9pm Mon-Fri, 9am-6pm Sat) is on the 7th floor of the Stockmann department store.

Post & Communications

The **main post office** (☎ 02045 14400; Mannerheiminaukio 1; open 10am-7pm Mon-Fri, 11am-4pm Sat & Sun) is in the large building between the bus and train stations. In the same building (at the rear opposite Finnair) is the **poste restante office** (open 8am-9pm Mon-Fri, 9am-6pm Sat, 11am-9pm Sun). Mail is held for one month.

The **main telephone office** (open 9am-5pm Mon-Fri), is on the 2nd floor in the main post office building. You can place calls from here, but it's cheaper to call overseas using a prepaid phonecard at any public telephone, or even a mobile phone.

Email & Internet Access

There are surprisingly few Internet cafés in Helsinki, but Internet access is free at public libraries. Half-hour slots can be prebooked by phone but there are usually a few terminals available on a first-come-first-served basis and even if you have to wait a while, there's plenty of reading matter around to keep you occupied.

Cable Book Library (Kirjakaapeli; ☎ 3108 5000, fax 3108 5700; e kirjakaapeli@lib.hel.fi; Mannerheimintie 22-24; open 10am-8pm Mon-Thur, noon-6pm Sat & Sun), on the 1st floor of the Lasipalatsi Multimedia Centre, is the best central place for Internet access – there are a number of half-hour terminals that are first-come, first-served, and the rest may be booked by telephone. There's also plenty of foreign reading material, including magazines and newspapers, to fill in waiting time.

The most central of Helsinki's public libraries is **Rikhardinkadun Library** (☎ 3108 5013; Rikhardinkatu 3; open 10am-8pm Mon-Fri, 10am-3pm Sat). It has a good selection of English-language books and several Internet terminals.

The impressive **University of Helsinki Library** is a serene place with a bank of quiet terminals on the 2nd floor which you can use to surf the Internet for 'information gathering' purposes – signs warn they are not for email and some email services are blocked.

Ateneum (see Museums & Galleries) has a peaceful reading room with two free Internet terminals. Access the rear entrance off

HELSINKI

PLACES TO STAY
2 Hostel Stadion
8 Hotelli Anton
14 Radisson SAS Hesperia;
   Europcar
35 Hotel Helka
36 Academica Summer Hostel
   & UniCafe
37 Radisson SAS Royal Hotel
38 Hostel Satakuntatalo
46 Lord Hotel
54 Scandic Hotel Grand Marina
55 Eurohostel

PLACES TO EAT
10 Chico's All American Bistro
26 Kolme Kruunua
30 Restaurant Bellevue
31 Sipuli
39 Mt Everest Restaurant
44 Kabuki
47 Konstan Mölja
49 Restaurant Satkar
59 Saslik
62 Cafe Carusel
68 Cafe Ursula

MUSEUMS
6 Museum of Worker Housing
11 Tram Museum
19 Hakasalmi Villa (City Museum)
20 Kansallimuseo
   (National Museum)
23 Natural History Museum
27 Military Museum
29 Maritime Museum
48 Cable Factory; Museums
50 Sinebrychoff Museum of
   Foreign Art
52 Museum of Art & Design;
   Museum of Finnish
   Architecture
65 Mannerheim Museum

OTHER
1 24-Hour Pharmacy
3 Olympic Stadium;
   Sports Museum of Finland
4 Olympic Swimming Stadium
5 Linnanmäki Amusement
   Park & Sea Life
7 Rytmi
9 Opera House
12 Sibelius Monument
13 Töölö Hospital
15 Easywash
16 Hertz
17 Boat Hire
18 Finlandia Talo
21 Storyville
22 Temppeliaukio Church
24 Parliament House
25 Burgher's House
28 Helsinki Zoo
32 Uspenski Cathedral
33 Casino Ray
34 Tennispalatsi Cinema
40 Budget Rent-a-Car
41 Vanha Maestro
42 Highlight
43 Orion Theatre
45 Saunabar
51 St John's Church
53 Kanava Ferry Terminal
56 Katajanokka Ferry Terminal
57 Olympia Ferry Terminal
58 Russian Embassy
60 Länsiterminaali
   (West Ferry Terminal)
61 Norwegian Embassy
63 Salomon Park (Skate Hire)
64 Cygnaeus Gallery
66 Estonian Embassy
67 American Embassy; French
   Embassy; British Embassy
69 Bungy Crane (Summer Only)

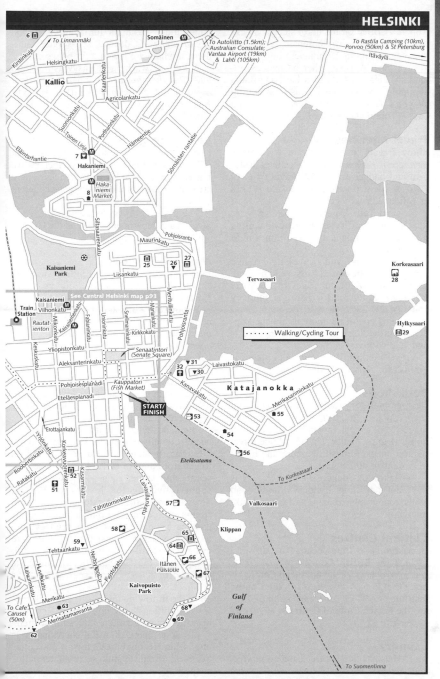

HELSINKI

Yliopistonkatu. **Netcup** is in the branch of Robert's Coffee on the north side of Stockmann's. There are two terminals free to customers (maximum 15 minutes) but they're always busy. Various other businesses, including cafés and some bars, have a terminal available for customer's use, including **Wayne's Coffee** (*Kaisaniemenkatu 3*) and **Lost & Found** (*Annankatu 6*).

Travel Agencies
Kilroy Travels (☎ *680 7811;* **W** *www.kilroy travels.com; Kaivokatu 10C*) specialises in student and budget travel. **STA Travel** (☎ *6812 7710;* **W** *www.statravel.fi; Mikonkatu 11*) has an office in the city centre.

Helsinki Tour Expert (☎ *2288 1599*), in the city tourist office, is an agency handling travel around Finland and to Tallinn and St Petersburg.

From Helsinki you can easily arrange trips to the Baltic States, Russia and beyond. Consult the 'Matkailu' pages of the daily *Helsingin Sanomat* for listings. **Finnsov Tours** (☎ *694 2001;* **W** *www.finnsov.fi; Eerikinkatu 3*) is one of the more established operators, providing tours, travel arrangements and help with visas.

Viro is Finnish for Estonia, and Pietari is Finnish for St Petersburg.

Bookshops
Akateeminen Kirjakauppa (*Academic Bookshop; Pohjoisesplanadi 39*) is easily the biggest bookshop in Finland and *the* place to go for reading matter. There's a huge travel section, maps, Finnish literature and books in more than 40 languages.

Karttakeskus Aleksi (*Unioninkatu 32*) is the main map shop. It stocks atlases, road maps, topographical maps and general hiking maps.

Cultural Centres
International cultural centres in Helsinki include the **British Council** (☎ *701 8731; Hakaniemenkatu 2*), the **American Center Library** (☎ *175 587; Vuorikatu 20*), the **Goethe Institute** (☎ *680 3550; Mannerheimintie 20A*) and the **French Cultural Centre** (☎ *622 0330; Keskuskatu 3*).

Laundry
Most Helsinki hotels offer laundry service, and some of the hostels have self-service facilities. Otherwise, look in the Yellow Pages under 'Pesuloita' for laundry services. *Isepalvelupesula* denotes self-service laundrettes, which are few and far between.

A load of washing at **Easywash** (☎ *406 982; Runeberginkatu 47; open 10am-8pm Mon-Thur, 10am-6pm Fri & Sat*) costs €3 to €4; drying is €2. Tram No 3 stops right outside.

Left Luggage
Lockers at the bus and train station cost €2/3 for small/large – the large lockers are big enough to hold most backpacks. There are similar lockers and left-luggage counters at the ferry terminals.

There are also very small lockers at the Stockmann department store and the University of Helsinki Library (free).

Medical Services
For medical assistance, English speakers should use the 24-hour clinic at **Töölö Hospital** (☎ *4711; Töölönkatu 40*).

Yliopistoni Apteekki (☎ *4178 0300; Mannerheimintie 96*) is the city's 24-hour pharmacy but the **branch** (*Mannerheimintie 5; open 7am-midnight daily*) in the city centre is more convenient.

MUSEUMS & GALLERIES
Unsurprisingly, Helsinki has Finland's best selection of museums and galleries. They represent the country's most famous painters, designers and architects, as well as an eclectic mix of historical and cultural exhibitions. It would take a good few days to get around all of Helsinki's 40 or so museums and some, such as the **News Museum** (covering the history of Finnish newspapers), the **Missionary Museum** (items collected by Finnish missionaries overseas) and the **Museum of the Deaf**, are too specialised for most visitors, but there are a few stand-out attractions. For a full list, pick up the *Museums* booklet from the tourist office.

The Helsinki Card allows admission to all of the following museums, although special exhibitions may cost extra. Note that opening hours are often reduced in winter.

In Espoo, the **Gallén-Kallela Museum** is one of the Helsinki area's top art museums. See the Around Helsinki section later in this chapter.

Kiasma Museum of Contemporary Art

Kiasma (☎ 1733 6501; W www.kiasma.fi; Mannerheiminaukio 2; adult/student €5.50/4, children under 18 free; open 10am-8.30pm Wed-Sun, 9am-5pm Tues, closed Mon) is in the curvaceous, quirky chalk-white building designed by American architect Steven Holl. It opened to much fanfare in 1998 and exhibits a rapidly growing collection of Finnish and international modern art from the 1960s to the present. The focus is definitely on the offbeat, and changing exhibitions feature striking visual arts and media exhibits with some bizarre themes. There's a growing permanent collection on the 3rd floor and a theatre with a changing programme (tickets usually cost extra) on the ground floor. Although many of the exhibits lack English text, there are infocomputers stationed around the gallery, as well as human guides who can provide artistic information. The free Kiasma magazine, available at the museum or from tourist offices, gives details of coming exhibitions.

Kiasma is a local meeting point in summer – its café and beer terrace are hugely popular, locals sunbathe on the grassy fringes and skateboarders do their thing around the Mannerheim statue.

Kansallismuseo

The impressive National Museum of Finland (☎ 4050 9544; W www.nba.fi/natmus /Kmeng.html; Mannerheimintie 34; adult/ student €4/3.50, children under 18 free; open 11am-8pm Tues-Wed, 11am-6pm Thur-Sun, closed Mon), just north of the parliament building, looks a bit like a Gothic church with its heavy stonework and tall square tower. It was actually designed and built specifically as a museum in National Romantic style and opened in 1916, but was extensively renovated in 2000. The museum is divided into rooms covering different periods of Finnish history, including prehistory and archaeological finds, church relics, ethnography and cultural exhibitions. Look for the imperial throne of Tsar Alexander I dating from 1809, and the display on the reindeer-herding Sami people of northern Lapland. There's plenty to see here, so allow a couple of hours.

From the entrance hall, or better still from the 1st-floor balcony, crane your head up to see the superb frescoes on the ceiling arches, depicting scenes from the epic Kalevala, painted by Aleksi Gallen-Kallela. The four scenes are well-known to most Finns and include one of the epic hero Väinämöinen plunging a stake into the giant pike.

Ateneum

The list of painters at Ateneum (National Gallery; ☎ 1733 6275; W www.fng.fi/ateneum .htm; Kaivokatu 2; adult/student €5.50/4; open 9am-6pm Tues & Fri, 9am-8pm Wed & Thur, 11am-5pm Sat & Sun) reads like a 'who's who' of Finnish art. It houses Finnish paintings and sculptures from the 18th century to the 1950s including works by Albert Edelfelt, Akseli Gallen-Kalleli, the Von Wright brothers and Pekka Halonen. There's also a small but interesting collection of 19th- and early-20th-century foreign art, pride of place going to Auguste Rodin's bronze The Thinker, and paintings by Van Gogh, Gaugin and Cezanne. Downstairs is a café, bookshop and reading room. The building itself dates from 1887.

Sinebrychoff Museum of Foreign Art

The largest collection of Italian, Dutch and Flemish paintings in Finland can be found on the premises of the old brewery (☎ 1733 6460; Bulevardi 40), but it was closed for renovation at the time of writing and due to reopen in spring 2003.

Kaapelitehdas

The massive Kaapelitehdas (Cable Factory; ☎ 4763 8305; W www.kaapelitehdas.fi; Tallberginkatu 1C), off Porkkalankatu and on the way to Espoo, was once used for manufacturing sea cable and later became Nokia's main factory until the 1980s. When Nokia moved out, artists moved in to the five-hectare site, eventually renting every spare space on offer. It's now a bohemian cultural centre featuring studios, galleries, concerts, theatre and dance performances, as well as the obligatory café and restaurant. Admission to most galleries and studios is free. Take tram No 8, bus Nos 15, 20, 21, 65A or 66A, or the metro to Ruoholahti stop.

Also here is the Finnish Museum of Photography (☎ 6866 3621; adult/child €4/free; open noon-7pm Tues-Sun), which mounts interesting temporary photographic exhibitions; **Hotel & Restaurant Museum** *(adult/child €1/free; open noon-7pm Tues-Sun)* showcasing Finnish cuisine; and the **Theatre Museum** *(adult/child €5.50/2.50; open noon-7pm Tues-Sun)*.

Cygnaeus Gallery

If you're looking for Finnish art from the 19th century, this gallery *(☎ 4050 9628;* W *www.nba.fi; adult/student €2.50/1.50;*

open 11am-7pm Wed, 11am-4pm Thur-Sun) is a great place to go. It opened in 1882 and is one of Finland's oldest art galleries. It's in an attractive wooden building (built in 1870) in Kaivopuisto Park, close to the Mannerheim Museum.

Amos Anderson Art Museum

The city centre Amos Anderson Art Museum *(☎ 684 4460; Yrjönkatu 27; adult/child*

Helsinki Walking & Cycling Tour

Helsinki is compact enough to be made for walking, especially in summer. And a network of cycling (or rollerblading) paths, plus free bikes provided by Helsinki City Transport, make it even better for cycling. The following tour is a combination of the two – if you're on foot you'll probably want to stick to the central Helsinki area and Kaivopuisto park, but with a bike it's a breeze to get out to the Olympic stadium, Seurasaari island and the Hietaniemi area west of the city.

The starting point for any tour of Helsinki is the bustling **kauppatori** (market square), also known as the fish market (see Markets in the Shopping section later in this chapter). It is surrounded by graceful 19th-century buildings – some of only a few remaining in the city after the devastation of WWII. As well as being a water transport hub, the market area is full or craft stalls and cheap food stalls. The stone obelisk topped by a golden eagle is the **Tsarina's Stone**, Helsinki's oldest monument, unveiled in 1835 in honour of a visit by Tsar Nicholas 1 and Tsarina Alexandra.

Havis Amanda, the lovely mermaid statue and fountain just west of the fish market, was designed in 1908 by one of Finland's most beloved artists, Ville Vallgren. The statue, also known as 'Manta', is commonly regarded as the symbol of Helsinki – if not all of Finland. During *Vappu* (May Day) students gather here to celebrate the coming of spring.

Across from the kauppatori is the **Presidential Palace**, guarded by colourful sentries. This is the president's official Helsinki residence – currently home to Tarja Halonen, Finland's first women president.

Heading east, cross the footbridge onto Katajanokka Island to visit the Orthodox **Uspenski Cathedral** on a hill above the harbour. This very photogenic red brick church, with its Eastern European 'onion domes', is one of the most recognisable landmarks in Helsinki. It was built in Byzantine-Slavonic style in 1868 and has an interior lavishly decorated with icons. **Katajanokka** itself is worth a stroll if you have the time – many of its narrow streets have fine Art Nouveau residential buildings.

Back on the mainland, turn right along Sofiankatu, a narrow cobbled street with interpretive boards explaining some early Helsinki history. It leads to **Senaatintori** (Senate Square), Helsinki's 'official' centre. Carl Ludvig Engel, a native of Berlin, was invited to design the square after the Finnish capital was moved from Turku in 1812. He had earlier worked in St Petersburg – so what you see today in Helsinki looks quite Russian, which explains why Helsinki has been used by Hollywood to shoot 'Russian scenes', such as those in the films *Reds*, *White Nights* and *Gorky Park*. The **statue of Tsar Alexander II** in Senaatintori was cast in 1894 and symbolises the strong Russian influence in 19th-century Helsinki.

Engel's stately chalk-white, blue-domed **Tuomiokirkko** (Lutheran Cathedral), completed in 1852, is the square's most prominent feature and Helsinki's most recognisable building. The inside is surprisingly plain, although the scale of the domes and the enormous pipe organ are well worth a look. Make the climb up the staircase for excellent views of old Helsinki.

The main **University of Helsinki** building is on the west side of Senaatintori, and the university's magnificent **library** is a little farther north along Unioninkatu. Two of Helsinki's **city museums** are along the south side of the square.

Walking back to the Eteläesplanadi and west on Pohjoisesplanadi, you're in the pleasant **Esplanade Park**, with a cobbled avenue and grassy verges. It's a favourite summer spot and there's often live music here. The Esplanade leads to the city's broad main thoroughfare, Mannerheimintie. On the northeast corner is the famous **Stockmann department store**, where seemingly every Helsinkian buys everything.

€7/1.50; open 10am-6pm Mon-Fri, 11am-5pm Sat & Sun) houses the collection of publishing magnate Amos Anderson, one of the wealthiest Finns of his time. It includes Finnish and European paintings and sculptures from the 15th century to the present, but the rather hefty admission fee means it's definitely best visited with the aid of the trusty Helsinki Card. Look out for special exhibitions here.

Mannerheim Museum

This fascinating museum (☎ 635 443; Kalliolinnantie 14; adult/student €7/free; open 11am-4pm Fri-Sun & by appointment) in Kaivopuisto Park was the home of CGE Mannerheim, former president, Commander in Chief of the Finnish army and Civil War victor. Such was the national regard for Mannerheim that the house was converted into a museum less than a year after his death in

Helsinki Walking & Cycling Tour

Continue two blocks north on Mannerheimintie to **Kiasma**, the daring Museum of Contemporary Art. An **equestrian statue** of Marshal CGE Mannerheim, the most revered of Finnish leaders, dominates the square next to the museum. Protests by war veterans delayed the building of Kiasma by almost a decade because many felt that it would degrade Mannerheim's memory to build a modern art gallery on the site – ironically, the Marshal was an avid collector of avant-garde art in his day.

Detour two blocks east to the Soviet-sized Rautatientori (Railway Square), where you'll find the train station, naturally, as well as the National Gallery, **Ateneum** (see Museums & Galleries). The museum building, long considered a masterpiece in progress, was completed in 1991.

Return to Mannerheimintie and continue walking northwest. The monolithic 1931 **Parliament House** dominates this stretch. Free guided tours are conducted at 11am and noon on Saturday, and noon and 1pm Sunday. Almost opposite is one of Alvar Aalto's most famous works, the angular **Finlandia talo**, a concert hall built in 1971. Guided tours in English can be arranged on ☎ 402 4246.

At this point you can detour east along Museokatu and Aurorankatu to Temppelikatu where you'll find **Temppeliaukio Church**, a modern church hewn from solid rock.

A few blocks further north on Mannerheimintie is the 1993 **Opera House**, home of the Finnish National Opera. From the Opera House, turn right on Helsinginkatu to reach the tiny and manicured **City Winter Garden** and the **Linnanmäki amusement park**. Continue a short distance north on Mannerheimintie to the 1952 **Olympic Stadium**. For some of the best views of Helsinki, take a lift to the top of the 72m **Stadium Tower** (adult/child €2/1; open 9am-7pm Mon-Fri, 9am-6pm Sat & Sun June–late Aug).

From the stadium, walk or cycle west to Sibelius park and the **Sibelius monument**. This kinetic modern sculpture was created by artist Eila Hiltunen in 1967 to honour Finland's most famous composer, Jean Sibelius. The organ-like cluster of steel pipes is said to represent the forest. Bus No 24 from the park can take you northwest to the **Seurasaari Open-Air Museum** (see Museums & Galleries), or south to the intersection of Mannerheimintie and Pohjoisesplanadi, its terminus.

Alternatively, continue walking or riding around the coast road to **Hietaniemi Beach**, Helsinki's most popular city beach. Continuing south along Mechelinkatu, detour east about 1km (along Porkkalankatu) to find the **Cable Factory**, an amalgam of studios, theatres, craft shops and cafés. Heading back towards the city centre, you'll pass **Hietalahti square** which has its own kauppahalli and a popular flea market where even rich and famous Helsinkians have been known to sell some of their designer duds.

From here you can either return to the city centre along Bulevardi, pausing in the summer park where there's a lovely **Old Church**, or continue around past the West Harbour to the south of the peninsula. This road follows the waterfront to **Kaivopuisto park**, a favourite place for Finns to picnic and laze around in summer. The park was designed in the early 19th century and was, for a time, a luxury spa retreat for Russian nobility. This strip is also popular for rollerblading and cycling and there are a couple of good seaside cafés along here. Note the small wooden jetties, erected for households to wash their rugs. On a summer's day you'll still see rugs hanging out to dry.

Continuing along the waterfront you pass the Olympia ferry terminal and eventually arrive back at the kauppatori.

1951. Among the souvenirs from Mannerheim's life are hundreds of military medals, as well as photographs from his trip to Asia, when he travelled 14,000km along the Silk Route from Samarkand to Beijing, riding the same faithful horse for two years. The results of his passion for game hunting adorn the walls and the floor – including two tiger skins shot in Nepal in the days when tigers were still plentiful on the Terai. Some of the Asian artefacts are displayed – others are in the collection of the National Museum. Admission is free on 4 June, Mannerheim's birthday. Entry includes a mandatory but enthusiastic guided tour (around one hour) in one of six languages, and free plastic booties to keep the hallowed floor clean.

Seurasaari Open-Air Museum

West of the centre, Seurasaari island is an open-air museum (☎ 4050 9660; adult/child €4/free; open 11am-5pm daily, 11am-7pm Wed June-Sept) with 18th- and 19th-century traditional houses, manors and outbuildings from around Finland. Guides dressed in traditional costume demonstrate folk dancing, and crafts such as spinning, embroidery and troll-making. There are guided tours in English at 11.30am and 3.30pm. You'll find similar sorts of museums all over Finland but this is up there with the best.

The buildings are deserted from October to May but the site is open year-round. On Easter Saturday, a festive bonfire is held here, following a Finnish tradition that the flames and 'bitter smoke' would drive away evil spirits disguised as witches. This is also a venue for Helsinki's biggest Midsummer bonfires.

Take bus No 24 from the Central train station.

Urho Kekkonen Museum Tamminiemi

Worth visiting on a trip to Seurasaari, this large house (☎ 4050 9652; Seurasaarentie 15, Tamminiemi; adult/child €3.50/free; open 11am-5pm daily, 11am-7pm Wed mid-May–mid-Aug) was a presidential residence for 30 years, right up until Urho Kekkonen's death, when it was turned into a museum. A visit includes a guided tour and the house is surrounded by a beautiful park. From central Helsinki, take bus No 24, or tram No 4 and walk.

Kaupunginmuseo

A group of small museums scattered around the city centre constitute the Kaupunginmuseo (Helsinki City Museum; admission per museum adult/student/child €3/1.50/free, free Thur; all open 11am-5pm Wed-Sun). All focus on an aspect of the city's past or present, and are free if you flash your Helsinki Card:

Burgher's House (☎ 135 1065; Kristianinkatu 12) Built in 1818, this is the oldest wooden townhouse in central Helsinki and has been preserved as a middle-class home.

Hakasalmi Villa (☎ 169 3444; Karamzininkatu 2) The villa features an historical exhibition on Helsinki.

Helsinki City Museum (☎ 169 3933; Sofiankatu 4; open 9am-5pm Mon-Fri, 11am-5pm Sat & Sun) This house museum just south of Senate Square has a historical exhibition and film about Helsinki.

Museum of Worker Housing (☎ 146 1039; Kirstinkuja 4) This museum shows how industrial workers in Helsinki lived earlier this century (closed October to April).

Sederholm House (☎ 169 3265; Aleksanterinkatu 16-18) Helsinki's oldest brick building dates from 1757 and is furnished to suit a wealthy 18th-century merchant.

Tram Museum (☎ 169 3576; Töölönkatu 51A) This delightful museum, in an old tram depot, displays vintage trams and depicts daily life in Helsinki's streets in past decades.

Tuomarinkylä Museum & Children's Museum (☎ 728 7458; Tuomarinkylä) In the suburb of Tuomarinkylä (Domarby), not far from the airport, this pair of museums occupies an 18th-century manor house and shows the city through the life of a modern family and a child. From central Helsinki take bus No 64 to its terminus and walk 1km.

Museum of Art & Design

This museum (☎ 622 0540; Korkeavuorenkatu 23; adult/student €6.50/free; open 11am-6pm daily, 11am-8pm Wed, June–end Aug) has a permanent collection and hosts changing exhibitions, mostly focusing on contemporary domestic and industrial design – everything from household furniture and appliances to tools.

Museum of Finnish Architecture

Strictly for trainspotting-type architecture buffs, this museum (☎ 8567 5100; Kasarmikatu 24; adult/student €3.50/1.70; open 10am-4pm Tues-Sun, 10am-7pm Wed year-round) has a display of photographs and models covering rural and urban Finnish architecture, as well as a reference library. Labelling is mostly in Finnish.

Natural History Museum

The Natural History Museum (☎ 1912 8800; Pohjoinen Rautatienkatu 13; adult/student €4.20/2.50; open 9am-5pm Tues-Fri, 11am-4pm Sat & Sun) houses the University of Helsinki's extensive collection of mammals, birds and other creatures – about seven million specimens in all, including all Finnish species.

Postimuseo

The Post Museum (☎ 0204-514 908; Asema-aukio 5; admission free; open 10am-7pm Mon & Wed-Fri, 11am-4pm Sat & Sun), in the main post office building next to the train station, may sound a bit dull, but it contains a fascinating collection of stamps, computerised data banks and other hi-tech exhibits.

Sports Museum of Finland

The sports museum (☎ 434 2250; Olympia-stadion; W www.stadion.fi; adult/child €3.50/1.70; open 11am-5pm Mon-Fri, noon-4pm Sat & Sun), in the 1952 Olympic Stadium, houses Finland's 'sporting hall of fame', and looks at the triumphs and defeats of its sporting heroes. Sport is a subject close to the heart and national identity of Finns and this is the place to see some of that pride on display. Tram Nos 3B, 3T, 4, 7A, 7B and 10 from the city centre all run past.

Military Museum

The Military Museum (☎ 1812 6211; Maurinkatu 1; W www.mpkk.fi; adult/child €2/1; open 11am-4pm Sun-Fri) has an extensive collection of Finnish army paraphernalia, including medals, photographs and weaponry.

HELSINKI ZOO & MARITIME MUSEUM

One of the world's northernmost zoos, the spacious Helsinki Zoo (☎ 169 5969; adult/child €5/3, with ferry ride €8/4; open 10am-8pm daily May-Oct) is located on Korkeasaari island – best reached by ferry from the kauppatori. Established in 1889, it has animals and birds from Finland and around the world housed in large natural enclosures, as well as a tropical house, small farm and a good café

and terrace. Ferries leave from the kauppatori and from Hakaniemi every 30 minutes or so in summer. An alternative to the ferry is to catch bus No 16 or the metro to Kulosaari and walk 1.5km through the island of Mustikka-maa, or take No 11 from Herttoniemi metro directly to the zoo.

On the adjoining Hylkysaari island, and only accessible by bridge from Korkeasaari island, is the Maritime Museum (☎ 4050 9051; adult/child €1.50/free; open 11am-5pm daily May-Oct). It's housed in a historic harbour building and has exhibitions on Finnish ship-building and seafaring.

CHURCHES

Helsinki has three notable churches and several imposing cathedrals. On Katajanokka island near the kauppatori is the unmistakable red-brick Uspenski Cathedral. This Russian Orthodox, with its Eastern European 'onion domes', was built in Byzantine-Slavonic style in 1868 and has an interior lavishly decorated with icons. Presiding proudly over Senate Square, the chalk-white Tuomiokirkko (Lutheran Cathedral) was designed by CL Engel but not completed until 1852, 12 years after his death. The steps at the front of the church are a favourite meeting place and the scene of New Year's revelry. There's a café in the crypt.

Temppeliaukio Church (Church in the Rock; Lutherinkatu 3; open 10am-8pm Mon-Fri, 10am-6pm Sat, noon-1.45pm & 3.30pm-5.45pm Sun), designed by Timo and Tuomo Suomalainen in 1969, remains one of Helsinki's foremost attractions. Hewn into solid rock, the church symbolises the modern meanderings of Finnish religious architecture and features a stunning 24m-diameter roof covered in 22km of copper stripping. There are regular concerts and a service in English at 2pm on Sunday. The entrance is at the end of Fredrikinkatu.

Helsinki's largest church is the soaring neo-Gothic St John's Church, in St John's Park off Korkeavuorenkatu. It's popular for local weddings and often hosts concerts and choral performances.

PARKS & GARDENS
City Winter Garden

The botanical gardens (Hammarskjöldintie 1; tram No 8 from Ruoholahti metro or Töölö; admission free; open noon-3pm daily) were founded in 1893 and contain cacti, palms and other sun-loving plants foreign to Finnish soil. There's a café.

University Botanical Gardens

These gardens (Unioninkatu 44; admission free) comprise Finland's largest botanical collection, with greenhouses and a park.

Linnanmäki Amusement Park

The Linnanmäki amusement park (☎ 773 991; Helsinginkatu; adult/child day pass €16/11, entry only €3.50; open 11am-10pm daily late May–Sept), on a hill just north of Kallio suburb, has all the usual kid-pleasing rides including a rollercoaster and the Peacock Theatre. Its profits are donated to child welfare organisations. Day passes allow unlimited rides, or you can pay the admission (free with Helsinki Card) and then buy individual ride tickets (€1). Also here is Sea Life (adult/child €9.50/6), a new state-of-the-art aquarium. Bus No 23 or tram No 3B, 3T or 8 takes you to Linnanmäki.

ACTIVITIES

No visit to Helsinki is complete without a sauna and swim at the Yrjönkadun Uimahalli (☎ 3108 7400; Yrjönkatu 21; admission €5-10). This sleek Art Deco complex was first opened in 1928, and its powerful Nordic elegance has been beautifully restored. There are separate hours for men and women, and bathing suits are not allowed in the pool or saunas.

Helsinki has several public swimming pools with inexpensive admission. Most convenient is the outdoor Olympic Swimming Stadium (open daily May–end Aug) near Hostel Stadion. However, the most impressive place to swim is the Itäkeskus swimming hall in the Itäkeskus shopping centre (take the metro to Itäkeskus Östra centrum station). The entire underground swimming hall – with several pools, saunas and a gym – is carved from rock and can also double as a bomb shelter for 3800 people.

Rollerblading is popular, especially in Kaivopuisto park. Inline skates can be hired at Salomon Park (☎ 040-525 7787), a kiosk on Merisatamanranta, west of Kaivopuisto park.

For information on bike rental see Getting Around later in this chapter. The bike and skate route map, Helsingin Pyöräilykartta, is free at the city tourist office.

In late July and August, a bungy crane is set up at the waterfront near Cafe Ursula. Benji Hippe (Finnish for bungy jump) is 30m high and costs €70.

ORGANISED TOURS

Helsinki Tour Expert (☎ 2288 1600; adult/child €19/10, with Helsinki Card €6) runs excellent 1½-hour sightseeing bus tours daily in summer on the hour from 10am to 2pm. They depart from the Esplanade Park, near the tourist office, and taped commentary (in 11 languages) is via a headset. In winter the tour departs only at 10am from the Olympia ferry terminal.

Open Top Tours also has hop-on hop-off tours aboard an open-top double decker bus. Tours leave from the kauppatori, follow a similar route and also have headphone commentary.

There are also several types of guided walking tours in summer, usually given once a week. Inquire at the city tourist office.

Cruises

Strolling through the fish market in summer, you won't have to look for cruises – the boat companies will find you. Royal Line (☎ 170 488), Sun Lines (☎ 727 7010; W www.sunlines.fi) and a number of smaller companies offer 1½-hour sea and canal cruises (adult/child €14/5) with regular daily departures in summer. The trip around the island of Laajasalo, run by Sun Lines, is probably the most interesting. There are also lunch (€24/10) and dinner (€36/15) cruises.

A visit to the Helsinki Zoo or Suomenlinna sea fortress is a good way to combine a scenic boat ride with other sightseeing (and they're free with the Helsinki Card). There are also longer day cruises by ferry and steamer from Helsinki to the Finnish town Porvoo; see the Getting There & Away section later in this chapter.

SPECIAL EVENTS

Vappu (May Day), the festival of students and workers, is taken very seriously in Helsinki – on 30 April at 6pm people gather in the centre around the Havis Amanda statue, which receives a white 'student cap'. On 1 May many students gather in Esplanade Park. Helsinki Day (12 June), celebrating the city's anniversary, brings many free and cheap activities to Esplanade Park.

CENTRAL HELSINKI

PLACES TO STAY
3 Gasthaus Omapohja;
  Matkakoti
  Margarita
4 Hotel Arthur
48 Hotel Kamp
63 Hotelli Finn
67 Sokos Hotel Torni
  & Ateljee Bar
94 Lonnrot Hostel
  & Cafe
96 Hostel
  Erottajanpuisto
110 Marttahotelli;
  Leningrad Cowboys

PLACES TO EAT
6 Eatz
20 Zetor;
  Ylioppilasaukio
  UniCafe
21 Alepa Supermarket
26 Wayne's Coffee
27 Cafe Krypta
30 Porthania
32 Amarillo
33 Papa Giovanni
34 Dick Tracy Diner
35 Hesburger
43 Cafe Engel
47 Fazer
49 Cafe Strindberg
50 Cafe Esplanade
52 Iguana
56 Iguana
57 Forum Shopping
  Centre, Food
  Court & Cinemas

64 Kosmos
70 Maithai
71 Long Wall
74 Lappi
75 Wrong Noodle Bar
79 Kappeli
85 Zucchini
86 Cantina West
87 Volga
90 Vespa
92 Tony's Deli
93 Cafe Ekberg
98 Chez Dominique
99 Ravintola Via
100 Limon
104 Bon Cafe
106 Labyrinth
107 Viva Café
111 Babushka Ira &
  St Petersburg Bar

OTHER
1 Ecobike
2 Greenbike
5 On The Rocks;
  Bar Fly
7 Pub Tram Sparåkoff
8 Forex & Hotel
  Booking Centre
9 Finnair Office &
  Finnair Buses
10 Main Post Office,
  Poste Restante &
  Telephone Office
11 Postimuseo
12 Kiasma Museum of
  Contemporary Art
13 Mannerheim Statue

14 Café Lasipalatsi
  Multimedia Centre;
  Cable Book Library;
  Cafe Lasipalatsi
15 Bus Station & Regional
  Buses
16 Kompassi
17 Sokos Department
  Store & Sokos
  Hotel Vaakuna
18 Pharmacy
19 Kilroy Travels
22 Wall Street Bar
23 Ateneum
  (National Gallery)
24 STA Travel
25 Molly Malone's
28 Tuomiokirkko
  (Lutheran Cathedral)
29 University of Helsinki
  Library
31 Copacabana
36 Club Helsinki
37 Thomas Cook
38 University of Helsinki
39 Sederholm House
40 Presidential Palace
41 Swedish Embassy
42 Helsinki City Museum
44 Karttakeskus Aleksi
  (Map Shop)
45 Helsinki City Tourist
  Office & Tour Expert;
  Tavex
46 Forex
51 Akateeminen
  Kirjakauppa
  Academic Bookshop

53 Stockmann Department
  Store, Western
  Union & Kitchen
54 Roberts Coffee; Netcup
55 Vanha
58 DTM
59 Finnish Youth Hostel
  Association (SRM)
60 Amos Anderson Art Museum
61 Yrjönkadun Uimahalli
62 Viking Line
65 Forex
66 Eckero Line
68 Mother Bar & Kitchen
69 Finnsov Tours
72 Corona; Moscow
73 Con Hombres
76 Old Church
77 Silja Line
78 Teaterri
80 Havis Amanda Statue
81 Cruise Boats
82 Local Ferries
83 Palace Hotel & Cafe
84 Finnish Tourist Board
88 Rikhardinkadun Library
89 Finnish Forest & Park
  Service (Tikankontti)
91 Tallink
95 Bar Tapasta
97 Erottaja
101 S-Market; Alko
102 Japanese Embassy
103 Makasiini Ferry Terminal
105 Gloria
108 Lost & Found;
  Hideaway Bar
109 Soda

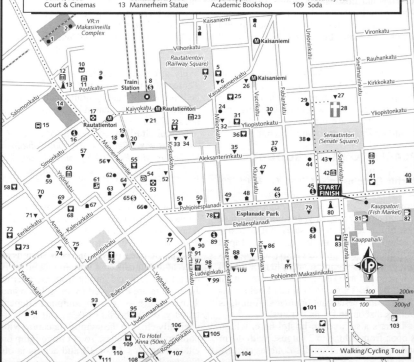

Surprisingly, Helsinki doesn't host any major summer festivals – they're scattered around the country – but there's something happening here most of the year. The **Regional Fair**, held in early June, spotlights a different region of Finland each year. From late August to early September, the **Helsinki Festival** is an elaborate arts festival with chamber music, jazz, theatre, opera and more. In early October the annual **Baltic Herring Market**, a 200-year-old tradition, takes place at the market square. Helsinki hosts an ethnic music festival, **Etnosoi**, in early November. Christmas is a special time in Helsinki, with the big Lucia parade taking place in mid-December.

The **Ice Hockey World Championships** in May are often televised on a big screen under a tent on Rautatientori – there's a great atmosphere here, especially if Finland makes the finals.

PLACES TO STAY

Bookings are advisable – if not essential – for Helsinki hostels and hotels from mid-May to mid-August, although July is usually a quiet time for mid-range and top-end hotels. The **Hotel Booking Centre** (☎ 2288 1400; e hotel@helsinkiexpert.fi; open 9am-7pm Mon-Fri, 9am-6pm Sat, 10am-6pm Sun June-Aug; 9am-5pm Mon-Sat Sept-May), in the central hall of the train station, can help in a pinch. There's also a branch at the city tourist office. There's a small booking fee, but room rates are often cheaper than you would be able to negotiate on your own.

PLACES TO STAY – BUDGET
Camping

Rastila Camping (☎ 321 6551, fax 344 1578; e rastilacamping@hel.fi; sites per person/group €9/14, cabins for 2/4 people €40/62, log cottages €95; open year-round) is 10km east of the centre in Vuosaari, but is easily reached by metro – the Rastila metro stop is only about 50m from the camp (turn right as you exit). The camping areas here are lush and peaceful and one section fronts onto a small beach. There are saunas, kitchen facilities and a restaurant open year-round, as well as discounted weekly rates.

There's also a **youth hostel** here, which is open from 3 June to 2 August, with dorm beds from €17 and singles/doubles costing €26/46.

Hostels

Helsinki has three year-round hostels and three that are open in summer only, plus there's a summer hostel on Suomenlinna island (see Around Helsinki later in this chapter). Most hostels offer a buffet breakfast which is either included in the rates, or €5 extra if you're in a dorm.

Eurohostel (☎ 622 0470, fax 655 044; e eurohostel@eurohostel.fi, w www.euro hostel.fi; Linnankatu 9; dorm beds €21, singles/doubles/triples €34.50/42/63; reception open 24hr), a high-rise place on Katajanokka island less than 500m from the Viking Line terminal, is an efficiently run and friendly HI hostel. The rooms are small and plain but well kept and there's a small self-catering kitchen on each floor. Rates include morning sauna. There's also a laundry and a good licensed café on the ground floor (lunch with buffet salad, soup, dessert and coffee is €7.40). It's about a 10-minute walk from the kauppatori, or take tram No 4 or 2 from the centre. Check-out is noon and check-in begins at 2pm.

Hostel Erottajanpuisto (☎ 642 169, fax 680 2757; Uudenmaankatu 9; dorm beds €25, singles/doubles €46/60; open year-round) is the most laid-back hostel in Helsinki, and has the best location on a lively street close to the heart of the city. There are comfortable, if a little pricey, six-bed rooms (linen and bedding included) and private rooms with shared bathroom. Check-out is 10am.

Hostel Stadion (☎ 477 8480, fax 477 84811; w www.stadionhostel.com; Pohjoinen Stadiontie 3B; dorm beds from €14.50, 4-5 bed rooms per person €17.50, doubles €39) is a 162-bed HI hostel in the Olympic Stadium. It's probably the least appealing of Helsinki's hostels – in a relatively dead part of town and a bit of a relic of the 'old school' of youth hostels, but you should have no trouble getting a bed here, particularly outside the peak months of July and August. In summer reception is open from 7am to 3am but from October to June hours are restricted (8am to 10am and 4pm to 2am). There's an equipped kitchen, laundry, buffet breakfast (€5) and it's conveniently close to the swimming centre with pool, gym and saunas. To get there jump on either tram Nos 3T or 3B and access is off Nordenskioldink.

Academica Summer Hostel (☎ 1311 4334, fax 441 201; [W] www.hostelacademica .fi; Hietaniemenkatu 14; dorm beds €16-21, singles/doubles/triples from €41/58/71), a student apartment building in winter, is an HI-affiliated hostel open to travellers from 1 June to 1 September. There are no large dorms as such but each room, with bathroom and kitchenette, can be used as a dorm (without linen) or as a private room (with linen and breakfast included). Rates include morning sauna and use of the swimming pool. It's in a quiet part of town but there's a UniCafe attached, a pub across the road and free off-street parking.

Hostel Satakuntatalo (☎ 6958 5231, fax 685 4245; [e] ravintola.satakunta@sodexho.fi; Lapinrinne 1A; dorm beds €13.50, singles/ doubles/triples/quads 39/56/66/76) is another student apartment building, originally built as accommodation for the 1952 Olympics, and is open to travellers from 1 June to 31 August. It's an austere place and the dorms are not flash but they are the cheapest in town at €11 with an HI card (linen not included). Private rooms are clean with fridge, phone, shared bathroom and buffet breakfast included and a morning sauna.

Tikkurilan Youth Hostel (☎ 8392 8050, fax 8392 8051; [e] hostel@urheilupuisto.fi; Valkoisenlähteentie 52; dorm beds from €10; open year-round) is the closest hostel to the airport in Vantaa. It's a clean HI-affiliated hostel, part of a large recreation complex called Tikkurilan Urheilupuisto.

PLACES TO STAY – MID-RANGE
Guesthouses
Gasthaus Omapohja (☎ 666 211, fax 6228 0053; Itäinen Teatterikuja 3; singles/doubles from €40/60, with bathroom €58/75), just around the corner from the train station, is a fine old guesthouse without any of the sleazy characteristics of some Helsinki guesthouses. Some rooms have shared bath, some have toilet and others a full bathroom, but they're all spotless and management is friendly.

Matkakoti Margarita (☎ 622 4261, Itäinen Teatterikuja 3; singles/doubles with shared bathroom €37/50), next door, is not quite as charming but again it's clean and reasonably good value.

Lönnrot Hostel & Café (☎ 6932 590; Lönnrotinkatu 16; singles/doubles/triples €49/ 64/74) is something of a last resort – it tends

to cater to lone Finnish men, and solo women might not feel comfortable here, but it's cheap enough. Rooms are basic, with shared bathroom, and include breakfast in the café.

Hotels
Marttahotelli (☎ 618 7400, fax 618 7411; [W] www.marttahotelli.fi; Uudenmaankatu 24; singles/doubles/triples €94/112/135, weekends & summer €70/80/100) is a spotless, friendly place with only 44 rooms. It's centrally located but most rooms (with bathroom and TV) face a quiet inner courtyard with free parking. Rates include a superb buffet breakfast and there's a small sauna.

Hotel Arthur (☎ 173 441, fax 626 880; [W] www.hotelarthur.fi; Vuorikatu 19; singles/ doubles/triples from €89/106/126, weekends & summer €71/88/108), near the train station, is a friendly place popular with groups. There are small twins with TV and attached bath as well as larger rooms and suites, and a good restaurant on the ground floor. Breakfast is included.

Hotelli Finn (☎ 684 4360, fax 6844 3610; [W] www.hotellifinn.fi; Kalevankatu 3B; singles/ doubles €65/80, weekends €55/70) is a small hotel occupying the top floors of a central city building. There are some cheaper rooms with shared bathroom.

Hotel Anna (☎ 616 621, fax 602 664; [W] www.hotelanna.com; Annankatu 1; singles/ doubles €100/135, superior rooms €115/150) is a popular mid-range hotel that fills up fast. Rates include buffet breakfast but sauna is extra. There are no set discounts, but ask about weekend and summer rates.

Hotel Helka (☎ 613 580, fax 441 087; [W] www.helka.fi; Pohjoinen Rautatiekatu 23; singles/doubles €109/135, weekends €75/ 99) is a smart business hotel. Rooms have wooden floors, private bathroom, TV, phone and minibar, and rates include breakfast and morning sauna.

Hotelli Anton (☎ 173 441; Paasivuorenkatu 1; singles/doubles from C05/100, weekends & summer €70/85) is a good-value option in an interesting location at Hakaniemi market square just north of the centre.

Airport Hotels
There are good transport connections from Vantaa airport to the city, but if you find yourself wanting to overnight here, there are

half a dozen choices that all offer shuttle services to the airport.

Good Morning Hotels Pilotti (☎ 329 4800; ⓦ www.choicehotels.fi; Veromaentie 1; singles/doubles from €85/100, weekends & summer €65/85) is 4km from the airport.

Airport Hotel Bonus Inn (☎ 825 511; ⓦ www.bonusinn.fi; Elannontie 9; singles/ doubles €100/140, weekends & summer €55/ 70) is 5km south of the airport. Sauna and shuttle is included, but not breakfast.

PLACES TO STAY – TOP END

Lord Hotel (☎ 615 815, fax 680 1315; ⓔ lord.hotel@co.inet.fi; Lönnrotinkatu 29; singles/doubles €134/164, weekends & summer €84/90) is in a lovely Art Nouveau building with stone facade and a distinctive turret. The rooms are modern, functional and good value when discounted. Rates include breakfast and a sauna, and there's an excellent restaurant attached.

Sokos Hotel Torni (☎ 131 131, fax 131 1361; Yrjönkatu 26; singles/doubles from €185/205) was Helsinki's first high-rise hotel (Torni translates as 'tower') and is still the tallest building in the city centre – the tiny rooftop bar has great views of Helsinki. It's quite elegant in an old-world, 1930s sort of way and there is a wing of newer, renovated rooms. All rooms have TV and the doubles have a fridge and sofa. The sauna costs extra. Summer rates (20 June to 8 August) are €76/93 for singles/doubles and weekend rates are €88/108.

The Radisson SAS group (ⓦ www.radis sonsas.com) has some quality hotels in Helsinki city, catering mainly to business clientele and groups. **Radisson SAS Royal Hotel** (☎ 69580, fax 6958 7100; Rune-berginkatu 2; singles/doubles from €230, weekends €97/114, June-Aug €86/95) is one of Helsinki's finest with a range of contemporary rooms in theme styles (Scandinavian, Oriental etc). Suites cost from €380 to €1060 a double! There are several good restaurants here (with breakfast and lunch buffets), a beer terrace on the forecourt, free sauna, and a gym. Less flashy but no less comfortable is **Radisson SAS Hesperia** (Mannerheimintie 50) with a popular nightclub.

Scandic Hotel Grand Marina (☎ 16 661, fax 664 764; Katajanokanlaituri 7; singles/ doubles €130/180, weekends & summer €75/ 85) enjoys a good location in a renovated

harbour building on Katajanokka island, a short walk from the Viking terminal. It has quality rooms and plenty of facilities.

Hotel Kamp (☎ 576 111, fax 576 1122; ⓦ www.hotelkamp.fi; Pohjoisesplanadi 29; doubles from €330) is Helsinki's finest, and most exclusive, hotel. The original hotel building dates from 1887 and it was restored and reopened in 1998, with much of the original architecture retained, including the grand central staircase. The rooms are pretty standard – even the luxurious Mannerheim Suite is way over the top at €2624 – but if you can afford it, this is where the elite hang out. There's a health club, conference rooms, a restaurant and bar.

PLACES TO EAT

Helsinki has by far the best range of restaurants in Finland, whether you're looking for fast food, authentic Finnish cuisine or international dinning. It also has a fabulous café scene, good markets and some great parks to set up a summer picnic.

The **kauppahalli** (covered market; Eteläranta) is one of the best in Finland and a great place to stock up on fresh produce, filled rolls (€3), salads, pastries and everything else you can think of. There's also a café and a tiny Alko store here. The **kauppatori**, also known as the fish market, is good for salmon chowder, cheap snacks and fresh produce such as berries. Most food stalls set up plastic chairs and tables on summer afternoons.

Restaurants

Finnish Traditional Finnish restaurants are in the minority in this cosmopolitan city, but there are a few gems.

Konstan Möljä (☎ 694 7504; Hietalahdenkatu 14; lunch/dinner buffet €7.50/11.50; open 11am-10pm Mon-Fri, 2pm-2am Sat) is the place to go for hearty home-style Finnish fare in a pleasant, rustic atmosphere. Much of the maritime decor comes from an old harbour near Vyborg (once Finnish but now in Russia). The buffet includes soup, salad, bread, meat and vegetable dishes, and always includes reindeer. Mains, such as fried Baltic herring and salmon, are priced from €7.50 to €22.

Kolme Kruunua (☎ 135 4172; Liisankatu 5; open at 4pm), a relic of the 1930s, is famous for its lihapullat (meatballs; €8).

Kiasma Museum of Contemporary Art, Helsinki

Toolonlahti River, Helsinki

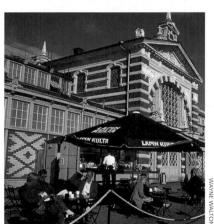

Kauppahalli (covered market), Helsinki

Central train station, Helsinki

Suomenlinna ferry

Cannon, Suomenlinna fortress

Seurasaari Open-Air Museum, Helsinki

Espoo chapel, Espoo

Old Town, Porvoo

Zetor (☎ 666 966; Mannerheimintie 3-5; mains €8-12) is a spoofy Finnish restaurant and pub with deeply ironic tractor decor ('Zetor' is a tractor manufacturer). It's owned by film maker Aki Kaurismäki and designed by those crazy guys from the Leningrad Cowboys. It's worth going in just for a drink and a ride on a tractor.

Leningrad Cowboys (☎ 644 981; Uudenmaankatu 16-20; mains €8-18), near Martta-hotelli, is a Tex-Mex saloon-style place with a touch of Soviet in the decor (same interior designers as Zetor). There's booth seating, reasonably priced food and a full bar.

Lappi (☎ 645 550; Annankatu 22; mains €15-30) serves up genuine Lappish specialities. It's a delightfully rustic restaurant with costumed staff. Dishes include breast of snowgrouse and sirloin of elk, as well as various reindeer dishes.

Russian The best Russian restaurants are said to be in Helsinki – try a blini (filled pancake; €8) at the romantic **Babushka Ira & St Petersburg Bar** (☎ 680 1405; Uudenmaankatu 28) to judge for yourself. It's a tiny, intimate place, so book ahead.

Volga (☎ 622 1717; Richardinkatu 1; lunch specials €8), near the main library, has a lovely summer terrace in an enclosed courtyard. There's entertainment in the evenings and good value weekday lunch specials.

Saslik (☎ 348 9700; Neitsytpolku 12; blinis from €13.50, mains €15-31; open noon-midnight Mon-Sat, 4pm-11pm Sun) is the city's top Russian restaurant. It offers live music nightly and seven private, themed dining rooms – all complete with plush velvet, stained-glass windows and chandeliers. Most mains are around €22 but blinis with Russian caviar is €64 (twice that with Iranian caviar).

Restaurant Bellevue (☎ 636 985; Rahapajankatu 3; mains €10-24), near the cathedral, is the oldest Russian restaurant in town. Bellevue specialises in Russian and Finnish food with a French accent.

International Although there are some good ethnic restaurants appearing around Finland, Helsinki definitely has the best range, so this is the place if you're after authentic Asian or Mediterranean flavours, occasionally with a Nordic touch and usually with a Finnish price tag.

Wrong Noodle Bar (Annankatu 21; dishes €6.50-7; open 11am-10pm Mon-Fri, 3pm-10pm Sun) is ultra-modern and trendy, and difficult to beat for a filling bowl of ramen noodles, laksa, satay or curry, including vegetarian.

Iguana (mains €4.50-10.50) is a modern, good value American-style Tex-Mex chain offering pizza, pasta and enchiladas. There are three branches in central Helsinki, including one on Keskuskatu and another on Mannerheimintie.

Cantina West (Kasarmikatu 23) is a popular Mexican restaurant and bar with a good buffet lunch.

Kitchen, in the basement of Stockmann department store, offers everything from €4 focaccia sandwiches to Asian stirfries.

Eatz (☎ 687 7240; Mikonkatu 15; sushi €3-8, mains €10-20) manages to serve up everything from Thai and Indian to Italian and even has a belt-driven sushi bar. It's also the cornerstone of Helsinki's biggest summer beer terrace.

Tony's Deli (☎ 641 100; Bulevardi 2; mains €8.50-11.50) is a stylish, low-key Italian place, with pasta from €10 and Helsinki's best antipasto. The antipasto buffet on Monday evenings is not cheap at €16, but it's really something special and includes tiramisu for dessert.

Maithai (☎ 685 6850; Annankatu 31-33; mains €10-16; open 11am-11pm Mon-Fri, noon-11pm Sat & Sun) is an intimate, authentic little place and a local favourite for Thai food.

Kabuki (☎ 694 9446; Lapinlahdenkatu 12; sushi €3-5) is a sushi specialist with probably the best Japanese food in town.

Long Wall (☎ 605 898; Annankatu 26; mains around €12) gets mixed reports but it's a popular Chinese restaurant with comfortable booth seating and reasonably priced takeaways.

Chico's All American Bistro (Mannerheimintie 68) is popular with families for its 'American' food – like pepperoni quesadillas and peanut butter chicken sandwiches.

Sipuli (☎ 179 900; Kanavaranta 3; mains €15-28; open dinner only), near the church on Katajanokka island, offers fine views back across the city. The speciality is gourmet wild game.

Papa Giovanni (☎ 622 6010; Keskuskatu 7; mains €10-22) is a real favourite among

Helsinki's pasta eaters. Downstairs is a spaghetteria with reasonably priced pasta dishes and an Italian-style café; upstairs is a stylish restaurant and wine bar with high-backed chairs and a tempting range of Italian soups, salads and mains.

Vespa (☎ 641 400; Eteläespanadi 22; pizza €8.50-10, pasta €10-12.50) is another good Italian restaurant with a bar and terrace close to the action at the northern end of the esplanade. There's a more expensive restaurant on the 1st floor, but the trick in summer is to secure a table on the terrace.

Kosmos (☎ 647 255; Kalevankatu 3; meals €8.50-12) is a Helsinki institution as far as cafés go and is a good place to fill up on Greek food.

Limon (☎ 622 5992; Rikhardinkatu 4; dishes €4-12) is essentially a café-bar where the beautiful people like to see and be seen, savouring finely flavoured Mediterranean-style concoctions.

Dick Tracy Diner (☎ 625 466; Keskuskatu 7; mains €10-20), just along from Papa Giovanni, is an American-style theme diner popular for pricey steaks, but also serves pasta, fish and even vegetarian dishes.

Amarillo (☎ 686 0000; Mikonkatu 9; mains €7-18) is Helsinki's central branch of the popular chain restaurant serving pasta, burgers and spicy Tex-Mex meals. The bar here is also a very popular nightspot (open until 4am on Friday and Saturday) and there's a good summer terrace.

Restaurant Satkar (☎ 612 077; Lonnrotinkatu 28; mains €9-17; open to 10pm daily) is an inexpensive Nepalese restaurant with plenty of North Indian dishes on the menu, including tandoori and thalis. There's a multicourse set menu for €19 (vegetarian €18).

Mt Everest Restaurant is another cheap Nepalese place close to the Academica Hostel. Meat kofta is €9.50 and chicken curry €9.

For fine Scandinavian-French cuisine, **Chez Dominique** (☎ 612 7393; Ludviginkatu 3; mains €13-40, set menus from €50) is the No 1 choice in Helsinki – it's one of the few Finnish restaurants to receive a Michelin star. There's an à la carte menu but the speciality is set menus of four courses or more.

Vegetarian Helsinki has a couple of fine vegetarian restaurants. **Zucchini** (☎ 622 2907; Fabianinkatu 4; lunch €6.50-9; open 11am-4pm daily) is the city's vegetarian café. It serves light meals such as vegetarian lasagne, quiche and soups.

Ravintola Via (☎ 681 1370; Ludviginkatu 8; mains €7-10.50) is a little more upmarket and specialises in vegie dishes with an Asian and Italian flavour.

Cafés

The Finns – long-time dedicated coffee drinkers – have passionately embraced the European notion of café culture and nowhere is this better expressed than in Helsinki. Most cafés are cosy retreats in winter, and have tables and terraces spilling out onto the footpath in summer. All serve coffee and usually some sort of pastry or sweet, most serve alcohol and some have cheap lunch menus. There are a number of good cafés around Esplanade Park – a great place for people-watching in summer.

Helsinki – Kahvi Drinking Capital of Europe

Time magazine recently predicted that Helsinki, with its street cafés full of coffee-guzzling, mobile-phone wielding go-getters, was poised to become the swinging London of the new millennium.

If mobile-phone ownership and coffee consumption have anything to do with success, this prediction could well come true. Finns consume 14kg of coffee per person annually, or the equivalent of nine cups a day each, and 50% of the Finnish population own a mobile phone.

Even outside the bustling big city, coffee is what drives Finland. There are dozens of cafés in every town and village; even petrol stations have cafés, and a cup of coffee is included with the lunch special at most restaurants.

Seldom will you visit a house without being served coffee. Traditionally you say 'no' three times and then accept, by saying 'OK, just half a cup', which in reality turns out to be four or five cups.

To do as the Finns do, pour your *kahvi* into a *kuppi* and add some *maito* (milk) or *kerma* (cream). Finns usually eat some *pulla* (wheat bun) with coffee.

Kappeli, in the park itself, is a café, restaurant and microbrewery/bar, but it's best known for its terrace and cellar pub – see Entertainment.

On any budget, **Cafe Esplanade** *(Pohjoisesplanadi 37; sandwiches €3-5)* is perfect, with oversized Danish pastries and Finnish *pulla* (wheat bun) for €2, and spectacular salads. **Cafe Strindberg** *(Pohjoisesplanadi 33)* is twice the price, but twice as classy; tables at the front (waiter service) are at a premium, and the upstairs lounge is all class.

Cafe Ekberg *(Bulevardi 9; buffet breakfast & lunch €7.20)* is Helsinki's oldest café (opened 1861) and one of the best places for breakfast in the city. The lunch buffet is also great value.

Fazer *(Kluuvikatu 3)* is another historical café worth delving into. Founded in 1891 by the Finnish confectionary-making family (you'll see Fazer sweets and chocolate everywhere), it does amazing ice cream sundaes.

Cafe Krypta *(Kirkkokatu 18; open 11am-5pm daily early June–mid-Aug)* is a reasonably pleasant subterranean café in the crypt of Tuomiokirkko.

Cafe Engel *(Senaatintori)*, directly opposite the cathedral, is popular with students popping across from the University of Helsinki. It's an arty place with a small gallery next door and a big notice board announcing coming events. There's a covered courtyard at the back and it's open until midnight daily.

Bon Cafe *(☎ 635 732; Korkeavuorenkatu 27; lunch buffet €7.40)* is simple on the decor but serves a cheap and hearty lunch buffet, including soup, dessert and coffee, as well as a selection of filled rolls and pastries.

Cafe Lasipalatsi, on the ground floor of the multimedia centre, specialises in Finnish food and has a €7 soup and salad buffet.

Down on Kaivopuisto Park, with great views over to Harakka island, is **Cafe Ursula** *(☎ 652 817; Ehrenströmintie 3)*, a popular summertime spot for tourists. A little further around the peninsular, **Cafe Carusel** is a cheaper, less pretentious waterfront café with excellent focaccias.

Wayne's Coffee *(Kaisaniemenkatu 3)*, part of the very successful Swedish café chain, has the best muffins in town, a laid-back environment and Internet access.

Another good spot to find cafés (and bars) is the pedestrian section of Roobertinkatu,

an animated strip just south of the centre. Popular spots include **Viva Café** and **Labyrinth**.

University Cafés The University of Helsinki operates dozens of student cafeterias around the city, known as **UniCafes** *(Ⓦ www.unifcafe.fi)*, where a full meal costs less than €5 and there's always a vegetarian main course on offer. They're also good places to meet Finnish students. Technically you should have a student card to get the cheap meals, but you may not be asked for it. Some of the best include **UniCafe** *(Hietaniemenkatu 14)*, below Academica Summer Hostel; **Porthania** *(Hallituskatu 11-13)*; and the huge **Ylioppilasaukio** *(Mannerheimintie 3B)*, next to Zetor in the city centre.

Fast Food & Self-Catering

There are plenty of hamburger restaurants (Hesburger, Carrols, McDonald's), pizza shops, kebab joints, hot-dog stands and grillis in Helsinki. For cheap fast food, it's hard to go past the basement of the sprawling **Forum shopping centre** *(Mannerheimintie 20)* which has an atrium-covered food court with everything from Asian noodles to burgers and kebabs.

Alepa supermarket *(Asematunneli; open 8am-10pm Mon-Sat, 10am-10pm Sun)* is in the train station pedestrian tunnel. A bigger supermarket is in the basement level of the **Forum shopping centre** *(Mannerheimintie 20)*. Another well-stocked central supermarket is **S-Market** on Fabiankatu, and there's a large **Alko** outlet here too.

ENTERTAINMENT

In many ways Helsinki has a typical capital city entertainment and nightlife scene, but in recent years the city's bars, cafés and clubs have blossomed into the envy of Scandinavia. As well as a full range of trends, from hole-in-the-wall bars and cafés to rock and jazz clubs to dance clubs, there's generally a sophisticated but down-to-earth air about Helsinki's nightlife. The Finns certainly know how to party, especially in summer when open-air beer terraces spill out everywhere to take advantage of the long hours of daylight. Helsinki's biggest summer terrace is along Mikonkatu where hundreds of chairs and tables crowd the sidewalk in front of Eatz, On the Rocks and Barfly. After about 4pm on a sunny day it's difficult to score a seat here, but the atmosphere is fantastic. Finally, being a compact city, it's easy to get around the city centre, where most nightspots are concentrated, on foot (or do as many Finns do and ride a bicycle).

For events, concerts and performances, see *Helsinki This Week* or inquire at the city tourist office. Major rock and pop concerts by touring bands are staged at the **Hartwall Arena** (☎ 020-494 076).

Terraces, Bars & Clubs

Kappeli, in the middle of Esplanade Park near the kauppatori, has one of the most popular summer terraces. It faces a stage where various bands and musicians regularly play in summer – if something is on, getting a table here is difficult. Inside, there's a medieval, vault-like brewery pub in the cellar, which is fantastic later in the evening or when the sun's not shining. Finnish composer Oskar Merikanto once wrote a song for Kappeli, his favourite drinking spot.

Ateljee Bar *(open 2pm-2am Mon-Thur, noon-2am Fri & Sat, 2pm-1am Sun)* is a tiny perch on the roof of the Sokos Hotel Torni, and is worth ascending just for the views of the city. Despite the location, drinks are almost reasonable (€5.50 for a beer). Take the lift to the 12th floor and the narrow winding staircase to the top. Another bar-with-a-view is the rooftop bar of the **Palace Hotel**, which actually has a better view, overlooking the harbour and church.

Vanha *(Mannerheimintie 3)*, a music bar in the beautiful 19th-century students' house, gets packed with students, though it's more interesting from the outside than within.

Molly Malone's (☎ *Kaisaniemenkatu 1C)* may not be very Finnish but it's a typically exuberant Irish pub and one of the best places in Helsinki to meet people – travellers, expats and Finns. There's live music on most nights upstairs – where it's shoulder-to-shoulder Guinness consumption – and a cosier, quieter bar down below.

Erottaja (☎ *611 196; Erottajankatu 15-17)*, a no-frills wine bar with reasonably cheap drinks, is well-patronised by locals in the know.

Bar Tapasta *(Uudenmaankatu)* is an intimate and welcoming bar that does genuine sangria (€3.70) and tapas from €2 to €4, including chilli olives.

Cosy **Wall Street Bar** *(Yliopistonkatu)* must be the smallest bar in Helsinki with only a handful of bar stools tucked into its corner location, near the back entrance to the Atheneum.

If you're young and/or beautiful, or just trying, **Soda** (Ⓦ *www.barsoda.fi; Uudenmaankatu 16-20)* is for you; its house and techno music draws shiny happy people most nights. The ultra chic club above **Teatteri** (☎ *681 1130, Pohjoisesplanadi 2)*, inside the Swedish Theatre, has space for 300 people and there's a beautifully designed bar on the middle level.

More down-to-earth is the stylish **Mother Bar & Kitchen** (☎ *612 3990; Eerikinkatu 2)*, with a wonderfully hip vibe and DJs playing drum and bass and acid jazz music four nights a week. The kitchen serves up sandwiches and Euro-Asian food.

Corona *(Eerikinkatu 15)* and **Moscow** next door are run by film makers Aki and Mika Kaurismäki; both attract a savvy, grungy crowd. Corona has about 20 pool tables and cheap beer, which makes it popular with students and travellers. Further down the street, the **Saunabar** (☎ *685 5550; Eerikinkatu 27)*, downstairs at the rear of the building, is popular with students and does indeed have saunas.

Vanha Maestro *(Fredrikinkatu 51-53)* is the place to go to experience first-hand the Finnish national passion for tango dancing. Live Finnish tango and humppa bands accompany the dancing.

Away from the centre, in the suburb of Kallio, **Rytmi** *(Toinen Linja 2)* is a funky little bar with DJs playing on weekends.

If you're partying late, **Club Helsinki** *(Yliopistonkatu 8, cnr Kluuvikatu)* is a mainstream dance club open until 4am and popular with a youthful Helsinkian crowd. As well as local DJs it occasionally hosts big names like Ministry of Sound. The minimum age on weekends is 22.

Highlight (☎ *734 5822; Fredrikinkatu 42)* claims to be a 'disco for demanding people' and attracts a young crowd looking for late-night action and cheap beer. It's open from 9pm to 4am but it's difficult to get in after 11pm on Friday and Saturday.

Copacabana (☎ *278 1855; Yliopistonkatu 5)* is a cavernous Latin American nightclub almost opposite Club Helsinki, with a mixture of DJs, salsa dancing and live music.

It's popular with a slightly older, well-heeled crowd, including the occasional Finnish celebrity, and at times, hosts big-name live acts.

Gloria (☎ 3104 5810; Roobertinkatu 12) is a youth *kulttuuriareena* (cultural arena) in a refurbished old theatre. It hosts an eclectic array of live music acts, club nights, theatre and jam sessions.

Gay & Lesbian By Scandinavian standards, Helsinki has a low-key gay scene, but **Lost & Found** (☎ 680 1010; Annankatu 6; open to 4am) and the associated **Hideaway Bar** is a sophisticated place that's open until 4am and gets busy around midnight. More vibrant are **DTM** (Annankatu 32), and the industrial 'eurobar' **Con Hombres** (☎ 608 826; Eerinkinkatu 14).

Pub Tram
In summer you can catch the bright red pub tram, **Spårakoff** (admission €7, beers €5) from the train station, with stops at the Opera House and kauppatori. It's a bit pricey but a quaint way to do a quick tour of town. It departs from its terminus on Mikonkatu on the hour between 2pm and 7pm Tuesday to Saturday.

Casinos
Gambling is certainly not frowned upon in Finland – quite a few bars have one or two casino-standard blackjack tables, complete with bow-tied dealer. **Casino Ray** (☎ 680 8000; ⓦ www.casino.ray.fi; Eteläinen Rautatiekatu 4; admission €5; open noon-4am daily) is the city's casino and the largest in Finland, though it's still not very big (five blackjack tables, seven roulette wheels and so on). The age limit is 18 and foreign travellers should carry their passport at all times for identification.

Jazz
Storyville (☎ 408 007; Museokatu 8) is one of Helsinki's best jazz clubs, housed in a converted coal cellar. An older crowd with deeper wallets groove to traditional, Dixieland and New Orleans jazz most nights. Bands start at 8pm and usually play to 4am. There's also a Creole restaurant here and a couple of bars.

Juttutupa (☎ 774 4860; Säästöpankinranta 6), west of Hakaniemi metro station, is one of

Helsinki's top live music bars, focusing on contemporary jazz and rock fusion. Arrive early as it gets pretty crowded with music-loving Helsinki students.

Opera, Theatre & Ballet
For concerts and performances, see *Helsinki This Week* or inquire at the tourist office. Opera, ballet and classical concerts are held at the **Opera House** (Helsinginkatu 58; tickets from €10), but not during summer. Performances of the Finnish National Opera are subtitled in Finnish. The opera and concert season is generally September to May (there are no indoor performances in summer). The Symphony Orchestra of the Finnish Broadcasting Corporation (RSO) features popular concerts in **Finlandia Hall**.

Cinemas
Tennispalatsi (☎ 0600-007 007; Salomonkatu 15) is one of Europe's largest multiplex cinemas and screens recent American movies; there are several other big cinemas in the centre. **Orion Theatre** (☎ 6154 0201; Eerinkinkatu 15) is the Finnish Film Archive's rep house, featuring film classics and the odd Woody Allen. You must purchase an annual membership card (€4), then admission is €3.50.

SPECTATOR SPORTS
Sporting events in Helsinki are numerous; between September and April ice hockey reigns supreme and the best place to see top level matches is the **Hartwall Arena** (☎ 020-494 076) about 4km north of the city centre (bus No 23 or 69, or tram No 7A or 7B). Built in 1997, Hartwell hosted the Ice Hockey World Championships that same year and has seating for more than 13,000 fans. It's the home of local Superleague side Jokerit Helsinki. Tickets cost €12.50 to €28.50. League matches are also played at the indoor arena at the Olympic Stadium off Mannerheimintie. Ask at the tourist office – or any bar – for match times.

SHOPPING
Prices are high at the shops on Pohjoisesplanadi, the main tourist street in town. Other notable shopping streets are Aleksanterinkatu and Fredrikinkatu. Mariankatu has many antiques shops, and Roobertinkatu is filled with funky boutiques.

Stockmann, the oldest and largest department store in Finland, is surprisingly well priced for Finnish souvenirs and Sami handicrafts, as well as Finnish textiles, Kalevala Koru jewellery, Lapponia jewellery, Moomintroll souvenirs and lots more. It offers an export service.

Arabia porcelain factory outlet & museum *(Hämeentie 135; open daily)* is rather bleakly located on the 9th floor of a suburban factory north of the centre. Take tram No 6 to its terminus and walk 200m farther north.

Dis 'n' Dat Records *(☎ 680 1118; w www .disndatrecords.com; Shop No 18 Kaisaniemi Metro Station)* is the place to look for CDs and other forms of music from Finland and abroad.

Markets

The famous **fish market** *(open 6.30am-2pm daily)* at the kauppatori is a must for anyone visiting Helsinki. Fish, seasonal fruit and berries, and *makkara* (sausages) are on sale at the produce stalls, and there are any number of stalls selling local handicrafts, unusual hats, Sami dolls, reindeer-related paraphernalia, knitwear such as gloves and hats, T-shirts and woodwork. There are evening markets in summer.

Hietalahti flea market *(tram No 6)* is the main second-hand centre in Helsinki: you'll find anything from used clothes to broken accordions. There is also a renovated **kauppahalli** *(open 8am-6pm Mon-Fri, 8am-3pm Sat)* here, which is not as touristy but rivals the gourmet pleasures of the main one at the harbour.

The **VR:n makasiineilla complex**, in the refurbished railway goods sheds off Mannerheimintie, house (among other things) a popular weekend second-hand market where you can pick up anything from a Russian soldier uniform to a pair of shoes. If you like junk markets, this is a good one and there are bars and food stalls set up in summer.

The **kauppahalli** at the Hakaniemi metro stop has a mix of craft and food stalls.

GETTING THERE & AWAY
Air

There are flights to Helsinki from the USA, Europe and Asia on many airlines. Finnair offers international as well as domestic service, with flights to 20 Finnish cities – generally at least once a day but several times daily to Turku, Tampere, Rovaniemi and Oulu. The **Finnair office** *(☎ 0203-140160 for reservations; Asema-aukio 1; open Mon-Sat)* is near the train station. The airport is in Vantaa, 19km north of Helsinki.

The quickest way to get to Tallinn is by helicopter. **Copterline** *(☎ 0200-18181; w www .copterline.com)* flies hourly between 8am and 10pm from Helsinki to Tallinn and back. The trip takes 18 minutes one way and costs from €86 for a limited ticket (book at least two days in advance) to €194 for a guaranteed seat. Everyday economy tickets are €120.

Bus

Purchase long-distance and express bus tickets at the **main bus station** *(between Mannerheimintie & Kamppi metro station; open 7am-7pm Mon-Fri, 7am-5pm Sat, 9am-6pm Sun)* or on the bus itself. Local and regional buses also depart from this station.

Train

The train station is in the city centre and is linked by pedestrian tunnel with the Helsinki metro system. Helsinki is the terminus for three main railway lines, with regular trains from Turku in the west, Tampere in the north and Lahti in the northeast. There is a separate ticket counter for international trains, including the ones that go to St Petersburg and Moscow.

Boat

International ferries travel to Stockholm, Tallinn, and Travemünde in Germany. There is also a regular catamaran and hydrofoil service to Tallinn. See the Getting There & Away chapter for more details.

Of the five ferry terminals in the city, four are just off the central kauppatori: Kanava and Katajanokka terminals are served by bus No 13 and tram Nos 2, 2V and 4, and Olympia and Makasiini terminals by tram Nos 3B and 3T. The fifth terminal, Länsiterminaali (West Terminal), is served by bus No 15.

Ferry tickets may be purchased at the terminal, from a ferry company's office in the centre or (in some cases) from the city tourist office. Book in advance during the high season (late June to mid-August). The cheapest ferries to Tallinn are with Eckero, while Tallink runs a reliable hydrofoil service.

Ferry company offices in Helsinki include:

Eckerö Line (☎ 228 8544) Mannerheimintie 10; Länsiterminaali
Linda Line (☎ 668 9700) Makasiini terminal
Nordic Jet Line (☎ 681 770) Kanava terminal
Silja Line (☎ 0203-74552) Mannerheimintie 2; Olympia terminal
Tallink (☎ 2282 1222) Erottajankatu 19; Kanava Terminal
Viking Line (☎ 123 577) Mannerheimintie 14; Katajanokka & Makasiini terminals

In summer there are daily ferries between Helsinki and Porvoo, through the scenic southeast archipelago. Although most people treat these as return day cruises, you can easily start or finish your travels this way, particularly as bicycles can be taken on board.

A great alternative to the long-distance, modern-day ferries is the leisurely pace of the former steamship MS *JL Runeberg* (☎ 019-524 3331; ⓦ *www.msjlruneberg.fi*). Built as a passenger ship in 1912, the *JL Runeberg* weaves its way through the archipelago east to Porvoo and west to Porkkala. It leaves for Porvoo daily except Thursday at 10am (adult one way/return €20/29, child €9/13; four hours). On Thursdays in late June and July it goes to Porkkala (one way/return €16/24).

A quicker way to reach Porvoo is aboard the MS *King*, operated by **Royal Line** (☎ 09-612 2950; ⓦ *www.royalline.fi*). It travels from

Tripping to Tallinn

Although Finland can seem very remote from the rest of Europe at times, Helsinki is remarkably close to the continental mainland and a day or overnight trip to the Estonian capital of Tallinn is a must. The contrast between modern Helsinki and the turrets and spires of Tallinn 's compact medieval Old Town is like chalk and cheese.

It's 80km across the Gulf of Finland to Tallinn and the catamarans and hydrofoils do the trip several times daily in 1½ hours and cost from €25 return. The ferry (with Eckero) costs as little as €12. At the other end of the scale, if you can afford it, you can even get there by scheduled helicopter. (Note that European citizens and most Western nationals don't require a visa for a short stay in Estonia, but Canadians do – contact the Estonian consulate in Helsinki for information.)

The trip itself is something of a 'booze cruise' for many Finns, but unlike the overnight trips to Sweden, it's not the cruise itself they are interested in, but the destination. Alcohol in Estonia is substantially cheaper than in Finland – less than half the price in liquor shops – so it's not unusual to see tipsy Finns tottering aboard with trolleys loaded up with beer and vodka (within customs limits of course). The ferries have the usual bars and cafeteria-style restaurants – check in early if you want a seat in one of the lounges.

The highlight of Tallinn is undoubtedly the walled **Old Town** – a Unesco World Heritage Site – and the lofty **Toompea Castle**. It's only about a 15-minute walk (follow the road Mere puiestee) from the ferry terminals to **Viru Gate**, the main entrance to Old Tallinn. A short walk along the cobbled, restaurant-lined Viru brings you to the central square **Raekoja plats**, which has been a marketplace since as early as the 11th century. Dominating the south side of the square is the Gothic **town hall**, dating from 1371, and opposite is the **tourist office** (☎ 645 7777), considerably younger but a great source of information and the place to buy your Tallinn Card if you intend to visit lots of attractions in the day.

The Old Town will seem pretty touristy after Helsinki, but with its tangle of narrow, cobbled streets and impossibly quaint medieval houses (many now studios, galleries, cafés, museums and craft shops), it demands to be explored on foot. Climb the hill to **Toompea**, dominated by the Alexandr Nevsky Cathedral, the Parliament building and Toompea Castle. Back in the Lower Town, take a stroll along **Pikk tanav**, lined with old merchants' houses and guilds and a couple of interesting museums and galleries.

Take the time to splurge at one of Tallinn's traditional restaurants or terrace cafés – although dining is generally a bit pricier in the Old Town, it's still much cheaper than Finland and the atmosphere is unbeatable. There are plenty along Viru and around Raekoja plats. If you plan to stay overnight there are a couple of youth hostels and inexpensive guesthouses nearby.

the Helsinki kauppatori at 10.20am daily from mid-June to mid-August, returning from Porvoo at 3.30pm. It costs €20/10 per adult/child one way. See the Porvoo Getting There & Away section for more information.

GETTING AROUND
To/From the Airport
Bus No 615 (€3, 30 minutes, Helsinki Card not valid) shuttles between Vantaa airport (all international and domestic flights) and platform No 10 at Rautatientori (Railway Square) next to the main train station.

Finnair buses (€4.90) depart from the Finnair office at Asemaaukio, also next to the main train station, every 20 minutes from 5am to midnight. There are also door-to-door **airport taxis** (☎ 106 464; W www.air porttaxi.fi) at €16.80 per person.

Public Transport
Central Helsinki is easy enough to get around on foot or by bicycle, but there's also a metro line and reasonably comprehensive local transport network. The city's public transport system, Helsingin Kaupungin Liikennelaitos (HKL; W www.hel.fi/HKL) operates buses, metro trains, local trains, trams and a ferry to the island of Suomenlinna. A one-hour flat-fare ticket for any HKL transport costs €2 when purchased on board, €1.40 when purchased in advance. The ticket allows unlimited transfers but should be validated in the stamping machine on board when you first use it. A single tram ticket (no transfers) is €1.50/1.

Tourist tickets are available at €4.20/8.40/12.60 for one/three/five days; 10-trip tickets will set you back €12.80. Alternatively, the Helsinki Card gives you free travel anywhere within Helsinki (see the Information section earlier for details).

There are also regional tickets for travel by bus or train to neighbouring cities such as Vantaa and Espoo which cost €3 for a single ticket, €7.50 for one day and €22 for the 10-trip ticket. Children's tickets are usually half price. The penalty for travelling without a valid ticket is €42.

HKL offices at the Rautatientori and Hakaniemi metro stations (open Monday to Friday) sell tickets and passes, as do many of the city's R-kiosks. Metro services run daily from about 6am to 11.30pm. The metro line extends to Ruoholahti in the

western part of the city and northeast to Mellunmäki.

The *Helsinki Route Map*, available at HKL offices and the city tourist office, is good for making sense of local transport.

Car & Motorcycle
Cars can be rented at the airport or in the city centre. The big companies include **Europcar** (☎ 7515 5444), which has an office at the Radisson SAS Esperia; and **Hertz** (☎ 555 2333; Mannerheimintie 44) also near the Radisson.

Some of the more economical rental companies include **Lacara** (☎ 719 062; Hämeentie 12) north of the centre and **Budget** (☎ 685 6500; Malminkatu 24) near the Radisson SAS Royal Hotel. Motorcycle rental is not common in Helsinki.

Parking in Helsinki is strictly regulated and can be a serious headache. Metered areas cost €0.50 to €1 per hour. There are a few free, long- or short-term parking areas scattered around the city; for locations consult the *Parking Guide for the Inner City of Helsinki*, a free map available at the city tourist office.

Taxi
Vacant taxis are hard to come by during morning and evening rush hours. If you need one, join a queue at one of the taxi stands – at the train station, bus station or Senaatintori. A trip across town from the kauppatori to somewhere like the Olympic Stadium costs about €10.

Bicycle
Helsinki is ideal for cycling: the inner city is flat, and there are well-marked and high-quality bike paths. Get hold of a copy of the Helsinki cycling map at the tourist office.

The city of Helsinki provides 300 distinctive green 'City Bikes' at stands within a radius of 2km from the kauppatori – although in summer you'll wonder where they're all hiding. The bikes are free: you deposit a €2 coin into the stand which locks them, then reclaim it when you return it to any stand.

For something a bit more sophisticated, **Greenbike** (☎ 8502 2850), in the old railway goods sheds, rents out quality bikes for €10 per day, or €15 for 24 hours. **Ecobike** is a smaller operation in the small yellow hut across the road from parliament house.

Around Helsinki

SUOMENLINNA

Suomenlinna, only a 15-minute ferry ride from Helsinki kauppatori, is an essential day or half-day trip from the city. Set on a tight cluster of islands, this Unesco World Heritage Site – the 'fortress of Finland' – was the scene of a major event in Finnish history when the Russians seized it from the Swedes in 1808.

The fields around Suomenlinna's stone ramparts are a favourite picnicking destination for locals – the boozing can get pretty serious on Friday and Saturday evenings in summer. There are some interesting museums, a few good cafés and even a youth

hostel if you want to stay overnight. You could easily spend the best part of a day wandering around and sightseeing here.

Every evening at 6.30pm dozens of people gather at Suomenlinna's main quay to wave as the Silja and Viking ferries sail through the narrow strait – it's quite a sight.

History

The greatest fortress of the Swedish empire was founded in 1748 to protect the eastern part of the empire against Russian attack. It was named Sveaborg (Swedish fortress).

Sveaborg was once the second largest town in Finland, after Turku. In 1806 it had 4600 residents whereas Helsinki had 4200.

After a prolonged attack, Sveaborg was surrendered to the Russians after the war of

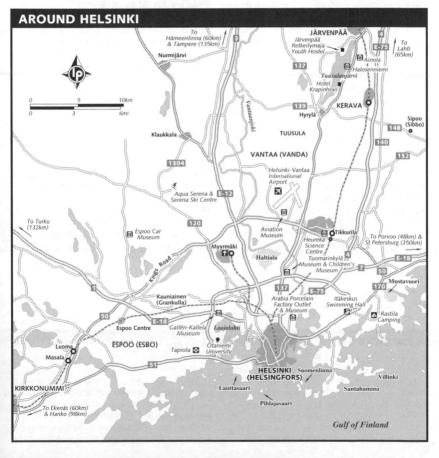

AROUND HELSINKI

1808, and renamed Viapori. Thanks in large part to the superb sea fortress, the Finnish capital was moved by the Russians from Turku to Helsinki in 1812. It remained Russian until Finland gained independence in 1917, and continued to have military significance until 1973 – it's still home to a naval base.

The present name was chosen in 1918, after Finland's independence.

Things to See & Do

Most attractions are on two main islands, Iso Mustasaari and Susisaari, connected to each other by a small bridge. At the bridge is the **Inventory Chamber Visitor Centre** (☎ 668 800) with tourist information, maps and guided walking tours in summer. In the same building is the **Suomenlinna Museum** (☎ 40501; adult/student/child €5/4/2.50; open 10am-6pm daily May-Aug, shorter hours rest of the year), covering the island's history. There's a scale model of Suomenlinna as it looked in 1808, and an illuminating 30-minute audiovisual display.

Most of Suomenlinna's museums are open 10am to 5pm daily in summer and weekends only in winter. All except the Doll & Toy Museum are free with the Helsinki Card. **Ehrensvärd Museum** (☎ 684 1850; adult/child €3/1; open 10am-5pm) preserves an 18th-century officer's home, and contains dozens of model ships, sea charts, portraits and blue-and-white tile Swedish stoves. Opposite Ehrensvärd Museum is the **shipyard** where sailmakers and other workers have been building ships since the 1750s. As many as two dozen ships are in the dry dock at any given time. They can be from 12m to 32m long and from as far away as the United Kingdom.

Three museums relating to Suomenlinna's military history can be visited with a combination ticket (adult/student €5.50/2). **Maneesi** (☎ 1814 5296) commemorates the battles of WWII and displays heavy artillery. **Coastal Defence Museum** (☎ 1514 5295) displays still more heavy artillery in a bunker-style exhibition. Finland was forbidden to possess submarines by the 1947 Treaty of Paris and the WWII-era *U-boat Vesikko* is one of the few submarines remaining in the country. You can take a look inside and sympathise with its wartime crew – it's not for the claustrophobic.

The delightful **Doll & Toy Museum** (adult/child €5/3; Helsinki Card not valid) is a private collection of hundreds of dolls – the personal achievement of Piippa Tandefelt. There's a café here serving delicious homemade apple pie. Next to the main quay, the **Jetty Barracks Gallery** (open 10am-5pm Tues-Sun) offers interesting temporary exhibitions.

Old bunkers, crumbling fortress walls and cannons are at the southern end of Susisaari island; poking around here gives the best impression of how the fortress once looked.

The **church** on Iso Mustasaari island was built by the Russians in 1854. It's the only church in the world to double as a lighthouse – the beacon was originally gaslight but is now electric and is still in use.

Places to Stay & Eat

Suomenlinna Hostel (☎ 684 7471; e leirik oulu@pp.inet.fi; dorm beds €23, singles/doubles €40/60), in an old red-brick building near the ferry quay on Suomenlinna island, is a peaceful and interesting alternative to staying in central Helsinki.

There are several good cafés and a couple of restaurants on Suomenlinna, but dining here is not all that cheap. Do as the locals and bring a picnic (carrying enormous quantities of cider and beer will help you blend in) and find a peaceful spot among the ramparts. There's a small Siwa **supermarket** near the Suomenlinna Hostel where you can pick up bread, groceries and light alcohol.

Cafe Viaporin, in an old wooden villa near the church on Iso Mustasaari, is the place for a light lunch or coffee. It's open from noon to 5pm. **Suomenlinna Panimoravintola**, further along at the main ferry quay, is an excellent brewery restaurant with a spectacular lunch buffet (€11.50). Three types of beer are brewed here – a lager, an ale and a stout – and the enclosed courtyard terrace is a good place to enjoy one.

Cafe Chapman (mains €6.90-9.50), near the dry dock on Susisaari, is a pleasant café in an old stone storehouse. Nearby, **Cafe Piper**, a delightful little wooden villa, has superb sea views.

Walhalla (☎ 668 552; mains €26-30; open 6pm-midnight, closed Sun & winter) is the island's gourmet restaurant and bookings are advised. Its location on the southwest side of Susisaari offers views of passing passenger ships from its open terrace. Next door,

Pizza Nikolai (*pizzas €8-10; open noon-8pm Sun-Thur, noon-10pm Fri & Sat*) has a similar outlook but is cheaper and more relaxed.

Getting There & Around

HKL ferries depart every 40 minutes from the passenger quay at the kauppatori in Helsinki, opposite the Presidential Palace. Buy tickets (€2) for the 15-minute trip at the pier. There is a less frequent and more expensive direct service to the Inventory Chamber Visitor Centre and to Walhalla restaurant (adult/child €5/2 return).

There's nowhere to hire bikes on the island, but they can be brought across on the ferries.

ESPOO

☎ 09 • pop 217,000

Espoo (pronounced **ehz**-poe; Swedish: Esbo) is an independent municipality just west of Helsinki and while it ranks as the second-largest city in Finland, it's virtually a suburb of the capital – most of its population works in Helsinki.

The most important sight in Espoo is **Gallën-Kallela Museum** (☎ 541 3388; W www.gallen-kallela.fi; Gallen-Kallelantie 27; adult/child €8/4; open 10am-6pm daily, closed Mon in Sept), the pastiche studio-castle of Aleksi Gallen-Kallela, one of the most notable of Finnish painters. The Art Nouveau building was designed by the artist and is now a museum of his work. Take tram No 4 from central Helsinki to Munkkiniemi, then walk 2km or take bus No 33 (Monday to Friday only).

Every architecturally minded person should visit **Otaniemi University** campus to see Aalto's main building and library, the Pietiläs' student building and Heikki Siren's chapel. **Tapiola** (Swedish: Hagalund), a modern shopping centre, was once a masterpiece of Finnish city planning. Now it's a rather embarrassing detour on several Helsinki bus tours.

Espoo Car Museum (☎ 855 7178; Pakankylän Kartano Manor; adult/child €5/2; open 11am-5.30pm Tues-Sun in summer) has more than 100 vintage motor vehicles dating from the early 20th century.

Espoo's annual **Jazz Festival** (☎ 8165 7234), held in late April, is topnotch.

Getting There & Away

You can catch buses to various parts of Espoo from the bus terminal in Helsinki. Local trains from Helsinki will drop you off at several stations, including central Espoo. Espoo also has its own bus system.

VANTAA

☎ 09 • pop 180,000

Vantaa is primarily of interest as the location of the **Helsinki-Vantaa international airport**. There's a **tourist office** (☎ 8392 3134; Ratatie 7, Tikkurila) and a handful of sights if you're killing time here.

Ilmailumuseo (Aviation Museum; ☎ 870 0870; W www.suomenilmailumuseo.fi; Tietotie 3; adult/child €5/2.50; open noon-6pm daily), near the airport, exhibits more than 50 old military and civil aircraft. Vantaa is also home to **Heureka** (☎ 85799; W www.heureka.fi; adult/child €17/11; open 10am-6pm Fri-Wed, 10am-8pm Thur), a fantastic hands-on science centre, IMAX theatre and planetarium next to the Tikkurila train station. To see the exhibitions only (without the theatre and planetarium) is €12.50/8.

For accommodation in Vantaa see Airport Hotels under Places to Stay in the Helsinki section earlier in this chapter.

There is frequent local train and bus service between Helsinki and Vantaa, 19km to the north. See To/From the Airport in Getting Around under Helsinki earlier in this chapter.

JÄRVENPÄÄ & TUUSULAN RANTATIE

The Tuusulan Rantatie (Tuusula Lake Road; W www.tuusulanrantatie.com) is a narrow road along Tuusulanjärvi (Tuusula Lake), about a 30-minute drive north of Helsinki. The region attracted a number of artists during the National Romantic era of the early 20th century. Sibelius, as well as the Nobel Prize-winning novelist FE Sillanpää and the painter Pekka Halonen worked here. A major stop along the 'museum road' is **Halosenniemi** (☎ 8718 3461; adult/child €5/2; open 11am-7pm Tues-Sun May-Sept, plus 11am-4pm Mon June-Aug; 11am-4pm Tues-Sun Oct-Apr), the Karelian-inspired, log-built National Romantic studio of Halonen, with a walking trail through his lakeside garden.

Sibelius' home, **Ainola** (☎ 287 322; W www.ainola.fi; adult/student/child €5/2/1; open 10am-5pm Tues-Sun May-Sept) is east of the lake near Järvenpää and is another popular stop with tour groups. The family home, designed by Lars Sonck and built on this beautiful forested site in 1904, contains original furniture, paintings, books and a piano owned by the Sibelius family. The graves of Jean Sibelius and his wife Aino are in the garden.

Järvenpää is a modern service centre with numerous restaurants and cafés but little to attract the traveller.

Places to Stay & Eat

Järvenpää Retkeilymaja Camping & Hostel (☎ 287 775; e marko.rantala@dlc.fi; Stålhanentie 5; tent sites €12, 2-5 person cabins €20-50, hostel rooms €20-63; open year-round) is a camping resort on the western shore of Tuusulanjärvi about 2.5km from Järvenpää town centre. The main building has a HI-affiliated hostel, but it's aimed at groups rather than solo travellers. There's a kitchen and sauna.

The unfortunately named **Hotel Krapinhovi** (☎ 274 841, fax 274 842; Rantatie 2; singles/doubles €90/113, weekends & summer €66/83), built in a brick cowshed, is a historic 1883 manor hotel on the Tuusula lake road south of Halosenniemi. It has modern rooms, three restaurants and a chance to steam up in a traditional smoke sauna.

Getting There & Away

Tuusulanjärvi is about 40km north of Helsinki. Take a local train to Kerava or Järvenpää or a bus to Hyrylä and proceed from there by bicycle.

PORVOO

☎ 019 • pop 44,000

With its quaint wooden riverside shore houses and rambling Old Town, historic Porvoo is a delightful place to visit and makes an easy day or overnight trip from Helsinki.

Porvoo (Swedish: Borgå), 50km east of Helsinki, is the second-oldest town in Finland after Turku. Officially it has been a town since 1346, but even before that Porvoo was an important trading centre. There are three distinct sections to the city: the Old Town, the new town and the 19th-century Empire quarter, built Russian style under the rule of Tsar Nicholas I of Russia. The Swedish Old Town, with its tightly clustered wooden houses, cobbled streets and riverfront setting, is one of the most picturesque in Finland. More than one-third of the residents in the area speak Swedish first.

Porvoo is easily reached from Helsinki by bus or car, but a more romantic choice is with an archipelago cruise on the steamship MS *JL Runeberg* (see Getting There & Away).

Information

The **tourist office** (☎ 520 2316, fax 520 2317; W www.porvoo.fi; Rihkamakatu 4; open 9am-6pm Mon-Fri, 10am-4pm Sat & Sun mid-June–end Aug, 9.30am-4.30pm Mon-Fri, 10am-2pm Sat & Sun rest of the year) has plenty of good information including the informative *Porvoo* booklet. There's also a **tourist information kiosk** (open 11am-5pm daily mid-June–mid-Aug) at the harbour.

Osuuspankki Bank, north of the market square, has foreign exchange and an ATM.

The modern **public library** (☎ 520 2417; Papinkatu 20; open 10am-8pm Mon-Fri, 10am-5pm Sat) has a couple of free Internet terminals which can be booked. There's also a terminal at the tourist office.

Porvoo Old Town

The Old Town district north of Mannerheiminkatu was largely built after the Great Fire of 1760. It's an alluring warren of narrow, winding cobblestone alleys and brightly coloured wooden houses. Craft boutiques and antique shops line the main roads, Välikatu and Kirkkokatu. The distinctive row of **shore houses** along the Porvoonjoki River were first painted with red ochre to impress the visiting King of Sweden, Gustavus III, in the late 18th century. They were originally used to store goods traded with German ships from the Hanseatic League, but many are now Porvoo's prime residential real estate.

The striking stone medieval **Kirkkotori** (cathedral; open 10am-6pm Mon-Fri, 10am-2pm Sat, 2pm-5pm Sun May-Sept; reduced hours other times) dominates the Old Town and has an important place in Finnish history: this is where the first Diet of Finland assembled in 1809, convened by Tsar Alexander I, thus giving Finland religious freedom. Free guides are on hand most days in summer to explain the history.

Porvoo Town Museum (☎ 547 7589; Vanha Raatihuoneentori; combined admission adult/child €5/1; both open 11am-4pm daily May-Aug, noon-4pm Wed-Sun Sept-Apr) is in two adjacent buildings on the Old Town

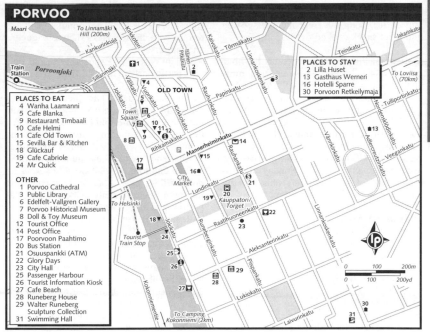

PORVOO

PLACES TO STAY
2   Lilla Huset
13 Gasthaus Werneri
16 Hotelli Sparre
30 Porvoon Retkeilymaja

PLACES TO EAT
4   Wanha Laamanni
5   Cafe Blanka
9   Restaurant Timbaali
10 Cafe Helmi
11 Cafe Old Town
15 Sevilla Bar & Kitchen
18 Glückauf
19 Cafe Cabriole
24 Mr Quick

OTHER
1   Porvoo Cathedral
3   Public Library
6   Edelfelt-Vallgren Gallery
7   Porvoo Historical Museum
8   Doll & Toy Museum
12 Tourist Office
14 Post Office
17 Poorvoon Paahtimo
20 Bus Station
21 Osuuspankki (ATM)
22 Glory Days
23 City Hall
25 Passenger Harbour
26 Tourist Information Kiosk
27 Cafe Beach
28 Runeberg House
29 Walter Runeberg
    Sculpture Collection
31 Swimming Hall

Hall Square. The more interesting of the two is the **Edelfelt-Vallgren Museum**, with paintings by Albert Edelfelt and sculptures by Ville Vallgren, two of Porvoo's most famous artists – Ville Vallgren designed the Havis Amanda statue that graces Helsinki's kauppatori. **Porvoo Historical Museum**, in the town hall building across the square, has old furniture and other paraphernalia.

Doll & Toy Museum (☎ 582 941; *Jokikatu 14; adult/child €2/1; open 11am-3.30pm Mon-Sat, noon-3.30pm Sun May–end Aug*) houses over 800 dolls and other toys and is the largest museum of its kind in Finland.

There are **guided walking tours** of Old Porvoo at 2pm on Saturdays from mid-June to late August. The one-hour tours, in Finnish, Swedish and English, begin at the passenger harbour and cost €5.

Linnamäki Hill

A five-minute uphill walk from the cathedral, Linnamäki Hill (Swedish: Borgbacken) was once a 14th-century fortress and Viking defence post (hence the town's Swedish name Borgå – 'castle by the river'). There's not much left to see, with thick pine trees

covering the hill, but there are a few good viewpoints over Porvoo.

Runeberg House

National poet Johan Ludvig Runeberg wrote the lyrics to the Finnish national anthem, *Maamme* (Our Country). His former home has been a museum (☎ 581 330; *Aleksanterinkatu 3; adult/child €4/2; open 10am-4pm Mon-Sat, 11am-5pm Sun May-Aug; closed Mon & Tues Sept-Apr*) since 1882. The interior has been preserved as it was when Runeberg lived in the house, and the house itself is one of the best preserved buildings in the Empire part of the town centre. The **Walter Runeberg Sculpture Collection** (*Aleksanterinkatu 5*) has 150 sculptures by Walter Runeberg, JL Runeberg's eldest son. Opening hours are the same and admission is good for entry to both museums.

Organised Tours

In winter, **Saaristolinja Ky** (☎ 523 1350; ⓦ *www.saaristolinja.com; Tuhtotie 1*) offers two-hour snowmobile safaris (€74) which are reasonable value if you want to get a feel for this popular activity. Departures are generally on demand so call in advance. A trip on ice along the river includes coffee and a hot snack cooked over a campfire.

Cruises Saaristolinja also operates 1½-hour cruises along the Porvoo River from mid-June to mid-August aboard MS *Ellan* or MS *Barkas Borgå*. They depart from the passenger harbour daily at 10.30am, noon, 1.45pm and 3.30pm (adult/child €6/2.50) and include some historical commentary. If you have more time, archipelago cruises aboard MS *Sandra* and MS *Fredrika* depart on Tuesday, Wednesday, Saturday and Sunday at 1pm (adult/child €11/5, three hours) and offer the chance to stop off at islands en route.

Places to Stay
Camping Kokonniemi (☎ 581 967; e] *myyn tipalvelu@lomaliitto.fi; tent sites €15, 4-person cabins €62; open June–mid-Aug)* is 2km south of Porvoo town.

Porvoon Retkeilymaja (☎/*fax 523 0012;* w] *www.porvoohostel.cjb.net; Linnankosken-katu 1-3; dorm beds €13, singles/doubles €27/32, linen hire €4; open year-round)*, an HI-affiliated hostel 800m southeast of Mannerheiminkatu, is in a lovely old house with spotless rooms and a well equipped kitchen. It's a bit old school – the doors close between 10am (check-out time) and 4pm, and curfew is 11pm – but it's popular so book ahead in summer. There's no sauna but there's an indoor pool and sauna complex over the road.

Gasthaus Werneri (☎ 524 4454, fax 524 4460; *Adlercreutzinkatu 29; singles/doubles €33/45, €30/35 from Sept-May)* is a central, family-run place with five rooms each with shared bathroom.

In the Old Town, the only accommodation is boutique and expensive, usually a room or two in an old home. **Lilla Huset** (☎ 524 8120; *Itäinen Pitkäkatu 3; doubles €100)* is in an 18th-century house in the heart of old Porvoo, but is open only in August. Ask tourist office for other possibilities.

Hotelli Sparre (☎ 584 455; w] *www.hotel li-sparre.fi; Piispankatu 34; singles/doubles €70/80, summer & weekends €60/70)* is a central, well-kept hotel with a sauna and a Thai restaurant attached.

Places to Eat & Drink
The cheapest places to eat are in the modern centre of town, particularly around the

kauppatori. On the riverfront, **Mr Quick** (*Jokikatu; meals €5-8)* is a popular grilli and terrace with cheap snacks such as baguettes and burgers.

Quaint cafés are a speciality of old Porvoo, particularly in the Old Town and on the waterfront. Try **Cafe Blanka** on the Old Town Hall Square, and the inexpensive **Cafe Old Town**, where young Porvoo sits outside and watches old Porvoo drift by. Although the surroundings are a bit stiff and formal, **Cafe Helmi** (*Välikatu 7)* specialises in Russian-style high tea and fresh pastries.

Cafe Cabriole (☎ 523 2800; *Piispankatu 30; dishes €6.40; open 11am-2.30pm daily)*, on the south side of the city market square, has pastries and a good-value lunch buffet.

Restaurant Timbaali (☎ 523 1020; *Välikatu 8; mains €8-18)* is a rustic place with a summer garden and perfect Old Town ambience. The menu is broad but the speciality here is snails. On the main street through town, **Sevilla Bar & Kitchen** (☎ 547 1291; *Mannerheiminkatu 9; mains €8-18)* is an upbeat, modern bar and restaurant serving Spanish and Mediterranean-inspired food.

The boat restaurant **Glückauf** (☎ 54761; *mains €10-20)*, a 19th-century sailing ship moored on the eastern riverfront, specialises in seafood, and there's a cheaper terrace menu (ie, you eat on the riverbank rather than the boat) from €6 to €8.

Wanha Laamanni (☎ 523 0455; *Vuorikatu 17; mains €17-23)*, in the Old Judges' Chambers, is the gourmet restaurant of Porvoo. It's in a splendid late-18th-century building with a fireplace for winter nights and a terrace for summer days. Game is a speciality, along with reindeer and Finnish fish dishes. Although prices are steep, it thoughtfully offers smaller portions and salads from €9.50 to €11.

In summer there are several **beer terraces** along this part of the river, including the eccentric **Cafe Beach**, Porvoo's biggest summer terrace with a range of fast food and a strangely diverse crowd.

Poorvoon Paahtimo (*Mannerheiminkatu 2)*, at the bridge, is primarily a cosy bar although sandwiches and cakes are available. There's a good range of beers and a great little balcony hanging over the water.

Glory Days, on the southeast side of the market square, is another café and bar popular with young locals.

Getting There & Away

Bus Buses depart for Porvoo from the Helsinki bus station at the market square every 30 minutes or so (€7.90, one hour), and there are frequent buses to/from towns further east, including Kotka (€11.40) and Lapeenranta (€23.10).

Train The old diesel *Porvoo Museum Train* (☎ 752 3262; one way/return €11/18) runs between Helsinki and Porvoo on Saturdays in summer (8 June to 31 August). The train departs from Helsinki at 10.16am and from Porvoo at 4.35pm, and takes 1½ hours; purchase tickets at the Helsinki or Porvoo train station or on board the train. In Porvoo, the train runs to a final stop near the main bridge, about 1km past the old train station. The trip can also be combined with a cruise on the MS *JL Runeberg* (see the following section).

Boat The MS *JL Runeberg* (☎ 524 3331; ⓦ www.msjlruneberg.fi; one way/return €20/29, child €9/13), a former steamship, travels between Helsinki and Porvoo in summer and makes an excellent day trip. It leaves Helsinki daily (except Thursday) at 10am, returning at 4pm. Since the trip takes four hours, you may want to return by bus or, on Saturdays in summer, on the vintage diesel train *(combined ferry & train ticket adult/child €27/11).*

An alternative is the modern, speedy MS *King*, operated by **Royal Line** (☎ 09-612 2950; ⓦ www.royalline.fi; adult/child one way €20/10). It travels from the Helsinki kauppatori at 10.20am daily from mid-June to mid-August, returning from Porvoo at 3.30pm, taking three hours each way and can be done as a day trip with an interesting archipelago cruise and two hours of sightseeing in Porvoo. If you do it in one day, the fare is €32 return or €43 with lunch on board.

South Coast

The Swedes settled the southern coast of Finland in medieval times, bringing their language and Scandinavian traditions with them. The area remained mostly Swedish until 1550, when King Gustav Vasa of Sweden established Helsingfors (Helsinki) at rapids on the Vantaa River, north of present-day Helsinki.

Another boost for the region came in 1812 when Finland's capital was transferred from Turku to Helsinki. To this day many south-coast towns remain predominantly Swedish-speaking further increasing the Swedish influence.

For travellers, this region to the west and east of the capital has beaches, attractive bays, slightly fading seaside resort towns and the convoluted islands and waterways of the southern archipelago. In summer, boat tours abound and are a great way to see this part of Finland. Some of the towns can be visited on a day trip from Helsinki.

Highlights

- Staying overnight in one of Hanko's charming Russian villas
- Spending a summer evening at the Mill Restaurant in Ruotsinpyhtaa
- Exploring the fascinating old ironworks at Fiskars, where Finland's industrial age meets contemporary design
- Drinking and dancing at Hamina's harbourside Pursiravintola Vantti, then spending the night on a historic steamship
- Fly-fishing at the Tsar's Imperial Fishing Lodge at Langinkoski, near Kotka, or walking in the surrounding nature reserve
- Taking in a summer evening concert at Raseborg Castle ruins near Ekenäs
- Boating around the islands of Ekenäs Archipelago National Park

West of Helsinki

The southwest is the most historic part of Finland, with medieval stone churches in every other village, and some notable castles and manor houses. The history of settlement in this region can be traced back to the Stone Age, and there are numerous Bronze Age burial grounds scattered around. The area also has plenty of idyllic little islands that are fun for camping, cycling and island-hopping in summer.

INKOO
☎ 019 • pop 4800

Inkoo (Swedish: Ingå) is a small, attractive seaside town where locals predominantly speak Swedish. Look for the unusual bell tower atop the medieval **St Nicholas church** *(open daily in summer)*, founded in the 13th century. There are rich fresco paintings on the church walls. Across the river, **Ingå Gammelgård** is the local museum.

About 8km west of Inkoo is the **Fagervik Ironworks** (☎ 295 151; road No 105), one of the most attractive *bruks* (early ironworks precinct) in Finland. It was established in 1646 by the Swedes and it was this industry that helped develop the region before anyone had thought of taking a holiday by the sea. The Russian army destroyed the area during the Great Northern War in the 1720s, but the factory was later rebuilt before ultimately closing in 1902. Guided tours of the grounds are available in summer. The site features an 18th-century wooden church, privately-owned manor, two restored blacksmith workshops, and the remnants of an orangery.

Inkoo is southwest of Helsinki on road No 51. There are several daily bus connections.

EKENÄS

☎ 019 • pop 14,600

The seaside town of Ekenäs (Finnish: Tammisaari), 96km southwest of Helsinki, is one of Finland's oldest – King Gustav Vasa conceived of it in 1546 as a trading port to rival Tallinn in Estonia. The idea failed, and many local business people were soon forcibly transferred to the newly founded Helsinki.

Present-day Ekenäs is a setting, popular with Finnish and Swedish holidaymakers and families, although it lacks the elegance and charm of Hanko further west. Predominantly Swedish-speaking, it has many well-preserved old buildings, including a quaint Old Town, and parts of the adjacent archipelago – with some 1300 islands – form a national park.

Information

The helpful **tourist office** (☎ 263 2100, fax 263 2212; W www.ekenas.fi; Rådhustorget; open 8am-5pm Mon-Fri, 10am-2pm Sat in summer, 8am-4.15pm Mon-Fri rest of the year), located on the main square, offers tourist information for the entire southwest region.

Located at the harbour, **Naturum Visitor Centre** (☎ 241 1198; open 10am-7pm daily May–end Aug) provides detailed information on Ekenäs Archipelago National Park, including a free slide show and the usual eco-exhibits.

The **public library** (☎ 263 2700; Raseborgsvägen 6-8; open 10am-7pm Mon-Fri, 10am-2pm Sat), just east of the centre, has three free Internet terminals.

SOUTH COAST

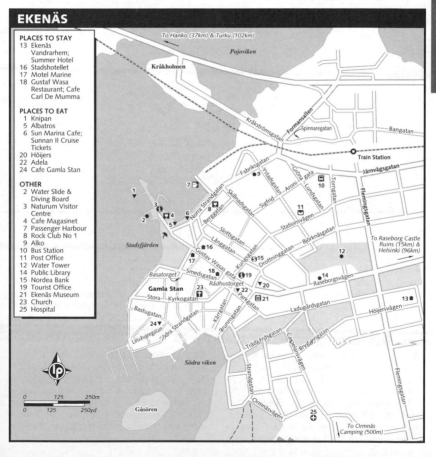

EKENÄS

PLACES TO STAY
13 Ekenäs Vandrarhem; Summer Hotel
16 Stadshotellet
17 Motel Marine
18 Gustaf Wasa Restaurant; Cafe Carl De Mumma

PLACES TO EAT
1 Knipan
5 Albatros
6 Sun Marina Cafe; Sunnan II Cruise Tickets
20 Höijers
22 Adela
24 Cafe Gamla Stan

OTHER
2 Water Slide & Diving Board
3 Naturum Visitor Centre
4 Cafe Magasinet
7 Passenger Harbour
8 Rock Club No 1
9 Alko
10 Bus Station
11 Post Office
12 Water Tower
14 Public Library
15 Nordea Bank
19 Tourist Office
21 Ekenäs Museum
23 Church
25 Hospital

To Hanko (37km) & Turku (102km)
Pojoviken
Kråkholmen
Kråkströmsgatan
Spinnaregatan
Bangatan
Formansallen
Train Station
Järnvägsgatan
Fabriksgatan
Lydgatan
Aroni gata
Gröna gata
Torngatan
Fleminggatan
Norra Strandgatan
Skillnadsgatan
Sigfrid
Lundsgatan
Berggatan
Stationsvägen
Slottsgatan
Långgatan
Björknäsgatan
To Raseborg Castle Ruins (15km) & Helsinki (96km)
Stadsfjärden
Gustav Wasas gata
Kungsgatan
Drottninggatan
Raseborgsvägen
Basatorget
Smedsgatan
Rådhustorget
Gamla Stan
Stora
Kyrkogatan
Ladugårdsgatan
Höijersvägen
Bastugatan
Strandgatan
Kanalstranden
Bryggvägen
Lillvikaregatan
Södra Strandgatan
Trädgårdsgatan
Södra viken
Strandgatan
Ormnäsvägen
Gåsören
Fleminggatan
To Ormnäs Camping (500m)

0   125   250m
0   125   250yd

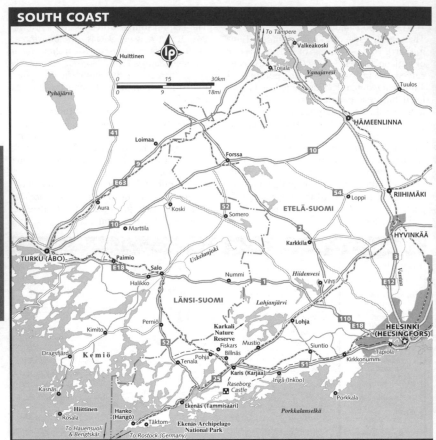

SOUTH COAST

Things to See & Do

The well-preserved **Old Town** (Gamla Stan) features wooden houses from the late 18th and early 19th centuries. They line narrow streets that are named after hatters, comb-makers and other artisans who once worked in the precinct. Some buildings contain artisans' shops, open in summer. The oldest buildings are on Linvävaregatan.

The stone **church** *(open 10am-6pm daily May-Aug)*, in Gamla Stan on Stora Kyrko-gatan, has a tower that can be seen from most parts of town. It was built between 1651 and 1680 and was renovated in 1990.

The main building of the **Ekenäs Museum** *(☎ 263 3161; Gustav Wasas gata 13; adult/child €2/1; open 11am-5pm daily in summer)*, built in 1802, displays the lifestyle of a wealthy artisan family in the 1800s. Other buildings have temporary exhibitions of modern art and photography, and perma-nent displays on local history, including a re-creation of a fishing village.

Bicycles can be hired from Cafe Sun Marina at the harbour. Rent rowing boats (€10/20 per half/full day) and bikes (€10 per day) at Ormnäs Camping.

Organised Tours

The former steamship MS *Sunnan II* *(☎ 241 1850)* has archipelago cruises daily in sum-mer, departing from the Sun Marina Cafe at the harbour. Cruises range from two hours (€10) to six hours (€25), and on Sunday there's a return cruise to Hanko (€27 return, seven hours).

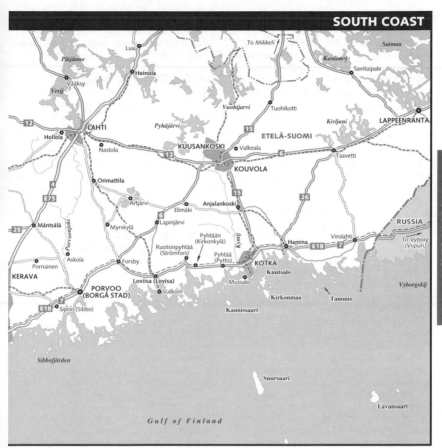

SOUTH COAST

Places to Stay

Camping At the seaside, **Ormnäs Camping** (☎ 241 4434; sites per person/tent €6.50/10, 2-/4-person cottages €31/42; open Apr–end Sept) is 1km from the town centre, next to Ramsholmen Natural Park. There's a café, and bikes and boats can be rented here.

Hostels An HI-affiliated summer hostel, **Ekenäs Vandrarhem** (☎ 241 6393, fax 241 3917; Höijersvägen 10; dorm beds from €12.50, singles/doubles €22/29; open mid-May–mid-Aug), offers tidy, modern apartment-style rooms (four rooms share a kitchen and bathroom). Breakfast is an extra €4.50 and sheets are €3.50 if you need them. Reception is open from 3pm to 9pm and there's a sauna and a laundry. On the same site is a **summer hotel** (singles/doubles €32/49); the apartments are exactly the same but breakfast and bed linen are included in the price.

Guesthouses & Hotels With just 10 rooms, **Gustaf Wasa** (☎ 241 1551; w www.gustaf-wasa.nu; Rådhustorget; singles/doubles from €65/83) is a small guesthouse overlooking the market square. All rooms have shower and toilet and breakfast is included. Rates drop by about 20% in winter.

There are two hotels near the harbour and Gamla Stan. **Stadshotellet** (☎ 241 3131, fax 246 1550; w www.stadshotell.nu; Norra Strandgatan 1; singles/doubles €69/92, weekends €62/87) is a little dated but still the top hotel in town – it even has a swimming pool and rates include breakfast and sauna. Double rooms have balconies.

Motel Marine *(☎ 241 3833; fax 241 3837; Kammakaregatan 4-6; singles/doubles with bathroom €55/75)* is a shabby-looking, weatherboard complex but the rooms are OK and range in price and quality. Some of the cheaper rooms (€45/65) share a bathroom, while others have been recently renovated.

Places to Eat
At the harbour, **Albatros** does a booming business in takeaway hamburgers, hot dogs and ice cream during summer, and it has a fine beer terrace serving light meals.

There are several good cafés and restaurants around the main square, Rådhustorget, including pizzerias and Chinese restaurants. **Cafe Carl De Mumma** is a bakery and café serving inexpensive sandwiches, cakes and pastries. Next door, **Restaurant Gustav Wasa** *(☎ 241 2050)* has a €6 lunch buffet as well as à la carte meals. Across the square, **Adela** *(mains €4-10; open 10am-midnight daily)* is good for cheap pizza and kebabs.

Around the corner from the market square, **Höijers** *(☎ 241 1792; Drottninggatan 1; mains €5.50-16.50; open 11am-5pm Mon-Thur, 11am-8pm Fri-Sun)* is a simple but very popular place specialising in tempting lunch specials from 11am to 2pm daily.

Cafe Gamla Stan *(☎ 241 5656; Bastugatan 5; open daily May–mid Aug)* is a beautiful garden café in the Old Town. The small house is a bit hard to find and has just a few seats, but is worth the effort. There's live music in the garden during summer.

Knipan *(☎ 241 1169; mains €11.50-19.50; open May–mid-Sept)*, in the old wooden building built in the harbour in 1867, is the best summer restaurant in town. As well as an à la carte menu there's a substantial lunch and dinner buffet (€9 and €14.50).

Entertainment
Knipan is a swank dance club and restaurant at the harbour. It was built on poles over the water because local laws allowed only one bar on town ground. There's live music on summer evenings and a floating beer terrace. Not far away, **Cafe Magasinet** has a good terrace overlooking the harbour, and reasonably priced beers.

The happening nightclub in town is **Rock Club No 1** *(☎ 241 2000; Norra Strandgatan 15)*, in a big old warehouse opposite the passenger harbour. The decor is American West, the music ranges from live rock bands to dance DJs.

Getting There & Away
Ekenäs is 96km southwest of Helsinki on road No 53. There are five to seven buses a day from Helsinki (€12.40, 1½ hours), Turku (€14.60, two hours) or Hanko (€5.70, 30 minutes).

Trains to Ekenäs from Helsinki and Turku go via Karis (Karjaa) where a change is required. There are seven to nine daily trains from Helsinki (€14, 1½ hours) and Turku (€18, 1½ hours), both continuing on to Hanko.

AROUND EKENÄS
Raseborg Castle Ruins
The Raseborg Castle ruins (Finnish: Raasepori), dating from the late 14th century, are fairly impressive thanks to restorations starting as early as 1890. The castle was of great strategic importance in the 15th century, when it protected the important trading town of Tuna. Karl Knutsson Bonde, three times the King of Sweden, was one of its most prominent residents. By the mid-16th century, Raseborg's importance had declined, and it was left empty for more than 300 years.

The castle *(☎ 234015; adult/child €1/0.50; open 10am-8pm daily)* is 15km east of Ekenäs, and about 2km from the village of Snappertuna. Free tours are given at 3pm on Saturday and Sunday from mid-May to August (also 3pm Wednesday and Friday from mid-June to the end of July), but you can visit the area at any time. During July there are evening concerts at Raseborg; contact the Ekenäs tourist office for details. There are occasional buses to Snappertuna from Ekenäs or Karis. The HI-affiliated **Snappertuna Youth Hostel** *(☎ 019-234 180; Kyrkoväg 129; dorm beds €13.50)*, in the village, is a quiet alternative to staying in Ekenäs.

Ekenäs Archipelago National Park
The beautiful archipelago surrounding Ekenäs includes a scattering of some 1300 islands, 50 sq km of which is a national park. The best way to visit the park is by boat from Ekenäs harbour. However, at the time of research there were no regular scheduled

tours into the park, only charter taxi boats including the MS *Panda* (☎ 241 2460), MS *Lea* (☎ 208629) or MS *Johanna* (☎ 210350).

If you visit the island of Älgö, you can see the old fishing house, use the cooking facilities or stay overnight at the camping ground. There are also camping grounds on the islands of Fladalandet and Modermagan. Visit the Naturum Visitor Centre in Ekenäs for more information about the park.

FISKARS
☎ 019

Northeast of Ekenäs along road No 111 is the village of **Pohja**, which is the centre of an area known for its historic *bruk*. Several small villages in this area can be visited in a day but the most outstanding by far is Fiskars (Swedish: Fiskari), a beautiful riverside village where the old brick buildings have been transformed into shops, galleries, design studios and cafés. During the last 10 years, Fiskars has gained a reputation as a centre of modern Finnish art and design, creating an absorbing mix of the old and the new.

The *bruk* was first established on the Fiskars River in 1649 and the village grew up around it. The main production here was tools, chiefly ploughs – more than a million horse-ploughs came out of here in the 19th century. In 1816, the mansion that was to house the owner of the *bruk* was built, and this is still the centrepiece of the village. A number of other buildings were designed by German architect Carl Engel.

There's a **tourist information office** (☎ 277 504; W *www.fiskarsvillage.net; open Mon-Sat May–end Aug*) in the workers' tenement buildings, near the distinctive clock-tower building.

Things to See
The best way to appreciate Fiskars is to walk through it, starting from the western end, with the river on your right. The first building on the left is the **Assembly Hall**, built in 1896 as a public hall. Opposite, encircled by a stream, is the **Granary** (1902), which now hosts various art, design and history exhibitions with changing themes. Across the river is **Copper Forge** (1818), with more exhibition space, a glass studio and a good restaurant with a riverside terrace. Continuing along, you pass the **Stone House**, the mansion originally occupied by factory owner John Julin, the old

mill on your right, and the distinctive **clock-tower building** on the left. It now houses shops, galleries and a café. Where the road forks is the marketplace with stalls, a café and terrace in summer. Continuing along the unpaved road towards Lake Degersjo, you pass more workers' housing and what remains of the Fiskars plant.

At the top of the road is **Fiskars Museum** (☎ 237 013; *adult/child €2.50/0.85; open 11am-4pm daily May-Sept*), which explains the fascinating local history of the ironworks and village.

Places to Stay & Eat
Fiskars can be visited as a day trip from Helsinki, but it also has a hotel and some boutique B&B accommodation.

Fiskars Wardshus (☎ 237 355) has six rooms and an excellent à la carte restaurant.

Parkvilla B&B (☎ 562 4012; *Teraskaari 4; rooms per person €20*), in an old wooden workers' cottage, has reasonably priced accommodation. **Wildrose B&B** (☎ 237 033; *Långdalintie 3; singles/doubles €35/55*) is a lovely guesthouse with two rooms, and an upper floor for groups (up to seven).

In the clock-tower building, **Cafe Antique** is a good spot for coffee and a light meal, and there's a summer café set up at the market square.

Restaurant Kuparipaja (☎ 237 0375; *mains €11-18*), in one of the old copper forge buildings, has a good à la carte restaurant, as well as a café-bar dispensing filled rolls, pasta dishes and a salad buffet. There's a charming terrace hanging over the river.

HANKO
☎ 019 • pop 10,000

Hanko (Swedish: Hangö) blossomed as a spa town in the late 19th and early 20th centuries, when it was a glamorous retreat for Russian nobles, tsars and artists. The grand seaside villas built by these wealthy summer visitors are now the town's star attraction – locals refer to them as 'the old ladies', as each has been given a woman's name. Many now operate as fancy guesthouses, which are Finland's most unique accommodation and very popular with tourists in summer.

Even before Hanko was founded in 1874, the peninsula on which the town lies was an important anchorage. Hanko has also been a major point of departure from Finland:

between 1881 and 1931, about 500,000 Finns left for the USA and Canada via the Hanko docks. During WWII, Hanko was annexed by the Soviet Union for one year.

Hanko is 127km southwest of Helsinki and is the southernmost town in Finland. The majority of its residents speak Finnish.

Orientation & Information

The main streets are Bulevardi and Esplanaadi, although Vuorikatu is the main shopping street. The East Harbour is the centre of the town's activity in summer; the West Harbour handles only commercial traffic. Russian villas are on Appelgrenintie, east of East Harbour. Most things are within walking distance of the adjacent bus and train stations.

The main **tourist office** (☎ 220 3411; **w** www.hanko.fi; Raatihuoneentori 5; open 9am-5pm Mon-Fri year-round) is in the town hall building. There's also a **tourist information booth** (open to almost midnight daily in summer) at the East Harbour.

The **public library** (Vuorikatu 3-5; open 11am-8pm Mon-Fri, 11am-2pm Sat) has several Internet terminals, and there's also a free terminal at Park Cafe in Spa Park.

Things to See & Do

Take a lift to the top of the 50m landmark **water tower** (Vartiovuori; admission €1; open daily mid-May–end Aug) in Kirkkopuisto Park for an excellent view across town and out to sea. The nearby neo-Gothic **Hanko church** (open 10am-6pm daily in summer), built in 1892, was damaged in WWII but has been thoroughly renovated.

Fortress Museum (Linnoitusmuseo; ☎ 220 3228; Nycanderinkatu 4; adult/child €2/0.50; open 11am-4pm Tues-Sun & 6pm-7pm Thur, shorter hours in winter) is the local museum housed in the brick-and-stone building near the East Harbour. Hanko is quite an artistic community and there are some half a dozen **art galleries** scattered around town, including changing exhibitions in the town hall. The tourist office has all the details of current exhibitions.

Just off the highway between Hanko and Ekenäs, **Front Museum** (☎ 244 3068; adult/child €3/1; open 11.30am-6.30pm daily in summer) covers the usual gamut of Finland's wartime involvement, specifically relating to this battlefront. There are original trenches, some foundations and a small scattering of

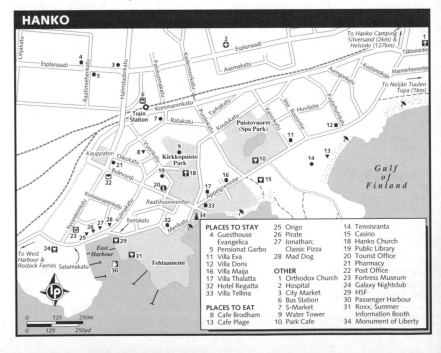

HANKO

PLACES TO STAY
4 Guesthouse Evangelica
5 Pensionat Garbo
11 Villa Eva
12 Villa Doris
16 Villa Maija
17 Villa Thalatta
32 Hotel Regatta
33 Villa Tellina

PLACES TO EAT
8 Cafe Brodham
13 Cafe Plage

25 Origo
26 Pirate
27 Jonathan; Classic Pizza
28 Mad Dog

OTHER
1 Orthodox Church
2 Hospital
3 City Market
6 Bus Station
7 S-Market
9 Water Tower
10 Park Cafe

14 Tennisranta
15 Casino
18 Hanko Church
19 Public Library
20 Tourist Office
21 Pharmacy
22 Post Office
23 Fortress Museum
24 Galaxy Nightclub
29 HSF
30 Passenger Harbour
31 Roxx; Summer Information Booth
34 Monument of Liberty

artillery, and an extensive tent exhibition. Although a serious subject, the use of shop dummies gives the exhibition a mildly comic aspect.

Hanko has 30km of sand beaches. The beach from Merikatu to the Casino is the best – it even has Victorian-style changing boxes. Near the beach is the **Monument of Liberty**, commemorating the landing of liberating German forces in 1918. The monument was taken down after WWII, but re-erected in 1960.

Bicycles are ideal for exploring the parkland and Russian villas east of the town centre – a ride or walk out to Neljän Tuulen Tupa on Little Pine Island is a good excursion. Bikes can be hired at **Sea & Fun Hanko** (☎ 248 6699) at the East Harbour, **Cafe Plage** (☎ 248 2776) or **Paul Feldt's bicycle shop** (☎ 248 1860; Tarhakatu 4; open year-round) in the town centre. **Sea & Fun** also rents mopeds, rowboats, canoes and water-skiing gear.

At **Tennisranta**, near Cafe Plage, there are eight outdoor tennis courts available to rent.

Organised Tours

Cruises The most interesting short cruise from Hanko is the 1¾-hour trip to **Hauensuoli** (see Around Hanko for more information). The MS *Marina* (☎ 0400-536 930; adult/child €15/7.50) departs from the East Harbour daily in summer at noon, 2pm and 4pm and includes commentary in English, Finnish and Swedish.

From mid-June to the end of August, several boats offer day cruises to the island of **Bengtskär**, all departing from the East Harbour. The cruises include lunch and entrance to the island. MS *Summersea* (☎ 0400-536 930; adult/child €40/20) sails at 10.30am, with an extra departure at 2pm in July. MS *Anna* (☎ 4692 500; adult/child €44/22) departs at 11am. MY *Marilyn* (☎ 728 9539; per person €40) operates from July to mid-August, departing at 11.30am. The cruises last between six and seven hours.

Special Events

Since Hanko claims to have Finland's largest marina, it's hardly surprising that the most important annual event is the **Hanko Regatta** in which more than 200 boats compete. The regatta takes place on the first weekend of July, attracts thousands of spectators and has a real carnival atmosphere.

Places to Stay

Bookings are advised during the summer months, particularly at any of the Russian villas. Many places raise their prices during the annual Hanko Regatta, and bookings must be made well in advance.

Camping About 3km northeast of the town centre, **Hanko Camping Silversand** (☎ 248 5500; W www.lomaliitto.fi, Hopeahietikko; tent sites €13.50, 4-person cabins €48-54, 6–8-person cabins €63-69; open June–mid-Aug) is set on a long beach. There's also a **motel** with single/double rooms for €51/73, as well as a café and sauna.

Guesthouses & Hotels The quirky **Pensionat Garbo** (☎/fax 248 7897; Raatimiehenkatu 8; singles/doubles/triples from €19/33/45, double with bathroom €69; open in summer, by prior arrangement rest of the year) is essentially a museum of celluloid kitsch. Each room commemorates a particular Hollywood star (we got the tragic Carole Lombard). It's nicely furnished with a garden and balcony. Unfortunately its future as a guesthouse was in doubt at the time of research.

Guesthouse Evangelica (☎ 248 6923; Esplanaadi 61; singles/doubles €26/39, with bathroom €40/52), diagonally opposite Garbo, is part of a school complex but is open year-round. Rooms are clean and well-priced and breakfast is available (€4).

Hotel Regatta (☎ 248 6491, fax 248 5535; Merikatu 1; singles €54-71, doubles €66-100) is the only standard hotel in Hanko. It's popular with tour groups and conferences. Breakfast is included in the rates and there's the obligatory sauna. You'll pay a little more for rooms with sea views.

Villas A unique feature of Hanko is its selection of old Russian-style villas that have been meticulously renovated and converted to guesthouses.

Villa Maija (☎ 248 2900, fax 248 3900; Appelgrenintie 7; singles/doubles from €50/70; open year-round), built in 1888, is a real beauty, with fine veranda windows and loads of ornate trim.

Villa Doris (☎ 248 1228; Appelgrenintie 23; singles/doubles from €53/65; open year-round), a charming *pensionat* dating from 1881, contains old furniture from various decades in all rooms. Rates are negotiable for longer stays and include breakfast.

Villa Tellina (☎ 248 6356; W www.tellina .com; Appelgrenintie 2; singles/doubles from €46/88; open June-Aug) is close to the beach and a ramshackle place with basic but comfortable rooms. The same owners run **Villa Eva** and **Villa Thalatta** (same contact and room prices), so this may be a good first port of call during busy periods.

Places to Eat

In summer, Hanko has enticing little cafés and the marina, packed with bobbing yachts, is the place to be and be seen. In the main shopping strip, **Cafe Brodhamn** (Vuorikatu), next to the cinema, is a good place for coffee, cakes and pastries and is open early for breakfast.

Cafe Plage (☎ 248 2776; Appelgrenintie; open May-Sept), part of the tennis complex, is a pleasant seafront café and terrace away from the bustle of the harbour area.

To take in Hanko's summer vibes, head to the East Harbour, where a row of quaint, red wooden buildings house a cluster of gourmet fish restaurants, all with crowded terraces, as well as cheaper pizza places and a grilli. There are restaurants facing the harbour on Satamakatu and the tiny lane behind.

Pirate (☎ 248 3006; Satamakatu 13; mains €8-18) is one of the most popular restaurants here and, unlike most, is open year-round. It's a down-to-earth place with occasional live music and big portions.

Origo (☎ 248 5023; Satamakatu 7; mains €15-18) is a charming place and arguably the best of the fish restaurants.

Jonathan (☎ 248 7742; Satamakatu 15) is a similar place with a varied menu served in a rustic stone-walled room. Adjacent and under the same management is **Classic Pizza** with reasonably priced pizzas.

For something cheaper, **Mad Dog** is a grilli and pub with a small terrace – it's a good spot for hamburgers and sandwiches with a beer.

Neljän Tuulen Tupa (House of the Four Winds; ☎ 248 1455; open mid-May–mid-Aug), on Little Pine Island 1.5km east of the centre, is where folks went to imbibe so-called 'hard tea' (alcohol) during the Finnish prohibition (1919–32). At the time, Field Marshal CG Mannerheim had his summer cottage on the neighbouring island. He found the merry-making disturbing and solved the problem

by buying the whole joint in 1926 – he fired the chef, imported tea sets from France and ran the place himself until 1931. Little Pine Island is now connected to the mainland by a bridge. These days, it's a pleasant café and summer terrace perched over the water.

Entertainment

The imposing green-and-white **Casino** (☎ 248 2310; Appelgrenintie 10), between Spa Park and the beach, is a classic seaside venue and Hanko's most famous nightspot. (It has more class than the name suggests!) There's music, dancing and a roulette table, and the cover charge depends on what's on. The restaurant here is good but a bit pricey.

Park Cafe (☎ 248 6182; Appelgrenintie 11), nearby in Spa Park, is an excellent Belgian café-bar with a casual atmosphere and free Internet access.

Good summertime beer terraces include **Roxx**, and the 2nd floor of **HSF**, both at East Harbour.

When it gets late, the sophisticated youth of Hanko head for **Galaxy Nightclub** (☎ 248 7700; Satamakatu 2). On Wednesday and Saturday nights DJs play techno and dance music until late.

Getting There & Away

Bus There are regular daily express buses to/from Helsinki (€17, 2¼ hours) via Ekenäs (€5.70).

Train Seven to nine trains travel daily from Helsinki or Turku to Karjaa (Swedish: Karis), where they are met by connecting trains or buses to Hanko (via Ekenäs). The two-hour ride from Helsinki costs €18.60.

Boat The MS Franz Höijer travels between Hanko and Turku (then on to Uusikaupunki) at 10am on Tuesday from mid-May to mid-August. The trip takes eight hours one way and costs only €12. From Turku, the boat departs at 10am, arriving in Hanko at 6pm.

On Sunday in summer MS Sunnan II cruises between Hanko and Ekenäs (€16 one way, 2½ hours), departing at 4.30pm. Call ☎ 241 1850 for information.

Superfast Ferries has an international service to Rostock in Germany at 9pm from Monday to Saturday (22 hours), departing from the West Harbour. The minimum charge for a passenger is €138/69 per adult/child.

AROUND HANKO
Hauensuoli

The narrow strait between the islands of Tullisaari and Kobben, called Hauensuoli (Pike's Gut), is a protected natural harbour where sailing ships from countries around the Baltic Sea used to wait out storms in days of yore. Many of the sailors who passed through here paused to carve their initials or tales of bravery on the rocks, earning Hauensuoli its other name, 'The Guest Book of the Archipelago'. Some 600 rock carvings dating back to the 17th century remain. Hauensuoli can be reached by charter taxi boat or on a cruise from Hanko – see Organised Tours under Hanko earlier.

Bengtskär

Bengtskär is an islet about 25km from Hanko at the bottom of Finland's southwestern archipelago. It's the southernmost inhabited island in Finland, chosen as a lighthouse station in 1906 to protect ships from the dangerous waters of the archipelago. At 52m the lighthouse is the tallest in Scandinavia, although it was extensively damaged during the Continuation War against the Red Army in 1941. It was restored and opened to the public in 1995 and now houses a museum, café, post office and **accommodation** (☎ 02-466 7227). Day cruises to Bengtskär leave from Hanko in summer (see the Organised Tours section under Hanko earlier), or you can charter boats from Hanko or the village of Rosala on the island of Hiittinen.

East of Helsinki

Beyond Porvoo (see the Around Helsinki section in the Helsinki chapter), there are fewer attractions along the coast east of Helsinki, but this is a more interesting alternative to the inland route if you're making your way to the southeastern Lakeland area at Lappeenranta. A night or two at the beautiful village of Ruotsinpyhtää is well worth considering.

As with the southwestern coast, there are numerous small islands dotting the coastline and this is a popular summer playground for the Finns. There's also plenty of historical significance as you near the present-day border with Russia – battles were fought and lost and new borders created.

LOVIISA
☎ 019 • pop 7700

Loviisa (Swedish: Lovisa) prefers to be known as the 'Queen's town' since it was named after the Swedish Queen Lovisa Ulrika in 1752, although there had been a settlement at this harbour site for almost a century before that. Although hurriedly fortified by the Swedes when they lost garrison towns (such as Hamina) to the east, Loviisa was surrendered to the Russians way in back in 1755.

In the 18th century Loviisa was one of three towns in Finland allowed to engage in foreign trade, and by the 19th century it was a flourishing port and spa town. Loviisa was devastated by fire during the Crimean War, so little of the original Old Town remains. These days it's very much a summer resort, when all the attractions are open and boat trips are operating from the marina – skip it out of season.

Orientation & Information

The *kauppatori* (market square) is bounded on the northern side by Mannerheiminkatu. The bus station is about 100m east of the square

The **tourist office** has two seasonal offices. The summer office (☎ 555 446; Aleksanterinkatu 8; open 9am-4pm Mon-Fri, longer hours Sat in July) operates from June to August; the head office (☎ 555 234; W www.loviisa.fi; Tullisilta 5), near Casino Camping, opens for the remainder of the year.

The **post office** is on the corner of the market square at Kuningattarenkatu 13, and the library, with free Internet access, is just north of Mannerheiminkatu – the entrance is via the small park off Kuningattarenkatu.

Things to See

The very small **Old Town** of Loviisa, just south of Mannerheiminkatu, is what's left of the wooden buildings following the disastrous fire of 1855. Don't expect another Porvoo, but the narrow streets around Degerby Gille restaurant are the quaintest in town, and the restaurant itself is in a building that predates the town (1662).

On the market square, the impressive red-brick neo-Gothic **Loviisa church** (open 10am-6pm daily in summer), built in 1865, is a dominant feature; guides are on hand in summer to give free tours.

The summer home of the family of Jean Sibelius, the great Finnish composer, is now the **Sibelius House museum** (☎ 555 499; Sibeliuksenkatu 10; admission €2; open early June–mid-August). The opening of the house generally coincides with Loviisa's biggest annual event, the **Sibelius Festival** in early June, which features a weekend of concert performances.

Loviisa Town Museum (☎ 555 357; Puistokatu 2; admission €2; open 11am-4pm June-Aug, noon-4pm Sun rest of the year) is in an old manor house about 200m north of the market square. There are three floors of historical exhibits, period furniture and costumes, and rather incongruous changing local art exhibitions, but there's no labelling in English so it's difficult to get a feel for the history.

In summer most of the action is at the **Laivasilta marina**, 500m south of the centre. A cluster of old rust-coloured wooden storehouses now contain galleries, craft shops, cafés and a small maritime museum, and this is from where boats to Svartholma Sea Fortress and the island of Hästholmen (see Around Loviisa) depart.

Places to Stay & Eat
The friendly **Casino Camping** (☎ 530 244; Kapteenintie 1; single/double tent sites €10/ 15.50, single/double rooms from €35/48; open mid-May–Aug) is in a delightful waterfront spot about 500m south of the marina. As well as camping, there are rooms in two renovated wooden houses, most with bathroom. A four-bed family room is €85.

Helgas Gasthaus (☎ 531 576; Sibeliuksenkatu 6; singles/doubles €25/45, 4-bed room €90) is a simple, old-fashioned, family-run guesthouse with a range of rooms and a large, peaceful garden at the back.

Hotel Degerby (☎ 50651, fax 505 6200; Brandensteininkatu 17; singles/doubles €78/ 91, weekends & summer €63/76), near the market square, is the best of the three hotels in town and it has the **Styrbord Restaurant**, with a decent bar and €7.50 lunch buffet.

Cheap kebabs, felafels and pizza (€4 to €6) can be found at the upstairs **Mehter Bazar** (Kuningattarenkatu 18).

Vaherkylä (Aleksanterinkatu 2) is an unassuming bakery and a pleasant café with quiche and cakes to go with the help-yourself coffee.

There are a couple of popular summer café-restaurants at Laivasilta marina. **Saltbodan Cafe & Restaurant** (☎ 532 572; meals €7-14) serves coffee and snacks in a rustic room or on the terrace and à la carte meals in a pleasant dining hall, as well as a €7.40 lunch buffet.

Degerby Gille (☎ 505 6300; Sepänkuja 4) is the most famous restaurant in Loviisa, mainly for the historic building with its charming, old-fashioned dining rooms. It's open for lunch only (11am to 2pm); dinner is by arrangement.

Getting There & Away
Loviisa is 90km east of Helsinki, reached by the motorway E18 or Hwy 7. There are up to 25 buses a day to/from Helsinki (€12.40, 1½ hours), as well as a regular bus service to/from Kotka (€6.70, 30 minutes) and Porvoo (€5.70, 30 minutes).

AROUND LOVIISA
An interesting short trip is to the **Svartholma Sea Fortress**, on an island 10km from the town centre. It was established in 1748 soon after Sweden had lost control of the eastern part of Finland and, along with Suomenlinna at Helsinki, was intended to defend Finland against further invasion from Russia. The fort was destroyed by the British during the Crimean War in 1855, but has since been reconstructed. From June to the end of August there are daily boats to the island from Laivasilta marina at noon and 2pm (adult/child €8.50/4, 45 minutes), and until early August you can go on **pirate cruises** (€10.50 per person) leaving at 10am, aimed specifically at families and kids. Guided walking tours of the fortress cost €3.50.

Loviisa Nuclear Power Plant (☎ 010-455 5011; adult/child €7/3.50) pumps away on Hästholmen, 15km from town, and in summer you can take a boat trip out there, tag along on a guided tour of the facility, then get the free bus back to town. Since this is mainly aimed at Finnish tourists you'll have to arrange in advance for a tour in English. This is one of two nuclear plants in Finland, but it won't be the last. While the governments of other EU countries such as Germany and Sweden are deciding to close existing nuclear plants, Finland intends to build more.

RUOTSINPYHTÄÄ
☎ 019 • pop 3200

Combining Finland's power struggles of the past and its industrial beginnings, the tiny, peaceful village of Ruotsinpyhtää (Swedish: Strömfors) is a great place to visit, and well worth an overnight stop. The long name means 'Pyhtää of Sweden', as it was here, along the Kyma River, that the Swedish–Russian international border split the town of Pyhtää into two in 1743. The western, oddly shaped section was Swedish property; Pyhtää proper was to become Russian for some time. The municipal and provincial border still follows the river, and nobody has had the courage or desire to unite these areas.

Although you could easily be forgiven for thinking Ruotsinpyhtää is a museum village, it's also a thriving community, thanks to the modern-day factory across the river. The tiny scattering of buildings includes a supermarket, bank (with ATM), library (with Internet access) and cafés. The annual **Bluegrass Music Festival** is held here on the first weekend in June.

There's an **information centre** (☎ 618 474; open 10am-6pm daily in summer, 8am-4pm Sept-May) at the café in the old forge building.

Things to See & Do
Strömfors ironworks (open 10am-6pm daily June–mid-Aug), founded in 1695, is one of the oldest of its kind in Finland. Today it's a picturesque open-air museum of wooden farm and industrial buildings, surrounded by forest, rivers and bridges. The rust-red and white wooden buildings reflected in the lake on a clear windless day is definitely the stuff of postcards. **Forge Museum** consists of an old smith's workshop and equipment. Across the road are some **craft workshops** – potters, silversmiths, textile makers and painters. One of the ironworks buildings serves as an **art gallery** in summer.

The octagonal wooden **church** dates from 1770; its altarpiece was painted in 1989 by Helene Schjerfbeck, a famous Finnish artist.

The area is ideal for **canoeing**, and you can rent rowing boats and canoes (around €20 a day) from either the tourist information office adjacent to Forge Museum or the hostel. There's also an 8km circular marked **walking trail** to lake Kukuljarvi – the information centre has a basic trail map.

Places to Stay & Eat
Finnhostel Krouvinmäki (☎ 618 474, 0400-492 161, fax 618 475; singles/doubles €25.50/50.50; open June–mid-Aug or by prior arrangement) is a wonderful HI-affiliated hostel in a renovated tavern house. All rooms are twins and there's a kitchen and laundry.

Kulma Kahvila is a cheap café and grilli just behind the hostel, while **Forge Café**, adjacent to Forge Museum and doubling as the information centre, has coffee and snacks.

The wonderful **Ravintola Ruukinmylly** (☎ 618 693; pizza & pasta €3.50-6, mains €10-14) is in a 17th-century former mill on a peaceful pond. In summer the restaurant has a terrace with live music and dancing. The menu includes light meals, wood-fired pizzas and some Finnish specialities – the salmon soup is something to be savoured.

Getting There & Away
Ruotsinpyhtää is 115km east of Helsinki, north of road No 7. Get to the village by bus from Loviisa, or from Ahvenkoski, 3km from the village. Daily buses from Helsinki, Loviisa and Kouvola stop at Ahvenkoski.

KOTKA
☎ 05 • pop 56,000

Kotka, built on an island 132km east of Helsinki, is Finland's most important industrial port, with massive pulp factories and stinking oil tanks as its major features. If that sounds like a reason not to go near the place, Kotka does have a couple of redeeming features in its vicinity – namely the new Maretarium, the Langinkoski Imperial fishing lodge, and as a jumping-off point for visits to outlying tiny islands.

Orientation & Information
The city centre is on Kotkansaari island. Keskuskatu and Kirkkokatu, with the small Sibelius Park between them, are the two main streets in the centre. To the west is the more rural island of Mussalo, a suburb of Kotka.

The **tourist office** (☎ 234 4424; W www .kotka.fi/matkailu; Kirkkokatu 3; open 9am-7pm daily July & Aug, 9am-5pm Mon-Fri rest of the year) can book tours and sells boat tickets to the islands.

The **library** (Kirkkokatu 24), near the Kotka church, has a free Internet terminal, and there's Internet access at **Cafe SoNetti** in the same building.

SOUTH COAST

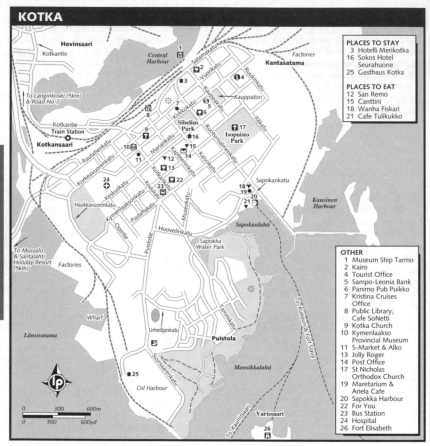

KOTKA

PLACES TO STAY
3 Hotelli Merikotka
16 Sokos Hotel
   Seurahuone
25 Gasthaus Kotka

PLACES TO EAT
12 San Remo
15 Canttini
18 Wanha Fiskari
21 Cafe Tulikukko

OTHER
1 Museum Ship Tarmo
2 Kairo
4 Tourist Office
5 Sampo-Leonia Bank
6 Panimo Pub Puikko
7 Kristina Cruises
  Office
8 Public Library;
  Cafe SoNetti
9 Kotka Church
10 Kymenlaakso
   Provincial Museum
11 S-Market & Alko
13 Jolly Roger
14 Post Office
17 St Nicholas
   Orthodox Church
19 Maretarium &
   Ariela Cafe
20 Sapokka Harbour
22 For You
23 Bus Station
24 Hospital
26 Fort Elisabeth

Maretarium

If you've ever wondered what swims beneath the surface of Finland's many lakes, rivers and surrounding seas, the impressive new **Maretarium** (☎ 234 4030; W www.mare tarium.fi; Sapokankatu 2; adult/student & child €9.50/6; open 10am-8pm daily late June–mid-Aug, 10am-6pm rest of the year) explains all in a series of giant fish tanks, each representing a particular body of water. The usual suspects are here: perch, salmon, bream, Arctic char and herring, but there are also a few strangers such as the lumpsucker and the heinous-looking, four-horn sculpin. Though not visually on a par with a tropical aquarium, it's a well-presented educational experience and there's English labelling, guided tours and a theatrette. And if all those

fish are making you hungry, the town's best fish restaurant is next door.

Sapokka Water Park

Just south of Sapokka harbour, this park is a lovely green oasis with bridges, walking trails, gardens and the **Rose Terrace** garden, illuminated every evening.

Museums & Churches

Kymenlaakso Provincial Museum (Maakuntamuseo; ☎ 234 4423; Kotkankatu 13; adult/child €2/1; open noon-6pm Tues-Fri, noon-4pm Sat & Sun) is the museum of regional history, with exhibits from the Stone Age to present day.

The world's oldest icebreaker, the **museum ship Tarmo** (☎ 234 4405; adult/child €2.50/1;

open daily in summer) is moored at the central harbour. Built at Newcastle-on-Tyne in 1907, it once kept Finnish shipping lanes open, and you can now go aboard and explore the cabins, bridge and engine room.

St Nicholas Orthodox Church *(open daily in summer)*, in Isopuisto Park, was built in 1801 and is the only building in Kotka to survive the Crimean War of 1853–56. It is believed to have been designed by architect Yakov Perrini, who also designed the St Petersburg Admiralty.

Activities

Archipelago cruises of all types depart from Sapokka harbour in summer, along with scheduled ferries to the outlying islands (see Around Kotka) – the tourist office has timetables and details.

Several operators offer **white-water rafting** (also called 'rapids shooting') on the Kymijoki. A three-hour trip costs around €40/25 per adult/child, including transportation. Contact **Eramys Ky** *(☎ 228 1244)* or **Keisarin Kosket Oy** *(☎ 260 9301)* or book at the tourist office.

You can go **fly-fishing** at the famous Langinkoski rapids (see the Around Kotka section).

Special Events

The **Kotka Maritime Festival** (Kotkan Meripäivät) is held annually in late July or early August. Events include boat racing, concerts, cruises and a market.

Places to Stay

Santalahti Holiday Resort *(☎ 260 5055; tent sites €9, cottages from €49; open May–late Sept)* is a sprawling resort on Mussalo, 5km from central Kotka. The facilities are good and some of the newer cottages are outstanding, but there's no regular public transport.

Gasthaus Kotka *(☎ 225 0622; Puistotie 24; beds €25.50)* is the cheapest place to stay in town, but it's in a thoroughly depressing area near the oil refinery. Rooms are basic but rates include breakfast.

Hotelli Merikotka *(☎ 215 222, fax 215 414; Satamakatu 9; singles/doubles €48/66)* is a small, friendly hotel in a good location facing the central harbour.

Sokos Hotel Seurahuone *(☎ 35035, fax 350 0450; Keskuskatu 21; singles/doubles €94/110, doubles weekends & summer €78)*

is the top hotel in Kotka and is in the thick of the action opposite the town park. There's a popular nightclub here.

Places to Eat

Canttiini *(☎ 214 130; Kaivokatu 15; mains €8-16)* is popular with locals and dishes up big serves of pasta and Mexican food in a casual atmosphere.

San Remo *(☎ 212 114; Keskuskatu 29; pizza & pasta €8-10, other mains €11-16)* is a more authentic, cosy Italian place, with chianti and reasonably priced pasta dishes.

Cafe Tulikukko, at Sapokka harbour, is a good place for coffee and snacks, while the nearby **Ariela Cafe** at the Maretarium is a good lunchtime spot with filled rolls, light meals and a large terrace.

Wanha Fiskari *(☎ 218 6585; Ruotsinsalmenkatu 1; mains €13-24)* is an elegant and pricey restaurant renowned for its Finnish fish specialities such as Baltic herring, perch and salmon (it's no small irony that the Maretarium was built next door). There are also meat dishes including reindeer (€24.30) and a good lunchtime salad buffet.

Entertainment

Most of Kotka's better pubs and clubs are near the centre, on Kotkankatu, Kirkkokatu and Keskuskatu.

Kairo *(☎ 212 787; Satamakatu 7)* is something of a legendary old sailors' pub facing the central harbour. Outrageous paintings adorn the walls, there's a large terrace in summer and frequent live music (often traditional Finnish dance). There are more tourists than sailors among its clientele these days but it still has plenty of character.

Panimo Pub Puikko *(Ruotsinsalmenkatu 14)* translates as a brewery but it doesn't actually brew its own stuff. Still, it's a popular pub facing one of the town's main squares.

Near the bus station, **Jolly Roger** *(Kymenlaaksonkatu 16)* is a convivial Irish bar with a lively terrace and, opposite, **For You** *(Kotkankatu 8)* is another popular drinking hole.

Getting There & Away

There are regular express buses from Helsinki (€16.80, two hours), via Porvoo, Loviisa and Pyhtää. Hourly buses make the 20-minute trip to Hamina (€4.50), 26km to the east.

SOUTH COAST

There are between four and six local trains a day to Kouvola (€7, 40 minutes) from where you can connect to trains with all major Finnish cities.

AROUND KOTKA
Archipelago Islands
Three interesting islands off the Kotka coast make for good day trips during the summer months. There are daily boat connections to each from Sapokka harbour during summer.

On **Kukouri** is Fort Slava, also known as the Fortress of Honour. It was built by Russians in 1794 as part of a chain of fortresses in the Gulf of Finland, then was destroyed by the British in 1855 before being renovated in 1993. There are five ferries daily in summer (adult/child return €6/2).

On **Varissaari**, Fort Elisabeth was another of the Russian fortresses built to defend the coast against the Swedes. A fierce naval battle was fought from here in 1789 and the fortress was abandoned in the late 19th century. It is now a popular venue for festivals, dances and open-air performances, and a favourite picnic spot. Ferries leave from Kotka hourly between 9am and 11pm from 25 May to 25 August (adult/child €5/2).

Kaunissaari is the most interesting island, with its own little community. There's a charming fishing village and a local museum, as well as a camping ground with some cabins. Evening cruises to Kaunissaari, with singing and live music, depart at 7pm Thursday and Friday from late May to late August. There are two regular ferries a day, three from Thursday to Sunday (adult/child €7/3.50).

Langinkoski
Imperial fishing lodge (☎ 228 1050; W www.langinkoskimuseo.com; Koskenniskantie 5C; adult/child €4/2; open 10am-7pm daily May–late Aug, Sat & Sun Sept & Oct) at the Langinkoski rapids, 5km north of the centre, is a worthwhile place to visit even if you're not interested in fishing haunts of the wealthy and powerful. The surprisingly simple wooden lodge was built in 1889 for Tsar Alexander III, who visited Langinkoski frequently. Most of the original furniture has been retained and the rooms look as they did at the end of the 19th century. In summer there are guided tours on the hour between 11am and 4pm on Sunday.

The riverside forest setting (now a 28 hectare nature reserve) is beautiful and there are many walking trails to soak up a few hours. **Fly-fishing** is still allowed at Langinkoski rapids, but for a permit you need to contact **Munkkisaaren Maju** (☎ 0770-95559; Munkholmantie 101, Karhula). The tourist office in Kotka may also be able to help. The lodge is not well signposted – turn off road No 15 at the signs (right if you're coming from Kotka) and drive about 1.5km to the road's end.

You can get almost all the way to Langinkoski on bus No 13 or 27. Alternatively, get off at the sign at the *pikavuoro* (express) bus stop and walk 1.2km.

HAMINA
☎ 05 • pop 10,000
Just 40km west of the Russian border, Hamina (Swedish: Fredrikshamn) is a small, harbourside town with an unusual octagonal plan at its centre.

Hamina was founded in 1653, when Finland was a part of Sweden. The crumbling fortifications that surround it were begun by panicky Swedes in 1722 after they lost Vyborg to Russia. Their fears were justified, but their efforts in vain – shortly afterwards the Russians marched in and took Hamina, too.

The unique town plan and pleasant, small-town atmosphere make this an enjoyable stop on the south coast, en route to Karelia or St Petersburg. It's also a favourite place for visiting Russians.

Information
The main **tourist office** (☎ 749 5251; W www.hamina.fi; open 9am-4pm Mon-Fri) is in the town hall building in Old Hamina, but there's a **summer office** (☎ 749 5252; open 9am-6pm Mon-Fri, 10am-3pm Sat & Sun June–mid-Aug) in the Lipputorni (Flagtower) at the kauppatori.

The **post office** is at Maariankatu 4, and the **public library** (Rautatienkatu 8; open 1pm-7pm Mon-Fri, 10am-2pm Sat), is just north of the bus station; you'll need to book to use the Internet terminals.

Things to See & Do
Restored 19th-century wooden buildings grace the eight radial streets of Hamina's octagonal town plan. From its centre – Hamina has a more literal centre than most towns,

dominated by the 18th-century **town hall** – most sights are a short walk away.

Highlights of Old Hamina include the neoclassical **Hamina church**, built in 1843 and designed by CL Engel; and directly opposite, behind the town hall, the 1837 **Orthodox Church of Saints Peter & Paul**, thought to have been created by architect Louis Visconti, who designed Napoleon's monument in France.

Hamina's three main museums all open from 11am to 3pm Wednesday to Saturday and noon to 5pm Sunday from May to August, and cost €2/1 per adult/child. Housed in Hamina's oldest building, **Town Museum** *(Kaupunginmuseo; ☎ 749 5242; Kadettikoulunkatu 2)* is the museum of local history. King Gustav III of Sweden and Catherine II

(the Great) of Russia held negotiations in one of the rooms in 1783.

Merchant's House Museum *(Kauppiaantalomuseo; ☎ 749 5244; Kasarminkatu 6)* is a former merchant's store and residence, and one of the best house museums in Finland. Kasarminkatu was a main shopping street in the 19th century.

Reserve Officers School Museum *(RUKmuseo; ☎ 181-66498; Kadettikoulunkatu 8)* is devoted to military uniforms and weapons. Nearby, **Gallery Ruutikellari** *(Roopertinkatu)*, an old gunpowder warehouse, has been converted to an art gallery with summer exhibitions.

Northwest of Old Hamina are remnants of the 18th century **Hamina Fortress**, including 3km of crumbling stone walls, and

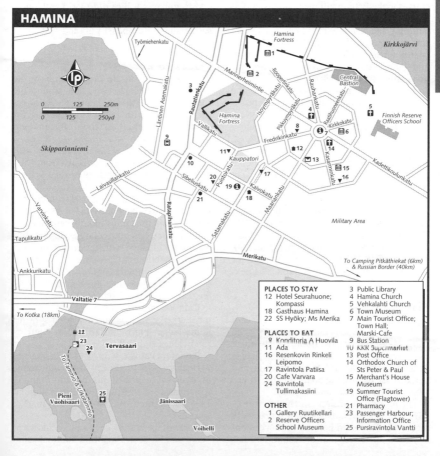

HAMINA

PLACES TO STAY
12 Hotel Seurahuone; Kompassi
18 Gasthaus Hamina
22 SS Hyöky; Ms Merika

PLACES TO EAT
8 Konditoria A Huovila
11 Ada
16 Resenkovin Rinkeli Leipomo
17 Ravintola Patiisa
20 Cafe Varvara
24 Ravintola Tullimakasiini

OTHER
1 Gallery Ruutikellari
2 Reserve Officers School Museum
3 Public Library
4 Hamina Church
5 Vehkalahti Church
6 Town Museum
7 Main Tourist Office; Town Hall; Marski-Cafe
9 Bus Station
10 KKK Supermarket
13 Post Office
14 Orthodox Church of Sts Peter & Paul
15 Merchant's House Museum
19 Summer Tourist Office (Flagtower)
21 Pharmacy
23 Passenger Harbour; Information Office
25 Pursiravintola Vantti

SOUTH COAST

the star-shaped bastions, but there really isn't much left to see. The **central bastion**, northeast of the centre along Raatihuoneenkatu, has been restored and covered by an enormous marquee. It is used for public events such as the Hamina Tattoo (see Special Events following).

A short walk southwest of the centre at Tervasaari harbour is the SS *Hyöky*, a 1912 steamship completed in the same year as the *Titanic*. It served both Russia and Finland in its colourful career, and was the last coal-burning steamship in commercial use in Scandinavia. During summer it's now a cluttered museum, bar and hotel (see Places to Stay). Moored alongside is the 1943 ice-breaker and tug MS *Merikarhu*.

Also from Tervasaari there are summer **cruises** to the fishing village on the island of Tammio. Departures take place on Tuesday, Saturday and Sunday from late May to late August. You can also reach Ulkotammio, an island further south, on weekends from mid-June to the end of July. The **information office** (☎ 040-594 4171; open 10am-4pm Mon-Fri, 10am-3pm Sat & Sun) at the harbour has timetables and sells tickets.

Special Events

Every two years in late July or early August, Hamina celebrates military music during the week-long **Hamina Tattoo**. This international event features not only Finnish and Russian military marching bands, but rock, pop, jazz and dance acts (Suzi Quattro was on the bill in 2002). Concerts are held under the canopy of the Central Bastion, in the streets of Old Hamina and under the market square marquee. Tickets range in price from €5 to €50. Contact ☎ 749 5510 or the tourist office for programme and ticket information. The next event is in 2004.

Places to Stay

Camping Pitkäthiekat (☎/fax 345 9183; tent sites €10, 4–6-person cottages €40-65; open daily May–late Aug, weekends in winter), 6km east of Hamina at Vilniemi, has a peaceful lakeside and forest setting, and you can use the rowing boats for free. It has a bar and café, sauna and laundry.

The historic steamship, SS **Hyöky** (☎ 040-763 3757; singles/doubles €30/40) is usually moored in Tervasaari harbour (but occasionally sails off to Helsinki or Kotka) and has

been partly converted into a floating hotel. There are nine tiny cabins, each with a set of bunks, plus the 'captain's cabin' above deck. It's not for the claustrophobic, but you stay here for the experience – the captain, 'Patu', is a well known local character and will make you feel part of the crew. If you're on a tight budget, ask about the dorm-style rooms. The ship also has a bar, a cluttered museum and even a tiny sauna (free for guests).

Gasthaus Hamina (☎ 354 1434; Kaivokatu 4; singles/doubles €37/55), on the corner of the market square, is a rustic little pub with 10 rooms upstairs. It's nothing flash but they have a bathroom and are reasonable for the price.

Hotel Seurahuone (☎ 3500 263; Pikkuympyräkatu 5; doubles €66), in the heart of Old Hamina, is full of old-world ambience, and summer discounts are available. The subterranean **Kompassi** pub and restaurant is also here.

Places to Eat

The **snack stalls** in the kauppatori have the usual array of cheap eats, and around the square are several inexpensive takeaways such as **Ada**, with kebabs and pizzas for around €5. In the Old Town, **Resenkovin Rinkeli Leipomo** (Kasarminkatu 8; open 9am-5pm Tues-Fri, 8.30am-1pm Sat), still owned and run by the Resenkovs from Russia, is a legendary pretzel bakery with a 100-year tradition.

Marski-Cafe (☎ 354 1600; Raatihuoneentori 1; open 10am-5pm Mon-Fri, 11am-4pm Sat & Sun), in the unmistakably central town hall building, has both a large, elegant dining room furnished with antiques, and a less formal lunchtime café. Also in Old Hamina, **Konditoria A Huovila** (Fredrikinkatu 1), in an old wooden house, is a great place for coffee, cakes and sandwiches.

Cafe Varvara (Puistokatu 2), just south of the market square, is another good spot for home-baked buns and cakes, as well as sandwiches and coffee.

Ravintola Patiisa (☎ 353 2444; Satamakatu 11; mains €8-15, pizzas €9), has a wide range of reasonably priced pizzas and Italian–American-style dishes, as well as a popular 1st-floor terrace overlooking the market square.

Some of the best places to eat are down at Tervasaari harbour. **Ravintola Tullimakasiini**

Savonlinna

Lake Saimaa

Olavinlinna Castle, Savonlinna

Savonlinna Opera Festival, Savonlinna

Kerimäki Church, Kerimäki

Linnoitus (Fortress) grounds, Lappeenranta

South Karelia Art Museum, Lappeenranta

Rauhalinna Villa, Savonlinna

(☎ 344 7470; mains €9-15, set menu €20), the quaint restaurant in an old customs house, specialises in Finnish fish and meat dishes.

Entertainment

The place to be on summer weekends is **Pursiravintola Vantti** (☎ 354 1063; open 3pm-late Tues-Sat, noon-late Sun), on the island of Pieni Vuohisaari just opposite Tervasaari harbour. There's drinking and dancing to live music in the friendly atmosphere of the yacht club, and food is available. To get to the island, press the buzzer at the little pier set up at Tervasaari harbour and a boat will come and pick you up (free).

In Old Hamina, **Kompassi** (☎ 350 0266; Pikkuympyräkatu 5) in the historic Hotel Seurahuone is a brooding basement pub once used by visiting seafarers. There's live music, karaoke, and a summer terrace at the side of the hotel.

Getting There & Away

You can reach Hamina by hourly bus from Kotka (€4.50, 20 minutes). Express buses from Helsinki (€20.90) make the 153km trip in less than three hours. The Russian border is only 40km to the east; buses pass through Hamina on the way to Vyborg and St Petersburg in Russia.

The Lakeland

Since lakes cover much of southern Finland, it's a bit of a misnomer to describe one area as the 'Lakeland', but that title undeniably goes to the waterlogged area in southeastern Finland to the south and west of Karelia. Much of this region encompasses the Savo district, the centre of which is the beautiful town of Savonlinna. The people of this lake area – the *savolaiset* – are among the most outspoken and friendly of all Finns: these are witty, open-hearted and easy-going people, who can laugh at themselves and are often lampooned by Finns from elsewhere – because of their distinctive Savo dialect, accent and humour, but perhaps also because they envy the locals their beautiful Lakeland.

A glistening patchwork of lakes, islands, narrow straits, canals and beaches, the Lakeland is one of the most popular summer holiday destinations among Finns, who come here en masse from late June to August to rent lakeside holiday cottages and enjoy fishing and boating. An exploration of the Lakeland in summer, particularly in and around Savonlinna and Kuopio, is a great way to immerse yourself in the Finns' love of nature. High culture is also in evidence here: in the west you'll find rock, blues and jazz festivals, but here the big events are Savonlinna's Opera Festival, Kuopio's Dance Festival and Mikkeli's Classical Music Festival.

An advantage of the lakes network is that many towns can be reached by boat, and here you'll find some of Finland's best steamboat routes. Public transport connections are good in this region, although to explore the out-of-the-way places, a car is the way to go.

Highlights

- Spending the night at Valamo, Finland's only Orthodox monastery
- Enjoying Olavinlinna Castle in Savonlinna, venue for the Opera Festival
- Descending into Retretti Art Centre at Punkaharju – a unique art museum inside a cave
- Steaming it up in the world's largest smoke sauna in Kuopio
- Hiring a canoe and seeking out the rare Saimaa ringed seal in Linnansaari National Park
- Paddling from Juva to Sulkava, an easy two-day canoe trip
- Taking the full-day ferry trip between Savonlinna and Kuopio, via lakes, lochs and canals

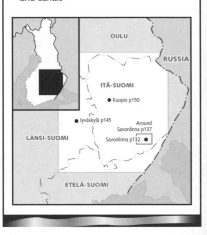

Eastern Lakeland

This is the heartland of the Savo region, and arguably the most scenic part of Finland's Lakeland.

SAVONLINNA
☎ 015 • pop 28,700

In the heart of the Lakeland and lorded over by a dramatic medieval castle, Savonlinna is the pick of the lake-region towns to visit during summer. Set on two islands between Lake Haapavesi and Lake Pihlajavesi, it offers the prettiest of waterscapes and the most stunning medieval castle in Finland.

In July, Savonlinna hosts the Opera Festival, the most popular of all Finnish festivals. It's a delightful experience, despite the high prices and crowds, with the operatic performances staged inside Olavinlinna Castle. Outside opera season, not much disturbs the peace in Savonlinna: there's a local joke that the definition of paranoia is walking down the main street of Savonlinna in January and thinking there's someone following you.

THE LAKELAND

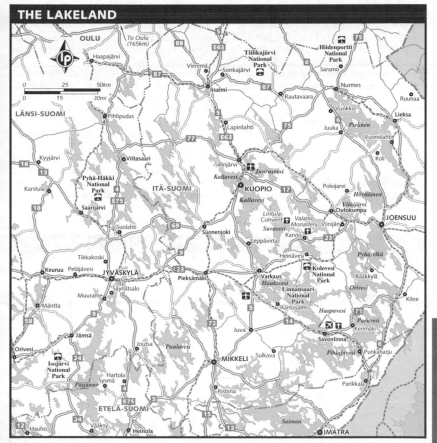

History

The slow growth of Savonlinna began in 1475 with the building of Olavinlinna Castle. In 1639, Savonlinna received a municipal charter at the instigation of Count Per Brahe, the founder of many towns around Finland. In 1743, this small market town was annexed to Russia; it was returned to the Finnish grand duchy in 1812. By the 1920s, Savonlinna was important as the major hub for steamboat traffic in the Lakeland, and has retained this important role today.

Orientation & Information

The tourist office, **Savonlinna Tourist Service** (☎ 517 510; e savonlinna@touristservice-svl.fi; Puistokatu 1; open 8am-8pm daily July, 8am-6pm daily June, 8am-6pm Mon-Fri Aug, 9am-5pm Mon-Fri rest of the year), is on the western side of town near the main bridge. It provides information about most places in the region, sells festival tickets, reserves accommodation and organises tours.

Nestori (☎ 0205-645 900; e saimaa@ metsa.fi; Aino Ackten puistotie l; open 11am-6pm daily July, 11am-5pm Tues-Sun May, June, Aug & Sept), near the castle, is the national parks visitor centre for the Saimaa region. There are slide shows, a nature exhibition and information on regional parks such as Linnansaari and Kolovesi.

Post & Communications The main post office is on Olavinkatu, near the bus terminal. Closer to the town centre there is a post office (Koulukatu 10) inside K-Market.

Savonlinna has several places where you can use Internet terminals for free, but predictably they're usually busy. The **public library** (Tottinkatu; open 11am-7pm Mon-Fri, 10am-2pm Sat) has one terminal you can book in advance. **Cafe Knut Posse** (Olavinkatu 55), joined to the bookshop of the same name, has one terminal, as does the café at **Hotel Seurahone**.

The city also has a **music library** (Kirkkokatu 12; open 1pm-7pm Mon-Thur, 10am-4pm Fri). It has a good collection of CDs, including opera.

Olavinlinna Castle

Olavinlinna (☎ 531 164; adult/child €5/3.50; open 10am-5pm daily in summer, 10am-3pm rest of the year) is the best-preserved medieval castle in northern Europe. These days it is famous as the setting for the month-long Savonlinna Opera Festival. If you visit in June you may be lucky enough to see some of the opera stars rehearsing.

Founded in 1475 by Erik Axelsson Tott, governor of Vyborg and the Eastern Provinces, Olavinlinna was named after Olof, a 10th-century Norwegian Catholic saint. The castle was meant to protect the eastern border of the Swedish empire. However, Russians occupied the castle from 1714 to 1721, and took control of it again from 1743 to the early half of the 20th century. Two museums within the castle have exhibits on its history plus displays of Orthodox treasures.

To tour the castle, including its original towers, bastions and chambers, you have to

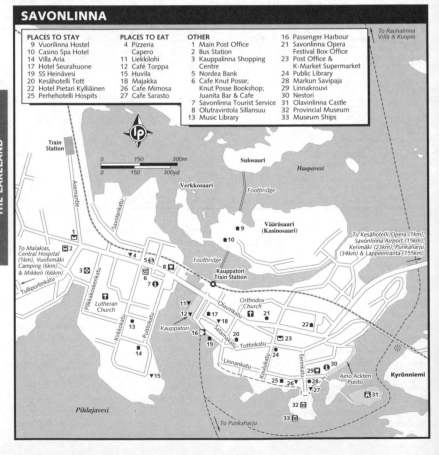

SAVONLINNA

PLACES TO STAY	PLACES TO EAT	OTHER	
9 Vuorilinna Hostel	4 Pizzeria	1 Main Post Office	16 Passenger Harbour
10 Casino Spa Hotel	Capero	2 Bus Station	21 Savonlinna Opera
14 Villa Aria	11 Liekkilohi	3 Kauppalinna Shopping	Festival Box Office
17 Hotel Seurahuone	12 Café Torppa	Centre	23 Post Office &
19 SS Heinävesi	15 Huvila	5 Nordea Bank	K-Market Supermarket
20 Kesähotelli Tott	18 Majakka	6 Cafe Knut Posse;	24 Public Library
22 Hotel Pietari Kylliäinen	26 Cafe Mimosa	Knut Posse Bookshop;	28 Markun Savipaja
25 Perhehotelli Hospits	27 Cafe Sarasto	Juanita Bar & Cafe	29 Linnakrouvi
		7 Savonlinna Tourist Service	30 Nestori
		8 Olutravintola Sillansuu	31 Olavinlinna Castle
		13 Music Library	32 Provincial Museum
			33 Museum Ships

join one of the excellent guided tours (around 45 minutes). Tours depart on the hour from 10am to 5pm daily from June to mid-August, and from 10am to 3pm at other times of the year. Guides speak English, Swedish, French, German, Japanese and Italian as well as Finnish. The guides are quite good at bringing the castle to life and can furnish you with some interesting stories: the soldiers, for instance, were partly paid in beer – 5L a day and 7L on Sunday, which makes you wonder how they were able to defend anything.

Provincial Museum & Museum Ships

The provincial museum (☎ 571 4712; Riihi-saari; combined ticket adult/student/child €3/2/free; open 11am-5pm Tues-Sun, 11am-8pm daily July) in an old Russian warehouse near the castle, has exhibits related to local history and the importance of water transport to trade and industry. There are plenty of old photographs and models, and upstairs is a changing art exhibition.

Moored alongside the museum are the historic ships *Salama*, *Mikko* and *Savonlinna*, all with exhibitions open from May to September during museum hours. The museum and ships can all be seen with a single ticket.

Rauhalinna Villa

This romantic Moorish-style wooden villa (☎ 517 640; Lehtiniemi; open June-Aug) was built in 1900 by Nils Weckman, an officer in the tsar's army, as a wedding-anniversary gift for his wife. It features an intricate wooden lattice trim and has a serene lakeside setting.

These days Rauhalinna warrants a visit for its café and fine restaurant, complete with banquet hall. For a real treat, try the excellent buffet. The café is open from 11am to 6pm Monday to Saturday in July, the restaurant from 11am to 8pm Monday to Saturday (until 6pm Sunday); both keep slightly shorter hours in June and August. Rauhalinna also houses a **summer hotel** (singles/doubles €61/71).

The villa is at Lehtiniemi, 16km north of Savonlinna. The best way to visit is by boat from Savonlinna passenger harbour (see Lake Cruises under Organised Tours). Alternatively, there are a few buses from the Savonlinna bus terminal to within 500m of the villa from Monday to Saturday.

Activities

The area around Savonlinna, with its quiet country lanes and gently sloping hills, is terrific for **bicycle touring**. Bikes can be carried on board local ferries for a small fee. The tourist office rents bicycles in summer, as does the camping ground. To rent **canoes and rowing boats**, visit the camping ground.

Organised Tours

There are numerous tour operators running tours that enable you to explore some of this Lakeland area. **Opera Safaris** (☎ 515 158; W www.operasafaris.com) operates a half-day kayaking trip off the waters of Casino Island (€42); traditional church longboat trips on Lake Haukivesi and around the castle (€32); and a full day adventure tour that includes mountain biking, kayaking, caving, sauna, lunch and dinner and a hydroplane flight (€252 per person).

Lake Cruises In summer, the Savonlinna passenger harbour is one of the busiest in Finland. There are a number of scenic cruises to choose from, with dozens of daily departures during the high season. These include cruises around the castle, to Rauhalinna villa, or through the archipelago. Most boats have café and/or bar facilities on board. Cruises include:

SS *Heinävesi* To Retretti jetty in Punkaharju at 11am daily mid-June to early August (adult/child €7/3.50 one way)

MS *Lake Star* One-hour scenic cruises in the Savonlinna area (adult/child €10/5) with five departures daily from June to the end of August

MS *Ieva* Daily trips to Rauhalinna in summer (adult/child €10/6 return) and guided lake cruises (adult/child €8/4)

MS *Faust* Daily scheduled lake cruises in July (adult/child €7/2)

Special Events

Savonlinna Opera Festival (☎ 476 750; W www.operafestival.fi, Olavinkatu 27, 57130 Savonlinna), held throughout July, is perhaps the most famous festival in Finland with an international cadre of performers that includes touring productions from Covent Garden in London. The setting is the most dramatic location in Finland: the covered courtyard of Olavinlinna Castle. It offers four weeks of high-class opera performances from early July to early August. If you're around in late June, you may get to see rehearsals at Olavinlinna Castle.

The first Opera Festival was held at Olavinlinna way back in 1912, the brainchild of Finnish soprano Aino Ackte. It was resurrected again in 1967 and has grown in stature with each passing year. The festival's excellent website details the programme of operas and concerts two years in advance and allows you to book seats in advance on the Internet.

Tickets cost from €30 to €95 for concerts, and from €72 to €170 for major opera performances (more for premieres), depending on the seats. Tickets for some shows can be picked up for as little as €25, particularly midweek. Tickets for same-night performances are sold after 6pm from the booth near the bridge, and at any time from the Savonlinna Tourist Service. Although opera dominates the festival calendar here, in August the castle hosts a **beer festival**, and in September a **theatre festival** takes place.

Places to Stay

Savonlinna is notoriously expensive in summer, and prices rise pretty sharply (between 30% and 50%) during the Opera Festival, when beds are scarce. Book accommodation well in advance – at least six months for hotels, less for hostels – if you plan to visit during opera season (any time in July). Even so, if you're not fussy about which day you visit, it's worth phoning ahead to see if any beds are free, particularly midweek.

Places to Stay – Budget

Camping About 7km west of town, **Vuohimäki Camping** (☎ 537 353; e myyntipalvelu@lomaliitto.fi; tent sites €15.50, bunk beds €17, cabins €70-80) has good facilities but fills up quickly in July.

Hostels There are no year-round hostels in Savonlinna. **Vuorilinna** (☎ 73950, fax 272 524; e casino.myynti@svlkylpylaitos.fi; Kylpylaitoksentie; dorm beds €22, singles/doubles €54/71; open June–late Aug), an HI-affiliated hostel near the spa hotel on Vääräsaari, is also known as Kasinosaari (Casino Island). Guests have access to all kinds of facilities: kitchen, laundry, sauna, café and restaurant. **Malakias** (☎ 739 5430, fax 272 524; Pihlajavedenkuja 6; dorm beds €21, singles/doubles

€42/57; open June–early Aug), 2km northwest of town, is another summer hotel with two-room apartments sharing a kitchen and bathroom.

During summer the SS *Heinävesi* (☎ 533 120; cabins upper/lower deck per person €19/17) offers cramped two-person cabin accommodation after the last cruise every evening. There's a good chance of getting a bed here, even during the Opera Festival.

There's another HI hostel near Kerimäki (see that section later), which is rarely full during the week (even in July), so can make a viable alternative to staying in Savonlinna if you have a vehicle.

Places to Stay – Mid-Range & Top End

Perhehotelli Hospits (☎ 515 661, fax 515 120; Linnankatu 20; singles/doubles from €70/80), a cosy place near the castle, is the best of Savonlinna's few year-round hotels. It has a pleasant garden with access to a small beach.

Casino Spa Hotel (☎ 73950, fax 272 524; e casino.myynti@svlkylpylaitos.fi; Kasinosaari; singles/doubles €78/115, weekends €64/88), near the *kauppatori* (market square) train station, is another good option. Guests have unlimited access to the pool, sauna and Turkish bath. Rates are higher during the opera season.

Hotel Seurahuone (☎ 5731, fax 273 918; Kauppatori 4-6; singles/doubles from €85/100, doubles €160 in July) is a stylish highrise hotel in the heart of town. Some of the doubles have glassed-in balconies with harbour views.

Kesähotelli Tott (☎ 575 6390, fax 514 504; Satamakatu 1; singles/doubles from €70/85; open early June–late Aug) is also near the kauppatori. Some rooms are apartmentstyle, with kitchens.

Hotel Pietari Kylliäinen (☎ 739 5500, fax 534 873; Olavinkatu 15; singles €54-72, doubles €61-90) is a nondescript, central hotel with 49 rooms.

Kesähotelli Opera (☎ 476 7515, fax 476 7540; e operafestival.ltd@operafestival.fi; Kyrönniemenkuja 9; doubles €75, with shared bathroom €70; open mid-June–early Aug), operated as a summer hotel by the Opera Festival, is across the bridge from the main part of town, about 1.5km from the centre. There are hotel and apartment-style rooms, some with kitchen.

Villa Aria (☎ 476 7515, fax 476 7540; Puistokatu 15; doubles €100-125) is another festival-run summer hotel on the western side of the town centre. It's a stylish wooden hotel with 20 comfortable, modern rooms.

Huvila, the brewery-restaurant (see Places to Eat for details), also has boutique accommodation with two modern rooms above the brewery. Similarly, **Cafe Mimosa** has comfortable guesthouse accommodation close to the castle – there are six double rooms, some with balconies facing the lake, for approximately €75.

Places to Eat

The lively market at the lakeside **kauppatori** is the place to find local pastries such as omena-lörtsy, a tasty apple turnover (€1.50). Also on the kauppatori, **Cafe Torppa** is a popular student-run kiosk for coffee and late night snacks.

Pizzeria Capero (Olavinkatu 51; pizza & pasta €6-8) is the best place in town for a quick pizza and it's open to 10pm nightly.

Majakka (☎ 531 456; Satamakatu 11; lunch specials from €7) opposite the harbour is a good restaurant with a nautical theme.

Near the castle, **Cafe Mimosa** (☎ 532 257; Linnankatu; light meals €6-10) has a fine terrace and bar, and serves salads, cakes and light meals. **Cafe Sarasto** (Linnankatu 10), also near the castle, has a pleasant garden.

Juanita Bar & Cafe (☎ 514 531; Olavinkatu 44; mains €7-12), upstairs next to Cafe Knut Posse, does reasonably priced burgers, fajitas and Tex-Mex, and is a popular bar later in the night.

Liekkilohi (Flaming Salmon; fish mains €7-8.50) is a bright-red, covered pontoon anchored just off the kauppatori. It serves portions of flamed salmon and fried vendace (tiny lake fish). It's open until 2am during summer – perfect for a very Finnish late night snack.

Huvila (☎ 555 0555; W www.savonniemi .com; Puistokatu 4; mains €11.50-21) is a brewery-restaurant and one of the finest places to dine or enjoy a beer in Savonlinna. It's across the harbour from the town centre.

Entertainment

With only a small student population, Savonlinna is quiet most of the year, but very lively in July. A good place for a drink is the brewery pub **Huvila** (see Places to Eat), with three types of beer brewed on the premises and some of the best sahti (a high alcohol sweet Finnish beer) in the country. It has a fine terrace looking out across the lake to the harbour area.

Olutravintola Sillansuu, just off Olavinkatu near the main bridge, is a cosy English-style pub with a big range of international beers and whiskeys.

Later in the night, **Juanita Bar & Cafe** (see Places to Eat) is the place to mix with young Savonlinnans – it's open, and usually jumping, until 4am.

Linnakrouvi, near the castle, has a beer terrace; the house is old and has heaps of style.

Shopping

At the kauppatori you'll find a lively summer **market** with handicrafts and souvenirs on sale. Linnankatu, the quaint back street running up towards the castle, is lined with old wooden houses, some of which are craft shops and studios selling local handicrafts at hefty prices. **Markun Savipaja** (Linnankatu 10) sells fine local ceramics.

Getting There & Away

Air Finnair flies to Savonlinna from Helsinki, Mikkeli and Varkaus. The airport is 15km from the centre and a shuttle bus operates during the opera festival (€6).

Bus Savonlinna is the major travel hub for the southeastern Savo bus network. There are several express buses a day from Helsinki to Savonlinna (€35.40, five hours), and buses run almost hourly from Mikkeli (€17, 1½ hours). There are also regular services to Joensuu (€18.50), Kuopio (€23.10, 2½ hours) and Jyväskylä (€29.40).

Train There are trains from Helsinki (€42.20, five hours) via Parikkala – note that you must change to a regional train or connecting bus service at Parikkala, otherwise you'll wind up in Joensuu (€21.40, 2½ hours). For Kuopio, you need to take a bus to Pieksämäki and a train from there. The main train station is a long walk from the centre; get off at the kauppatori platform instead.

Boat In summer there is scheduled ferry service from the Savonlinna passenger harbour to Punkaharju and to Kuopio. The SS

Heinävesi travels to the Retretti jetty in Punkaharju daily from mid-June to mid-August. It departs from Savonlinna at 11am and from Punkaharju at 3.40pm (adult/child €7/3.50 one way, two hours).

In summer the lake ferry MS *Puijo* travels to Kuopio on Monday, Wednesday and Friday at 9.30am (€60, 11½ hours), returning on Tuesday, Thursday and Saturday. The boat passes through scenic waterways, canals and locks, and stops along the way at Oravi (€17), Heinävesi (€37), Karvio canal (€39) and Palokki (€41) among others. Meals are available on board but are expensive, so consider bringing your own food.

Getting Around

The Savonlinna airport is 15km northeast of the centre. An airport taxi shuttle meets arriving flights during the opera season; in town it picks up at the bus station and Hotel Seurahuone. The 20-minute trip costs €6 one way.

The city bus service costs €1.80 per ride within the Savonlinna area.

Several car rental agencies have offices in the centre and at the airport, including **Europcar** (☎ 730 8292) and **Hertz** (☎ 510 995; Rantakatu 2).

Land of Lakes

Lakes are the life force of southeastern Finland, with 10% of Finland consisting of water. Many of its 187,888 lakes are linked by rivers, and the towns, villages, factories and hydroelectric plants along these lakes and rivers rely on them for drinking water, and as a means of transportation. Finns cross the lakes by boat in summer and snowmobile in winter, and build summer cottages and saunas beside them.

Finnish lakes are shallow – only three are deeper than 100m. This means their waters warm quickly in summer, freeze over in winter, and also makes them susceptible to pollution.

Throughout Finland you will often hear the words *järvi* (lake), *saari* (island), *ranta* (shore), *niemi* (cape), *lahti* (bay), *koski* (rapids), *virta* (stream) and *joki* (river). All these words form some of the most common Finnish family names, especially Järvinen, Saarinen, Rantanen, Nieminen, Lahtinen, Koskinen, Virtanen and Jokinen.

AROUND SAVONLINNA

The area around Savonlinna, with its scenic islands, peninsulas, bays and straits, is the most beautiful part of the Lakeland.

Punkaharju Region

☎ 015 • pop 4500

Between Savonlinna and Parikkala is Punkaharju, the famous pine-covered sand esker (sand or gravel ridge) that ranks as one of the most overrated attractions in Finland, although in summer it's certainly a pretty area for walking or cycling. The village of Punkaharju has a post office, bank, bus and train stations, and several shops. There's a **tourist office** (☎ 734 1233; W *www .punkaharju.fi; Kauppatie 20)* in the village, and a small **information centre** in the old *vanha asema* (train station) next to Lusto Museum.

Punkaharju Ridge During the Ice Age, formations similar to this 7km-long sand ridge were created all over the country. Because the Punkaharju ridge crosses a large lake, it has always been an important travel route. Just a few hundred metres of the original unsealed road along the top of the ridge remain – this was once part of a route to Russia. To take a stroll on the famous Punkaharju Ridge, get off at the Retretti train station and walk east towards Punkaharju village.

Retretti Art Centre Retretti (☎ 775 2200; *adult/senior/student/child €15/12/9/5; open 10am-5pm daily June & Aug, 10am-6pm July)* is Finland's most unusual gallery – an art exhibition inside a man-made subterranean cave. This ambitious creation features waterfalls, a concert hall and special effects, including lights, sounds and shadows, using the natural elements of the cave – the walls, water and the darkness – to good effect. Above the cave (at ground level) is a more conventional exhibition space displaying art exhibitions on loan from elsewhere – in 2002 it was Russian and French masterpieces. The entire exhibition changes each summer. Admission is steep but it's a unique look at Finnish modern art.

About 100m away is the popular **Kesämaa Water Park** (*admission €10; open 10am-7pm daily June–mid Aug)*, with water slides and pools.

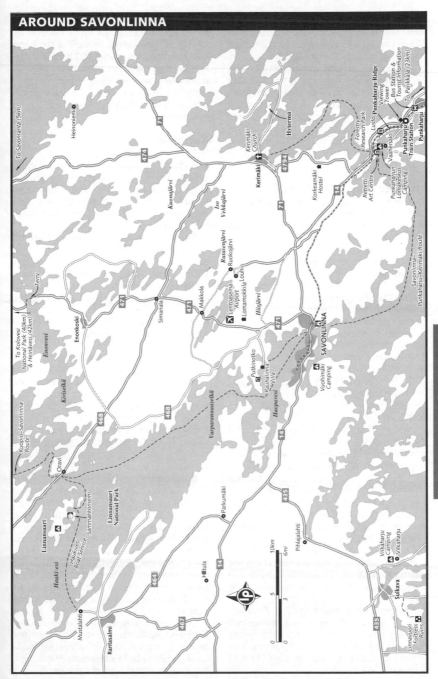

Lusto Forest Museum Lusto (☎ 345 1030; adult/student/child €7/6/3.50; open 10am-7pm daily) is devoted to that most Finnish of industries – forestry. It's actually quite good in an educational sort of way, with displays not only about the industry and resource that has provided Finns with heat, power and export income for many years, but also on the natural forests and their habitats. The building itself is an interesting timber structure with the main display hall designed to represent the trunk of a tree.

Places to Stay & Eat Next to the Kesämaa Water Park and near Retretti, **Punkaharjun Lomakeskus Camping** (☎ 739 611; W www.lomaliitto.fi/punkaharju; tent sites €15.10, 2-/4-person cabins €33.50/52, selfcontained cottages from €113; open yearround) is one of the largest such complexes in Finland. It has more than 150 lakeside cottages and is very crowded in summer.

Gasthaus Punkaharju (☎ 473 123; e naar anlahti@kolumbus.fi; Palomäentie 18; singles/ doubles €45/65), is in the village about 2km from the bus station. You can use the sauna and swimming pool for an additional fee. The owners also run a quiet farm estate **Naaranlahti**, with 12 well-equipped rooms at the same price. This is a place where you can relax and take part in rural activities, including canoeing, fishing or gathering berries in the woods. It's about 15km from Punkaharju but transport is provided from the guesthouse.

Valtionhotelli (☎ 739 611, fax 441 784; singles/doubles €73/96; open year-round), on the ridge just west of the Lusto museum, is a romantic hotel dating from 1845, and the first tourist hotel in Finland. As well as rooms in the main house, there are two villas built for the wife of the tsar, and there's a fine restaurant attached. Rates are lower in winter.

For a cheap meal in the village, try the **Punkero Baari** at the bus station. There are relatively pricey **cafés** at both Retretti and Lusto, mainly catering to the mid-afternoon sightseers.

Ravintola Finlandia (☎ 644 255; Finlandiantie 98; lunch buffet €12), a few hundred metres from Lusto, is in a beautiful house built in 1914 and surrounded by forest. The superb lunch buffet is served from 11am to 6pm daily in summer.

Getting There & Away All trains between Parikkala and Savonlinna stop in the village of Punkaharju, as well as the Lusto and Retretti train stations. There are also regular buses to/from Savonlinna (€5, 20 minutes). In summer there is a ferry service from Savonlinna; see the Savonlinna Getting There & Away section for more information.

Kerimäki
☎ 015 • pop 6500

Kerimäki is a small and very unassuming village, yet it's dominated by the world's largest wooden church. The information booth opposite the church entrance sells souvenirs, and the staff are more than happy to reel off some historical facts.

The nearby protected island of **Hytermä** celebrates one of the weirdest of human achievements: it has a monument to RomuHeikki (Junk Heikki), a man who built large structures with millstones. The island is also quite beautiful, and it's easily visited by hiring a rowing boat (€10 for around three to four hours) through the tourist office (☎ 541 423) across from the church.

There are hourly buses along route 71 between Savonlinna and Kerimäki.

Places to Stay & Eat An attractive old wooden house not far from the church, **Gasthaus Kerihovi** (☎ 541 225; Puruvedentie 28; singles/doubles €34/54) has spotless, comfortable rooms each with shared bathroom. There's a restaurant-bar on site and breakfast and a sauna is included in the room rate.

Korkeamäki Hostel (☎ 442 186, 050-215 817; Ruokolahdentie 545; singles/doubles €25/34, 3-/4-/5-bed rooms €40/50/57; open June–late Aug), 8km south of Kerimäki village on the road to Punkaharju, is a very friendly HI-affiliated farmhouse and cottages run by a Savonian family. This road is not well served by public transport (two buses a day to Savonlinna), but if you have a car, this is an excellent option for cheap accommodation during the Opera Festival.

There are a couple of pleasant cafés in Kerimäki. **Katriania** (☎ 541 102; Puruvedentie 63) is a good spot for a Finnish buffet lunch, while **Kahvila Kaivopirtti** (Halvantie 1) has a sunny terrace facing the church.

Kerimäki Church

Finland has plenty of notable churches, but few are as visually striking as Kerimäki's – the largest wooden church in the world. Built in 1847, it was designed to seat more than 3000 people and to accommodate 5000 churchgoers if all standing room was used.

The oversized church was no mistake, but was deliberately inflated from original plans by overexcited locals. At the time the church was built, Kerimäki's population was around 12,000, and the parish reverend felt that half of the residents should be attending church on any given Sunday. Worshippers would visit the church from all around the region, crossing the lake in their *kirkkovene* (church longboats).

As stunning as the yellow-and-white church appears from the outside (it dominates tiny Kerimäki), the scale doesn't become apparent until you step inside and survey the massive interior – the height of the nave is 27m. You soon realise it would have been impossible to heat this building. It originally had eight stoves inside (now there are four) but it still wasn't enough and a smaller, 300-seat winter chapel had to be built at the rear. The main church is still used for services in summer, but the last time it was full was in 1972 when a charity concert was held here.

The church (☎ 578 9111) is open 10am to 4pm mid-May to late August (later in June and July). There's an information and gift shop in the separate bell tower in front of the church, and for €2 you can climb the tower for a better view.

Linnansaari National Park

☎ 015

This scenic park consists of Lake Haukivesi and 130 uninhabited larger islands and hundreds more smaller ones; the main activity centres around the largest island, Linnansaari, which has several short hiking trails. Lurking in the park's waters is a tiny population of the nearly extinct Saimaa ringed seal; in 1999 there were 50 known seals in the park, although there are around 200 in Lake Saimaa further south. Rare birds, including osprey, can also be seen and heard in the park.

In summer, there's a regular daily boat service to Linnansaari from Mustalahti quay, 3km from Rantasalmi village. However, the best way to see the park is to pack camping gear and food, rent a rowing boat in Rantasalmi or Oravi (on the eastern shore of the lake) and spend a few days exploring. Boats, kayaks and canoes can be hired from **Saimaan Erapalvelu Oravi Oy** (☎ 050-563 3257, Oravi) or **Saimaan Eraelamys** (☎ 64303; Rantasalmi).

Lakeland Centre (☎ 0205-645 916; open 10am-6pm daily June-Aug, 10am-4pm Tues-Fri, 10am-2pm Sat Feb-May & Sept-Nov) in Rantasalmi acts as a visitor information centre for the park and also has environmental displays.

On the island you can stay at the established **camping areas** for free, or there's a private **camping ground** (☎ 0500-275 458) with huts, tent sites and sauna. A canteen at Sammakkoniemi harbour sells provisions.

Several smaller islands also have designated camping sites.

Getting There & Away The main entrance to Linnansaari National Park is Mustalahti quay, but there is no bus stop, only boat connections. There is a regular boat service to the island of Linnansaari from Mustalahti quay in Rantasalmi and from Oravi.

There are regular buses to Oravi and Rantasalmi leaving from Savonlinna. From Rantasalmi, it's an extra 3km to Mustalahti quay – hitch, walk or catch a taxi. The Savonlinna–Kuopio ferry MS *Puijo* stops at Oravi.

Kolovesi National Park

This fine national park to the northeast of Linnansaari was founded in 1990 and covers several islands featuring unusually well-preserved pine forests. There are high hills, rocky cliffs and caves, and even prehistoric rock paintings dating back 5000 years. The rare Saimaa marble seals live in the park's waters (there are about 20 here).

Motor-powered boats are prohibited in the park. A rowing boat is practically the only way to see the fantastic scenery, and groups get to travel in an old *kirkkovene* or 'church longboat' with up to 10 pairs of oars. A guide is an unavoidable expense if you want to find the best places. There are also several restricted areas within the park, and access to the islands is prohibited during winter. Check details at the small **information cabin** (☎ 015-479 040) in the village of Enonkoski.

There are two marked **walking trails** in the park. The 3.3km Nahkiaissalo nature trail is in the south of the park and accessible without a boat. There's a 3.9km nature trail on the northern island of Mantysalo.

Kolovesi Retkeily (☎ 673 628) is the main tour operator for the park. It also rents boats and canoes, as well as cottages in the park area. To get to the Kolovesi office, drive north from Savonlinna towards Heinävesi on road No 471 and look out for the sign 'Kolovesi Retkeily' after Enonkoski village. Boats can also be hired at the Neste petrol station in Enonkoski.

Inside the national park there are three **camping grounds**, one at Lohilahti near the southern access road No 471; one at Lapinniemi; and the other on the island of Pitkäsaari.

Kievari Enonhovi (☎ 479 431, fax 479 531; Urheilukentantie 1; beds from €25) is a hotel-restaurant and HI-affiliated hostel in Enonkoski village, close to the national park.

Sulkava
☎ 015 • pop 3800

Scenic, sleepy Sulkava, 39km from Savonlinna, is known among Finns for its rowing-boat competitions (which some locals say is as much about the after-race partying as the rowing itself). It's the finishing point for the two-day Oravareitti canoe route leaving from Juva.

The **Sulkava Rowing Race** attracts big crowds in early July. Competitors row around the island of Partalansaari over a 65km (one-day) course, or 75km (two-day) course, then get thoroughly hammered. There's also an 'armada race' of 12m boats.

The protected **Vilkaharju Ridge**, along road No 438, has two *luontopolku* (nature trails), 3km and 3.6km long, marked by yellow ribbons. On Lake Pöllälampi you can rent boats and purchase fishing permits to fish for salmon.

The prehistoric **Linnavuori Fortress Ruins** is probably the most interesting sight in the Sulkava area. It's well signposted. The view from the top is of idyllic Lakeland scenery and old fortifications.

Vilkaharju Camping (☎ 471 223; tent sites €12, cottages €30-47), in the Vilkaharju area 7km from the village, is on a scenic headland across a pedestrian bridge (road access is possible). **Homeyard Camping** (☎ 471 444; Urheilukentantie 5), closer to the centre of the village, is a great little place to stay with tent sites, four-bed rooms and nature trails.

Partalansaaren Lomakoti (☎ 478 850; Hirviniementie 5; dorm beds €14) is an HI-affiliated hostel not far from the Sarsuinmäki WWII battery site. Facilities include a sauna, meals, and bicycles and boats for hire.

Juva
☎ 015 • pop 7800

The village of Juva, 60km west of Savonlinna and on the highway midway between Mikkeli and Varkaus, is mainly of interest to travellers as the starting point for the two-day Oravareitti canoeing trip. While you're here (or if you're passing through), check out the bizarre **Puutaitonäyttely** (adult/student €7/3.50; open 10am-6pm daily June-Sept) just off the highway junction. It's an exhibition space of more than 500 wooden sculptures made by 40 artists, many using chainsaws. It's Finland timber industry turned fine art. There are quite a few sculptures out front if you want to avoid the steep admission.

The village centre is along the main street, Juvantie, where you'll find plenty of services and the **tourist office** (☎ 755 1224; Juvantie 13) in the town hall building.

There's an interesting combined museum in the imposing Partala manor area. **Juva Museum & Carelian Museum** (☎ 755 1297; Huttulantie 1; adult/child €2/1; open 11am-5pm Tues-Sun in summer) displays local history, and items from Soviet-occupied Karelia.

Places to Stay Just off the main road, **Juva Camping** (☎ 451 930; w www.juva camping.com; Hotellitie 68; tent sites €11, cabins for 2 people from €27, for 4 €35.50; open early June–late Aug) is right beside Jukajärvi. You can rent rowing boats and canoes here.

Hotelli Juva (☎ 755 0100; Hotellitie 3; singles/doubles €50/70) is a flash hotel and restaurant complex near the highway junction (at the turn-off to Juva Camping).

There are dozens of B&Bs in this area – contact the Juva or Mikkeli tourist offices for information.

Canoeing the Squirrel Route

The scenic 52km Juva to Sulkava canoeing route, known as Oravareitti ('squirrel') route, is a high-light of this area and the perfect way for travellers to experience the lake region. Starting on the lake Jujajärvi (at Juva Camping; see Places to Stay), it traverses lakes, rivers and rapids on the way to Sulkava. Only one section of rapids is impassable – at Kuhakoski rapids, where canoes must be carried 50m past a broken dam. However, they should be carried at two other points along the way. Otherwise the rapids are relatively simple, though the water level drops 25m between Juva and Sulkava.

Juva Camping provides everything you need: it rents two-person Canadian canoes (€25 per day) or single kayaks (€17), gives you a waterproof map, and can arrange to pick you up (or just the canoe) at Sulkava for an additional fee. The route is signposted with information boards and there are two designated rest stops with fireplaces and toilets, as well as a midway camping area. It's also possible to start or break the route at Toivo, where there's a **hostel** (☎ 015-459 622).

It's 8km from the camping ground across the lake to the first river section, Polvijoki. Along here you must carry your canoe to the right of the dam. Passing through the small lakes, Riemio and Souru, you come to the first rapids, the gentle 200m Voikoski, which is followed by the first rest area to the left of a small island. Continue along the canal, carrying the canoe across the road at the end, before negotiating the Karijoki River.

There's a camping ground called **Oravanpesat** on the 2km long Lake Kaitijärvi with tent sites and cot-tages. Next comes a series of rapids including Kissakoski and the strong currents of the Kyrsyanjoki River. You continue through the Rasakanjoki and Tikanjoki Rivers before coming to the large lake Halmejärvi, at the end of which is another resting place. The route continues on the western shore of Lohnajärvi to the Lohnankoski rapids, at the end of which the canoes must be carried past the broken concrete dam. From here it's a leisurely paddle down the Kuhajärvi lake, past a final set of rapids and into Sulkava, where you pull in at the Kulkemus Boat Centre. There's a camping ground and a café here.

MIKKELI & AROUND

☎ 015

Mikkeli is a sizeable provincial town on Lake Saimaa and an important transport hub for eastern Lakeland, but it's a dull, modern centre with little to attract travellers. Mikkeli was the headquarters of the Finnish army during WWII, and it was from here that the great military leader CGE Mannerheim directed the Winter War campaign against the Soviets. Museums relating to those years are the main sights in town.

For information on local attractions contact the Mikkeli **tourist office** (☎ 194 3900; *Porrassalmenkatu 15; open 9am-5pm Mon, 9am-4.30pm Tues-Fri*), near the kauppatori.

Päämajamuseo (*Headquarters Museum;* ☎ 194 2427; *Päämajamkuja 1-3; adult/child €4/free*) was the army's command centre during the war; and **Jalkaväkimuseo** (*Infantry Museum;* ☎ 369 666; *Jaarkarinkatu 6-8; adult/child €3.50/1.50*) is one of the largest military museums in Finland.

The area around Mikkeli is excellent for **freshwater fishing** – its many lakes teem with perch, salmon and trout, and ice-fishing

is popular in winter. The tourist office can help with information, fishing permits, guides and equipment rental.

Mikkeli Music Festival (Ⓦ *www.mikkelimusic.net*), held here in late June/early July, is a week-long classical music event featuring top Finnish and Russian conductors.

Ristiina

☎ 015

Ristiina, 18km south of Mikkeli, is one of the region's historic villages, founded by Count Per Brahe in 1649 and named after Kristina, his wife (subsequently the queen of Sweden). Little remains of the village's glorious past, though there are several places that reflect Per's aspirations.

The **tourist office** (☎ 661 401; *Brahentie 53; open 10am-6pm Mon-Fri, 10am-2pm Sat & Sun, shorter hours in winter*), 2km from the main road, can provide a map, and you can rent bicycles from Gasthaus Brahe nearby.

There's a distance between the main road and Ristiina's principal attraction, the castle ruins, but most shops and places to stay and eat are on the main street, Brahentie.

THE LAKELAND

Brahelinna is the castle that was built by Per Brahe; its ruin is on a hill 2km from the village. The castle's high crumbling walls and the surrounding forest make for lovely walking. A sign saying 'Dunckerin kivi' points to a stone that was erected to honour a local, Mr Duncker, who fought and died during the 1809 battles against Russia.

The **rock paintings** of Astuvansalmi (Astuvansalmen Kalliomaalaukset), estimated to be 3000 to 4000 years old, are some of the finest prehistoric rock paintings in Finland. They are on a steep rock cliff, 20km east of Ristiina village, reached by a walking track from the road. You'll need a vehicle or bicycle to get there.

Close to the rock paintings, the open-air **Pien-Toijolan Talomuseo** (☎ *416 103; open 10am-4pm Thur-Sun*) is an estate dating from 1672, and consists of over 20 old houses.

Places to Stay & Eat

Visulahti Camping (☎ *18281; Visuahdenkatu 1; tent sites €13.50, cabins €50-140; open late May–end Aug*), next to the Visulahti amusement park, is the closest camping ground to Mikkeli. It's about 5km east of the town centre and has lakeside tent sites and a wide range of cabins.

There are no HI hostels in Mikkeli itself, but the summer hotel **Metsätähti** (☎ *173 777; Metsäkouluntie 10; dorm beds from €15*) fits the bill for cheap accommodation.

Gasthaus Brahentie (☎ *661 078; Brahentie 54; beds from €12; open year-round*) is affiliated with HI and is the only place to stay in Ristiina itself. It's on the main street about 100m from the tourist office. It also has a decent restaurant and provides some local nightlife. The rooms are in a separate building, previously used as a school dormitory. There are bicycles, boats and canoes to rent.

Löydön Kartano (☎ *664 101; Kartanontie 71; dorm beds €13.50-22*), 5km north of Ristiina near the öytö, is a pleasant year-round HI-affiliated hostel in an old manor house. There's a bus stop at Kartanontie, the gravel road that takes you to the hostel.

Getting There & Away

Mikkeli is a transport hub between Helsinki and eastern Lakeland or Kuopio to the north, so plenty of buses pass through in all directions. The bus station is on the northern side of the kauppatori.

There are up to five trains daily from Helsinki and a similar number of connections from towns in the north. From other directions, change at Pieksämäki or Kouvola.

There are lake cruises between Mikkeli and Ristiina in summer; the Mikkeli tourist office has schedule and fare information.

VARKAUS
☎ 017 • pop 24,000

The town of Varkaus is a small transport hub in a decent location, surrounded by water and spread over several islands cut by canals. It's this location, however, that led to the establishment of the timber and pulp industry and the smoke-belching factories that blight the town. Much of the population works for the local paper and pulp industries.

The **tourist office** (☎ *551 555; Kauppatori 6; open 9am-4.30pm Mon-Fri*) is in the town centre near the market square.

If you have a vehicle, it's well worth driving the 2km from the town centre to **Mekaanisen Musiikin Museo** (Museum of Mechanical Music; ☎ *558 0643; Pelimanninkatu 8; adult/child €10/5; open Tues-Sun early Mar–mid-Dec*). A Finnish-German couple runs this delightful collection of 250 unusual musical instruments, and admission includes an eccentric tour of the house and its lovingly renovated mechanical instruments from the USA and Europe.

East of the town centre is the **Taipale canal area**. The new canal was built by Russians, and the old canal area includes **Keskuskanavamuseo** (admission €1.50), a café and canal museum with information on the history and use of Finnish canals. The new canal is worth a look when logs are floated through. There are canal cruises on weekends in summer.

Places to Stay & Eat

Camping Taipale (☎ *552 6644; Leiritie; tent sites per person/family €10/16, cottages €42-96; open May–mid-Aug*), on the lake and near the canal, is a very family-oriented camping ground with the usual facilities.

The HI **Varkauden Retkeilymaja** (☎ *579 5700; Kuparisepänkatu 5; apartments per person €15-22; open June–mid-Aug*) is a cheap option for cyclists or backpackers who get stuck in Varkaus. It's a student apartment building with self-contained rooms.

Hotel Oscar (☎ *579 011, fax 579 0500; Kauppatori 4; singles/doubles €121/148,* *doubles weekends & July €83)* is a flash business hotel on the market square next to the tourist office. There are rooms in the older wing for €66/93, or €58/68 in July.

Kauppakatu near the train station is a street with several cheap eateries, such as **Herkkupizza** and **Kahvila Aaretti**. There's also a good **restaurant** at Hotel Oscar.

One of the best places to dine out in Varkaus is a little way out of town next to the Museum of Mechanical Music. **Restaurant Zeppelin** (☎ 558 0644; *Pelimanninkatu 8; mains €14-20; open 11am-late Tues-Sat)* is a stylish German-run restaurant with an appealing continental menu.

Getting There & Away
There are daily flights from Helsinki to Varkaus. Keskusliikenneasema is the central station, which includes train and bus terminals. Trains between Joensuu and Turku stop in Varkaus.

HEINÄVESI & AROUND
☎ 017 • pop 4500
The village of Heinävesi lies amid hilly country some way off the main Lakeland routes, but some of the most scenic lake routes in Finland pass through here and canals provide a means of local transport.

The village itself is not at all quaint but there's a huge wooden **church** on a hill at the end of Kirkkokatu. It was built in 1890, seats 2000 people, and offers good lake views over Kermajärvi from the tower. Nearby is the local **museum** and a **handicrafts centre**.

The main **activities** in the Heinävesi region are fishing, walking, cruising on the lakes and canals and, in winter, Nordic skiing. The **tourist office** (☎ 578 1273; ⓦ *www .heinavesi.fi; Kermanrannantie 7; open 9am-3.45pm Mon-Fri)*, in the town hall building, can provide copious information about sights and activities in the region.

On the northern side of Kermajärvi, 28km by road from Heinävesi, **Karvio village** has scenic rapids that are good for fishing, and the canal serves as a jetty for lake ferries. This is a stopover for the Savonlinna–Kuopio ferry and a jumping-off point for the Valamo Monastery and Lintula Convent.

Karvio is central enough to serve as a base for covering the northern side of Heinävesi. You can rent bicycles and rowing boats here, and obtain fishing permits.

Places to Stay
Viitalahti Camping (☎ 568 710; *Lomakylantie 10; tent sites €9, cabins €20-32; open June-Sept)*, on the western side of Kermajärvi, is on the road about halfway between Heinävesi and Karvio.

Karvio Camping (☎ 563 603; ⓦ *www.loma karvio.fi; Takunlahdentie 2; tent sites €11.50-13, cottages €22-60; open May–mid-Sept)* is well located near the Karvio rapids. **Uittotupa** (☎ 563 603; *Uitontie 1; 4–6-person cabins €60-75)* is across the road, and part of Karvio Camping. There's a café here renowned for its home-made bread, which can be eaten at lunch or bought by the loaf.

Hotel Heinävesi (☎ 562 411; *Askeltie 2; singles/doubles €55/75)*, in the village centre opposite the bus terminal, has clean and comfortable rooms plus an excellent breakfast. There's a pub and restaurant here, which makes it the social heart of town.

At Karvio, **Karvio Kievari** (☎ 563 504; *Lepikkomaentie 3A; doubles €30-50)* is a good-value, intimate manor house. There are 10 beds and rooms have shared facilities. Breakfast is included.

Getting There & Around
Being off the main roads, transport connections to Heinävesi are bad – even worse in summer when school is out. There are sporadic departures for villages around the lake, five a day to/from Varkaus (€6.20, 40 minutes), one to Kuopio (€12.40, two hours) and two a week to Savonlinna (€11.40, 1½ hours). There are also direct buses from Helsinki via Varkaus. For Valamo Monastery you need to get to Karvio and take another bus from there. The unmanned Heinävesi train station is 5km south of the village. Bus and train tickets must be purchased on board.

In summer, the passenger ferry MS *Puijo* from Kuopio or Savonlinna calls at the Heinävesi jetty, just below the village. The southbound ferry (heading to Savonlinna) arrives at 2.20pm Tuesday, Thursday and Saturday, and the northbound ferry arrives at 4pm Monday, Wednesday and Friday. They pass through Karvio canal 40 minutes before or after. There are also ferries to Karvio.

A boat and/or bicycle are ideal ways to explore this region. Bikes can be hired at the Heinävesi harbour, and boats and canoes can be hired at the Karvio or Viisalahti camping grounds.

THE LAKELAND

VALAMO ORTHODOX MONASTERY

The Valamo monastery (☎ 017-570 111, fax 570 1510; W www.valamo.fi; Valamontie 42, 79850 Uusi-Valamo) – Finland's only Orthodox monastery – is one of Savo's most popular attractions. Its history goes back 800 years to the Karelian island of Valamo on Lake Lagoda.

The original Valamo Monastery was annexed by the Red Army during WWII. Most of its treasures were brought to Finland, and some of them remain here (others are in Kuopio).

The Valamo Monastery has grown considerably over the last several decades, partly because of increased tourism, which is the monastery's main source of income. It's now quite a commercialised place, with crowds of summer tourists flocking to buy souvenir beeswax candles, icons and CDs at the Tuohus gift shop.

The two churches at the monastery contain a number of priceless icons. The new church was finished in 1977, while the old one was built in 1940. Down at the riverside, the small *tsasouna* (chapel) of St Nicholas, is also worth a look. The **museum**, inside the cultural centre is open 10am to 5pm (noon to 5pm Sunday) from mid-June to mid-August, and with the guided tour at other times of year.

Guided tours of the monastery are conducted regularly (€3.50), although for tours in English you may have to contact the monastery in advance for times. Services are open to the public and are given at 6am and 6pm Monday to Friday, 9am and 6pm Sunday and also at 1pm from June to August.

Like any good monks, the clergy at Valamo produce their own **wine** using berries such as crowberries, raspberries, strawberries and blackcurrants. You can purchase bottles (around €9) at the wine shop in the reception building.

Taking photos in the churches, or of the monks, is forbidden without permission, and shorts and singlet tops should not be worn in the monastery complex.

A good way to appreciate the monastery is to stay overnight. You can stay in the simple **Valamo Guesthouse** (2–5-bed rooms per person €20, singles €22,) or the more comfortable **Valamo Hotel** (singles/doubles €32/47).

Breakfast is included and there's a sauna available to hotel guests.

Also in the complex is **Trapesa**, the monastery café-restaurant. There's a good lunch and dinner buffet for €9.50, a Russian-style 'high tea' in the evenings (€6, bookings required) and the usual sandwiches, cakes, coffee and monastery wine.

See Getting There & Away under Lintula Orthodox Convent for transport information.

LINTULA ORTHODOX CONVENT

The only Orthodox convent in Finland, **Lintula** (☎ 017-563 106, open 9am-6pm daily June–late Aug, other times by arrangement) is much quieter than the popular Valamo monastery. It's a serene contrast that is well worth the short detour.

Lintula was founded in Karelia in 1895 and transferred during WWII to Savo and then Häme. The nuns founded a convent at the present location in 1946. A souvenir shop on the premises sells wool and candles manufactured at the convent, and there's a pleasant coffee shop open 10am to 6pm.

Lintulan Vierasmaja (☎ 017-563 225; singles/doubles €18/28) is a small red house at the back of the convent. There are simple but clean rooms, with separate bathroom, and it's open to men and women.

Getting There & Away

There are buses direct to Valamo from Joensuu, Mikkeli and even Helsinki, but the services aren't frequent. From Heinävesi you need to change at Karvio. For Lintula, daily buses from Kuopio stop in the nearby village of Palokki, but if you're coming from the south, the nearest bus stop is on the highway 9km away.

The most pleasant way to get to either place in summer is on a **Monastery Cruise** from Kuopio. The cruise uses a combination of the regular Kuopio–Savonlinna ferry and car or bus transport. The ferry departs from Kuopio at 9.30am Tuesday, Thursday and Saturday, then there's car transport from Palokki to Lintula and Valamo, then a bus back to Kuopio. On Monday, Wednesday and Friday, transport is reversed with a bus to Valamo and a ferry back from Palokki. The cost is €51/25 per adult/child.

There are also canal cruises on the MS *Sergei* (☎ 570 111; €8-15) from Valamo to Palokki and on Joujärvi lake.

Central Lakeland

JYVÄSKYLÄ
☎ 014 • pop 75,300

Jyväskylä (pronounced **yuh**-vah-skuh-lah), the bustling provincial capital of central Lakeland, is known among architecture lovers for its Alvar Aalto buildings, particularly the university campus. It was founded in 1837 and its reputation as a nationalistic town goes back to the earliest days, when the first Finnish-language schools were established here. In 1966 the University of Jyväskylä was inaugurated, and Jyväskylä was to become renowned for its architecture, though this could come as a surprise to the average traveller who might be more inclined to think that the town consists of a cluster of drab cement boxes crowded around a lake.

Although a little light-on for interesting attractions, Jyväskylä's youthful student population gives it plenty of energy. It's also popular as a winter sports centre with some frightening ski jumps near town, and you can get here in style by lake ferry from Lahti.

Information

The **tourist office** (☎ 624 903; ☒ www
.jyvaskyla.fi; Asemakatu 6; open 9am-6pm
Mon-Fri, 10am-3pm Sat & Sun June–late Aug,
9am-5pm Mon-Fri, 10am-3pm Sat rest of the
year) publishes an excellent free guide to events and activities in the region, rents bicycles and sells fishing permits.

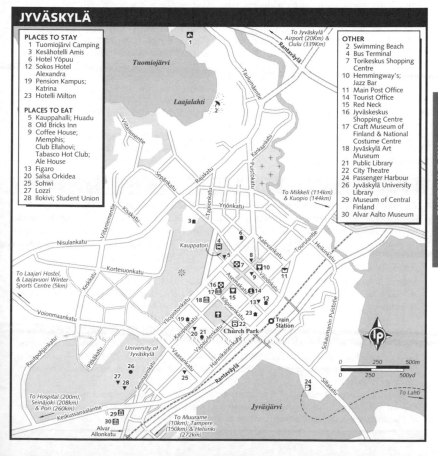

JYVÄSKYLÄ

PLACES TO STAY
1 Tuomiojärvi Camping
3 Kesähotelli Amis
6 Hotel Yöpuu
12 Sokos Hotel Alexandra
19 Pension Kampus; Katrina
23 Hotelli Milton

PLACES TO EAT
5 Kauppahalli; Huadu
8 Old Bricks Inn
9 Coffee House; Memphis; Club Ellahovi; Tabasco Hot Club; Ale House
13 Figaro
20 Salsa Orkidea
25 Sohwi
27 Lozzi
28 Ilokivi; Student Union

OTHER
2 Swimming Beach
4 Bus Terminal
7 Torikeskus Shopping Centre
10 Hemmingway's; Jazz Bar
11 Main Post Office
14 Tourist Office
15 Red Neck
16 Jyväskeskus Shopping Centre
17 Craft Museum of Finland & National Costume Centre
18 Jyväskylä Art Museum
21 Public Library
22 City Theatre
24 Passenger Harbour
26 Jyväskylä University Library
29 Museum of Central Finland
30 Alvar Aalto Museum

THE LAKELAND

The **Jyväskylä Card**, as with similar cards in Helsinki and Turku, offers admission to most attractions in the town, includes travel on local transport, and discounts on various goods and services including restaurants and sporting activities, over a specified period. The card costs €10/4 per adult/child for 24 hours, €15/6 for 48 hours. It's available from the tourist office.

The **main post office** *(Vapaudenkatu 60)* is a few blocks past the church park. The **public library** *(Vapaudenkatu 39-41; open 11am-8pm Mon-Fri, 11am-3pm Sat)* has several Internet terminals on the 3rd floor, and there's a free terminal at the tourist office.

Architecture

At times Jyväskylä is crawling with architecture buffs, curiously pointing wide-angled lenses at every Alvar Aalto building. The list includes the university's main building and the **theatre** *(Vapaudenkatu 36)*. On the corner of Kauppakatu and Väinönkatu is the old Workers' Club building, designed by Alvar Aalto in 1925. It now houses restaurants and nightclubs. If you're into architecture, the best time to visit Jyväskylä is Tuesday to Friday, as many buildings are closed on weekends and the Aalto Museum is closed on Monday. You can pick up a brochure with details in English on Aalto-designed buildings at the Alvar Aalto Museum.

Museums

Jyväskylä has four main museums. They can all be visited free with the Jyväskylä Card, although several are free on Friday anyway. If you're serious about visiting museum here, avoid Monday when most are closed.

Alvar Aalto Museum Without a doubt Alvar Aalto is Finland's most famous architect. The **museum** *(☎ 624 809; Alvar Allonkatu 7; adult/student €6/2; open 11am-6pm Tues-Sun)*, in a building designed by the man himself, chronicles the life, work and philosophy of Aalto and contains models and photographic exhibits, as well as Aalto-designed furniture. Indeed, it shows as much about his interior design as exterior. Even for those totally uninterested in architecture the museum is engaging and worth a visit.

Keski-Suomen Museo The Museum of Central Finland *(☎ 624 930; Alvar Allonkatu 7; adult/child €4/free; open 11am-6pm Tues-Sun)*, adjacent to the Alvar Aalto Museum, has artefacts and displays from various parts of the province, including an exhibition on the history of Jyväskylä. The building was designed by Aalto and finished in 1961.

Jyväskylän Taidemuseo Opened in 1998, the Jyväskylä Art Museum *(☎ 626 855; Kauppakatu 23; adult/child €5/free; open*

Alvar Aalto – Architect, Designer, Sculptor

The churches, town halls, museums and concert halls designed by Alvar Aalto can be seen across Finland from Helsinki to Rovaniemi. Aalto's buildings tread the line between the unadorned functionalism of the International Style (so-called because its designs spoke the universal language of the machine) and the people and materials orientation of the Organic Style. His designs emphasise the qualities of wood, brick and glass, the role of the building and its relationship to the people using it.

Aalto was born in 1898 just outside Seinäjoki in the town of Kuortane. He practised in central Finland, Turku and Helsinki until gaining an international reputation for his pavilions at the World Fairs of 1937 (Paris) and 1939 (New York). He was professor of architecture at the Massachusetts Institute of Technology from 1945 to 1949 and president of the Academy of Finland from 1963 to 1968.

His most famous work is probably Helsinki's Finlandia Hall (1962–71), but the House of Culture (1952–58), with its convex wall of wedge-shaped bricks, and the Helsinki University of Technology in Espoo (1953–66) are also fine examples of his work. Jyväskylä is chock-a-block with Aalto-designed buildings including the Workers' Club (1952) and the Alvar Aalto Museum (1971–73). A comparison of the Civic Centre in Seinäjoki with the Church of the Three Crosses (1955–58) in Imatra highlights the range of Aalto's work.

Aalto also achieved a reputation as an abstract painter, sculptor and furniture designer. In 1925 he married Aino Marsio, with whom he collaborated on Artek furniture designs. Their work on bending and laminating wood revolutionised furniture design. Marsio died in 1949 and Aalto in 1976.

11am-6pm Tues-Sun) houses the modern art and sculpture collection of Ester and Salo Sihtola. There are Finnish and international works on display, with changing exhibitions.

Suomen Käsityön Museo The permanent collection at the Craft Museum of Finland & National Costume Centre (☎ 624 946; Kauppakatu 25; adult/child €5.50/free; open 11am-6pm Tues-Sun) is all about Finnish handicrafts and their history. There are also temporary displays, and a room with materials for children to play with. The costume centre displays regional dress from around Finland. There is a small permanent collection plus temporary exhibitions.

Activities

Skiing Northwest of the city centre, **Laajavuori Winter Sports Centre** (☎ 624 885; w www.laajavuori.com; Laajavuorentie) has five modestly sloped ski runs, 65km of cross country trails (of which 15km is illuminated) and a number of very scary ski jumps (for which it is famous). There is a good ski area for children and the resort is popular with families.

Organised Tours

Lake Cruises Jyväskylä is a popular cruise centre in summer because of the Keitele canal route north of town. This runs through some impressive canals constructed by Russians in the early 1990s. You can return to Jyväskylä the same day for €35, or travel one way to Suolahti for €23.50. The one-way trip to Suolahti takes five hours.

Short cruises on northern Lake Päijänne are also available from early June to early August, with daily departures. Some of these are evening cruises with dinner and dancing. Try to catch the SS *Suomi*, one of the oldest steamers still plying the Finnish lakes, which goes at 3pm Tuesday to Friday (adult/child €12/6, three hours).

Tickets can be purchased at the **Jyväskylä passenger harbour** (☎ 218 024; Siltakatu 4). Take bus No 18, 19 or 20 from the centre.

For information about the Jyväskylä to Lahti route, see the Getting There & Away section.

Special Events

In early July, the **Jyväskylä Arts Festival** has concerts, exhibitions, theatre and dance.

Places to Stay

Tuomiojärvi Camping (☎ 624 896; Taulumäentie 47; tent sites €14-16, cottages €38-50; open June-Aug), a pleasant place 2km north of town, has several four-bed cottages scattered in the lakeside woods. Take bus No 8 from the centre.

Laajari (☎ 624 885; Laajavuorentie 15; dorm beds from €17-21, singles/doubles €28/42; open year-round) is an HI hostel in the Laajavuori ski-centre complex.

More central is the 3rd-floor **Pension Kampus** (☎ 338 1400; e pensionkampus@kolumbus.fi; Kauppakatu 11; singles/doubles €52/70, weekends & summer €43/60). It has just eight spotless rooms, and guests can use the kitchen.

Kesähotelli Amis (☎ 443 0100, fax 443 0121; Sepänkatu 3; singles/doubles/triples €42/58/66; open June–mid-Aug), on a hill behind the bus terminal, offers plain but tidy rooms with private facilities.

Hotelli Milton (☎ 337 7900, fax 631 927; Hannikaisenkatu 27-29; singles/doubles from €54/71) is a family-run hotel opposite the train station.

Hotel Yöpuu (☎ 333 900, fax 620 588; Yliopistonkatu 23; singles/doubles from €77/114, in summer €61/71, weekends €65/81) is a superb old-world hotel with two fine restaurants and plenty of style. There are 26 rooms, all individually decorated.

Sokos Hotel Alexandra (☎ 651 211, fax 651 200; Hannikaisenkatu 35; singles/doubles €65/93, weekends & summer €52/74), directly across from the train station, is a reasonably priced business hotel with plenty of facilities and breakfast included.

Places to Eat

The cheapest meals in town are available at university cafés. The building housing **Lozzi** was designed by Alvar Aalto. Meals, available in summer, are excellent value. **Ilokivi** in the Student Union building has meals from €5. The modern **kauppahalli** (covered market) is a good place to pick up fresh produce and snacks. Another good spot for fast food is **Rodin**, a cheap pizza and kebab place opposite the train station.

Katrina (mains €7-8.50) is a cute little vegetarian café next to Pension Kampus, with veggie pasta, curries and ratatouille.

The pedestrian Kauppakatu has plenty of good cafés. The open-fronted **Coffee House** has a big range of filled rolls, croissants and bagels, and pretty good coffee. Next door, **Memphis** (Kauppakatu 30; lunch €7-11) offers everything from spring rolls and curry to pasta and steak.

Huadu (Yliopistonkatu 15; lunch from €6), above the kauppahalli, is a good place for Chinese food. It offers filling lunch specials from 11am to 3pm Monday to Friday. For big servings of pasta, salads, tortilla and kebabs, it's hard to beat **Salsa Orkidea** (☎ 611 557; Kauppakatu 10; mains €6-12). There's a €6 lunch buffet and most mains are under €10.

Old Bricks Inn (☎ 616 233; Kauppakatu 57; meals €5-13.50) ranks as one of the best places to eat in town with filling meals and a big range of international beers.

Sohwi (☎ 615 564; Vaasankatu 21; meals €6.50-14), between the town centre and the university, is a great little café-bar with tapas (€2 to €3), pizza and internationally-inspired light meals (felafel, curry, pastas etc).

Figaro (Asemakatu 4; mains €10-29) is an intimate little Finnish-Italian restaurant with a broad menu. There are several vegetarian options, as well as pasta and fish from €10 to €15, and more expensive à la carte dishes.

Entertainment

Jyväskylä has the sort of animated nightlife you only find in a busy university town, and the compact nature of the centre emphasises this. Kauppakatu, the main pedestrian strip, is a great place for bar-hopping, and in summer terraces spill out along here.

Good pubs in this vicinity include the **Old Bricks Inn**, the **Ale House**, and **Hemingway's**, with a popular summer terrace. **Jazz Bar** (Kauppakatu 32) is the place for relaxing live music, with regular jazz slots and jam sessions during the week.

Red Neck (Asemakatu 7) has Finnish music, a heavy farming motif, and happy hour from 3pm to 9pm daily.

Sohwi (see Places to Eat), a short walk from the town centre, is an ambient bar with Belgian beers on tap, tapas on the table and great music. It's open till 3am Wednesday to Saturday and until midnight Sunday to Tuesday.

The old Aalto-designed Workers' Club, above Coffee House/Memphis, houses some late-night action, including **Club Ellahovi**, with retro nights, and **Tabasco Hot Club**.

Getting There & Away

Air There are several flights from Helsinki to Jyväskylä each weekday and fewer on weekends. The Jyväskylä airport is 21km north of the town centre; buses meet each arriving flight. In the centre, catch the airport bus on Vapaudenkatu.

Bus The bus terminal (Koulukatu 2) just north of the town centre serves the entire southern half of Finland, with many daily express buses connecting Jyväskylä to the big cities.

Train The train station is between the town and the harbour. There are regular trains from Helsinki (€36.30, 5½ hours) via Tampere, and some quicker direct trains.

Boat There is a regular ferry service on Lake Päijänne between Jyväskylä and Lahti, operated by the **Päijänne Risteilyt Hildén Oy** (☎ 263 447, fax 665 560) at the harbour. Boats depart from Jyväskylä at 10am on Wednesday and Friday, and from Lahti at 10am on Tuesday and Thursday (adult/child €36/18, 10½ hours) from June to mid-August.

AROUND JYVÄSKYLÄ
Säynätsalo

The large **Säynätsalo Civic Centre** southeast of Jyväskylä is one of Aalto's most famous works, the architect winning an international competition in 1949 to design it. The building was completed in 1952. On the small island of **Juurikkasaari**, just off Säynätsalo, Alvar Aalto's boat (his own design) features a humble note 'Nemo Propheta in Patria' (No-one is a prophet in one's own land). Follow the sign that says 'Aallon vene'.

Muurame

Along the main Tampere road, about 10km south of Jyväskylä, Muurame is home to the **Sauna Village** (Saunakylä; ☎ 014-373 2670; Virastotie 8; adult/child €4/3; open 10am-6pm daily in summer), a Finnish attraction if ever there was one. This open-air museum is a rather dull tribute to a great Finnish institution, with a variety of old saunas, plus smoke saunas you can hire for private use (from €85).

The white **church** (open 10am-6pm in summer) was designed by Alvar Aalto during the 1920s.

Petäjävesi

If you're heading west from Jyväskylä, it's worth pausing at the tiny village of Petäjävesi, 35km away, to see the Unesco World Heritage-listed, cross-shaped wooden church. Built in 1764, **Petäjävesi church** (admission €2; open 10am-6pm June–mid-Aug) is probably the most notable example of 18th-century peasant architecture in Finland. Prior to its construction, there had been some debate about whether this village should get a church at all. While a reply to applications (sent to Stockholm for approval) was delayed, Jaakko Leppänen started the job minus permission and properly drawn instructions. The result was a combination of Renaissance and Byzantine architecture. It's a marvellous, though awkward, wooden building. Since 1879, the church has functioned only as a museum.

Northern Lakeland

KUOPIO

☎ 017 • pop 87,350

Of all the northern Lakeland towns, Kuopio is certainly the most satisfying. It's a vibrant place with lots to see and do and enjoys a beautiful location, surrounded by forest and lakes. The ferry trip between Savonlinna and Kuopio also makes this a prime destination in summer. Time your visit for a Tuesday or Friday so you can steam it up in the world's biggest smoke sauna.

Although not a huge population, Kuopio sprawls over a large area and manages to exude the atmosphere of a city while retaining the charm of a lake town. The annual international dance festival adds to Kuopio's sophistication.

The first Savonian people entered the area at the end of the 15th century, and in 1552 the first church was built. In 1652 Count Per Brahe founded the 'church village' of Kuopio, which had little significance until 1775, when Gustav III of Sweden incorporated Kuopio as a provincial capital. A few important figures of the National Romantic era lived here from the 1850s, but the main growth of Kuopio was in the 20th century.

Information

Tourist Office The helpful tourist office, **Kuopio Travel Shop** (☎ 182 585, fax 261 3538;

w www.kuopioinfo.fi; Haapaniemenkatu 17; open 9.30am-5pm Mon-Fri, 9am-3pm Sat in July, 9.30am-4.30pm Mon-Fri rest of the year) is behind the impressive town hall on the northern side of the market square. It has information on attractions and accommodation in the entire Kuopio region. If you're planning to do a bit of sightseeing in town, the museum card (€11), available from the tourist office, gets you into six city museums. . Good-quality bikes can be hired from **Leosport** (☎ 262 8559; Haapaniemenkatu 27) for €15 a day.

Post & Communications The **post office** is situated just west of the market square on Tulliportinkatu.

The **public library** (☎ 182 111; Maaherrankatu 12; open 10am-7pm Mon-Fri, 10am-3pm Sat) has free Internet terminals on the 2nd floor; book ahead. There are also a few terminals at **Net Café** on Haapaniemenkatu.

Puijo Hill

In a country with few hills, Puijo Hill is the pride of Kuopio – the spectacular panoramic lake and forest views from the 75m **Puijo Tower** (adult/child €3/2; open year-round) are said to represent 'the national ideal of Finnish scenery'. There's a revolving restaurant on the 12th floor, a café on the 13th and an open-air viewing deck at the very top.

Surrounding Puijo Hill is one of the best-preserved **spruce forests** in the region. It's a popular local spot for walks and picnicking. Also here is an all-season ski jump and chairlift. Even in summer you can often see ski jumpers in training. Unfortunately there are no public buses to Puijo – walk or take a taxi.

Jätkänkämpällä Smoke Sauna

It's hardly surprising that the world's largest smoke sauna is in Finland, and it's as good a reason as any to visit Kuopio, but call ahead to check times since it's only open to the public two days a week. The lakeside Jätkänkämpällä sauna (☎ 473 473, admission €10; open 5pm-10pm Tues & Fri year-round) is at a former loggers' camp near the Rauhalahti Tourist Centre. The 60-person, mixed sauna (record capacity is 103 people) is heated a full 24 hours in advance with a big wood fire, hence the name 'smoke sauna'. Guests are given towels to wear but bring a swimsuit for a dip in the lake. The technique is to sweat it

THE LAKELAND

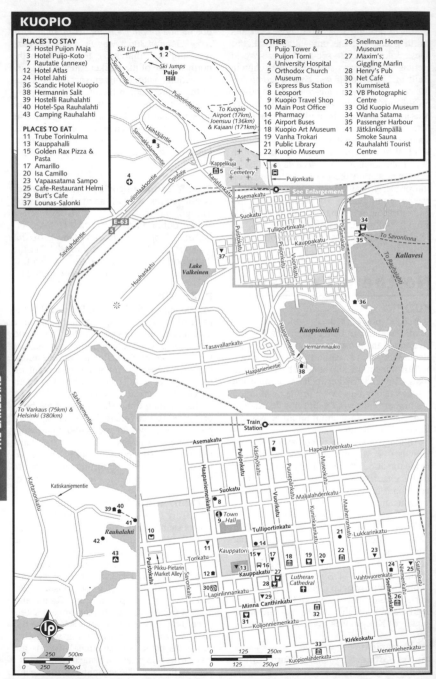

KUOPIO

PLACES TO STAY
2 Hostel Puijon Maja
3 Hotel Puijo-Koto
7 Rautatie (annexe)
12 Hotel Atlas
24 Hotel Jahti
36 Scandic Hotel Kuopio
38 Hermannin Salit
39 Hostelli Rauhalahti
40 Hotel-Spa Rauhalahti
43 Camping Rauhalahti

PLACES TO EAT
11 Trube Torinkulma
13 Kauppahalli
15 Golden Rax Pizza & Pasta
17 Amarillo
20 Isa Camillo
23 Vapaasatama Sampo
25 Cafe-Restaurant Helmi
29 Burt's Cafe
37 Lounas-Salonki

OTHER
1 Puijo Tower & Puijon Torni
4 University Hospital
5 Orthodox Church Museum
6 Express Bus Station
8 Leosport
9 Kuopio Travel Shop
10 Main Post Office
14 Pharmacy
16 Airport Buses
18 Kuopio Art Museum
19 Vanha Trokari
21 Public Library
22 Kuopio Museum
26 Snellman Home Museum
27 Maxim's; Giggling Marlin
28 Henry's Pub
30 Net Café
31 Kummisetä
32 VB Photographic Centre
33 Old Kuopio Museum
34 Wanha Satama
35 Passenger Harbour
41 Jätkänkämpällä Smoke Sauna
42 Rauhalahti Tourist Centre

out for a while, cool off in the lake, then repeat the process several times – devoted sauna-goers do so even when the lake is covered with ice.

There is a restaurant in the loggers' cabin serving traditional meals when the sauna is fired up, and live music and storytelling at a small outdoor theatre on summer evenings (adult/child €17/8). Bus No 7 goes every half-hour from the market square direct to Rauhalahti, or take the lake ferry from the passenger harbour in summer (adult/child €10/5, 6pm and 8pm Tuesday and Friday, June to August).

Museums

Kuopio has some worthwhile museums so if you're planning on a bit of cultural sightseeing, pick up a **museum card** (€11) from the tourist office or any of the participating museums. It gets you into the following six city museums (one visit to each), and is valid for a year.

Kuopio Museum The beautiful Art Nouveau 'castle' (☎ 182 603; Kauppakatu 23; adult/student & child €4/2; open 9am-4pm Mon-Sat, 11am-8pm Sun) was built in 1907 and houses the Kuopio Museum, with interesting archaeological and cultural displays. There are also frequent special exhibitions.

Old Kuopio Museum This block of old town houses (☎ 182 625; Kirkkokatu 22; adult/child €2.50/free) forms another of Kuopio's delightful museums. It consists of several homes – all with period furniture and decor – seven of which are open to the public. Apteekkimuseo in building No 11 contains old pharmacy paraphernalia. There is also a pleasant museum café, where you can have coffee and taste the delicious *rahkapiirakka* (a local pastry).

Kuopio Art Museum The art museum (☎ 182 633; Kauppakatu 35; adult/child €2.50/ free; open 10am-5pm Tues, Thur & Fri, 10am-7pm Wed, 11am-4pm Sat & Sun) features mostly modern art in temporary exhibitions, but also displays works by Finnish painters such as Pekka Halonen.

Snellman Home Museum This museum (☎ 182 624; Snellmaninkatu 19; adult/student/ child €1.50/1/free; open 10am-5pm daily,

10am-7pm Wed mid-May–late Aug) is a branch of the Kuopio Museum. JV Snellman, an important cultural figure during the National Romantic era of the 19th century, used to live in this old house from 1854 to 1849. It has been converted into a museum of interest mainly to students of Finnish history.

Orthodox Church Museum A fascinating, well-presented museum, the Orthodox Church Museum (☎ 287 2244; Karjalankatu 1; adult/child €5/3; open 10am-4pm Tues-Sun May–late Aug, noon-3pm Mon-Fri, noon-5pm Sat & Sun rest of the year) holds collections brought here from monasteries, churches and *tsasouni* (chapels) in USSR-occupied Karelia. Today it is the most notable collection of eastern Orthodox icons, textiles and religious objects outside Russia. The oldest artefacts date from the 10th century.

The museum is in a plain brown building about 1km west of the train station; take bus No 7 from the market.

VB Photographic Centre The Photographic Centre (☎ 261 5599; Kuninkaankatu 14-16; adult/child €4/2; open 10am-7pm Mon-Fri, 11am-4pm Sat & Sun, closed Mon in winter) is devoted to Victor Barsokevitsch, who was a local portrait photographer regarded as one of the pioneers of Finnish photography. His studio is now a photo gallery, but there are enough old cameras and photos to call this a museum. In the garden, you can enjoy a cup of coffee in summer, and be astounded by the camera obscura.

Pikku-Pietari Market Alley

Just off Puistokatu, about 200m west of the kauppatori, Pikku-Pietarin Torikuja is a narrow lane of renovated red shop-houses stocking jewellery, clothing, handicrafts and other items. There's also a café with a terrace. It's a charming little arcade, open 10am to 5pm Monday to Friday and to 2pm Saturday and Sunday from June to August.

Activities

Rauhalahti Tourist Centre (☎ 187 718; w www .rauhalahti.com) has grown around Rauhalahti Manor (Kartano Rauhalahti), an area converted into a year-round family park. The whole Rauhalahti area is full of amusements and activities for children and families, including boating, cycling, tennis and

Sauna – Smoke & Steam but No Sex

The ancient Romans had their steam and hot-air baths, the Turks and Persians had their *hammams*, and the Finns gave the world the sauna (pronounced **sow**-oo-nah not **saw**-nuh). It's one of the most essential elements of Finnish culture. Finns will prescribe a sauna session to cure all ills, from a head cold to sunburn. Finnish soldiers posted in desert regions have even been known to build themselves a sauna.

The earliest written description of the Finnish sauna dates from chronicles of Ukrainian historian Nestor in 1113. There are also numerous references to sauna-going in the Finnish national epic, the *Kalevala*.

Today there are 1.6 million saunas in Finland, which means that practically all Finns have access to one. Most are private, situated in Finnish homes. An invitation to bathe in a family's sauna is an honour, just as it is to be invited to a person's home for a meal. The sauna is taken in the nude, a fact that most Westerners find uncomfortable and confronting, but Finns consider perfectly natural.

There are also public saunas, often found on the edge of a lake or by the sea. Usually these have separate sections for men and women and if there is just one sauna the hours are different for men and women. In unisex saunas you will be given some sort of wrap or covering to wear. Indeed, Finns are quite strict about the nonsexual character of the sauna bath and this point should be respected. The sauna was originally a place to bathe, meditate and even give birth. It's not, as many foreigners would believe, a place for sex.

The traditional *savusauna*, or 'smoke sauna', is marvellous if you can find one; the modern electric sauna stoves used by most hotels and hostels are very dry and lack the authentic smell of burning wood, heated stones and *löyly* (steam). Look for authentic, log-heated *savusauna* in the countryside. The world's biggest *savusauna* at Jätkänkämpällä is adjacent to the Rauhalahti camping ground and hostel in Kuopio – it seats up to 100 and is unisex.

Proper sauna etiquette dictates that you use a *kauha* (ladle) to throw water on the *kiuas* (sauna stove), which then gives off the *löyly*. At this point, at least in summer in the countryside, you might take the *vihta* or *vasta* (a bunch of fresh, leafy *koivu*, or birch, twigs) and lightly strike yourself. This improves circulation and gives your skin a pleasant smell. When you are sufficiently warmed, you'll jump in the sea, a lake, river or pool, then return to the sauna to warm up and repeat the cycle several times. If you're indoors, a cold shower will do. The swim and hot-cold aspect is such an integral part of the sauna experience that in the dead of winter, Finns cut a hole in the ice and jump right in!

If you want to know more about the sauna and the part it plays in Finnish life, check out **W** www .sauna.fi, the Finnish Sauna Society website.

minigolf in summer, skating, ice-fishing, snowmobile safaris, snowshoeing and a snow castle in winter. In summer there's also **Uppo-Nalle House** (Uppo-Nallen koti) for the kids. Take bus No 7 from the town centre. There are also lake ferries from the passenger harbour in the town centre in summer.

You can rent bikes from around €10 a day, rowing boats, canoes, inline skates, and even hire Icelandic ponies for gentle trail rides.

At Puijo Hill, there are also mountain-biking and walking tracks, including a marked nature trail. During winter there are cross-county ski trails, and equipment rentals are available.

Organised Tours
During summer there are daily departures for several different types of lake cruises.

Standard two-hour cruises from the harbour cost €10 to €12 (half price for children) and depart hourly from 11am to 6pm. Special theme cruises include dinner and dancing, wine tasting, or a trip to a local berry farm (adult/child €10/5). There are also canal cruises and a monastery cruise to Valamo.

There are cruises to Rauhalahti tourist centre Tuesday to Saturday in summer (and Sunday in July); the best one is the smoke-sauna cruise on Tuesday and Friday (adult/child €12/6), including sauna and towel.

Tickets for all cruises are available at the passenger harbour. Schedules are available at the harbour or from the tourist office.

Special Events
Tanssii ja Soi is the **Kuopio Dance Festival** (☎ 282 1541; **W** *www.kuopiodancefestival.fi*)

in mid- to late June, the most international and the most interesting of Kuopio's annual events. This is where you'll see unusual performers like the Finnish All Star Afro-Cuban Jazz Orchestra, as well as talented performers from many other countries. There are open-air classical and modern dance performances, comedy and theatre gigs, and the town is generally buzzing at this time.

In addition to performances, dance lessons are also given during the festival, but these must be booked well in advance (☎ 182 586).

The **Kuopio International Wine Festival**, held in early July, celebrates a different international wine-producing region each year.

Places to Stay – Budget
Camping Adjacent to the Rauhalahti spa complex, **Camping Rauhalahti** (☎ 361 2244; *Kiviniementie; tent sites €10/16 per person/family, 2–4-person cabins €30-54; open mid-May–Sept*) has a pleasant lakeside location and plenty of facilities. It's well set up for families.

Hostels Perched on top of Puijo Hill is **Hostel Puijon Maja** (☎ 255 5250, 255 5266; *Puilontornintie; dorm beds without/with linen & breakfast €17/28, singles/doubles €50/56; open year-round*). It's popular with groups, including practising ski jumpers, so book ahead. Unfortunately, there's no public transport from the town centre.

Hostelli Rauhalahti (☎ 473 111, fax 473 470; *Katiskaniementie 8; dorm beds €33, singles/doubles €57/66; open year-round*) is next to the spa hotel in the Rauhalahti Tourist Centre complex, 5km southwest of the town centre. It's handy for the smoke sauna if you're there on the right days, but a long way from town and overpriced for backpacker accommodation. You do get to use the hotel facilities though, which include a gym, spa and pool. Groups of two to four rooms share a well-equipped kitchen and bath. Take bus No 7 from town.

Hermannin Salit (☎ 364 4961, fax 364 4911; *Hermanninaukio 3A; dorm beds €15.50, singles/doubles €28/40*) is the city's most central hostel, about 1.5km south of the market square. It's a small, friendly place with a small shop and cafeteria offering cheap breakfast and lunch. Linen is included in the rates.

Places to Stay – Mid-Range & Top End
Rautatie (☎ 580 0569, fax 580 0654; *Asemakatu 1; singles/doubles €46/75*) is in the train station building but is a surprisingly comfortable and peaceful guesthouse.

About 50m away is another, cheaper **Rautatie** (☎ 580 0569, fax 580 0654; *Vuorikatu 35; singles/doubles €36/56*) run by the same owner (the name simply means 'station').

Hotel Puijo-Koto (☎ 282 8333; *Hiihtäjäntie 11; doubles from €54/64*) is a small, private hotel northwest of the town centre with modern, clean rooms. Breakfast and morning sauna are included in the room rates.

Hotel Jahti (☎ 264 4400; *Snellmaninkatu 23; singles/doubles €50/65*), near the passenger harbour, is a pleasant, intimate mid-range hotel with a good restaurant.

Hotel Atlas (☎ 211 2111, fax 211 2103; *Haapaniemenkatu 22; singles/doubles €64/78, weekends & summer €61/68*) is an ageing but comfortable hotel right on the kauppatori. Rates skyrocket during festivals such as the Kuopio Dance Festival.

Scandic Hotel Kuopio (☎ 195 111, fax 195 170; *Satamakatu 1; singles/doubles €100/120*) is a big hotel on the shores of Lake Kallavesi, about 1km from the kauppatori. It has the usual restaurants, saunas and a pool.

Hotel-Spa Rauhalahti (☎ 473 111, 473 473, fax 473 470; *Katiskaniementie 8; singles/doubles €81/100 June-Aug, €90/116 rest of the year*) at the Rauhalahti Tourist Centre, is a superb place to stay. In addition to the spa facilities, the hotel has a restaurant, café and popular dance club. Bookings are advised.

Places to Eat
At the **kauppatori** you'll find stalls selling fresh produce, coffee and snacks. Look for *kalakukko*, a sandwich, eaten hot or cold, that is made with locally caught fish baked inside a rye loaf. The **kauppahalli** at the southern end of the kauppatori is a classic Finnish indoor market hall with fresh produce and food stalls.

Trube Torinkulma (*Tulliportinkatu*), at the Sokos building near the kauppatori, has the best pastries and cakes, as well as sandwiches and other light fare.

Lounas-Salonki (*Kasarminkatu 12; lunch specials €8*), another good spot for lunch, is a charming place in a neighbourhood of wooden houses just west of the centre.

THE LAKELAND

Golden Rax Pizza & Pasta *(Puijonkatu 45; buffet lunch & dinner €7)* serves the usual all-you-can-eat cardboard.

Burts Cafe *(☎ 262 3995; Puijonkatu 15)* is the best place in town for coffee and home-made cakes and pastries. **Cafe-Restaurant Helmi** *(Kauppakatu 2; pizzas €7-10)*, in an old stone building near the harbour, is an atmospheric bar and restaurant specialising in great pizzas. There's often live music in the courtyard at the side.

Vapaasatama Sampo *(☎ 581 0458; Kauppakatu 13; meals €8-13)* is the spot for a truly local taste. This is the town's oldest restaurant – it's been in Kuopio for almost 70 years – and is famous all over Finland for its *muikku* and *vendace* (both whitefish), served in various forms. Outside meal times Sampo is very much a typical Finnish pub.

Puijon Torni *(☎ 209 111; mains €14-21; open summer only)* is the revolving panorama restaurant at the top of the Puijo observation tower. Views aside, the food here is expensive but the menu puts a lot of emphasis on Finnish specialities. The summer three-course, set menu *(€28)* includes roast reindeer fawn, trout roe and cloudberry melba with arctic-bramble liqueur.

Isa Camillo *(☎ 581 0450; Kauppakatu 25; mains €9-21)*, in a beautifully renovated bank, is one of Kuopio's finest restaurants, but is reasonably informal and affordable. The menu is international with plenty of Finnish specialities and there's a good enclosed terrace at the side.

Entertainment

Most of Kuopio's nightlife is conveniently strung along Kauppakatu, running east from the market square to the harbour.

Wanha Satama *(☎ 197 304)*, down at the harbour, is a lively pub with a sprawling terrace during the summer, and occasional live music. **Vanha Trokari** *(Kauppakatu 29)* is another popular pub and brewery with a busy summer terrace and a jazz bar attached.

Kummisetä *(Minna Canthinkatu 44)* is a very popular pub-cum-restaurant, a rustic place like a little red barn. On sunny summer days its terrace gets pretty crowded. The branch of the chain restaurant **Amarillo** *(☎ 197 337, Kirjastokatu 10)* is a particularly lively place for a drink and is open late.

Henry's Pub *(Käsityökatu 17)* is one of the best rock music venues in town with live bands Friday and Saturday nights. Around the corner, **Maxim's** *(Kauppakatu)*, draws a younger late-night crowd, combining a happening music bar on two levels, with a nightclub playing house and drum & bass.

Giggling Marlin *(☎ 288 8100; Kauppakatu 18; open 10pm-4am Tues-Sat)* is a frenetic 'Suomi pop' club with DJs, dancing on the table, theme nights and plenty of youthful enthusiasm.

For good old-fashioned Finnish dancing and karaoke, the **Hotel-Spa Rauhalahti** has a dance-restaurant open every night and usually packed to the hilt. The biggest nights are Friday and Saturday, when there's a live dance band and cover charge, and Wednesday is 'ladies-choice' night.

Getting There & Away

Air There are half a dozen direct flights from Helsinki to Kuopio daily (€166, one hour).

Bus The busy bus terminal, just north of the train station, serves the entire southern half of Finland, with regular departures to all major towns and villages in the vicinity. Each destination has its own platform. Express services to/from Kuopio include: Helsinki (€44.20, five hours), Joensuu (€19.20, two hours), Kajaani (€23.10, 2½ hours), Jyväskylä (€20.90, two hours) and Savonlinna (€23.10, 2½ hours).

Train Five trains a day run to Kuopio from Helsinki (€40, 4½ to five hours). Kouvola, Pieksämäki, Iisalmi and Kajaani also have direct trains to/from Kuopio. From Savonlinna you'll need to change to a bus connection at Pieksämäki.

Boat Ferries and cruise boats depart from the passenger harbour, about 600m east of the kauppatori. In summer, the lake ferry MS *Puijo* departs for Savonlinna on Tuesday, Thursday and Saturday at 9.30am (€60, 8½ hours), going via Heinävesi and Oravi. It returns from Savonlinna on Monday, Wednesday and Friday.

Getting Around

To/From the Airport Kuopio airport is 17km north of town. Buses depart from the kauppatori. The 30-minute trip costs €5 one way. Airport **taxis** *(☎ 106 400)* cost €10 and must be booked three hours in advance.

Bus The local bus network is extensive. A single ticket costs €2.20 Monday to Saturday, €2.70 Sunday. Some buses travel beyond Kuopio city limits, with higher rates.

LAPINLAHTI
☎ 017 • pop 8000
Lapinlahti is a peaceful rural town just off the main highway between Kuopio and Iisalmi. It enjoys a typically scenic location surrounded by Savonian waters, and there are a couple of worthy museums that may warrant a stop if you're taking a leisurely tour of this region.

The **Finnish Cattle-Calling Championships**, on a weekend in early July, proves that Lapinlahti can hold its own with the rest of the strange festivals in this region. There's also a **Cheese & Wine Festival** in early August.

Lapinlahti's main claim to fame is as the home of the Halonen family. National Romantic artist Pekka Halonen was the most famous of them, but it's the sculpture work of his cousin Eemil that is displayed here in the **Eemil Halonen Museum** (☎ 732 288; Eemil Halosentie; admission €2.50; open 10am-6pm Sun-Fri, 10am-5pm Sat June-Aug). Eemil was one of the most notable Finnish sculptors of the early 20th century, and many of the works depict scenes from the *Kalevala*. An enormous number of sculptures are on display in this converted old cow shed, not far from the village centre.

Virtually across the road, **Taidemuseo** (Art Museum; ☎ 732 288; Suistamontie; adult/child €5/1) shows high-quality temporary art exhibitions. It has the same hours as the Halonen museum and a combined ticket for both is €6.

Portaanpää (☎ 768 860; dorm beds €13-15, singles/doubles €24/30, apartments €30-48; open June–mid-Aug) is an HI-affiliated summer hostel in an old manor-like building used as a boarding school most of the year. The facilities are good but it's a bit remote (3km southwest of Lapinlahti) – best if you're looking to get away for a few days.

There's a train station in Lapinlahti and trains between Kuopio and Iisalmi stop here.

IISALMI
☎ 017 • pop 24,000
Iisalmi, 85km north of Kuopio, is known as the home of the Olvi Brewery and, naturally,

for its annual beer festival. Aside from this and a handful of oddball festivals in the district there's not much to draw travellers here, though there's an Orthodox church and a couple of local museums. During the 18th century, the area became known for the Runni 'health springs', and in 1808 a successful battle against the Russians was fought in Koljonvirta, near Iisalmi.

Information
The **tourist office** (☎ 830 3391; W www.iisalmiregion.com; Kauppakatu 22; open 9am-6pm Mon-Fri,9am-5pm in winter) is across the road from the bus terminal. The **public library** has Internet access, and you can store bags in a locker at the train station (€3) or the left luggage counter at the bus station (€3.40 per 24 hours).

Things to See
The **Karelian Orthodox Cultural Centre** (☎ 816 441; Kyllikinkatu 8; adult/child €2.50/1.20; open 9am-6pm daily) displays icons, murals and miniature models of Orthodox churches and *tsasouni* (chapels) from Russian Karelia. Some of the icons had lain forgotten in attics and barns, and were later discovered to be valuable. The adjacent **Orthodox church** (open 10am-4pm Tues-Sun in summer) has beautiful illustrations painted in 1995 by a Russian.

Kuappi, at the harbour's edge, bills itself as the world's smallest restaurant – it has one table, two seats, a bar and a toilet. You can't actually eat in here, but in summer the owners may open up the bar (it's listed in the Guinness Book of Records as the world's smallest pub). The building dates back to 1907 when it was a hut for railway workers.

Special Events
Unsurprisingly for the home of one of Finland's largest brewers, there's a **Beer Festival** (Oluset) in early July. The Iisalmi region has made an art-form of staging oddball festivals: in early May there's a **Fishing By Hand** competition in the Rajajoki River, and then there's the **Wife-Carrying World Championships** (see the boxed text on the following page) and **Finnish Barrel-Rolling Championships** in nearby Sonkajärvi. Another nearby village, Pielavesi, hosts the annual **Finnish Boot-Throwing Championships**, usually in July.

She Ain't Heavy, She's My Wife

If the thought of grabbing your wife by the legs, hurling her over your shoulder and running for your life sounds appealing, make sure you're in Sonkajärvi in early July, because you won't want to miss the World Wife-Carrying Championships. What began as a heathenish medieval habit of pillaging neighbouring villages in search of nubile women has become one of Finland's oddest – and most publicised – events.

The championship is a race over a 253m obstacle course, where competitors must carry their 'wives' through water traps and over hurdles to achieve the fastest time. Dropping your cargo means a 150-second penalty. The winner gets the wife's weight in beer and, of course, the prestigious title of World Wife-Carrying Champion. To enter, you need only find a consenting woman – but all borrowed wives must be returned.

The championship is accompanied by a weekend of drinking, dancing and typical Finnish frivolity.

Places to Stay & Eat

NMKY Hostel (☎ 823 940; Sarvikatu 4C; beds per person from €20; open June–late July) is HI-affiliated and typically austere, but cheap and clean. You can use the sauna for an additional fee. There is a shared kitchen and bathroom for every three rooms. The reception is open from 5pm to 11pm.

Hotel Artos (☎ 812 244, fax 814 941; e hotel.artos@co.inet.fi; Kyllikinkatu 8; singles/doubles from €54/65, weekends & July €46/54) is the best of the town's hotels. It's run by, and adjacent to, the Orthodox church, although the modern rooms have no more character than the usual Finnish hotel. The restaurant here has an €8 lunch buffet.

The **kauppatori** has the usual cheap grillis and snack stands, including **Ti Amo**, which has kebabs and burgers from €2.50 to €4.50. Savonkatu, running east from the kauppatori to the train station, has a string of restaurants and pubs, including a branch of **Rosso** and **Nelly's Corner Pub**.

Olutmestari (☎ 8381 430; mains €8-18; open 11am-11pm Mon-Fri, 11am-2am Sat & Sun), at the harbour, is an atmospheric bar and restaurant with a good summer terrace. The pizzas are good value at €8.50.

Getting There & Away

Iisalmi is a centre for bus traffic in the region, and a link between the west coast and North Karelia, so you can catch buses to/from Joensuu in the east or from Oulu in the west. Services include Kuopio (€11.40, 1½ hours), Joensuu (€24.70, four hours), Nurmes (€16.80, two hours), Oulu (€27.10, three hours) and Helsinki (€52.80, eight hours). There are local buses to surrounding towns and villages like Sonkajarvi (€4.20).

There are five trains a day from Helsinki to Iisalmi, via Lahti, Mikkeli and Kuopio. Coming from the north, you can reach Iisalmi from Oulu or Kajaani.

AROUND IISALMI
Sonkajärvi
☎ 017 • pop 5800

This unassuming village, 18km northeast of Iisalmi, has gained an international reputation for hosting one of Finland's wackiest summer events, the **Wife-Carrying World Championships**. Competitors pour in from all over Europe, so accommodation can be tight over that particular weekend, but the Kuopio and Islamic tourist offices can usually help out, often putting visitors up in local homes.

Sonkajärvi's other attraction is the **International Bottle Museum** (Pullomuseo; ☎ 761 470; admission €2; open 10am-8pm Tues-Sun June–late Aug). There are hundreds of bottles on display from all over the world.

The 30km **Volokki Nature Trail** begins in the village and goes through the countryside.

Karelia

There is no region of Finland more controversial, or guaranteed to stir up as much nationalistic emotion as Karelia. It was here that the famous Winter War and Continuation War were fought against the Soviet Union during WWII. For travellers, this is a fascinating region where folklore and pre-war culture still hold strong. You'll see Karelian food at markets, hear Karelian music at festivals and see the scars of the Winter War along the Russian border. The North Karelian wilderness is also a great place for trekking and canoeing.

South Karelia

If you study the map, you may come to the conclusion that just a tiny fraction of South Karelia is Finnish territory. There is barely 10km between Lake Saimaa and the Russian border at the narrowest point, near Imatra. The once-busy South Karelian trade town of Vyborg (Finnish: Viipuri) and the Karelian Isthmus reaching to St Petersburg are now part of Russia.

Wars have been a feature in this troubled region, and the evidence of Russian fortifications can be seen in South Karelia, particularly the garrison town of Lappeenranta.

LAPPEENRANTA
☎ 05 • pop 58,400

Lappeenranta (Swedish: Villmanstrand), the capital of South Karelia, is an old spa and garrison town at the southern end of Lake Saimaa, near the Russian border. With some interesting sights, a bustling harbour and visa-free canal cruises across the border into Russia, Lappeenranta is one of the most visited cities in Eastern Finland. It's a relaxed, friendly place and like other border cities is increasingly popular with Russian visitors popping across to shop for luxury goods.

The building of the Saimaa Canal in 1856 made this an important trading port, and Lappeenranta is now the largest inland port in Finland. The waterway from Lake Saimaa to the Gulf of Finland is 43km long and has eight locks. A day cruise along the Saimaa Canal to Vyborg, Russia – Finland's second-largest city until it was lost in WWII – is one of Lappeenranta's main attractions.

Highlights

- Taking a day cruise along the Saimaa canal from Lappeenranta to Vyborg in Russia
- Listening to a kantele performance at the Parppeinvaara in Ilomantsi
- Enjoying a couple of relaxing nights at Imatra's lakeside Ukonlinna Hostel
- Cycling around Lake Viinijärvi, with its scenic backroads, old houses and Karelian churches

History

The early Lappeenranta area on Lake Saimaa was a busy Karelian trade centre. It was established as a town by Count Per Brahe in 1649. Queen Kristina of Sweden accepted the coat of arms depicting a primitive man, after whom the Swedish 'Villmanstrand' was unflatteringly adopted (Villmanstrand means 'Wild Man's Shore' in Swedish). Apparently jealous, Vyborg businesses lobbied against their emerging rival, and Lappeenranta lost its town status in 1683.

Following a Russian victory on 23 August 1741, and the town's complete destruction, Lappeenranta was ceded to Russia in 1743, and it remained part of tsarist Russia until independence in 1917. Fortified during the 1780s, Lappeenranta was still a small village of only 210 people in 1812. A spa was founded in 1824, but it was only after railways and industries were developed that

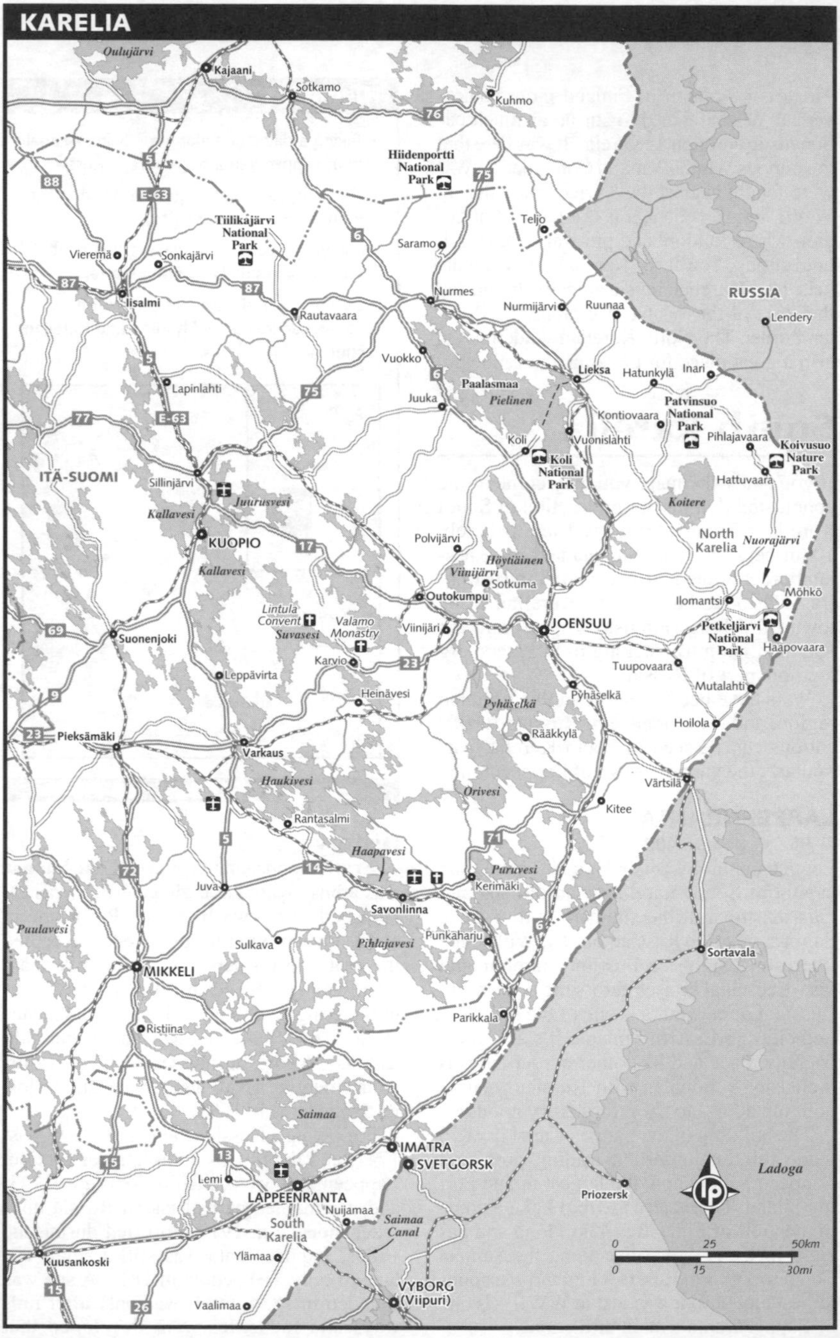

KARELIA

Oulujärvi
Kajaani
Sotkamo
Kuhmo
76
Hiidenportti National Park
75
Teljo
88
E-63
Tiilikajärvi National Park
Saramo
Vieremä
Sonkajärvi
Nurmes
RUSSIA
87
Iisalmi
87
Rautavaara
Nurmijärvi
Ruunaa
Lendery
Vuokko
5
6
Lieksa
Hatunkylä
Inari
Lapinlahti
75
Juuka
Paalasmaa
Pielinen
Kontiovaara
Patvinsuo National Park
Pihlajavaara
Koivusuo Nature Park
77
E-63
Koli
Vuonislahti
Hattuvaara
ITÄ-SUOMI
Sillinjärvi
Juurusvesi
Koli National Park
Koitere
Kallavesi
North Karelia
Nuorajärvi
KUOPIO
17
Polvijärvi
Höytiäinen
Kallavesi
Viinijärvi
Sotkuma
Ilomantsi
Möhkö
Lintula Convent
Suvasesi
Valamo Monastry
Outokumpu
Petkeljärvi National Park
Haapavaara
69
Suonenjoki
Viinijäri
JOENSUU
Leppävirta
Karvio
23
Tuupovaara
Mutalahti
9
Heinävesi
Pyhäselkä
Pyhäselkä
Hoilola
23
Pieksämäki
Varkaus
Rääkkylä
Värtsilä
Haukivesi
Orivesi
Kitee
Rantasalmi
5
Haapavesi
71
72
14
Puruvesi
Juva
Kerimäki
Sortavala
Savonlinna
Puulavesi
Sulkava
Punkaharju
6
Pihlajavesi
MIKKELI
Ristiina
Parikkala
Saimaa
15
13
IMATRA
Ladoga
Lemi
SVETGORSK
Puulavesi
LAPPEENRANTA
Priozersk
South Karelia
Nuijamaa
Kuusankoski
Saimaa Canal
Ylämaa
15
26
VYBORG (Viipuri)
Vaalimaa

0   25   50km
0   15   30mi

Lappeenranta began to grow. Today the beautiful lakeside setting is marred by oversized industries, such as timber milling, that provide work and wealth to many.

Orientation & Information

Kauppakatu and Valtakatu are the main streets. The train station is about 1km south of their intersection. The cheapest places to stay are west of the town centre.

The **main tourist office** (☎ 667 788; e mat kailuoy@lappeenranta.fi; open 9am-6pm Mon-Fri June–late Aug, 9.30am-4.30pm Mon-Fri rest of the year) is on the southern side of the kauppatori (market square). A **summer tourist office**, in the wooden restaurant and theatre building at the harbour, is open 9am to 9pm daily from June to late August.

The **main post office** is at Pormestarinkatu 1. The **public library** (☎ 616 2346; Valtakatu 47; open 10am-8pm Mon-Fri, 10am-3pm Sat, noon-3pm Sun) has free Internet terminals but they book up quickly. **I@Cafe** (☎ 223 3700; Kauppakatu 63; per hour €5) is a better bet for Internet access.

Linnoitus

The fortifications in the Linnoitus (Fortress) area of Lappeenranta above the harbour were started by the Swedes and finished by the Russians in the 18th century. Some of the fortress buildings have been turned into interesting **museums** (W www.lappeenranta .fi/linnoitus; combined ticket adult/student/child €5/4.20/3.40; open 10am-6pm Mon-Fri, 11am-5pm Sat & Sun June–late Aug, 11am-5pm Tues, Thur, Sat & Sun Sept–late May).

The **South Karelia Museum**, at the northern end of the fortress, displays folk costumes and a scale model of Vyborg as it looked before it fell to the Russians in 1939. Before WWII, Vyborg was the capital of Karelia and the second biggest town in Finland.

South Karelia Art Museum has a permanent collection of paintings by Finnish and Karelian artists, and a space devoted to temporary exhibitions

The cavalry tradition is cherished in Lappeenranta – from the 1920s to the 1940s, cavalrymen in their red trousers and skeleton jackets were a common sight on town streets. The town's oldest building (erected 1772), a former guardhouse, houses the small **Cavalry Museum**, which exhibits portraits of commanders, uniforms, saddles and

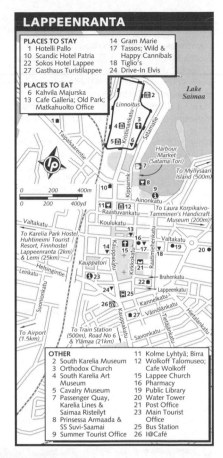

LAPPEENRANTA

PLACES TO STAY
1 Hotelli Pallo
10 Scandic Hotel Patria
22 Sokos Hotel Lappee
27 Gasthaus Turistilappee
14 Gram Marie
17 Tassos; Wild & Happy Cannibals
18 Tiglio's
24 Drive-In Elvis

PLACES TO EAT
6 Kahvila Majurska
13 Cafe Galleria; Old Park; Matkahuolto Office

OTHER
2 South Karelia Museum
3 Orthodox Church
4 South Karelia Art Museum
5 Cavalry Museum
7 Passenger Quay, Karelia Lines & Saimaa Risteilyt
8 Prinsessa Armaada & SS Suvi-Saamai
9 Summer Tourist Office
11 Kolme Lyhtyä; Birra
12 Wolkoff Talomuseo; Cafe Wolkoff
15 Lappee Church
16 Pharmacy
19 Public Library
20 Water Tower
21 Post Office
23 Main Tourist Office
25 Bus Station
26 I@Café

guns. Riders in old cavalry costumes parade between the fortress and the kauppatori for several hours each day from Tuesday to Friday between June and mid-August.

Other fortress buildings now house a variety of **artists' workshops** selling ceramics, paintings and hand-knitted garments during summer. The jewel-like **Orthodox church** (open noon-4.30pm Tues-Sun June–mid-Aug) is Finland's oldest. It was built in 1785 by Russian soldiers.

City Centre

The city centre also has several attractions worth exploring.

Wolkoff Talomuseo (Kauppakatu 26; adult/student/child €3.40/2.50/1.20; open 10am-6pm Mon-Fri, 11am-5pm Sat & Sun June–late

Aug, 11am-5pm Fri & Sat Sept-May) is the preserved home of a Russian emigrant family. The house, built in 1826, was owned by the Wolkoff family from 1872 to 1986. There are 10 rooms that have been maintained as they were; you must join one of the hourly guided tours (around 40 minutes) to see them.

Laura Korpikaivo-Tamminen's Handicraft Museum *(Kantokatu 1; admission €2; open 11am-4pm daily June–late Aug, 11am-3pm Tues-Thur, 11am-5pm Sat & Sun Sept-May)* focuses on textile art and has a permanent collection of more than 2000 hand-made pieces, donated by the late Laura Korpikaivo-Tamminen. The ticket to any of the fortress museums can also be used here.

Organised Tours & Activities

Cruises on Lake Saimaa and the Saimaa Canal are popular and there are daily departures from late May to late August from the passenger quay near the fortress.

Saimaa Risteilyt *(☎ 415 6955; adult/child €10/5)* at the harbour offers two-hour cruises aboard the 95-passenger MS *El Faro*, either around the archipelago or down the Saimaa Canal. Canal cruises depart daily at noon from June to September, with an additional 3pm cruise and a 6pm archipelago cruise from June to early August. **Karelia Lines** *(☎ 453 0380; adult/child €11/6)* has two-hour cruises on Lake Saimaa aboard the spacious MS *Camilla* at noon and 6pm from Tuesday to Saturday (there are also cruises on Monday in July).

There's a public **beach sauna** *(adult/child €3.50/1.50)* on Myllysaari island, just east of the harbour area. Hours for women are 4pm to 8pm Wednesday and Friday, and the same hours Tuesday and Thursday for men.

Places to Stay

Camping About 2km west of the centre, **Huhtiniemi Tourist Resort** *(☎ 451 5555;* Ⓦ *www.huhtiniemi.com; Kuusimäenkatu 18; tent sites & van sites €17.50, 2-/4-person cottages €30/41, apartments €34-74; open mid-May–Sept)* is a well-kept, slightly officious camping ground on the shores of Lake Saimaa, (bus No 6 runs past). As well as cottages and self-contained apartments on the mainland, there are eight upmarket cottages (from €170 for four people) on the island of Nuottasaari, which is accessible from Huhtiniemi by rowing boat.

Hostels There are two HI hostels on the Huhtiniemi camping site, with the same contact details as Huhtiniemi Tourist Resort. **Huhtiniemi Hostel** *(dorm beds €10; open June–mid-Aug)*, with six-bed dorms, is the cheapest accommodation in town but it books up fast. It has a café, kitchen, laundry and indoor swimming pool.

Finnhostel Lappeenranta *(singles/doubles €45/57; open year-round)* is a bit flash to be called a hostel, and that's reflected in the price. Tidy rooms with bathroom include linen, breakfast and a morning swim and sauna.

Cruising to Russia

One of the highlights of a visit to Lappeenranta is a boat trip along the Saimaa Canal, and the best way to experience it is the cruise across the border to Vyborg in Russia. No visa is required for the trip (you must return on the same cruise), but you need to carry your passport and provide passport details to the cruise operator a week in advance. Because the cruises are so popular, you'll need to book at least a week ahead anyway.

The return cruise aboard the MS *Carelia* departs at 8am (Wednesday to Saturday in June, August and September, Tuesday to Saturday in July), arriving in Vyborg at noon. You get about 3½ hours to sightsee and shop in the Russian city before returning on the ferry. A return ticket costs €40/20 adult/child (€50/25 on Saturday and from 24 June to 10 August). Although you leave from the passenger harbour, the cruise itself begins at Nuijamaa on the border. The **Karelia Lines** *(☎ 453 0380;* Ⓦ *www.karelialines.fi)* office at the harbour sells tickets.

Kristina Cruises *(☎ 05-21144;* Ⓦ *www.kristinacruises.com)*, based in Kotka, has overnight cruises between Lappeenranta, Vyborg and Kotka, or from Lappeenranta to Vyborg and back, staying on board the boat. Cruises are on selected days from June to August and range from €68 to €180 per person in a cabin.

Karelia Park (☎ 675 211, fax 452 8454; Korpraalinkuja 1; dorm beds €17.50, singles/doubles €43/50; open June–late Aug), an HI-affiliated summer hotel 300m west of Huhtiniemi, is good-value budget accommodation. It's in a rather austere student apartment block but there are no large dorms – the spotless two-bed rooms each have kitchen facilities and attached bathroom. Breakfast is €2.50 if you're paying the dorm rate and there's a communal kitchen, sauna and laundry. Linen hire is €4 but you can use sleeping bags here.

Guesthouses & Hotels Not far from the train station, **Gasthaus Turistilappee** (☎ 415 0800; Kauppakatu 52; singles/doubles/triples €33.70/50.50/57.20) is a homey place that offers tidy rooms with bathroom and TV. Breakfast and sauna are included in the rates.

Hotelli Pallo (☎ 411 8456; Pallonkatu 9; singles/doubles €50/66) is a small and pleasant guesthouse consisting of several cottages in a quiet residential area west of the fortress. Breakfast is included.

Scandic Hotel Patria (☎ 677 511; Kauppakatu 21; singles/doubles €102/125, doubles weekends & summer €75), close to the harbour, is Lappeenranta's top hotel, with good views, sauna, restaurant and bar.

Sokos Hotel Lappee (☎ 67861, fax 678 6545; e markku.makela@sok.fi; Brahenkatu 1; singles/doubles €118/140, doubles weekends & summer €80) is convenient to the centre and is the largest business hotel in town, with five restaurants, five saunas, a gym and covered parking.

Farmhouses Many farmhouses in the countryside around Lappeenranta offer B&B accommodation, a unique opportunity to meet local people and participate in their way of life. In some cases no English is spoken on these farms, so it may be easier to make bookings or inquiries through the tourist office at Lappeenranta.

Lahtela Farmhouse (☎ 457 8031; Lahtolantie 120; rooms per person €28.50; open year-round) near Ylämaa, south of Lappeenranta, is a dairy farm run by Hellevi and Lauri Lahtela. Rates include breakfast, sauna and use of a rowing boat on their small lake.

Asko's & Maija's Farmhouse (☎/fax 454 4606; Suolahdentie 461; adult/child €27/13.50; open mid-May–late Sept) is a dairy farm 27km north of Lappeenranta in the village of Peltoi. Accommodation is in a traditional log outbuilding, and breakfast is included.

Places to Eat

Lappeenranta offers many good dining options in all price ranges. At the **kauppatori** stalls sell local Karelian specialities such as vety (bread roll or pie with smoked ham, sliced boiled egg and spices), potato pie, or waffles with jam and whipped cream. There are a dozen more snack stands at the harbour during summer.

Drive-In Elvis (Kauppakatu 45) is a classic grilli with pizzas, burgers and kebabs from €2.

One of the most charming cafés in Finland, **Kahvila Majurska** (Kristiinankatu 7), is in an 18th-century wooden building at the fortress complex, with antique furniture and an abundance of delicious home-made cakes and quiches. **Cafe Galleria** (Koulukatu 15; mains €6-8), downstairs next to the Matkahuolto bus office in the centre, is more of a standard café and a good choice for breakfast and lunch.

Gram Marie (☎ 451 2625; Kauppakatu 41; lunch buffet €7.20) is a lunch restaurant specialising in Finnish food with an all-you-can-eat buffet. It's on the 5th floor.

Lappeenranta has a surprisingly decent range of international restaurants. **Tiglio's** (☎ 411 8311; Raatimiehenkatu 18; pasta & pizza €9-11, other mains €12-22) is a pleasant find – an authentic Italian restaurant with reasonably priced meals, including a free starters buffet of fresh bread, Italian dressings, olives and vegetables. It's spacious enough to be informal but nice enough for a night out.

Tassos (☎ 678 6565; Valtakatu 41; mains €12-22) is a fine Greek place, which is a bit pricier for dinner but has a good-value lunch special served 11am to 2.30pm Monday to Friday. Dishes range from traditional mezedes (€10.40) and souvlaki to Greek lamb specialities and vegetarian dishes.

Cafe Wolkoff (☎ 415 0320; Kauppakatu 26; mains €16-25) adjacent to the Wolkoff Museum, is a stylish restaurant specialising in Finnish cuisine such as whitefish, reindeer, elk and cloudberry soup.

The small village of Lemi, 25km west of Lappeenranta, is famous for its lemin särä (roast mutton). This traditional dish – cooked in a wooden trough – has been described as 'one of the seven wonders of Finland'. And so it should – it takes nine hours to cook and must be ordered at least two days in advance. **Säräpirtti Kippurasarvi** (☎ 414 6470; *Rantatie 1)*, on the lakeside at Lemi, is the place to try *lemin särä*. Phone ahead for a booking.

Entertainment
In summer, the SS **Suvi-Saamai** and the **Prinsessa Armaada**, at the harbour, are cheerful beer terraces.

Kolme Lyhtyä *(Kauppakatu 21)*, across from Cafe Wolkoff, is a typical eastern Finland pub, and next door is **Birra** *(Kauppakatu 19)*, an ugly, modern bar where Lappeenranta's student population congregates to drink cheap beer.

Old Park *(Valtakatu 36)* is a boisterous Irish pub that gets very crowded most nights. **Wild & Happy Cannibals** *(☎ 678 6565; Valtakatu 41; open 10pm-4am)* is Lappeenranta's most popular nightclub – revellers from the preceding pubs head here after closing.

Getting There & Away
Air There are daily flights between Helsinki and Lappeenranta on **Finnair** *(☎ 0203-140 140)*. Bus No 4 travels the 2.5km between the city centre and the airport.

Bus All buses along the eastern route, between Helsinki and Joensuu, stop in Lappeenranta. Bus and train tickets can be booked at the central office of **Matkahuolto** *(☎ 0200-4053)*, next to Cafe Galleria, or at the bus station. Regular services include: Helsinki (€27.10, four hours), Savonlinna (€18.50, three hours via Parikkala), Mikkeli (€14.60, 2½ hours) and Imatra (€5.70, 45 minutes). For Kuopio (€30.90) change at Mikkeli.

There are local connections to smaller places in South Karelia, although some buses only run once a day, on weekdays.

Train Seven to eight trains a day between Helsinki and Joensuu will take you to Lappeenranta. There are frequent direct trains to/from Helsinki (€33, 2¾ hours), and to Savonlinna (€18.40, 2½ hours; change at Parikkala).

AROUND LAPPEENRANTA
Ylämaa
☎ 05 • pop 1650
Ylämaa, 21km south of Lappeenranta, is a rural municipality best known for the gemstone spectrolite, a special kind of labradorite found only here. Spectrolite is a dark stone which glitters in all the colours of the spectrum. The local **tourist information office** *(☎ 613 4259)* is in Jewel Village.

Jewel Village *(museum & shops open daily June–late Aug)*, on the No 387 Lappeenranta–Vaalimaa road, is Ylämaa's main attraction. The village consists of a restaurant, two stone grinderies, quarries, a goldsmith's workshop and gem museum. The **gem museum** *(adult/child €2/1; open 11am-5pm daily)* has a collection of spectrolites and precious minerals and fossils from around the world, many in their raw, uncut state.

At the workshops you can buy spectrolite pieces fashioned into clocks, paperweights, pen-holders, pendants and jewellery boxes.

Ylämaa church *(Koskentie; open daily in summer)*, in the municipal centre, was built in 1931 and has an unusual facade made partially of spectrolite.

In summer, catch the afternoon bus from Lappeenranta that runs Monday to Friday only. There are a number of farmstays in the area – contact the Ylämaa or Lappeenranta tourist offices for information.

IMATRA
☎ 05 • pop 30,400
Close to the Russian border, Imatra is a strange city sprawling around the southeastern shores of Lake Saimaa. It bears a legacy of wars, industrial pollution and human greed, though Imatrans are still justifiably proud that in 1894 one of its citizens invented a revolutionary machine for gutting herring.

Among Imatra's four centres, scattered across a large area, are several attractions unfortunately marred by industrial progress. The raging torrent of the waterfall, once the prime 19th-century tourist attraction in Finland, was harnessed to produce hydroelectricity in 1929, while pulp factories blot the landscape. Still, Imatra and its foaming rapids (which once again foam daily in summer) remain popular with vacationing Finns, and you'll pass through here on the route between Lappeenranta and Savonlinna. It's also possible to cross into Russia from here.

Orientation & Information

Although Imatra has four dispersed 'centres', the one of most interest to travellers is Imatrankoski at the rapids (or the power station), where you'll also find the best restaurants and hotels. A little way north, Mansikkala is the administrative centre, with architecture not dissimilar to the Soviet ideal, and the bus and train station. Vuoksenniska, to the northeast, is an industrial area (surrounded by two gigantic pulp factories) and former independent municipality, while the budget accommodation (and one of Finland's best-located hostels) is in Saimaanranta, on Lake Saimaa northwest of the centre.

The main **tourist office** (☎ 681 2500; Koskenparras 6; w travel.imatra.fi; open 9am-5pm Mon-Fri, 10am-2pm Sat in summer, 9am-4.30pm Mon-Fri rest of the year) is on the main pedestrian mall in Imatrankoski.

The **public library**, in the Kaupungintalo (Cultural Centre) in Mansikkala, has free Internet access.

Things to See & Do

Probably the highlight in Imatra is the 3km stroll along the mighty **Vuoksi River**, from the bus and train station in Mansikkala to the power station in Imatrankoski. Until the hydroelectric power station was built and the river dammed in 1929, Imatra's **rapids** were one of the highest waterfalls in Finland and drew hundreds of tourists (as well as a fair number of people bent on committing suicide by jumping). These days, the water is allowed to flow free only for the 20-minute **Rapids Shows** from Midsummer to September. There's a daily show at 7pm from mid-June to mid-August. There's an accompanying sound and light show (to the strains of Sibelius music) at 1am nightly in July. The same show is on at 10pm Saturday evening in August, and at 9pm on Saturday in September.

Vuoksen Kalastuspuisto (☎ 432 3123; Kotipolku 4; open 9am-9pm daily May-Sept) is a fishing park on Varpasaari island in Mansikkala. Pike and salmon can be caught in the river here. A kiosk sells permits (€6/10 a day/week) and rents equipment and boats. You can also camp here (€13 per tent site).

Karjalainen Kotitalo (open Tues-Sun June & July), signposted as 'Ulkomuseo', is an open-air museum with a dozen Karelian houses gathered at the riverfront.

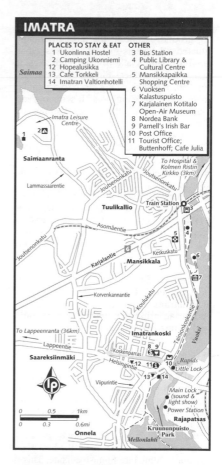

IMATRA

PLACES TO STAY & EAT
1 Ukonlinna Hostel
2 Camping Ukonniemi
12 Hopealusikka
13 Cafe Torkkeli
14 Imatran Valtionhotelli

OTHER
3 Bus Station
4 Public Library & Cultural Centre
5 Mansikkapaikka Shopping Centre
6 Vuoksen Kalastuspuisto
7 Karjalainen Kotitalo Open-Air Museum
8 Nordea Bank
9 Parnell's Irish Bar
10 Post Office
11 Tourist Office; Buttenhoff; Cafe Julia

Kolmen Ristin Kirkko (Church of the Three Crosses; Ruokolahdentie; bus No 1; open daily year-round) in Vuoksenniska was designed in 1957 by Alvar Aalto. As an interesting detail, only two of the 103 windows of the church are identical.

Places to Stay

Camping Ukonniemi (☎ 472 4055; e myyntipalvelu@lomaliitto.fi; Leiritie 1; tent & caravan sites €16, 3-/4-/5-person cabins €30/35/49; open June–early Aug) is a pleasant lakefront camping ground near the Imatra Leisure Centre. It has two saunas (for hire) and a camp kitchen. Bus No 3 travels from the bus station to the Imatra Spa every hour.

Ukonlinna Hostel (☎ 432 1270; Leiritie 8; dorm beds €13.50, family room per person

€20; open year-round), alongside the camping ground, is one of the most idyllically situated HI hostels in Finland. Nestled in the forest with a lake frontage and lakeside sauna, this is typical Finland. It's a small, cosy place and since it's close to a popular cross-country skiing area, it's open year-round – in winter there's ice fishing and skating on the lake.

Imatran Valtionhotelli (☎ 68881, fax 688 8888; Torkkelinkatu 2; singles/doubles Mon-Fri €104/127, Sat & Sun €77/86, summer €89/98) is an Art Nouveau place overlooking the rapids in Imatrankoski and is the city's most famous building. Built in 1902 and called The Grand Hotel Cascade, it was a favourite spot of the St Petersburg aristocracy. The decor is definitely lost in the past but has a certain elegance – especially the tower suite at €340.

Places to Eat

Imatra's centre for cafés and restaurants is at Imatrankoski, particularly along the pedestrian strip Koskenparras, where you'll find a supermarket, bars, outdoor cafés and beer terraces set up in summer. There are several cheap **grillis** and restaurants along Lappeentie and Helsingintie.

Cafe Torkkeli (Torkkelinkatu 1), opposite Valtionhotelli, is a good spot for coffee and it sells local produce and handicrafts. **Hopealusikka** (Lappeentie 18) is good for a cheap lunch.

Buttenhoff (☎ 476 1433; Koskenparras 4; lunch €7-11, mains €14-26) is the best place to sample some rare Finnish cuisine. This is the most legendary restaurant in Imatra, with a 100-year history. Downstairs, **Cafe Julia**, decorated with teddy bears, is the place for coffee and tempting cakes.

Parnell's Irish Bar (Koskenparras 5), also on the pedestrian strip, is the pick of the pubs along here.

Getting There & Away

Imatra is well served by eastbound trains and buses from Helsinki, and by hourly buses from Lappeenranta (€5.70, 45 minutes). There are seven trains a day from Helsinki to Imatra (€34.60, three hours). The central train station is near the river at Mansikkala; it also has four bus platforms for various destinations and a number of travel-related services.

North Karelia

There is no area in Finland like North Karelia, or Karjala as it is called in Finnish. When Finland lost the Karelian Isthmus and the Salla region to the Soviet Union after WWII, this province was the only part of Karelia to remain Finnish territory. Some 500,000 Karelian refugees had to be settled in Finland after WWII.

Under the shadow of the Soviet Union, Karjala was a taboo subject. Starting a discussion about how and when Karelia should be returned to Finland was a definite end to any political career.

All nations have their symbols and their nationalistic dawn. For Finns, Karelia provided both. The wild Karelian 'outback' inspired artists during the National Romantic era, from Sibelius, the composer, to Gallen-Kallela, the painter. This sparsely populated frontier region (population 175,000) does its best to live up to all Karelian legends.

For the traveller, it is a unique region where you can meet friendly people, visit beautiful Orthodox churches and explore wilderness trekking paths.

History

In 1227, a crusade from Novgorod (situated in present-day Russia) forcibly baptised Karelians into the Orthodox faith, sparking skirmishes that did not end until the Treaty of Nöteborg in 1323 established Novgorod's suzerainty over the region.

Karelians have survived repeated wars with Sweden and Russia. In 1617 Swedes annexed much of Karelia. North Karelia was constantly attacked by Russia and religious intolerance forced Orthodox believers across the border into Russia. The Treaty of Uusikaupunki in 1721 resulted in North Karelia remaining Swedish territory and South Karelia falling to Russian feudalism.

JOENSUU

☎ 013 • pop 52,100

Joensuu is both the capital of the province of North Karelia and its major travel hub. It has a flourishing university, lively cultural life, a good market and abundant services, which compensate somewhat for the lack of any major tourist attraction (with the exception of Carelicum). You'll probably find yourself

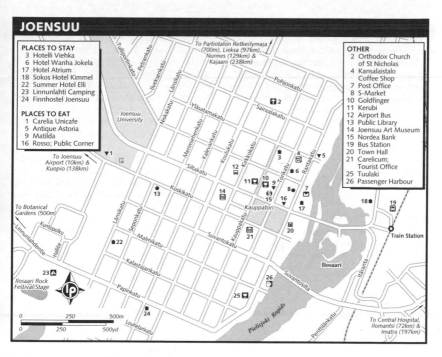

JOENSUU

PLACES TO STAY
3 Hotelli Viehka
6 Hotel Wanha Jokela
17 Hotel Atrium
18 Sokos Hotel Kimmel
22 Summer Hotel Elli
23 Linnunlahti Camping
24 Finnhostel Joensuu

PLACES TO EAT
1 Carelia Unicafe
5 Antique Astoria
9 Matilda
16 Rosso; Public Corner

OTHER
2 Orthodox Church of St Nicholas
4 Kansalaistalo Coffee Shop
7 Post Office
8 S-Market
10 Goldfinger
11 Kerubi
12 Airport Bus
13 Public Library
14 Joensuu Art Museum
15 Nordea Bank
19 Bus Station
20 Town Hall
21 Carelicum; Tourist Office
25 Tuulaki
26 Passenger Harbour

in Joensuu anyway if you're heading into North Karelia, and as a base for hiking in surrounding Karelian wilderness areas.

The city was on the receiving end of a bad reputation some years ago after some well-publicised race-related attacks. Although a youth culture of 'skinheads' remains, things have quietened down enough that this is no more alarming than in other Finnish cities.

Joensuu was founded in 1848 at the mouth of the Pielisjoki, hence its name ('joen' is a genitive form of 'joki', or river; 'suu' means 'the mouth'). Joensuu soon became an important trading post for the region, and an international port after the completion of the Saimaa Canal in the 1850s.

Orientation & Information

The gentle Pielisjoki rapids divide Joensuu into two parts. The train and bus stations are in the east; the town centre, including the market square and most accommodation, is in the west. Siltakatu and Kauppakatu are the two main streets.

The **tourist office** (☎ 267 5300; Ⓦ www .kareliaexpert.com, Ⓦ www.jns.fi; Koskikatu 5) is in the Carelicum, which also has a café,

free Internet and the town's best museum. It handles tourism information for the town and the region.

The **public library** (Koskikatu 25), near the university campus, has several free Internet terminals. Another good place for Internet access is **Kansalaistalo coffee shop** (cnr Torikatu & Ylasatamakatu), where you can also hire bikes for €6 a day.

Things to See

Carelicum (☎ 267 5222, fax 267 5232; Koskikatu 5; adult/student/child €4.20/2.50/ 1.70; open 9am-5pm Mon-Fri, 11am-4pm Sat) is a fine conceptual museum focussing on Karelia – its history, people and customs. This is an excellent place to get acquainted with Karelia before heading further east or north. There's one main floor of photographic exhibits and static displays, an interactive area for kids modelled on part of old Joensuu, and a miniature model of Sortavala (now in Russia) upstairs. There is also a gift shop and a good café on the ground floor.

The unusual **town hall** (Rantakatu 20) dominates the town centre, between the kauppatori and the river. It was designed by

KARELIA

Eliel Saarinen, who also designed Helsinki's train station, and was built in 1914. Part of the building now houses the local theatre.

Near the kauppatori, **Joensuu Art Museum** (☎ 267 5388; Kirkkokatu 23; adult/child €3/1; open noon-6pm Tues-Sun) displays art from the Mediterranean, Asia and Scandinavia, including a few old religious icons.

The most interesting church in Joensuu is the wooden **Orthodox church of St Nicholas** (Kirkkokatu; open 10am-4pm Mon-Fri mid-June–mid-Aug), built in 1887. The icons were painted in St Petersburg in the late 1880s.

In summer, the **kauppatori** is a good place to shop for Karelian handicrafts.

Organised Tours

In summer there are **scenic cruises** on the Pielisjoki, a centuries-old trading route. The MS *Koli III* has day and evening cruises (adult/child €15/7, two hours), departing from the passenger harbour south of Suvantosilta bridge. You can book and check timetables with **Saimaa Ferries** (☎ 481 244) or the city tourist office.

For ferry cruises to Koli and Lieksa, see the Getting There & Away section later.

Special Events

The **Ilosaari Rock Festival** (ⓦ www.ilosaari rock.fi) is a highly charged annual rock concert held over a weekend in mid-July. It draws up to 20,000 young concert-goers and a line-up of mainly Finnish rock acts to the huge festival area set up in the southwest of the city. The **Kajakka Festival** in early June is a Karelian folk music and dancing festival featuring markets and street performances.

Places to Stay

Camping Just south of the centre, **Linnunlahti Camping** (☎ 126 272; Linnunlahdentie 1; camping per person/tent site €7/12, 4–6-person cabins €35-42) has a pleasant lakeside location and is near a vast open-air stage, so expect occasional free concerts and lost sleep.

Hostels There are three hostels in Joensuu; all are affiliated with HI but only one has genuine dormitory accommodation. **Partiotalon Retkeilymaja** (☎ 123 381; Vanamokatu 25; dorm beds €10-14; open June–late Aug) provides basic accommodation in the slightly

run-down old scout hall, but it's certainly the cheapest in town. Reception is open from 9am to 11am and 4pm to 10pm.

The year-round **Finnhostel Joensuu** (☎ 267 5076; ⓔ finnhostel@islo.jns.fi; Kalevankatu 8; shared rooms per person €26, singles/doubles €42/52) is HI-affiliated, but at the high end of hostel accommodation. Very comfortable twin rooms include linen and TV, and have their own bathroom and fully equipped kitchen.

Summer Hotel Elli (☎ 225 927; Länsikatu 18; singles/doubles €36/52; open mid-May–mid-Aug) is a student apartment building that becomes a summer hotel. There is a sauna and laundry.

Hotels Cheap and cheerful, **Hotel Wanha Jokela** (☎ 122 891; Torikatu 26; singles/doubles €25/50) is a busy pub with basic rooms upstairs. Bathrooms are shared and it can get noisy below.

Hotelli Viehka (☎/fax 256 2200; Kauppakatu 32; singles/doubles €59/76, weekends & summer €49/65) is a comfortable, central hotel, and its nightclub is one of the most popular in town. There are also triples and family rooms.

Hotel Atrium (☎ 225 888, fax 225 8300; ⓦ www.hotelliatrium.fi; Siltakatu 4; singles/doubles €68/97, weekends & summer €62/73) is a pleasant central hotel with a restaurant, sauna and a cheeky pet parrot in the lobby.

Sokos Hotel Kimmel (☎ 277 111, fax 277 2112; Itäranta 1; singles/doubles €107/129, doubles weekends & summer €82), the largest hotel in Joensuu, is on the eastern side of the river, close to the bus and train stations. It has a pool, restaurant and a nightclub.

Places to Eat & Drink

At the busy **kauppatori** look for Karelian sweets such as *Karjalan piirakka*, a rice-filled pastry. There are all sorts of food stalls set up here, along with cheap **grillis**.

The University of Joensuu has several student cafeterias, most notably **Carelia Unicafe** (open 11am-2pm Mon-Fri) in the main building. A buffet meal costs less than €4.

Matilda (Torikatu 23; lunch from €4.50), just north of the kauppatori, is a good bakery, restaurant and café. There's a popular branch of **Rosso** (Siltakatu 8; mains €7-12) nearby, with a good people-watching terrace.

Antique Astoria (☎ 229 766; mains €8-20) is a stylish little restaurant with a riverfront terrace. It specialises in hearty Hungarian dishes (heavy on the meat and paprika), but also has cheaper pizza and pasta.

The oldest and best-known pub is the rustic **Wanha Jokela** (Torikatu 26), and in summer there's plenty of drinking at the harbour café **Tuulaki**, where the passenger ferries dock.

The pedestrian section of Kauppakatu between the kauppatori and Niskakatu has a handful of late-night bars and clubs where you can usually catch live bands and DJs on weekends. **Kerubi** (Kauppakatu 23A) has original live acts, while **Goldfinger** (Kauppakatu 26), across the mall, is a popular nightclub and bar with DJ action and cover bands.

Getting There & Away

Air There are several flights a day between Helsinki and Joensuu. The airport is 11km west of town; bus service is €4 one way and departs from Kirkkokatu 25.

Bus Joensuu is a transport hub for North Karelia so there are regular buses to all points, departing from the bus terminal east of the river. Tickets are sold from 8am to 4pm Monday to Friday, but you can pay on the bus. Services include Kuopio (€19.20), Savonlinna (€18.50), Jyväskylä (€29.10), Helsinki (€48.40), Kuhmo (€27.10), Ilomantsi (€10.40) and Nurmes (€16.80).

Train Direct trains run frequently to/from Helsinki (€41.80, 5¼ hours), Turku, Jyväskylä and Kajaani. From Savonlinna you have to change at Parikkala.

Boat In summer the MS *Vinkeri II* operates twice weekly from Joensuu to Koli (€30/40 one way/return, 6½ hours), from where you can connect with another ferry to Lieksa, across Lake Pielinen. The ferry departs at 9.30am on Thursday and Saturday, returning from Koli at 12.30pm Wednesday and Friday. Book with **Saimaa Ferries** (☎ 481 244).

JOENSUU TO ILOMANTSI
Outokumpu
☎ 013 • pop 9000

Outokumpu, about 50km west of Joensuu, was a wealthy copper mining town until the 1980s, when all three mining operations were permanently closed, turning this area into a shadow of its former industrial self. The abandoned **Vanha Kaivos Mine** (☎ 554 794;

Cycling the Lake Viinijärvi Loop

Roads around Lake Viinijärvi are scenic, with beautiful churches and old houses. In August, you can find blueberries in the nearby forests. If you have a bicycle (you can hire one in Joensuu or Ilomantsi), you can bring it to Viinijärvi by train or bus from Joensuu, Varkaus or Kuopio, and ride the 60km loop between Viinijärvi, Sotkuma, Polvijärvi and Outokumpu in a day. Another option is to take a bus from Joensuu to Polvijärvi, bypassing Sotkuma.

The tiny village of **Viinijärvi**, on the southern shore of the lake, is quite famous domestically for its champion women's *pesäpallo* (baseball) team. The local field gets pretty packed on Sunday during matches. A colourful Praasniekka Festival (a Karelian religious holiday) is held on 26 June each year. The beautiful **Orthodox church** is west of the village centre. Its 19th-century icons are copies of those in Kyiv Cathedral.

The narrow 14km road from Viinijärvi north to **Sotkuma** is scenic. The small *tsasouna* (chapel), built in 1914, has interesting 19th-century icons inside. The Praasniekka Festival is held here on 20 July each year.

A further 14km, **Polvijärvi** is a larger town with an interesting background. When a canal was being constructed at the southern end of Lake Höytiäinen in 1859, the embankment collapsed and the water level sank 10m, revealing fertile land. Polvijärvi was soon incorporated as a municipality and its population soared. The **Orthodox church**, built in 1914, is not far from the village centre. Its icons are from St Petersburg and were probably painted in the early 20th century. The church has its Praasniekka Festival on 24 June.

It's another 22km along road No 504 to Outokumpu. There are several buses a day from Joensuu and a few others from Kuopio and Juuka. Buses from Outokumpu run on school days only.

Kiisukatu 6; adult/child €8/4; open 10am-6pm daily), on a hill overlooking the town centre, is now an extensive mining museum and there's an adjacent tunnel with mining equipment. You can climb the tower for a bird's-eye view. There's also an underground restaurant and a café.

One of the best bird-nesting lakes in Finland, Lake Sysmäjärvi Bird Sanctuary, lies south of Outokumpu. Sysmäjärvi was declared dead in the 1950s, due to polluted mining deposits that flowed freely into the lake. Since rehabilitated, the lake is now surrounded by lush vegetation, and birds have returned here in large numbers; a recent study found 72 species. There are several bird-watching towers. May and June are the best months to visit.

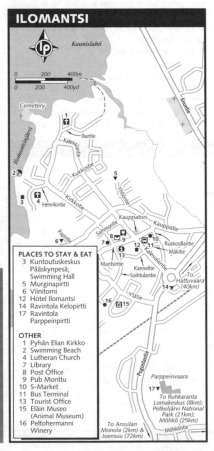

ILOMANTSI
☎ 013 • pop 8500

Ilomantsi, 72km east of Joensuu, is the centre of a charming region and Finland's most Karelian, Orthodox and eastern municipality. It is one of three regions with a nonmainstream indigenous culture (the others being Åland and the Sami culture of northern Lapland) and indigenous Karelians see themselves as distinct from Russians and Finns.

This is the ideal place to base yourself for hiking and other activities in the Karelian wilderness. It's a friendly region and a good place to witness local culture in the form of Praasniekka festivals. The village centre itself is modern and quite ugly, having been trampled by the Russians, but it's the surrounding region that demands exploration, on foot or by bicycle.

Information
The excellent **tourist office** (☎ 881 707; W www.travel.fi/fin/ilomantsi; Mantsintie 8; open 8.30am-5pm Mon-Fri year-round) can help with just about everything from cottage reservations to information on trekking routes and hire of camping equipment (tents €8.50 per day), bikes (€6.80/25.30 per day/week), snowshoes and cross-country ski gear. This should be your first stop if you're planning trips into the Karelian countryside.

The **library** (open 1pm-7pm Mon-Thur, 10am-3pm Fri), about 100m from the tourist office on Mantsintie, has Internet access.

Parppeinvaara
One of the most famous of Ilomantsi's historical characters was Jaakko Parppei (1792–1885), a bard and a player of the *kantele*, a traditional Karelian stringed instrument. He is the namesake of Parppeinvaara hill (where he lived), which now features a re-created **Karelian village** (☎ 881 094; adult/child €3.50/1; open 10am-6pm daily mid-June–mid-Aug). Built since the 1960s, it is the oldest of the Karelian theme villages in Finland and one of the most interesting. To qualify for their job, guides wearing *feresi* (traditional Karelian work dress) must know how to play the *kantele* and be fluent in several languages. A highlight is the regular performance of folk singing accompanied by the *kantele*. Runonlaulajan pirtti, the main building, has exhibitions on the *Kalevala* epic and Orthodox arts.

ILOMANTSI

Kaunislahti

0   200   400m
0   200   400yd

Cemetery

Iliantie

Kalevalantie

Kukkostie

Kirkkotie

Henrikintie

Kauppatori

Kauppatie

Ruskosillantie

Mäkitie

Mantsintie

Kannettie
Soihtulantie

To Hattuvaara (40km)

Ylätie

Enontie

Pogostantie

Parppeinvaara

To Ruhkaranta
Lomakeskus (8km);
Petkeljärvi National
Park (21km);
Möhkö (25km)

To Ansslan
Monola (2km) &
Joensuu (72km)

Möhköntie

PLACES TO STAY & EAT
3 Kuntoutuskeskus
  Pääskynpesä;
  Swimming Hall
5 Murginapirtti
6 Viinitorni
12 Hotel Ilomantsi
14 Ravintola Kelopirtti
17 Ravintola
  Parppeinpirtti

OTHER
1 Pyhän Elian Kirkko
2 Swimming Beach
4 Lutheran Church
7 Library
8 Post Office
9 Pub Monttu
10 S-Market
11 Bus Terminal
13 Tourist Office
15 Eläin Museo
  (Animal Museum)
16 Peltohermanni
  Winery

An Orthodox **tsasouna** (chapel) stands behind the Matelin museoaitta, a tiny museum commemorating female rune singer Mateli Kuivalatar, renowned in the 19th century for her renditions of the *Kanteletar* epic.

To get to Parppeinvaara, take the road south towards Joensuu. Turn left and follow the 'Runonlaulajan pirtti' sign.

Peltohermanni Wine Tower & Winery

The local water tower was reborn in 1994 as a **viinitorni** *(wine tower; adult/child €2/1; open 10am-10pm daily June–late Aug)* when some enterprising locals started a café at the top and specialised in serving their own wine. Strawberry, blackcurrant, whitecurrant, crowberry and blueberry are used as raw materials to produce the half-dozen varieties of wine sold here by the glass (€3.30). The tower has a panoramic viewing deck, which is a great place to sit on a summer afternoon or evening. Admission includes a cup of coffee, tea or fruit juice, but it's free after 6pm.

If you want to buy the wine by the bottle, you have to visit the **Peltohermanni winery** *(open 9am-5pm daily)* about 200m down the road from the wine tower.

Eläin Museo

The Animal Museum *(☎ 2183; adult/child €3.50/2; open 10am-5pm June–mid-Aug)* contains the stuffed results of many years of hunting. On display are most of the furry and feathered animals of Finland's forests, including wolves, bears, lynx, badgers, owls (including the huge Lapp owl), moose, seals and beavers. Pride of place goes to a 215kg male bear shot in 1968. It's as close as you'll get to most of these forest animals.

Churches

Ilomantsi features two interesting churches. **Pyhän Elian Kirkko** is the large and beautiful Orthodox church of Ilomantsi, 1km west of the village centre, towards Lake Ilomantsinjärvi. The *kalmisto* (graveyard) sign near the church will lead you to the old graveyard at the waterfront. It is a peaceful place, where old trees give shade to a few graves.

The large **Lutheran church**, dating from 1796, is almost as impressive as the Orthodox church. Following the Swedish conquest, a Lutheran congregation was established here

in 1653 and the new religion soon overshadowed the eastern one. Colourful paintings from 1832, an achievement of Samuel Elmgren, are the highlight of this church.

Special Events

As Ilomantsi has so many (Russian) Orthodox believers, several **Praasniekka** festivals are held here. Originally, these were strictly religious events, but these days they also attract tourists. Sometimes there is dancing afterwards. Ilomantsi village celebrates Petru Praasniekka on 28 and 29 June and Ilja Praasniekka on 19 and 20 July every year.

Not quite a festival, but the annual **Kantele Camp** is an annual event where you can spend 10 days learning to play this uniquely Karelian instrument. The course is intensive and includes accommodation and meals.

Places to Stay

Lomakeskus Ruhkaranta *(☎ 843 161; Ruhkarannantie 21; tent sites €7-12, cottages €33-74; open May-Sept)* is 9km east of Ilomantsi. In a thick pine forest, it has spectacular views of several lakes. There's a traditional smoke sauna here, but it takes six hours to heat up and costs €200 a session (only worthwhile for a large group). There's also an electric sauna. The restaurant is open only on weekends.

Anssilan Monola *(☎ 881 181; Anssilantie; singles/doubles €25/46, cottage €86)* is a former dairy farm on a hill 3km south of the village centre and about 500m off the main road. The friendly family rents rooms in a converted farmhouse building. Breakfast and linen are included.

Hotel Ilomantsi *(☎ 881 707, fax 883 270; Kalevalantie; singles/doubles €58/78, small twin €66)*, in the centre of the village, is a clean, comfortable hotel which is also a pub, restaurant, karaoke bar and local disco. This is where you should find Ilomantsi on a Saturday night.

Kuntoutuskeskus Pääskynpesä *(☎ 682 1200, fax 682 1444; e myyntipalvelu@paaskynpesa.fi; Henrikintie 4; singles/doubles €69/100)*, is an anonymous-looking spa hotel, popular with older Finns and families. It's right on Lake Ilomantsi and facilities include a pool, saunas (naturally) and various therapy treatments.

KARELIA

Places to Eat

There are several cheap **grillis** in the centre. For a real *pitopöytä* (Karelian buffet) go to **Ravintola Parppeinpirtti** *(☎ 881 094; lunch €10; open noon-3pm daily)* in Parppeinvaara, where there's a daily lunch buffet. Try the *vatruska* (Karelian pies of pastry and potato), and the slightly sweet *vuassa* (milk-malt drink).

On the main-road roundabout, **Ravintola Kelopirtti** is a log cabin with a café (lunch buffet €8) and an interesting Karelian craft shop.

Murginapirtti *(☎ 881 250; Yhtiöntie)* is an old-style Finnish farmhouse restaurant with a delicious lunch buffet for around €8.

Hotel Ilomantsi *(mains from €6.10)* has a restaurant open for lunch and dinner, and serving an unexciting range of meals. The town nightclub is downstairs. A little further along Kalevalantie, **Pub Monttu** is a local bar that gets busy on weekends and also serves food.

Getting There & Away

Buses run frequently between Joensuu and Ilomantsi from Monday to Friday (€10.40, one hour). There are fewer buses on weekends. The bus terminal is in the village centre. During school term there are Monday to Friday buses from here to surrounding villages, but in summer you'll have to rely on taxi buses, which you might have to charter. To get to Nurmes, Lieksa or other major towns, you have to go first to Joensuu and change there.

AROUND ILOMANTSI

From Ilomantsi, road No 5004 heads east towards the Russian border, through a patchwork of lakes and into the start of some fine wilderness trekking country.

Petkeljärvi National Park

The turn-off to Finland's smallest (6.3 sq km) national park is about 14km east of the main highway. The main reason to visit Petkeljärvi is to walk the nature trails that cover birch and pine forest and *eskers* (wooded ridges). The marked 35km 'Taitajan Taival' trek starts here and runs northeast to the village of Mekrijärvi, about 13km north of Ilomantsi. More than one-third of the park is water, with two sizeable lakes dominating.

Petkeljärvi Camping *(☎ 013-844 199; single/family tent sites €7/12, lodge singles/doubles/triples €29/39/51; open June-Aug)*, in the heart of the park, is an excellent retreat. As well as tent and caravan sites, there's a modern lodge building with kitchen, a café, sauna and boats and canoes for use on the lake. Park information, including maps, is also available here.

Möhkö

☎ 013

The tiny village of Möhkö, only a few kilometres from the Russian border, is at the southern end of the Wolf's Trail (see the boxed text 'Karelian Treks').

This remote outpost was once the unlikely scene of heavy industry. An ironworks was established here in 1849 and at its peak it employed more than 2000 people and was one of the largest ore-processing works in Finland. The site included a sawmill and tar works, and a canal was dug in 1872 to transport ore and timber out of the wilderness. Part of the original canal and lock can still be seen. The small **ironworks museum** *(☎ 844 111; admission €3.50; open 10am-6pm daily May-Aug, 10am-8pm July)* explains the story

Möhkön Karhumajat *(☎ 844 180; tent sites from €7, 2-person cabins €30, cottages €68; open June-Sept)* is a fine lakeside camping ground with pleasant cottages, a small beach, a couple of saunas, friendly owners and Finland's 'easternmost beer terrace'. Nearby is **Möhkön Manta**, a café in an old, grounded canal boat. Traditional Karelian pies, soups and sweets are dished up here from May to August.

HATTUVAARA

☎ 013

Hattuvaara, about 40km northeast of Ilomantsi, is a convenient base for exploring easternmost Finland. The village is the main landmark along the little-travelled *Runon ja rajan tie* route. Experiencing a summer night in this quaint little village is therapeutic: birds sing and cow bells tinkle. Winter is quieter, with a great deal of snow falling.

The main attraction here is the **Taistelijan Talo** *(Fighters House; ☎ 830 111; open 10am-10pm daily in summer)*, designed by Joensuu architect Erkki Helasvuo to symbolise the meeting of East and West. There is a

Karelian Treks

Some of the best trekking routes in North Karelia have been linked up to create **Karjalan Kierros** (Karelian Circuit), an 800km loop of marked trails between Ilomantsi and Lake Pielinen. The best known are the Bear's Trail (not to be confused with the more famous Bear's Ring in Oulanka National Park) and the Wolf's Trail, which link up in Patvinsuo National Park (see that section later in this chapter). These can be walked in either direction, but are described here in a north–south direction. You'll need to arrange transport to trailheads, including Patvinsuo National Park, in advance, although there is a bus service to Möhkö village.

Although there are wilderness huts and lean-to shelters along the way, it's advisable to carry a tent. Hiking equipment can be rented at the Ilomantsi tourist office. Much of the Ilomantsi region is boggy marshland, so waterproof footwear is essential.

For more information on these and other routes contact the Lieksa or Ilomantsi tourist offices, or **Metsähallitus** (☎ 0205-645 500; Urheilukatu 3A, Lieksa), the information office for the Forest & Park Service's eastern region. See also the Activities chapter earlier for general information about trekking.

Sustaival (Wolf's Trail)

The 90km Wolf's Trail is a marked three-day trek running north from Möhkö village to the marshlands of Patvinsuo National Park. The terrain consists mostly of dry heath, pine forest and swampy marshland which can be wet underfoot. This trail runs close to the Russian border in places and it was here that many of the battles in the Winter War and Continuation War were fought. Early in the trek, at Lake Sysmä, you'll see a memorial and anti-tank gun. There are wilderness cabins at Sarkkajärvi, Pitkajärvi and Jorho, and farm or camping accommodation in the village of Naarva. In the Ilomantsi wilderness area there are about 100 bears and 50 wolves – chances of running into one are slim but not impossible.

Karhunpolku (Bear's Trail)

The Bear's Trail is a 133km marked hiking trail of medium difficulty leading north from Patvinsuo National Park near Lieksa, through a string of national parks and nature reserves, including Ruunaa Recreation Area, along the Russian border. Because of this accessibility, the trail can be walked in relatively short stages. The trail ends at Teljo, about 50km south of Kuhmo. You'll need to arrange transport from either end.

From Patvinsuo, the trail crosses heathland and boardwalks 15km to the first wilderness hut at Kangas-Piilo, then another 14km to a hut and lean-to at Valkealampi. From here there's a short trail detouring to the WWII battle line of Kitsi. The trail then heads northwest to the Ruunaa Recreation Area, where there are several choices of accommodation, and opportunities for fishing canoeing and rafting.

Beyond Ruunaa it's around 42km to Änäkäinen, another WWII battlefield. The trail follows the Jongunjoki River on its final leg to the Ostroskoski wilderness hut, about 6km from Teljo.

Tapios Trail (Tapion Taival)

The easternmost trekking route in Finland, Tapion Taival (Fighter's Trail) gives you the choice of a 13km wilderness track along the Koitajoki River, or an 8km northern extension across the Koivusuo Nature Reserve, or yet another extension north of Koivusuo to Kivivaara. The Koitajoki section is certainly the highlight. The path is marked by orange paint on tree trunks.

You will need a private car and good local map to reach the trekking area, or you can negotiate with Jouni Puruskainen in Hattuvaara about transport and price.

---

fascinating **WWII museum** (admission €3.50) downstairs, with a short film in several languages, multimedia, photo exhibitions, weapons and displays relating chiefly to the Winter War and Continuation War fought along the nearby border. There are also *puhde-esineitä* (handicrafts) made

by Finnish soldiers during wartime. The house is run by Irma Anttonen and Jouni Puruskainen, who are also the contacts for information and accommodation in the village.

Hattuvaara has the oldest **Orthodox tsasouna** (chapel) in Finland. Built in the

1720s, it has several old Russian icons inside. Its small tower was used as a watchtower during WWII. On 29 June, a colourful **Praasniekka festival** takes place here, with a *ristinsaatto*, or Orthodox procession commemorating a saint, beginning at the *tsasouna*.

Places to Stay & Eat
Arhipanpirtti *(☎ 830 111, 0400-17367; Hatunraitti 5B; rooms per person €18.50)* is the main place to stay in Hattuvaara. There are rooms in several buildings, plus a four-person cottage at €70 a night, and the price includes linen and sauna. There are also some cottages and self-contained flats nearby for the same price.

Taistelijan Talo serves a fabulous all-day Finnish buffet (€10) in a pleasant dining room. As well as hearty meat and fish dishes, salads, bread, cheese and Karelian pies, there's a range of desserts. In summer, food is served until 10pm.

AROUND HATTUVAARA
Easternmost Point
With a vehicle you can journey east to the Finnish–Russian border crossing at **Lake Virmajärvi**, the easternmost point of Finland and therefore of the European Union (at least until Turkey is accepted as an EU member). You need a permit from the **Border Guards Station** *(open 8am-4pm Mon-Fri)* next to Taistelijan Talo in Hattuvaara, issued free on the spot provided you have your passport details with you. It's then a 15km drive down a fairly rough gravel road, signposted by blue 'EU' markers. There's not much to see and nothing to do at the end – it's sort of a spiritual (for Karelians) and geographical pilgrimage to say you've been.

The actual border is marked by two posts on a small island in the lake. About 2km back is the **log house**, which contains nothing of interest but you can stay here overnight with permission from Taistelijan Talo, and along the way you pass several WWII *sotapaikka* (battle locations) and memorials.

If you're in a group, Jouni Puruskainen at Taistelijan Talo in Hattuvaara runs tours out to Lake Virmajärvi (€35 per person, minimum five people) including a coffee stop at the log house.

Lake Pielinen Region

In a region so dominated by lakes, Pielinen – Finland's fourth largest – is something of a standout. A main road and numerous minor roads encircle the lake, ferries cross it in several directions, and some of the most interesting attractions in North Karelia can be found around its shores. Highlights include Koli National Park on the western shore, Lieksa and Vuonislahti on the east, and Nurmes in the north.

LIEKSA
☎ 013 • pop 16,000
The small centre of Lieksa, on Lake Pielinen about 100km north of Joensuu, is an important service centre and potential base if you plan to hike, bicycle, fish, paddle or raft in this very active corner of North Karelia. It has good transport links, including lake ferries across to Koli, accommodation, services and the primary tourist organisation for the region.

Count Per Brahe founded the town of Brahea in 1653 but it didn't survive long. The present Lieksa township was founded in 1936 and incorporated as a town in 1972.

Information
The local tourist office is **Lieksan Matkailu Oy** *(☎ 689 4050; w www.lieksa.fi/travel; Pielisentie 7; open 8am-6pm Mon-Fri, 9am-2pm Sat June-Aug, plus 11am-3pm Sun July, 8am-4pm Mon-Fri rest of the year)*. It has loads of information on accommodation, fishing, paddling, smoke saunas and national parks, and sells trekking maps for local routes. Staff can also book tours and accommodation.

The **post office** is at the northern end of Pielisentie, the main street. The **library** *(Urheilukatu)* has Internet access.

Pielisen Museo
Pielisen Museo *(☎ 689 4151; Pappilantie 2; adult/child €4/1.50; open 10am-6pm daily 15 May–15 Sept)* is a huge complex of almost 100 Karelian buildings and open-air exhibits, divided into several sections according to the century or the trade featured (eg, farming, milling, fire-fighting, forestry). The timber

buildings are set up in such a way that you don't get the feeling of a re-created village, but it's certainly a comprehensive display in a relatively small area – the collection comprises some 100,000 objects and 15,000 photographs. The separate **indoor museum** features photographs and static displays on Karelian folk history. It's also open in winter *(adult/child €3/1, open 10am-3pm Tues-Fri)* when the open-air display in closed.

Lieksa Church
The modern Lieksa church *(open 10am-6pm daily in summer)*, also known as the Church of Lake Pielinen, was built in 1982 to replace the old wooden church that burnt down on a freezing New Year's night in 1979. The huge cross-shaped ceiling dominates the hall, and large windows at the altar enable you to view the surviving bell tower.

Activities
Pony-trekking on hardy Icelandic horses can be arranged through the tourist office. **Ahaa Horse Stables** *(☎ 040-525 7742)* has riding lessons *(from €12)* and cross-country treks for more experienced riders.

In winter, husky-dog and snowmobile **expeditions** along the Russian border are popular – Lieksan Matkailu Oy has a list of tour operators. **Fishing** is good in Lake Pielinen, Pudasjoki River and the Ruunaa and Änäkäinen recreational fishing areas. They each require separate permits, available from local sports shops or the Lieksa tourist office.

Special Events
Lieksa Brass Week *(☎/fax 689 4144;* **w** *www .lieksabrass.com; Koski-Jaakonkatu 4)*, held during the last week in July, attracts quite a number of international musicians. There's a programme of concerts each day, with ticket prices ranging from €5 to €20.

Places to Stay & Eat
There are a few places to stay in Lieksa, but it's also worth considering the surrounding options in Vuonislahti, Koli and Ruunaa – see those sections later.

Timitraniemi Camping *(☎ 521 780;* **e** *ilkka .uusitupa@pp.inet.fi; tent sites €11, cabins €30-80; open 1 June–31 Aug)*, at the river mouth, has log cabins, cottages of varying sizes, plenty of tent sites and facilities like lakeside saunas and bikes and boats for hire.

Aikuikoulutuskkeskus *(☎ 244 3674; Oravatie 1; beds €14.60)* is a mouthful to pronounce but it's basically apartment-style student accommodation. Call ahead to book as there's no-one on site.

Hotelli Puustelli *(☎ 511 5500;* **e** *lieksa@ hotellipuustelli.inet.fi; Hovileirinkatu 3; singles /doubles €70/90, weekends & summer €65/ 80)* is a pleasant riverside hotel in the town centre, and rates include breakfast and sauna.

Most places to eat and drink are on Lieksa's main street, Pielisentie. **Cafe Sanna** *(Pielisentie 2-6; meals €6-8)* offers reasonably priced, home-cooked lunches. **Brahea Pizza** is across the street from Sanna.

Tinatahti *(☎ 521 914; Pielisentie 28)* is a lively pub that also serves meals.

Getting There & Away
Buses from Joensuu are frequent (€12.40, 1½ hours). There are two trains a day to Lieksa from Helsinki, via Joensuu. The more scenic mode of transport is by ferry from Joensuu, via Koli; see the Joensuu Getting There & Away section for more information.

The car ferry MF *Pielinen* from Lieksa to Koli operates twice daily in summer (June to mid-August), departing from Lieksa at 9.30am and 3.30pm, and returning from Koli at 11.30am and 5.30pm. The trip takes 1¾ hours and costs €14/7 per adult/child, €7 for a car, €4 for a motorcycle and €2 for a bicycle.

PATVINSUO NATIONAL PARK
Patvinsuo is a large marshland area between Lieksa and Ilomantsi. Swans, cranes and other birds nest here, and bears and other mammals can be seen if you're lucky (or unlucky in the case of a bear). With the excellent *pitkospuu* (boardwalk) network, you can easily hike around, observing the life of a Finnish marshland.

If you have little time, go to the southern shore of Lake Suomu. It's 3.5km from the main road to Teretin lintutorni, a birdwatching tower. This is a good walk through forests and wetlands, and you will see some birds. Get a free map at the park headquarters and use it for planning. There are lakes and pine forests between the wetlands. Come in May or June to hear birds sing, or from June to September for the best trekking conditions.

KARELIA

There are three nature trails and several good hiking routes along the boardwalk path. You can walk around Lake Suomu or follow *pitkospuu* trails through the wetlands.

Suomu Park Centre (☎ 548 506) has a warden in attendance from May to mid-September, for advice, fishing permits and free maps. There is a dormitory with nine beds, including the use of a small kitchen. You can use the telephone and the sauna for a fee. There are seven camping sites and one *laavu* (an open shelter with sloping roof) within the park boundaries; all have toilets and firewood and are free of charge.

Getting There & Away

There is no public transport. From Lieksa, drive 18km east towards Hatunkylä, then turn right to Kontiovaara. It is a dangerously narrow but very scenic road, which runs along small ridges. When you reach a sealed road (Uimaharjuntie), turn left, drive a few hundred metres and turn right. If you drive along the eastern Runon ja rajantie route, turn west as you see the small 'Uimaharju' sign, just south of the Lieksa–Ilomantsi border. If you are trekking, the Karhunpolku (Bear's Trail) and Susittaival (Wolf's Trail) both lead here, as the park is where these trails meet.

RUUNAA RECREATION AREA
☎ 013

Ruunaa, 30km northeast of Lieksa, is adventurous Finns' most sought-after destination east of Lake Pielinen, mainly for the huge variety of outdoor activities that can easily be arranged here. It boasts 38km of waterways with six white-water rapids, plus unpolluted wilderness, excellent trekking paths and good fishing. The area is run by the Forest and Park Service, which puts more than 6000kg of fish into the waters every year. Designated camp sites (with fire rings) are also provided and maintained.

There's an observation tower situated at Huuhkajavaara.

Information

Ruunaa Nature Centre (☎ 0205-645 757; *open 9am-7pm daily in summer, 9am-9pm July*) is near the bridge over the Naarajoki, where most boat trips start. There are exhibitions, maps, a library and a free slide show in English. This is a good stop to find out about rafting operators and hiking trails.

Activities

Ruunaa is busy all year round, as it hosts skiing and other snow sports in winter.

Boating, Canoeing & Rafting There are six rapids, and you can shoot them in wooden or rubber boats. There are several launches daily in summer from Naarajoki bridge (near the Nature Centre). A two- to four-hour trip costs €34/17 per adult/child (including lunch) and the Nature Centre or **Lieksa tourist office** (☎ 689 4050) can line you up with an operator. If you're coming from Lieksa and time is short, it pays to check at the tourist office there about which tours are going out, since all trips require a minimum of eight people and should be booked in advance. Transport can also be arranged from Lieksa if you book a tour. **Erasteely** (☎ 546 550) organises canoeing expeditions from the Nature Centre for €70/35 per adult/child. Rafting operators include:

Karjalan Eramatkat (☎ 312 970) adult/child €59/29.50; departures on demand; wooden boat or rubber raft; includes smoke sauna and fried salmon
Koski-Jaako (☎ 533 122) adult/child €34/17; noon departure; wooden boat
Lieksan Koskikierros (☎ 521 645) adult/child €35/17; 10am & 3.30pm departure; wooden boat or rubber raft
Ruunaan Matkailu (☎ 533 130) adult/child €35/17; 10am & 2.30pm departure; wooden boat

Fishing Ruunaa is one of the most popular fishing spots in North Karelia. Trout and salmon fishing is excellent in the numerous rapids, and good fishing spots are accessible along a long wooden walkway. One-day fishing permits cost €13 in summer and are available in Lieksa and at the Ruunaa Nature Centre. There is also a fishing-permit machine near the Neitijoki rapids. Fishing is allowed from June to early September and from mid-November to late December, and only lures and flies may be used.

Trekking There are two trekking routes within the Ruunaa area. The **Karhunpolku** (Bear's Trail), a longer trekking route, passes through Ruunaa. You can find it just 50m north of the Naarajoki bridge. The path is marked with round orange symbols on trees. See the boxed text 'Karelian Treks' earlier in this chapter for more details.

Around the river system, and over two beautiful suspension bridges, runs **Ruunaan koskikierros**, a marked 29km loop along good *pitkospuu* paths. If you have more time, there are another 20km of side trips you can take. If you start at the Naarajoki bridge, you will have to walk 5km along the Bear's Trail to reach the Ruunaan koskikierros trail. Another 3.3km brings you to the **Neitikoski rapids**, where you'll find commercial services. Neitikoski also has road access and a parking area.

Places to Stay & Eat

There are at least 10 *laavu* shelters and another 10 designated camp sites in the area. Camping and sleeping in a *laavu* is free of charge. Get the free *Ruunaa Government Hiking Area* map and guide for accommodation information. You will need a lightweight mattress, a sleeping bag and some mosquito repellent. Lighting a fire is allowed, except during fire alerts (watch for posted signs).

Ruunaan Matkailu (☎/fax 533 130; **w** www .ruunaanmatkailu.fi; Siikakoskentie 47; singles/ doubles from €17/26, cabins €36-83), 5km east of Naarajoki bridge, has tidy accommodation, as well as a café, lakeside sauna, smoke sauna, rental boats and various snowmobile and boating tours.

Neitikoski Hiking Centre (☎ 533 170; tent sites/cabins €10/75), near the Neitikoski rapids, has a large café, camping area, kitchen, sauna and luxurious four- to six-bed cabins. There are mountain bikes, canoes and rowing boats for hire. The boardwalk to the rapids starts near here.

Lomapirtti Sillankorva (☎/fax 533 121; rooms from €32-80) offers superb accommodation right at the Naarajoki bridge. You can rent the entire farmhouse if you have a large group (sleeps at least 12; €121/467 a night/week), or either floor of two renovated apartments (from €62/239), plus there's an outbuilding sleeping four (€32). Everything is extremely clean and beautifully designed. There's a smoke sauna and a summer restaurant.

Getting There & Away

Infrequent minibuses make the trip from Lieksa – inquire at the tourist office for timetables. The best way to reach the area is on an organised rafting tour from Lieksa, by hitching or by private car.

NURMIJÄRVI AREA
☎ 013

Known for its canoeing routes, the Nurmijärvi area is wild and remote. Nurmijärvi village has enough services to get you to the Jongunjoki or Lieksajoki canoeing routes, or to the Änäkäinen area for fishing and trekking.

Änäkäinen Fishing Area

Änäkäinen is a government fishing area, with the Bear's Trail running through it. The Forest and Park Service controls fish quantities in three lakes in the area. Fishing is allowed year-round, except in May. The Aunen Kahvila and Jongunjoen Lomapirtti (see Places to Stay) have boats and fishing permits (€10/35 a day/week in summer). Permits are also available in Lieksa.

Änäkäinen experienced fierce fighting during the early weeks of the Winter War in December 1939. Finnish soldiers held their positions here, leaving a large number of Russians dead. In order to stop enemy tanks, the Finns built large rock barriers; when the war erupted again in 1940, even larger rocks were added.

Canoeing the Pankasaari Route

While in Nurmijärvi, you can rent a canoe from the **Erästely Company** (☎ 546 550; Nurmijärventie 158A). The paddle route starts across the road. Get yourself a free route guide, which is widely available at brochure outlets (tourist offices or roadside shopping areas), or at Lieksan Matkailu in Lieksa. The route follows the Lieksajoki downstream to Lake Pankajärvi. From there, you paddle southeast under a road bridge to Lake Pudasjärvi. Avoid the dangerous Pankakoski power station in the south and paddle upstream to the upper part of the Lieksajoki. Heading northwest from this point, you first reach Naarajoki at Ruunaa and then pass a few tricky rapids, especially Käpykoski (pull the canoe with a rope here, unless you are experienced), before returning to Nurmijärvi.

Canoeing the Jongunjoki

This beautiful wilderness river has more than 40 small rapids, but none of them is very tricky. Lieksan Matkailu has a good English-language guide to the route. You can start at Jonkeri up north (in the municipality of Kuhmo), or further south at Teljo bridge, or

KARELIA

at Aittokoski, or even at Lake Kaksinkantaja. Allow four days if you start at Jonkeri and one day from the last point. The Räsänen shop in Nurmijärvi will take care of transportation to Jonkeri, Teljo or Kaksinkantaja, and will also rent canoes.

Places to Stay & Eat

Aittokoski Cabin (☎ 546 500; Nurmijärventie 158A), at Erästely Company, the main canoe rental company, also offers accommodation in the village, usually rented out to groups – call ahead to see if there's a spare bed.

Jongunjoen Lomapirtti (☎/fax 546 531; Kivivaarantie 21; beds per person €22) is 2km from the main road towards Änäkäinen and the Russian border. If you come by bus, you can walk here. There are two- to six-person rooms, tent sites, smoke saunas and bicycles, canoes and boats for rent.

Aunen Kahvila (☎ 546 503; Nurmijärventie 154) is a popular roadside café in Nurmijärvi, 15km from the Russian border. There are meals, and you can buy fishing permits and pick up keys for the Änäkäinen rented fishing boats.

VUONISLAHTI
☎ 013

Vuonislahti is a rural lakeside village, with little more than a train station and a great hostel – which is enough to justify a stay if you have the time.

There is a **war memorial** on a small hill across the road as you come from the train station. This is where Russians were stopped by Finnish soldiers in 1808. The nearby *tanssilava* (dance stage) house has dancing in summer on Saturday evenings.

The brilliant lakeside HI hostel, **Kestikievari Herranniemi** (☎ 542 110; W www.herranniemi.com; Vuonislahdentie 185; dorm beds €12.50, cabins €25-68, B&B singles/doubles €42/58) is about 2km south of the train station. The quaint 200-year-old farm building has a restaurant, a range of comfortable accommodation, including cheap dormitories in an old *aitta* (storage) building, two lakeside saunas and rowing boats. The owners even offer a range of treatment therapies such as herbal baths and *turvesauna* (a cross between a sauna and a mud bath). To get to Herranniemi, walk straight from the Vuonislahti train station to the main road, turn left and proceed 500m.

In Vuonislahti, **Hotelli Pielinen** (☎ 544 144; Lapikaytavantie 54; dorm beds €21, singles/doubles €27/48, hotel doubles €58) is a modern hostel/hotel, with a restaurant, smoke sauna and a range of activities.

There are daily trains to Vuonislahti from Joensuu and Lieksa. The small Vuonislahti train station keeps short hours, but you can always buy tickets on the train.

Paateri

Paateri is best known for the **church and gallery** (☎ 543 223; adult/child €4.20/2.50; open 10am-6pm daily May-Sept) at the studio-home of Eva Ryynänen, a respected wood-carver, on Lake Vuonisjärvi. Born in 1915, she has been a sculptor since her teens and became widely recognised in Finland in the 1970s. This isolated property, surrounded by pine trees, is the childhood home of her husband, Paavo. The Paateri wilderness church was built in 1991 with walls and floor made of Russian pine, and huge doors carved from Canadian cedar. The altar was created using a stump that once belonged to the largest pine tree in Finland. The place also has a café.

One way to get to Paateri is to row a boat from the Herranniemi hostel, but it's a 1½-hour trip one way – not for the faint-hearted or lazy. By motor boat, also available from the hostel, it takes about 20 minutes. If you are driving or cycling, follow the road signs from the main road or from the secondary road north of Vuonislahti. You can also rent a bicycle at the Herranniemi hostel.

KOLI NATIONAL PARK

The views from the top of 347m Koli Hill offer some of Finland's finest Lakeland scenery – it was these views that inspired many of the famous artists from Finland's National Romantic era, including Pekka Halonen and Eero Jarnefelt. The composer Jean Sibelius is said to have played a piano at the top of the hill on his honeymoon.

Rising above Lake Pielinen and accessible by ferry from Lieksa, Koli has been dubbed the first-ever tourist attraction in Finland and it continues to draw holiday-makers year-round – as a winter sports resort and for hiking, boating and its unique scenery in summer. Although the lake views are panoramic and the nature trails in the national park are good, don't expect too much – it's a hill covered in pine and birch.

Koli Hill was declared a national park in 1991 after hot debate between environmentalists and landowners. The owners agreed to sell their land and environmentalists dropped their demand that the Hotel Koli, up on the hill, be demolished. Most of the area remains relatively pristine and there are some 90km of marked walking tracks.

The hill has road access and from the lower car park there's a short funicular railcar up to the hotel (free). **Koli Heritage Centre** (☎ 013-688 8400; **w** koli.metla.fi; open 9am- 7pm daily June-Aug, 10am-5pm Jan-June) is a modern visitor centre with exhibitions on history and geology of the park (adult/child €5/2), and information on hiking. There's also tourist information available at **Art-Cafe Kolin Ryynanen** (☎ 013-422 000; Kolintie 2A) adjacent to the supermarket in Koli village.

Ukko-Koli is the highest point and 200m further is **Akka-Koli**, another peak. **Mammutti** is a huge stone with a 'Temple of Silence', which is used for religious events. The solid rock peak nearby is called **Pahakoli**, or 'Evil Koli'. Further south is **Mäkrävaara**, a hill that offers the best views.

In winter, Koli attracts skiers with two slalom centres (Loma-Koli and Ukko-Koli, served by a total of nine lifts) and more than 60km of cross-country trails, including 24km of lit track. If you can't make it up to Lapland, this is one of Finland's most accessible winter ski resorts. Contact the **Koli Ski Centre** (☎ 013-672 275) for lift tickets, equipment hire and more information.

Places to Stay

There are several basic **huts** in the national park. They each cost €17 per night and can be booked through the heritage centre.

Loma-Koli Camping (☎ 013-673 212; tent sites €10-12; open June–late Aug), near the Hiisi Hill slopes, has excellent facilities, including cottages, and rents mountain bikes.

Kolin Lomaranta (☎ 040-729 5030; Merilänrannantie 15; tent sites €10, cabins €20-34; open June-Aug) has camping areas and 'outbuildings' for two to five people.

The family-run **Koli Hostel** (☎ 013-673 131; Niinilahdentie 47; dorm beds from €12; open year-round), on a gravel road 5km from the bus stop, has a kitchen and smoke sauna. It's a great getaway and one of the most relaxing hostels in Finland – if you call ahead you may be able to arrange a pick-up.

Hotel Koli (☎ 013-688 7100, fax 688 7200; Ylä-Kolintie 39; singles/doubles from €83/ 100), at the top of Koli Hill, is a huge concrete-and-glass place dominating the hill top. Although it does nothing to enhance the scenery, the views from the **Hillside Cafe** and **Scenic Restaurant** are pretty special.

Getting There & Away

There are buses to Koli from Joensuu, Juuka and Nurmes, including at least one a day to the top of Koli Hill. The best way to arrive in summer is by lake ferry from Joensuu or Lieksa (see those sections). Buses to the top of Koli Hill meet all arriving ferries.

JUUKA
☎ 013

Juuka, just off the main highway about halfway between Nurmes and Koli, is known for its soapstone mining and handicrafts. It has a small **Puu-Juuka** (old town) of wooden houses, some more than 100 years old. They were preserved from demolition largely through the efforts of local individuals and have now been restored as shops, galleries and homes. There's also the **Mill Museum** and the **Village Museum**.

Piitterin Lomakylä (☎ 472 000; Piitterintie 144; tent sites €10-11.50, cabins €30-40), on the shore of Lake Pielinen, has a marina and swimming beach. There is a typical Finnish huvilava (dancing stage) here, where minor Finnish celebrities sometimes sing on Saturday nights.

PAALASMAA ISLAND
☎ 013

The largest island in Lake Pielinen is connected to the mainland by a free ferry that winds through smaller islands. The island is noted for its scenery and peaceful atmosphere, and is the highest island in Finland – its tallest point is 132m above water level. There is a wooden **observation tower** on the island, 3km from the camping ground via a marked trail. If you follow the signs that say 'tornille', you will see some **old houses** that tell the long history of Paalasmaa.

The ferry terminal is 15km east of the main road and the turn-off is about 2km north of Juuka. **Paalasmaan Lomamajat** (☎ 479 516; tent sites €8; open June–late Aug) is a camping ground at the eastern end of the island with a nice lakeside spot.

KARELIA

NURMES
☎ 013 • pop 11,000

Nurmes, at the northwestern tip of Lake Pielinen, is probably the most picturesque of the Karelian-heritage eastern towns. Much like Lieksa, this is a base for wallet-draining activities such as dog-sledding, snowmobiling, ice-fishing and cross-country skiing tours in winter, and canoeing and farmhouse tours in summer. It's a more pleasant town in its own right though, with a terraced Puu-Nurmes (Old Town) area of historical wooden buildings, rows of beautiful birch trees lining Kirkkokatu, and a delightful re-creation of a Karelian village.

Nurmes was founded in 1876 by Tsar Alexander II of Russia and the Old Town still has the character approved of by the 19th-century Russian ruler.

Orientation & Information
The train and bus stations are in the town centre. The main street is Kirkkokatu, at the northwestern end of which is Puu-Nurmes, while the Bomba (a Karelian theme village) and most places to stay are a few kilometres southeast of the centre.

For local information and to book activities, the efficient **Loma-Nurmes tourist office** *(☎ 481 770;* w *www@nurmes.fi; open 8am-10pm daily in summer, 8am-5pm Mon-Fri rest of the year)* is at the Hyvärilä Holiday Centre 3km southeast of town, which is also a good place to stay.

The **post office** is at Torikatu 5. The **public library** *(☎ 689 5125; Kötsintie 2)*, in the Nurmes-talo building at the northeastern end of town, has free Internet access, a reading room and a collection of the *Kalevala* in various languages.

Things to See
Just north of the kauppatori, the **Lutheran church** *(open 10am-6pm in summer)* from 1896 is the largest in North Karelia, with 2300 seats. Inside are some miniature models of earlier Lutheran churches.

Continue northwest from the church to reach **Puu-Nurmes**, the Old Town area on the *esker* (ridge) above the train station. It's a pleasant neighbourhood for a stroll among the traditional wooden houses, which are protected by law and surrounded by birch trees. The plan dates back to 1897.

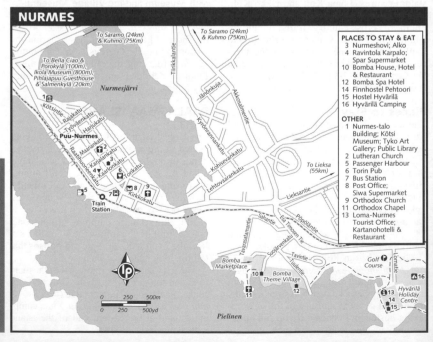

NURMES

PLACES TO STAY & EAT
3 Nurmeshovi; Alko
4 Ravintola Karpalo; Spar Supermarket
10 Bomba House, Hotel & Restaurant
12 Bomba Spa Hotel
14 Finnhostel Pehtoori
15 Hostel Hyvärilä
16 Hyvärilä Camping

OTHER
1 Nurmes-talo Building; Kötsi Museum; Tyko Art Gallery; Public Library
2 Lutheran Church
5 Passenger Harbour
6 Torin Pub
7 Bus Station
8 Post Office; Siwa Supermarket
9 Orthodox Church
11 Orthodox Chapel
13 Loma-Nurmes Tourist Office; Kartanohotelli & Restaurant

Kötsi Museum (☎ 689 5117; Kotsintie 2; adult/child €1.70/0.85; open noon-6pm Mon-Fri), the local museum of history, is in the large Nurmes-talo building. Artefacts on display include some from the Stone Age. With the same ticket you can visit the Ikola Museum, an agricultural museum in Tuupala northeast of the centre. It features an open-air exhibit of Karelian wooden buildings. Also in the Nurmes-talo building is the free Tyko Art Gallery with changing monthly exhibitions.

Nurmes' biggest tourist draw is Bomba House, 2.5km southeast of the town centre. The imposing main building – with its high roof and ornate wooden trim – is a replica of a typical Karelian family house that was built in 1855 by Jegor Bombin, a farmer from Suojärvi (now in Russian Karelia). It now houses a restaurant. The surroundings include a charming re-creation of a Karelian village, with an Orthodox tsasouna (chapel) and a summer theatre. The village also has shops, craft studios and a summer market, and you can buy locally made wines, homemade ice cream, handicrafts and more.

Activities & Organised Tours
Perfect for those with lots of money but little time, Nurmes offers a well-organised schedule of tours with daily departures – dog-sledding, snowmobiling, ice-fishing and cross-country skiing from January to the end of March, and canoeing, rapids-shooting (at Ruunaa) and farmhouse tours from June to the end of August. Nurmes is a popular holiday spot for Finns so there are usually enough people to form a tour.

Contact the Loma–Nurmes tourist office for an updated schedule, pricing information and other details. Bookings at least 24 hours in advance are often required for the tours.

Saimaa Ferries (☎ 481 244) has cruises on Lake Pielinen in summer (€14) from the passenger harbour near the train station.

Special Events
The Bomba Festival Week, held in early or mid-July, is a Finno-Ugrian cultural spectacle, with theatre performances and concerts. It's a fascinating event for those who have a special interest in Finnic cultures. There's an ice-fishing championship on Lake Pielinen in March.

Places to Stay
The main choice for accommodation in Nurmes is Hyvärilä Holiday Centre (☎ 481 770; Lomatie), a sprawling lakeside complex 4km southeast of town, with a camping ground, two youth hostels, an upmarket hotel, restaurant and a golf course. There's also a small swimming beach, tennis courts, bike and boat rentals and plenty of other activities. You can walk from here to Bomba Spa along marked walking routes. Not surprisingly, this is a very popular vacation destination for Finnish families and school groups, and if you're tired of travelling, it's not a bad place to pull up stumps and relax for a while.

Hyvärilä Camping (tent sites per person/family €7/12, cabins €30-48; open mid-May–mid-Sept) is a spacious area of lawn on the lake.

Hostel Hyvärilä (dorm beds €14, linen €6; open year-round) is a purpose-built hostel with dormitory accommodation, communal kitchen and laundry and access to all resort facilities. Breakfast is €5 extra. Finnhostel Pehtoori (singles/doubles €35/50) is a better standard of hostel accommodation in a building with four double rooms. Bathrooms are shared but breakfast and linen is included

Finally, Kartanohotelli (singles/doubles €52/70, suites from €120) is the resort's hotel and restaurant, with comfortable rooms with TV and breakfast included.

About 1km back towards town near the Karelian theme village, Bomba Spa Hotel (☎ 687 200, fax 687 2100; Suojärvenkatu 1; singles/doubles from €78/95) is a stylish set-up where you can pamper yourself with the spa and sauna facilities, then sleep in modern hotel rooms. Nonguests can use the spa facilities for €10. About 200m away Hotel Bomba (apartments €120-177) is a group of attractive apartments in Karelian cabins decorated by local artisans.

In Nurmes town itself, Nurmeshovi (☎/fax 480 750; Kirkkokatu 21; singles/doubles €58/80, weekends & summer €41/64) is a bit of a travelling salesperson's joint, but it's central with a decent restaurant and functional rooms.

Pihlajapuu Guesthouse (☎ 440 090; Joensuuntie 50), in Salmenkylä village, some 20km from Nurmes, gets rave reviews from travellers. It's a friendly, family-run guesthouse with kitchen facilities and activities arranged by the owners.

Places to Eat

In the town centre, you can rely on the **grilli** at the kauppatori, or do your grocery shopping at the **Spar supermarket** on Kirkkokatu.

Ravintola Karpalo *(☎ 480 651; Kirkkokatu 18)* is an unpretentious place behind the supermarket. It serves burgers, pizzas, kebabs and steaks and has a €7 lunch buffet. It's doubles as a local nightspot with karaoke and dancing nightly.

Bella Ciao *(☎ 461 332; Porokylänkatu 14; mains from €6)*, in the commercial centre of Porokylä, is a good Italian restaurant, popular with families, and with reasonably priced pizza and pasta.

Bomba House *(☎ 678 200; lunch buffet €13, mains €10-23)* has an expensive but fantastic Karelian smorgasbord abounding in Karelian pies, *muikku* (fried whitefish) and varieties of *karjalanpaisti* (stew), served throughout the day in summer.

For a beer with the local crowd it's hard to beat the **Torin Pub** *(Kauppatori 7)*, a rustic joint opposite the market square.

Getting There & Away

Nurmes is quite a transport hub for this side of Lake Pielinen. Buses run regularly to Joensuu (€16.80, two hours), Kuhmo (€10.40, one hour), Kuopio (€14.60, two hours) and Lieksa (€7.90, 40 minutes).

Regional trains from Joensuu (€15.20, two hours) via Lieksa, stop in Nurmes.

Saimaa Ferries *(☎ 481 244; W www .saimaaferries.fi; Kirkkokatu 16)* operates ferries on Lake Pielinen in summer. As well as cruises, there are scheduled ferries to Koli and Joensuu. The MS *Vinkeri II* travels to and from Joensuu (via Koli) twice weekly, departing from Nurmes at 9am on Wednesday and Friday (€35, 10 hours).

On Sunday a ferry goes only to Koli, departing from Nurmes at 10am (€20, 3½ hours).

AROUND NURMES
Saramo
☎ 013

This small, remote village, 24km north of Nurmes, is where the *Korpikylien tie* (Road of Wilderness Villages) begins. At the far end of the village, the **Kalastajatalo** *(Fishers House; ☎ 434 066; Saramontie 77; open daily in summer, Sat & Sun rest of the year)* serves as an information centre and restaurant. There is a shop and a post office in Saramo.

Saramo can be used as a base for the marked 75km **Saramo Jotos Trek**. Between Saramo and Peurajärvi, there are two campfire sites in addition to Kourukoski, a spot named after rapids there. Between Peurajärvi and road No 75, at Jalasjärvi, there's a *laavu*. Between road No 75 and Lake Mujejärvi, there are three *laavu* sites. South of Lake Mujejärvi, there's a *laavu* at Markuskoski and cottages for rent at Paalikkavaara. Ask for a trail map in Nurmes or Saramo.

It is also possible to paddle the Saramojoki River, starting from Peurajärvi or Mujejärvi lakes. Contact Kalastajatalo in Saramo for canoe rentals (€50 a day) and transport (around €15).

Tampere & Häme Region

The Häme (Swedish: Tavastland) district is a place of great contrasts: from the energetic industrial city of Tampere and the fortress town of Hämeenlinna, to countless old villages such as Hattula and Kangasala; from the wilderness of the north to the flat farmland in the south.

The people of Häme built a chain of fortresses that had its heyday around 1000 years ago. In 1249 Earl Birger, on a Catholic crusade, arrived in Häme. He attacked the Hakoinen fortress and founded the Swedish stronghold of Tavastehus (Finnish: Hämeenlinna). The Swedish settlers who followed established large estates – causing irritation among locals who had traditionally been hunters and fishers. During the 19th century a workers' movement began in industrialised Tampere, which spread to other provinces.

Tampere

☎ 03 • pop 198,000

Tampere (Swedish: Tammerfors), Finland's third-largest city, is the largest Nordic city without access to the sea. Once known for its textile industry, dozens of red-brick chimneys from former factories point skyward in this 19th-century manufacturing centre; most have now been transformed into superb cultural centres, bars or restaurants – notably the former Finlayson and Tampella mills.

Long known as the 'Manchester of Finland', on a grey day Tampere takes on a sort of Dickensian (or maybe Orwellian) quality, with steam rising from the ground and hanging in the air like industrial fog. But if this paints a bad picture, don't be put off: Tampere works beautifully, somehow combining working-class energy with Finnish sophistication. With a large student population and growing technology industry, Tampere is one of Finland's liveliest and energetic cities.

History

In the Middle Ages, the area around Tampere was inhabited by the notorious Pirkka tribe which collected taxes as far north as Lapland. At that time, the 'town' consisted of a number of Swedish-run estates around the forests and the two lakes that surround

Highlights

- Exploring the bars and clubs of Tampere, one of Finland's most exciting cities, especially during Tammerfest
- Cruising the 'Poet's Way' from Tampere to Virrat
- Touring the imposing medieval Häme Castle, pride of Hämeenlinna
- Cycling the Häme Ox Road, an ancient trade route which once linked Turku with Hameenlinna
- Watching two of Finland's best ice-hockey teams do battle at Tampere's Hakametsä stadium
- Taking in the view from Lahti's Ski Jump Observation Terrace

Tampere. Modern Tampere was founded in 1779 during Gustav III of Sweden's reign.

In the 19th century, the Tampere Rapids, or Tammerkoski, which today supply abundant hydroelectric power, were a magnet for textile industries. Finnish and foreign investors flocked to the busy town, including the Scottish industrialist James Finlayson, who founded the cotton mill in 1820.

The Russian Revolution in 1917 increased interest in socialism among Tampere's large working-class population. It became the capital of the 'Reds' during the Civil War that followed Finnish independence.

TAMPERE & HÄME REGION

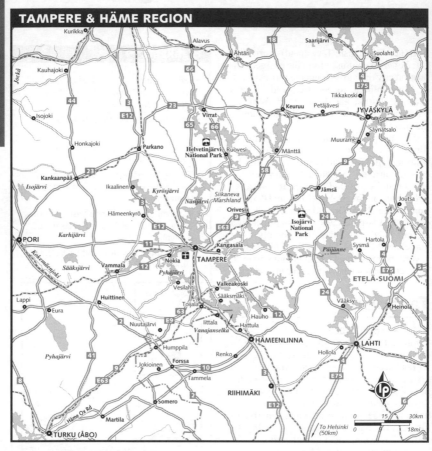

Orientation & Information

Tampere is set between Lake Näsijärvi and Lake Pyhäjärvi, which are connected by the Tammerkoski Rapids. Just about everything is conveniently arranged along one street, the cobbled Hämeenkatu, with the train station at the eastern end.

Tourist Offices The excellent **Tampere City Tourist Office** (☎ 3146 6800, fax 3146 6463; ⓦ www.tampere.fi; Verkatehtaankatu 2; open 8.30am-8pm Mon-Fri, 10am-5pm Sat & Sun June–late Aug, 10am-5pm Mon-Fri rest of the year) has lots of information, Internet terminals and helpful staff. Pick up the free guide This is Tampere & Surroundings. The office has a **hotel booking hotline** (☎ 342 5700, fax 342 5736; open 8.30am-4.30pm Mon-Fri).

Money The best place to change money is the **Forex currency exchange office** (Hämeenkatu 1; open 9am-7pm Mon-Fri, 9am-5pm Sat year-round, plus 10am-4pm Sun in summer) opposite the train station.

Post & Communications The **main post office** (Rautatienkatu 21, 33100 Tampere; open 9am-8pm Mon-Fri, 10am-2pm Sat) is near the train station.

Tampere City Library (Metso; ☎ 314 614; Pirkankatu 2; open 9.30am-8pm Mon-Fri, 9.30am-3pm Sat, noon-6pm Sun, shorter hours in summer) is called 'Metso' (Wood Grouse) by locals because of its unusual organic architecture. It has several Internet terminals, some of which are first-come-first-served (15 minutes). There are two free terminals in the tourist office. **Nettikahvila Vuoltsu** (*Vuolteen-katu;* [e] *nettikahvila@info1.info.tampere.fi; open noon-6pm Mon-Fri*) is an Internet café opposite the bus station.

Bookshops For an extensive selection of English-language fiction and nonfiction, head to **Akateeminen Kirjakauppa** (*Tuomiokirkonkatu 28*).

Left Luggage The train station has lockers for €2 to €3, depending on size. It also has a left-luggage counter. Lockers at the bus station cost €2 for 24 hours.

Medical Services About 2km east of the train station, **Tampere University Hospital** (☎ 247 5111) deals with emergencies.

Vapriikki Museum Centre
Vapriikki (☎ 3146 6966; *Veturiaukio 4;* [w] *www.tampere.fi/vapriikki; adult/child & student €4/1; open 10am-6pm Tues-Sun, 11am-8pm Wed*) is Tampere's premier exhibition space – a bright, modern glass and steel gallery in the renovated Tampella textile mill. As well as regularly changing art and photography exhibitions, there's a permanent display on Tampere's history from prehistoric times to the present. Also here is the small but cluttered **ice hockey museum**, which will no doubt inspire some emotion if you're familiar with the players and teams that star in Finland's national sporting passion. On display are photos, trophies, pucks, jerseys and other hockey memorabilia.

There's a pleasant café on the ground floor of the complex.

Lenin Museum
The small Lenin Museum (☎ 276 8100; [w] *www.tampere.fi/culture/lenin; Hämeenpuisto 28; adult/child €4/2; open 9am-6pm Mon-Fri, 11am-4pm Sat & Sun*) is one of Tampere's more interesting attractions. There are just two rooms packed with photographs, documents and relics from the life of the Russian revolutionary, who spent some time in Tampere. Since 1946, the museum has been maintained by the Finnish-Soviet Friendship Society. There's a crazy gift shop where you can buy Lenin pens, badges, T-shirts and other souvenirs.

Vladimir Lenin lived in Finland from November 1905 to December 1907, and was a popular figure for championing Finnish independence, while shaping socialism in the Soviet Union. Among the displays is the threadbare couch that Lenin slept on at Helsinki Library. The building itself is where Lenin convened Russian revolutionaries in 1905 and 1906.

Moomin Valley Museum
Tove Jansson, the Finnish artist and writer, created her Moomin figures decades ago, but the popularity of the comical cartoon figures never seems to wane – at least not in Finland. The museum (*Hämeenpuisto 20; adult/child €4/1; open 9am-5pm Mon-Fri, 10am-6pm Sat & Sun in summer, closed Mon rest of the year*), in the basement of the public library building, contains original drawings by Ms Jansson, plus elaborate tableaux models depicting stories from Moomin Valley (English language explanations are available), computer displays, toys and other memorabilia. Naturally there's a gift shop.

Adjacent is the small **Museum of Minerals** (*Kivimuseo; adult/student €4/1*), devoted to rare stones and fossils. It has the same hours as Moomin Valley – but not the same crowds.

Sara Hildén Art Museum
The museum (☎ 214 3134; *Sarkanniemi; adult/child €4/1; open 11am-6pm daily, closed Mon in winter*), on the shore of Lake Näsijärvi, contains a collection of international and Finnish modern art and sculpture amassed by Sara Hildén, a local business person and art collector. There are also changing art exhibitions. The concrete building was designed by Pekka Ilveskoski and was opened in 1979. There are good views from the café, which has Alvar Aalto furniture. Take bus No 4 or 16 from the centre.

Hiekka Art Museum
The Hiekka museum (☎ 212 3975; *Pirkankatu 6; adult/child €4/2; open 3pm-6pm Tues-Thur, noon-3pm Sun*) contains the collection of Kustaa Hiekka, a wealthy industrialist. There are paintings, furniture and fine old gold and silver items in the impressive building.

Työväen Keskusmuseo
The Central Museum of Labour (☎ 253 8800; [w] *www.tkm.fi; Vaino Linnan aukio 8; adult/*

child €4/2; open 11am-6pm Tues-Sun) is dedicated to revolutionary aspects of the workers' movement. You will find changing exhibitions covering social history and labour industries. The museum is in the old **Finlayson Factory**, a massive red-brick building that was once a textile mill, and is now partially a glitzy mall of cafés and shops. This was the first building in northern Europe to have electric lighting, which was installed on 15 March 1882.

Amurin Työläismuseokortteli

The Amuri Museum of Workers' Housing *(☎ 3146 6690; Makasiinikatu 12; adult/child €4/1; open 10am-6pm Tues-Sun May–mid-Sept)* preserves an entire block of 19th-century wooden houses, including 32 apartments, a bakery, a shoemaker, two general shops and a café. It's the most realistic home museum in Finland – many homes look as if the tenant had left just moments ago to go shopping.

Museum of Dolls & Costumes

This fascinating museum *(☎ 222 6261; Hatanpaanpuistokuja 1; adult/child €5/1; open 11am-5pm Tues-Sat Apr-Sept)* at Hatanpää Manor, south of the city, has more than 4000 dolls on display. The oldest and rarest date from the 12th century. There are also temporary exhibitions on various doll-related themes.

The old manor house is surrounded by the large **Arboretum Park** with about 350 species of flora. Bus No 21 runs from the city centre to Hatanpää.

Spy Museum

This off-beat museum *(☎ 212 3007; w www.vakoilumuseo.fi; Hatanpaanpuistokuja 32; adult/child €6/4; open noon-6pm Mon-Fri, 10am-4pm Sat & Sun)* exposes some of the secrets of international espionage from KGB documents to James Bond–style devices. There are plenty of photos but also a few interactive gadgets – including a working lie detector machine.

Särkänniemi Amusement Park

The park *(☎ 248 8111; w www.sarkan niemi.fi; adult/child day pass €27/16; usually open 10am-8pm mid-May–mid-Aug)* just north of the city centre is enormously popular with Finnish families. A day pass is good for all sights and unlimited rides. Alternatively, you can pay for each ride or attraction separately as you go along (€3.50). To get to Särkänniemi, take bus No 4 from the train station.

Inside the amusement park are 30 **carnival rides** including the 'Tornado super rollercoaster', plus cafés and restaurants. The **aquarium** is the largest in Finland, with 200 species of sea creatures. The **children's zoo**, with gentle domestic animals, and a **planetarium** *(open year-round)*, with daily shows, are nearby.

The **Dolphinarium** *(open year-round)* has Finland's only dolphin show. There are one to five dolphin shows in summer and an entertaining dolphin training show (in Finnish) daily at other times.

At 168m, **Näsinneula Observation Tower** *(admission €3.50; open noon-midnight daily)* is the tallest in Finland and has a revolving restaurant near the top (at 124m).

Pyynikki Ridge

Rising between Tampere's two lakes, this ridge is a forested area of walking trails with fine views on both sides. The surrounding pine forests stretch to the suburb of Pispala. There's an old stone **observation tower** *(open 9am-8pm daily; adult/child €1/0.50)* on the ridge, which also has a great café serving Tampere's best donuts. You can easily walk or drive to the tower, or take westbound bus No 15 to its terminus and walk back from there along the ridge.

Churches

The landmark **old wooden church** *(open daily in summer)* just north of Keskustori Square has occasional gospel concerts on Saturday evenings.

The wonderful **Tampere Cathedral** *(Tuomiokirkonkatu; open 10am-6pm daily)* is one of the most notable examples of National Romantic architecture in Finland. It was designed by Lars Sonck and was finished in 1907. Inside are the weird frescos and inspired stained glass windows of Hugo Simberg.

The small but ornate, onion-domed **Orthodox church** *(open 10am-4pm Mon-Sat, noon-4pm Sun June-Aug)*, near the train station, is also worth a visit. During the Civil War, White troops besieged the church, which had been taken over by the Reds.

Tallipiha Stable Yards

In the attractive Näsinpuisto park, Tallipiha (☎ 223 4311; Kuninkaankatu 4; admission free; open 10am-6pm Mon-Sat, 11am-5pm Sun mid-May–mid-Aug, shorter hours in winter) is a restored collection of 19th-century stable yards and staff cottages that now house artists and craftworkers making handicrafts, chocolates, ceramics and shoes. Traditional Midsummer and Christmas celebrations are held here and you can recharge your batteries at the Russian-style **Vatruska Cafe**.

Activities

There's an **indoor swimming pool** (☎ 215 5812; Joukahaisenkatu 7; adult/child €3.50/2; open 6am-7.45pm Mon-Fri, 10am-4.45pm Sat & Sun, closed Tues mornings) about 1.5km east of the train station.

The older **Pyynikki swimming hall** (☎ 3146 6863; Kortelahdenkatu 26; adult/child €3.50/2; closed Tues & Sun & in summer) is adjacent to Hostel Uimahallin Maja.

To **fish** in the Tammerkoski Rapids in the town centre, you will need a daily or weekly permit, available from the tourist office.

You can rent **rowing boats** and **canoes** from Camping Härmälä (see the Places to Stay section). Roller blades can be hired from **K2 Rullaluisteluvuokraus** at Mustalahti quay.

Organised Tours

You can get an overview of Tampere's attractions on a **bus tour** (adult/child €9/3.50; 2pm daily 1 June–31 Aug). The guided tours depart from the tourist office and cover the main sights, the Tammerkoski Rapids industrial area and Pyynikki Ridge.

Cruises Lake cruises on Tampere's two magnificent lakes are extremely popular in summer and there are plenty of options. Trips on Lake Näsijärvi leave from Mustalahti quay, while Laukontori quay serves Lake Pyhäjärvi.

Tammerlines Cruises (☎ 254 2500) offers short cruises on Lake Pyhäjärvi from mid-June to mid-August, with departures from the Laukontori quay on Monday and Friday (adult/child from €8/2). On Wednesday and Saturday the cruise goes further to Nokia and the Spa Hotel Rantasipi Eden (adult/child €13/4).

Tammerlines Cruises also has a shuttle service to nearby **Viikinsaari Island**, a pleasant picnic spot, from Tuesday to Sunday in summer. Departures from Laukontori quay are every hour on the hour (adult/child €5/2 return).

The SS *Tarjanne* (☎ 212 4804), a steam ship, departs from Mustalahti quay for eight-hour excursions on Lake Näsijärvi three times a week in summer (Tuesday, Thursday and Saturday, 10.45am). The route, from Tampere to Ruovesi and Virrat, is known as the **Poet's Way** and is one of the finest lake cruises in Finland. A one-way ticket costs €31 to Ruovesi and €42 to Virrat. For €20 per person, you can sleep in this old boat before or after your trip, and get free day-use of the cabin. Bicycles can be taken on board for a small fee.

For information about cruises with Finnish Silverline between Tampere and Hämeenlinna see the Getting There & Away section later.

Special Events

There are festivals and annual events in Tampere almost year-round. Usually held in early March, the **Tampere Film Festival** (W www.tamperefilmfestival.fi) is a respected international festival of short films. The **Tampere Biennale** is a festival of new Finnish music, held in the spring (April) of even-numbered years only. The **Pispala Schottishce** (W www.sottiisi.net), an international folk-dance festival, takes place in early June.

Tammerfest (W www.tammerfest.net) is the city's premier music festival, held over five days in mid-July and featuring rock concerts at the Ratina Stadium and various smaller gigs around town. Also in July, **Pirkan Soutu** is a widely attended rowing competition. The **Tampere International Theatre Festival**, held over a week in early August, is a showcase of international and Finnish theatre. Most works are in Finnish, and there's also a fringe festival called **Off-Tampere** held at the same time. October or early November brings the **Tampere Jazz Happening**, a high energy, award-winning event featuring Finnish and international jazz musicians.

Twice a year in autumn and mid-winter, the **Tampere Illuminations** light up the city streets with 40,000 coloured lights.

TAMPERE

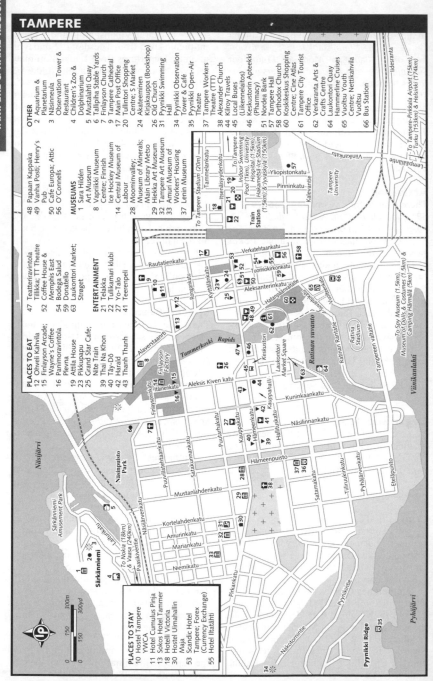

PLACES TO STAY
10 Hostel Tampere
     YWCA
11 Hotel Cumulus Pinja
13 Sokos Hotel Tammer
18 Hotelli Victoria
30 Hostel Uimahallin
     Maja
53 Scandic Hotel
     Tampere; Forex
     (Currency Exchange)
55 Hotel Iltatähti

PLACES TO EAT
12 Ohveli Kahvila
15 Finlayson Arcade;
     Wayne's Coffee
16 Panimoravintola
     Plevna
19 Attila House
23 Pikkupapu
25 Grand Star Cafe;
     Nite Train
39 Thai Na Khon
40 Täy-Dö
42 Harald
43 Thanh Thanh

47 Teatteriravintola
     Tillikka; TT Theatre
52 Coffee House &
     Memphis East
54 Bodega Salud
59 Donatello
63 Laukontori Market;
     Stroget

ENTERTAINMENT
21 Telakka
22 Tullikamari klubi
27 Yo-Talo
41 Teerenpeli

48 Papaan Kappaka
49 Vanha Posti; Henry's
     Pub
50 Cafe Europa; Attic
56 O'Connells

MUSEUMS
1 Sara Hildén
    Art Museum
3 Vapriikki Museum
    Centre; Finnish
    Ice Hockey Museum
14 Central Museum of
     Labour
28 Moominvalley;
     Museum of Minerals;
     Main Library Metso
29 Hiekka Art Museum
32 Tampere Art Museum
33 Amuri Museum of
     Workers' Housing
37 Lenin Museum

OTHER
2 Aquarium &
    Planetarium
3 Näsinneula
    Observation Tower &
    Restaurant
4 Children's Zoo &
    Dolphinarium
5 Mustalahti Quay
6 Tallipiha Stable Yards
7 Finlayson Church
9 Tampere Cathedral
17 Main Post Office
     Tullintori Shopping
     Centre; S Market
24 Akateeminen
     Kirjakauppa (Bookshop)
26 Old Church
31 Pyynikki Swimming
     Hall
34 Pyynikki Observation
     Tower & Café
35 Pyynikki Open-Air
     Theatre
37 Tampere Workers
     Theatre (TTT)
38 Alexander Church
44 Kilroy Travels
45 Local Buses
     (Liikennelaitos)
46 Keskustorin Apteekki
     (Pharmacy)
51 Nordea Bank
57 Tampere Hall
58 Orthodox Church
60 Koskikeskus Shopping
     Centre; Cine Atlas
61 Tampere City Tourist
     Office
62 Verkaranta Arts &
     Crafts Centre
64 Laukontori Quay
     Hammerline Cruises
65 Vuoltsu Youth
     Centre; Nettikahvila
     Vuoltsu
66 Bus Station

Places to Stay

Camping About 5km south of the centre (take bus No 1) is **Camping Härmälä** (☎ 265 1355, 6138 3210; Leirintäkatu 8; tent sites €13.50, 3-5 person cabins €27-60). There are lakeside saunas and rowing boats, and an adjacent **summer hostel** (singles/doubles €34/51) with self-contained rooms.

Hostels There are two HI-affiliated hostels at opposite ends of town. **Hostel Tampere YWCA** (☎ 254 4020, fax 254 4022; Tuomiokirkonkatu 12A; dorm beds €13.50-15, singles/doubles €31/44; open June-Aug) is simple and clean, with kitchen and laundry facilities.

Hostel Uimahallin Maja (☎ 222 9460, fax 222 9940; [e] sales@hosteltampere.com; Pirkankatu 10-12; dorm beds €19, singles/doubles €33/50; open year-round), adjacent to the swimming complex, has a slightly higher standard of rooms with twin beds and washbasins. There's a cheap café and bar here, as well as kitchen facilities.

Hotels Tampere has plenty of mid-range and top-end business hotels in the city centre.

Hotel Iltatähti (☎ 315 161, fax 3151 6262, Tuomiokirkonkatu 19; singles/doubles €37/45.50, with bathroom €55.50/63; reception 9am-7pm Mon-Fri, noon-6pm Sat & Sun) is a friendly guesthouse in a reasonably quiet but central street near the train station.

Hotelli Victoria (☎ 242 5111, fax 242 5100; [w] www.hotellivictoria.fi; Itsenäisyydenkatu 1; singles/doubles weekends & summer €70/75, rest of the year €90/110) has good rooms.

Hotel Cumulus Pinja (☎ 241 5111, fax 241 555; Satakunnankatu 10; singles/doubles €108/129, weekends & summer €89), near the cathedral, is one of three Cumulus hotels in the city. It's a relatively small Art Nouveau building in a quiet but central location with garage parking.

Scandic Hotel Tampere (☎ 244 6111, fax 222 1910; Hämeenkatu 1; singles/doubles from €99/132) is opposite the train station. It has plenty of facilities, including sauna, gym, restaurants and a cocktail bar.

Sokos Hotel Tammer (☎ 262 6265, fax 262 6266; Satakunnankatu 13; singles/doubles €129/147, weekends & summer €85/103) is one of the oldest and finest hotels in Tampere. Modern facilities are combined with an old-fashioned elegance.

Places to Eat

The scary-looking Tampere speciality, *mustamakkara*, a thick black sausage made with cow's blood, can be found lurking at any of the city's several markets, including the *kauppahalli* (indoor market). Some locals insist mustamakkara tastes best with milk and cranberry jam.

From Monday to Saturday, visit the **kauppahalli** (Hämeenkatu 19) for fresh produce and quick, cheap meals.

Laukontori market (open to 2pm Mon-Sat) is a produce and fish market at Laukontori, also called *alaranta* (lower lakeside).

Keskustori, the central market, is busy only on the first Monday of each month, and on weekday evenings in summer.

The cheapest food stores in Tampere are the numerous **Vikkula** shops, which have a *tarjous* (special price) on almost everything. **Koskikeskus Shopping Centre** (Hatanpäänvaltatie) just south of the tourist office, is good for fast food – it has pizza, kebab, taco and hamburger outlets.

Cafés There are dozens of cafés lining Hämeenkatu, but one of the best in town – certainly for coffee – is **Pikkupapu** (Little Bean; Tuomiokirkonkatu). It's a nice little European-style café with espresso, cappucino, great smoothies and crepes and sandwiches. **Coffee House** (Hämeenkatu 3) is another good place specialising in various styles of coffee.

Wayne's Coffee, in the renovated Finlayson buildings, suffers from a bit of a shopping mall setting (despite the historic building) but it's a reliable place for great muffins.

Ohveli Kahvila (Ojakatu 4) is a quaint place specialising in Tampere's best fresh waffles (the name means waffle café).

Strøget (Laukontori 10; sandwiches €3-7) is a small café at the quay specialising in spectacular Danish open sandwiches, as well as burgers, and American-style tuna and club sandwiches. It's not cheap but the sandwiches are big.

The Tampere University student cafeteria at **Attila House** (Yliopistonkatu 38; open 8.30am-5pm Mon-Fri, lunch Sat), just north of the main campus, is a good place to meet and eat with local students. Substantial set meals (changing daily) are served from 10.30am to 3pm. Coffee and snacks are also inexpensive.

Finnish In the old Finlayson textile mill, **Panimoravintola Plevna** (*☎ 260 1200, Itäinenkatu 8; mains €7-17; open daily*) is a brewery pub and restaurant and is the most enjoyable place to dine in Tampere. As well as Finnish-style fish and steak dishes, the speciality here is German sausages such as bratwurst and bockwurst (€6.70 to €9.80). Wash down a plate of this hearty fare with a pint of Plevna's award-winning strong stout (€5.60).

For the best view in Tampere, **Näsinneula** (*☎ 248 8212; meals €12-27; open 11am-midnight daily*) is the revolving restaurant atop the observation tower (124m) at Särkänniemi amusement park. It serves gourmet Finnish cuisine.

Teatteriravintola Tillikka (*☎ 254 4700; Teatteritalo; lunch from €7*), wedged between the river and the TT (Tampere Theatre), serves a fine buffet-style lunch.

Harald (*☎ 213 8380; Hämeenkatu 23; mains €11-21; 3-course set meals from €24*) is a Viking theme restaurant, which isn't really Finnish though much of the food is, with game specialities such as reindeer. It's identical to the one in Turku.

International There are some good vegetarian dishes on offer at **Thai Na Khon** (*Hämeenkatu 29; lunch from €6*) and **Tây-Do** (*Hämeenkatu 22*), a tiny Vietnamese restaurant across the street. Equally good and very cheap is **Thanh Thanh** (*Hämeenkatu 16; mains €3.50-6.50*), which serves Asian meat and veg curries until 5am most nights.

Donatello (*Aleksanterinkatu 37; buffet €6*) sets out a lavish all-you-can-eat pizza and pasta buffet for lunch and dinner, which is cheap and tasty.

Bodega Salud (*☎ 366 4460; Tuomiokirkonkatu 19; mains €6-17*) is a long-standing favourite for gourmet Spanish food. The signature dish is 'coyote casserole' – made with pork, chicken and alligator. Paella and seafood dishes are also a feature, and there's a tapas bar. The salad buffet is terrific.

Entertainment
Pubs & Bars Easily the coolest bar in Tampere is **Cafe Europa** (*☎ 223 5526; Aleksanterinkatu 29*), but it gets impossibly crowded on weekend evenings. Furnished with 1930s style couches, it is a romantic old-world European type of place complete

with Belgian and German beers and an excellent summer terrace. Upstairs is a small but hip dance club called **Attic**, which opens at 10pm.

Tucked down an alley near the train station, **O'Connell's** (*Rautatienkatu 24*) is an unpretentious Irish pub with a strong local following. It's a good place to meet travellers, expats and Tampere locals.

Panimoravintola Plevna (see Places to Eat) is a superb brewery pub in the converted Finlayson cotton mill buildings. It brews four beers, including an award-winning strong stout, two ciders and even has a distillery. Plevna attracts an older, more refined crowd than some other places. **Teerenpeli** (*Hämeenkatu 25*) is another good pub with home-brewed beer and cider and a cavernous club downstairs.

Of the many bars on Hämeenkatu, **Vanha Posti** (*Hämeenkatu 13A*) is a perennial favourite with a good terrace. **Henry's Pub**, in the basement of the same building, has live music (country and rock bands) and is even more popular. You'll probably have to queue to get into either place late on a Friday or Saturday.

Clubs & Live Music The cavernous **Tullikamari klubi** (*Tullikamarinaukio 2*) near the train station is Tampere's main indoor venue for rock concerts. Big name Finnish bands sometimes perform here and the cover charge varies from free to €15. This is also the venue for the film festival and jazz happening. It's open nightly and till 4am from Wednesday to Saturday.

Yo-Talo (*Ylioppilastalo; ☎ 223 5974; Kauppakatu 10*) is a student-oriented nightclub that frequently holds rock or blues concerts, and dance DJs.

Telakka (*☎ 225 0700, Tullikamarinaukio 3*) is a bohemian bar-theatre-restaurant in another of Tampere's restored red-brick factories. There's live music here regularly, theatre performances and a brilliant summer terrace.

Papaan Kappaka (*☎ 211 0037; Koskikatu 9*) is a small bar in the heart of town (across from the tourist office) with regular live jazz and blues and a swinging terrace.

For classical concerts, the **Tampere Hall** (*☎ 243 4500 ticket office; W www.tamperetalo.fi; Yliopistonkatu 55*) is the city's modern concert hall. It hosts classical concerts by the Tampere Philharmonic Orchestra on Fridays from September to May. In addition to this it also puts on regular chamber music concerts, and visiting opera and ballet performances.

Theatre & Cinema Tampere is a thriving centre for the performing arts. There are several theatres in the city and a programme of what's on where is available from the tourist office. The biggest are the **TT** *(Tampere Theatre;* ☎ *216 0500; Keskustori)*, just off Hameenkatu near the river; and the **TTT** *(Tampere Workers' Theatre;* ☎ *217 8222; Hameenpuisto 32)*. Both present major Finnish and international shows, including musicals, but as is the case elsewhere in the country, almost all performances are in Finnish.

Pyynikki Open-Air Theatre *(☎ 216 0300 ticket office)* is a summer theatre on the shores of Lake Pyhäjärvi south of Pyynikki Ridge. A Finnish play is performed here on summer evenings from mid-June to mid-August.

There are several cinemas around the city, including **Cine Atlas** *(☎ 273 2180)* at the Koskikeskus shopping centre. Films are usually recent American releases subtitled in Swedish and Finnish.

Spectator Sports
Tampere has two ice-hockey teams in the national league – Ilves and Tappara – both of which are among the best in the country, and the city is generally regarded as the home of the sport. Finland's first artificial hockey rink was opened here in 1955. The **Hakametsä Ice Stadium**, about 2km east of train station, just off the Hervannan Valtaväya freeway, is the venue for matches on Thursday, Saturday and Sunday from September to March. Take eastbound bus No 25 to get there.

Tampere United, the local football (soccer) team, is also quite successful in the national league. They play their games in summer at the **Tampere Stadium** and at the **Ratina Stadium**.

Shopping
Kehräsaari, a converted brick factory building just east of Laukontori market square, is your one-stop souvenir shopping centre, with many boutiques selling authentic Finnish

glassware, handicrafts, knitted clothing and T-shirts.

Verkaranta Arts & Crafts Centre *(Verkatehtaankatu 2)*, a smaller former factory building located near the tourist office, exhibits and sells extraordinary textiles and handicrafts.

Getting There & Away
Air You can fly to Tampere direct from Stockholm; all other international flights are via Helsinki. There are several daily Finnair flights to Tampere from Helsinki and other major Finnish cities.

Bus The main bus station *(Hatanpäänvaltatie 7)* is a block from the Koskikeskus shopping centre. Regular express buses run from Helsinki (€23.10, 2½ hours) and Turku (€16.80, two hours).

Local buses are most conveniently taken from Keskustori (central square).

Train The train station is at the city centre. Express trains run hourly to/from Helsinki (€21.40, two hours). Intercity trains continue to Oulu (€50, five hours) and there are direct trains to Turku, Pori, Jyväskylä, Vaasa and Joensuu.

Boat You can cruise to Hämeenlinna by lake ferry in summer. **Suomen Hopealinja** *(Finnish Silverline;* ☎ *212 4804;* www .finnishsilverline.com*)* operates cruises from Tampere's Laukontori quay daily (€37 one way, eight hours), and north to Virrat along the 'Poet's Way' (€42, eight hours).

Getting Around
To/From the Airport The Tampere–Pirkkala airport is 15km southwest of the city centre. Each arriving flight is met by a bus to Tampere. Bus No 61 to the airport stops at Pyynikintori and several points in the city centre (€2, 30 to 45 minutes).

There are also shared **taxis** *(☎ 10041; per person €10)* carrying up to eight passengers.

Bus The city transport and ticket office is **Liikennelaitos** *(Keskutori 5A)*. The local bus service is extensive and a one-hour ticket costs €2. A 24 hour Traveller's Ticket will set you back €4. You can pick up a free bus-route map at the city tourist office or at Liikennelaitos.

North of Tampere

ROUTE 66
☎ 03

Road No 66, starting northeast of Tampere and winding north, is one of the oldest roads in Finland. When the famous song – the chorus of which goes 'Get your kicks on Route 66' – was translated into Finnish, the popular rock star Jussi Raittinen adapted the lyrics to this highway. There are a few sights along the way between Tampere and Virrat but it's not as romantic as the name suggests.

Orivesi
Road No 66 begins in Orivesi. There's nothing spectacular in the village itself, but it is at a major crossroads. The village's silolike modern **church** (open Mon-Fri in summer) was controversial when built, one reason being the Kain Tapper woodcarving in the altar. The old bell tower remains, with its *vaivaisukko* (pauper statue).

Kallenautio Roadhouse
This wooden roadhouse (☎ 335 8915) is the oldest building along Route 66 and dates back to 1757. It has always been a *kievari*, or roadside guesthouse. Around 200 years ago, when transport was by horse and cart or on foot, kievari were nearly as common as petrol stations are today. However, there are few such places left.

The building houses a rustic café and a museum. There are sometimes handicraft exhibitions – you can see how *päre* is made from wood. *Päre* is a thin sheet of wood once burnt to shed light in a house. It was often the reason for fires that destroyed entire towns.

Siikaneva Marshland
This large protected marshland accommodates some unusual bird species, including owls. Staying overnight is not allowed, but if you have a vehicle, it may be worth driving to either starting point of the 6km loop path, which can be walked in a few hours. The duckboard path crosses an open peat bog and forest area. The entrance is at the 'Varikko' sign on the Orivesi to Ruovesi road.

Kalela House
The most celebrated artist of the National Romantic Era, Aleksi Gallen-Kallela painted most of his famous *Kalevala* works in this studio, which he also designed and helped build, in the wilderness near Ruovesi. Exhibitions are held here in summer, although the studio was closed for renovations in 2002. To get here, follow main road No 66 5km south from the village of Ruovesi, then turn east. It's 3km to Kalela along a gravel road.

Ruovesi
Once voted the most beautiful village in Finland, Ruovesi, just off Route 66, retains much of its charm. There is not much to see or do in the village, but if you have a car the journey through the surrounding countryside is scenic. The **local museum** (admission €2) covers local history and includes an open-air museum of 18th-century farm buildings.

Haapasaari Holiday Village (☎ 486 1388; *Haapasaarentie 5; tent sites €13.50, cottages €27-93; open mid-May–early Sept)* is on the small islet north of the village, connected by a causeway. The box-like **Hotel Ruovesi** (☎ 476 2273; *Ruovedentie 44; singles/doubles €37/57)* is one of two hotels in the village.

Several buses a day connect Ruovesi with Tampere and other places in the region. The SS *Tarjanne*, travelling along the 'Poet's Way' between Tampere and Virrat, stops at Ruovesi; see the Tampere Lake Cruises section for more information.

Helvetinjärvi National Park
The main attraction of this national park, often called 'the Hell' for short (Helvetinjärvi means 'Hell's Lake'), is the narrow **Helvetinkolu gorge**, probably created as the ice moved the huge rocks apart some 10,000 years ago. The scene inspired the design of the Finnish pavilion at the Seville World Exhibition in 1992. There are a numerous trails to follow, including a walk to **Haukanhieta**, a sandy beach and popular camping spot on the shores of Lake Haukkajarvi. You can pitch a tent for the night at designated camp sites in the park and there's a free hut at Helvetinkolu. To get there from Route 66, take the signposted road via Pohtio village.

Toriseva
One of the best gorges in the region surrounds three lakes, together constituting a 5km **walking trail**. Start from the small café on the top of the hill, near the car park, 5km south of Virrat. The café has a trail map.

Virrat

pop 8200

The town of Virrat is the end point for some ferry cruises from Tampere. It is useful to have a bicycle with you to continue exploring the region. There's a **tourist office** (☎ 485 111; Virtaintie 26) in the town hall building.

Lakari Camping (☎ 475 8639; Lakarintie; open late May–late Aug), outside the town centre, is a well-equipped camping ground with tent sites and cottages.

Domus Virrat (☎ 475 5600; Sipiläntie 3; dorm beds €18, singles/doubles €37/58; open June–mid-Aug), close to the harbour and the church, is an HI-affiliated summer hostel with facilities including kitchen, tennis court and sauna.

Several buses a day connect Virrat to Tampere and other towns in the region. The 'Poet's Way' cruises from Tampere end here; see Boat under Getting There & Away in the Tampere section for more information.

Virtain Perinnekylä

The 'Tradition Village' (☎ 472 8160, Herrasentie 16; guided tour adult/child €5/2.50; open noon-6pm daily mid-June–mid-Aug), about 5km northwest of Virrat along road 23, is a sprawling open-air museum featuring four main museum buildings, handicraft shops and a restaurant with a lavish buffet lunch. Most attractions are open daily from late May to late August.

The **Talomuseo** has furniture, traditional Sunday decorations from the 1840s and a smoke sauna. The **Metsäkämppämuseo** features a large house and two small huts once used by loggers. The **Sotaveteraanien museo-huone**, or War Veteran Museum Room, has guns and other things that were used during WWII. The **Kanavamuseo** has an exhibition relating to the canal.

Tuulimylly is a restored windmill dating from 1828. The nature trail or the gravel road (old road No 66) will take you to **Herrasen Lintutorni**, a bird-watching tower that provides a good view of birdlife on Lake Toisvesi bay.

Kenttälinnoitusalue, the area near the canal, was used by Russian troops as a depot during the war in 1808. In 1915, when Finland was part of tsarist Russia, a ditch system was dug as a large strategic defence system against expansionist Germany. Today the area has renovated ditches and a bunker. A French 19th-century cannon completes the attraction. You can pick up a map from the information centre and wander around yourself, or join a guided tour. Set aside half a day for this area and bring a picnic if the weather is fine. There's also a **camping ground** here.

KEURUU

☎ 014

The little town of Keuruu is on the northern shore of Lake Keurusselkä and boasts one of the most interesting wooden churches in Finland. There is a **tourist office** (☎ 751 7144; Multiantie 5; open in summer) in the town hall.

Keuruu's fascinating old **wooden church** (admission €2; open 10am-5pm daily June–mid-Aug), built in 1758, has superb portraits of Bible characters, and photos of the mummified corpses that are buried below the chancel.

There are **lake cruises** on the MS *Elias Lönnrot*, a paddle boat, from early June to mid-August. It has service to the town of Mänttä once weekly, more frequent service to other destinations.

MÄNTTÄ

☎ 03 • pop 6900

The main reason for visiting the industrial town of Mänttä, about 30km south of Keuruu, is to see the Serlachius art museum, one of the best art collections in Finland. The **tourist office** (☎ 474 0070; Lansitorikatu 5) is open from 11am to 6pm daily in summer.

Mänttä is dominated by the huge Serlachius paper factory. The Art Nouveau 1928 **church** (open daily) was financed by the factory, and has unique woodcarvings on the altar and pulpit.

Joenniemi Manor, the private home of the late industrialist Gösta Serlachius, now houses the **Gösta Serlachius Museum of Fine Arts** (☎ 474 5511; ⓦ www.serlachiusartmuseum.fi; adult/child €6/1; open 11am-6pm Tues-Sun in summer, noon-5pm Sat & Sun rest of the year). Its large collection features art and sculptures from various European countries but the highlight is the Finnish section, which includes all the major names from the 'Golden Age' of Finnish art, including Gallen-Kallela and Edelfelt.

Honkahovi Art Centre (☎ 474 7005; open year-round) is a mansion belonging to the Serlachius family. It's a 1938 Art Deco building containing temporary art exhibitions.

You can walk between Honkahovi and the Joenniemi Manor via a trail around Lake Melasjärvi.

The HI-affiliated **Mantta Hostel** (☎ 488 8641; Koulukatu 6; dorm beds €17; open June–mid-Aug) is in the modern dormitory building of a school, not far from the centre.

Getting There & Away

In summer, you can catch the MS *Elias Lönnrot* from Keuruu. Otherwise, there are several buses a day to Mänttä from Tampere. The bus station is 700m west of the centre.

Häme Region

HÄMEENLINNA

☎ 03 • pop 46,300

Dominated by its namesake, the majestic Häme Castle, Hämeenlinna (Swedish: Tavastehus) is the capital of the Province of Häme and the oldest inland town in Finland, founded in 1649. However, there had been a trading settlement at this location on Lake Vanajavesi from the 9th century. After the Swedes built the castle on a crusade to Finland in the 13th century, Hämeenlinna developed into an administrative, educational and garrison town.

Hämeenlinna's town centre is pleasantly small and navigable, there are enough sights to keep you busy for a day, and its location on the motorway between Helsinki and Tampere keeps it firmly on the tourist route. A great way to arrive or depart from here is by lake ferry from Tampere.

Orientation & Information

Hämeenlinna lies on both sides of Lake Vanajavesi. The town centre is a compact area between the lake in the south and east, the main Helsinki to Tampere road in the west and Häme Castle in the north. Raatihuoneenkatu is the partly pedestrianised main street. A large area, including the town centre, castle environs and Aulanko National Park, was recently designated a 'national urban park'.

Tourist Office You'll find plenty of information and a free Internet terminal at **Häme Tourist Service** (☎ 621 2388, fax 621 2716; Linnankatu 6; open 9am-5pm Mon-Fri, plus 9am-2pm Sat mid-June–mid-Aug). In the

same building, **Kastelli** is a travel agency that sells tickets for lake cruises and books accommodation at hotels and cabins throughout the region.

Post & Communications The **post office** (Palokunnankatu 13-15, 13100 Hämeenlinna; open 9am-8pm Mon-Fri) is near the bus station. As well as the Internet terminal at the tourist office, the **public library** has half a dozen terminals that can be prebooked. **Hannibal**, a music bar on Hallistuskatu, also has a couple of Internet terminals and it's open late.

Häme Castle & Museums

The red-brick **Häme Castle** (☎ 675 6820; adult/child €4/2.50; open 10am-6pm daily May–mid-Aug, 10am-4pm daily rest of the year) is the symbol of Hämeenlinna (the town was named after it) and also its most significant attraction. Construction of the castle was started during the 1260s by Swedes, who wanted to establish a military base in Häme. In 1837 the castle was converted into a jail. The last prisoners were hurried out in the 1980s and extensive renovations of the castle were finally completed in 1991.

The inside has been substantially rebuilt and now houses a museum displaying period costumes and furniture and various exhibitions, some related to the castle (its history and archaeology), others temporary exhibitions simply using the castle as a venue. Free guided tours in English are given every hour.

Around the castle are three **museums** which can be visited with the castle on a combined ticket (€12).

National Prison Museum The old prison block near the castle has been converted into a museum (☎ 621 2977; adult/child €4/1; open 11am-5pm daily) where you can visit a solitary confinement cell or admire the graffiti left by former inmates. The most interesting bit is the three cells, left more or less as they were when the inmates departed, along with a brief description of their occupants' crime and lifestyle. There's also a sauna, where prisoners would sometimes violently settle disputes as they were not accompanied by guards. The building was last used as a prison in 1997.

Historical Museum Next to the Prison Museum, the historical museum (☎ 621 2979; adult child €4/1; open 11am-6pm daily) is a relatively new display showcasing the local Häme area through the ages – from around the 18th century to the present – through models, photographs, costumes and bits of memorabilia. There's a replica of an early bank, and lots of pop culture memorabilia.

Artillery Museum There are numerous museums devoted to the Finnish involvement in World War II, but this one takes the cake. It's huge. The **museum** (☎ 682 4600; adult/child €6/3; open 10am-6pm daily May-Sept) consists of three floors packed with cannons, guns, shells, old photos, models and medals, and outside is a collection of heavy artillery big enough to start a war – including a rocket launcher.

Sibelius Museum

Jean Sibelius, the most famous of Finnish composers, was born in Hämeenlinna in 1865 and went to school here, but surprisingly the town makes little fuss about this fact. His childhood home has been converted into a small and unassuming museum (☎ 621 2755, Hallituskatu 11; adult/child €3/1; open 10am-4pm daily in summer, noon-4pm rest of the year) with only a small plaque on the side to alert you to the fact that there's something of interest inside. The four rooms contain photographs, letters, his upright piano and some family furniture. Sibelius music plays in the background and you can request a particular piece of music. Concert performances are sometimes given here.

Hämeenlinna Art Museum

The town's art museum (☎ 621 2669; Viipurintie 2; adult/child €5/2.50; open noon-6pm Tues-Sun, 6pm-8pm Mon) has an interesting collection of Finnish art from the 19th and 20th centuries, including some well-known works. The building's ceiling frescos are by famous Finnish painter Akseli Gallen-Kallela.

House of Tropical Animals

This small tropical zoo (☎ 676 5773; Viipurintie 4; adult/child €6/3.50; open 11am-7pm daily), next to the art museum, is something different for Finland. It houses an interesting collection of reptiles – including snakes and alligators – as well as birds and fish in a hothouse environment.

Jean Sibelius

Born in 1865 in Hämeenlinna, Jean Sibelius started playing piano when he was nine and composed his first notable work at age 20. During the cultural flowering that inspired Finland's independence, Sibelius provided the nation with music that complemented its literature and visual arts. Sibelius was fascinated by mythology and one of his greatest inspirations was the *Kalevala*, the Finnish epic compiled by Elias Lönnrot in 1833.

In 1892 Sibelius gained international recognition for his tone poem *En Saga*, and in 1899 composed the *Finlandia* symphony, a piece which has come to symbolise the Finnish struggle for independence.

Sibelius experimented with tonality and rejected the classical sonata form, building movements from a variety of short phrases that grow together as they develop. His work, particularly the early symphonies, is notable for its economical orchestration and melancholic mood.

In 1892 he married Aino Järnefelt (sister of the painter Eero Järnefelt) and together they had six daughters. The family moved to a new home, Ainola, north of Helsinki, in 1904; this is where Sibelius composed five of his seven symphonies. Ainola is now preserved as a museum that is open to the public in summer.

Sibelius studied in Berlin and Vienna and visited the USA in 1914 as an honorary doctor at Yale University. In later life he wrote incidental music for plays and a number of choral works and songs. He died in 1957, at the age of 92.

Sibelius' birthplace in Hämeenlinna, the family's summer residence in Loviisa, and his former home, Ainola, in the town of Järvenpää, now function as museums. The excellent Sibelius Museum in Turku is devoted to the composer and his musical instruments, and frequently holds concerts. It's a terrific introduction to the music of Finland's greatest composer.

House of Cards

Hundreds of postcards are displayed at this small, quirky museum of postcards *(Korttien talo; ☎ 616 9502; Niittykatu 1; admission €2; open 10am-4pm daily June-Aug, closed Mon rest of the year)*. Some of the cards on display date back almost a century and contain the original handwritten 'wish you were here…' messages. The museum gift shop sells reproductions of the best postcards in the collection, as well as stamps.

Palanderin Talo

The historic Palander House *(☎ 621 2967; Linnankatu 16; adult/child €3/1; open noon-3pm daily in summer, Sat & Sun only in winter)* is an upper middle-class home built in 1861 and filled with period furnishings, including Art Nouveau furniture and copper utensils. A guided tour (every half hour) is included with admission.

Hämeenlinna Church

The town church dates from 1798 and was designed by Jean-Luis Desprez, court painter for King Gustav III of Sweden. It is modelled after the Pantheon Temple in Rome.

Aulanko National Park

This beautiful park, northeast of the town centre, was founded early in the 20th century by Hugo Standertskjöld, who dreamt of a Central European–style park with ponds, swans, pavilions and exotic trees. He spent a fortune to achieve his goal and the result was Aulanko. In 1930, it was declared a nature

HÄMEENLINNA

PLACES TO STAY & EAT
9 Rantakasino
10 Sokos Hotel Vaakuna
13 Dragon
14 Piparkakkutalo;
   O'Maggies
16 Kimene Kebab
20 Laurell; Tawastia Bank
21 Hotelli Emilia
24 Popino
26 Cafe Kukko

OTHER
1 Artillery Museum
2 Häme Castle
3 Historical Museum
4 National Prison Museum
5 House of Cards

6 Palander House
7 Public Library
8 Passenger Harbour
11 House of Tropical
   Animals
12 Hämeenlinna Art
   Museum
15 Hämeenlinna Church
17 Hannibal
18 Sibelius Museum
19 Metropol
22 Sirkus
23 Häme Tourist
   Service & Kastelli;
   Laurell
25 Bus Station
27 Post Office
28 Tyne

conservation area and today is one of the most varied urban parks in Finland. Although the best way to get around it is on foot, the sealed one-way road (loop) is accessible by private car. An observation tower in a granite, fortress-style building is open daily in summer (free) and gives superb views of the surrounding forests and lakes. There's a nature trail in the park and a lakeside golf course next to Rantasipi hotel.

Bus Nos 2, 13 or 17 will take you to Aulanko from Hämeenlinna centre, but it's only 6km away (turn left on Aulangontie just east of the railway tracks) so it's a pleasant bike ride.

Organised Tours

Hämeenlinna is on Lake Vanajavesi at the southern tip of a lake network that stretches north to Tampere. See the Getting There & Away section that follows for details of lake ferries.

From Thursday to Saturday in summer there's a one-hour evening cruise around the lake at 6pm from the passenger harbour. Essentially it's a booze cruise, but a great way to start the evening! The MS *Wanaja* (☎ 682 1400; cruises €10) has two-hour evening cruises on Wednesday in summer. Book at Häme Tourist Service.

Places to Stay

Aulanko Camping (☎ 621 3373; tent/van sites €15, cabins €43-61; open May-Sept) is the closest camping ground to the city. It's on the edge of the beautiful nature park and as well as cabins there are fully self-contained five-person cottages for €70.

There are no hostels in Hämeenlinna. **Hotelli Emilia** (☎ 612 2106, fax 616 5289; Raatihuoneenkatu 23; singles/doubles €58/79, weekends & summer €53/70) is the cheapest hotel in town and is a welcoming, tidy little place with free parking and a good buffet breakfast.

Sokos Hotel Vaakuna (☎ 65831, fax 658 3600; Possentie 7; singles/doubles €97/115, doubles weekends & summer €78), across the river from the town centre and near the train station, is a large, modern hotel designed to resemble Häme Castle. There are 121 rooms, three saunas and several restaurants.

The lakeside **Rantasipi Aulanko** (☎ 658 801, fax 682 1922; singles/doubles €120/144, doubles weekends & summer €89), in Aulanko

National Park, has a long tradition and is considered one of the best hotels in the region. Its location, between the lake and the forest park, could not be better, but it's essentially just a big conference hotel with lots of facilities, including five saunas, restaurants and an adjacent golf course.

Places to Eat

Kimene Kebab (Sibeliuksenkatu 11; kebabs €2-6) is the place to grab a cheap kebab or pizza.

Cafe Kukko (Palokunnankatu 11; open daily), near the bus station, is a good café with a fine selection of filled rolls. **Laurell** (Raatihuoneenkatu 11A), in the same building as the tourist office, is the place for cakes, pastries and coffee. There's another branch opposite the *kauppatori* (market square) in Sibeliuksenkatu.

Popino (☎ 653 2555; Raatihuoneenkatu 11; mains €7.50-15), tucked away where the steps divide Linnankatu into two levels, is a fine mid-range pizza and pasta restaurant. As well as pizza there are meat and fish dishes and lunch specials for €7.50.

Piparkakkutalo (☎ 648 040; Kirkkorinne 2; mains €8-20), one block east of the church, is easily the best restaurant in Hämeenlinna and everyone's favourite for a gourmet meal. Dishes range from inexpensive pasta and vegetarian to reindeer, wild boar and ostrich. The restaurant is in a historic 1906 shingled house with period decor, formerly the home of artist Albert Edelfelt. The name means 'gingerbread house'.

Dragon (☎ 612 1858; Raatihuoneenkatu 8A; mains €7-12) is a decent Chinese restaurant in a cellar. Rice and noodle dishes are inexpensive and there are seafood and vegetarian choices.

Down at the passenger harbour, **Rantakasino** (meals €3.50-12) is a lakefront summer restaurant with a good beer terrace and a cheap lunch buffet.

Entertainment

O'Maggie's (☎ 648 0450; Kirkkorinne 2) is a very cosy Irish pub in the same building as Piparkakkutalo. Since there's no terrace it fills up later in the evening during summer, but it's definitely the place to be in winter when there's weekly live Irish music. **Tawastia Bank**, on the pedestrian mall near the kauppatori, is another popular pub with a terrace spilling onto the pedestrian street. In summer, the floating boat-bar **Tyne**, south of the bus station, is a fun place for a beer.

Metropol *(Sibeliuksenkatu; open Tues-Sun)* at the kauppatori, is a lively bar and club popular with locals who have recently graduated to the drinking age. **Sirkus** *(Sibeliuksenkatu 2; open 10pm-4am Fri & Sat; admission €5-7)* is the main live music and nightclub venue with regular rock acts.

Hannibal *(Hallituskatu 20; open noon-3am Mon-Thur, noon-4am Fri-Sun)* is a grungy music bar featuring Finnish heavy rock.

Getting There & Away

Bus Hourly buses between Helsinki and Tampere stop in Hämeenlinna at the central bus station. From Turku, there are eight buses daily (€18.50, two hours).

Train The train station is 1km northeast of the town centre. Hourly trains between Helsinki (€15.80, one hour) and Tampere (€11.20, 40 minutes) stop at Hämeenlinna. From Turku (€21, 1¾ hours), change trains in Toijala.

Boat Leaving from Hameenlinna's passenger harbour, **Finnish Silverline** *(☎ 03-212 4804 in Tampere)* has a daily ferry to Tampere in summer at 11.30am. The route goes via Visavuori, where there's a one-hour stopover. See the Tampere Getting There & Away section for more information.

The passenger harbour is on Arvi Karistonkatu 8, just north of the Rantakasino beer terrace.

HÄMEENLINNA TO TAMPERE

There are several interesting sights just off the main highway between Tampere and Hämeenlinna.

Pyhän Ristin Kirkko *(Church of the Holy Cross; admission €2; open daily in summer)* in Hattula, only 5km north of Hämeenlinna, was built in the 14th century. It is one of the oldest churches in mainland Finland and has beautiful paintings and a number of old statues. The old grain store built in 1840, close to the old church, houses the tourist office and sells handicrafts.

Iittala

Iittala, a village on the highway 23km northwest of Hämeenlinna, is best known for its glass factory, which sells its products under the brand name 'Iittala'.

Glass Centre *(☎ 0204-393 512; Lasikeskus; open 10am-8pm daily in summer, 10am-5pm rest of the year)* is opposite the bus terminal. The **glass museum** *(☎ 0204-396 230; admission €2)* exhibits objects designed and manufactured locally. It also gives an insight into the history of Finnish design. It's free to watch craftspeople blowing glassware in the back room. The shop sells second-grade products at a 35% discount. Nearby is a small **chocolate factory** and shop.

Sääksmäki

This historical and scenic area northwest of Hämeenlinna is one of the highlights of the region.

Rapolan Linnavuori on Rapola Hill is the largest prehistoric fortress in Finland. There are fine views and you can follow a marked trail that will take you to 100 burial mounds on the western side of the hill. You can get to Rapola either by following the signs from the main road, or by taking the narrow road, Rapolankuja, that passes by the privately owned Rapola estate.

Once the studio of Emil Wickström, a sculptor from the National Romantic era, **Visavuori** *(adult/child €6/4; open 11am-7pm daily in summer, Tues-Sun rest of the year)* is the best-known sight in the region. It consists of three houses, the oldest of which was the home of Wickström, built in 1902 in Karelian and Art Nouveau styles and containing fantastic Art Nouveau furniture. The beautiful studio with hundreds of sculptures was built in 1903 and later expanded. Kari Paviljonki is dedicated to Kari Suomalainen, Emil Wickström's grandson. One of the most famous political cartoonists in Finland, in the early 1960s he received an award from the US National Cartoonist Society for his daring cartoons on communism. Ferries from Hämeenlinna and Tampere stop at Visavuori in summer.

Visavuori is about 4km east of the Hämeenlinna–Tampere motorway, just off Toijala road.

HÄME OX ROAD

One of the oldest roads in Finland and still partly unpaved, the Ox Road (Härkätie) winds its way through rural landscape between Hämeenlinna and Turku. Since the

13th century, this path developed as a trade route, linking the port of Turku – and therefore Sweden – with the inland Häme region. In spite of the present-day name, early travel was on foot, with goods carried on horseback rather than by ox. As well as being a link between western Finland's two most important castles, the Ox Road was a path of pilgrimage since it connected the Turku Cathedral, Church of St James in Renko and the Church of the Sacred Cross in Hattula.

Härkätie runs roughly parallel to, or south of, Hwy 10 (which opened in 1962), passing through Renko, Porras, Somero, Marttila and Lieto. At around 160km, the route can be cycled in two or three days.

Just west of the village of Porras and on the south side of lake Ruostejarvi is the **Häme Visitor Centre** (☎ 0205-644 630) with information on hiking and the natural environment. For more information see **w** www .harkatie.net.

Renko

Renko, 15km southwest of Hämeenlinna, is the first stop along the Ox Road and is also on Hwy 10. The local museum, **Härkätien Museo** (open 11am-2pm Sun in summer) is devoted to the Ox Road and its history.

Tammela

Tammela village is on the shores of Lake Pyhäjärvi. The old **Tammela church** dates from the early 16th century. It was enlarged in 1785 and is almost like a museum: there are medieval sculptures and old coats of arms.

Tammela provided King Gustav II Adolf of Sweden with 24 soldiers during the Thirty Years' War in 1630 (the largest number of such soldiers from anywhere in Finland) and the 'Hakkapeliitat' are now honoured by a **statue** near the church.

North of Tammela village, the impressive **Mustiala Manor** (☎ 03-646 5519) was originally owned in the 16th century by Marshal Klaus Horn, a Swede. Now the estate houses an agricultural school, a small museum devoted to farming tools, and a brewery and restaurant.

Saari Park

The scenery in Saari Park (☎ 03-434 1833), south of Tammela, inspired many painters during the National Romantic era. The attractive sand ridge is part of the estate of Saari, which includes a private manor nearby. The park allows public access to anyone, any time. For the best view, climb the 20m **observation tower**. You can get the keys from the restaurant on the eastern side of the park.

Somero

The Ox Road town of Somero was founded in the 15th century. The **kivisakasti**, a stone building on the grounds of the old **church**, dates from that time. The church dates from 1859. **Someron torpparimuseo** (open daily in summer), the local museum, which is north of the centre, includes a windmill and some very old peasants' houses.

Jokioinen

The town of Jokioinen, north of the Ox Road, has a unique history. In the 16th century, King Erik XIV of Sweden (who later went insane) gave exclusive rights to the Swedish war hero Klaus Horn to establish an estate in the Jokioinen region. At the time of independence, in 1917, it had grown to be the largest such estate in Finland. The main estate, in the town centre, now houses an agricultural research institute. There is also an odd-looking red granary, with three floors and a clock tower. The granary was stolen from the nearby Humppila in the 18th century. Today it's open in summer as a gallery.

The little **church** of Jokioinen (1631), 1km past the granary, is the second-oldest wooden church in Finland but renovations hide the original architecture.

A **museum train** runs from Jokioinen to Humppila. The 14km trip takes one hour and runs on summer Sundays at 12.15pm, 2.50pm and 5.10pm from June to September and six trains each Sunday in July. A one-way ticket costs €10.

There's also a **vicarage museum**, which looks like a haunted house, near the Jokioinen centre.

Getting There & Away

There are regular buses from Hämeenlinna to Renko, the first village on the Ox Road route. At the other end, there are buses between Jokioinen and Helsinki. Local buses connect the rest of the towns, mainly coming from the large industrial town of Forssa. However, it's easiest to explore the Ox Road by private car or bicycle.

LAHTI

☎ 03 • pop 97,500

About 100km north of Helsinki by motorway, Lahti is in some ways a satellite of the capital and thus has a modern, business city feel compared to other lake region towns. Its claim to fame is being a winter sports centre: the sports complex close to the centre has three frighteningly high ski jumps which are used in winter and summer (for training), and five world championships in Nordic skiing have been staged here.

Although there are a few formal attractions, Lahti is not very interesting in other respects. Founded in 1905, it lacks anything that could be called 'old town'. The 10,000 Karelian refugees who arrived here after WWII have contributed their entrepreneurial spirit to what the locals call the 'Business City'.

Surrounded by a network of bicycle routes, Lahti does make a good base for visiting nearby attractions. Its location by Lake Vesijärvi (which is connected to Lake Päijänne) makes it the obvious place to start a ferry trip to Jyväskylä. One of the largest lakes in Finland, Päijänne provides Helsinki with drinkable tap water and everyone else with scenic waterways.

Information

Tourist Centre Aleksi (☎ 877 677, fax 877 6700; Ⓦ www.lahtitravel.fi; Aleksanterinkatu 13; open 9am-5pm Mon-Fri June-Aug & 10am-2pm Sat) is opposite the kauppatori. It has a free Internet terminal and makes hotel and

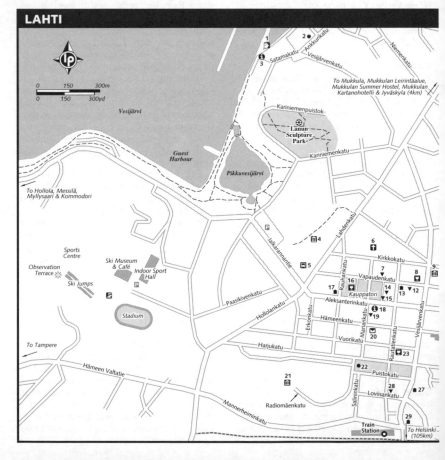

transport bookings. There's a summer tourist booth at the harbour.

The **public library** *(☎ 812 511; Kirkkokatu 31; open 10am-8pm Mon-Fri, 10am-3pm Sat)* has several free Internet terminals.

Things to See

Ski Jump Observation Terrace *(chairlift & terrace €5/2; open daily in summer, Sat & Sun only in winter)*, at the Sports Centre, provides a fine view over the jumps and the town and surrounding lakes. A chairlift takes you to the top. The small **Ski Museum** *(☎ 814 4523; adult/child €4.30/2; open 10am-5pm Mon-Fri, 11am-5pm Sat & Sun)* at the Sports Centre is worth a visit. There are skis that were used 2000 years ago and skis that belonged to the Samis of Lapland. The

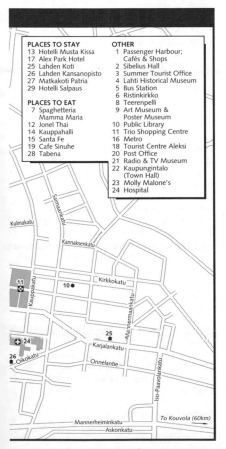

PLACES TO STAY
13 Hotelli Musta Kissa
17 Alex Park Hotel
25 Lahden Koti
26 Lahden Kansanopisto
27 Matkakoti Patria
29 Hotelli Salpaus

PLACES TO EAT
 7 Spaghetteria
     Mamma Maria
12 Jonel Thai
14 Kauppahalli
15 Santa Fe
19 Cafe Sinuhe
28 Tabena

OTHER
 1 Passenger Harbour;
     Cafés & Shops
 2 Sibelius Hall
 3 Summer Tourist Office
 4 Lahti Historical Museum
 5 Bus Station
 6 Ristinkirkko
 8 Teerenpeli
 9 Art Museum &
     Poster Museum
10 Public Library
11 Trio Shopping Centre
16 Metro
18 Tourist Centre Aleksi
20 Post Office
21 Radio & TV Museum
22 Kaupungintalo
     (Town Hall)
23 Molly Malone's
24 Hospital

ski jump simulator is great fun. A combined ticket to the terrace and museum is €6/3.50.

Lahti Historical Museum *(Lahden Histo-riallinen Museo; Lahdenkatu 4; adult/child €2.50/free; open 10am-5pm Mon-Fri, 11am-5pm Sat & Sun)* is in a beautiful old manor house. Exhibits include the Klaus Holma collection of French and Italian furniture and medieval and Renaissance art.

Art Museum & Poster Museum *(☎ 814 4547; Vesijärvenkatu 11; adult/child €4.30/2; open 10am-5pm Mon-Fri, 11am-5pm Sat & Sun)* has temporary exhibitions of sculpture and paintings, and an off-beat collection of advertising posters from yesteryear.

Radio & TV Museum *(Radiomäki Hill; adult/child €4.30/2; open 10am-5pm Mon-Fri, 11am-5pm Sat & Sun)* has a collection of old radios and a working broadcasting studio from the 1950s. You can film and appear in your own TV broadcast or radio programme, which is great fun for kids.

Ristinkirkko *(Church of the Cross; Kirk-kokatu 4; open 10am-3pm daily)* was designed by Alvar Aalto and finished in 1978. Although the exterior is made of brown brick, the interior is typically Aalto: wooden benches, white walls and, on the ceiling, four concrete structures which look like rays emanating from the cross.

The Art Nouveau **Kaupungintalo** *(town hall; Harjukatu 31)* was designed by another famous Finnish architect, Eliel Saarinen. There are guided tours of the building at 2pm on Friday. **Sibelius Hall** *(☎ 81418; [W] www .lahti.fi/sibeliustalo; Ankkurikatu 7)*, near the harbour on Lake Vesijärvi, is a huge new concert hall creation made from wood and glass.

Activities & Cruises

Sports Centre *(☎ 814 4570)* just west of the centre has three sky-high ski jumps that are the landmark of Lahti. Thrill-seekers note that these are not open to the general public. Even in the summer you'll often see high-level ski-jumpers in training here.

There's still plenty for the average visitor to do. In winter, there is an ice-skating hall and a total of 145km of cross-country ski tracks, 35km of which are illuminated. Skiing and skating gear can be rented in the main building. In summer the centre offers bike trails and a large outdoor swimming pool.

There's also plenty to do out at **Mukkula** in summer. The lakefront location, 5km from

Lahti, has boat and canoe hire, tennis, mini-golf, beach volleyball and bicycles for rent.

In summer there are several daily 1½-hour return **cruises** from the passenger harbour on the MS *Enon Elli* (☎ 787 2660; *adult/child €5/3)* around Lake Vesijarvi via Mukkula, Enonsaari and Messilä. There are also 3½-hour cruises to the Vaaksy Canal and back on the MS *Soumetar (adult/child €13/7.50)*.

Special Events

Unsurprisingly, Lahti hosts several annual winter sports events including the **Ski Games** in early March. There are also some good summer music festivals such as **Jazz at the Marketplace**, a week-long street festival in early August, and the **Sibelius Festival**, with performances by the Lahti Symphony Orchestra in mid-September.

Places to Stay

Camping & Hostels In the scenic grounds of Mukkula manor house is **Mukkulan Leirintäalue** (☎ 874 1442, fax 874 1413; *Ritaniemenkatu 10; tent sites €14, cottages €34-85)*. Also here is HI-affiliated **Mukkulan Summer Hostel** (☎ 882 3602; ⓦ *www.mukkulankesahotelli.fi; singles/doubles/family €39/52/80; open June–early Aug)*, which has self-contained rooms though there are no dorms.

Lahden Kansanopisto (☎ 878 1181, fax 878 1234; *Harjukatu 46; dorm beds from €18, singles/doubles €32/46, with bathroom €38/56; open June–mid-Aug)*, the local folk college, is an HI summer hotel with a variety of rooms and an equipped kitchen.

Matkakoti Patria (☎ 782 3783; *Vesijärvenkatu 3; singles/doubles from €28/42)* is a bit run-down but it's a cheap guesthouse close to the train station.

Hotels In a renovated apartment building is **Lahden Koti** (☎ 522 173; *Karjalankatu 6; single/double studios or apartments from €59/69)*, which has been converted into a very nice small hotel. All apartments are tastefully decorated and come with a well-equipped kitchen and a bathroom. In summer prices are lower.

Hotelli Musta Kissa (☎ 85122, fax 851 4477; *Rautatienkatu 21; singles/doubles €69/79, weekends & summer €59/70)* is in the heart of town.

Mukkulan Kartanohotelli (☎ 874 140, fax 874 1444; ⓦ *www.mukkulankartano.net; Ritaniemenkatu 10; singles/doubles €66/81, weekends & summer €45/66)* is in the old manor house at Mukkula, 5km north of Lahti. It is a romantic place to stay, the lakeside location is superb and the price is very reasonable.

The modern **Hotelli Salpaus** (☎ 813 411, fax 813 4711; ⓦ *www.salpauslahti.fi; Vesijärvenkatu 1; singles/doubles €94/117, doubles in summer €78)* is the closest hotel to the train station. It has a restaurant and two saunas.

Alex Park Hotel (☎ 52511, fax 525 1200; ⓦ *www.alexpark.fi; Aleksanterinkatu 6; singles/doubles €96/115, weekends & summer €77 doubles)* is a very central, slightly 1970s hotel is very comfortable and great value in summer.

Places to Eat

Lahti is reasonably-well endowed with good places to dine and drink. The kauppatori, and the nearby **kauppahalli**, are good places to start looking for cheap snacks. Being a popular winter sports centre, some restaurants and cafés in Lahti have an interesting feature – glassed-in terraces for winter dining.

For fantastic pastries and good coffee, **Cafe Sinuhe** (*Mariankatu 21)* is a pleasant street-style café.

Jonel Thai (*Vapaudenkatu; mains €6.50-11.50)* is one of a couple of decent Thai restaurants near the centre. There's a filling lunch special for €7.

Sante Fe (☎ 781 8007; *Aleksanterinkatu 16; mains €8-15)*, on the southeast corner of the kauppatori, is a busy Tex-Mex restaurant with a bar and terrace downstairs and dining room on the 1st floor. The menu features the usual nachos, fajitas, steaks and pastas.

Spaghetteria Mamma Maria (☎ 751 6716; *Vapaudenkatu; mains €6.50-9; open Tues-Sun)* is an Italian-Finnish restaurant with authentic homestyle food including pastas and home-made gelati. For inexpensive Greek cuisine, **Tabena** (☎ 734 6494; *Rautatienkatu 3; lunch specials €6)* is a tasty place for a filling lunch that makes a change from the usual Finnish buffet.

Entertainment

Teerenpelli (*Vapaudenkatu 20)* is a great brewery-pub-restaurant with a glassed-in

Sahti – Finnish for Beer

It won't take you long to realise that Finns love beer. But the most Finnish of beers – and the father of all beers – is the one that's hardest to find these days. *Sahti* is a sweet, high-alcohol beer (a nectar to connoisseurs) that was traditionally made by farmer's wives in a small pocket of central Finland just north of Helsinki.

The history of beer-making in Finland dates back to at least the 13th century, but what made Finnish sahti unique was the use of juniper berries and twigs, alongside hops, as the major ingredient. Sahti was a home brewery tradition (and still is) and the easy cultivation of barley and hops in south-central Finland made it prosper – even during the period of prohibition in Finland (1919–1932). These days traditional sahti can be made using wheat, malt, barley, hops, rye, juniper or a combination of these ingredients. But you won't find sahti on tap in Finnish pubs for two reasons: one, it is a time-consuming and exacting art to make; and two, because of the high tax on alcohol in Finland (good sahti is upwards of 9% alcohol volume), it is expensive.

The best places in Finland to sample sahti are in city pubs close to the traditional brewing areas, notably Lahti, Tampere, Vantaa and Helsinki. In Savonlinna, the brewer at Huvila, Markku Pulliainen, won Finland's sahti brewing award in 2000, and he continues to make this traditional beer available at his brewery-restaurant. The main commercial brewer in Finland is the Lammin Sahti Brewery, about 50km from Lahti, and you can sample these brews at pubs in Lahti. For more information, check out W www.sahti.com (Finnish only) or www.posbeer.org/oppaat/sahti.

terrace. It brews four beers on the premises, and sells *sahti*, the sweet Finnish beer. **Metro** is an unusual underground bar and club on the western side of the kauppatori. It attracts a more grungier crowd than the Teerenpeli.

Molly Malone's *(Vuorikatu 35)* is a laid-back Irish pub with live music on Friday and Saturday nights.

Getting There & Away

Bus There are regular daily buses along the motorway from Helsinki (€14.60, one hour), and frequent services to/from Tampere (€19.20, two hours); Jyväskylä (€23.10, 2½ hours) and Turku (€27.10, three hours).

Train There are at least 15 direct trains per day from Helsinki (€15, 1½ hours) and Riihimäki. Travellers from Tampere change trains at Riihimäki.

Boat From early June to mid-August **Päijänne Risteilyt Hildén Oy** (*☎ 263 447, fax 665 560)* operates daily ferries from Lahti's passenger harbour to Heinola at 10am (€15.50/25 one way/return, 4½ hours). The cruise goes via Vaaksy and Kalkkinen canals. It also has a twice-weekly ferry to Jyväskylä at 10am on Tuesday and Thursday (adult/child €36/18, 10½ hours) from June to mid-August.

AROUND LAHTI
Hollola Region
☎ 03 • pop 20,000

Hollola, west of Lahti, is the most historical place in this area. It's close enough to Lahti for a leisurely bicycle tour – take the narrow road (No 2956) around Lake Vesijärvi. Although the modern town centre is only about 7km from Lahti via the highway, most of the attractions are 15km to 18km northwest on the southern shores of Vesijärvi.

In the village centre, a small **tourist office** (*☎ 880 111; W www.hollola.fi; Virastotie 3*) provides information about local attractions.

Things to See & Do Taking the loop road north of Hollola, the first place you come to is **Messilä**, a fine old estate with a golf course, guest harbour and winter ski slopes (see also the following Places to Stay & Eat section). **Messilän Pajat** is a separate building featuring local craft (and a bakery).

Pirunpesä (Devil's Nest) is a steep rock cliff, near Messilä. A marked trail takes you there, or you can walk the entire 7km *luontopolku* (nature trail) that goes via a series of hills and offers some good views. One of these hills, **Tiirismaa**, is a downhill-skiing resort in winter.

Between Pirunpesä and the other attractions in Hollola lies **Lake Kutajärvi**, a resting place for migratory birds. In May, plenty of local people gather to scan the lake for rare species.

Pyhäniemi Manor *(☎ 788 1466; adult/child €7/3.50; open 11am-6pm daily June-Aug)* in Pyhäniemi is one that deserves a visit. This wooden mansion, dubbed the 'Hollywood of Hollola' in the 1930s, when many Finnish films were shot here, has had quite a colourful history since being established in the 15th century. Swedish king Gustav III granted the estate to the Schmiedefelt family in 1780 and even visited it himself in 1783. The estate grew to enormous proportions; its industries included a sawmill, a wheel factory and a Swiss-run dairy that exported its products to St Petersburg.

On the shores of Vesijärvi, the large **Hollola church** *(☎ 788 1351; open 11am-6pm daily June–mid-Aug, 11am-4pm Sun mid-Aug–May)* dates from 1480. In the main hall are 10 sculptures from the 15th century, and coats of arms from the von Essen family. The bell tower from 1831 was designed by Carl Engel. The church is marked 'Hollola kk' on signs and bus timetables.

The local museum of Hollola consists of two separate museums, both open Tuesday to Sunday. **Esinemuseo**, the large red building not far from the church, contains a collection of local paraphernalia, including a Stone Age axe. **Hentilä museum** features old buildings that have been transferred from nearby locations.

Places to Stay & Eat

Camping Messila *(☎ 753 7006; ⓦ www .campingmessila.fi; tent sites €14, cottages €50-185)* is a beautifully equipped holiday park next to the estate on Lake Vesijärvi. It's open year-round and offers a host of summer and winter activities.

Messilä Estate *(☎ 86011, fax 860 123; ⓦ www.messila.fi; singles/doubles €98/115, 3-/4-person cottages €135/185)* offers plenty of choices. There are modern hotel rooms, plus a holiday village with self-contained cottages. The several restaurants here serve everything from gourmet cuisine to burgers and beers, and this is a popular venue in summer for live music and dancing.

Vääksy
☎ 03

Vääksy is mostly known for **Vääksy Canal**, the busiest canal in Finland – more than

15,000 vessels pass through it every summer and you must pass through it on the lake ferry between Lahti and Jyvaskyla. A local **tourist office** *(☎ 888 6232)* in the commercial centre has information about local attractions, and arranges accommodation in the pleasant lakeside surroundings. **Vääksyn Vesimyllymuseo** *(☎ 766 0860; open in summer)* is a small water-mill museum.

Urajärven Kartano estate *(☎ 766 7191; open daily June-Aug)*, one of the finest in Finland, was the property of the von Heideman family. It has a museum, a café and an attractive garden. You'll need a private car to visit the estate as it is east of the Vääksy Canal.

Vääksy is busy in summer, with plenty of buses, or you can catch one of the canal boats that ply their way between Lahti and Heinola in summer (see the Lahti Getting There & Away section).

HEINOLA
☎ 03   •   pop 21,000

Heinola is today overshadowed by Lahti to the south but is a much older town. It has a scenic waterfront setting, with the Jyrängönvirta River flowing through it. In addition to summer cultural attractions, Heinola serves as a starting point for scenic summer lake cruises. There's a **tourist office** *(☎ 849 3615; Kauppakatu 10-12)*.

Heinola Ridge has a few attractions. The 1900 Harjupaviljonki pavilion is meant to look like a Japanese temple. In summer there is an art exhibition here. Nearby, the tower offers good views. The **Heinola Bird Zoo** *(☎ 715 2916; admission free; open 10am-4pm daily)* is an aviary housing more than 500 species. It also acts as a hospital for sick or injured birds.

Places to Stay & Eat

Heinäsaari Camping *(☎ 849 3644; tent sites/cottages €10/30)* is on Heinäsaari island, 1.5km from the town centre.

Finnhostel Heinola *(☎ 714 1655; Opintie 3; dorm beds from €15; open June–early Aug)* is an HI-affiliated summer hostel with a café and kitchen facilities. Reception is closed from 10am to 3pm.

Harjupaviljonki on the hill is a most attractive place to enjoy a cup of coffee in summer. There are several **restaurants** on Kauppakatu, the main road.

Getting There & Away

There are buses roughly every 30 minutes from Lahti (€4.50, 20 minutes). Heinola is 136km north of Helsinki. Ferries from Lahti sail to Heinola in summer; see the Lahti section for details.

AROUND HEINOLA
Onkiniemi

Situated around 25km north of Heinola on the road to Hartola, Onkiniemi is home to **Musta & Valkea Ratsu Nukketalot** *(Black & White Horse Puppet House;* ☎ *03-718 6959; Onkiniementie 222; open noon-4pm daily year-round).* *Nukketalot* (puppet houses) are extremely popular with Finnish kids, and here you can meet the puppets and even make your own.

A very eccentric family has created more than 350 hand puppets – some appearing regularly on TV – and give daily theatre performances (adult/child €7/5). Most people fall totally in love with the place, the people and the puppets. Some items are for sale, and the building contains a self-service café.

Turku & the Southwest

For travellers, the southwest region of Finland is an appealing and accessible destination. Turku, a likeable port city and gateway to Finland, provides a base for exploring the island-studded waters of the southwest archipelago, and the historic coastal towns to the north such as Rauma and Pori are virtually a window into the settlement and founding of Finland.

Turku

☎ 02 pop ● 173,700

The oldest city in Finland and its first capital, Turku (Swedish: Åbo) has plenty to offer the visitor, especially in summer when the riverside comes to life. You can easily spend hours strolling the banks or relaxing in a floating bar between visits to museums and the medieval Turku Castle. For many travellers Turku is their first taste of Finland, since frequent and inexpensive ferries ply between here and Stockholm via the Åland islands.

Turku was named Åbo by Swedish settlers because it was a *bo* (settlement) on the Aura River *(å)*. The Finnish name, Turku, means 'marketplace' – the city's market has long been one of the largest and finest on the south coast. Turku has a thriving university, a cultural spirit and its residents are a proud lot – some are still irked that Helsinki took over as Finland's capital way back in 1812. The longstanding joke among its loyal residents is that after Turku spread culture to the rest of Finland, it never returned.

The region had its beginnings in 1229 when a Catholic settlement was founded at Koroinen, near the present centre of Turku. Work soon started on the new church (consecrated in 1300) and the Turku Castle. Both the early Catholic Church and the Swedish administration ran what is present-day Finland from Turku, which was at times the second-largest town in Sweden. Fire has destroyed Turku several times during the centuries.

Orientation

The centre of Turku town is a few kilometres northeast of Turku harbour, and is

Highlights

- Reliving the past in medieval Turku Castle, with its dungeons, extensive museums and magnificent banquet halls
- Strolling around Luostarinmäki open-air museum, with costumed artisans and musicians in summer
- Cruising the archipelago from Turku to Naantali or Hanko
- Browsing in Naantali's quaint Old Town, then dining on the marina or taking the kids to Moominworld
- Meeting the ghosts of the past at Louhisaari Manor in Askainen village – one of Finland's grandest manors
- Taking a walking tour of historic Vanha Rauma, a Unesco World Heritage listed living museum
- Partying at the annual week-long Pori Jazz Festival in July – one of Finland hottest summer events

reached by bus from each arriving ferry. The city centre straddles the Aurajoki River, and everything is within easy walking distance – it's only about a 20-minute walk from the harbour or castle to the centre of town. Aurakatu, Kauppiaskatu, Eerikinkatu and Yliopistonkatu around the *kauppatori* (market square) are the main streets in Turku.

Information

Tourist Offices The busy **Turku City Tourist Office** (☎ 262 7444; W www.turku touring.fi; Aurakatu 4; open 8.30am-6pm Mon-Fri, 9am-4pm Sat & Sun), near the kauppatori, is an excellent place for information on the entire Turku region. It rents bikes and sells the Turku Card.

Money Offering better rates than banks, **Forex** (Eerikinkatu 12; open 8am-7pm Mon-Fri, 8am-5pm Sat) is the best place to change cash and travellers cheques. Several banks located on the market square have 24-hour ATMs.

Post & Communications The **main post office** (Humalistonkatu 1; open 9am-8pm

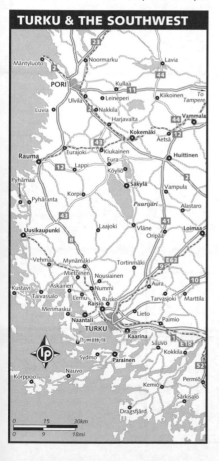

TURKU & THE SOUTHWEST

Mon-Fri) is situated two blocks west of the kauppatori. There are two types of public phones that accept phone cards in Turku – some accept a phone card that works all over Finland, while others require a card that works only in Turku. Both these types of cards can be purchased at any city R-kiosk.

Internet Resources & Library There are several Internet terminals on the 2nd floor of the **public library** (☎ 262 3611; Linnankatu 2; open 10am-8pm Mon-Fri, 10am-3pm Sat), and there's one free terminal (15 minutes) at the tourist office. **Surf City** (Aninkaistenkatu 3) is an Internet café charging €2 for 30 minutes, with discounts for students.

Reading-Room Julin (Eerikinkatu 4; open 10am-8pm Mon-Fri, 10am-4pm Sat & Sun), on the basement level of Hotel Julia, has an enormous selection of Finnish and foreign daily papers and periodicals, including the *International Herald Tribune*.

Travel Agencies For all your travel needs head straight to **Kilroy Travels** (☎ 273 7500; Eerikinkatu 2; open 10am-6pm Mon-Fri, 10am-2pm Sat) specialises in student and budget travel.

Bookshops In the Hansa Shopping Arcade are **Akateeminen Kirjakauppa** and **Suomalainen Kirjakauppa** bookshops. They stock maps, English-language books and foreign periodicals.

Left Luggage The train station offers a left-luggage counter and locker service, and there are more lockers (€2) located at the ferry terminal and Silja and Viking Line buildings.

Turku Card

Like the Helsinki Card, the Turku Card gives admission to most museums and attractions in the region, public transport and various other discounts for a set period. The 24-hour card costs €21, the 48-hour card is €28. You can buy the card at the tourist office or from most participating attractions, and it's valid from the first time you use it.

TURKU & THE SOUTHWEST

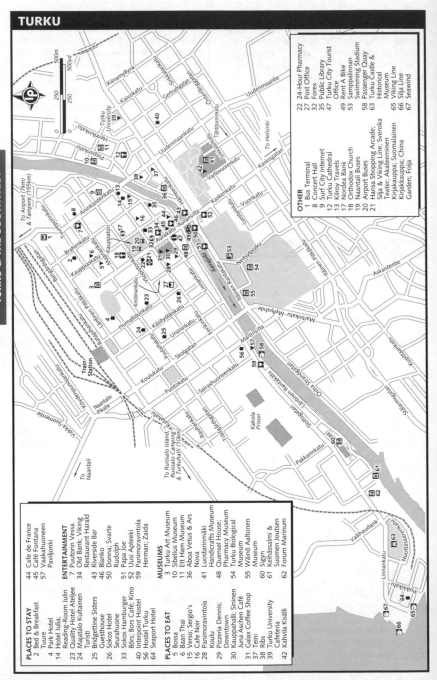

TURKU

PLACES TO STAY
2 Bed & Breakfast Tuure
4 Park Hotel
14 Hotel Julia; Reading-Room Julin
23 Quality Hotel Ateljee
24 Majatalo Kultainen Turisti
25 Bridgettine Sisters Guesthouse
26 Sokos Hotel Seurahuone
33 Sokos Hamburger Börs; Bors Café; Kino Rudolph
40 Interpoint Hostel
56 Hostel Turku
64 Seaport Hotel

PLACES TO EAT
5 Bossa
6 Baan Thai
15 Verso; Sergio's
16 Café Noir
28 Panimoravintola Koulu
29 Pizzeria Dennis; Downtown
30 Kauppahalli; Sininen Juna Aschen Café
31 Galax Coffee Shop
37 Teini
38 Ribs
39 Turku University Cafeteria
42 Kahvila Kisälli

44 Cafe de France
45 Café Fontana
57 Vaakahuoneen Paviljonki

ENTERTAINMENT
7 Puutorin Vessa
34 Old Bank; Viking Restaurant Harald
43 Riverside Bar
46 Blanko
50 Donna; Svarte Rudolph
51 Papa Joe
52 Uusi Apteeki
59 Panimoravintola Herman; Zaida

MUSEUMS
3 Turku Art Museum
10 Sibelius Museum
11 Ett Ham Museum
36 Aboa Vetus & Ars Nova
41 Luostarinmäki Handicrafts Museum
48 Quensel House; Pharmacy Museum
54 Turku Biological Museum
55 Wäinö Aaltonen Museum
60 Sigyn
61 Keihässalmi & Suomen Joutsen
62 Forum Marinum

OTHER
1 Bus Terminal
8 Concert Hall
9 Surf City Internet
12 Turku Cathedral
13 Kilroy Travels
17 Nordea Bank
18 Orthodox Church
19 Naantali Buses
20 Airport Buses
21 Hansa Shopping Arcade; Silja & Viking Line; Svenska Teater; Akateeminen Kirjakauppa; Suomalainen Kirjakauppa; China Garden; Foija

22 24-Hour Pharmacy
27 Post Office
32 Forex
35 Public Library
47 Turku City Tourist Office
49 Rent A Bike
53 Samppalinnan Swimming Stadium
58 Passenger Quay
63 Turku Castle & Historical Museum
65 Viking Line
66 Silja Line
67 Seawind

Turku Castle & Historical Museum

The mammoth Turku Castle (☎ 262 0300; adult/child €6.50/4.50, guided tours €1.50; open 10am-6pm daily mid-May–mid-Sept, shorter hours in winter), near the ferry terminals, is a must for everyone visiting Turku and is one of the country's most popular tourist attractions. Founded in 1280 at the mouth of the Aurajoki, the castle has been growing ever since. Notable occupants have included Count Per Brahe, founder of many towns in Finland, who lived here in the 17th century, and Sweden's King Eric XIV, who was imprisoned in the castle's Round Tower in the late 16th century, having been declared insane.

Highlights include two dungeons and magnificent banqueting halls, as well as a fascinating historical museum of medieval Turku in a maze of restored rooms in the castle's old bailey. A series of models in the main part of the castle shows its growth from a simple island fortress to medieval castle.

Guided tours of the stronghold area are given in English at 11am, then hourly from 12.10pm to 4.10pm. They give a good account of the castle's history but do not visit the Renaissance rooms on the upper floor, or the extensive museums in the bailey section of the castle, so you should allow time to explore those yourself, before or after a tour.

Luostarinmäki Handicrafts Museum

The name 'handicrafts museum' gives little indication of how interesting this open-air museum (☎ 262 0350; adult/child €3.40/2.60, guided tours €1.60/1.40; open 10am-6pm daily mid-Apr–mid-Sept, 10am-3pm Tues-Sun rest of the year) really is. It is made up of the only surviving 18th-century area of this medieval town – Turku has been razed by fire 30 times – and all the buildings are still in their original locations, unlike most Finnish open-air museums where the buildings are moved from elsewhere, or re-created. Carpenters, stonemasons, jewellers and other workers built homes and shops in the area, beginning in 1779. When the great fire of 1827 destroyed most of Turku, Luostarinmäki neighbourhood was one of the few that survived.

Since 1940 it has served as a museum. There are about 30 furnished workshops altogether, including a printing press, silversmith, watchmaker, bakery and cigar shop.

In summer, artisans in period costume work inside the old wooden houses and musicians stroll its paths. There are guided tours in English given roughly hourly from 10.30am to 4.30pm.

Turku Cathedral

The most notable of all Finnish churches, the Turku Cathedral (cathedral & museum open 9am-7pm daily), looming over the river, is the national shrine of the Evangelical-Lutheran Church of Finland. Its oldest parts date back to the 13th century. In the Middle Ages, the cathedral was extended by the addition of side chapels for Catholic bishops; these side chapels became resting places for Swedish war heroes after the Lutheran reformation. In one chapel rests Catherine Månsdotter, Queen of Sweden, wife of the unfortunate Erik XIV.

The **cathedral museum** (adult/child €2/1) displays models showing different stages of the cathedral's construction from the 14th century, as well as medieval sculptures and other religious paraphernalia.

Most Tuesday evenings the cathedral offers live music, and English-language services are held at 4pm on the last Sunday of each month.

Forum Marinum

This superb new maritime museum (☎ 282 9511; Ⓦ www.forum-marinum.fi; Linnankatu 72; adult/child €6/3, with museum ships €10/4; open 11am-7pm daily May-Sept, 10am-6pm Tues-Sun Oct-Apr) is set back from the riverfront near the castle. The museum itself is a better-than-average exhibition space devoted to Turku's shipping and naval background, including scale models, some full-size ships, WWII mines, multimedia displays and a theatrette. It's housed in an old granary built in 1894. There's a good café and shop in the foyer.

Outside, anchored in the river, are three **museum ships** which you can climb aboard and poke around, above and below deck. The WWII mine layer Keihässalmi gives an insight into wartime conditions at sea; the beautiful three-masted barque Sigyn, originally launched from Gothenburg in 1887, has well preserved cabins; and the impressive 1902 sailing ship Suomen Joutsen (Swan of Finland), which was built in France, was used by the Finnish Navy during WWII as a mother ship for submarines and as a hospital. The ships can be visited independently of the museum for €4/2 per adult/child.

Aboa Vetus & Ars Nova Museums

These twin museums (☎ 250 0552; *Itäinen Rantakatu 4-6; adult/child to each museum €7/5, combined ticket €9.50/7; open 11am-7pm daily May–mid Sept, Thur-Sun Sept-Dec)* are under one roof. Ars Nova is a museum of contemporary art with permanent and temporary exhibitions. Aboa Vetus is a museum of archaeology that is built around an excavated housing plot from the 14th century. The treasure hunt (11.30am daily from 1 July to 11 August, Sunday only at other times) is great for kids. There are free guided tours in English at 11.30am in July and August.

Sibelius Museum

The Sibelius Museum (☎ 215 4279; *Piispankatu 17; adult/child €3/1; open 11am-4pm Tues-Sun, 11am-3pm & 6pm-8pm Wed)*, near the cathedral, displays some 350 musical instruments from around the world, and exhibits memorabilia of the famous Finnish composer Jean Sibelius. It is the most extensive musical museum in Finland. You can listen to Sibelius' music on record or, better still, attend a Wednesday evening concert.

Qwensel House

This oldest wooden house in Turku (☎ 262 0280; *Läntinen Rantakatu 13; adult/child €3.40/2.60; open 10am-6pm daily Apr-Sept, 10am-3pm Tues-Sun Sept-Apr)*, on the riverfront, was built around 1700, and now houses the small **Pharmacy Museum**. You can see an old laboratorium with aromatic herbs, fine 18th-century furnishings with hints of 'Gustavian' (Swedish) style, and an exhibition of bottles and other pharmacy items.

Turku Biological Museum

In a beautiful 1907 Art Nouveau building, this museum (☎ 262 0340; *Neitsytpolku; adult/child €3.40/2.60; open 10am-6pm daily Apr-Sept, 10am-3pm Tues-Sun Sept-Apr)* is surprisingly interesting and superbly presented, if you don't mind staring at stuffed beasts. There are 30 mammal and 140 bird species native to Finland on display in their natural habitats – from the tundra of Lapland to the forests of Karelia.

Ett Hem Museum

Ett Hem means 'a home' and this museum (☎ 215 4279; *Piispankatu 14; adult/child €3/1; open noon-3pm Tues-Sun May–late Sept)* re-creates a wealthy 18th-century home, with old furniture of various styles, valuable works by famous Finnish painters Albert Edelfelt and Helene Schjerfbeck, and collections of china and glass.

Wäinö Aaltonen Museum

Wäinö Aaltonen was one of the leading sculptors of the 1920s, in the era of Finnish independence. The museum (☎ 262 0850; *Itäinen Rantakatu 38; adult/child €3/2; open 11am-7pm Tues-Sun)* has permanent exhibitions of Aaltonen's paintings and sculptures; temporary exhibitions are of contemporary art. The museum is on the south bank of the river. Special fees may apply for temporary exhibitions.

Turun Taidemuseo

The Turku Art Museum (*Aurakatu 26)* was under renovation at the time of research and was not expected to reopen with its collection of Finnish art works until at least 2004.

Orthodox Church

The church facing the market square was designed in the 1840s by German architect CL Engel, who is best known for creating Senate Square in Helsinki.

Activities

Cruises Archipelago cruises are a popular activity in Turku during summer. There are day trips around the islands as well as evening dinner-and-dance cruises. Departures are from the quay at Martinsilta bridge.

The historic steamship SS *Ukkopekka* (☎ 515 3300; Ⓦ *www.ukkopekka.fi)* cruises to Naantali daily at 10am and 2pm from June to August (one way/return €13/18). The trip takes 1½ hours and you can have lunch on board (€10 to €13). If you'd rather party on board, there's an evening 'gourmet' cruise, departing at 7pm Monday to Saturday from mid-June to late August (€17 for cruise only). The meals, which cost an extra €22, take on a different theme each night (but always involve fish) and are served on dry land – on the island of Loistokari.

The MS *Lily (Rosita Oy;* ☎ 469 2500; Ⓦ *www.rosita.fi)* cruises out to Vepsa island three times daily from mid-June to mid-August (adult/child €9/4, two hours) and as far as Maisaari on Friday and Sunday evening (€14.50/6, four hours). In May and September, cruises are Friday to Sunday only. Rosita also has cruises to Bengtskar island aboard the MS *Anna* on scheduled Saturdays in May, June and August (adult/child €44/22, 15 hours). The full-day return cruise includes guide fees and entry to the island.

SS *Franz Hoijer* sets sail north to Uusikaupunki and south to Hanko once a week – see the Getting There & Away section later for information.

Cycling The city tourist office can suggest cycling routes and publishes an excellent free *pyörätiekartta* (bike route map) of the city and surrounding towns. You can rent bikes from **Rent A Bike** (☎ 041-512 3430), on the river just around the corner from the tourist office for €9/45 a day/week, or from the tourist office itself (€10 a day).

Swimming & Sauna At the **Samppalinnan outdoor swimming stadium** (admission €3; open late May–late Aug), the entry fee includes a sauna and use of the 50m pool with diving boards. In winter, go to the indoor **Impivaara swimming hall** for swimming and sauna, north of the city centre (take bus No 13 to Impivaara).

Special Events

The **Turku Music Festival**, held during the second week of August, is a feast of classical and contemporary music and opera. Venues include the Turku Castle and the cathedral, and tickets cost €10 to €30. For further information contact the **Turku Music Festival Foundation** (☎ 251 1162, fax 231 3316; ⓦ www.turkumusicfestival.fi; Uudenmaankatu 1, 20500 Turku).

Quite different is **Ruisrock** (ⓦ www.ruisrock.fi), Finland's oldest and largest annual rock festival, held since 1969. The festival takes place over two days in early June at the recreational park on Ruissalo island. Tickets cost from €35 to €50.

Keskiajan Turku, held in late July or early August, is the festival of medieval Turku. It's a fantastic week of pageantry, banqueting, fencing and outrageous costumes. Events take place at the market square, Turku Castle, the cathedral and Aboa Vetus

museum. Inquire at the city tourist office about the festival programme and tickets.

Paavo Nurmi Marathon, named after the legendary distance runner, one of Turku's favourite sons, is a big event in late June/early July. It attracts an international field as well as hundreds of marathon-mad Finns. The course begins in the town centre and goes out to Ruissalo island. There's a statue of Nurmi on the south side of the river.

Flying Finns

There's a proud dynasty of Flying Finns, athletes who have excelled in fields like running, ski-jumping, motor racing, and ice hockey.

The first Flying Finn, distance runner Paavo Nurmi, was born in Turku in 1897. He won the 10,000m and cross-country at the 1920 Antwerp Olympics, picked up four gold medals for various races in Paris in 1924, and scored another gold in the 10,000m in Amsterdam in 1928. From 1920 to 1931 he set 20 world records. There's a bronze statue of him in Turku and a marathon named after him.

Nurmi was a hard act to follow, but successive generations of Finnish athletes have certainly tried. Finnish rally driving champions like Ari Vartanen, four-time world champion Juha Kankkunen, and the 1998 World Rally Drivers Champion Tommi Makinen have each in their time earned the nickname 'Flying Finn'. The Olympic ski-jumper Matti Nykanen, when he won gold in 1990, was known as a Flying Finn, as was the whole ice-hockey team which beat Sweden in May 1995 to gain the world ice-hockey championship. Mika Häkkinen was the toast of the nation when he won the 1998 Formula One Drivers Championship.

Success in *Olympiakisat* (the Olympic Games) is the goal for many more would-be Flying Finns, and the towns of Helsinki, Lahti and Kuopio are currently dreaming of hosting the Winter Olympic Games. Even the smallest rowing boat competitions are treated with great enthusiasm. Every town has sports fields, indoor sports halls, swimming pools, tennis courts, downhill slopes and jogging and skiing tracks. Large crowds gather to watch locals compete in *pesis* (Finnish baseball), *futis* (soccer or football), *koris* (basketball), and especially *lätkä* (ice hockey).

TURKU & THE SOUTHWEST

Places to Stay

Camping Situated on Ruissalo island, 10km west of the city centre, **Ruissalo Camping** (*☎ 262 5100, fax 262 5101; camp sites €9, double rooms €23, villa €59; open June–late Aug*) doesn't have any cabins, but there is a villa, as well as saunas, a cafeteria and nice beaches – including a nude beach. Bus No 8 runs from the market square in the centre to the camping ground.

Hostels HI-affiliated **Hostel Turku** (*☎ 231 6578, fax 231 1708; Linnankatu 39; dorm beds €13.50, singles & doubles €37; reception open 6am-10am & 3pm-midnight daily*) is well located on the river close to the town centre and is one of the busiest hostels in Finland, though there's nothing particularly special about it. Finnish families, school groups and backpackers arriving from or departing to Sweden help fill the 120 beds – book ahead in summer, especially for a private room. Facilities include a well-equipped kitchen, laundry (€1 per hour), lockers and bike hire. Linen and breakfast each cost €4.50 extra. From the train station take bus No 30 (or walk about 10 minutes), and from the bus station and harbour take bus No 1.

Interpoint Hostel (*☎ 231 4011, fax 231 2584; Vähä-Hämeenkatu 12A; dorm beds €8.50-10.50*) is a friendly, central YMCA place open only for a month between 15 July and 15 August, and it certainly fills a need during that busy period. It's the cheapest place in Turku but for good reason – 30 mattresses on the floor and one shower!

Guesthouses & B&Bs Turku has a handful of guesthouses that make a reasonable alternative to the hostels.

Bed & Breakfast Tuure (*☎ 233 0230; Tuurkeporinkatu 17C; singles/doubles €34/47*) is a tidy and friendly guesthouse in a quiet street close to the bus station and market square. Plain but bright rooms have shared bathroom.

Majatalo Kultainen Turisti (*☎ 250 0265; Käsityöläiskatu 11; singles/doubles/triples €34/47/67*) is a basic but comfortable guesthouse, close to the train station. It's above a set of shops.

Bridgettine Sisters Guesthouse (*☎ 250 1910; Ursininkatu 15A; singles/doubles €42/61*) is run by the nuns of a Catholic convent. The clean, simple rooms are a bargain and include breakfast. Silence is expected around the corridors and reception areas after 10pm. It's wise to book ahead.

Hotels In a lovely Art Nouveau building dating from 1904, **Park Hotel** (*☎ 251 9666, fax 251 9696; Rauhankatu 1; singles/doubles €105/130, weekends & summer €80/105*) is Turku's most romantic and ambient hotel by a long shot. All rooms are slightly different in character, so ask to see a few (the top-floor room is gorgeous).

Sokos Hamburger Börs (*☎ 337 381; Kauppiaskatu 6; singles/doubles €120/140, weekends & summer €70*), overlooking the market square, is the town's swishest business hotel with an assortment of popular nightclubs and restaurants attached. **Sokos Hotel Seurahuone** (*☎ 337 301, fax 251 8051; Eerikinkatu 23; singles/doubles €90/108, doubles weekends & summer €73*), the quieter sister hotel, has rustic decor and the popular Memphis bar.

Hotel Julia (*☎ 336 311, fax 233 6699; Eerikinkatu 4; singles/doubles €87/110, weekends & summer €73/82*), just off the market square, is one of the finest hotels in Turku. It has 130 rooms and plenty of class.

Quality Hotel Ateljee (*☎ 336 111, fax 233 6699; Humalistonkatu 7; singles/doubles €75/92, weekends & summer €55/60*) is in a landmark (ugly) building designed by Finnish architect Alvar Aalto. The inside is more appealing than the exterior but it's a standard business hotel.

Seaport Hotel (*☎ 230 2600, fax 230 2169; Matkustajasatama; singles/doubles €80/90, weekends & summer €65/80*) is an attractive hotel in a restored harbour warehouse, right in front of the Viking Line terminal. There's a restaurant here.

Places to Eat

Cheap eats abound in the city centre, in the **kauppahalli** (*covered market; Eerikinkatu*) and around the **kauppatori** (market square). In particular, the outdoor market (held daily in summer) is superb for produce and smoked fish. Look for kebab stands and **grillis** around the market square, on Aurakatu and Yliopistonkatu. Hesburger restaurants – Finland's answer to McDonald's – are everywhere in Turku, which is hardly surprising since the chain was born here. Turku is a university city, so it is always possible to get a €4 breakfast or lunch at the Turku

University **cafeteria**. The university campus is a short walk northeast of the cathedral.

Restaurants There are plenty of fine restaurants and bars in the city, including some of the best ethnic restaurants outside Helsinki, as well as popular boat restaurants in summer.

Finnish There are some very good traditional Finnish restaurants around town.

Teini *(☎ 223 0203; Uudenmaankatu 1; mains €7-12)* is a city institution for traditional Finnish food. It has a boggling array of dining halls and smaller rooms.

Panimoravintola Koulu *(☎ 274 5757; Eerikinkatu 18; mains €11.60-15)* is in an enormous former schoolhouse built in 1889. Upstairs is an upmarket restaurant, downstairs a brewery pub, beer garden and wine bar serving decent €7 lunches.

While the floating bars may be good for drink and socialising, the riverfront **Vaakahuoneen Paviljonki** *(☎ 515 3324; Linnankatu 38; mains €7-15, fish buffet €8)* is *the* place to go for great value food and entertainment. As well as an à la carte menu of snacks, pasta, pizzas and steak, there's a daily 'archipelago fish buffet' (11am to 10pm), plus a changing ethnic buffet (Thai, Vietnamese, Indian etc). Combined they cost €12. On top of this there's live music, usually traditional jazz, most days in summer.

Viking Restaurant Harald *(☎ 276 5050; Aurakatu 3; mains €11-21)* is a theme restaurant where you get to mix it with Norse warriors and eat with your hands. There are three-course set meals from €24.

Svarte Rudolph *(☎ 250 4567; mains €8.50-18)* is the fanciest of the floating restaurants moored on the south side of the Aurajoki. The speciality is seafood, which goes well with the nautical theme, and the below deck dining room is elegant.

International Facing the river, opposite the cathedral, **Ribs** *(☎ 251 7557; Itäinen Rantakatu 2; mains €12-20)* is a popular steakhouse with a summer terrace; the speciality is ribs and wings though they're not cheap.

Pizzeria Dennis *(☎ 469 1191; Linnankatu 17; dishes €8-11)* doesn't look much from the outside, but within is a warren of cosy rooms adorned with chianti bottles and strings of garlic. The traditional Italian menu includes a big and innovative range of pizzas and pasta (try pasta Finlandia, with meatballs, sausage, onion and tomato-mustard sauce), plus bagels, burgers and buffalo wings.

China Garden *(Aurakatu 10; mains from €6.50)*, inside the Hansa Shopping Arcade, is generally rated the best of Turku's Chinese restaurants and offers a discount on takeaway. **Foija** *(☎ 251 8665; Aurakatu 10; mains €8-18)*, also at the Hansa centre, is a very popular place serving steaks, pastas and more. Food is good, portions are big and prices are OK.

Baan Thai *(☎ 233 8290; Kauppiaskatu 15; mains €7.50-13)* is an authentic and intimate little Thai restaurant a short walk north of the kauppatori.

Almost opposite, **Bossa** *(☎ 251 5880; Kauppiaskatu; mains €11-16)* is probably the only Brazilian restaurant in Finland. It's an intimate place with spicy food and live Latin music most nights.

Sergio's *(Linnankatu 1; mains €8.50-10)* is a great little Italian restaurant/café concentrating on fine pasta, and excellent coffee. The outside tables are perfectly poised to have a drink and watch Turku go by.

Verso *(Linnankatu 3; lunch specials from €6)* is a nice vegetarian restaurant that offers filling lunch specials from 11am to 2pm Monday to Friday. There are hot dishes as well as salads and home-made breads.

Cafés There are several good cafés in the area around the market square, including the large, open-fronted **Bors Café** on Kappiaskatu, and **Galax Coffee Shop** around the corner on Aurakatu. The latter serves breakfast as well as filled rolls and croissants.

Cafe Fontana *(cnr Aurakatu & Linnankatu)*, in the heart of the city, is an Art Nouveau café with delicious pastries and pies.

At the entrance to the Luostarinmäki Handicrafts Museum, **Kahvila Kisälli** is a large, cheery café in a historic 1851 building. It's a good spot to stop for coffee after visiting the museum.

Sininen Juna Aschen Café, in the kauppahalli, is a neat little café where you sit in a converted train carriage. The name translates as 'blue train'.

Cafe Noir *(Eerikinkatu; meals €6-10)* is not fancy but it's one of the cheapest sit-down places for pasta and other dishes. The eclectic menu also includes pizza, schnitzel, chicken curry and omelettes.

Cafe de France (*Läntinen Rantakatu 5*), on Turku's most pleasant stretch of street (along the river between Auransilta bridge and Kauppiaskatu) is a fine Euro-style café with espresso and great sweets.

Entertainment

In summer the heart of Turku's nightlife is along the river. The evening usually begins on many of the **boats** lining the south bank of the river. Although some of these also serve food, they are primarily floating beer terraces with music and lots of shipboard socialising. Hard-up young locals drink on the grassy riverbank nearby. Popular boats on the south side of the river include *Donna*, *Papa Joe* and *Cindy*. *Zaida*, a small wooden boat on the north side of the river outside Herman brewery pub, has some of the cheapest beer in town – €2.70 for a large beer.

Pubs & Clubs Next to the bridge and opposite the tourist office is the ultra-chic **Blanko** (*☎ 233 3966; Aurakatu 1*), where Turku's gorgeous young things shake their booty to DJs on Friday and Saturday night; when not striking a sullen pose the staff whip up an excellent tapas menu. Across the river near the boat bars, **Riverside Bar** is another good spot with street dancing on Tuesday evening in summer.

South of the river, **Uusi Apteeki** (*Kaskenkatu 1*) is a wonderful bar in a converted old pharmacy; the antique shelving and desks have been retained, but they are filled with hundreds of old beer bottles. For pure novelty value, **Puutorin Vessa**, in the middle of a small square near the bus station, is worth popping into. It was once a public toilet!

Old Bank (*Aurakatu 3*), on the corner of Aurakatu and Linnankatu, was once a bank but is now a boisterous Irish pub that attracts a slightly older drinking crowd, and has a huge range of beers to satisfy connoisseurs.

Panimoravintola Koulu (see Places to Eat) is a great brewery pub in the town centre. There's a big, comfortable front bar, a lively summer beer garden (big enough to boast a minigolf course) and there are three homegrown brews on tap including a fine stout. **Panimoravintola Herman** (*Läntinen Rantakatu 37*) is another brewery pub/restaurant fronting the river near Hostel Turku. It's a lot smaller than Koulu but is part of a busy little waterfront area that includes the passenger

quay for local cruises and the jazz restaurant Vaakahuoneen Paviljonki.

One of the most popular nightclubs is **Bors** (*☎ 337 381; Kappiaskatu 6*) at Sokos Hamburger Bors, opposite the market square. Next door, **Kino** (*☎ 469 3433; Kappiaskatu 8*) is a chic, Euro-style bar with a modern, minimalist decor and a pumping nightclub downstairs. Both places are open late.

Music & Theatre The Turku Philharmonic Orchestra is one of the oldest in Europe – it was founded in the 1790s. The orchestra performs in the **Concert Hall** (*Aninkaistenkatu 9*).

There's live jazz most days at **Vaakahuoneen Paviljonki** (see Places to Eat) at the passenger quay. For live rock music, the slightly down-at-heel **Downtown** (*Linnankatu 17*), on the corner near Pizzeria Dennis, is worth a look.

Svenska Teater (*☎ 277 7377; Eerikinkatu 13*), next to the Hansa Shopping Arcade, is one of the oldest theatres in Finland and it hosts well known musicals with performances in Swedish.

Spectator Sports

Turku is a hot town as far as ice hockey is concerned. Games are played in Turkuhalli stadium, near Ruissalo island.

Getting There & Away

Air Finnair has flights to Turku from a number of Finnish cities and some European capitals, including Stockholm. Domestic flights are generally at least once a day but several times daily to Helsinki, Mariehamn, Tampere, Rovaniemi and Oulu.

The **Finnair office** (*☎ 415 4909*) is at the airport.

Bus Purchase long-distance and express bus tickets from the bus terminal at Aninkaistentulli. There are hourly express buses to Helsinki (€20.90, 2½ hours), and frequent services to Tampere (€16.80, two hours), Rauma (€11.40, 1½ hours) and other points in southern Finland. Regional buses depart from the market square.

Train Turku is the terminus for the southeastern railway line. The train station is a short walk northwest of the centre; trains also stop at the ferry harbour and at Kupittaa train station east of the centre and Bus No 30 shuttles between the centre and the train station. Express trains run frequently to and from Helsinki (€19.80, two hours), Tampere (€16.60, 1¾ hours), Oulu (€60.20, seven hours), Rovaniemi (€67.40, 10 hours). For Oulu and Rovaniemi change in Tampere.

Boat Turku is a major gateway to Finland from Sweden and Åland and smaller boats ply the waters up and down the coast.

Sweden & Åland The harbour, southwest of the centre, has terminals for **Silja Line** *(☎ 335 255)*, **Viking Line** *(☎ 33311)* and **Seawind** *(☎ 210 2800)*. Ferries sail to Turku from Stockholm (9½ hours) and Mariehamn (six hours). Prices vary widely according to season and class of service, but Viking Line offers the cheapest tickets (deck class).

Purchase tickets from one of the offices at the harbour or from the Silja or Viking Line offices in the Hansa Shopping Arcade; you should book ahead during the high season (late June to mid-August), especially if you plan to take a car and if you're travelling on a weekend (or Friday night). Bus No 1 travels between the market square and harbour.

See the main Getting There & Away chapter for more details about international ferry travel.

Mainland Finland From mid-May to mid-August the MS *Franz Höijer* travels between Turku and Hanko at 10am on Tuesday (€12, eight hours) and Turku and Uusikaupunki at 10am on Thursday (€12, eight hours). All departures are from the passenger quay just west of Martinsilta bridge.

Getting Around
To/From the Airport Bus No 1 runs between the market square and the airport, about 8km north of the city, every 15 minutes from 5am to midnight Monday to Friday, from 5.30am to 9.30pm Saturday and from 7am to midnight Sunday (€1.80, 25 minutes). This same bus also goes from the market square to the harbour.

Bus City and regional buses are frequent and you pay €1.80 for a single journey or €4.20 for a 24-hour ticket. Important city bus routes include bus No 1 (harbour–market square–bus station–airport) and bus Nos 32 and 42 (train station–market square).

Around Turku

☎ 02
The area surrounding Turku is simply called 'Turku Land'. This region is among the most historical in Finland, with medieval churches dotting the landscape every 10km or so.

NAANTALI
pop 12,500
Naantali (Swedish: Nådendal) is perhaps Finland's most idyllic port town and at only 17km from Turku, it's a hugely popular destination for daytrippers.

Once you get over the shock of the summertime crowds – and the fact that the majority of them are Finnish families making a beeline for a children's theme park – it's difficult not to like Naantali. The compact boat-filled harbour is ringed with pleasant cafés and restaurants, the cobbled Old Town has a quaint (if slightly dressed up) old-world feel, and there's plenty of sights and shopping to occupy for an afternoon. The main attraction for all those Finnish families is Moominworld, a theme park celebrating characters from the storybooks by Tove Jansson.

History
Naantali grew around the Catholic Convent of the Order of Saint Birgitta, which was founded in 1443. After Finland became Protestant in 1527, the convent was dissolved and Naantali had to struggle for its existence; the convent had been important not only spiritually but also economically. When the pilgrims no longer came to town, people had to find other means of making a living, notably by knitting socks, which became Naantali's main export.

Orientation & Information
Naantali sprawls on both sides of the channel Naantalinsalmi. The island of Luonnonmaa is on the southwest side of the channel, accessible by bridge, and the mainland, with the town centre, is on the northeast side. The old part of Naantali surrounds the harbour, 1km west of the bus terminal.

Tourist Service *(Naantalin Matkailu; ☎ 435 9800, fax 435 0852; Kaivotori 2; open 9am-6pm Mon-Fri, 10am-3pm Sat & Sun June–mid-Aug, 9am-4.30pm Mon-Fri rest of the year)*, is near the harbour. There's plenty of local information here and it can book tours some private accommodation (for a fee of course).

There's free Internet access at the tourist office and at the **library**, on the 2nd floor of the post office building.

Muumimaailma (Moominworld)

Undoubtedly one of Finland's most popular family attractions, this island-based Disney-like theme park brings to life the characters and stories of children's writer Tove Jansson. Even kids who haven't grown up with the books (or seen the Moomin film or TV series) will warm to the whimsies of the **Muumimaailma** (☎ 511 1111; W www.muumimaailma.fi; admission €13; open 10am-6pm daily June–mid-Aug).

The main attraction is on Kailo island, accessible by bridge from the mainland. Costumed characters inhabit its Moominhouse, Pirate Fort, Moominmama's Doughnut House and Whispering Woods. There is a safe swimming beach and a minigolf course. There's also **Väski Adventure Island** with pirate adventures that will suit older children. It's accessible by regular boat and admission is €9, or €4 if you already have a ticket for Moominworld.

Old Town

The Old Town of Naantali is like a big open-air museum. The town grew around the convent, without any regular town plan, and new buildings were always built on the sites of older ones. The result is a delightfully

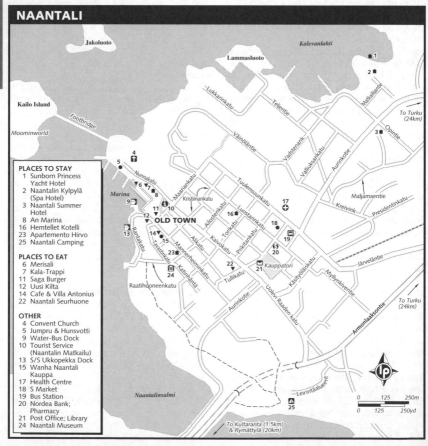

NAANTALI

PLACES TO STAY
1 Sunborn Princess Yacht Hotel
2 Naantalin Kylpylä (Spa Hotel)
3 Naantali Summer Hotel
8 An Marina
16 Hemtellet Kotelli
23 Apartemento Hirvo
25 Naantali Camping

PLACES TO EAT
6 Merisali
7 Kala-Trappi
11 Saga Burger
12 Uusi Kilta
14 Cafe & Villa Antonius
22 Naantali Seurhuone

OTHER
4 Convent Church
5 Jumpru & Hunsvotti
9 Water-Bus Dock
10 Tourist Service (Naantalin Matkailu)
13 S/S Ukkopekka Dock
15 Wanha Naantali Kauppa
17 Health Centre
18 S Market
19 Bus Station
20 Nordea Bank; Pharmacy
21 Post Office; Library
24 Naantali Museum

Ms Moomin

The late Tove Jansson, creator of the much-loved Moomin children's books, was born on 9 August 1914 in Helsinki to Swedish-speaking parents. The talented young Tove was an artist almost from birth – her first drawings were published in a magazine when she was a mere 14 years of age. The first book featuring Moomin trolls came out in 1945, and a new Moomin adventure followed every two years or so.

Despite almost immediate Moomin fever in Finland, it was more than 40 years before the lovable Moomin family attracted worldwide attention. The big break was a Japanese-made cartoon which has been shown on TV in several countries.

Today, the Moomin world comprises four picture books, eight novels and one short story collection, which have been translated into many languages – including English. Apart from Naantali's Moomin-world theme park, you can get acquainted with the characters at the Moomin Valley Museum in Tampere, and at galleries and bookshops around Finland.

Tove lived most of her life on various islands off the Finnish south coast. Whenever she tired of the journalists who frequently visited her studio, she moved to a more isolated island. She passed away in June 2001 in Helsinki, aged 86.

photogenic district of old narrow cobbled streets and low wooden houses – many of which now house handicraft shops, art galleries and cafés. Only the old windmills and storehouses along the shore have disappeared. The main thoroughfare is Mannerheiminkatu and at No 13, **Wanha Naantali Kauppa** is a shop selling old-fashioned Finnish sweets, bottled soft drinks, stamps, postcards and souvenirs – it's one of those nostalgic places you can easily get lost in.

Naantali Museum *(☎ 434 5324; Katinhäntä 1; adult/child €2/1; open noon-6pm daily mid-May–late Aug)* is housed in three old wooden buildings dating from the 18th century. Displays include old furniture and exhibitions on the history of Naantali as a ritzy spa town.

Convent Church
The only building remaining from the Convent of the Order of Saint Birgitta is the massive Convent Church *(open noon-7pm daily May–mid-Aug, noon-3pm daily Apr & mid-Aug–late Sept, noon-3pm Sun & holidays Nov–Mar)*, which towers above the harbour. The church was completed in 1462 and its fine baroque stone tower dates from 1797. Until this century, the clock face on the tower had painted hands which always pointed to 11.30 – local people used to joke that the end of the world would come when the clock struck 12.

During summer the church offers a programme of organ music; the tourist office can provide a schedule. At 8pm on summer evenings you'll hear the 'vespers' (evensong) played by a trumpeter from the belfry of the church.

Kultaranta
The summer residence of the president of Finland is a fanciful stone castle on Luonnonmaa island, across Naantali Bay. The castle, designed by Lars Sonck, was built in 1916 and is surrounded by a 56-hectare estate with beautiful, extensive rose gardens. If you don't have children to drag you into Moomin World, this is the top attraction in Naantali.

The Kultaranta grounds can only be visited in summer (24 June to 11 August daily) by guided tour only. The 45-minute tour costs €5/2.50 per adult/child if you start from Kulturanta gate (3pm), or €8/4.50 for the bus tour from Naantali. Book through the tourist office.

Activities
Naantali's **spa** traditions date from 1723, when people took health-giving waters from a spring in Viluluoto. Even if you can't stay there, Naantalin Kylpylä, the town's top-class spa hotel and one of the finest in Scandinavia, allows nonguests to use its pool and sauna area – including several pools and a Turkish bath – during daytime hours. The fee for two hours is around €18. Various spa and sauna treatments, including massage, clay and peat saunas, hydrotherapy and shiatsu, cost from €20 for 15 minutes to €117 for a day package. Phone ☎ 445 5800.

You can rent **bicycles** at **Jumpru & Hunsvotti** (*☎ 533 2242; per day €10*), a small marine shop at the harbour near the bridge to Moomin World.

Special Events
The week-long **Naantali Music Festival**, held over two weeks from early June, features chamber music by Mozart, Bach, Rautavaara and others, with international participants. Many of the concerts are at the Convent Church. Tickets are available through the tourist office, or by phoning ☎ 434 5363.

One of the more unusual Finnish festivals is **Sleepyhead Day** (27 July), a Naantali tradition that goes back more than 100 years. Townspeople elect a 'Sleepyhead of the Year' who is woken early in the morning by being tossed into the sea! A carnival with music, dancing and games follows.

Places to Stay
Although Naantali can easily be visited on a day trip from Turku, it's worth staying overnight to enjoy it away from the afternoon crowds. This is also one of the few towns in Finland to offer accommodation in quaint B&Bs, many of them in historic homes. None of these places are particularly cheap, especially in summer.

Naantali Camping (*☎ 435 0855, 435 0850; Kuparivuori; tent sites €13-17, cabins €30-100; open Apr-Oct*), 400m south of the town centre, is an exceptional camping ground with good facilities, including a beachside sauna.

Naantali Summer Hotel (*☎ 445 5660; Opintie 3; rooms per person €31; open June–mid-Aug*) is a modern hostel-type place near to and run by the spa hotel. The per-person rate means it's reasonable value for solo travellers but not so much for groups.

Apartemento Hirvo (*☎ 435 1619; Mannerheiminkatu 19; doubles €60, children half price*), well-placed in the Old Town, has friendly staff, a quiet garden, and guests can use the kitchen.

An Marina (*☎ 435 6066; Nunnakatu 5; singles/doubles €50/70*), the closest accommodation to the harbour, is a lovely little place with six rooms. It's open year-round and there are good discounts outside summer.

Villa Antonius (*☎ 435 1938; Mannerheiminkatu 9; doubles from €85*), in the heart of the Old Town, has about a dozen

romantically decorated rooms (with hints of Art Nouveau).

Hemtellet Kotelli (*☎ 435 1419; Luostarinkatu 13; singles/doubles €55/60, breakfast €5*) is a fine early 19th-century villa, well-kept and furnished. The dining room has heaps of style and the garden is pleasant.

For the ultimate in indulgence, look no further than **Naantalin Kylpylä** (*Spa Hotel; ☎ 44550, fax 445 5622; W www.naantalispa.fi; Matkailijantie 2; singles/doubles from €124/144, €134/184 Sat & in summer*). This sprawling, upmarket spa hotel trades partly on Naantali's history as a spa town but does it in style. Guests have unlimited use of the spa, sauna, pool and gym facilities. For real jetset-types, moored in the harbour alongside the hotel is **Sunborn Princess Yacht Hotel** (*☎ 445 5660; singles/doubles from €154/184, €164/224 Sat & in summer*), a luxurious cruiser with 140 rooms.

Places to Eat
Naantali caters for tourists, with a variety of places to try good food. However, prices are higher than in other small towns in Finland.

Saga Burger is the cheapest place around the waterfront area with burgers from €2. If nothing else it makes a change from Hesburger. Near the kauppatori, **Naantali Seurhuone** is a cheap restaurant with a grilli and kebab section.

Kala-Trappi (*☎ 435 2477; Nunnakatu 3; pizzas €8.70, mains €12.50-16*), at the harbour, has a large patio, good-value wafer-thin pizzas and a few off-beat dishes such as 'chicken with fruits' and pan-fried snails.

Uusi Kilta, on the other side of the harbour, has an international menu, great outdoor seating and cold beer.

If you have an appetite, **Merisali** (*☎ 435 2451; Nunnakatu 1; buffet lunch/dinner €9/10.50, Sun lunch €12*), just below the Convent Church, is without question the best on the Naantali dining scene. The historic restaurant has a shaded terrace and a mind-blowing smorgasbord for lunch and dinner, including staggering quantities of salads and fish. If you value your waistline, beware the Sunday lunch.

Cafe Antonius (*Mannerheiminkatu 9*), an unbeatable café in Villa Antonius, has gingerbread and other mouth-watering sweets. The cosy interior is an endearing combination of style, kitsch and fine pastries.

Getting There & Away

There are buses to Naantali every 15 minutes from the bus terminal in Turku (€3.40, 20 minutes). Virtually all routes to Naantali go via Turku.

SS *Ukkopekka* sails between Turku and Naantali in summer, arriving at the passenger quay on the south side of the harbour. For more information see the Turku Getting There & Away section earlier.

RYMÄTTYLÄ

Rymättylä, a sleepy island village 20km southwest of Naantali, is the ideal place to escape to when you've tired of 'big cities' like Turku and Helsinki. Worth a look is the large stone **church** which dominates the village centre and has one of the most colourful of all Finnish medieval church interiors.

Päiväkulma (☎ 252 1894, fax 252 1794; *Kuristentie 225; beds per person from €16.50*), formerly a youth hostel but now a guesthouse popular as a weekend retreat, is in a big, old former schoolhouse on the seafront in farming country. There are rooms in the main house and two cottages, as well as a kitchen, laundry facilities and a seaside sauna. The house is on an unpaved road about 3km from the village – take the turnoff to Heinainen then follow the signs. It's open year-round but call ahead as it's often full in summer.

LOUHISAARI MANOR

The village of **Askainen**, 30km northwest of Turku, is the setting for stunning Louhisaari Manor (*adult/child €3.50/1; open 11am-5pm daily mid-May–end Aug*), its lavishly decorated rooms including a 'ghost room', and its extensive museum and gardens. The manor, locally referred to as a castle, was built in 1655 in the Dutch Renaissance style. The five-storey manor was purchased by the Mannerheim family in 1795, and Finland's greatest military leader and president, Marshal CGE Mannerheim, was born here in 1867. Soon after that the family lost its fortune and the property. Louhisaari was later acquired by the National Board of Antiquities; it's now an attraction rivalling the castles at Turku and Savonlinna. Tours are in Finnish only.

The village and manor are located just off road No 193. There are three to four buses daily from Turku to Askainen.

NOUSIAINEN

Nousiainen is 25km north of Turku, and is worth a visit for the **Nousiainen church** (*open noon-6pm Tues-Sun*). In a country with seemingly limitless medieval churches, this one is notable as the eternal resting place of St Henry, the first (Catholic) Bishop of Finland, who died in the early 15th century. The church was built in the 14th century and restored in the 1960s. It has a triple-aisle hall design with early 15th-century murals.

KUSTAVI

The island village of Kustavi (Swedish: Gustavs) offers scenic seascapes, a peaceful rural setting and a jumping off point for the Åland islands. Its wooden **church** (*open daily early June–mid-Aug*), built in 1783, features the votive miniature ships common in coastal churches – sailors offered these in exchange for divine blessings.

Kustavin Lomakeskus ja Camping (☎ 876 230; e *myyntipalvelu@lomaliitto.fi;* tent sites €12.50-14, rooms €36-44; open late May–mid-Aug) is a large holiday village 2km south of Kustavi. It has a café-restaurant, many cottages and a host of activities.

Kustavi is on road No 192, about 70km from Turku, and there are many buses. To reach Åland, continue 8.5km west to the passenger pier of Osnäs (Finnish: Vuosnainen) on Vartsala island. From there ferries depart regularly for the island of Brändö.

Most buses from Turku travel direct to Osnäs, and some continue to Brändö. If you have a private vehicle, expect delays during the high season. Taking a car by ferry to Brändö will cost money; bicycles travel free. See the Åland chapter for more details.

South of Turku

TURUNMAA ARCHIPELAGO
☎ 02

The Turunmaa archipelago is a tightly clustered chain of islands that begins south of Turku at Parainen, then stretches southwest to Korppoo. Free local ferries – especially for those travelling by bicycle or bus – can be taken all the way out to Galtby harbour on Korppoo island. From there, you can catch one of the frequent ferries plying the southern archipelago route to Mariehamn, Åland; see the Åland chapter for more details. Local ferries on the route between Parainen, Nauvo and Korppoo offer a continuous service.

Parainen

The de facto 'capital' of the archipelago is Parainen (Swedish: Pargas), about 25km south of Turku. With a population of 12,000, it's the largest town with all facilities. There's a **tourist office** (☎ 458 5942) at Runeberinkatu 6. The **old town**, with wooden houses, is behind the church.

Solliden Camping (☎/fax 485 5955; W www.solliden.fi; Norrby; tent sites €14, 4-8 person cottages €39-70; open June-Oct) is the seaside camping ground of Parainen, 1.5km north of the centre. It has camp sites, cottages, saunas, and the HI-affiliated hostel **Norrdal** (dorm beds €10) in a rustic old building with a kitchen and a TV room.

Sattmark, halfway between Parainen and the island of Nauvo, is worth a stop for the **Sattmark Coffee Shop**, a charming 18th-century red wooden crofter's cottage serving home-made wheat buns and cakes.

Parainen is on road No 180 from Turku. There are one to three buses an hour from Turku to Parainen, and five or six buses a day from Helsinki.

Nauvo

Nauvo (Swedish: Nagu) is an idyllic island community between Parainen to the east and Korppoo to the west. It is connected to both by free ferries. **Nagu church** (open daily June–late Aug) dates from the 14th century and contains the oldest Bible in Finland.

From Nauvo harbour it's possible to island-hop around the Turunmaa archipelago on free local ferries.

Korppoo

Korppoo (Swedish: Korpo) is the most distant island in the Turunmaa archipelago, and the final stop before entering the Åland archipelago. A highlight is the medieval **Korppoo church** (open daily in summer) built in the late 13th century. Treasures in this church include naive paintings on the ceiling and a statue of St George fighting a dragon.

Korppoo has plenty of B&Bs and cottages. **Faffas B&B** (☎ 464 6106; beds per person €26), about 4km from the harbour near Osterretais, is a comfortable year-round guesthouse. The main hotel in the village centre is **Forellen** (☎ 463 1202; Kyrkbyn).

Korppoo is 75km southwest of Turku on road No 180 and is connected to Nauvo by continuous ferry. Galtby is the passenger harbour, 4km northeast of Korppoo centre. A number of free ferries depart from Galtby for Åland but as this is a popular route in summer, expect to wait a few extra hours on Friday going to Åland and on Sunday going to Turku if travelling by car. There are also regular ferries to smaller, nearby islands of the Turunmaa archipelago, such as Houtskär.

KEMIÖ ISLAND
☎ 02 • pop 3400

Kemiö Island offers excellent possibilities for bicycle tours. The access point is the village of Kemiö (Swedish: Kimito), which has a **tourist office** (☎ 423 572; Arkadiantie 13). Swedish is still predominantly spoken here, so Kimito is commonly used.

The village has a 14th-century **church** (open daily mid-May–mid-Aug) with a grandiose interior. **Sagalund Museum** (adult/child €4/free; open 11am-6pm Tues-Sun), 2km west of the church, is an open-air museum with more than 20 old buildings. There are guided tours every hour.

Dragsfjärd
pop 3800

Dragsfjärd, in the southwest of Kemiö Island, is a quiet, rural village with a **church** dating from the 1700s. **Söderlångvik** (☎ 424 662; adult/child €3.50/free; open 11am-6pm daily in summer) is a manor house that belonged to local newspaper magnate and art collector Amos Anderson until 1961. There are paintings, furniture and special exhibitions in this beautiful manor, as well as an extensive garden and a café. The best reason to stick around in Dragsfjärd, however, is the excellent hostel.

Pensionat och Vandrarhotell (☎ 424 553; Kulla; dorm beds €18, singles/doubles €20/31, with bathroom & breakfast €39/64; open Mar-Dec), at the turn-off to Dragsfjärd, is one of the most comfortable hostels in Finland. It's beautifully furnished like a private home, has several common areas, kitchen, a big garden, sauna and bicycles and boats for rent. The sea is just steps away.

Dragsfjärd is on road No 183, 18km south of Kemiö village. Take a bus from Salo, Turku or Kemiö village; there are several daily.

Kasnäs

The Kasnäs harbour, on a small island south of Kemiö Island, is the main jumping-off point for regional archipelago ferries. Visit **Sinisimpukka** *(Naturum; ☎ 466 6290; open 10am-6pm daily in summer)* for information on the South-West Archipelago National Park. The centre organises tours to some of the islands in June, July and August, depending on demand. There's also a nature trail from Sinisimpukka.

At the road's end **Hotel Kasnas** *(☎ 521 0100;* W *www.kasnas.com; singles/doubles €74/102, weekends €65/83)* is a sprawling hotel at the harbour. The rooms are overpriced but there's a good restaurant and terrace, a beach sauna and water-sports hire kiosk. It's worth it for the €8 lunch buffet.

Ferries MS *Rosala II* and MS *Aura* ferry to nearby islands, including Hiittinen, daily in summer. Even if you don't want to visit the islands, they make a pleasant day cruise.

There are just one or two daily bus-and-ferry connections from Dalsbruk (Taalintehdas) on Kemiö Island, about 3km south of Dragsfjärd on road No 183.\

North of Turku

Heading north from Turku, there are several coastal towns worth visiting before going inland to Tampere, or heading up the west coast to the Pohjamaa region. This southwest region is known as Vakka-Suomi, and refers to the *vakka* (wooden bowls) that have been made here for centuries.

UUSIKAUPUNKI

☎ 02 • pop 17,600

Uusikaupunki (Swedish: Nystad) is a relaxing seaside town 77km north of Turku. The name translates as 'New Town' – ironic because Uusikaupunki is now one of the oldest towns in Finland, first founded in 1617 by Gustav II Adolf, the king of Sweden.

Uusikaupunki's main claim to fame is the treaty of 1721 which brought an uneasy peace between Sweden and Russia after the devastating Great Northern War. Today, almost nobody in the town speaks Swedish and Nystad is merely a historical name – use Uusikaupunki (oo-see-**cow**-poonki).

Uusikaupunki has a lively marina at its rivermouth, some good restaurants, and an oddball museum – otherwise it's a fairly typical Finnish summer resort, albeit less touristy than similar places like Naantali or Hanko.

Information

The **tourist office** *(☎ 8451 5443;* W *www .uusikaupunki.fi; Rauhankatu 10; open 8.30am-6pm Mon-Fri, 9am-3pm Sat late June–early Aug, 8.30am-4pm Mon-Fri rest of the year)*, across from the market square, has a free Internet terminal and rents bikes for €2/5 per hour/day.

The **public library** *(Alinenkatu 34; open 11am-7pm Mon-Fri, 10am-2pm Sat)* also has free Internet access and a newspaper reading room.

Things to See

Is the **Bonk Dynamo Centre** *(☎ 841 8404; Siltakatu 2; adult/child €5/2; open 10am-6pm daily mid-May–late Aug)* a science and history museum, or a practical joke? The creation of local artist Alvar Gullichsen (who even the staff describe as 'a bit nuts'), this tiny museum tells the story of a Mr Per Bonk (who made a fortune on 'Garum Superbe' anchovy spice in 1900) and his strange 'fully defunctioned' machines. It's elaborate, offbeat humour and a spoof on the power and seduction of advertising.

Three museums concentrate on the region's seafaring history and can be visited on a combined ticket (€3). **Kulttuurihistoriallinen Museo** *(Museum of Cultural History; ☎ 874 118; Ylinenkatu 11; adult/child €2/ 0.50; open 10am-5pm Mon-Fri, noon-3pm Sat & Sun June–mid-Aug, noon-3pm Tues-Sun rest of the year)* is in an old house built by a powerful shipowner and tobacco manufacturer. Rooms are furnished in the style of a wealthy 19th-century home and exhibit seafaring memorabilia.

Merimiehen Koti *(Seaman's Home; ☎ 8451 5413; Myllykatu 18; adult/child €1/0.50; open 11am-3pm Tues-Fri, noon-3pm Sat & Sun June–mid-Aug)* is a home museum of a local sailor. **Luotsitupa** *(Pilot Museum; ☎ 8451 5450; Vallimäki hill)* is a small house devoted to maritime navigation. Admission and hours are the same as for the Seaman's Home.

Automobile Museum *(☎ 484 8086; Autotehtaantie 14; adult/child €5/2; open 11am- 5pm daily)* is dedicated to old Saab cars – Saab

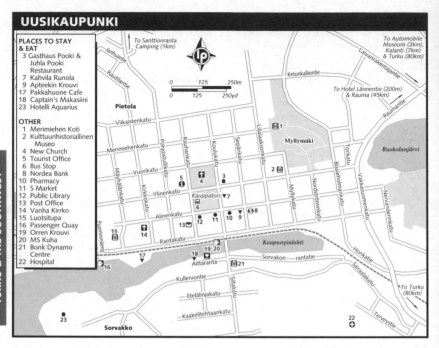

UUSIKAUPUNKI

PLACES TO STAY
& EAT
3 Gasthaus Pooki &
  Juhla Pooki
  Restaurant
7 Kahvila Runola
9 Apteekin Krouvi
17 Pakkahuone Cafe
18 Captain's Makasiini
23 Hotelli Aquarius

OTHER
1 Merimiehen Koti
2 Kulttuurihistoriallinen
  Museo
4 New Church
5 Tourist Office
6 Bus Stop
8 Nordea Bank
10 Pharmacy
11 S Market
12 Public Library
13 Post Office
14 Vanha Kirrko
15 Luotsitupa
16 Passenger Quay
19 Orren Krouvi
20 MS Kuha
21 Bonk Dynamo
  Centre
22 Hospital

and Porsche models are still manufactured in Uusikaupunki. If you're a fan of Scandinavian automobiles, you'll love it.

Vanha Kirrko *(Old Church; Kirkkokatu 2; open 11am-3.30pm Mon-Sat, noon-4pm Sun June–mid-Aug)* is worth a look. Completed in 1629, it's the town's oldest building. Its ornate barrel-vaulted roof is meant to resemble a ship's hull.

Myllymäki (Windmill Hill), northeast of the centre, is a hilltop park with four lovely windmills – the sole survivors of the dozens that used to exist in Uusikaupunki.

The village of **Kalanti**, about 7km east of Uusikaupunki on road No 43, is where the first sizable party of Swedes, led by Bishop Henry of the Catholic Church, arrived on a crusade in 1155. Thus, the Swedish chapter of Finland's history began. The medieval **Kalanti Church** dates from the late 14th century; its interior paintings depict Bishop Henry meeting a pagan on the Finnish coast.

Cruises

There are plenty of charter boats and water taxis available for archipelago cruises from Uusikaupunki's harbour. From late June to early August, MS *Rosita* cruises daily (adult/child €35/17, seven hours) to the **Isokari Lighthouse**. The cost of the full-day cruise is a bit excessive, but it includes lunch, a guided walk and 3½ hours at Isokari. Cruises just to the lighthouse and back (adult/child €5/2) are also arranged in summer – book through the tourist office.

MS *Kuhu* offers archipelago cruises on Monday, Wednesday, Friday and Sunday in summer (€5/3).

The MS *Franz Höijer* sails to Turku once a week in summer; see the Getting There & Away section later.

Places to Stay

Santtionranta Camping *(☎ 842 3862; Kalalokkikuja 14; tent sites €12, cottages €30-42; open late May–mid-Aug)*, an attractive seaside camping ground, is 1km northwest of the town centre.

Gasthaus Pooki *(☎ 847 7100, fax 847 7110; Ylinenkatu 21; singles/doubles €66/ 88)* is reason enough to stay in Uusikaupunki. This sturdy granite building on the corner of the kauppatori was once a bank but is now a charming inn with just four spacious, stylish rooms (book ahead in summer). Rates include breakfast, and there's a good restaurant, courtyard and evening entertainment here.

Hotel Lännentie (☎ 845 6100, fax 845 6200; Levysepänkatu 1; singles/doubles from €55/65), east of the centre on the road to Rauma, is a hotel-motel with basic but tidy rooms. There's a slight discount in summer and on weekends.

Hotelli Aquarius (☎ 841 3123, fax 841 3540; W www.hotelliaquarius.fi; Kullervontie 11; singles/doubles €85/100, doubles weekends & summer €69), the largest and most business-like hotel in town, is in a park-like setting with tennis courts and a pool.

Places to Eat & Drink

The **kauppatori** is in full swing from Monday to Saturday in summer with snack stalls and grillis. **Kahvila Runola** is an inexpensive lunch café across from the kauppatori.

Apteekin Krouvi (☎ 844 2244; Alinenkatu 28; pizza & pasta €8-13) is a fine Irish pub and restaurant in a historic building that was once a pharmacy. There's a great courtyard terrace at the back. Pizza is the speciality.

Perhaps the best restaurant in Uusikaupunki is **Juhla Pooki** (☎ 847 7100; Ylinenkatu 21; mains €6.50-17, lunch grill €10), the gourmet kitchen at Gasthaus Pooki (see Places to Stay). The lunch grill is excellent value. This is also the place for summer entertainment with music and dancing on Friday and Saturday and the **Bonk Theatre** (€40) on Wednesday and Friday.

The place to dine – or just sun yourself over a drink – on a summer afternoon is at one of the red wooden shophouses lining the south bank of the kaupunginlahti (town bay). All have enticing terraces and among the restaurants are some interesting craft and souvenir shops.

Captain's Makasiini (☎ 841 3600; Aittaranta 12; mains €6-15) is the pick of these if you want to have just one big meal in Uusikaupunki. The menu ranges from inexpensive burgers and pizza to big €15 steaks – but you're really here to soak up the terrific nautical atmosphere. **Orren Krouvi**, next door, is a great pub with a popular terrace.

On the other side of the marina, **Pakkahuone Cafe** (☎ 842 4822) services the visiting yachties at the guest harbour, and is the town's liveliest café, with a nice waterfront terrace.

Getting There & Away

Uusikaupunki is 75km north of Turku and 50km south of Rauma, off the main north–south road (road No 8) – take road No 43 west to reach Uusikaupunki.

Buses to Turku (€10.40, one hour) run from the kauppatori in the centre of town once or twice per hour on weekdays, less frequently on weekends. There are five to eight buses per day from Rauma (€6.70, 45 minutes). Buses from Helsinki run via Turku.

The MS *Franz Höijer* (☎ 262 7444) travels between Uusikaupunki and Turku weekly from mid-May to mid-August. It departs from the passenger harbour on Friday at 10am (€12, eight hours). It stops at Kustavi, a jumping-off point for the Åland islands' northern archipelago. From Turku it departs on Thursday at 10am, arriving in Uusikaupunki at 6pm. The same ship also goes to Hanko – see the Turku or Hanko sections for details. There's a restaurant and bar on board.

RAUMA
☎ 02 • pop 38,000

Rauma (Swedish: Raumo) was founded in 1442 and came of age in the 18th century, when it became famous throughout Europe for its production of beautiful hand-made lace. Locals still celebrate their heritage of lacemaking with an annual festival.

Although Rauma is not as attractive as many south coast seaside towns, it certainly merits a stop for its **Vanha Rauma** (Old Town) district. The old town area of more than 600 low wooden houses won a spot on the Unesco World Heritage list as Finland's first entry and is the largest wooden town preserved in the Nordic countries.

Orientation & Information

Rauma is really two towns – Vanha Rauma, with historic houses and shops; and the new district, which virtually swallows the Old Town and has most services and hotels. The main street is Valtakatu, in new Rauma.

The **tourist office** (☎ 834 1551, 834 1552; W www.rauma.fi; Valtakatu 2; open 8am-6pm Mon-Fri, 10am-3pm Sat, 11am-2pm Sun June–late Aug, 8am-4pm Mon-Fri rest of the year) publishes a free map and a self-guided walking tour.

The **public library** (☎ 834 4531; Ankkurikatu 1; open 10am-7pm Mon-Fri, 10am-2pm Sat) has two Internet terminals, and the

Sky Cafe (*Tehtaankatu 4*) has Internet access at €1 for 15 minutes.

Special Events
Rauma's biggest event sounds pretty staid on paper, but it's a good time to be in town. **Rauma Lace Week**, beginning in the last week in July, celebrates the town's lacemaking heritage. Lace-trimmed caps were in vogue in Europe during the 18th century – heady days indeed for Rauma's 600 or so lacemaking women, many of whom started learning the craft when only six. Museums hold lace-related exhibitions, and lacemakers in period costume can be seen sewing in shops around Vanha Rauma. Lace Week culminates with the 'Night of Black Lace', a carnival that draws party-minded Finns.

There are also several music festivals worth looking out for: the **Rauma Blues Happening** is for one day only in late July, but it draws a decent line-up of international and Finnish performers to the main venue at the ice hockey stadium (tickets €45 at the door); **Festivo** is a week of classical and choral music at various venues held in early August; and **Raumanmeren Juhannus** is a three-day rock festival held during Midsummer.

Places to Stay
Poroholma Camping & Hostel (*☎ 8388 2500, fax 8388 2502; Poroholmantie; camping per person/site €8/13.50, dorm beds from €9.50, singles/doubles €20/30, cottages €42-51; open mid-May–late Aug*) is on Otanlahti

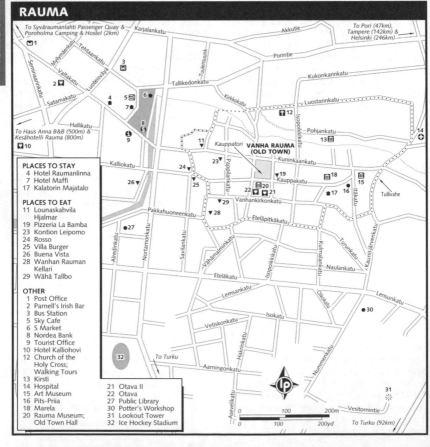

RAUMA

PLACES TO STAY
4 Hotel Raumanlinna
7 Hotel Maffi
17 Kalatorin Majatalo

PLACES TO EAT
11 Lounaskahvila Hjalmar
19 Pizzeria La Bamba
23 Kontion Leipomo
24 Rosso
25 Villa Burger
26 Buena Vista
28 Wanhan Rauman Kellari
29 Wähä Tallbo

OTHER
1 Post Office
2 Parnell's Irish Bar
3 Bus Station
5 Sky Cafe
6 S Market
8 Nordea Bank
9 Tourist Office
10 Hotel Kalliohovi
12 Church of the Holy Cross; Walking Tours
13 Kirsti
14 Hospital
15 Art Museum
16 Pits-Priia
18 Marela
20 Rauma Museum; Old Town Hall
21 Otava II
22 Otava
27 Public Library
30 Potter's Workshop
31 Lookout Tower
32 Ice Hockey Stadium

bay about 2km northwest of the town centre. It's a pleasant waterside location with plenty of boats around. The HI-affiliated hostel section is in two parts – one a cheaper, very basic building with dormitory accommodation, the other a nice old villa that also houses a café and the reception. Kitchen, sauna and laundry are available. There is no local bus service.

Kesähotelli Rauma (☎ 824 0130; Satamakatu 20; twin rooms €9.50, singles/doubles €33/52; open June-Aug) is a summer hostel with typical twin-share student rooms with private kitchen and bathroom shared between two rooms. The dorm beds are extremely cheap – the difference between them and a double is that linen and breakfast are not included, and you must be an HI member.

Haus Anna (☎/fax 822 8223; Salamakatu 7; singles/doubles €47/60) is a modern and tidy family-run B&B not far from the town centre. Rooms have private bathroom and TV.

Hotel Raumanlinna (☎ 83221, fax 8322 2111; e raumanlinna@raumanlinna.fi; Valtakatu 5; singles/doubles €93/113, weekends & summer €62/72) is a central hotel with reasonable summer rates and a good restaurant and bar.

Hotel Maffi (☎ 533 0857, fax 822 6049; Valikatu; singles/doubles €50/60) is a small, friendly, reasonably priced hotel just off Valtakatu.

Kalatorin Majatalo (☎ 8378 6150, fax 822 2535; Kalatori 4; singles/doubles €85/105, weekends & summer €66/76), the most pleasant hotel in town, is in a beautifully

A Walk Around Vanha Rauma

Vanha Rauma, the World Heritage listed Old Town in the heart of modern Rauma, is not a museum but a living centre, with low-key cafés, hardware shops, residences and a smattering of artisans and lacemakers working in small studios.

Most of the low wooden buildings of Vanha Rauma were erected in the 18th and 19th centuries. There are some 600 houses and 180 shops, and each building has a name – look for it on a small oval sign near the door. You can spend a pleasant half day wandering around Vanha Rauma's cobbled streets and visiting its shops and museums.

Start at the **kauppatori** in the heart of Old Rauma. It's a typically lively market square teeming with food and craft stalls, buskers and tourists. On the south side is Rauma's most imposing building, the Vanha Raatihuone (old town hall), built in 1776. It now houses the **Rauma Museum** (☎ 834 3532; Kauppakatu 13), with exhibits relating to seafaring and the city's lacemaking heritage, including model ships, paintings, baroque furniture and lace costumes.

North of the kauppatori is the attractive stone **Church of the Holy Cross** (Pyhän Ristin Kirkko; Luostarinkatu 1; open daily May-Sept), a 15th-century Franciscan church set in a picturesque churchyard; a Catholic monastery functioned here until 1538.

The four main museums in Vahna Rauma, including Rauma Museum, can be visited on a single ticket (€4), available at any of the museums. They are all open 10am to 5pm daily from mid-May to mid-August, and 10am to 5pm Tuesday to Saturday the rest of the year.

Marela (☎ 834 3528; Kauppakatu 24) is the most interesting of Rauma's museums. The preserved home of a wealthy 18th-century shipowner is furnished with turn-of-the-century antiques, wall paintings and Swedish ceramic stoves.

Kirsti (☎ 834 3529; Pohjankatu 3) is another 18th-century house museum – this was once the home of a sailor. **Savenvalajan Verstas** (☎ 533 5526; Nummenkatu 2) is a small museum of pottery, and a workshop where you can see potters at work and have a go yourself. It's open in summer only.

Art Museum (☎ 822 4346; Kuninkaankatu 37; adult/student €3.50/2.50, open 10am-6pm Mon-Thur, 10am-4pm Fri, 11am-4pm Sat & Sun), in the heart of Vanha Rauma on Hauenguano Square, features changing exhibitions of traditional and modern art. Note the old town well in the middle of the square.

Walking tours of Vanha Rauma are coordinated by the city tourist office. Tours in English are held only on Saturday at 1pm from mid-June to early August (€4,1½ hours). Tours depart from the Church of the Holy Cross.

renovated Art Deco warehouse in Vanha Rauma. The owners are very friendly and know a lot about the history and sights of the area. There's also a good restaurant here.

Places to Eat & Drink

The bright **kauppatori** is the heart of the Old Town and it's packed with inexpensive food stalls. **Villa Burger** is a grilli and cheap snack kiosk just outside the old town on Kalliokatu.

Buena Vista *(Kanalinranta 5; lunch mains €7-10)* is an often crowded restaurant very popular with locals for its Mexican-Finnish menu and generous lunch buffet.

Lounaskahvila Hjalmar *(Kuninkaankatu 6; lunch specials €6.30; open lunch only)* is a hearty home-cooking kind of place in Vanha Rauma.

Pizzeria La Bamba *(mains €6-9.50)*, at the kauppatori, serves reasonably priced pizzas and pastas and has a festive, family atmosphere. There's 15% off for students. There's a branch of **Rosso** with a good terrace just outside the Old Town on Savilankatu.

Charming cafés are plentiful in Vanha Rauma. **Kontion Leipomo** *(Kuninkaankatu 9)* is a perennial favourite – a great place for coffee, cakes or pastries, and there's a large garden at the back. **Wähä Tallbo** *(Vanhankirkonkatu 3)*, in a relatively quiet street south of the kauppatori, is another alluring café with a €6 lunch special.

On the edge of Vanha Rauma, **Wanhan Rauman Kellari** *(☎ 866 6700; Anundilankatu 8; lunch €9.50, mains €10-21)* is a very popular cellar restaurant with a terrific rooftop beer terrace open in summer. Steaks and fish dishes are big on the menu.

Rauma doesn't have the liveliest nightlife on the west coast. **Parnell's Irish Bar** *(Valtakatu 4)* draws a young crowd on weekends and has occasional live music. **Hotel Kalliohovi** *(Kalliokatu 25)* has a nightclub open most nights and Wednesday is student night.

In the old town you'll find **Otava** *(Isoraastivankatu)*, a typical Finnish tango dance club open from 9pm to 3am Friday and Saturday, and just around the corner on Vanhankirkonkatu is **Otava II**, a rustic local drinking venue with an older clientele.

Shopping

Rauma is famous for its bobbin lace. The best place to buy it is **Pits-Priia** *(Kauppakatu 29)* where you can see bobbin lace being made.

Getting There & Away

There are frequent daily direct buses between Helsinki and Rauma (€26.70, four hours). Between Rauma and Pori, there are buses every hour or so (€6.70, 40 minutes). From the south, Turku and Uusikaupunki are connected by buses every two hours or so. There are direct buses to Tampere (€16.80, two hours) or you can take any Helsinki-bound bus to Huittinen and change there. The bus station is northwest of Vanha Rauma, a block north of the main street, Valtakatu.

Get off the Tampere-to-Pori train at the Kokemäki train station, and transfer to a connecting bus. Your train pass will be valid on the bus.

AROUND RAUMA
Lappi

The small village of Lappi (Finnish for Lapland) is particularly pleasant, with the Lapinjoki running through it, and more importantly it's a base for visiting a couple of prehistoric sites, including one World Heritage listed site. In the village an old stone bridge survives, and nearby is a **church** dating from 1760. It has medieval sculpture and a separate bell tower.

The main attraction is the prehistoric site, by the name **Kirkonlaattia** (Church Floor), which is a plain stone tableau in a seemingly Lappish setting. The prehistoric site is 4km from the main road No 12 – turn north to Eurajoentie and then follow the signs.

Köyliö

Köyliö, now a quiet hamlet, was an important estate in medieval times. It also was the scene of a terrible crime: in 1156 a local peasant, Lalli, killed the crusading Bishop Henry – the first Catholic bishop to voyage into the Finnish wilderness – on frozen Lake Köyliönjärvi. In the local **church** are paintings – created later and intended to teach a lesson – that depict Lalli under the foot of a saint, his inevitable fate in the afterlife. The church and its paintings are on an island in Köyliönjärvi lake and are accessible by a small causeway. This is the finishing point of Catholic pilgrimages from Turku.

Köyliö is about 35km east of Rauma, south from road No 12 at the town of Eura. There is no bus service.

PUURIJÄRVI-ISOSUO NATIONAL PARK

Lake Puurijärvi, 65km due east of Rauma, is one of the best bird-watching lakes in Western Finland. The lake and surrounding marshlands have been protected since 1993 and are a favourite nesting site for migrating waterfowl of many varieties, totalling about 500 pairs in season. The lake itself can be reached by a 800m nature trail from the main road. A boardwalk makes a loop of the open marshland, where there's an observation tower. The Näköalapaikka (a viewing cliff) also offers a good general view. Visitors are required to stay on marked paths during breeding season, and camping is not allowed in the park at any time.

PORI

☎ 02 • pop 76,000

Pori (Swedish: Björneborg) would be an unremarkable west coast town for travellers, if not for its internationally renowned Jazz Festival which sets the town ablaze for a week in July. Domestically it's one of the most important deep-water harbours in Finland, and is kept prosperous by numerous industries including textiles, timber industries, oil-related industries, manufacturing and technology.

In 1558, Duke Juhana, who was then ruler of Finland, decided to establish a trading town on the eastern coast of the Gulf of Bothnia. As a result, Pori was founded at the mouth of the Kokemäenjoki. For a brief shining moment in 1726 a Professor Israel Nesselius championed Pori as the new capital of Finland – but it was not to be.

Pori has few Swedish speakers. The Swedish name Björneborg translates as Fort of the Bear.

Information

The helpful **tourist office** (☎ 621 1273; Ⓦ www.pori.fi; Hallituskatu 9; open 8am-6pm Mon-Fri, 10am-3pm Sat June–mid-Aug, 8am-1.15pm Mon Fri rest of the year) is in the old town hall. In the same building is a private accommodation office operating in the lead-up to the jazz festival.

The **public library** (Gallen-Kallelankatu 12) has several free Internet terminals (bookings required).

There are 24-hour luggage lockers at the train and bus stations.

Things to See

Despite being one of the oldest towns in Finland, Pori has few historic buildings or other attractions, although the local tourism body has made a good fist of playing up what is here by producing a free detailed map and brochure entitled *Architectural Map of Pori* – it shows 101 'points of interest' in and around the town.

Pori Taidemuseo (Pori Art Museum; ☎ 621 1080; Eteläranta; admission €2-3.50; open 11am-6pm Tues-Sun, 6pm-8pm Wed) is a fine modern art museum with a good permanent collection. Finnish and international art is exhibited in the airy, elegant space, a former warehouse, and there are various changing exhibitions.

The neo-Gothic **Keski-Pori Church** (Yrjönkatu) was built in 1863 and lovingly renovated in 1998. It has a steeple with unusual iron fretwork.

Satakunta Museum (☎ 621 1063; Hallituskatu 11; admission €2; open 11am-5pm daily) is a museum of regional history and archaeology – it has an interesting miniature of Old Pori, before the devastating fire of 1852.

Juselius Mausoleum (Käppänä Cemetery; ☎ 623 8746; Maantiekatu; admission free; open noon-3pm daily in summer), west of the centre, is the most poignant sight in Pori. FA Juselius, a wealthy businessman, had the mausoleum built as a memorial to his daughter, who died of tuberculosis at the age of 11. The original frescoes were painted in 1898 by famous Finnish artist Akseli Gallen-Kallela (who had just lost his own daughter). The ones you see now were painted by Akseli's son, Jorma Gallen-Kallela, after his father's death.

Special Events

Spanning nine days in mid-July, **Pori Jazz Festival** is one of the most appreciated summer events in Finland. It's a great time to be in Pori, even if you don't attend any of the major concerts – the free jam sessions and electric atmosphere alone make it worthwhile. The festival started in 1966 when some local musicians arranged a two-day event with an audience of 1000 people. Now the Jazz Festival features more than 100 concerts held in tents, outdoors or in old warehouses. Performers – and thousands of visitors – pour in from all over the world,

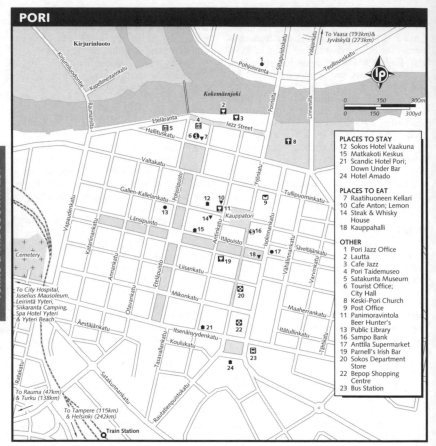

PORI

To Vaasa (193km)&
Jyväskylä (273km)

Kirjurinluoto

Kokemäenjoki

Jazz Street

PLACES TO STAY
12 Sokos Hotel Vaakuna
15 Matkakoti Keskus
21 Scandic Hotel Pori;
   Down Under Bar
24 Hotel Amado

PLACES TO EAT
7 Raatihuoneen Kellari
10 Cafe Anton; Lemon
14 Steak & Whisky
   House
18 Kauppahalli

OTHER
1 Pori Jazz Office
2 Lautta
3 Cafe Jazz
4 Pori Taidemuseo
5 Satakunta Museum
6 Tourist Office;
   City Hall
8 Keski-Pori Church
9 Post Office
11 Panimoravintola
   Beer Hunter's
13 Public Library
16 Sampo Bank
17 Anttila Supermarket
19 Parnell's Irish Bar
20 Sokos Department
   Store
22 Bepop Shopping
   Centre
23 Bus Station

To City Hospital,
Juselius Mausoleum,
Leirintä Yyteri,
Siikaranta Camping,
Spa Hotel Yyteri
& Yyteri Beach

To Rauma (47km)
& Turku (138km)

To Tampere (115km)
& Helsinki (242km)

Train Station

and hotels are fully booked up to a year in advance. Although the emphasis is on jazz, the musical styles include blues, soul and mainstream performers. The line-up in recent years has included Paul Simon, Garry Moore, Robert Cray and Chick Corea

The main venue is Kirjurinluoto Concert Park, on the north side of the river, where an open-air stage is set up for an audience of up to 25,000. Jazz Street, the closed off section of Etelranta along the riverfront, is where a lot of the action happens, with stalls, free concerts, makeshift bars and street dancing.

Day passes range from €60 to €70, but individual concert tickets (around €12) are also available.

For more information and to purchase tickets contact **Pori Jazz** (☎ 626 2200, fax 626 2225; W www.porijazz.fi; Pohjoisranta 11, 28100 Pori), or the Pori tourist office.

Places to Stay

If you are planning to visit Pori during the Jazz Festival it's advisable to book hotel accommodation up to a year in advance, particularly for the final weekend – and expect to pay double the regular rates (at least €150 for a double at the big hotels). Guesthouses are worth a try even in the weeks leading up to the festival. A private accommodation service also operates from the same building as the tourist office, with beds in private homes going for €30/45 a single/double, but you have to get in early. You can book and get more information on the Web at W www.pori jazz.fi. Finally, the city tourist office can direct you towards basic mattress-on-the-floor accommodation, which is sometimes held on a first-come, first-served basis.

At the time of writing, there were no hostels operating in Pori, and the closest camping grounds are some way out of town.

Camping A fair way from Pori, but in a great location at the popular Yyteri beach, **Leirintä Yyteri** (☎ 634 5700, 634 5747; |e| leir inta.yyteri@pori.fi; Yyterinsatojentie; tent sites €13-15, 4-bed cabins €34-42, 4-6 bed cottages with sauna €72-100; open year-round) is usually full around Jazz Festival time.

Siikaranta Camping (☎ 638 4120; bus No 30 or 40 from centre; camp sites €10-17, cabins €35; open June–late Aug) is on Reposaari island, just northwest of Yyteri beach. The island is connected to the mainland by bridge.

Guesthouses & Hotels Centrally located **Matkakoti Keskus** (☎ 633 8447; Itäpuisto 13; singles/doubles €29/39) is a very basic guesthouse with simple rooms and shared bathrooms. There's no breakfast.

Matkakoti Musa (☎ 637 0153; Putimäentie 69; singles/doubles €31/51), some 3.5km west of the centre in the Musa area, is a nicer guesthouse with pleasant rooms.

Hotel Amado (☎ 631 0100, fax 633 8175; Keskusaukio 2; singles/doubles €73/93, weekends & summer €63), close to the bus station, is the most reasonably priced of the city's hotels and is perfectly comfortable, with a good à la carte restaurant.

Scandic Hotel Pori (☎ 624 900, fax 6249 2211; Itsenäisyydenkatu 41; singles/doubles €92/115, weekends & summer €68/78, suites €168) is a reasonably stylish hotel within walking distance of the centre. Downstairs is a little slice of Australian Outback (see Entertainment).

Sokos Hotel Vaakuna (☎ 528 100, fax 528 182; Gallen-Kallelankatu 7; singles/doubles €95/120, weekends & summer €74), in the town centre and with the usual array of nightclubs, wine bars and Fransmanni restaurant attached, is Pori's biggest hotel.

Spa Hotel Yyteri (☎ 628 5300, fax 628 3776; singles/doubles €66/86), at Yyteri beach, has a spa, pool and sauna.

Places to Eat

Grillis around town sell the local speciality, *Porilainen* (Pori burger), best enjoyed late at night after a few pints of Porin Karhu (Bear of Pori) beer. The finest Porilainen is made with *Korpelan Metsästäkänwurst* (Korpela onion sausage), pickles and a fluffy bun. At the **kauppahalli** *(Isolinnankatu)* look for another local specialty, smoked river lamprey (a fish that looks like an eel).

For burgers and other fast food, there's plenty of choice in the futuristic **Bepop Shopping Centre** at the end of the pedestrian strip on Yrjönkatu.

Lemon *(Antinkatu; meals €3-9.50)*, across from the kauppatori, is a popular place for pizza and kebab, eat-in or takeaway.

The **cafeteria** at the public library offers bargain basement lunch specials (from €5) from 11am to 1pm Monday to Friday. **Cafe Juselia**, a sunny café diagonally across from the post office, has a lunch buffet (€7) and light meals.

Cafe Anton (☎ 641 4144; Antinkatu 11), on the corner of the market square, is more pub than café but it has a €7 lunch special and bar snacks such as nachos, wedges or pizza from €2 to €8.

Steak & Whisky House (☎ 648 2170; Gallen-Kallelakatu 6) is a lot classier than it sounds. Attached is a music café with live jazz. The restaurant is reasonably elegant with a Finnish-continental menu of steaks, fish and salads.

Raatihuoneen Kellari (☎ 633 4804; Hallituskatu 9; meals €13.50-19.50, lunch from €9) is an elegant cellar restaurant in the vaulted bowels of the old town hall. There's a superb weekday buffet luncheon, and Finnish cuisine is the speciality.

Entertainment

Pori is pumping around the time of the Jazz Festival, with the eastern section of Eteläranta being converted into 'Jazz Street', a pulsating and infectious strip of makeshift bars and food stalls. The rest of the year it's a typical mid-size university town with plenty of bars and a few popular nightclubs in the big hotels.

Cafe Jazz (☎ 641 1344; Etelaranta) is the most dynamic venue along Jazz Street. It has a perfect location on the river, a warm ambience and regular jazz slots and jam sessions. There's a good summer terrace and food is served here.

Panimoravintola Beer Hunter's *(cnr Gallen-Kallelankatu & Antinkatu)* is a great brewery-pub and one of the most popular drinking spots in town. Of the three beers brewed on the premises, the 'Mufloni stout', was recently voted Finland's beer of the year.

Down Under Bar, in the Scandic Hotel Pori, is a little piece of Australiana up near the Arctic – this must be the only Aussie theme bar in Finland! Along with the crocodile and Kombi van decor, there are some disturbing 'Aussie' cocktails and plenty of music and dancing.

Punainen Kukko (*Pohjoispuisto*) is a lively dance club catering to the slightly older 'humppa' crowd, but there's also a nightclub section.

Getting There & Away

Air There are daily flights between Pori and Helsinki.

Bus There are frequent daily buses between Pori and Helsinki (€27.10, four hours), Rauma (€7.90, 1¼ hours), Turku (€19.20, 2¼ hours) and Tampere (€13.60, 1¾ hours). Some Tampere-bound buses require a change at Huittinen and take considerably longer, so avoid those. There are also direct connections with Vaasa, Oulu and Jyvaskyla.

Train All trains to Pori go via Tampere, where you often have to change. There are frequent daily trains (regional and Intercity) between Tampere and Pori (€13.60 to €18.60, 1½ hours), all of which have good connections with trains from Helsinki (€30, 3½ hours).

Getting Around

An extensive bus service operates in the town area; route maps are available at the tourist office. Most buses pass the market square. Ask at the tourist office for bicycle rental.

AROUND PORI
Yteri Beach

Yyteri beach, 15km northwest of Pori town centre, is still something of a playground in summer, though like many Finnish beach resorts it has been in a decline ever since charter flights to Spain were invented. Stands at the beach offer all kinds of activities, and the white sand stretches quite a distance. There is a good camping ground and a spa hotel here; see Places to Stay in the Pori section earlier.

Leineperi

This fine village received the Europe Nostra award in 1993 for careful preservation of 18th-century buildings. The area was first developed in 1771 by the Swedish as a *bruk* (early ironworks precinct) for making household items, and was in operation for about a century. Today it is a lively place, at least on summer weekends. Attractions along the scenic Kullaanjoki riverside include **Masuuni ironworks**, now renovated, a blacksmith's shop, now a **museum**, and some **artisans' workshops**. **Museo Kangasniemi** is devoted to Kaarlo Kangasniemi, the 1968 Olympic weight-lifting champion (he is Finnish, of course). On weekends you may be lucky enough to meet the champion. Most of these museums charge a €1 admission and are open on summer weekends. Free town maps are available at most attractions.

Leineperi is on an unpaved road that runs parallel to the Tampere to Pori road No 11. Buses between Pori and Kullaa stop at Leineperi; there are usually two daily.

Åland

☎ 018 • pop 25,000

The Åland islands are a unique, autonomous island group, with their own flag, culture and *lagting* (local government). Several dialects of Swedish are spoken, and few Ålanders speak Finnish. Though technically still a part of Finland, Åland took its own flag in 1954 and has issued its own stamps – prized by collectors – since 1984.

The islands are popular with both Swedes and Finns for cycling, camping and cabin holidays – and Midsummer celebrations are particularly festive here. There are medieval parish churches and quaint fishing villages dotted around, while Kastelholm castle, which was established in the 14th century, is Åland's most striking attraction.

Åland is also the name of the main island. Surprisingly, Åland translates as 'river land', although the region is better known for its islands and islets, which number more than 6400. You can take your wheels almost anywhere around the islands using the bridges and the network of car and bicycle ferries. Regular ferries connect Åland to both Sweden and the Finnish mainland.

The centre of Åland is Mariehamn, a port with two harbours, in the south of the main island group.

History

The first settlers set foot on Åland 6000 years ago, and more than a hundred Bronze and Iron Age *fornminne* (burial sites) have been discovered. These are all clearly signposted, though they aren't much to look at. Åland was an important harbour and trading centre during the Viking era, and evidence has been found of six fortresses from that time.

During the Great Northern War of 1700–21 (nicknamed the 'Great Wrath'), most of the population fled to Sweden to escape the Russians, who were bent on destroying Åland. The Russians returned during the 1740s (a period known as the 'Lesser Wrath'), and again in 1809.

When Finland gained independence in 1917, Ålanders were all too familiar with Russians and feared occupation by Bolsheviks. There were strong moves for Åland to be incorporated into Sweden, which was not only the Ålanders' former mother country

Highlights

- Grabbing a bicycle and island-hopping around the archipelago on the mostly free inter-island ferries
- Enjoying the slow pace of island life and the unique Swedish-speaking culture – this isn't Finland, but neither is it Sweden
- Taking a tour of the medieval Kastelholm castle in Sund, followed by a picnic beside the river
- Gorging on Åland pancakes with jam and cream
- Returning to 'city' life in colourful Mariehamn, with its rows of linden trees maritime history and bustling harbour area
- Midsummer celebrations, when the colourful Midsummer poles are erected
- Summer cruises on the wooden schooner *Linden*

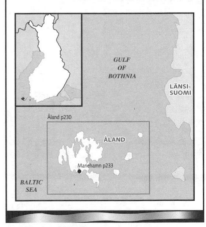

but also their source of language and cultural identity (not the case for the majority of Finns). But Finland refused to give up its island province. The Swedish–Finnish dispute only came to an end in 1921, when Åland was given its status as an autonomous, demilitarised and neutral province within the Republic of Finland by a decision of the League of Nations. Today Åland is almost like a Little Sweden, and locals are more aware of events in Stockholm than Helsinki.

ÅLAND

Gulf of Bothnia

NORTHERN ARCHIPELAGO

To Jumo
Långö
Åva
Björnholma
BRÄNDÖ

To Osnäs
To Turku
To Galtby

Torsholma
Lappo

KÖKAR
Hellsö
Karlby
Källskär

Krokarno
Husö

Enklinge
KUMLINGE
Remmarina stugor
Snäckö
Sandvik Camping
Hamnö

Ledholm Camping
Seglinge

Skaget
SOTTUNGA
SOUTHERN ARCHIPELAGO

Simskäla
Hummelvik
Överö
Finholma
FÖGLÖ

VÅRDÖ
Vargata
Långnäs
Degerby

Sveden
Prästö
Lumpo
Svinö
Herrön

Orrdals Klint
SALTVIK
Kvarnbo
Borgboda
Bomarsund
Kastelholm
SUND
Finby
LUMPARLAND

Nääs
Odkarby
FINSTRÖM
Godby
Önningeby
Lemström Canal
Norrby
LEMLAND

Getabergen
GETA
Bastö
JOMALA
Jomala
Lemböte
Lemböte

Dånö
Hällö
Skarpnåtö
Ingbyberget
Järsö

Sällis
Mörby
Kattby
HAMMARLAND
ÅLAND
Gottby

Skag
ECKERÖ
Kyrkoby
Storby
Torp
Degersand
Marsund

ÅLAND SEA

To Stockholm & Kapellskär

Mariehamn

To Grisslehamn

0   5   10km
0   3   6ml

--- International ferry
····· Inter-island ferry
····· Bicycle ferry

Although Åland joined the EU along with Finland in 1995, it was granted a number of exemptions, including duty-free tax laws that allowed the essential ferry services between the islands and mainland Finland and Sweden to continue operating profitably.

Warning

Ticks carrying infectious diseases that may cause rash and fever (and may sometimes even lead to hospitalisation) are a concern in rural areas of Åland. The simplest way to deal with this problem is to take proper precautions – do not walk barefoot outside, wear trousers or long pants when hiking, and always conduct a swift 'tick check' after spending time outdoors.

Information

The main tourist office is **Ålands Turistinformation** (☎ 24000; w www.goaland.net; Storagatan 8) in Mariehamn, and there are smaller offices at the ferry terminal in Eckerö, at Godby and at Långnäs.

Both the euro and Swedish krona can be used in Åland. Branches of Nordea Bank and Andelsbanken in Mariehamn have ATMs that accept international cards, and credit cards are easily used here.

Åland operates on the same time as Finland – that is, one hour ahead of Sweden.

Post & Communications The telephone code for Åland is 018. Finnish telephone cards can be used on Åland, but there are also local cards. Åland uses the Finnish mobile phone network – Sonera and Radiolinja work here but Telia (even if purchased in Finland) does not.

Mail sent in Åland must have Åland postage stamps – Finnish ones won't work.

Medical & Emergency Services For emergencies call ☎ 112, for police ☎ 10023 and for medical service ☎ 10023. The main **hospital** (☎ 5355, Norragatan 17) and **police** (cnr Styrmansgatan & Strandgatan) are in Mariehamn.

Accommodation For accommodation bookings, **Ålandsresor** (☎ 28040; w www.alandsresor.fi; Torggatan 2, Mariehamn) handles hotel, guesthouse and cottage bookings for the entire island and is often the *only* way to secure accommodation other than camping

grounds. Viking Line and Eckerö Linjen also make bookings.

Getting There & Away

Air The airport is 4km northwest of Mariehamn and there is a bus into the centre. A taxi to the centre costs about €10. **Finnair** (☎ 634 500) has a direct service to Åland from Stockholm Monday to Friday and a daily service from Helsinki (€155, one hour) via Turku. There's a Finnair office in **Hotell Arkipelag** (Strandgatan 31, Mariehamn).

Skärgårdsflyg Air (☎ 13880; w www.sflyg .com; Flygfältsvägen 69, Mariehamn), at the airport, has two regular flights on to Stockholm Monday to Friday.

Boat Viking and Silja lines have year-round daily ferries to Mariehamn from Turku as part of their links with Stockholm; you can stop off 'between' countries or sail return from either. Viking also sails to Mariehamn from Kapellskär (north of Stockholm) in Sweden. Birka Cruises sails only between Stockholm and Mariehamn.

Eckerö Linjen (☎ 28000; w www.eckero linjen.fi; Mariehamn) sails from Grisslehamn in Sweden to Eckerö – this is the cheapest and quickest route from Sweden to Åland. There are five connections a day from Grisslehamn during the high season and two or three during the low season. Most of the tours have a bus connection to/from Stockholm and Mariehamn. The boat trip takes two hours, and a combined boat and bus trip from Stockholm to Mariehamn takes five hours.

Ferry fares vary widely by season and class of travel, so contact the local ferry offices for more information (see Getting There & Away in the Mariehamn section). As a guide, the passenger fare from Grisslehamn to Eckerö is €8.90 in high season.

Free travel for pedestrians and cyclists on the archipelago ferries all the way to the central Åland islands is possible from mainland Finland via Korppoo (southern route, from Galtby passenger harbour) or Kustavi (northern route, from Osnäs passenger harbour), but only if you break your journey to stay on one or more islands.

Getting Around

Bus Five main bus lines depart from Mariehamn's regional bus terminal on Torggatan in front of the library. No 1 goes to

Hammarland and Eckerö; No 2 to Godby and Geta; No 3 to Godby and Saltvik; No 4 to Godby, Sund and Vårdö (Hummelvik); and No 5 to Lemland and Lumparland (Långnäs). The one-way fare from Mariehamn to Storby (Eckerö) is €4.50; from Mariehamn to Långnäs is €4.20. Bicycles can be carried on buses (space permitting) for €4.

If you plan to use the bus a lot, you can buy a 24-hour bus pass valid for the whole island (adult/child €12/6), or a three-day pass (€24/12).

Ferry There are three kinds of inter-island ferry. For short trips across straits, flat-bottom vehicle ferries ply nonstop and are always free. For longer routes, ferries run according to schedule, and take cars, bicycles and pedestrians. There are also three bicycle ferries in summer – a ride is €6 to €9 per person with a bicycle. The bike ferry routes are Hammarland–Geta, Lumparland–Sund and Vårdö–Saltvik.

Timetables for all inter-island ferries are available at the main tourist office in Mariehamn and at the local transportation office, **Ålandstrafiken** (☎ 25155; ⓦ www.aland strafiken.aland.fi; Strandgatan 25, Mariehamn).

Bicycle Cycling is a great way to tour these flat, rural islands. The most scenic roads have separate bike lanes that are clearly marked. RO-NO Rent has bicycles available at Mariehamn and Eckerö harbours with rates ranging from €7/35 per day/week to €13/65 for a quality mountain bike.

Mariehamn

pop 12,000
Mariehamn will seem a bustling metropolis if you've arrived from some of the other entry points in Åland or have spent some time in the archipelago. But if you come directly to Mariehamn from either Sweden or mainland Finland, you'll find the capital an attractive, low-key town framed on either side by marinas full of gleaming sailing boats. With its wide, tree-lined boulevards, Mariehamn is sometimes called the 'town of a thousand linden trees'. It is hectic here in summer – when it becomes the town of a thousand tourists – but outside the peak season Mariehamn reverts to its somnolent, local self.

Mariehamn was founded in 1861 by Tsar Alexander II, who named the town after his wife, Tsarina Maria. Today, Mariehamn is the administrative and economic centre of Åland. It is the seat of the *lagting* and *land-skapsstyrelse*, the legislative and executive bodies of Åland.

Orientation & Information
Mariehamn is situated on a long, narrow peninsula and has two harbours – Västra Hamnen (West Harbour) and Östra Hamnen (East Harbour). Ferries from Sweden and mainland Finland dock at Västra Hamnen, but just about everything else is at Östra Hamnen. Torggatan is the colourful pedestrian street, while the broad, tree-lined Storagatan is the main thoroughfare roughly connecting the two harbours. The airport is 4km northwest of the centre.

Tourist Office The main tourist office is **Ålands Turistinformation** (☎ 24000, fax 24265; ⓦ www.goaland.net; Storagatan 8; open 9am-6pm daily June-Aug, 9am-4pm Mon-Fri, 10am-3pm Sat Sept-May). It stocks material about Åland and books tours (but not accommodation).

A **tourist information booth** (☎ 531 214; open daily July, Mon-Sat June & Aug, closed Sept-May) is at the ferry terminal, Västra Hamnen.

Post & Communications The main post office (☎ 6360; open 9am-5pm Mon-Fri, 11am-2pm Sat) is on Torggatan. There are several Internet terminals at the **Mariehamn Library** (Strandgatan; open 10am-8pm Mon-Fri, 10am-4pm Sat) at Östra Hamnen. Some must be booked in advance, but there are a few first-come-first-served (15 minutes maximum) and a few foreign newspapers. The tourist office has one free Internet terminal that you can use for 15 minutes, as does the Ålands Konstmuseum.

Left Luggage You can store luggage in the lockers (€2) at the ferry terminal for up to 24 hours. Ålandstrafiken will store backpacks for longer periods.

Museums
The stalwarts of Åland are mariners and the **Sjöfartsmuseum** (Ålands Maritime Museum; ☎ 19930; ⓦ www.maritime-museum.aland.fi;

ÅLAND

MARIEHAMN

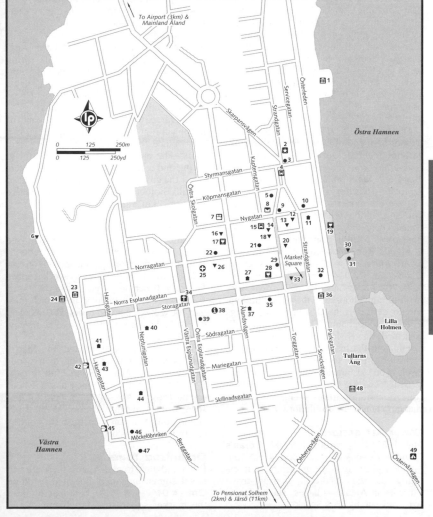

PLACES TO STAY
11 Hotell Arkipelag;
   Finnair Office
27 Park Alandia Hotell
37 Hotell Esplanad
40 Gästhem Neptun
41 Kaptensgarden
43 Hotell Adlon
44 Gästhem Kronan
49 Gröna Uddens
   Camping

PLACES TO EAT
6 ÅSS Segelpaviljongen
12 Buffalo Saloon

13 Bagarstugan 7
   Hantverkare
14 Cafe La Strada
16 Dixie Grill
18 Cafe Julius
20 Nikolaj Brasserie
26 Kaffestugan Svarta
   Katten
30 FP von Knorring
33 Eat

OTHER
1 Sjökvarteret
2 Police Station
3 Library

4 Regional Bus Terminal;
   Ålandstrafiken
5 Ålandsresor; Eckerö
   Linjen
7 Bio Savoy Cinema
8 Post Office
9 Svalan Art & Handicrafts
10 Jussis Keramik
15 Local Bus Terminal
17 Alvas Bar
19 Club Marin
21 Silja Line
22 Fäktargubben
23 Sjöfartsmuseum
24 Museum Ship Pommern

25 Hospital
28 Buffalo After Beach Bar
29 Silja Line
31 RO-NO Rent
32 Sjaavstyrelsgården
34 St Göran's Church
35 Viking Line
36 Ålands Konstmuseum
38 Ålands Turistinformation
39 Birka Line
43 Birka Line Terminal
45 Ferry Terminal
46 RO-NO Rent
47 Ålandsparken
48 Köpmannagården

ÅLAND

Västra Hamnen; adult/child €4.50/2.50; open 9am-5pm daily May-Aug, 9am-7pm July, 10am-4pm rest of the year), a kitschy museum of sailing and maritime commerce, is devoted to them. There are heaps of items from old boats, including figureheads that once graced local ships, model ships, ships in bottles, sea chests and nautical equipment. The central part of the museum is a re-creation of a ship with mast, saloon, galley and cabins, but to see the real thing, go outside.

The **museum ship Pommern** *(adult/child €4.50/2.50; open 9am-5pm daily Apr-Sept, 9am-7pm July)*, anchored behind the Sjö-fartsmuseum, is a beautifully preserved old sailing ship and a symbol of Mariehamn. The four-masted barque was built in 1903 in Glasgow, Scotland, and once carried tons of cargo and a 26-man crew on the trade route between Australia and England. An audio guide (available in English; €3.50) can help bring the old ship to life. A combined ticket to the ship and the museum is €7/3.50.

On the opposite side of the peninsula, at the northern end of Östra Hamnen, is **Sjök-varteret** *(Maritime Quarter; ☎ 16033; w www .sjokvarteret.com; adult/child €4/free; open 10am-6pm daily mid-June–mid-Aug, 9am-1am Mon-Thur rest of the year)*, where you can see the modern-day approach to boat-building, along with traditional wooden boats. There's also a museum with exhibitions on shipbuilding and a café.

Ålands Konstmuseum *(Ålands Museum & Art Museum; ☎ 25426; Stadhusparken; adult/child €2.50/1.70; open 10am-4pm daily, 10am-8pm Tues, closed Mon Sept-Apr)*, two museums housed in the same building, should definitely head your list of things to see in Mariehamn. The lively and well-presented Ålands Museum gives an absorbing insight into the history of the islands from prehistoric times to the present, including displays on local music, culture, industry and festivals. The Art Museum has a permanent collection of art from Åland, as well as changing temporary exhibitions.

Other Attractions

The 1927 copper-roofed **Sankt Göran's Church** *(St George's Church; open 10am-3pm Mon-Fri)* in the town centre is not as interesting as the medieval treasure-trove churches in Åland's villages. The design is Art Nouveau, by Lars Sonck.

Köpmannagården *(Merchant's House; Parkgatan; admission free; open 1pm-3pm Mon-Fri mid-June–mid-Aug)* has trade and handicraft displays.

Sjaavstyrelsegården *(Self-Government Building; ☎ 25000; cnr Österleden & Storagatan)* is home of the Åland parliament. Free guided tours are given at 10am every Friday from mid-June to mid-August. The tour ends with a slide show about Åland.

The small **Ålandsparken** amusement park *(☎ 13413; rides €1.20 or 10 for €10; open noon-9pm daily July, shorter hours May, June & Aug, closed Sept-Apr)*, next to the ferry terminal, has rides and arcades best suited to small children.

South of Östra Hamnen is **Tullarns Äng**, a small park that is prized for its spring wildflowers. **Lilla Holmen** island, connected to Tullarns Äng by a bridge, has a café, a decent swimming beach and peacocks strolling through the grounds.

The **Järsö** recreational area, 12km south of Mariehamn at the tip of the peninsula, is a good place for short bicycle and walking tours. The area is at its most beautiful in spring and early summer, when wildflowers cover the ground. Nåtö nature trail (trailhead at Nåtö Biological Station) and Järsö trail are two easy 2km walking tracks.

Activities

In additional to bicycles, RO-NO Rent (see Getting Around later in this section) rents all kinds of fun outdoor equipment. You can rent fishing rods for €7/15 per day/week; canoes for €10/20 per hour/day; rowing boats for €35/50 per two hours/day; and beach buggies for €25/45 per two hours/day. Scooters can be had from €17/45 per two hours/day, including free mileage and a full tank.

With so many boats packed into Mariehamn's harbours it's tempting to try your hand at sailing. **Åland Sailing Club** *(☎ 040-724 5797)* at Västra Hamnen has one-hour sailing trips on Monday from 6pm to 7pm June to early August. It costs €15/10 per adult/child. You can also organise courses and private lessons here.

Organised Tours

From mid-June to mid-August there are two novel sightseeing tours operated by **Rode Orm** *(☎ 0457-548 3554)*, both leaving from the market square in Mariehamn. A red

London double-decker bus does a 45-minute tour to Järsö and back, departing at 11.15am and 3.15pm from mid-June to mid-August. For a tour of Mariehamn itself, a 'minitrain' leaves from the market at 1.15pm and 4.15pm. Both tours cost €7 and run daily except Sunday.

In summer (July to early August) there are cruises aboard the traditional wooden schooner *Linden*. There's a two-hour **lunch cruise** at 2pm from Thursday to Saturday (€33 per person) and a four-hour **dinner cruise** at 5pm (€45 per person) on the same days. They both sail between Sjökvarteret and Västra Hamnen. Call ☎ 12055 or look up w www.linden.eget.net for information and bookings. If you have time and money, a great way to experience Åland is on an overnight archipelago cruise. The *Linden* sails for two full days departing every Tuesday from 4 July to 10 August. The cost is €298 per person, which includes meals and cabin accommodation.

Places to Stay

Mariehamn has no youth hostels, and while hotel prices drop in mainland Finland during summer, Mariehamn's hotels generally raise their rates between mid-June and the end of August. You can usually find a bed at short notice, even in peak season, but it pays to book ahead on weekends.

Camping Just 1km south of the centre, **Gröna Uddens Camping** (☎ 21121; e grona udden@aland.net; Östernäsvägen; tent/family sites €11.50/17.50; open mid-May–Aug) is a seaside camping ground. The camping areas are pleasant, if sometimes a bit cramped, and the beach is good for swimming. There are cooking and laundry facilities and a café – but no sauna, and no cottages.

Guesthouses & Hotels The cheapest accommodation in town is **Gästhem Kronan** (☎ 12617, fax 19580; Neptunigatan 52; singles/doubles in summer €37/55; open year-round) – it's a pity it's not more welcoming. The owners operate two basic guesthouses in the same street. **Gasthem Neptun** (Neptunigatan 41) is newer and the rooms are cleaner.

Pensionat Solhem (☎ 16322, fax 16350; Lökskärsvägen; singles/doubles in summer €41/59; open year-round), one of the more peaceful places to stay in Mariehamn, is

pleasantly situated by the sea, 3km south of the centre. Rooms drop to €30/42 outside the high season, and guests can use the rowing boats and sauna.

Hotell Esplanad (☎ 16444, fax 14143; Storagatan 5; singles/doubles €53/66; open mid-June–end Aug) is one of the cheapest hotels in Mariehamn. It's not flash but it's friendly, central and the buffet breakfast is good.

Hotell Adlon (☎ 15300, fax 15077; Hamngatan 7; singles/doubles €95-110; open May-Sept) is a modern hotel close to the ferry terminal, and attempting a nautical theme in its decor. Across the road **Kaptensgarden** (doubles without/with bathroom €68/85), in an old wooden house, is a cheaper annexe, but rates include use of facilities at Adlon such as the sauna.

Park Alandia Hotell (☎ 14130, fax 17130; Norra Esplanadgatan 3; singles/doubles €74/92.50) is on the main boulevard and has a popular terrace facing the street. Rates are €65/78 out of season.

Hotell Arkipelag (☎ 24020, fax 24384; w www.hotellarkipelag.com; Strandgatan 31; singles/doubles €105/130, suites €185), overlooking Östra Hamnen, is the largest hotel in Åland and one of the brighter lights of Mariehamn's nightlife.

Places to Eat

The best dining on the islands is found in Mariehamn, so this is the place to splurge.

Many cafés in town serve the local speciality, *Ålandspannkaka* (Åland pancakes), for around €2.50. They're fluffy square puddings made with semolina and served with stewed prunes or strawberry jam and whipped cream. One of the best places to try one (though not the cheapest) is at cosy **Kaffestugan Svarta Katten** (Norragatan 15). Another tasty local speciality, Åland dark bread, is available at local markets – this fruity type of bread takes four days to make.

Cafe Julius (Torggatan 10), on the pedestrian strip, opens early and has plenty of cheap sandwiches, pastries and snacks, including fresh pancakes, and tables out the front.

There are several other good places along the busy Torggatan, including **Cafe La Strada** (pizzas & pasta from €6-10), and **Eat** (meals €4-7.50), at the market square, an incredibly popular lunchtime café. For cheap snacks, **Dixie Grill** (Ålandsvägen 40) is an established burger and pizza joint.

ÅLAND

Bagarstugan 7 Hantverkare (☎ 19881; Ekonomiegatan 2), just off Torggatan, is one of Mariehamn's more charming cafés. Its home-made soups and sandwiches have a strong local following and there are also local crafts for sale.

Buffalo Saloon (☎ 13939; Strandgatan 12; mains €8-15) is a popular meeting spot with enormous hamburgers, pasta and pizza, and a great outdoor deck.

Nikolaj Brasserie (☎ 22560; mains €8.50-12), in the Galleria shopping centre on Torggatan, has huge pizzas and vegetarian dishes.

The boat restaurant **FP von Knorring** (☎ 16500; Östra Hamnen; mains €15-27) has classy seafood meals served in intimate surroundings below deck, plus a busy beer terrace on the deck. It's one of the local restaurants adhering to the 'taste of the archipelago' scheme, providing local produce prepared in traditional ways.

ÅSS Segelpaviljongen (☎ 19141; Västra Hamnen; lunch €13, mains €22-24), north of the Sjöfartsmuseum, is the oldest restaurant in town, and also one of the most atmospheric. It's in a lovely old wooden building on the water's edge. The speciality is seafood and the set lunch buffet (11am to 6pm) is good value.

Entertainment

Mariehamn is busy with holidaying people of all ages in summer, so there's a reasonably varied nightlife on offer.

Hotell Arkipelag (☎ 24020; Strandgatan 31) is an evening hotspot, especially for the big-spending boat-owners. It has a lively disco and a casino.

Club Marin (Östra Hamnen) is an attractive, slightly upmarket, harbour pavilion serving beer and meals, and is very popular on weekend nights in summer when there's dancing and live music.

Buffalo After Beach Bar (Norra Esplanadgatan) is a chic little open-fronted bar and club popular with a young crowd. **Buffalo Saloon** (see Places to Eat) is a down-to-earth pub with live entertainment in summer.

Alvas Bar (☎ 16141; Ålandsvägen 42) is the most popular late-night bar and disco with the younger crowd, particularly on weekends.

Bio Savoy cinema (cnr Nygatan & Ålandsvägen), west of the centre, usually shows films in English with Swedish subtitles.

Shopping

Mariehamn is a great place to shop for quality handicrafts – pick up a map of craft shops in Mariehamn and around mainland Åland at the tourist office.

Jussis Keramik (☎ 13606; Nygatan 1) sells interesting ceramics and glassware, and you can watch the objects being made. **Svalan Art & Handicrafts** (☎ 13470; Torggatan 5), around the corner from Jussis Keramik, specialises in knitting, needlework and related items.

Bagarstugan 7 Hantverkare (☎ 19881; Ekonomiegatan 2) is a crafts collective representing nearly a dozen artists. It also has a lovely café (see Places to Eat). **Fäktargubben** (☎ 19603; Norragatan 13) sells assorted Åland handicrafts and art.

Getting There & Away

See the main Getting There & Away section at the beginning of this chapter for information on travelling to and from Mariehamn by plane or ferry.

Viking and Silja ferries depart from the ferry terminal at Västra Hamnen. Just north of it is a smaller terminal used only by Birka Line.

All ferry lines have offices in Mariehamn: **Viking Line** (☎ 26011; W www.vikingline.fi; Storagatan 2), **Silja Line** (☎ 16711; W www.silja.com; Norragatan 2), **Eckerö Linjen** (☎ 28000; W www.eckerolinjen.fi; Torggatan 2) and **Birka Line** (☎ 27027; W www.birkaline.com; Östra Esplanadgatan 7).

Regional buses depart from the **terminal** (Torggatan) in front of the library; for route and fare information see the main Getting Around section at the start of this chapter, or contact **Ålandstrafiken** (☎ 25155; W www.alandstrafiken.aland.fi; Strandgatan 25).

Getting Around

A free local bus services the town, departing from Nygatan.

For bicycles, **RO-NO Rent** (☎ 12820; open 9am-noon & 1pm-6pm daily June–end Aug) is the main rental firm and it has outlets at Mariehamn's Östra Hamnen and Västra Hamnen. There are daily/weekly rates for standard bicycles (€7/35), three-speed models (€9/45) and mountain bikes (€13/65), as well as tandem bikes (€20/100) and motor scooters (€45/135). At other times of the year, arrangements can be made by phone.

ÅLAND

Mainland Åland & Around

The largest islands of the archipelago form a core group, which is the most popular destination in the province. This is where many of the oldest historical landmarks in Finland are found. Eckerö is particularly loved by Swedish families, given its proximity by ferry to Sweden, while Saltvik and Sund have the most well-known sights.

Bicycle tours around this part of Åland are very popular in summer because there are marked paths, distances are not too great, and bridges or ferries connect the various islands to make up an area large enough for an interesting week of touring.

JOMALA
pop 3000
The Jomala region, just north of Mariehamn, has two main centres: Jomala village, with a range of facilities, and the smaller Gottby.

The locally famous landscape painter Victor Westerholm had his summer house in Önningeby, a tiny village in eastern Jomala. Other artists followed him there, and for two decades around the turn of the 20th century, the area was known as the 'Önningeby colony'. There's an interesting **museum** (☎ 33710; adult/child €3/free; open 10am-4pm Fri-Wed, 6pm-8pm Thur May-Aug, noon-4pm Sat & Sun Aug-Oct) here that is dedicated to the artist and the village, with local historical memorabilia on display. The building itself was once a stone cowshed. The art collection and exhibitions include works by many of the artists influenced by the Önningeby School, but none by Westerholm himself. The area around the museum forms a photogenic scene of red wooden farm buildings, windmills and Midsummer poles.

From Mariehamn, catch bus No 5 to Önningeby or bus No 1 to Gottby.

FINSTRÖM
pop 2150
Finström is the central municipality in Åland. Godby is the island's second biggest town and offers all facilities, including a **tourist office** (☎ 41890; open 10am-8pm Mon-Fri, 10am-4pm Sat, noon-4pm Sun June–mid-Aug) in the main shopping centre.

The medieval **Sankt Mikael Church** (open Mon-Fri in summer), with a wealth of frescoes and sculptures, is in a small village 5km north of Godby along a picturesque secondary road and is perfect for a stopover on a bicycle tour.

The Café Uffe på Berget (see Places to Stay & Eat), just south of the bridge to Sund, has a 30m-high **observation tower** with superb views of the archipelago. Across the road is **Godby Arboretum**, a tiny park with native and exotic trees along a short, marked nature trail. There is no charge to visit the tower or the park.

Places to Stay & Eat
Bastö Hotell & Stugby (☎ 42382, fax 42520; singles/doubles €72/91; open May–end Aug) is on a headland at Bastö, 12km northwest of Godby. It has cottages, hotel rooms, a sauna and a restaurant.

Café Uffe på Berget (☎ 41190; open May-Aug), near the bridge on the Mariehamn–Sund road, is a popular stopover with outdoor seating and great views.

Getting There & Away
Road No 2 from Mariehamn takes you to Godby. Bus Nos 2, 3 and 4 from Mariehamn all go via Godby (€2.80). To get to other parts of Finström, take bus No 6.

SUND
pop 950
Sund, just east of the main island group and connected by bridge to Saltvik, is one of the most interesting municipalities in Åland. Attractions include a medieval castle and church, the ruins of a Russian stronghold and a large open-air museum. Sund is just 30km from Mariehamn, which makes it an ideal first overnight stop on a slow-paced bicycle

---

Midsummer Poles

The most striking manmade feature in the Åland landscape is the Midsummer pole. It's a long flagpole decorated with leaves, miniature flags, small boats and whatever else is available to add a splash of colour. Each village usually has one or more poles, decorated in a public gathering the day before Midsummer. The pole then stands until the next Midsummer.

ÅLAND

tour. Finby, in the centre of Sund, is the largest town, with all services.

Things to See & Do

The relatively small but impressive **Kastelholm** castle (☎ 432 150; adult/child €5/3.50; open 10am-5pm daily May-Aug, 10am-5.30pm July, 10am-4.30pm Sept) is one of Åland's top sights. Its exact age is not known, but it was mentioned in writings as early as 1388. To visit the castle you must join one of the regular guided tours, conducted in English, Finnish and Swedish.

Just around the corner from Kastelholm is **Jan Karlsgården Museum** (admission free; open 10am-5pm daily May-Sept), a delightful open-air museum. Traditional buildings, including windmills, from around the archipelago have been gathered here, and the old Åland culture is alive and well. It's one of the best places in all Finland to witness the Midsummer festival.

Close to the entrance of the Jan Karlsgården Museum is **Vita Björn** (☎ 432 156; admission €2; open 10am-5pm daily May-Sept), a prison museum that's worth a visit. The building was used as a jail from 1784 to 1974.

Also near Kastelholm is Åland's oddest tourist attraction, the **snail safari** run by **Alandia Escargots** (☎ 43964; adult/child €5.50/2; open Tues-Sun June-Aug). The snail farm opens only for the one-hour tours at 11am, 2pm and 4pm Monday to Friday, 11am and 2pm Saturday and noon and 2pm Sunday. For €9 you get the tour and a taste of snail in garlic butter and a glass of strong cider.

Åland's original **golf course** (☎ 43883), boasting 36 holes, is across the bay from Kastelholm.

North of Kastelholm, **Sankt Johannes Church** (open daily in summer) is the biggest church on Åland. It is 800 years old and is decorated with beautiful paintings. Note the stone cross with the text 'Wenni E'. According to researchers, it was erected in memory of the Hamburg bishop Wenni, who died here when on a crusade in AD 936.

East of Kastelholm are the ruins of the Russian fortress at **Bomarsund**. After the war of 1809, Russian troops began to build Bomarsund as a defence against the Swedes. Construction was halted during the Napoleonic Wars – when Russia allied itself with Sweden against France – but the mammoth

building was finally completed in 1842. Ultimately, Bomarsund was destroyed by the French and the English during the Crimean War (1854). The ruins of Bomarsund can be seen on both sides of road No 2 between Kastelholm and Prästö island. The small **Bomarsund museum** (☎ 44032; admission by donation; open 10am-5pm Tues-Sun in summer, shorter hours in winter) has more information and displays bits and pieces excavated from the site of the fortress ruins. It's on Prästö island, which is joined to the mainland island by a bridge.

There are four **graveyards** – Greek Orthodox, Jewish, Muslim and Christian – on the island of Prästö. All date back to the Russian occupation.

Prästö is also an entry point to the main island group from the island of Vårdö.

Places to Stay & Eat

Puttes Camping (☎ 44016, 44040; [e] puttes .camping@aland.net; tent sites per person €2.50, plus per tent or vehicle €1.70, cabins €27; open May–end Aug), at Bomarsund, has reasonably priced cabins, a café, beach sauna and canoe jetty.

Prästö Stugor & Camping (☎/fax 44045; tent sites €2, cabins €39-59; open mid-June–mid-Aug) is another camping ground with cabins on Prästö island, not far from Bomarsund. There is a grilli and a sauna.

Kastelholms Gästhem (☎ 43841; singles/ doubles €43/60; open Apr-Oct), 1.5km from Kastelholm in Tosarby village, has good-value rooms and cottages but it's unlikely you'll get a room without booking well in advance.

The **restaurant** opposite the Jan Karlsgården Museum serves light snacks and meals. This is one place to stuff yourself with those incredibly tempting Åland pancakes.

Getting There & Away

Road No 2 and bus No 4 from Mariehamn to Vårdö will take you to Sund. The bus goes via Kastelholm (€3.40), Svensböle, Bomarsund and Prästö (€4.60).

The bicycle ferry *Nadja* (☎ 35592) operates between Prästö, Sund, and Lumpo, Lumparland, from June to mid-August. There is one departure daily in June and August, and two daily departures in July (€7 one way).

SALTVIK
pop 1600

Was the 10th-century Viking capital, Birka, situated in Saltvik? Though there's no evidence – and stronger proof exists that the Viking stronghold was near the Swedish Lake Mälaren – one Ålandese archaeologist is convinced of Saltvik's former glory.

Whatever the case, many signs of Viking occupation have been unearthed around Saltvik, more so than elsewhere on the Åland archipelago. There just isn't much to look at.

East of Kvarnbo, the central village of Saltvik, is the Viking fortress of **Borgboda**. On the main Saltvik bicycle route, it is thought to have been built at the end of the Iron Age (AD 400–1000). Some stone outcroppings remain, but otherwise it's just a cow field with a nice view.

Kvarnbo has the large **Sankta Maria Church** that dates from the 12th century and is probably the oldest church in Finland. There are some wall paintings and sculptures from the 13th century, but most of the paintings are from the Lutheran era, in the 1500s.

Opposite the church look for the Birka monument on an old *tingsplats* (meeting and cult site).

Orrdals Klint
The highest 'mountain' in Åland, 129m above sea level, is really no more than a big hill. Two short, well-marked walking tracks (1km and 2.5km long respectively) lead to the top, where there's a viewing tower and a four-bed hut. There is no charge to sleep in the hut, but bring sheets or a sleeping bag, a torch (flashlight), water and food, and do not take wood from living trees. There is no public transport to Orrdals Klint.

Getting There & Away
Bus No 3 runs from Mariehamn to Kvarnbo (€3.40) and other villages in Saltvik.

The bicycle ferry *Kajo* plies between Tengsödavik (Saltvik) and Västra Simskäla (Vårdö) mid-June to mid-August. There is one daily departure each way in June and August, and two in July. It's €9 one way.

GETA
pop 450

The northern municipality of Geta is quiet and isolated. The only real attraction is **Getabergen** – at 98m above sea level, the archipelago's second highest 'mountain'. Explore the surroundings via a 2km marked nature trail.

On the island of Dånö is an open-air **museum** *(adult/child €2/free; open 1pm-4pm Sat & Sun June-Aug only)* with well preserved old buildings, including a fisherman's home.

Granqvist Stugor *(☎/fax 49610; 2/3/4 people €31/36/41)*, on road No 4, is a guesthouse with five clean and reasonably priced two- and four-bed cottages. **Soltuna Stugor** *(☎ 49530; 2/3/4 people €30/35/40)*, at the top of Getabergen, is a pleasant, well-located group of 10 cottages and a popular stop for cyclists. **Soltuna restaurant** at the top of Getabergen serves breakfast, lunch and dinner during summer.

To get to Geta from Mariehamn, take bus No 2, along road No 4 via Godby. The bicycle ferry *Silvana* (☎ 37212) travels between Hällö, Geta, and Skarpnåtö, Hammarland, from June to mid-August. There is one departure daily in early June and two daily departures during the rest of the season (€6 one way).

HAMMARLAND
pop 1200

The northwestern section of mainland Åland is called Hammarland. This is one of the oldest inhabited areas in Åland; almost 40 burial mound sites have been discovered. Kattby is the main village, with all facilities.

Sankta Catharina Church *(open daily in summer)* in Kattby was probably built in the 12th century. There's an **Iron Age burial site** to the west of the church, with more than 30 burial mounds.

North of Kattby, on the road to Skarpnåtö, is **Ålands Wool Spinnery** and shop. It sells homespun yarn and handmade sweaters. The spinnery is in the town of Mörby, 1.5km north of road No 1 to Eckerö. Further north in Lillbolstad is a ceramics shop, **Lugnet Ceramics** (☎ 37780). All products are handmade. West of the village of Sålis, **Bovik** is a nice fishing harbour.

Activities in Skarpnåtö centre around **Södergård Estate** *(closed in winter)*, a museum and handicrafts shop. The owners of the estate rent fishing boats.

Places to Stay & Eat
Kattnäs Camping *(☎ 37687; tent sites per person €2.50, plus per tent or vehicle €1.65,*

ÅLAND

cabins €37.50; open May–mid-Sept) is 3km south of the Eckerö–Mariehamn road, a bit west of Kattby. It has a café and sauna.

Gäddvikens Turisthotell (☎ 37650; singles/doubles €41/67; open mid-June–early Aug), north of Sålis, has comfortable rooms, a restaurant and sauna.

Kvarnhagens Stugor (☎/fax 37212; 2/3/4 people €41/46/51; open May-Sept) at Skarpnåtö has six sturdy timber cottages.

Getting There & Away
Bus No 1 from Mariehamn to Eckerö runs through Hammarland. For information on the bicycle ferry between Hammarland and Geta that section earlier.

ECKERÖ
pop 800
The island of Eckerö is the westernmost municipality in Finland, just a two-hour ferry ride from mainland Sweden. Eckerö has been a popular holiday spot since the 1800s. Today this area of Åland is almost a Little Sweden, and vacationing Swedish families constitute the majority of the population during the summer season.

Eckerö has also been an important communication link across the Baltic since Viking times. In 1638, the farmers of Eckerö were divided into *rotas*, groups of eight men who were responsible for maintaining mail services between Eckerö and mainland Sweden. Mail was transported in small boats until 1910. During the 272 years that the post *rota* system operated, more than 200 men lost their lives. On the second Saturday in June in odd-numbered years, old-fashioned boats are rowed to Eckerö from Grisslehamn in Sweden.

Storby (Big Village), at the ferry terminal, is the main centre. The distance from Mariehamn to Storby (40km) makes this a suitable day trip by bicycle.

Things to See & Do
The historic **Post och Tullhuset** (Post & Customs House; ☎ 38689) in Storby was designed by German architect Carl Ludwig Engel, who also designed parts of central Helsinki. It was completed in 1828, during the era of Tsar Alexander I of Russia. The building was meant to be a bulwark against the West and, for that reason, is far more grandiose than a post office in a small village should be. It

also now houses a café (open 10am-4pm daily June–mid-Aug), bank, art gallery and the small **mailboat museum** (☎ 39000; admission €1.70; open 10am-4pm daily June–mid-Aug). The museum tells the story of the dedicated men whose job it was to get the mail through to mainland Sweden and Finland by boat. The post office, bank and art gallery are open daily in summer and Monday to Friday only in winter.

Also in Storby, the **Labbas Homestead & Bank Museum** (☎ 38507; admission €1.70; open noon-4pm Wed late June–early Aug) is the local museum of Eckerö, though it's only open four hours a week. It has old archipelago houses with local furniture, maritime displays and a section devoted to banking history.

Just north of Storby is the attractive **Käringsund harbour**. On summer evenings the quiet, small-boat harbour, with its rustic old wooden boathouses reflected in the water, is so scenic it's almost unreal. There's an 800m **naturstig** (nature path) from Käringsund west to the larger ferry harbour. There's a small **beach** here and canoes and rowing boats can be hired from a kiosk nearby.

At Käringsund harbour is **Ålands Hunting & Fishing Museum** (☎ 38299; adult/child €4.20/1.70; open 10am-5pm or 6pm daily May-Aug, Sat & Sun only Sept) with photographs, stuffed animals, pearl-digging displays and the history of the hunting and fishing industries.

Viltsafari (☎ 38000), also at Käringsund harbour, is a fenced-in forest with typical Finnish fauna like red and fallow deer, black swans and wild boar, as well as a few ostriches. The 45-minute tour (€4) departs from the Hunting & Fishing Museum hourly in summer and by arrangement during other seasons.

In the village of Kyrkoby, about 5km east from Storby on the road to Mariehamn, the 13th-century **Sankt Lars Church of Eckerö** (open daily in summer) has beautiful 18th-century interior paintings and a 14th-century Madonna sculpture.

Kyrkoby is also home to the **Kyrkoby golf course** (☎ 38370), a short-hole course with 18 holes.

Degersand, about 9km south of Storby beyond the village of Torp, has a good **beach** for swimming and sunning, and it's also possible to camp right on the beach.

Volleyball, Tampere

Industrial buildings, Tampere

Kauppahalli (covered market), Turku

Traditional wooden houses, Rauma

Crane *(Grus grus)*

Oulankajoki River, Oulanka National Park

Liminganlahti Bird Sanctuary, near Oulu

Nature Centre, Liminganlahti Bird Sanctuary

There's a branch of RO NO Rent near the harbour for bicycle, scooter and canoe hire. See the Mariehamn Getting Around section for details of prices.

Places to Stay
Eckerö has more cabin and cottage rentals than any other Åland province – contact Ålandsresor for details.

Camping At Käringsund harbour, **Käringsunds Camping** (☎ 38309; e yvonnee@aland.net; tent sites €6-8, cabins €33-44; open mid-May–end Aug) is a down-to-earth place with camping and lots of cabins. There are all kinds of activities available, and the restaurant is busy at weekends with Swedes dancing to live music.

Alebo Stugor & Camping (☎ 38575; e alebo@aland.net; Alebovägen 24; tent sites per person/family €4/7; cabins €37; open May–end Sept) in Storby, 200m north of the main road, has canoe hire and a network of nature trails among its facilities. In July most of its cabins are rented only by the week.

Notvikens Camping (☎ 38020, fax 38329; tent sites €12, cabins €25-60; open May–end Sept) is a camping ground with a café and sauna and it also rents boats and fishing equipment. From Överby village on road No 2, turn south and go 2km.

Uddens Camping (☎ 38670, fax 38547; tent sites per person €1.20, cabins €54; open May–end Sept) is in the isolated village of Skag on the northern coast.

Guesthouses & Hotels In an 18th-century wooden house in Storby, **Ängstorp Gästhem** (☎ 38665; singles/doubles high season €51/59; open Apr–end Oct) is one of the best places to stay on Åland, but it's often full. There are just six rooms, and they're well equipped and attractive. Rates vary throughout the season.

Granbergs Gästhem (☎ 39462; doubles high season €49; open Apr-Nov) is another attractive place in Storby with five doubles. Breakfast is included.

Storby Logi (☎ 38469; singles/doubles €27/52; open year-round), opposite the Labbas Museum, is another central guesthouse with 10 rooms that are reasonably priced.

Hotell Havsbandet (☎ 38200, fax 38305; singles/doubles €65/83; open Apr-Dec), between the Post & Customs House and the

sea, is a friendly 29-room hotel with a nice restaurant.

Hotell Eckerö (☎ 38447, fax 38247; singles/doubles Mon-Fri high season €86/97), also in Storby, is a favourite of visiting Swedes. It has 40 rooms and a restaurant with daily specials. Weekend rates are slightly higher.

Österängens Hotell (☎ 38268, fax 38356; singles/doubles high season €66/78; open Apr-Sept), on the quiet beach of Torp, has a good restaurant and sea views.

Places to Eat
In addition to the hotel restaurants, you can eat in Storby village at **Pirjo Cafe** at the Esso petrol station opposite the supermarket, or at the **Hem Bagarn** bakery, which is a bit closer to the harbour. **Jannes Bodega** is an attractive little café at the Käringsund harbour, open from June to August.

Cafe Lugn & Ro at the Post & Customs House serves sandwiches and hamburgers.

Restaurant Rusell (☎ 38499), one of the best eateries in the whole province, is in Kyrkoby on road No 2 – just look for the pink house. Lunch (€8) is available until 3pm, but evenings see plenty of locals gossiping downstairs at the pub.

Getting There & Away
Road No 2 runs from Mariehamn to Eckerö. If you use public transport, take bus No 1 (€4.50, 40 minutes). For information on ferries between Eckerö and Grisslehamn, Sweden, see Getting There & Away at the beginning of this chapter.

LEMLAND
pop 1300
Lemland municipality is between Lumparland and the Lemström Canal, 5km east of Mariehamn on road No 3 (take bus No 5). The canal was built in 1882 by prisoners of war. Norrby village is Lemland's centre.

In Norrby, **Sankta Birgitta Church** (open Mon-Fri in summer) has 13th- to 14th-century wall paintings that were rediscovered in 1956. **Burial mounds** from the Iron Age are nearby. At **Lemböte** on the western side of the island are the ruins of a 13th-century chapel and more ancient burial mounds. Near the crossing to Lumparland, **Skeppargården Pellas** (☎ 34001; adult/child €2.50/free; open 10am-4pm daily June–mid-Aug) is the homestead museum of a local shipmaster.

Herrön, at the southernmost tip of Lemland, is a popular picnic spot. There is a small observation tower here for bird-watching.

Herro Cafe & Pensionat *(☎ 35311; singles/doubles €34/51; open May-Aug)*, in the southern village of Herro, is a five-room guesthouse with shared facilities and a café-restaurant.

LUMPARLAND

pop 300

Many travellers pass through Lumparland in southeastern Åland because of its two ferry harbours, Svinö and Långnäs. Otherwise, there's little reason to visit.

Sankt Andreas Church *(open daily in summer)*, built in 1720, is one of the 'newer' churches of Åland. This little wooden church is in a beautiful seaside spot along the road to Lumparby village and Lumpo.

Långnäsbyn *(☎ 35557; singles/doubles €41/44; open May-Aug)*, near the Långnäs ferry terminal, has nine reasonably priced cottages. **Svinö Stugby** *(☎ 35781; doubles €29; open May-Sept)* is a rustic group of 10 good-value cottages in Svinö.

From Mariehamn take bus No 5 to Svinö and Långnäs (€4.20, 45 minutes). For information on the bicycle ferry to Prästö see Getting There & Away under Sund.

VÅRDÖ

pop 400

The island of Vårdö was on the old mail route from Sweden to Finland, and some of the ancient 'milestones' have been resurrected for tourists.

The main settlement is Vargata, which has a bank, a shop and a post office. Northeast of Vargata, Lövö village was the scene of a peace conference in 1718 between representatives of King Karl XII of Sweden and Tsar Peter I (Peter the Great) of Russia, during the Great Northern War. Judging by what has been dug from the earth here, the 1200 participants in this high-class event consumed French wine and oysters in frightening quantities. The event ended with few positive results, and there was no peace until 1721.

On the main road between Vargata and Lövö, **Seffers Homestead Museum** *(☎ 47605; adult/child €2/free; open noon-3pm Tues, Thur & Sat June & July)* has a windmill, farm equipment and a Midsummer pole on display. A little further along the same road, **Åland School Museum** *(☎ 0457-548 3934; adult/child €1.50/1; open 11am-3pm Tues-Sun May-Aug)*

Places to Stay

Sandösunds Camping *(☎/fax 47750; W www.sandocamping.aland.fi; tent sites per person €2, plus tent or vehicle €2, cabins €35)* is on the beach in the north of the island. There are pleasant two- and four-bed cottages, and a café, restaurant and canoe and bike rentals.

Getting There & Away

Bus No 4 will take you to Vårdö from Mariehamn. Ferries on the northern archipelago route depart from the village of Hummelvik on Vårdö. For more details see Getting There & Away under Brändö later. For information on the bicycle ferry between Saltvik and Vårdö, see Getting There & Away under Saltvik earlier.

Northern Archipelago

The northern group of the Åland islands consists of the archipelago municipalities of Kumlinge and Brändö. They are very quiet and offer less for the traveller than the southern group, but you're certainly away from it all exploring these far-flung islands. If you're coming to Åland from Kustavi on the Finnish mainland through Osnäs, you'll arrive at Långö in the north of the Brändö island group. You can also depart from here, but confirm ferry times in advance to avoid getting stuck.

KUMLINGE

pop 450

About 1½ hours by ferry from Vårdö, Kumlinge municipality isn't exactly a thrumming tourist hotspot. The main island, Kumlinge, is flanked by Enklinge island to the north and Seglinge island to the south. All services can be found on Kumlinge, and a bank is on Enklinge. There is no accommodation on Seglinge and no restaurant – only a shop in the main village.

The ferry to Seglinge departs from the island of Snäckö, 8km from Kumlinge village. Local ferries to Enklinge from the main island depart from the village of Krokarno.

A marked cycling route runs from Snäckö north to Krokarno, with bridges between the islands. On Enklinge there is a signposted route from the harbour to the local museum.

Many consider **Sankta Anna Church** *(open daily in summer)* on Kumlinge island to be one of Finland's most beautiful churches, with 500-year-old Franciscan-style paintings. The church is some 2km north of Kumlinge village.

On Enklinge is the small open-air **Hermas Farm Museum** *(☎ 55334; adult/child €2/ free; open 9am-4pm Mon-Fri mid-June–early Aug, 9am-7pm July)*, 3.5km from the pier, with 20 buildings that are all original to this island.

On Seglinge there is a **fishing village** near the ferry pier, and a 2km **nature trail**.

Places to Stay & Eat
Ledholm Camping *(☎/fax 55647; tent sites per person €2.50; open May-Aug)* is on the island of Snäckö near the ferry pier. It also has cheap cabins and a small grocery.

Remmarina Stugor *(☎ 0400-529 199; 2/ 3/4 people €40/45/50; open May-Sept)*, at the guest harbour 2km from Kumlinge village, has 12 clean, reasonably priced cottages on a small hill, plus a sauna and a small canteen for snacks.

Getting There & Away
Ferries on the route between Hummelvik and Torsholma on Brändö stop at both Enklinge (one hour) and Kumlinge islands (1½ hours).

One or two ferries a day go from Långnäs in Lumparland to Snäckö in Kumlinge, via Överö in the Föglö island group (two hours).

BRÄNDÖ
pop 550
The municipality of Brändö consists of a group of 1180 islands, the largest and most important of which are connected by bridges. Banks and other services are on the main island and in the villages of Lappo and Torsholma on smaller islands.

The peculiar shape of the main island makes for interesting cycling – no matter where you go, you will always be riding by the sea. A signposted bike route runs from the harbour at Torsholma north across the main island to the harbour at Långö.

St Jakobs Church, the wooden place of worship on the main island of Brändö, dates

from 1893. On Lappo island further south (and connected to the main island by ferry), **Archipelago Museum** *(☎ 56689; adult/child €3.50/free; open 10am-noon & 2pm-4pm daily mid-June–early Aug)* has exhibits of local history, boats and nature.

Places to Stay & Eat
There's camping on Brändö at **Brändö Stugby** *(☎ 56221, fax 56606; open May-Sept)*, which also has log cabins and rowing boats for hire.

Hotell Gullvivan *(☎ 56350, fax 56330; singles/doubles high season €63/80)* is a top-end hotel on Björnholma island with 16 rooms. There's a restaurant and minigolf course here.

Getting There & Away
From Mariehamn, take bus No 4 to Hummelvik harbour on Vårdö. There are three ferry connections a day from Vårdö to Lappo and Torsholma. The trip from Hummelvik takes about three hours.

From Turku on mainland Finland, take a bus to Kustavi, and on to Vartsala Island to reach the harbour of Osnäs (Finnish: Vuosnainen). There are five to seven connections a day from Osnäs to Långö on the northern Brändö island of Åva.

Southern Archipelago

The southern group of Åland islands consists of the municipalities of Föglö, tiny Sottunga and remote Kökar. Kökar is the most quaint and appealing island, and is also the jumping off point for archipelago ferries from Galtby harbour on Korppoo on the Finnish mainland (see Kökar Getting There & Away later).

FÖGLÖ
pop 600
The Föglö island group was first mentioned in 1241 by a Danish bishop who landed here en route to Tallinn. An inn was founded in 1745 at Föglö at Enigheten Estate.

A signposted bike route runs from Degerby northeast to Överö, and there is a regular bus service. Both villages are served by archipelago ferries. Degerby has a bank, post office and grocery.

ÅLAND

The 'capital' of Föglö is Degerby, a small village noted for its unusual **architecture**. Many Föglöites have traditionally been civil servants, not farmers, and have chosen to build their houses in Art Nouveau or Empire styles instead of the traditional archipelago style.

In the red building at the harbour is the local **museum** (☎ 50156; admission €1.70; open 1pm-4.30pm & 5pm-8pm Tues-Sun mid-June–early Aug). **Sankta Maria Magdalena Church** (open Mon-Fri in summer) is on an island south from Degerby, connected by a bridge. Getting there is half the fun, as the road is scenic. The simple 14th-century church is not very impressive but the way it rises from the plain rock bed is dramatic.

Places to Stay & Eat

CC Camping (☎ 51440; tent sites €3, cabins €28-47; open June-Aug) is on the small Finholma island northeast of Degerby. It's on the Degerby–Överö cycle route.

Enigheten Gästhem (☎/fax 50310; singles/doubles €37/54; open May-Sept), a rustic retreat 1km from the Degerby ferry terminal, is a fine place to stay. Booking is essential. It has a café and good breakfasts.

Seagram (☎ 51092) in Degerby is a good licensed restaurant with dancing in summer.

Getting There & Away

From Mariehamn, bus No 5 goes to the Svinö and Långnäs ferry harbours, both in Lumparland. A dozen or so ferries a day make the one-hour trip between Svinö and Degerby. There are one or two ferries a day on the Långnäs–Överö–Kumlinge route.

SOTTUNGA
pop 130

Somnolent Sottunga island has more cows than people. Despite the small population, the island has its own bank, shop, school, health-care centre, library and church.

The wooden **Sankta Maria Magdalena Church** was built in 1661 and renovated in 1974. A short **nature trail** starts at the fishing harbour, and a marked cycling route runs north from the harbour to the village of Skaget.

Strandhuggets Stugor (☎ 55255; doubles €30; open May-Sept) near the harbour has six cottages for two people available for overnight or longer stays, as well as a café.

Ferries on the southern archipelago route from Lumparland or Föglö, as well as occasional ferries from Kumlinge, will take you to Sottunga.

KÖKAR
pop 300

The Kökar island group, with its strikingly barren landscape, is one of the most interesting in Åland. Many of the inhabitants live in and around the quaint little town of Karlby, which has a bank, post office and grocery.

Though it feels quite isolated from the rest of the world, Kökar is not difficult to reach by ferry. A signposted cycle route runs from the harbour to Karlby and Hellsö.

Things to See & Do

Historic **Hamnö island** is connected to the main island by a bridge. Since time immemorial, boats have been anchored at its shores, many of them plying the Hansa trade route between Germany and Turku. A very small – a dozen members at most – Jesuit Franciscan community built a monastery here in the 14th century. The main building is long gone, but the present **church** (open daily in summer), from 1784, was built on the same site.

The small **Kökar Homestead Museum** (☎ 55763; admission €1.80; open noon-5pm daily mid-June–mid-Aug) of local history is on the east side of the main island, in the village of Hellsö. A short **nature trail** starts near Hellsö.

During summer there are two cruises from Kökar to the tiny island of Källskär. The MS *Kristina* (☎ 55737) charges €20/15 adult/child for a return cruise.

Places to Stay & Eat

Sandvik Camping (☎ 55911; tent sites €7.60; open May–end Sept) is at the harbour. There are also cabins, a grilli and bike rentals, and lone cyclists pay €4.20 for a site.

Antons Gästhem (☎ 55729, fax 55938; singles/doubles in summer €64/68), the red building along the road south from the harbour, has 11 simple rooms. It's open year-round and rates are one-third cheaper outside the June-to-August high season.

Hotell Brudhäll (☎ 55955, fax 55956; singles/doubles in summer €91/108; open year-round) in Karlby has a very impressive location on the waterfront. It has a highly regarded restaurant serving traditional archipelago dishes. There's entertainment and dancing on summer evenings.

Klobbars Gasthem (☎ 55709; W www .klobbars.com; singles/doubles in summer €53/73; open Apr-Oct) is a 20-room guesthouse in the village of Hellsö.

Getting There & Away
On mainland Finland ferries depart for Kökar once or twice daily from the harbour of Galtby on Korppoo Island, 75km from Turku (take the Saaristotie bus from Turku). This is a popular route – if you're travelling with a car expect to wait a few extra hours on Friday heading to Åland and on Sunday to Turku. The trip from Galtby to Kökar takes two hours.

It is much easier to get to Kökar from mainland Åland. There are three to five connections a day from Långnäs (take bus No 5 from Mariehamn) to Kökar, via Föglö and Sottunga. The ferry also stops at the tiny island of Husö. Travel time is 2½ hours from Långnäs.

Pohjanmaa

Western Finland comprises a region known as Pohjanmaa in Finnish, Österbotten in Swedish and sometimes as Ostrobothnia (from the Latin). It stretches along the Gulf of Bothnia (Pohjanlahti), roughly from Pori in the south to Kalajoki in the north, and includes the flat farming region around Seinäjoki.

Swedes first developed trading towns on the west coast in the 17th century to exploit the surrounding rich forests – sources of tar for Sweden's war fleet. After the tar trade dried up, many Swedish settlers remained and, in the centuries since, a proud farming culture has grown up in the flat but fertile Pohjanmaa.

For travellers, this is largely a flat, dry, dull and unremarkable-looking region – especially away from the coast. True, it lacks the mystery and grandeur of Lapland or the riverine beauty of the Lakeland. But skipping the coastal towns along here would be a mistake for anyone wanting to get a full picture of Finland. Between Kristinestad and Jakobstad you'll find yourself on the 'Swedish Coast', a predominantly Swedish-speaking area of quaint fishing villages and islands. Language is the distinctive feature here; a magazine booth in a local supermarket will have a collection of imported Swedish papers that keep locals gossiping about Sweden's TV stars, and the radio station is more likely to be playing Stockholm's 'P3' than the Finnish Rundradion. People from Sweden treat this region of lost brethren with curiosity and call it *Parallelsverige*, or 'Parallel Sweden'.

Highlights

- Pitching a tent for the Kaustinen Folk Music Festival in July; with 250 folk and blues concerts in eight days, it's Finland's answer to Woodstock
- Enjoying summer drinks at Strampen or one of Vaasa's other lively terrace-bars
- Cycling around the fishing villages on the island of Replot
- Exploring the 'parallel Sweden' phenomenon in Jakobstad with its quaint Old Town, eccentric museums and beautiful nearby coastline
- Relaxing in the quiet fishing village of Kaskinen, with its friendly hostel
- Finding out what a seaside holiday experience at a latitude of 64° is like at Kalajoki Beach in summer – Mediterranean meets the Arctic!

Vaasa

☎ 06 • pop 55,000

Vaasa (Swedish: Vasa) has a culture all of its own. Some 27% of the population speak Swedish and the surrounding countryside is largely inhabited by Swedish speakers, making Vaasa the largest distinctively bilingual town in Finland. Some travellers use this as an entry or exit point between Finland and Sweden (see Getting There & Away later) and, as the largest town along the west coast between Turku and Oulu,

Vaasa has a lively, bustling air, especially in summer. However, it lacks the character and charm of some of the smaller places along the 'Swedish Coast'. More interesting than the city itself is the surrounding countryside and nearby islands.

The town began in the 14th century as a village called Korsholm. In 1606 Swedish King Charles IX created Vasa, named after the royal Swedish Wasa family. During the Civil War that followed Finnish independence, Vaasa was the capital of the 'Whites'.

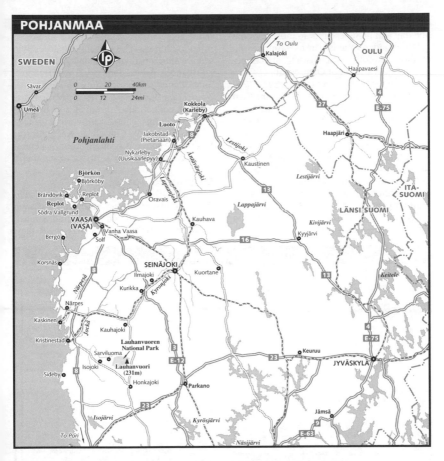

POHJANMAA

Orientation & Information

Vaasanpuistikko is the main street through the centre of Vaasa. Vaskiluoto to the west and Palosaari to the north are two islands connected to central Vaasa by bridges. The town centre is small enough to walk around.

The busy **tourist office** (☎ 325 1145; W www.vaasa.fi; Kaupungintalo; open 8am-8pm Mon-Fri, 10am-6pm Sat & Sun, shorter hours in winter), in the town hall building just off Raastuvankatu, books accommodation and rents bikes.

The **main post office** (Hovioikeudenpuistikko 23A; open 10am-6pm Mon-Fri) is opposite the train station. The modern **public library** (Kirjastonkatu) has several free Internet terminals, while **Oliver's Inn** (see Entertainment later) also has Internet access.

Things to See & Do

Vaskiluoto is a big holiday destination for Finnish families, with beaches, boating, a popular camping ground and **Wasalandia Amusement Park** (☎ 211 1200; W www.wasalandia.fi; day pass adult/child €15/10; open noon-8pm daily late June–early Aug), the Finnish answer to Disneyland. From early May to mid-June and from mid- to late August the park runs on a reduced schedule.

Just south of the amusement park is the 'tropical bathing paradise' **Tropiclandia** (☎ 211 1300; W www.tropiclandia.fi; adult/child €13/9; open daily mid-June–mid-Aug), a water park and spa. It keeps similar hours to Wasalandia.

If you plan on visiting a few museums in the Vaasa region, pick up an **Art City Pass**

POHJANMAA

(€5) from the tourist office. It's valid for one day and includes entry to most regional galleries and museums. The most interesting of the numerous museums and art collections is the **Museum of Ostrobothnia** (☎ 325 3800; Museokatu 3; adult/child €4/2, free Wed; open 10am-5pm daily, 10am-8pm Wed), with one of the best collections of art from Finland's Golden Era. The general collection displays some of the cultural wealth for which Pohjanmaa is famous: decorations, traditional wedding items and colourful artefacts. In the basement level is the **Bothnia Straits Nature Centre**, with displays on the region's geology, flora and fauna.

Bragegården (☎ 317 2271; admission €3.50; open 11pm-5pm Tues-Fri, noon-4pm Sat & Sun June–late Aug) is an open-air history museum 1km south of the centre, at Hietalahti. There are old saunas and a dozen or so other buildings. The museum is accessible via a walking path off Hietalahdenkatu.

Tikanoja Art Gallery (☎ 325 3916; Hovioikeudenpuistikko 4; adult/student €4/3; open 11am-4pm Tues-Sat, noon-5pm Sun) has a good collection of Finnish and international paintings, and is well worth a visit.

The **Orthodox Church** at Kasarmintori has some old icons brought from St Petersburg; contact the tourist office to see them.

Organised Tours

The MS *Tiira* (☎ 315 4047; adult/child €10/5) cruises the Vaasa archipelago at noon and 4pm daily from mid-June to mid-August, departing from the Kalaranta passenger quay.

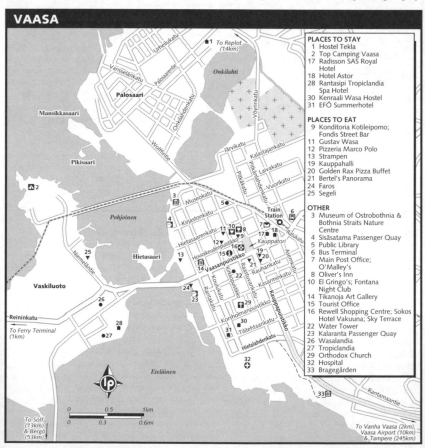

VAASA

PLACES TO STAY
1   Hostel Tekla
2   Top Camping Vaasa
17 Radisson SAS Royal Hotel
18 Hotel Astor
28 Rantasipi Tropiclandia Spa Hotel
30 Kenraali Wasa Hostel
31 EFÖ Summerhotel

PLACES TO EAT
9   Konditoria Kotileipomo; Fondis Street Bar
11 Gustav Wasa
12 Pizzeria Marco Polo
13 Strampen
19 Kauppahalli
20 Golden Rax Pizza Buffet
21 Bertel's Panorama
24 Faros
25 Segeli

OTHER
3   Museum of Ostrobothnia & Bothnia Straits Nature Centre
4   Sisäsatama Passenger Quay
5   Public Library
6   Bus Terminal
7   Main Post Office; O'Malley's
8   Oliver's Inn
10 El Gringo's; Fontana Night Club
14 Tikanoja Art Gallery
15 Tourist Office
16 Rewell Shopping Centre; Sokos Hotel Vakuuna; Sky Terrace
22 Water Tower
23 Kalaranta Passenger Quay
26 Wasalandia
27 Tropiclandia
29 Orthodox Church
32 Hospital
33 Bragegården

Special Events

The **Korsholm Music Festival**, an international chamber music festival, is held in late June; see W www.korsholm.fi/music or call ☎ 322 2390 for more information.

The Vaasa shoreline reverberates to **Rantarock**, a major summer music festival held on Hietasaari island in mid-June. It attracts plenty of well known alternative international acts.

Vaasa Rules is a big Midsummer party with music and concerts; and during the **Vaasa Carnival** in early August, there is dancing, music and beer drinking.

Places to Stay

Camping For happy campers there's **Top Camping Vaasa** (☎ 211 1255; Niemeläntie; tent sites €7 plus per person €4, cabins €9 plus per person €4; open June–late Aug), a well-kept, family-friendly camping ground about 2km from the town centre, on Vaskiluoto. It also rents bicycles and boats, and offers discount coupons for the Tropiclandia spa and free admission to Wasalandia Amusement Park.

Hostels & Hotels Housed in part of an old military complex, **Kenraali Wasa Hostel** (☎ 0400-668 521, fax 3121 394; Korsholmanpuistikko 6-8; singles/doubles/triples €37/46/50) is the best of the few budget places in Vaasa. It's a friendly place with a well-equipped kitchen and cosy rooms (shared bathrooms).

Hostel Tekla (☎ 327 6411, fax 321 3989; W www.hosteltekla.net; Palosaarentie 58; beds in summer €22.50, singles/doubles/triples €42/60/77), on Palosaari island in northern Vaasa, is more like a hotel for sporting enthusiasts than a hostel, but it has great facilities including a gym, squash courts and a café. Rooms have shower and toilet and some have TV. Take bus No 1 from the centre.

EFÖ Summerhotel (☎ 317 4913; Rantakatu 21-22; singles/doubles €40/47; open mid-June–mid-Aug) is a summer hotel run by an evangelical folk school. Rooms should be booked in advance. Use of kitchens, gym and sauna is included in the price.

Hotel Astor (☎ 326 9111, fax 326 9484; W www.astorvaasa.com; Asemakatu 4; singles/doubles €100/125, weekends & summer €75/93) is a stylish, intimate hotel with just 32 rooms and is popular with foreign tour groups

in summer and well-to-do business types in winter. Rates include breakfast and sauna, and rooms with private sauna cost €18 more.

Radisson SAS Royal Hotel (☎ 212 8111; Hovioikeudenpuistikko 18; doubles €134, weekends & summer €83) is the biggest of Vaasa's business hotels, boasting not only rooms on both sides of the street but a pub, nightclub and two restaurants.

Rantasipi Tropiclandia Spa Hotel (☎ 283 8000; W www.rantasipi.fi; Lemmenpolku 3; singles/doubles €101/118) is a large spa hotel attached to Tropiclandia on Vaskiluoto island. Rates include all kinds of spa and resort activities so it's popular with families and anyone wanting a relaxing time out.

Places to Eat

There are cheap grillis, pizzerias and hamburger restaurants around the **kauppatori** (market square) and in the **Rewell shopping centre**. The **kauppahalli** (covered market) on Kauppapuistikko has stalls selling fresh bakery products and the usual market fare.

Bertel's Panorama (Vaasanpuistikko 16; lunch buffet €7.40; open 11am-4pm Mon-Fri, 11am-3pm Sat) is a great place for lunch with a view over the kauppatori. The daily buffet is not gourmet but is very generous.

There's a **Golden Rax Pizza Buffet** (Kauppapuistikko 13; buffet €7.50) serving the usual cheap all-you-can-eat option of pizza, pasta, salad and chicken wings.

Konditoria Kotileipomo (Hovioikeudenpuistikko 13), on the kauppatori in the city centre, is a pleasant café with outdoor seating in summer.

Pizzeria Marco Polo (☎ 317 5922; Hovioikeudenpuistikko 11; pizzas €6-9) is a traditional little Italian place serving cheap pizzas and pastas.

Vaasa has several good summer restaurants. On Vaskiluoto, and part of the local sailing club, **Segeli** (☎ 317 2037; Niemeläntie 14; mains €9-16, lunch buffet from €6.50) is a stylish but surprisingly reasonably priced restaurant. It has a terrace overlooking the marina and features dishes such as reindeer, and whitefish fillet in lobster sauce.

On the opposite side of the harbour, **Strampen** (☎ 320 0355; Rantakatu 6; Sisasatama; mains €9.50-18, lunch buffet €6-9.50) is a summer beer terrace in the waterfront park, with a good restaurant serving a range of meals.

POHJANMAA

Faros (☎ *312 6411; Kalaranta; meals €9-12)* is a boat restaurant moored in Kalaranta Harbour on the southern side of the bridge. It's a good place for lunch or an evening drink and snack, with decent burgers, pasta and salads.

Gustav Wasa (☎ *326 9200; Raastuvankatu 24; €16.50-27)*, around the corner from the tourist office, is a cellar restaurant with a small but gourmet menu of Finnish cuisine including wild duck and sirloin of reindeer. Unusually for a restaurant, there's a sauna in an adjoining building so patrons can cook themselves.

Entertainment
For a drink with a birds-eye view of the city, head to the **Sky Terrace** on the rooftop of the Sokos Hotel Vaakuna, adjacent to the Rewell Shopping Centre. Probably the most popular and well-positioned summer beer terrace is **Strampen** (see Places to Eat) in the waterfront Hovioikeuden Park. The deck of the boat restaurant **Faros** is another good place to take in the summer maritime breeze over a few beers, and there's often live music here.

O'Malley's *(Hovioikeudenpuistikko 18)* is an Irish bar popular with visiting business people since it's part of the Radisson Hotel. With international beers and stout on tap, booth seating and a cosy atmosphere, it's a good place to be in winter. **Oliver's Inn** *(Kauppapuistikko 8)* bills itself as a party pub and draws a younger crowd with live music, DJs, karaoke and theme nights.

Fondis Street Bar *(Hovioikeudenpuistikko 15)*, next door to Konditoria Kotileipomo, has live music such as jazz or blues a couple of times a week and a good pavement terrace. Around the corner in Raastuvankatu, **El Gringo** is a basement saloon bar that packs them in with cheap beer (€2.50). When that closes everyone heads upstairs to **Fontana Night Club**.

Getting There & Away
Air Finnair offers daily flights from Vaasa to Helsinki, Kokkola and Stockholm. The airport is situated 12km southeast of the centre; airport buses depart from the city bus station.

Bus There are daily bus services from the terminal on Vöyrinkatu to all major western and central towns, and there are several express buses a day from Helsinki and Turku via Pori. Buses run up and down the west coast pretty much hourly from Monday to Friday.

Train Vaasa is off the main train lines, but there is a connecting line from Seinäjoki to Vaasa and there are half a dozen trains per day from Helsinki (€35.60, five hours) via Tampere or Seinäjoki. The fastest IC train to/from Helsinki covers the 420km in four hours.

Boat In summer there are daily ferries (€41, three hours) between Vaasa and the Swedish town of Umeå (Uumaja) with **RG Lines** (☎ *320 0300;* Ⓦ *www.rgline.com).* **Botnia Link** (☎ *322 6600; Reininkatu 3)* is a vehicle and cargo ferry service that also takes passengers for €35 per person. It sails four times a week to Umeå and also to Harnosand. The ferry terminal is on the western side of Vaskiluoto (take bus No 10).

Getting Around
Local buses come in handy if you want to reach areas of town outside the centre. Take bus No 5 or 10 to Vaskiluoto island and bus No 1, 3 or 4 to the hostel on Palosaari island. The fare is €2.20 (€2.70 on Sunday). The Lilliputti tram runs between the kauppatori and Wasalandia (€3) daily in the summer months.

Bicycles can be rented at the tourist office or Top Camping Vaasa for around €3.50 for two hours.

AROUND VAASA
Vanha Vaasa
The Old Town of Vaasa developed around a harbour, southeast of the modern centre, but the harbour became unsuitable for large vessels. The medieval church is now in ruins and, although the old fortress area has been protected, not much remains. Probably the most interesting sight is the **Church of Korsholm**, built in 1786. It looks very pompous; it was originally a judges' palace. **Köpmanshuset Wasasferne** (☎ *356 7578; Kauppiaankatu 10; adult/child €2/1; open 11am-5pm daily mid-June–mid-Aug)* is a museum of local history.

Bus Nos 7, 9, 12A and 12B travel between Vanha Vaasa and the town centre.

Solf

One of the most attractive villages in Finland, Solf (Finnish: Sulva) is best known for its **Stundars Handicraft Village** (☎ 344 2200; W www.stundars.fi; adult/child €4/2; open noon-6pm daily mid-May–mid-Aug, noon-6pm Sat & Sun mid-Aug–late Aug), an open-air museum and crafts centre boasting 60 traditional wooden buildings, progressively moved here from surrounding villages. The whole place hums with activity in summer, when artisans demonstrate crafts such as wool dyeing and wood carving. On some days the workers dress in national costume (phone for the schedule). Lots of handcrafted items are available for sale and there's a café. The entrance fee includes a guided tour.

Regional buses from Vaasa make the 15km trip south to Solf.

Replot

Replot (Finnish: Raippaluoto) is a large island that lies just off the Vaasa coast. It's easy to reach and ideal for exploring by bicycle. On the island there are several small fishing communities in addition to the main village, which is also called Replot. The total population is 2000.

Södra Vallgrund village is on the southwestern corner of the island, some 10km from the village of Replot. It has a small museum. **Klobbskat** village, at the western end of the island, is in a barren, Lappish-like setting. **Björkön** (Swedish: Björköby) is a fishing village on a smaller, northern island, accessible from Replot by bridge.

In 1997 a 1045m bridge – the longest bridge in Finland – was completed connecting Replot with the mainland.

Bulleråsin Holiday Village (☎ 352 7613; Bulleråsvägen 330; tent sites €10, cottages €42-58) in Södra Vallgrund has camping, cottages and a restaurant in a 1920s villa.

South of Vaasa

KRISTINESTAD
☎ 06 • pop 8600
Kristinestad (Finnish: Kristiinankaupunki) is a small, idyllic seaside town and like many along this coast it's bilingual – some 58% of the locals speak Swedish.

Named after Queen Kristina of Sweden, Kristinestad was founded in 1649 by the great Count Per Brahe. By the 1850s, the town had become one of the main ports in Finland and an important centre for shipbuilding. With the arrival of steamships, Kristinestad's importance declined, and many of its inhabitants moved to Sweden.

Kristinestad is quite small, with a village feel and everything except the camping ground within a block or two of the market square. The tourist office (☎ 221 2311; W www.krs.fi; Sjögatan 47) is almost opposite Cafe Alma and is open from 10am to 5pm Monday to Friday and 10am to 3pm Saturday in summer.

Things to See
The most interesting thing in Kristinestad is the town itself, with its rows of colourful, old, painted wooden houses. In its heyday as a key port, every traveller entering the town had to pay customs duty, collected at the **Old Customs House** (Staketgatan).

Adjacent to the customs house is the striking **Old Church** (Ulrika Eleonora Kyrka; open Tues-Sat mid-May–late Aug), which was constructed from 1698 to 1700 and retains many of its original detail. The church, named after the 17th-century Swedish Queen Ulrika Eleonora, wife of Karl XI, is now among the oldest wooden churches in Finland. The red-brick **New Church** (Parmansgatan), holds some relics from the original church.

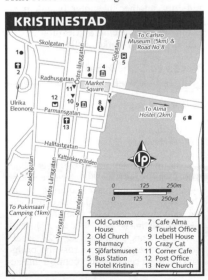

KRISTINESTAD

1 Old Customs House	7 Cafe Alma
2 Old Church	8 Tourist Office
3 Pharmacy	9 Lebell House
4 Sjöfartsmuseet	10 Crazy Cat
5 Bus Station	11 Corner Cafe
6 Hotel Kristina	12 Post Office
	13 New Church

POHJANMAA

Sjöfartsmuseet *(Maritime Museum; ☎ 221 2859; Salutorget 1; adult/child €3.40/1; open noon-4pm Tues-Sun mid-May–mid-Aug)* displays sea-related items collected by an old sea captain and portrays Kristinestad's proud maritime history – the whole town seems to have pitched in to help put this place together, and they've done a fine job.

Lebell House *(Lebellska Köpmansgården; ☎ 221 2159; Strandgatan 51; adult/child €4/1; open noon-4pm Tues-Sun June–late Aug)*, a block south of the market square, is a home museum that once belonged to a wealthy merchant. Dating from the early 19th century, it's an excellent representation of upper-class life in old Kristinestad.

About 5km north of town, **Carlsro Museum** *(☎ 222 3144; Carlsrovägen 181; adult/child €4.20/1; open 11am-6pm Tues-Sun June–late August)* is in an old villa (1896) and is quite delightful, with a collection of bric-a-brac and toys from the tsarist era.

Three blocks south of the market square is **Kattpiskargränden** (Cat Whipper's Alley). It's the narrowest street in town, a mere 299cm wide. In the 1880s the town employed a cat catcher, whose job was to kill sick cats in order to prevent the spreading of plague – hence the name of the street.

Special Events
The town has three big **market fairs**; one in mid-July, another in winter (Candelmas) and the third in autumn (Michaelmas). They feature music, dancing and exhibitions as well as the usual market stalls.

Places to Stay & Eat
Pukinsaari Camping *(☎ 221 1484; Salavägen 32; tent sites €12, cabins €32-55; open June-Sept)* is a pleasant place at a small beach, 1.5km southwest of the town centre. There are bicycles for rent.

Alma Hostel *(☎ 221 3455; Högåsen; singles/doubles/triples €30/43/60; open June- Aug)* is a summer hostel across the river about 2km east of the centre. There's no reception – you can book and make inquiries at Cafe Alma, which also offers B&B accommodation in the town centre for €45/58.

Hotel Kristina *(☎ 221 2555, fax 221 3250; Stortorget 1; singles/doubles €54/74, weekends & summer €46/65)*, across the bridge from the town centre, offers comfortable accommodation with a nice view over the bay.

There is dancing and live music here in the evenings.

Fabulous **Cafe Alma** *(☎ 221 3455; Sjögatan; lunch soup & salad €5.50, full buffet €9)* on the waterfront has a bright atrium dining area at the front and a terrace. Dominating the interior is a sizeable scale model of the ship *Alma*. There's a fine buffet lunch from 11am to 5pm on weekends.

Corner Cafe *(lunch buffet €6)*, on the market square, has a relaxing garden terrace at the back.

Crazy Cat *(☎ 221 3100, Östralånggatan 53-55; lunch special €7.50)* is a small pizzeria just off the market square. As well as the lunch special there is the usual range of pizzas.

Getting There & Away
Kristinestad is on road No 662, 100km south of Vaasa. Buses between Pori and Vaasa stop at Kristinestad. There are two daily buses from Tampere (200km, five hours).

KASKINEN
☎ 06 • pop 1650
Kaskinen (Swedish: Kaskö) – mainland Finland's smallest town – is a relaxing and peaceful island village and a good place to break your journey. Finnish is spoken by the majority of people, many of whom work in the enormous pulp factory at the southern end of the town. This may be the only factory area in Finland that is actually larger than the town itself.

Although there's not a lot to see in Kaskinen, there's a very friendly hostel and opportunities for boating and fishing. Naturally there's a **local museum** *(Raatihuoneenkatu 48)*, as well as a small **fishing museum** at the northern end of the island, at the Kalaranta boat dock. The 18th-century **Bladh House**, on Kaskinen Sound, is a restored burgher house and the most important building in Kaskinen.

Two bridges connect the island town to the mainland. There's a small tourist office down at the harbour, and a post office, supermarket, library and pharmacy on the market square. Raatihuoneenkatu is the main road, and runs north–south.

Places to Stay & Eat
Marianranta Camping *(☎ 220 7311; tent sites €10, cabins €20-27; open June-Aug)* is small, but is by the seaside at the northeastern tip of the island. There are a few cottages.

Björnträ Vandrarhem (☎/fax 222 7007; Raatihuoneenkatu 22; rooms per person €18-23; open June–mid-Aug or by prior arrangement) is a very friendly HI-affiliated hostel with six rooms almost of hotel standard. It's run by a very helpful and hospitable Swedish-speaking couple. Guests have use of a well-equipped kitchen and TV room.

Hotel Kaskinen (☎ 222 7771; Raatihuoneenkatu 41; singles/doubles €61/78), the only hotel in the village, is a comfy, if slightly overpriced, place opposite the kauppatori.

Cafe Kung Gustav, on the market square, does triple duty as the town's only café-pub-restaurant, although there's also a restaurant at Hotel Kaskinen.

NÄRPES
☎ 06 • pop 1000

Närpes (Finnish: Närpiö), 85km southwest of Vaasa, is the tomato basket of Finland. It has one of the highest ratios of Swedish to Finnish speakers in the country – 93% speak Swedish as their native language, with a local accent that is hard to understand.

Some 150 *kyrkstallar*, or 'church stables' (though they were designed for the use of people not horses), surround the medieval **Närpes Church**. This is the only place in Finland where these temporary shelters have been preserved. In the past, people from outlying districts used these to stay overnight when visiting the church. The interior of the church is richly decorated.

Öjskogsparken, just down the road from the church, includes a pharmacy museum, a dozen old wooden houses and a 'country store' with goods more than 100 years old.

North of Vaasa

NYKARLEBY
☎ 06 • pop 7650

Nykarleby (Finnish: Uusikaarlepyy) is a small town 20km south of Jakobstad where 91% of the population speak Swedish, making it one of the most Swedish of all mainland Finnish towns.

The town was founded in 1620, the same year as Karleby (Kokkola); despite the identical founding dates, this place got the name Nykarleby which means 'new Kokkola'. Today Nykarleby is a peaceful riverside town and it makes a pleasant stop on the road

between Vaasa and Jakobstad or Kokkola – if nothing else you should try the local waffles.

In summer, you can get tourist information and town maps from the Cafe Kyrktuppen.

The yellow **Nykarleby Church** (open 9am-6pm daily in summer) on the riverside was built in 1708. Its walls, pulpit and ceiling are covered with 18th-century paintings. **Nykarleby Museum**, to the north along the main street, has plenty of local flavour. It features bric-a-brac, old costumes and furniture.

Cafe Kyrktuppen is a pleasant little café specialising in the local *våfflor* (waffles) with cream and strawberry jam. **Brostugan**, across the river opposite the church, is also worth a waffle stop.

JAKOBSTAD
☎ 06 • pop 20,000

Although the international ferries have ceased, the pretty town of Jakobstad (Finnish: Pietarsaari) is distinctively Swedish (55% of the population speak Swedish), and the most interesting place to stop and sample the curious world of *Parallelsverige* ('Parallel Sweden'). There is a well-preserved historic Old Town filled with 18th- and 19th-century wooden houses, some off-beat museums and easy access to some interesting coastal area. As charming as this harbour town may be, it has a history of industry and the nearby pulp factory exudes that familiar bad smell.

Jakobstad was founded in 1652 by Ebba Brahe, wife of war hero Jacob de la Gardie. The surrounding region, Pedersöre, gave the town its Finnish name, which translates as Peter's Island. Russians sacked Jakobstad twice in 1714; despite the repeated drubbings, it became the leading shipping town in Finland during the 18th century. Later, in 1844, Finland's first round-the-world sailing expedition started from Jakobstad harbour.

Information
The **tourist office** (☎ 723 1796; ⓦ www .jakobstad.fi; Kauppiaankatu 12; open 8am-6pm Mon-Fri, 9am-3pm Sat, shorter hours in winter) is just off the kauppatori.

The **public library** (2nd floor, Rådhusgatan 3; open 11am-7pm Mon-Thur, 11am-4pm Fri in summer, 11am-8pm Mon-Fri rest of the year) has an Internet terminal but a better bet is the four free terminals at **After Eight**, a café and youth drop-in centre on Storgatan.

POHJANMAA

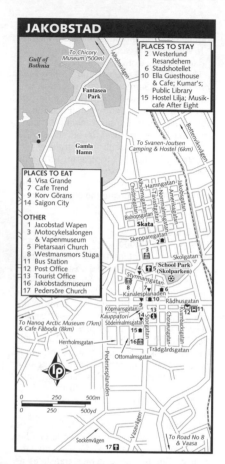

JAKOBSTAD

PLACES TO STAY
2　Westerlund Resandehem
6　Stadshotellet
10　Ella Guesthouse & Cafe; Kumar's; Public Library
15　Hostel Lilja; Musik-cafe After Eight

PLACES TO EAT
4　Visa Grande
7　Cafe Trend
9　Korv Görans
14　Saigon City

OTHER
1　Jacobstad Wapen
3　Motocykelsalongen & Vapenmuseum
5　Pietarsaari Church
8　Westmansmors Stuga
11　Bus Station
12　Post Office
13　Tourist Office
16　Jakobstadsmuseum
17　Pedersöre Church

Jacobstad Wapen

In Gamla Hamn (the old harbour area) is the pride of Jakobstad, the **Jacobstad Wapen** (adult/child €4/2; open when in dock daily mid-May–late Aug), modelled after a 17th-century galleon. There's a small museum explaining the history of the ship and the building of the replica, which was started in 1987 from original drawings dating back to 1758. Public sailings on the *Jacobstad Wapen* are given only a couple of times a year; inquire at the tourist office.

Skata

The Old Town section of Jakobstad has around 300 wooden houses that have been beautifully preserved. Most of them were built in the 19th century and were occupied by sailors and workers; the 18th-century houses along Hamngatan are the oldest in town.

Museums

Jakobstad has a truly eclectic collection of small private museums, some of the quirkiest in Finland.

Motocykelsalongen (Motorcycle Salon; ☎ 724 3262; Alholmsgatan 8; adult/child €4/2; open noon-5pm Mon-Fri, noon-4pm Sat & Sun May-Sept), in the city hall complex, is a private museum with a fascinating collection of over 120 motorcycles – from old Harley Davidsons and Nortons to homemade, motor-powered bicycles. Some of the bikes date back to the early 1900s and there's one motorcycle built entirely by the museum's collector in 1920.

In the same group of buildings, **Vapenmuseum** (Weapons Museum; ☎ 723 2974; Alholmsgatan 8; adult/child €4/2; open noon-5pm Mon-Fri, noon-4pm Sat & Sun May-Sept) is the small private collection of Jakobstad resident Bengt Ena. There are more than 300 old guns, hunting rifles, machine guns and military pistols dating back to the 1740s.

Jakobstadsmuseum (☎ 758 1111; Storgatan 2; admission €2; open noon-4pm daily) includes the old main building (Malmska Gården, dating back to 1904) with local-history displays on the shipping industry and town itself, as well as several historic houses scattered around the town centre. They include **Westmansmors Stuga** (Mother Westman's Cottage; Visasbacken 4; open on request), which was once a private school attended by Finland's national poet JL Runeberg in the early 19th century.

Chicory Museum (☎ 0204-161 113; Alholma; admission free; open noon-4pm Tues-Sat June-Aug, noon-6pm July) is in the old chicory factory, founded in 1883 and preserved pretty much as it was when it closed in 1960. It was built by local entrepreneur Wilhelm Schauman who saw the market for making chicory into an additive for coffee, which at the time was an expensive commodity. The machinery for roasting, grinding and hardening the chicory root is still in place along with old photographs and other factory hardware. It's free to visit the old factory and it includes an interesting guided tour.

POHJANMAA

Fantasea Park

This amusement park (☎ 365 9272; admission €2.50; open 11am-6pm daily June–mid-Aug) at Gamla Hamn has water slides, arcade games, pools and a good swimming beach.

Pedersöre Church

Pedersöre Church (Vasavägen 118) was originally built in the 1400s, but the bell tower dates from the 1760s. During the reign of King Gustav III the church was greatly enlarged to become a cross-shaped structure. Thankfully, the architect thumbed his nose at the king's plan to demolish the 85m spire.

Places to Stay

Camping About 6km north of town in Nissasörn, **Svanen-Joutsen Camping** (☎ 723 0660; Luodontie 50; tent sites €14, 2-person cabins €22-28, 4-person cabins €38-65; open mid-May–late Aug) is a family camping ground (take a bus from the city bus station). You can hire bikes, boats and canoes.

Hostels At the camping ground, **Svanen-Joutsen Hostel** (Luodontie 50; doubles per person €10.50; reception open 9am-10pm daily in summer) is HI-affiliated and offers cheap beds in basic twin cabins. It has a kitchen, sauna and laundry.

Hostel Lilja (☎ 786 6500; Storgatan 6; shared room per person €22.50, singles/doubles €40/45) is a stylish new HI hostel attached to **Musikcafe After Eight** in the town centre. Although part of a historic building, the rooms and facilities are brand new.

Guesthouses & Hotels Run by a friendly Swedish-speaking family, **Westerlund Resandehem** (☎ 723 0440; Norrmalmsgatan 8; singles/doubles €27/43) is a charming B&B in the heart of old Jakobstad. Spotless rooms all have shared bathroom, but it's only a small place so book ahead.

Ella Guesthouse (☎ 723 5049; Rådhusgatan 3; singles/doubles €30/46) is above the lunchtime café of the same name – call or book before 2pm when the café closes. Rooms are simple but good value.

On the main pedestrian street, **Stadshotellet** (☎ 788 8111; fax 788 8222; [e] stadshotellet@multi.fi; Kanalesplanaden 13; singles/doubles €87/105, summer €75/90) is Jakobstad's top hotel, with comfortable rooms, two restaurants and a nightclub.

Places to Eat

Korv Görans (Kanalesplanaden), on the pedestrian mall, is a busy little pizza, fried food and kebab kiosk that has been in business more than 25 years and is a Jakobstad institution. Most options are under €5.

Cafe Trend, also on the pedestrian mall, lives up to its name – Jakobstad's beautiful people crowd the terrace or read magazines over coffee inside.

Ella Cafe (☎ 723 5049, Rådhusgatan 3; buffet lunch €6; open 11am-2pm) is a 3rd-floor lunch restaurant with a typically generous Finnish buffet of hot and cold meats, soups and salads.

Saigon City (Storgatan 8; lunch specials from €6) is an appealing and authentic Asian restaurant – possibly the only one in the world to offer wok-fried fillet of reindeer! Lunch specials are served from 11am to 3pm weekdays.

Visa Grande (☎ 723 4150; Storgatan 20; pizza & pasta buffet €7-9; open Mon-Sat) is an authentic Italian place with an excellent-value pizza and pasta buffet as well as an à la carte menu.

Kumar's (☎ 723 7559, Storgatan 11; mains €6-12), near Ella, is an interesting restaurant combining Indian and Asian flavours with pizzas and sandwiches. It's reasonably priced and popular with locals.

Getting There & Away

There are regular buses to Jakobstad from Vaasa (€12.40), Kalajoki (€14.60) and other towns along the west coast.

Bennäs (Finnish: Pännäinen), 11km away, is the closest railway station to Jakobstad. A shuttle bus meets arriving trains.

AROUND JAKOBSTAD
Fäboda

About 8km west of Jakobstad, Fäboda is a small recreational area facing the Gulf of Bothnia. There are small lovely, sandy beaches, rocky inlets and forest walks, and this is a favourite spot for swimming, surfing and windsurfing. It's an easy cycle out to Fäboda along a narrow country road.

Nanoq Arctic Museum (☎ 729 3679; Pörkenäsintie 60; adult/child €6/3.50; open noon-6pm daily June-Aug) is 7km west of Jakobstad in the village of Fäboda. While the concept might seem incongruous here (the Arctic Circle is, after all, several hundred

POHJANMAA

kilometres to the north), this little museum is surprisingly good, and worth a detour. Housed in a model of a Greenlandic peat house, the collection is the private achievement of Pentti Kronqvist who has made several expeditions to the Arctic. There are Eskimo tools, fossils, authentic Arctic huts from Greenland and elsewhere, and various other Arctic souvenirs.

Cafe Fäboda (☎ 729 3510; mains €11-17; open 10am-11pm daily May-Aug), near the beach, is a wonderful café and restaurant and worth the trip. There's a generous lunch buffet, and international menu, sunny summer deck and children's playground. In the evenings the bar is popular and there's often entertainment in summer.

KOKKOLA
☎ 06 • pop 35,500
When seen from the train station, Kokkola (Swedish: Karleby) looks uninspiring, with box-like supermarkets, factories and a busy highway obscuring the pleasant Old Town and riverside parks hidden behind. Although the central part of the town is pretty enough, there's not a lot to see in Kokkola and not a lot of reason to stop here if you're in a hurry – it's primarily a transportation hub.

In 1620, the village of Kokkola was founded as Karleby as an essential west-coast port for the tar trade, which flourished in the 17th century. Today only a few people speak Swedish.

Orientation & Information
The train station is south of the centre on Rantakatu, the main street, while most places of interest are within walking distance of the riverside kauppatori, at the intersection of Rantakatu and Torikatu.

The **tourist office** (☎ 828 9402; w www .kokkola.fi; Kauppatori; open 8am-5pm Mon-Fri, 9am-1pm Sat June-Aug, shorter hours in winter) is on the northern side of the square. There is an Internet terminal at the **public library** (Isokatu 2), one block north of the train station, plus **Net Cafe** at Pitkänsillankatu 33.

Things to See
Neristanis is the Old Town district, hemmed in by the more modern parts of town. The most colourful streets are Itäinen Kirkkokatu, Läntinen Kirkkokatu and Isokatu, and at least one old house is open to the public. Pick up a walking-tour brochure from the tourist office, which also has information on the town's historical attractions. In the area are several museums that come under the umbrella of the **Renlund Museum** (adult/child €3.40/1.60; open Tues-Sun): they include the **Historical Museum** (Pitkänsillankatu 28), the **Renlund Art Gallery** (Pitkänsillankatu 39), and the **Camera Museum** (Pitkänsillankatu 26).

The **riverfront** area through town is nice for strolling.

Places to Stay & Eat
Camping Suntinsuu (☎ 831 4006; w www .kokkolacamping.com; Pikiruukki; camping per person/tent site €5.50/12, cabins €31.50-38.50, self-contained cottages €44-68; open June–late Aug) is a pleasant riverside camping ground about 2km northwest of the centre. At the same place is **Tankkari** (dorm beds €18, singles/doubles €28/32), an HI hostel.

Sokos Hotel Kaarle (☎ 826 2111, fax 826 6490; Kauppatori 4; singles/doubles €110/132, doubles weekends & summer €75) is one of a number of big hotels in the centre. It has a couple of restaurants and a popular night-club. Breakfast and sauna are included in the room rates.

Wanha Lyhty & Kellari (☎ 868 0188; Pitkänsillankatu 24; mains €10-20) is a café, restaurant and beer cellar cheerfully decorated in the spirit of the Old Town. The beer cellar offers live music on weekends.

Cafe Kahvipuu (Isokatu 11), around the corner from Wanha Lyhty, is a lovely little café with home-made pastries, strong cappuccino and a summer terrace.

The deck of the **Sientin Krunni**, an old Danish fishing boat now aground in the kauppatori, is a great place for a drink, overlooking the river and square.

Getting There & Away
The Kronoby airport is 22km southeast of Kokkola and served by a regional bus service. There are several flights a day to/from Helsinki.

Regular buses run to/from all coastal towns, especially Vaasa (€17.50) and Jakobstad (€5.10). The bus station is one block west of the train station.

There is a major train station in Kokkola and all trains using the main western line stop here. The daytime journey from Helsinki takes less than five hours.

If you're driving to or from Jakobstad, a scenic (and quicker) alternative to the main highway is to take road No 749, which crosses the island of Luoto.

KALAJOKI
☎ 08 • pop 10,000

Most Finns know Kalajoki for its long, sandy beaches. Over the years, as package charter flights to Spain have become cheaper than a holiday in Kalajoki, the region has sought new ways to attract Finnish tourists. As a result Kalajoki is again one of Finland's fastest-growing resort regions, with a building boom of summer cottages and many services for tourists, including a huge spa and amusement park, resort-style hotels, and a new 18-hole golf course. Essentially all this adds up to a family holiday place for Finns; travellers may be more interested in a side trip to the rocky, windswept islets of Maakalla and Ulkokalla nearby.

Things don't close down completely in winter – there are plenty of cross-country skiing trails and many of the cottages are available for rent.

Orientation & Information
The bus terminal, supermarkets, banks, a post office and a large travel and booking agency are all in Kalajoki village, on the banks of the Kalajoki just off the highway. The resort area, with the beach and most of the accommodation, is 6km south of the village along Hwy 8.

The **tourist office** (☎ 460 505; open 11am-6pm daily in summer, 10am-4pm Mon-Fri in winter) is the small white building on the highway at the turn-off to the beach.

Things to See
About 1km north of Kalajoki village, the Plassi area has 17th-century wooden houses and a small **fishing museum** (☎ 460 505; Kalastusmuseo; admission free; open Tues-Sun in summer).

Kalajoki Särkät (Kalajoki Beach) is one of the country's most popular holiday spots for Finns. It has a lot to offer: **Jukujukumaa Amusement Park** (admission €10), spa, golf course, holiday villas, beaches, restaurants and cafés, hotels and discos. It's billed as a 'Mediterranean-style holiday experience at a latitude of 64°', but it's all very Finnish – saunas, summer cottages and humppa music.

Places to Stay & Eat
The beach, 6km south of the village, is the place to look for accommodation. Dozens of sturdy summer cottages dot the forest behind the beach. Something basic costs €35 to €50 a night for two to four people, while a self-contained cottage is around €150 for up to eight to 10 people. The best place to book is through the **Kamusenliikenne** travel agency (w www.kamusenliikenne.fi) in Kalajoki.

Camping Hiekkasärkät (☎ 469 2400; e markkinointi@hiekkasarkat.fi; tent sites €15, cabins €30-85; open mid-May–late Aug) is a huge and very busy place fronting the beach and adjacent to the amusement park.

Hostel Kalajoki (☎ 4639 421; Opintie 2; 2-bed rooms €15 per person, weekends €30) is a summer hostel close to the township, with kitchens and shared bathrooms.

Tapion Tupa (☎ 466 622, fax 466 699; Hiekasarkat; singles/doubles/triples €19/36/54, apartment doubles from €104), near the main road and close to the beach, has a range of accommodation including an HI-associated hostel, log cabins and self-contained holiday apartments.

Hotelli Rantakalla (☎ 466 642, fax 466 617; singles/doubles €74/103) is one of many hotels at the beach. Rates drop considerably outside the summer high season.

Ravintola Lokkilinna has a fine summer terrace overlooking the beach, a big lunch buffet for €9 and a casual bar-restaurant with ocean views.

Getting There & Away
There are several buses a day from Oulu, Raahe, Kokkola and other coastal places to Kalajoki and the beach. The easiest way to reach Kalajoki by train is to get off at Kokkola and catch a bus from there.

AROUND KALAJOKI
Maakalla & Ulkokalla Islets
An isolated islet that has only existed since the 15th century, Maakalla has retained a genuine fishing-village feel. There are no roads, shops or electricity – in fact, there are no permanent humans – but you will find an interesting wooden **church**, abundant plant and birdlife and some old **fishing huts**. The owners of the huts gather regularly and vote to keep the islet exactly as it is.

For the most isolated accommodation in Finland, ask the boat operator about cottages on the island of Ulkokalla, a rocky islet 5km west of Maakalla. There is no electricity, and fresh water for the sauna stove is brought from the mainland! There are rooms in the lighthouse-keepers cottage for €20 to €25.

From mid-June to August there are three-hour cruises (adult/child €14/7 return) to Maakalla from the pier at Kalajoki. To get to Ulkokalla you'll need to charter a boat (☎ 0400-382 652).

Central Pohjanmaa

What's Central Pohjanmaa? It's flat – as flat as can be. Farmer's fields stretch as far as the eye can see, some splashed with bright yellow canola (rapeseed) and each one dotted with dozens and dozens of grey or rust-red, weathered hay barns.

It's an unlikely area for travellers – but if you find yourself passing through, pause to enjoy some of its subtle delights. The undisputed capital of the area is Seinäjoki, only really worth a visit during the Tango Fair in mid-July or the Provinssrock Festival in mid-June. Kaustinen is a town to pencil in on your summer itinerary for its outstanding Kaustinen Folk Music Festival in July.

SEINÄJOKI
☎ 06 • pop 29,000
Seinäjoki, the commercial centre of the region, is a train junction for travellers. However, it hosts two of Finland's major summer festivals – the Tango Fair and Provinssrock Festival, perhaps as far apart in the music spectrum as you can get. The town is also known for its modern centre designed by Alvar Aalto, and there's a large open-air museum area at the southern edge of town.

Information
The **tourist office** (☎ 420 9090, fax 420 9092; [e] matkailu@epmatkailu.fi; open 9am-5pm Mon-Fri) is in the bus and train station complex. This is the regional tourist office and, although short on English-language literature, the staff are very helpful. This is the place to book accommodation in private homes during the festivals.

The **public library** (Koulukatu 21; open 10am-7pm Mon-Fri, 11am-3pm Sat) has three Internet terminals, and **Du:ni** café also has a couple of terminals.

Aalto Centre
The monumental Aalto Centre (1960) is one of the most important works of architect Alvar Aalto, who was born in nearby Kuortane in 1898. It's a must-see for students of modern architecture but a likely miss for most travellers. The complex's stark white buildings include the **Lakeuden Risti Church**, **town hall** and **public library**. The massive **church** (open noon-6pm daily), with its oddly secular steeple-clock tower, is the most recognisable building. Take a lift to the top (€1) for a view of the region.

Etälä-Pohjanmaan Maakuntamuseo
South Pohjanmaa Provincial Museum (☎ 416 2642, fax 416 2646; adult/child €2/1; open noon-6pm Tues-Fri & Sun, noon-4pm Sat mid-May–Aug) is an open-air museum in the leafy suburb of Törnävä, 7km south of town. The wealthy Wasastjerna family first settled this area in 1806 and built a mansion, Törnävä, that still stands. Elsewhere on the grounds, a large number of old wooden buildings, including some that have been transferred from elsewhere, constitute an open-air museum.

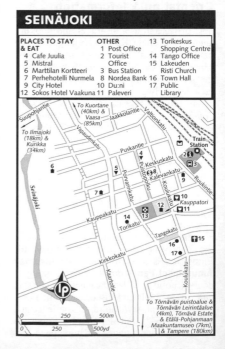

SEINÄJOKI

PLACES TO STAY & EAT	OTHER	
4 Cafe Juulia	1 Post Office	13 Torikeskus Shopping Centre
5 Mistral	2 Tourist Office	14 Tango Office
6 Marttilan Kortteeri	3 Bus Station	15 Lakeuden Risti Church
7 Perhehotelli Nurmela	8 Nordea Bank	16 Town Hall
9 City Hotel	10 Du:ni	17 Public Library
12 Sokos Hotel Vaakuna	11 Paleveri	

On your right, when coming from the town centre, is the **Agriculture Museum** and the **Mill Museum**. On your left in the old yellow building is the **Gunpowder Museum**. Behind is a smoke house and a smith's house from the 17th century.

Local bus No 1 runs from Seinäjoki bus station to Törnävä.

Special Events

Seinäjoki's two major summer festivals attract very different crowds, but both are enormously popular, so book accommodation in advance.

Provinssirock (W *www.provinssirock.fi*) is a classic, open-air international rock concert held mainly at Törnävän puistoalue (Törnävä park area), 4km south of town, over three days in mid-June. Day passes cost €35 to €45, a three-day pass is €70. International names over the years have included Black Sabbath, Garbage, Manic Street Preachers, Limp Bizkit, Prodigy, The Cure, Iggy Pop, Moby, Lou Reed and The Ramones, along with plenty of established and up-and-coming Finnish bands.

Tangomarkkinat (W *www.tangomarkkit.fi*) appeals to a generally older and almost exclusively Finnish crowd but, in terms of audience, it's one of Finland's biggest festivals. It opens with a huge open-air dance and party in 'Tango Street' and continues over four days with dance competitions, tango classes, and other festivities, culminating with the awarding of the 'Tango King & Queen'. The competition here is not to find the best dancer, though, but the best tango singer – the performers to which the people dance.

Places to Stay & Eat

Törnävän Leirintäalue (☎ 412 0784; Törnäväntie 29; tent sites €10, cabins €30-75; open June-Aug) is south of the centre towards Törnävä. A temporary camping area is set up near the festival site during Provinssirock. To pitch a tent costs €6 per person for the weekend.

Marttilan Kortteeri (☎ 420 4800; Puskantie 38; shared room per person €21, singles/doubles €42/60; open June–early Aug) is an HI-affiliated summer hostel with two- and three-bed rooms. Rates include linen and breakfast, and there's a good café. You'll need to book well ahead during the festivals but at other times it's virtually empty.

Perhehotelli Nurmela (☎ 414 1771; Kalevankatu 29; singles/doubles from €35/55) is a cosy, family-run guesthouse west of the centre. Some rooms have private bathroom, others are shared; all rates include breakfast.

City Hotel (☎ 215 9111; e cityhotel@bw-cityhotel.net; Kalevankatu 2; singles/doubles €79/96, weekends & summer €62/72) is a comfortable place opposite the bus station. There's a good restaurant and café here.

Sokos Hotel Vaakuna (☎ 419 3111, fax 419 3112; Kauppatori 3; singles/doubles €110/138; weekends & summer €78) is one of two big business hotels in Seinäjoki.

There are plenty of fast-food places in and around the **Torikeskus Shopping Centre** on the kauppatori. **Cafe Juulia** (Puistopolku 15) is a reliable little lunch place that has home-cooked specials from €7.

Mistral (☎ 419 3111, Keskuskatu 1; mains €9-25) is the fanciest restaurant in Seinäjoki. It specialises in Finnish and Mediterranean

---

Tango

Seinäjoki is the undisputed tango capital of a country that is certifiably tango-mad. In the rest of the world the tango craze was swept away by Elvis, but in Finland it never died.

The world's first tango was danced in the suburbs of Buenos Aires towards the end of the 1900s. Argentinean musicians and dancers brought tango to Europe around 1910. A Finnish version of tango developed soon after, championed by the composer Unto Mononen and Olavi Virta, the Finnish king of tango dancing.

No other music could epitomise the melancholic Finn better than this Argentinean music. If Finns lack the electrifying tension that Latin Americans bring to the tango, they lack none of the enthusiasm. Finnish tango music is usually performed with a live band and the lyrics deal with loneliness, unrequited love and desperation. The best place and time to dance is during the *Tangomarkkinat* festival held in Seinäjoki every July. However, many younger Finns might disagree about tango being the thing; they would rather stick to *rokki* or *jatsi* or *tekno* or whatever the latest dance craze may be.

POHJANMAA

cuisine and has attractive inside and outside dining areas.

Du:ni *(cnr Kauppakatu & Koulukatu)* is a loungy café-bar with a great terrace, free Internet access and a popular club downstairs. A block away, **Palervi** is another popular bar and Provinssrock venue.

Getting There & Away

There are buses to towns and villages throughout western Finland, and frequent service to points such as Vaasa (€10.40), Jyväskylä (€19.20), Tampere (€17), Turku (€29.10) and Helsinki (€29.10).

Seinäjoki is the rail hub of Pohjanmaa. The fastest intercity trains from Helsinki cover the 346km in just over three hours (€38.40).

AROUND SEINÄJOKI
Kurikka

Kurikka, 34km southwest of Seinäjoki, is a great place to learn something about Pohjanmaa's traditions. The **museum** *(admission €1; open Sun-Fri June-Aug)* has good coverage of local traditions, including a collection of *kurikka* tools, items used to dry clothes. Samuli Paulaharju, an important 'cultural explorer', was born in Kurikka in 1875 and there's a room devoted to his travels.

Kuortane

The town of Kuortane was the birthplace of architect Alvar Aalto in 1896. Although his childhood home still exists, it is privately owned and not open to visitors.

Kuortane Church is exceptionally beautiful and dates back to 1777. The yellow bell tower is equally attractive, and there's an old longboat nearby. Kuortane is surrounded by a wealthy farming region with several examples of the typical *kaksifooninkinen* farmhouse (literally 'one house with two floors').

KAUSTINEN
☎ 06 • pop 4500

Kaustinen is a small inland village 47km southeast of Kokkola. There isn't much to see in the village itself, so plan your visit around the superb Kaustinen Folk Music Festival in July. Such is the renown of this festival, the Peanuts cartoon character 'Woodstock' is called 'Kaustinen' in the Finnish translation.

The small **tourist information office** *(Kaustintie 1)* is easy to find in the centre. Nearby is the festival office, which handles accommodation during the event. The bus station, shops and services are all easily reached on foot.

Folk Music Instrument Museum *(admission €1; open 10am-7pm daily in summer)* at the festival area has a small but interesting display. **Pauanne** is an off-beat centre that combines shamanism, handicrafts and much more. There's a popular smoke sauna here. Pauanne is on a small hill about 3km from the centre of Kaustinen.

Special Events

The **Kaustinen Folk Music Festival** *(☎ 860 4111, fax 860 4222; ⓦ www.kaustinen.net; PL 11, 69601 Kaustinen)* is one of the most beloved of summer festivals in Finland, attracting huge crowds. It's *the* place to be if you're interested in Finnish folk music and dance, since some 300 Finnish bands (and many international acts) perform more than 250 concerts during the week in mid-July. At any time between 10am and 3am there are several official concerts and half a dozen impromptu jam sessions going on. Folk dance performances are also an integral part of the festival, with everything from Celtic and Latin dancing alongside Finnish dance. Daily festival passes cost €12 to €20. For more details visit the website or contact the festival office.

Places to Stay

The festival office organises accommodation during the busy periods. Camping and dormitory beds cost around €10, accommodation in private homes is around €25 per person. Call ahead to see what's available.

Koskelan Lomatalo *(☎ 861 1338; Känsäläntie 123; beds per person €25-50; open year-round)*, an HI-affiliated place about 5km north of Kaustinen, offers kitchen, sauna and laundry facilities.

Getting There & Away

There are several buses daily from Kokkola, which has a railway station. There are express buses from other cities during the festival season.

Oulu, Kainuu & Koillismaa

Oulu Province

Wedged between the Lakeland and Lapland, the central strip of Finland is a transitional region comprising the province of Oulu to the west, the wilderness area of Kainuu to the east, and Koillismaa in the northeast. Administratively, the entire region is called Oulu Province.

Finns entered the Kainuu region in the 16th century, violating the earlier border treaty between Sweden and Russia. In the late 16th century, the region witnessed fierce frontier wars between Russians and citizens of the Swedish Empire. After these bloody wars, Swedish territory was pushed further east, to where the border stands today.

By the 19th century tar had become the salvation of the economically depressed Kainuu region, but most of the profits were sent downriver to Oulu, along with the barrels of tar. During WWII, bloody battles were fought against the Red Army in the area around Kuhmo, and soon after the war a flood of emigrants escaped poverty-stricken Kainuu for Sweden and elsewhere. The region has only recently recovered from this exodus but remains sparsely populated.

Kainuu is a heavily forested wilderness area traversed by the famed UKK trekking route close to the border with Russia.

Koillismaa, near the Russian border, is the transitional region between the south and Lapland, and includes the rugged Kuusamo area and Oulanko National Park – one of the natural highlights of Finland. It is an area of tumbling rivers, isolated lakes and dense forests. Fells and wandering reindeer herds make this the most Lappish area of Oulu Province. This is also where northern and southern fauna meet, and there are more species to be found here than almost anywhere else in the country. Add to this the fierce local pride, abundance of summer and winter activities and excellent services and you have an interesting – if sometimes forgotten – pocket of Finland.

Oulu, surrounded by a flat region with many historical attractions, is the undisputed provincial capital, and a natural stopover on the way north.

Highlights

- Cycling on Oulu's bike paths, then enjoying the energetic nightlife in the city's cafés and bars
- Bird-watching in Liminka Bay during the 'great migration' of May, August and September
- Trekking the Karhunkierros (Bear's Ring) route in Oulanka National Park – some of the best wilderness scenery in Finland
- Fishing for salmon, trout and perch at Hossa, Finland's 'fisher's paradise'
- Rafting, sledding, trekking or skiing – in Kuusamo or Ruka, the adventure capital of the region
- Experiencing high culture in the middle of nowhere at Kuhmo's Chamber Music Festival

OULU
☎ 08 • pop 123,200

Oulu (Swedish: Uleåborg) is a lively, fast-growing and affluent university town, the largest city north of Tampere and the sixth biggest in Finland. The extraordinary number of outdoor bars, lively market and waterfront, and terrific network of bike paths, plus a generous dollop of off-beat festivals, make this an exciting, fun place to visit in summer. In June and July, it never gets dark in Oulu, even at midnight. In winter, Oulu is

OULU, KAINUU & KOILLISMAA

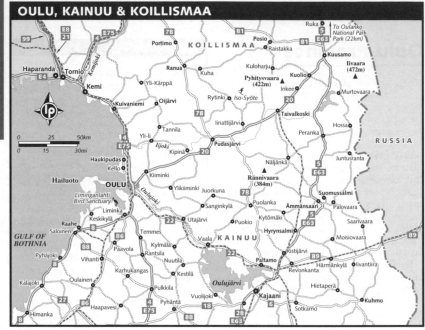

OULU, KAINUU & KOILLISMAA

a reasonably convenient base for downhill skiing at Iso-Syöte, and there's a big network of cross-country skiing tracks around town.

Locals will often point out to you that Oulu is the only town with 'a university built on a swamp, a theatre on the sea, a ship in the market place and a science centre in a factory'.

With the highly-regarded Oulu University and School of Technology turning out top-notch graduates, hi-tech companies such as Nokia were soon drawn to this northern capital.

In recent years a couple of corporate science and technology 'parks' have set up in Oulu, and with more than 10,000 people employed in this sector, you're almost as likely to run into expat IT workers here as in Helsinki. This being Finland, there's also a stinky pulp factory not too far from the city centre.

While Oulu lacks any 'must see' sights and suffers a dearth of budget accommodation, its summertime energy, cosmopolitan air and frenetic nightlife make it well worth a stop on the road north.

History

Oulu was founded by King Karl IX of Sweden in 1605. It wasn't long before industrious and hard-working Swedish pioneers descended upon the Kainuu forests in search of tar, which was floated in barrels to Oulu – the sticky stuff was essential to the building of unsinkable wooden ships. By the late 19th century Oulu boasted the largest fleet in Finland.

In 1822 Oulu burned to the ground, and was rebuilt, although very few old buildings now remain.

Orientation

Oulu is situated at the mouth of the Oulujoki, with bridges connecting the riverbanks and several islands. Although the entire city covers a very large area, you can easily walk from the train and bus stations to most places in the centre and the town centre is very compact.

The main street is Kirkkokatu, running north-south, with a pedestrian section called Rotuaari in the middle. Kauppurienkatu is also pedestrianised from Isokatu to the *kauppatori* (market square).

Information

The city **tourist office** (☎ 5584 1330; [W] www
.oulutourism.fi; Torikatu 10; open 9am-6pm
Mon-Fri, 10am-3pm Sat in summer, 9am-4pm
Mon-Fri rest of the year) publishes the useful
guide *Look at Oulu*.

The **main post office** (Hallituskatu 36; open
9am-8pm Mon-Fri) is near the train station.

The impressive **public library** (☎ 558 410;
Kaarlenväylä; open 10am-8pm Mon-Fri, 10am-
3pm Sat) is on the waterfront opposite the
Oulu Theatre. It has a few Internet terminals,
including three first-come-first-served, and a
reading room with foreign newspapers. There
are also two Internet terminals (€1 for 10
minutes; free to customers) at **Pint Netti
Baari**, a pub on the pedestrian Rotuaari.

There is a **pharmacy** at Kirkkokatu 23 and
is open from 9am to 9pm.

Kauppatori

Oulu has one of the liveliest market squares
in Finland, and its position at the waterfront
makes it all the more appealing. The square
is bordered by several old wooden storehouses that now serve as restaurants, bars
and craft shops selling woven pine baskets,
carved wooden cups and other typical Finnish souvenirs. Look for the squat *Toripol-
liisi* statue, a humorous representation of
the local police. At the southern end of the
square is the **kauppahalli** (covered market),
with fresh produce and food stalls.

Oulu Cathedral

The rather imposing 19th-century cathedral
(Kirkkokatu 36; open 11am-8pm daily June–
late Aug, noon-1pm daily Sept-May) has
Finland's oldest portrait (dating from 1611)
in its vestry. A much older church, built in
1777, stood here until the great fire of 1822.
This version was designed by the German
architect CL Engel.

Tietomaa Science Centre

The mammoth Tietomaa Science Centre
(☎ 5584 1340; [W] www.tietomaa.fi; adult/child
€10/8.50; open 10am-6pm daily Aug-June,
10am-8pm July), in an old factory building, is
Scandinavia's oldest and largest science museum; at any given time it's mobbed with
hundreds of school children bussed in from
all over Finland. Many of the exhibits are in
Finnish only (as is the Omnimax film), but
it's one of those places you can poke around

for half a day, and the interactive exhibits are
good for kids. As well as the UFO exhibit,
hologram hall, junior science centre, 'world
of sport', weather exhibition and display of
the workings of the human body, you can
take a lift to the top of the tower for a view
over Oulu.

Taidemuseo

The Taidemuseo (Oulu Art Museum; ☎ 5584
7450; Kasarmintie 7; adult/child €3/1, free Fri;
open 11am-6pm Tues & Thur-Sun, 11am-8pm
Wed) is a bright gallery opposite Tietomaa.
It has intriguing temporary exhibitions of
both international and Finnish contemporary
art, as well as a good permanent collection.

Merimiehen Kotimuseo

The small Sailor's Home Museum (☎ 5584
7185; Pikisaarentie 6; admission €1; open
10am-6pm Mon-Thur, 11am-5pm Sat & Sun
June-Aug) on Pikisaari island formerly belonged to a local sailor. Built in 1737, it is
the oldest house in Oulu and was transferred
here from the town centre in 1983.

Ainola Provincial Museum

The small provincial museum (adult/child
€1.60/0.50; open 8am-4pm Mon-Thur, 11am-
5pm Sat & Sun June-Aug), in Ainola Park on
Hupisaaret island, has displays dealing with
everything from old Finnish coins to Sami
culture – but unfortunately there are no English translations.

Oulunlinna

There's not much left of Oulu Castle, although you can clearly see the remaining
fort-like structure from the main road, dominating the small park near the bridge. The
observation tower of the castle, rebuilt in
1873, now houses a café, but you can go
below and look in the cellar, which has a
small interpretive display. The original castle was built in 1590 as a base for the
Swedish army moving east towards Russia.
The whole thing blew up in 1793 when a
lightning strike hit a powder magazine.

Turkansaari Open-Air Museum

In summer you can take a boat out to
the folksy Turkansaari Open-Air Museum
(☎ 5586 7191; admission €2.50; open 11am-
8pm daily June–late Aug, 11am-5pm daily
early–mid-Sept) on Turkansaari island, 13km

southeast of the city. Originally the island was a trading post for Russians and Swedes and many of the old buildings remain. There are regular displays of tar-burning, log-rolling and folk music and dancing. The MS *Sympaatti* departs from Värtto Pier in Oulu from Tuesday to Sunday at noon (€17 return) from June to August. Otherwise take bus No 3 or 4, or drive or cycle along road No 22 east in the direction of Muho.

Automuseo

The collection at the Atomise *(Car Museum; ☎ 552 1600, Automuseontie 1; adult/child €4/2.50; open 9am-6pm Mon-Fri & Sun, 9am-3pm Sat June-Sept; 9am-4pm daily other times)* includes more than 50 old vehicles, from a 1910 German Vomag to Cold War

East German cars. Most cars and motorcycles here are privately owned. It's on the Oulu–Kempele road, 5km south of Oulu.

Parks & Gardens

Oulu University Botanical Gardens *(Kaitovayla 5; open 8am-8pm daily year-round, greenhouses open 8am-3pm Tues-Fri, 11am-3pm Sat & Sun)*, in Lineman north of the centre, are pleasantly landscaped with thousands of exotic plants – including hardy 5m-tall cacti. A pair of greenhouses, named Romeo and Juliet, house tropical species.

Just north of the town centre and connected by small bridges, **Hupisaaret Island** is a pleasant city park with bike paths, greenhouses, a summer café and the **Ainola Park**. It's a popular place for strolling in summer.

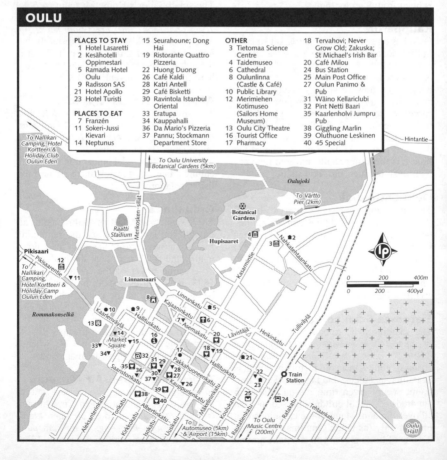

Cycling & Rollerblading

One of Oulu's best features is the extensive network of wonderful **bicycle paths** – routinely praised as the best local cycling routes in Finland. Nowhere is the Finns' love of two-wheeled transport more obvious than here in summer. Bike paths cross bridges, waterways and islands and can take you all the way out to surrounding villages. A good easy ride is from the kauppatori, across the bridge to Pikisaari and across another bridge to Nallikari where there's a good beach facing the Gulf of Bothnia.

Bikes can be hired from the train station, and bikes and rollerblades can be hired from shop 24 at the kauppatori. Nallikari Camping rents out bikes but only to guests. An excellent cycling route map is available (free) from the tourist office.

Organised Tours

The 'Potnapekka' – a tourist trolley – travels around Oulu's pedestrian streets and bike paths in summer, from Rotuaari pedestrian street to Hupisaaret island or Nallikari beach. The fare is €3.40/1.70 per adult/child to either, or €5/2.50 for both routes; departures are from Rotuaari every hour on the hour, daily from mid-June to mid-August.

From May to October the MS *Alexandra* (☎ 528 2190; 1½ hours adult/child €10/5; four hours adult & child €15) cruises the Oulu archipelago, with daily departures from the kauppatori. A smaller boat, MS *Happy Days* (adult/child €6/4.50) also has cruises out to Nallikari and Varjakka Manor from the market.

Special Events

In a country that wrote the book on oddball festivals, Oulu hosts more than its fair share. Take the **World Air Guitar Championships**, which is part of the **Oulu Music Video Festival** in late August. Contestants – with no musical ability required – from all over Finland and overseas take the stage to show what they can do with their imaginary instruments. The winner receives a real guitar.

There are two unusual winter events, both the largest of their kind anywhere in the world. The **Oulu Tar Ski Race**, held in early March, is a 70km skiing race (40km for women) that is entering its 113th year. The **Ice-Angling Marathon** is a 48-hour contest held on the open sea in early April (when the

ice is still quite thick) and draws more than 400 participants.

The biggest summer event is **Tar-Burning Week**, a festival that takes place in late June, around midsummer. **Elojazz & Blues** is a two-day music festival in early August.

Garlic Night is one of Oulu's strangest but most popular festivals. Held for one day and evening in mid-July, this event draws huge crowds to Rotuaari and the kauppatori. The focus is eating or tasting garlic – everything from garlic potatoes, pizzas and bread to garlic-flavoured beer and ice cream – all enhanced by festivities and live entertainment.

Places to Stay

Strangely enough for a provincial capital with reasonable tourist appeal, Oulu has no youth hostels and only one inexpensive summer hotel. Book ahead if you're staying in hotels on a weekday outside summer: because of the burgeoning technology industry in the town, business and conference travellers book out hotels months in advance.

Camping Oulu's saviour for budget travellers is **Nallikari Camping** (☎ 5586 1350; e nallikari.camping@ouka.fi; Hietasaari; tent sites €10/15.50 per person/family, 2-4-bed camping cabins €29, cottages from €58; open year-round), not only because you can pitch a tent or rent a cheap cabin, but because it's mercifully close to the city centre. It's on Hietasaari island, 5km northwest of the city centre – but only 2.5km by foot or bicycle via the pedestrian bridges. Nearby is the good Nallikari beach.

Hotels The cheapest rooms in Oulu are at **Kesähotelli Oppimestari** (☎ 884 8527, fax 884 8772; Nahkatehtaankatu 3; singles/doubles €35/50; open June–early Aug), across from the Tietomaa Science Centre. All rooms are nonsmoking and equipped with kitchenettes, and breakfast is included.

Hotel Kortteeri (☎ 550 9700, fax 550 9843; e uluotsi@pohto.fi; Vellamontie 12; doubles €57; open mid-June–mid-Aug) is a summer hotel in the Pohto college campus on Hietasaari island. Rooms are hotel-style (ie, no kitchen) with TV and a good buffet breakfast included, but there's no single discount.

Hotel Lasaretti (☎ 884 8300, fax 884 8301; Kasarmintie 13; singles/doubles €65/85; open June–mid-Aug), near Oppimestari, is Oulu's newest summer hotel and is a spotless, efficiently run place with modern, allergy-free rooms (no smoking and no carpets).

Directly opposite the train station, **Hotel Turisti** *(☎ 563 6100, fax 311 0755; Rautatienkatu 9; singles/doubles/triples €70/85/95)* is in a slightly seedy area but it's a surprisingly bright and tidy place with decent-sized rooms. Breakfast is included in the rates and there are some four- and five-bed rooms handy for groups.

Hotel Apollo *(☎/fax 52211, fax 372 060;* e *hotel@apollo.inet.fi; Asemakatu 31-33; singles/doubles from €78/100, weekends & summer €64/78)* is a small but reasonably stylish hotel with attractive summer rates. Rooms with private sauna cost €83/100 in summer. The hotel has a popular **karaoke bar** *(open until 4am daily)*.

Radisson SAS *(☎ 887 7666, fax 887 7888;* W *www.radisson.com/oulufi; Hallituskatu 1; standard/superior doubles €147/167, weekends & summer €83/92)* is the slickest business hotel in Oulu, ideally located near the riverfront and kauppatori. Rates include breakfast, pool and sauna, and there's a popular nightclub and restaurant here.

Ramada Hotel Oulu *(☎ 883 9111, fax 883 9100; Kirkkokatu 3; singles/doubles €120/145, weekends & summer doubles €79)* is slightly older but still a good choice, with a good location overlooking the cathedral. Some of the 154 rooms have private sauna and there's a nice atrium restaurant.

Holiday Club Oulun Eden *(☎ 550 4100, fax 554 4103;* W *www.holidayclub.fi; Nallikari; singles/doubles €115/128)* is a deluxe spa hotel on Hietasaari island, near Nallikari Camping and the beach. Discounts are available for longer stays, and there are various holiday packages. Accommodation prices include unlimited use of saunas, water slides and lushly landscaped indoor pools, plus you can call on the services of various massage and hydrotherapy treatments.

Places to Eat

Oulu is the most cosmopolitan city in western Finland, and offers a good variety of restaurants in all price ranges. The best and cheapest snacks and local specialities can be found in the lively **kauppatori** and the classic indoor **kauppahalli** on the southern side of the square. In summer there are stalls selling fresh salmon, paella and Oulu specialities,

such as *rieska* (flat bread), *leipäjuusto* (cheese bread), and *lohikeitto* (salmon soup).

Oulu's hungry student population means there are plenty of cheap kebab and pizza places (including no fewer than 11 branches of Koti Pizza!). The best pizzas are at **Da Mario's Pizzeria** *(Torikatu 24; pizzas €6)*, while some of the cheapest can be found at **Ristorante Quattro Pizzeria** *(Asemakatu 20)* where you can get pizza, salad and a drink for €5.

For grillis and fast-food restaurants, try Rotuaari (the pedestrian street) or the blocks surrounding the train station.

Cafés Oulu has some fine cafés and in summer tables clutter the pedestrian streets and market square. **Café Bisketti** *(Kirkkokatu 8)*, on the north–south section of Rotuaari, is a great spot for lunch. It has filled rolls, croissants, quiche and cakes (€2.50 to €5), and a small terrace facing the pedestrian square. Opposite Bisketti, **Katri Antell** *(Kirkkokatu 17)* has been an Oulu institution for a very long time; the first Katri Antell was founded in 1880. Come for its freshly baked pastries and cakes.

The hip young things of Oulu sip their green tea in the dazzling Nordic elegance of **Café Kaldi** *(Isokatu 25)*; it has great sweets as well.

Restaurants The area east of the train station has a number of cheap ethnic eateries, including Chinese, Italian and Turkish. **Huong Duong** *(☎ 311 3362; Asemakatu 26)* is a small Vietnamese place with inexpensive lunch specials from €5. Another good Vietnamese restaurant is **Dong Hai** *(Rantakatu 5)* near the market square.

Pannu *(☎ 815 1600; Kauppurienkatu 12; mains €6.50-19.50)*, in the basement of Stockmann, is an informal grill restaurant with a huge range of dishes including snails, ostrich and various steaks. It manages to blur the lines between informal, affordable dining and gourmet restaurant, and does it well.

Zakuska *(☎ 379 369; Hallituskatu 13)*, in the busy strip of bars and cafés, is a popular place for fine Russian cuisine.

Neptunus *(☎ 372 572; meals €13-30)*, at the kauppatori, is an old sailing ship, converted into a pricey gourmet restaurant. Fish dishes are the speciality but there are also game dishes such as reindeer and pheasant.

Ravintola Istanbul Oriental (☎ 311 2922; Kauppurienkatu 11; dishes €12-24) is a Turkish restaurant with style and flair. Kebab meals, such as Iskender and Anatolian, cost €12 to €15, and there's a good range of veg options, including felafels (€11 to €13).

Sokeri-Jussi Kievari (Sugar John; ☎ 376 628; Pikisaarentie 2), on Pikisaari island, is a big, old, timbered place with icy beers and outdoor tables that have good views of the centre. The recently reopened restaurant gets rave reviews from locals.

Eratupa (☎ 881 1300; mains €18.50-30), in one of the red storehouses on the waterfront, is a pricey restaurant but the food is high quality and includes everything from whitefish to wild boar.

Franzén (☎ 311 3224; Kirkkokatu 2; mains €16-29) is one of Oulu's finest restaurants. The cuisine is French and Finnish, with fish (salmon, whitefish etc) and reindeer featuring on the menu. The building, diagonally opposite the cathedral, dates back to 1829 and has a German-style beer cellar (Johanneksen kellari).

Entertainment

There's plenty going on in Oulu at night – the number of bikes lined up outside pubs and bars on summer weekends has to be seen to be believed. Perhaps more than any other city in Finland, Oulu is a place where locals brave the elements and drink their ice cold beer outside, basking in the first rays of spring sun, the minute the snow melts from the footpath. Wall-to-wall beer terraces flourish in summer on Rotuaari, the pedestrian section of Kirkkokatu, and around the kauppatori, where you'll often find live music and other entertainment.

Pubs & Bars The Oulu institution, Kaarlenholvi Jumpru Pub (Kauppurienkatu 6), is a great place for meeting locals. It has an enclosed terrace, a perennial favourite, and a warren of cosy rooms inside.

Oluthuone Leskinen (Saaristonkatu 15) is a friendly bar with an extraordinary range of Finnish and international beer. This is where expats working for Nokia start (and often end) their night, so it's a good place to find out where to head next.

The main pedestrian strip between the kauppatori and Isokatu is called Rotuaari and it's here you'll find bars and cafés, including

Oulun Panimo & Pub (Kauppurienkatu 13), a brewery pub with three home-grown tap beers and a lively atmosphere.

On Hallituskatu is a small strip of bars and cafés, including Never Grow Old, a reggae bar that hits its stride after 10pm; Tervahovi, a typically Finnish pub popular with a slightly older crowd; and St Michael's, an Irish bar.

Café Milou (Asemakatu 21) is away from the main strip but is one of the hippest bars in town, packing in students with its cheap beer, 'way gone' vibe and bookshelves filled with comics (Tin Tin among others).

Clubs The grungy 45 Special (☎ 881 1845; Saaristonkatu 12) is Oulu's best rock venue, with free entry most nights and wall-to-wall patrons. Giggling Marlin (Torikati 21-22) is one of a new brand of 'Suomi pop' clubs, featuring two dance floors with contemporary Finnish pop and international music and young Finns dancing on the tables.

Wäino Kellariclubi (☎ 522 1437; Kauppurienkatu 9), a basement-level club with a pub at street level, is another great spot for live rock.

Classical Music & Theatre The Oulu Symphony Orchestra – the world's northernmost professional symphony orchestra – holds concerts at Oulu Music Centre (Madetoja Hall; ☎ 5584 7212; Lintulammentie 1-3) most Thursdays.

Oulu City Theatre (☎ 5584 7600; Kaarlenväylä 2) has classical music, contemporary theatre and the occasional Shakespearian performance, almost all of it in Finnish.

Spectator Sports

Sporting events – including ice hockey, football, volleyball and Finnish baseball – take place at Raatti Stadium and Oulu Hall. Contact the tourist office for information.

Getting There & Away

Air Oulu airport is one of the busiest in Finland. Finnair has daily direct flights to/from Helsinki, other major Finnish cities, and from Stockholm.

Bus The bus station, near the train station, has express services connecting with Oulu from all the main centres. These include Rovaniemi (€26.70), Tornio (€19.20) and

Kajaani (€20.90). To reach nearby villages, catch a local Koskilinjat bus from the centre.

Train The train station is just east of the centre. Six to 10 trains a day run from Helsinki to Oulu; the fastest direct train from Helsinki takes only six hours (€53.40). There are also trains via Kajaani.

Getting Around
The airport is 15km south of the centre. Arriving flights are met by a Finnair bus to Oulu (€4.40). From the bus or train station you can catch local bus No 19 to the airport (€2.20; 30 minutes).

There is a good network of local buses. Each ride costs about €2.20, and route maps are displayed at bus stops.

The main roads north and south from Oulu are oversized motorways (freeways) which are off-limits to cyclists – fortunately there are many minor roads and bikeways. Pick up a bike route map at the Oulu tourist office.

AROUND OULU
The area around Oulu was a sea bed after the Ice Age and until a few thousand years ago. These days, it is relatively fertile farmland, which is still rising a centimetre every year.

Hailuoto Island
☎ 08 • pop 970
Hailuoto is the opposite of Atlantis – it rose from the sea about 2000 years ago. This flat island is 200 sq km in size, and growing. These days Hailuoto's main appeal is its sleepy fishing villages, as traffic is effectively regulated by ferries. Artists come here to seek inspiration, vacationers to bask on sandy beaches. Grey lichen, used for reindeer food on the mainland, is the main produce of Hailuoto. Most of the island can be explored only on foot.

The island is 30km long and has just one main road. Hailuoto village has shops and a bank. The **tourist information office** (☎ 810 1133) at the ferry harbour distributes free maps.

The open-air **Kniivilä Museum** (admission €1; open daily June & July), in Hailuoto village, has a collection of old houses. Marjaniemi is the westernmost point of Hailuoto, with a lighthouse and a cluster of old homes.

Ranta-Sumppu Camping (☎ 810 0690; tent sites €10, cottages €35; open year-round) is at

Marjaniemi, 30km west of the ferry pier. There are cottages for rent, camping and a simple lunch restaurant. There is a **café** at the ferry pier.

Bus No 18 from Oulu crosses the 7km strait from the mainland on a free *lossi* (ferry) and continues across Hailuoto island to its westernmost point, Marjaniemi. There are two or three buses daily. If you are coming from Oulu by car, take road No 816.

Haukipudas
☎ 08 • pop 14,600
Haukipudas is 20km north of Oulu at a scenic spot along the Kiiminkijoki river. The buttercup-coloured **church** (open year-round) is one of the most notable 'picture churches' in Finland, with superb naive frescoes on the walls and a small, wooden *vaivaisukko* (pauper statue) outside.

Virpiniemen Retkeilyhotelli (☎ 561 4200, fax 561 4224; e virpiniemi@mail.suomi.net; Hiitomajantie 27; beds €13-22; open year-round), at the seashore near Kello village, is 6km from the main road and 20km from Oulu. It is an HI-affiliated Finnhostel. There is a kitchen and sauna.

Särkyneen Pyörän Karjatila, next to the church in Haukipudas village, is a 150-year-old cowshed now wonderfully transformed into a cosy restaurant serving 'country-style' gourmet Finnish food.

To get here take bus No 1 to Kello from Oulu or bus No 15 or 20 to Haukipudas.

Liminka
☎ 08 • pop 5400
Liminka has always been a wealthy municipality, so it has many attractive old buildings. Dozens of weathered, wooden hay barns dot the flat, ploughed fields in this farming region. The town centre, off the main highway, has a wide range of services, including supermarkets.

The three museums of the Museum Area (Museoalue) are at Limingan Ranta, the old 17th-century centre located 500m off the main road, and are all open from noon to 6pm daily from June to August. In **Lampi Museo** there are paintings by Vilho Lampi, a local artist. **Muistokoti Aappola** features furniture and other items once owned by an opera singer, Abraham Ojanperä. Admission is €2, valid for both museums. Nearby is the **local history museum** (admission free).

Liminka lies along road No 8. Several daily Raahe-bound buses make the 30km trip from Oulu to Liminka.

Liminganlahti Bird Sanctuary
The bird sanctuary at Liminka Bay attracts more avian species than any other similar place in Finland. The wide bay is protected and funded by the World Wide Fund for Nature (WWF).

The 'great bird migration' is best seen in May, August and September. Several rare species of birds nest here during summer months, and up to 70 species of birds can be seen in a single summer day. Prominent species include the yellow-breasted bunting, a variety of wader, and the Ural Owl. There are several observation towers in the sanctuary, boardwalks and a couple of designated camp sites.

Your first stop should be the **Liminka Bay Nature Centre** (☎ 562 0000; W www.limin ganlahti.net; Rantakurvi 6), about 600m from road No 813 between Liminka and Lumijoki, and about 6km from Liminka village. As well as a nature display explaining the birdlife, migrations and flora, there's an observation tower, café and information desk. A guide is in attendance from 9am to 5pm daily from May to August and you can borrow a telescope to use at any of four bird-watching towers – the nearest is just 400m away.

The nature centre also has a new **accommodation wing**, with comfortable, modern rooms sleeping two to six people, a sauna and a guest kitchen.

KEMI
☎ 016 • pop 23,400
Kemi is an industrial town surrounded by huge pulp factories creating a strong, distinctive sulphur smell. That may not sound terribly appealing – and in summer you could certainly skip the town altogether – but Kemi is home to two of Lapland's blockbuster winter attractions: the authentic Arctic icebreaker ship, *Sampo*, and the Lumilinna (Snow Castle).

Information
The well-stocked **tourist office** (☎ 259 690; W www.kemi.fi; Kauppakatu 19; open 8am-6pm Mon-Fri, 10am-6pm Sat & Sun daily June-Aug, 8am-4pm Mon-Fri rest of the year) is in the Gemstone Gallery at the town harbour.

The **public library** (open 11am-8pm Mon Thur, 11am-6pm Fri, 10am-4pm Sat), at the kauppatori, has free Internet access.

The Arctic Icebreaker *Sampo*
The highlight of a visit to Kemi in winter is a trip aboard the *Sampo*, the only Arctic icebreaker ship in the world that accepts passengers. The four-hour cruise includes ice swimming in special drysuits, as well as a walk or snowmobile trip on the ice – a remarkable experience. The *Sampo* sails at noon on Thursday, Friday and Saturday from mid-December to late April and costs €162 per person. The best time to go is when the ice is thickest, which is usually in March. Contact **Sampo Tours** (☎ 256 548, fax 256 361; W www.sampotours.com; Torikatu 2).

Departures are from Ajos Harbour, 15km south of Kemi, where you'll also find the *Sampo* out to pasture in summer.

Lumilinna
Kemi's Snow Castle (☎ 259 502, W www .snowcastle.net; adult/child €5/2.50; open 10am-6pm Mon-Thur, 10am-8pm Fri-Sun, Feb–mid-Apr) is another big winter drawcard. In 1996 the 'World's Largest Snow Castle' – 13,500 sq metres – was built here. It was such a success that the castle is now constructed every year and features an **ice restaurant**, with bar, ice tables covered with reindeer fur, and ice sculptures. The restaurant opens from 30 December. It's also possible to stay overnight in the **snow hotel**, where heavy-duty Arctic sleeping bags keep you warm in -5° room temperature!

Jalokivigalleria
The Gemstone Gallery (☎ 220 300; Kauppakatu 29; adult/child €5/2.50; open same hours as tourist office), in an old seaside customs house, has an internationally notable collection of over 3000 beautiful, rare stones and jewellery, including a crown that was meant for the king of Finland. The crown was made in the 1980s by the gallery's founder, who created the 'first and only' crown of the king of Finland from original drawings.

Historiallinen Museo
Kemi History Museum (☎ 259 366; Sauvosaarenkatu 11; open noon-6pm daily) does not have permanent collections, just

frequently changing exhibitions. The admission fee depends on the current exhibition.

Special Events
Every May, Kemi hosts Arctic Comics, an international cartoon festival.

Places to Stay & Eat
Kemi has no hostel, but in summer **Hotel Relletti** (☎ 233 541; Miilukatu 1; singles/doubles €25/40), 1.5km southeast of the train station, provides reasonably priced rooms with private bathroom.

Hotel Palomestari (☎ 257 117; Valtakatu 12; singles/doubles from €67/71) is more central – only a few hundred metres from the bus and train stations – and is the cheapest hotel in the town centre.

Hotel Yopuu (☎ 232 034; W www.hotelli yopuu.com; Etelantie 227; doubles from €45), a little way out of town on road E4, is a pleasant guesthouse-style hotel with comfortable rooms and a good restaurant.

There are plenty of grillis and pizzerias on Valtakatu and around the kauppatori.

Cafe Sufe (Kauppakatu 15) is best for coffee and cake, and there's a €6 lunch buffet.

Hullu Pohjola (☎ 458 0250; Meripuistokatu 9; open year-round) is a pub offering Tex-Mex dishes like burritos and fajitas.

Sampo (mains €12-15) serves as an atmospheric daytime restaurant in summer, but you'll need your own transport to get to Ajos Harbour, 15km away.

Kemin Panimo (Keskuspuistokatu) is one of the liveliest pubs in town, with a large terrace and international beers.

Getting There & Away
The Kemi/Tornio airport is 6km north of town, and there are regular flights from Helsinki.

Buses from Tornio will take you to Kemi train station, and they are free with a train pass. There are also some departures to Muonio to the north and Oulu to the south.

There are trains from Helsinki (€64.20, 8½ hours) and Rovaniemi (€15, 1½ hours).

TORNIO
☎ 016 • pop 22,500
Tornio (Swedish: Torneå) is not an overly attractive or lively town, but its position on the Swedish border and the ease of visiting its twin across the Tornionjoki river – the Swedish town of Haparanda (Finnish: Haaparanta) – give it some interest for travellers. The two towns are geographically, if not culturally, melded into one so you can easily explore them both in a day or so. They share a tourist office and a famous golf course, where you can tee off into another country and another time zone. Nearby, the rapids at Kukkolankoski are another highlight.

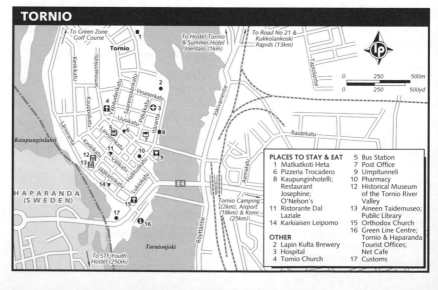

TORNIO

PLACES TO STAY & EAT		5	Bus Station
1	Matkatkoti Heta	7	Post Office
6	Pizzeria Trocadero	9	Umpitunneli
8	Kaupunginhotelli; Restaurant Josephine; O'Nelson's	10	Pharmacy
		12	Historical Museum of the Tornio River Valley
11	Ristorante Dal Laziale	13	Aineen Taidemuseo; Public Library
14	Karkiaisen Leipomo	15	Orthodox Church
		16	Green Line Centre; Tornio & Haparanda
OTHER			Tourist Offices; Net Cafe
2	Lapin Kulta Brewery	17	Customs
3	Hospital		
4	Tornio Church		

Midnight at the Green Zone Golf Course

You walk up to the first hole and place your ball on the tee. The sun is hanging low on the horizon. The time is five minutes to midnight, but you know it doesn't really matter how badly you play, how long it takes to get around 18 holes: fading light won't be an issue. You're standing on one of the most unique golf courses in the world – the Green Zone Golf Course at Tornio-Haparanda.

This is the world's northernmost golf club, and playing at this latitude (a few degrees south of the Arctic Circle) brings with it a few advantages. For a start, in summer you can play all night. Secondly, the course straddles the border of Finland and Sweden, beautifully laid out on either side of the Tornionjoki river, with nine holes in each country.

Of the 18 holes on this remarkable course, four cross the international border. Given the one-hour time difference, this technically means that if you tee off on the par 3 sixth hole, your ball remains in the air for at least an hour before it lands on the green (eight iron required here, hole-in-one possible). If you tee off from the par 4 third hole at 12.30am on Saturday, you'll hit the ball into Friday (driver or 3 wood). Play a short nine-iron from the 18th onto the green at a similar time on a Sunday, and you'll have smacked the ball into next week.

All this golfing novelty can be yours for €22 green fees (18 holes) plus around €10 if you need to hire a rather shoddy set of clubs. To play after 10pm (and get the full novelty benefit) you need to book in advance, since the clubhouse closes at 10pm.

All this may sound a bit trite, but golfers should note that this is a pretty decent course: lush fairways; well-maintained, solid greens; and with former PGA tour winner Bobby Mitchell, who scored a hole-in-one in the 1972 US Open, as club professional. How can you deny yourself this story when you're on the 19th green back home?

Otherwise there's not really a lot to see. Swedish day-trippers help to keep Tornio busy, frequently crossing the river to take advantage of the cheaper alcohol.

Don't forget – Finland's clocks are one hour ahead of those in Sweden.

History

The area along the Tornionjoki has been inhabited since medieval times, when it was the centre for Pirkka tax collectors (who worked for the king of Sweden). The town of Tornio was founded in 1621, and the entire Tornionjoki valley was administered by Sweden until 1809, when it was incorporated into Finland, under Russian suzerainty. In 1821, Haparanda was founded as a Swedish trading town to replace the loss of Tornio to Russia.

Information

Green Line Centre (☎ 432 733; w www .tornio.fi; open 8am-8pm Mon-Fri, 10am-8pm Sat & Sun June–mid-Aug, 8am-11.30am & 12.30pm-4pm Mon-Fri rest of the year), near the bridge on the Tornio side of the border, acts as the tourist office for both towns, with information on Finland and Sweden. There's a small tourist office in the foyer of the Stadt Hotel in Haparanda.

There's a free Internet terminal in the tourist office; a couple of machines at the **public library**, next to the Aine Art Museum; and **Net Cafe** (open 9am-4.30pm daily; 30 mins €1) in the Green Line Centre (adjacent to the tourist office).

There's a **hospital** (☎ 43211; Sairaalakatu 1) and a **pharmacy** (Hallituskatu 14).

Things to See & Do

Tornio church was completed in 1686 and is one of the most beautiful wooden churches in Finland. It is dedicated to the Swedish Queen Eleonora. The unusual 19th-century **Orthodox church** in the town centre was built by order of Tsar Alexander I of Russia.

Aineen Taidemuseo (Aine Art Museum; ☎ 432 438; Torikatu 2; admission €2; open 11am-6pm Tues-Thurs, 11am-3pm Fri-Sun) features a private collection of Veli Aine, a local business tycoon. It features Finnish art from the 19th and 20th centuries, and has a good café.

Historical Museum of the Tornio River Valley (☎ 432 451; Keskikatu 22; adult/child €2/1; open noon-5pm Mon-Fri, noon-3pm Sat & Sun, closed Sat in winter) has a collection of interesting old artefacts and costumes, although all displays are labelled in Finnish.

Lapin Kulta Brewery, founded in 1873, was the original brewery producing the ubiquitous Lappish lager. Free tours of the brewery plant are offered on Monday and Thursday at 2pm, starting at the front gate.

River-rafting trips are popular in summer on the Kukkolankoski Rapids (see the Around Tornio section). Rafting tours are run by Safaris Unlimited (☎ 253 405; w www .safarisunlimited.fi) and Nordic Safaris (☎ 040-755 1858; w www.nordicsafaris.com) from around €35 to €60 per person. Various trips use either inflatable rubber rafts or traditional wooden boats. Safaris Unlimited also has kayaking trips, and both companies offer winter excursions such as snowmobile, reindeer and husky safaris. The Tornio tourist office can make bookings for all trips.

Places to Stay
Tornio Camping (☎ 445 945; e sirkka.hyry@ pp.inet.fi; Matkailijantie; camp sites €10, cabins €54) is about 3km from town on the road to Kemi.

Hostel Tornio (☎ 211 9244; e pptoimis to@ppopisto.fi; Kivirannantie 13-15; singles/ doubles €13.50/27, with bath €25/40; open June-Aug) is an HI-affiliated summer hostel in a poor location east of the river about 3km from the centre. Facilities are good, including kitchen, lounge, laundry and a gym. On the same site is the summer hotel Joentalo (singles/doubles €45/55) with comfortable rooms including sheets and breakfast.

A better choice for hostellers is the STF Youth Hostel (☎ 0046 61171, fax 0046 61784; Strandgatan 26; dorm beds from Skr110; open year-round) in Haparanda – if there's one thing the Swedes do better than the Finns it's youth hostels. Reception is open from 5pm, euros are accepted and there's a good café here.

Matkatkoti Heta (☎ 480 897; Saaren-päänkatu 39; singles/doubles/triples €27/42/ 60) is an eccentric family-run guesthouse north of the centre. It's very simple but friendly and cheap enough.

Kaupunginhotelli (☎ 43311, fax 482 920; Itäranta 4; singles/doubles €97/117, doubles weekends & summer €82) is the only hotel in Tornio. It's a huge, ageing place with a swimming pool, decent restaurant and a couple of pubs.

A nicer choice is the Stadshotell (☎ 0922-61490; Torget 7) in Haparanda.

Places to Eat
There are plenty of grillis and fast-food places on Hallituskatu and Länsiranta.

Opposite the bus station, Pizzeria Tro-cadero (Kemintie 11) has lunch specials and decent pizzas.

Karkiaisen Leipomo (Länsiranta 9) has the best fresh pastries, cakes and donitsi (donuts) in town.

Ristorante Dal Laziale (☎ 481 009; Kaup-pakatu 12; pasta €7-10, pizza €4-8) is a popular Italian place with reasonably priced meals. It's open until 11pm.

For a quality sit-down meal, Restaurant Josephine (mains €7-20), in the Kaupungin-hotelli, is a good choice. The menu is broad, with Finnish specialities and international dishes, and prices are reasonable.

Entertainment
For entertainment Finnish-style, head to Umpitunneli, near the bridge on Hallituskatu. It's an open-air dance pub where you can enjoy a drink and feel the humppa music in full swing from Wednesday to Saturday (€5).

Then there's a lively, Irish-style pub, O'Nelson's, at the Kaupunginhotelli (see Places to Stay).

Getting There & Away
The Kemi/Tornio airport is 18km south of town, and there are regular flights to and from Helsinki.

There are a few daily buses from Rovaniemi (€16.80) and north to Muonio (€30.90), and buses from Kemi (€4.50) run almost hourly. Most continue to Haparanda. There are also frequent shuttle buses between Haparanda and Tornio, although the distance is so short you can walk. There are buses direct to Stockholm four times a week (Skr450).

AROUND TORNIO
Kukkolankoski Rapids
The Kukkolankoski Rapids on the Tornion-joki, 15km north of Tornio on road No 21, are the longest free-flowing rapids in Finland. The length is 3500m and the fall is just under 14m. Kukkolankoski has been a favoured fishing place since at least the Middle Ages. Today, locals still catch white-fish the traditional way, using long-handled nets. An annual whitefish festival is celebrated on the last weekend of July.

Arctic Circle, Kuusamo

Snowmobile

Partly frozen river, Kuusamo

Kemijoki River, Lapland

Feeding reindeer, Rovaniemi

Ho ho ho!

Forest road, Lapland

You can sample grilled *siika* (whitefish) at either Cafe Myllynpirtti or Kukkolankoski Grill Cafe.

On the Swedish side of the rapids is a **fishing museum** *(open daily in summer)*, but there's no bridge across the river here.

Kainuu Region

KAJAANI
☎ 08 • pop 36,400

Kajaani is the centre of the Kainuu region, and although a pleasant riverside city, it's mainly a transport hub and stopover between the Lakeland and Oulu or Rovaniemi. What little there is to see is related to Kajaani's long position as an important station on the Kainuu tar transportation route – until the 19th century this region produced more tar than anywhere else in the world.

Count Per Brahe founded the town of Kajaani in 1651. Soon after, King Karl IX had a castle built on an island in the Kajaaninjoki and Kajaani became a vital regional stronghold. Russians attacked in 1716 and destroyed the castle after five weeks of fighting.

One of Kajaani's claims to fame is that Elias Lönnrot, creator of Finland's national epic, the *Kalevala*, stayed here for a period in the 19th century, using it as a base for his travels. The long-reigning president Urho Kekkonen also lived here as a student (his house stills stands at Kalliokatu 7).

Locals are proud of their town, which boasts good fishing in the centre, a lively pedestrian strip and a friendly atmosphere.

Information
The tourist office **Kajaani Info** *(☎ 615 5555; w www.kajaani.fi; Kauppakatu 21; open 9am-6pm Mon-Fri, 9am-2pm Sat June-Aug, 9am-4.30pm Mon-Fri rest of the year)*, on the small town square at the end of the pedestrian strip, is a useful place for regional information, hotel bookings and fishing permits.

The **public library** *(Kauppakatu 35; open 10am-8pm Mon-Fri, 10am-3pm Sat)* has free Internet access.

Things to See & Do
In town, the beautiful wooden **church** *(Pohjolankatu; open daily in summer)* from 1896 is a rare example of neo-Gothic architecture.

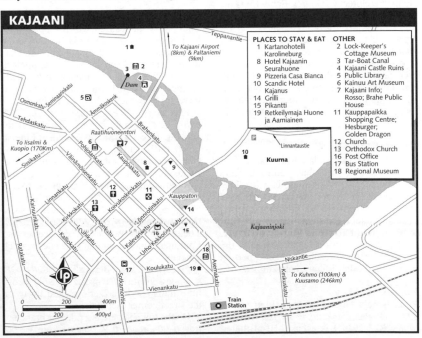

KAJAANI

PLACES TO STAY & EAT
1 Kartanohotelli Karolineburg
8 Hotel Kajaanin Seurahuone
9 Pizzeria Casa Bianca
10 Scandic Hotel Kajanus
14 Grilli
15 Pikantti
19 Retkeilymaja Huone ja Aamiainen

OTHER
2 Lock-Keeper's Cottage Museum
3 Tar-Boat Canal
4 Kajaani Castle Ruins
5 Public Library
6 Kainuu Art Museum
7 Kajaani Info; Rosso; Brahe Public House
11 Kauppapaikka Shopping Centre; Hesburger; Golden Dragon
12 Church
13 Orthodox Church
16 Post Office
17 Bus Station
18 Regional Museum

It's typically Karelian, with lots of ornate wooden trim. Nearby is an **Orthodox church** (*Kirkkokatu; open daily in summer*). See the Around Kajaani section for details of the Paltaniemi church, 9km north of town.

Across the Kajaaninjoki from the town centre is what's left of **Kajaani Castle**, built in the 17th century and thoroughly damaged by war, time and some more recent mischief. It's not much to see, admission is free and it's easily viewed from the bridge.

At the Ämmäkoski waterfall, near the castle ruins, is a **tar-boat canal**, a type of lock built in 1846 to enable the boats laden with tar barrels to pass. There's a small **museum** (*open 11am-5pm Tues-Sun; admission free*) in the old lock-keeper's cottage, and tar boat shows at 11am on Saturdays in July.

Kainuu regional museum (*Asemakatu 4; adult/child €2/1; open noon-4pm Mon, Tues, Thur & Fri, noon-8pm Wed, noon-5pm Sun*), near the train station, is a good place to get acquainted with local history, including the *Kalevala* and its author, Elias Lönnrot. There is no information in English.

Facing the small *raatihuoneentori* (town square) is the old **town hall**, designed by German architect CL Engel. Behind it is the former police station, which now serves as the **Kainuu art museum** (*Linnankatu 14; adult/child €2/1; open noon-4pm Mon, Tues, Thur & Fri, noon-8pm Wed, noon-5pm Sun*).

Walking tracks can be found around Pöllyvaara Hill, just above the Kartanohotelli Karolineburg. You can **fish** for trout, char and salmon right in town on the Kajaaninjoki river; permits (€6) are available from the tourist office.

Special Events

Kainuun Jazzkevät in late May is a festival of international jazz, blues and rock. Stars have included Dizzie Gillespie, Mick Taylor and the Phil Woods Quintet, and many Finnish performers. For information and tickets contact the Kajaani tourist office.

If you're interested in Finnish literature, **Poetry Week** draws a lot of people to the town for recitals, readings, theatre performances and other literary happenings.

Places to Stay

Retkeilymaja Huone ja Aamiainen (*☎/fax 622 254; Pohjolankatu 4; singles/doubles/triples €27/39/51*) is a basic HI-affiliated place but the rooms are clean and it's the cheapest in town, with breakfast and linen included. Dormitory beds are not advertised, but if you're on your own you could ask for a share bed in one of the larger rooms. Reception opens at 4pm.

Hotel Kajaanin Seurahuone (*☎ 623 076, fax 613 4495; Kauppakatu 11; singles/doubles €80/95, doubles weekends & summer €75*) is very central and has standard rooms. There's an Irish bar and restaurant downstairs.

Scandic Hotel Kajanus (*☎ 61641, fax 616 4505; Koskikatu 3; singles/doubles €90/112, doubles weekends & summer €78*), across the river from Hotel Kajaanin Seurahuone, is one of the largest and flashiest hotels in Northern Finland, with 235 rooms, five restaurants and five saunas.

Kartanohotelli Karolineburg (*☎ 613 1291, fax 613 1296;* **w** *www.karolineburg.com; Karoliinantie 4; singles/doubles from €70/80, doubles with sauna €117, suites €100-250*) is easily the most romantic place to stay in Kajaani. It's an elegant 19th-century wooden manor house across the river from the centre, with rooms in the main building and two outbuildings.

Places to Eat

The partly pedestrianised Kauppakatu – leading northwest from the kauppatori to the raatihuoneentori – is the main street and has many restaurants and cafés. The **kauppatori**, at the southeast end of Kauppakatu, has stalls selling smoked fish and other goodies and there are a couple of cheap **grillis** nearby.

Pikantti (*☎ 628 870; Kauppakatu 10; lunch buffet €8.60*), on the corner of Urho Kekkonenkatu, offers a typically excellent Finnish lunch buffet until 5pm weekdays. It includes vegetable soup and a main course, salads, bread, milk, dessert and coffee.

Kauppapaikka Shopping Centre (*Kauppakatu 18*) has some cheap eating options, including a branch of **Hesburger** and the **Golden Dragon** (*☎ 627 776; mains €6-10*), a better-than-average Chinese place serving Cantonese and Szechuan and cheap lunch specials.

Pizzeria Casa Bianca (*☎ 628 498; Koivukoskenkatu 17D; pizzas €6-8*) is a cosy little Italian-style pizzeria tucked away on the street corner facing the river.

On the town square is a popular branch of **Rosso** (*Kauppakatu 21; mains from €6.50*) with the usual array of pizzas, pastas and steaks. Opposite is a rustic **stall** where Finnish pancakes are whipped up while you wait.

When it's warm, the terrace at the **Brahe Public house** (cnr Kauppakatu & Linnankatu) in the cute cobbled town square, is Kajaani's best spot to sit with a beer or coffee and watch the passing parade.

Getting There & Away
Finnair has daily flights from Helsinki to Kajaani. The airport is 8km northwest of town; take bus No 4 (€2.50).

Kajaani is the major travel hub in the Kainuu district. There are frequent departures for Kuhmo and other towns in the region during the week, but few departures on weekends. The local bus service is useful if you want to visit Paltaniemi.

Kajaani is on the main Helsinki to Oulu line. There are four daily trains from Helsinki, via Kouvola and Kuopio; the fastest train takes less than seven hours (€56). The night train from Helsinki takes approximately 10 hours.

AROUND KAJAANI
Paltaniemi
The village of Paltaniemi is considered a suburb of Kajaani, although it has its own distinctive history. The first church was built here in 1599. In the centuries that followed, Paltaniemi became the regional centre for the Lutheran Church. You'll see some of the most exciting church paintings in Finland here.

The old wooden **church** (☎ 615 5555; open 10am-6pm daily May-Aug) was built in 1726, and its bell tower dates from 1776. The church is known for its wonderful old murals and ceiling paintings (some were altered and repainted in 1940). The Hell scene has been partly covered, apparently to avoid disturbing the locals. An information tape in English is available on request.

Keisarintalli, an old wooden stable, was used as a boarding house for Tsar Alexander I when he toured Finland in 1819. This simple building was actually the best available for the exalted visitor. Ask at the church to be shown around.

Eino Leino Talo (Eino Leino House; ☎ 687 5210; admission free; house & café open 10am-7pm daily June-Aug) was built in 1978

to commemorate the centenary of the birth of Finland's famous poet Eino Leino, who was born in Paltaniemi.

Take local bus No 4 (the airport bus) from Pohjolankatu in Kajaani to Paltaniemi. There are hourly departures on weekdays, less often on weekends.

KUHMO
☎ 08 • pop 11,200
Kuhmo, like Kajaani, was once a major tar producer, but is now a modern service town in the heart of accessible wilderness territory – it makes an excellent jumping off point or natural base for hiking the UKK route, Finland's longest marked trek.

Kuhmo is well known in Finland for its annual chamber music festival, and has several connections to the Finnish epic the *Kalevala* – including the Kalevala Village theme park. Greater Kuhmo covers a massive area of 5458 sq km, stretching to the Russian border, while the town itself is small but unusually pleasant, at least for a frontier town.

Information
Kuhmo tourist office (☎ 655 6382, fax 655 6384; W www.kuhmonet.fi; Kainuuntie 82; open 8am-6pm Mon-Fri, 10am-4pm Sat June– late Aug; 8am-5pm Mon-Fri rest of the year) is in the town centre, opposite the kauppatori. The office stocks good maps and walking guides to the region.

Kainuu Nature Centre (☎ 0205-646 380; e kainuu@metsa.fi; Lentiirantie 342A), near the Kalevala Village theme park, is a national park information centre run by the Metsähallitus (Forest and Park Service). As well as providing hiking advice, there's a free nature exhibition.

The modern **public library** (Pajakkakatu 2; open 10am-7pm Mon-Wed & Fri, 2pm-7pm Thur) has free Internet access, as does **Osku**, a small office on Koulukatu opposite the bus terminal.

Kalevala Village Theme Park
The theme park (☎ 652 0114; adult/child €10/5; open 9.30am-6pm daily June–late Aug), 3km from the centre, is the main attraction in Kuhmo. Although named after the Finnish national epic, the *Kalevala*, it is essentially an open-air museum of Karelian folk history and log buildings, with cultural

exhibitions, artisan displays and costumed staff demonstrating tar-making, woodcarving, fishing and so on. You can walk around the marked *Kalevalakierros* (Kalevala Circuit) alone, or time your visit to coincide with a guided tour (10am and 1.30pm Monday to Saturday from mid-June to mid-August). Along the way you will see a recreation of the cabin and desk Elias Lönnrot worked at, and Pohjola House, which includes the Sampo Gallery and a good café.

The site becomes a **Christmas Village** in mid-December.

The adjacent **Winter War Exhibition** (*adult/child €3/2; open 9am-6pm daily May–late Sept*) displays artefacts found in the Kuhmo wilderness.

Juminkeko

If your interest in the *Kalevala* has been piqued, Juminkeko (☎ 653 0670; W *www.ju minkeko.fi; Kontionkatu 25; adult/child €4/2; open noon-6pm Sun-Thur*) is worthy of a visit. It features a gallery, theatre and multimedia library devoted to the national epic and to Karelian culture. On display is Finland's largest collection of *Kalevala* books translated into almost 50 languages. With the multimedia programme you can view extracts from the epic in audio and pictures in 43 languages.

Tuupala Museum

This charming Karelian farmhouse (☎ 655 6283; *Tervatie 1; adult/child €2/1; open 9am-6pm Tues-Sun June-Aug*) has been, in

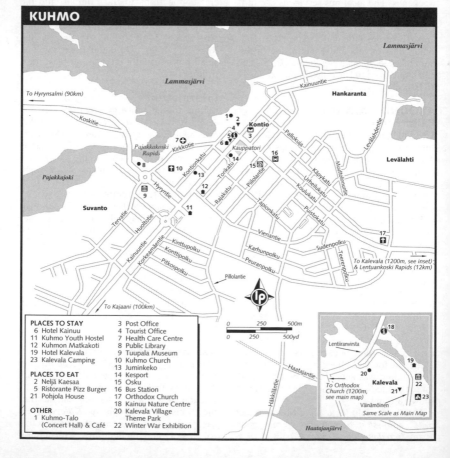

KUHMO

Lammasjärvi

Lammasjärvi

To Hyrynsalmi (90km)

Hankaranta

Koskitie

Kirkkotie

Kontio

Kauppatori

Levälahti

Pajakkakoski Rapids

Pajakkajoki

Kontionkatu

Torikatu

Piilolantie

Käpykatu

Multitienmäntie

Urhelukatu

Kolukatu

Levälahdentie

Pallokuja

Suvanto

Hyryntie

Rajakatu

Tapionkatu

Piostokatu

Tervatie

Huoltotie

Kainuuntie

Korkeamäentie

Kinttupolku

Konttipolku

Pitkospolku

Vienantie

Karhunpolku

Peuranpolku

Sudenpolku

Teerenpolku

To Kalevala (1200m, see inset) & Lentuankoski Rapids (12km)

Piilolantie

To Kajaani (100km)

Häkkiläntie

Haatajantie

To Orthodox Church (1200m, see main map)

Lentiiranvirsta

Kalevala

Väinämöinen

Same Scale as Main Map

Haatajanjärvi

0   250   500m
0   250   500yd

PLACES TO STAY
6 Hotel Kainuu
11 Kuhmo Youth Hostel
12 Kuhmon Matkakoti
19 Hotel Kalevala
23 Kalevala Camping

PLACES TO EAT
2 Neljä Kaesaa
5 Ristorante Pizz Burger
21 Pohjola House

OTHER
1 Kuhmo-Talo
   (Concert Hall) & Café

3 Post Office
4 Tourist Office
7 Health Care Centre
8 Public Library
9 Tuupala Museum
10 Kuhmo Church
13 Juminkeko
14 Kesport
15 Osku
16 Bus Station
17 Orthodox Church
18 Kainuu Nature Centre
20 Kalevala Village
   Theme Park
22 Winter War Exhibition

its past lives, a general store, pharmacy, inn, post office and home to the town's police chief. It now houses the museum of local history.

Churches
The striking 1816 wooden **Kuhmo Church** *(open 11am-6pm daily in summer)* in the town centre is a venue for concerts during the chamber music festival (see under Special Events). The **Orthodox Church**, 1km from the centre on the road to the theme park, is only 35 years old. It contains several 18th-century icons that were painted in the Valamo Monastery before it was annexed by the Soviet Union, plus a 300-year-old Madonna icon. The church is open on request only; inquire at the tourist office for more details.

Activities
There's plenty to do in and around Kuhmo. White-water rafting trips to Lentuankoski Rapids, 15km north of Kuhmo, are arranged on weekends in June and August and daily during July, with a minimum of two persons. The cost is €8.50 per person (two or three people), €7 per person (four or more). Book through the Kuhmo tourist office.

Fishing for perch and pike is popular at Pajakkakoski Rapids near the town centre and at Lentuankoski Rapids north of town. Check with Kainuu Nature Centre or the tourist office about permits.

The tourist office also has brochures and maps describing various easy hikes in the Kuhmo region.

Bicycles can be hired from **Kesport** *(Kainuuntie 87)* for €10 a day.

Special Events
The **Kuhmo Chamber Music Festival**, held over two weeks from mid-July to August each year, attracts top musicians from around the world. It's been going since 1969 and more than 100 musicians participate each year. Most of the concerts are held at Kuhmo-Talo (Kuhmo Arts Centre), a spacious, modern concert hall. Tickets are €5 to €15, with most costing €12. There are also a few free concerts every day. For advance bookings contact the Kuhmo tourist office or the **Kuhmo Chamber Music Festival** *(☎ 652 0936, fax 652 1961; W www.kuhmofestival.fi; Torikatu 39)*.

Places to Stay
Most places charge a premium during the Chamber Music Festival (mid-July) and you'll need to book well ahead for a bed then anyway.

Kalevala Camping *(☎ 655 6388, fax 655 6384; tent sites €11, 2-/4-person cabins from €26/34; open June–late Aug)*, on the lake near the theme park, has good facilities including a smoke sauna and boats.

Kuhmo Youth Hostel *(☎ 655 6245; Kainuuntie 113; dorm beds €12, singles/doubles €26/30; open July)* is an HI place in the Piilolan school building, but it's open only in July when the town is crowded with music lovers.

Kuhmon Matkakoti *(☎/fax 655 0271, Vienantie 3; singles/doubles/triples €25/44/56)* is a friendly, good value guesthouse near the town centre.

Hotel Kainuu *(☎ 655 1711, fax 655 1715; Kainuuntie 84; singles/doubles Mon-Fri €54/71, Sat & Sun €48/64)* is the nicest hotel in the town centre.

About 4km from the centre, **Hotel Kalevala** *(☎ 655 4100, fax 655 4200; Väinämöinen 9; W www.hotellikalevala.fi; singles/doubles €76/101, weekends & summer €59/74)* is Kuhmo's top hotel – a modern, upmarket place in a lakeside location near the theme park. It handles most rental services, including canoes.

Places to Eat
The small **kauppatori** is busy in summer, daily until late afternoon. Look for local specialities like karjalanpiirakka pies.

Ristorante Pizz Burger *(☎ 652 0144; Kainuuntie 84; mains €6.50-12)*, despite the naff name, is a reasonably good pizza, pasta and salad restaurant with a filling lunchtime buffet (€7.20), booth seating and a small terrace.

Neljä Kaesaa *(Koulukatu 3)*, around the corner from the tourist office, is a pleasant café with €6 lunch specials. There are also good cafés at the **Kuhmo-Talo** and **Pohjola House** at the Kalevala Village.

Probably the best restaurant around is out at the **Hotel Kalevala** *(☎ 655 4100; mains €13-19)*, where the a la carte menu features Finnish, Lappish and international dishes.

Getting There & Away
A taxi minibus runs from Kajaani airport to the town of Kuhmo after the arrival of each

Trekking the UKK

Pockets of the now-rare Finnish wilderness still exist – in pristine condition – along the eastern border of Finland. They are best seen and experienced on a trek along the Urho K Kekkonen (UKK) route. This 240km trail is the nation's longest and greatest trekking route. It was named after President Urho K Kekkonen, and it has been in development for decades, with new shelters and boardwalks regularly being constructed.

The trail starts a long way south at Koli Hill in North Karelia and continues along the western side of Lake Pielinen, ending at Iso-Syöte Hill far to the north of Kuhmo.

However, two of the finest sections of the UKK route are easily accessible from Kuhmo: the Kuhmo to Hiidenportti leg and the Kuhmo to Lentiira leg. The trek east from Kuhmo to Lentiira village via Iso-Palonen park takes at least four days and offers superb scenery.

The trail is well maintained in the Kuhmo area, with clear markings, and *laavu* (simple shelters) are spaced every 10km to 20km. Each laavu is near water and has an established campfire place, firewood and a pit toilet. Carry a sleeping bag and *plenty* of mosquito repellent to take advantage of this free open-air accommodation.

Pick up route maps at the Kuhmo tourist office or the **Kainuu Nature Centre** (☎ 877 6380; e *kaapalinna@metsa.fi)*, also in Kuhmo.

---

flight, and there is also a regular service the other way (€25, 1½ hours).

There are numerous daily buses to/from Kajaani (€14.60, 1½ hours), where you can get connections to other towns west and south, and less frequent direct buses to Nurmes (€10.40, 1½ hours) and Joensuu (€27.10, four hours). Trains arriving in Kajaani (102km to the west) connect with buses to Kuhmo.

HOSSA
☎ 08

Hossa, dubbed the 'fisher's paradise', is one of the most carefully maintained fishing areas in Finland. Trekking is also excellent, and some of the paths take you to beautiful ridges between lakes.

To visit Hossa you will need to plan in advance where to stay and where to purchase fishing permits. See Fishing in the Activities chapter for more information on permits.

Hossa visitor centre (☎ 0205-646 041; *Jatkonsalmentie 6)*, on Lake Ollori, provides everything for a successful stay. It rents out cottages, boats, hiking gear and fishing equipment; sells fishing permits and hiking maps; and has a café/restaurant and lakeside sauna. In winter the centre rents out cross-country skis as well.

On the steep cliffs at Somero, in the northwest corner of the Hossa preserve, is **Värikallio** (Colour Rock). Its rock paintings, estimated to be 4000 years old, are the most

northern ones in Finland. You can only reach the site via a marked hiking trail.

Hossa offers 100km of marked **hiking trails** in summer and 70km of cross-country ski tracks in winter. Those who are interested in exploring by **canoe** can choose to paddle from Julma Ölkky or Iijärvi to Hossa. Each route is 10km, and longer trips are possible.

Fishing is one of the main drawcards here and there are designated fly-fishing and spear-fishing areas within Hossa, designated fishing areas for children and the disabled, as well as special waters for fishing trout and salmon, pike and perch and rainbow trout. In winter, ice-fishing for salmon is popular.

Places to Stay & Eat
Karhunkainalo Leirintäalue is a camping area adjacent to and run by the Hossa visitor centre, with tent and caravan spaces and a lakeside sauna.

On the road south from the information centre, **Hossan Lomakeskus** (☎ 732 322; *doubles from €60)* is a large hotel with double rooms, and many kinds of cottages at the waterfront. Buffet lunch is available.

Getting There & Away
The best way to reach Hossa is by car. There are also daily buses to Hossa from Kuusamo. You can reach Hossa from Kajaani by changing buses at Ämmänsaari; these buses run only on weekdays.

OULU, KAINUU & KOILLISMAA

Koillismaa Region

KUUSAMO
☎ 08 • pop 17,700

Kuusamo is a frontier town about 200km northeast of Oulu and similar in feel to the towns of Lapland. There is little to see in Kuusamo itself, but it's perfectly situated as a base for planning and launching treks or canoeing trips into the surrounding area and it's close to one of Finland's most popular ski resorts. There are good services, including shops with trekking supplies.

A Lutheran parish for over 300 years, Kuusamo was incorporated as a municipality in 1868. By 1900, its population had grown to 10,000, and it had close relations with nearby Russia. During WWII, the village was a command centre for German troops, who also supervised the construction of the 'Death Railway' that operated for 242 days. When the Soviet army marched into Kuusamo on 15 September 1944, the Germans burned the town and blew up the railway. The Soviets retreated, after occupying Kuusamo for about two months, and the inhabitants of Kuusamo returned to their shattered town. A large number of refugees from the Soviet-annexed Salla region were settled around Kuusamo just after WWII.

Information

The **Kuusamo tourist office** (☎ 850 2910, fax 850 2901; W www.kuusamo.fi; Torangintaival 2; open 9am-8pm Mon-Fri in summer, 9am-5pm Mon-Fri rest of the year) is in the Karhuntassu (Bear's Paw) Tourist Centre on road No 5 (the main highway), 2km southwest of the town centre. A **Forest and Park Service office** (☎ 852 3241) is also here, with maps and information on nearby trekking routes and national parks.

The **public library** (Kaiterantie 22; open noon-8pm Mon, Wed & Thur, 10am-8pm Tues, 10am-2pm Fri, 10am-3pm Sat), opposite the bus terminal, has free Internet access, and there's one free terminal at the tourist office. There's a **Net Cafe** at the local sports centre at Kitkantie 42.

Things to See

About 500m southeast of the town centre is the local **open-air museum** (☎ 850 6027; Kitronintie 6; admission free; open noon-6pm

daily mid-June–mid-Aug 9am-3pm Mon-Fri mid–late Aug), with a cluster of old, grey farm buildings brought together from the Kuusamo region.

The **water tower** (Joukamontie 32; open noon-9pm, noon-1pm Fri-Sat, closed Thur) has an observation platform with a good view over Kuusamo, and the Torni café. On the other side of the bus terminal, **Kuusamotalo** (☎ 850 6560; Kaarlo Hännisentie 2) is a concert hall and cultural centre – the pride of Kuusamo. Check with the tourist office or call direct for coming performances and exhibitions.

There are quite a few craft shops and studios in Kuusamo, which means you can pick up some good buys. **Bjarmia** (☎ 853 869; Vienantie 1) is a ceramics factory and studio

KUUSAMO

PLACES TO STAY
1 Holiday Club Kuusamo Tropiikki
2 Rantatropiikki Camping
11 Kuusamon Kansanopisto
22 Hotel Kuusanka
23 Sokos Hotel Kuusamo

PLACES TO EAT
13 Ampan Pizza Bar
14 Kauppakulma Shopping Centre
20 Tori Grilli

21 Martina; Parnell's Irish Bar
25 Baari Martai
26 Supermarkets

OTHER
3 Kuusamon Uistin
4 Net Cafe; Sports Centre
5 Greenline Safaris
6 Ruka Palvelu
7 Kuusamotalo Concert Hall
8 Bus Station
9 Public Library
10 Water Tower & Torni Cafe
12 Matka-Ruka Travel Agency
15 Bjarmia Ceramics Factory & Café
16 Music House Circus; Havana
17 Post Office
18 Health Care Centre
19 Pharmacy
24 Open-Air Museum
27 Karhuntassu Tourist Centre; Forest and Park Service; Stellar Polaris; Kuukkeli Café
28 White Studio Ceramics

right in the centre. There's a ceramics and textiles 'museum' here (€2) or you can just visit the shop and café. Just behind the tourist office building, **White Studio** (☎ 852 3170, Torangintaival 2B) is another fine ceramics studio.

Kuusamon Uistin, north of the centre on main road No 5 to Ruka, sells beautifully crafted fishing lures and sheath knives from its factory. Some of these products are exported throughout the world under the brand name Kuusamo. Again there's a shop and café here.

Organised Tours

There are a dozen or more independent tour operators based in Kuusamo, offering activities as diverse as ice climbing, river rafting, mountain biking, ice fishing, snowshoe hiking and more. If you're travelling alone or in a small group, it's worth checking with the bigger agencies as they often round up individuals for trips that require a larger group. **Matka-Ruka** (☎ 852 1395, fax 852 2015; W www.matkaruka.com; Kitkantie 15) is a major travel agency that organises activities and also arranges reservations at any of over 600 accommodation units scattered around Kuusamo.

One of the largest companies is **Ruka Palvelu** (☎ 860 8600, fax 860 8601, W www .rukapalvelu.fi). It offers regular weekly programmes during summer and winter high seasons: river rafting, fishing, canoeing and climbing from June to September, and dogsledding, ice-fishing, snowmobiling and snowshoeing from November to March. Tours are priced from €42 per person for two-hour bike or walking trips to €117 for a full-day canoe trip. Worth trying are **Stellar Polaris** in the same building as the tourist office; and **Green Line Safaris** (☎ 852 3041; W www.greenlinesafaris.fi; Kitkantie 38-40).

Places to Stay

Rantatropiikki Camping (☎ 859 6404, fax 852 1901; e mypa.kuusamo@kt.inet.fi; Kylpyläntie; tent sites €7.50-14) is 5km north of the centre, but since it's associated with the neighbouring Holiday Club (see later in this section), you can take advantage of the spa and pool facilities as well as the restaurant and bar. There are also stylish cottages.

Kuusamon Kansanopisto (☎ 852 2132, fax 8521 1134; Kitkantie 35; dorm beds from

€10-12, singles/doubles €18/30, with bathroom €30/40; open Midsummer–end Aug), close to the centre, is a rambling summer HI hostel with a range of rooms. There is a kitchen and a satellite TV in the common room, as well as sauna and laundry facilities. Reception is open for check in between 5pm and 10pm only, but you can store your bags here during the day.

Hotel Kuusanka (☎ 852 2240; Ouluntie 2; singles/doubles €50/65) is a small, familyrun hotel that feels more like a guesthouse. It's on the main street but there's off-street parking and a good breakfast included.

Sokos Hotel Kuusamo (☎ 85920, fax 852 1263; Kirkkotie 23; singles/doubles Mon-Fri €108/136, Sat & Sun €84/102), near the centre, is a big, box-like structure topped by a glowing kota (Lappish hut).

Holiday Club Kuusamon Tropiikki (☎ 85 960, fax 852 1909; W www.holidayclub.fi; Kylpyläntie; singles/doubles €100/115), some 5km north of Kuusamo, is a modern hotel and spa complex in a forest setting. Rooms are plain but comfortable (apartments are also available) and you get full use of the spa, sauna, pool and other services (the spa is a plastic tropical wonderland with a 45m water slide). Non guests can use the spa for a modest fee.

Places to Eat

Most of Kuusamo's eating options are crowded along the main streets Kitkantie and Ouluntie, the intersection of which is where you'll find the kauppatori. **Ampan Pizza Bar** (Kitkantie 18; pizzas €6-10) is popular for its reasonably priced pizzas, while the **Tori grilli** at the kauppatori is open past midnight.

There are several good cafés tucked away in town. **Torni Cafe** at the top of the water tower serves coffee and cakes with a view; **Bjarmia** (Vienantie 1) is a quaint little coffee shop above the ceramics factory of the same name. **Baari Martai** (☎ 851 4199; Airotie) is in an unattractive industrial area between the town centre and the tourist office, but it's well known for its excellent lunches on weekdays in summer.

Martina (☎ 852 2051; Ouluntie 3; meals €8.50-18.50) is one of those Finnish family restaurants that has a go at everything – pasta, steaks, fish and a salad buffet. It's a comfortable and accommodating place for an informal dinner.

Adjacent to the tourist office are several giant **supermarkets** where you can stock up on trekking supplies.

Entertainment

Likewise, the two main streets offer most of the nightlife spots. **Parnell's Irish Bar** (*Oluntie 5*) is the top pub in town, with international brews on tap.

Sokos Hotel Kuusamo (☎ 85920; *Kirkkotie 23*) has a good à la carte restaurant, as well as a nightclub and dance floor. If you're up for a party, **Music House Circus** (*Kitkantie 1*) kicks on late; next door is **Havana**, a Latin bar and club.

Getting There & Away

Finnair flies daily from Helsinki to Kuusamo airport, which is 7km northeast of the town centre.

Buses run daily from Kajaani (€28.90), Oulu (€27.10) and Rovaniemi (€22.90). There are frequent services to the ski centre at Ruka (€4.50). In summer (June to mid-September) an excursion bus travels between the Karhuntassu tourist office in Kuusamo and the Oulanka Visitor Centre (€9.30, 1½ hours), stopping at the Kuusamo bus terminal, Tropiikki spa centre, Ruka and Juuma village. It departs at 8.45am from Monday to Saturday. At the Juuma road junction (Käylä) you can change buses to get to Ristikallio, Hautajärvi visitor centre and Sallo.

RUKA
☎ 08

Only 30km north of Kuusamo, Ruka is one of the most popular winter sports resorts in Finland – you'll see *Ruka!* bumper stickers on cars all over the country. Ruka is also a protected nature area, with abundant wildlife.

Prices and demand for accommodation keep Ruka somewhat off-limits for budget travellers in winter, but in summer it is a fine place to start or finish the Karhunkierros trek because there are good bus connections from Kuusamo. **Valtavaara hill**, adjacent to the Ruka ski slope, is the best place in the region for bird-watching: some 100 species of birds nest here, and an annual bird-watching competition is held in the area in June. In this competition – called 'Pongauskilpailu', from the Swedish *poeng*, meaning 'point' – you score a point for every bird species you spot.

Information

The resort has two main centres, west and east, with most of the facilities at the main square on the west side. The Kuusamo tourist office can also provide information on Ruka activities and accommodation. The main information centre at the ski resort is **Rukakeskus Oy** (☎ 860 0200; **w** *www.ruka.fi*) in the Rukaklubi building in the main village parking area. In the same area there are ski rental shops, lift ticket outlets, postal services, a supermarket and accommodation booking services. A helpful tourist booklet, *Ruka!*, is published in Finnish and English.

Tour operators in Ruka include **Ruka-palvelu Oy** (☎ 860 8600, fax 860 8601) in the Safaritalo building. It arranges fishing tours, canoe safaris, white-water rafting expeditions and guided treks.

Skiing

There are 28 downhill ski slopes and 18 lifts on Ruka fell. The vertical drop is 201m and the longest run is 1300m – not bad averages at all for Finland, where hills are small and slope gently. Ruka also boasts cross-country trails totalling 250km. There are special areas for snowboarders.

The ski season runs from early November to mid-May, depending on snowfalls. During holiday periods such as Christmas and Easter it seems that almost the entire population of Finland can be seen on Ruka's slopes.

A single ride up on the ski lift costs €4/2 per adult/child, a day/weekly pass is €26/120 (€16/72 for children). Rates are slightly lower in the shoulder seasons. Alpine skis, including poles and boots, rent for €21/50/80 for one/three/seven days; €12/28/42 for children. Snowboards (boots included) rent for €25/85 a day/week, and cross-country skis are €18/70. Ski lessons are available at Ruka for adults or children for around €27 a day.

Places to Stay

Ruka is a very busy winter sports centre, and in season it may be difficult to find a bed, especially at reasonable prices. Book accommodation in advance, or stay in Kuusamo. In summer, rooms can be good value, though some of the village services close down completely.

For **cottage rentals** in Ruka, contact the Kuusamo tourist office or the Matka-Ruka travel agency in Kuusamo (see that section earlier). For apartments and chalets also try **Ruka-ko** (☎ *866 0088;* W *www.ruka-ko.fi; Postibaari)* at the resort. You can make online accommodation bookings for cabins on the website W www.ruka.fi.

Viipus Camping (☎ *040-586 6251; Viipuksentie; camping per person/site €5/10, 2-4-person cabins from €25; open June–mid-Sept)* is a very small rustic camping ground at lake Viipusjärvi, several kilometres north of Ruka. It's a good spot in summer, with camp sites, a few cabins, a shop, sauna and boats for hire.

Hotel Omena (☎ *868 660;* W *www.om ena.com; apartments €67-72, €47 May-Aug),* next to the Ski Bistro at the Ruka East parking area, is easily the best value accommodation at Ruka. The small, self-contained apartments have four beds, so even in high season a group of four pays only €18 per person.

Hotel Rantasipi Ruka (☎ *85910, fax 868 1135; singles/doubles €112/140, in high season €135/164, all rooms €79 June-Aug),* at the foot of the Ruka West ski slopes, is the largest hotel in Ruka. It has three parts: an old wing, the new wing (built in 2001) and apartments, along with a couple of restaurants, bars, nightclubs and karaoke – in many ways it's the thumping heart of the resort.

Royal Hotel Ruka (☎ *868 6000, fax 868 6100;* W *www.royalruka.fi; doubles €116),* down at the foot of the fell at the turn-off to Rukajärvi, is a well-appointed hotel with a restaurant, and breakfast and sauna included. Rates are slightly lower out of season.

Places to Eat

There are a few **cafés** and **grillis** in Ruka's main square, including one in the Rukaklubi building. Also on the square and part of the Safaritalo building, **Zone Restaurant** has a great terrace and is a lively spot for *apres ski* or relaxing after summer activities. **Pizzeria Montagna Di Ruka** (☎ *868 1445; pizzas €8-10; open 11am-11pm daily),* down at the Kelo ski-lift, is the place for Italian-style pizzas.

Riipisen Riistakauppa (☎ *868 1219; mains €12.50-34),* just up from Pizzeria Montagna, is a meat-lover's dream and a classic restaurant – popular with Finnish celebrities in winter. It's speciality is pricey game dishes, including sauteed wild boar, reindeer pepper steak, and hare or woodgrouse stew.

Kaltio Kivi *(mains €9.50-21.50),* the restaurant at the Rukahovi hotel, is unpretentious

and has reasonably priced pizza and pasta as well as an a la carte menu. The hotel also has plenty of nightlife in winter.

At Ruka East, **Ski Bistro** (☎ *860 0300)* offers a menu with an Alpine touch – dishes such as fondue – and live music during high season.

Getting There & Away

Ruka is 30km north of Kuusamo on main road No 5. Most regular bus services to Kuusamo continue further north to Ruka. During ski season (early November to early May) a skibus shuttles between Kuusamo and Ruka, stopping at all of the big hotels. In summer there's an excursion bus (see the Kuusamo Getting There & Away section for details).

KARHUNKIERROS TREK & OULANKA NATIONAL PARK

The 80km Karhunkierros (Bear's Ring), one of the oldest and best-established trekking routes in Finland, offers some of the country's most varied and breathtaking scenery. It's extremely popular during the *ruska* (autumn) period, but it can be walked practically anytime between late May and October.

Because the loop runs through some isolated areas within Oulanka National Park, getting there – or at least to and from the trailheads – will require some strategic planning. There are four possible starting points: the northern access point is from Hautajärvi visitor centre on the road to Salla; further south on road No 950 is the Ristikallio parking area where there's another starting point; in the south you can start the walk at Ruka ski resort; or further northeast at Juuma village. The best section of the trail runs from Ristikallio to Juuma. Also at Juuma there's a short but demanding marked loop trail, the 9km Little Bear's Ring (see that section later).

Information

Oulanka visitor centre (☎ *0205-646 850;* e *oulanka@metsa.fi; open 10am-8pm daily June-Aug, shorter hours Apr-May & Sept-Oct)* at Kiutaköngäs Rapids in the middle of Oulanka National Park is accessible by car or by bus along a partly sealed road from Käylä on road No 950. The centre has nature exhibits and a slide show, and sells trekking

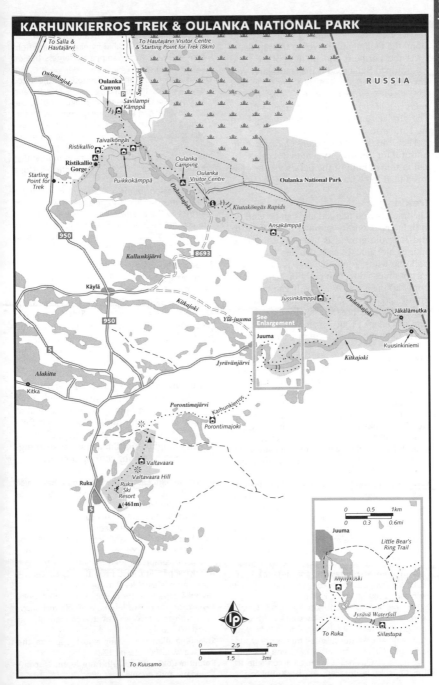

KARHUNKIERROS TREK & OULANKA NATIONAL PARK

To Salla & Hautajärvi

To Hautajärvi Visitor Centre & Starting Point for Trek (8km)

RUSSIA

Oulankajoki

Oulanka Canyon

Savilampi Kämppä

Taivalköngäs

Ristikallio

Ristikallio Gorge

Puikkokämppä

Oulanka Camping

Oulanka Visitor Centre

Oulanka National Park

Starting Point for Trek

Oulankajoki

Kiutaköngäs Rapids

Ansakämppä

950

Kallunkijärvi

8693

Käylä

Kitkajoki

Jussinkämppä

Oulankajoki

Jäkälämutka

Ylä-juuma

See Enlargement

Juuma

Kuusinkiniemi

950

5

Jyrävänjärvi

Kitkajoki

Alakitta

Kitka

Porontimajärvi

Karhunkierros

Porontimajoki

Ruka

Valtavaara

Valtavaara Hill

Ruka Ski Resort

▲(461m)

Juuma

0   0.5   1km
0   0.3   0.6mi

Little Bear's Ring Trail

Myllykoski

Jyrävä Waterfall

To Ruka

Siilastupa

0   2.5   5km
0   1.5   3mi

To Kuusamo

supplies, maps and fishing licences. There's also a café, and easy walking trails take you along the Oulankajoki river to the rapids.

At the northern end of the park on the Kuusamo to Salla road is the **Hautajärvi visitor centre** (☎ 0205-646 870, fax 0205-646 871; open 9am-6pm daily June-Aug, shorter hours rest of the year), in Hautajärvi village. The services and information provided here are similar to Oulanka.

The 1:40,000 *Rukatunturi-Oulanka* map is useful for treks of any length. It costs €12 and is sold at both of the park's visitor centres and at the Kuusamo tourist office.

Trekking

The track is well marked and can be walked in light shoes on dry summer days. Prior to mid-June the ground is too soggy to make hiking enjoyable. Even if you don't intend to walk the whole route, if you have a vehicle it's possible to do relatively short return treks from parking areas. A day walk can take you from Ristikallio to Oulanka Canyon, for example. It's also possible to drive to within 1km of Oulanka Canyon along a signposted dirt road about 12km north of Ristikallio.

Day 1 Start your trek at the parking area at the Ristikallio parking area. After 15 minutes you will reach the national park border. You can stop at a camp site at Aventojoki or proceed further to Ristikallio, which offers some breathtaking scenery. Proceed less than one hour further to reach Puikkokämppä hut at a small lake. Continue another kilometre past the lake to reach Taivalköngäs waterfall (near the wilderness hut of the same name), with two sets of rapids and three suspension bridges.

Northern extension If you really enjoy hiking, begin your trek further north at the Hautajärvi visitor centre – this adds an extra 22km to the hike. The landscape is unimpressive until the path reaches the Savinajoki river. The deep Oulanka Canyon is a highlight of this part of the trek. A wilderness hut, Savilampi kämppä, is at the Oulanka riverfront near Lake Savilampi, 18km south of Hautajärvi. The distance from Lake Savilampi to Taivalköngäs – where you'll join the Ristikallio trail – is 4km.

Day 2 The first leg is an 8km trek from Taivalköngäs through some ordinary scenery although there are a few beautiful lakes. After 4.2km, you can camp at Lake Runsulampi; there's dry wood available. About 4km further east, you can stay overnight at Oulanka Camping, or continue to the Oulanka visitor centre. The Kiutaköngäs

Rapids, just 800m from the visitor centre, are noted for the rugged cliffs nearby. It's possible to reach Ansakämppä cabin by early evening from here, or even Jussinkämppä wilderness hut on Lake Kulmakkajärvi.

Day 3 This is the most strenuous of the three days. A hike through ridges and forests (and boardwalks across wetlands) takes you to the Kitkajoki river, in another deep gorge. After following the river, you can choose between several routes, either walking directly to Juuma or crossing the river at Myllykoski to see the mighty Jyrävä waterfall (3km from Juuma) that has an elevation of 12m. There's the Siilastupa hut at Jyrävä.

Ruka extension Juuma is a convenient end point to the trek, but it's also possible to walk 23km further to Ruka, which has an excellent choice of accommodation and better road connections to Kuusamo. There are wilderness huts and designated camping grounds en route.

Places to Stay

Camping The Bear's Trail runs right though **Oulanka Camping** (☎ 863 429; Liikasenvaarantie 139; tent sites €10, 4-person cabins €37; open June–late Aug), 500m from the park visitor centre. It rents out canoes and rowing boats, and has a café and sauna.

There are a few camping grounds in Juuma; see Places to Stay under Juuma.

Wilderness Huts There is a good network of wilderness huts along the Karhunkierros route. They are all pretty similar and tend to be crowded in the high season. Dry firewood is generally available, but you'll need to carry a lightweight mattress for sleeping. From north to south, your options are:

Ristikallio 5km east of the main road, has a nice lakeside location. It accommodates 10 people and has dry firewood.

Puikkokämppä 2.5km further east, is a basic lakeside hut that sleeps 10 people.

Taivalköngäs 1.3km east, accommodates 15 people on two floors. You can cook on the gas stove or at the campfire.

Ansakämppä 7km east from the visitor centre, accommodates at least 10 people.

Jussinkämppä 9km further on, sleeps 20 people.

Myllykoski 2km from Juuma, is an old mill building with few facilities but it accommodates at least 10 people.

Siilastupa 4km from Juuma just opposite the Jyrävä waterfall, sleeps 12 people.

Porontimajoki – 8km south from Juuma, accommodates four people.

Getting There & Away

There are daily buses along the main road between Salla and Kuusamo, departing from either town and stopping at both the Ristikallio starting point and the Hautajärvi visitor centre. In summer there is an excursion bus Monday to Saturday from Kuusamo to the Oulanka visitor centre, Oulanka Camping and Kiutaköngäs Rapids. It also goes to Juuma – see the Kuusamo Getting There & Away section for details. In winter, take the daily school bus.

PADDLING THE KITKAJOKI

The rugged Kitkajoki offers some of the most challenging canoeing and kayaking in Finland. There are plenty of tricky rapids, including the class IV, 900m Aallokkokoski.

The village of Käylä, on the Kuusamo to Salla road, is a starting point for whitewater rafting along the Kitkajoki. There is a shop, a fuel station and a post office. You can also start the trip from Juuma, where it's about a 20km trip to the exit point near the Russian border. You can do this trip as an organised white-water adventure, or hire canoes or kayaks from the operators, who will also arrange transport at either end. Most of the operators are based in Kuusamo (see that section earlier). **Kitkan Safarit** (*☎/fax 853 458; Juumantie 134*), in Juuma, also arranges trips.

Käylä to Juuma

The first 14km leg of the journey is definitely the easier of the two and does not involve any carrying at all. You start at the Käylänkoski Rapids, and continue 3km to the easy Kiehtäjänniva, and a further kilometre to the Vähä-Käylänkoski Rapids. These are both class I rapids. After a bit more than 1km, there are three class II rapids spaced every 400m or so. A kilometre further, there's the trickiest one, the class III Harjakoski, which is 300m long. The rest of the journey, almost 7km, is mostly lakes. The road bridge between lakes Ylä and Ala-Juumajärvi marks the end of the trip. It is 1km to Juuma from the bridge.

Juuma to the Russian Border

This 20km journey is the most dangerous river route in Finland. You should be an expert paddler, and you *must* carry your canoe at least once – around the 12m, class VI Jyrävä waterfall. Inspect the tricky rapids before you let go and ask for local advice in case the water level is unfavourable.

The thrill starts just 300m after Juuma, with the class II Niskakoski. From here on, there is only 1km of quiet water. Myllykoski, with a water-mill, is a tricky class IV waterfall. Right after Myllykoski, the 900m Aallokkokoski Rapids mean quick paddling for quite some time. The Jyrävä waterfall comes right after this long section. Pull aside before Jyrävä, and carry your canoe. You might want to carry it from Myllykoski to well beyond the Jyrävä waterfall, skipping the Aallokkokoski Rapids.

After Jyrävä things cool down considerably, although there are some class III rapids. After about 6km, there is a wilderness hut, the Päähkänäkallio. When you meet the Oulankajoki, 7km downriver from the hut, paddle upriver to Jäkälämutka or downriver to Kuusinkiniemi, 100m from the Russian border. At either spot you can access a 4WD forest road that will take you back to civilisation. You must arrange return transport from this point in advance, as traffic is nonexistent.

PADDLING THE OULANKAJOKI

Equally impressive, and demanding, among the great Kuusamo river routes, the Oulankajoki gives you a chance to see mighty canyons from a canoe or kayak. You *must* carry your canoe at least four times – past parts of the Oulanka Canyon, and waterfalls at Taivalköngäs and Kiutaköngäs. Study a river map before starting out.

The first leg, an 18km trip, starts from road No 5, north of Ristikallio. The first 7km or so is relatively calm paddling, until you reach the impressive Oulanka Canyon. The safe section extends for about 1km, after which you should pull aside and carry your canoe past the dangerous rapids. You can overnight at Savilampi hut.

Some 3km after Savilampi are the Taivalköngäs Rapids. You'll need to carry your canoe, and there's a hut here, too. The next 6km are quiet, until you reach Kiutaköngäs Rapids, where you'll again need to carry your canoe. The park visitor centre and a camping ground are near here.

The second leg of the journey, a full 20km long, starts on the other side of Kiutaköngäs waterfall. You pass through 500m of quiet waters, then there's another water-fall, and it's carrying-time again!

On the final leg, the river becomes smooth and there is little to worry about as far as rapids go. This leg is suitable for families with children.

JUUMA
☎ 08

The village of Juuma is the most popular base for treks along the Karhunkierros route. It's a convenient place to stock up on supplies, has several basic accommodation options, and there's daily transport from Kuusamo.

If you have only a little time for trekking, you can take the **Little Bear's Ring**, a 9km loop trail, to Myllykoski Rapids and Lake Jyrävänjärvi. The trail is short but crosses varying terrain, and has several interesting sights, including the 12m Jyrävä waterfall. The walk can be done in four hours and takes in some of the best of the entire Bear's Ring. There are two wilderness huts on this trail – Myllykoski and Siilastupa (see Places to Stay in the Karhunkierros Trekking Route & Oulanka National Park section) – and a couple of swing bridges.

Kitkan Safarit (☎/fax 853 458; W www .kitkansafarit.fi; Juumantie 134), near the car park, arranges white-water rafting along the Kitkajoki and Oulankjoki rivers, and rents out canoes and kayaks. A short 'family' paddle costs €25 per person, the 1½-hour 'wild route' is €35, the four-hour complete route is €68, and canoeing on the Oulanka-joki is €43.

Places to Stay & Eat
There are numerous accommodation choices in Juuma from June to August, and some places stay open throughout September. Cottages can be rented year-round; contact the Kuusamo tourist office or Matka-Ruka travel agency in Kuusamo for assistance.

Lomakylä Retkietappi (☎ 863 218; Ju-umantie 134; tent sites €10, 4-person cabins €30; open June–late Sept), on the Karhun-kierros trail and at the start of the Little Bear's Ring, is the most convenient place to stay. The café serves snacks and meals. It also has a sauna, and rents out rowing boats and bicycles.

Juuman Leirintä (☎ 863 212; Riekamontie 1; tent sites €10, cabins €22, self-contained cottages €53; open year-round) has a lakeside

location, a sauna and a café-grilli that's open until 9pm.

Getting There & Away
In summer, the excursion bus makes the 50km trip from Kuusamo to Juuma, via Ruka, twice daily (except Sunday).

ISO-SYÖTE & PIKKU-SYÖTE
☎ 08

Just two decades ago, Syöte, the southern-most fell in Finland, was covered by virgin forest. Not any more. Syöte's twin peaks, Iso-Syöte and Pikku-Syöte ('Big Syöte' and 'Little Syöte', respectively), are now dotted with ski lifts, ski tracks, hotels and restaurants. The proximity to Oulu, about two hours by car, makes this a popular winter ski destination.

In addition to its winter sports facilities, the Syöte area offers the visitor access to the protected government recreational area to the north and southwest of Iso-Syöte, with a network of walking tracks and wilderness huts.

Pudasjärven Matkailu Oy (☎ 823 400, fax 823 421, Varsitie 7; open 8am-5pm Mon-Fri), in Pudasjärvi, is a travel agency that provides tourist information and assistance for the Syöte region. For online accommodation bookings and detailed information go to W www.syote.net.

Activities
At Iso-Syöte, there are 21 downhill slopes and 11 lifts. The vertical drop is 192m and the longest run is 1200m. There are some 110km of cross-country trails, all clearly marked. You can rent skiing equipment and purchase lift passes at Romekievari station.

Relatively few trekkers take advantage of the excellent walking tracks and free wilderness huts around Syöte. The majority of trekkers use the Ahmatupa hut as a base, and do a loop around the northern part of the trekking area. Another route, indicated by yellow markings on trees, makes a loop around Iso-Syöte hill. Additionally, the UKK route crosses through Syöte; see the UKK Trekking Route section earlier in this chapter.

There are three fishing areas near Syöte, and the Forest and Park Service stocks them all. On the Pärjänjoki and Livojoki Rivers, fishing is from June to mid-September. In lakes Hanhilampi, Kellarilampi and Lautta-lampi, near Iso-Syöte, you can fish at any time except May.

Places to Stay & Eat

Practically all accommodation in the Syöte region can and should be arranged through Pudasjärven Matkailu Oy (see earlier in this section). Daily, weekly and weekend rates are available and in summer the places that remain open offer bargain rates, from around €200 a week.

Hostel Syote (☎ *838 172, fax 838 173;* Ⓦ *www.syotekeskus.fi; dorm beds €14; open year-round*) is a five-bed HI Hostel and eas-ily the cheapest accommodation in the region. It's in the village centre near Pikku-Syote and has a café.

There are dozens of *kelo* (pine) log cabins on top of Syöte Hill, and the most luxurious are equipped with kitchenettes and TVs. In the spring high season (the weeks surround-ing Easter), these cabins cost from €100/500 per night/week and accommodate six people.

There are three **wilderness huts** and sev-eral kota or laavu shelters around the Syöte area, all of which can be used free of charge.

Bring food supplies with you in summer, as many places are shuttered once the ski season winds down.

Getting There & Away

There is a bus service from Oulu to Syöte (140km, 2½ hours) each weekday afternoon. The bus back to Oulu departs each weekday morning.

Lapland & Sapmi

There's a romance and intrigue about Lapland that makes it one of the 'must-sees' on any Finnish travel itinerary. It's inextricably linked with the midnight sun and the aurora borealis (northern lights), with wandering herds of reindeer and the Santa Claus legend. It conjures up images of a pristine and serene land, more often than not blanketed in snow. To say it's a land of contrasts is cliched but inevitable – winter and summer here are as different as night and day.

Covering almost half of the entire country, the sparsely populated northernmost region is *the* great wilderness adventure in Finland. Here you'll find some of the best preserved wilderness in Europe – though much of it really is barren, lifeless tundra. Whether you just drive through it or do extensive trekking around the region, set aside enough time to get off the main roads.

The far northern part of Lapland is known as Sapmi, home of the Sami people and their reindeer herds. The main Sami communities are around Inari and Hetta.

Lapland has a population of 200,000, or 2.1 people per sq km, and much of that population lives in a few of towns in southern Lapland. The true wilderness is further north. Rovaniemi is the capital of and gateway to Lapland and the best place to start a tour.

HISTORY

Finnish Lapland was inhabited as early as the Stone Age, but was probably not as heavily settled as the Finnmark region in northern Norway. When Sami peoples were pushed north by migrating Finns, traditions evolved and developed. Many legends remain, including those of miracle-working witches who could fly and transform themselves into strange creatures. Conspicuous lakes or rocks became *seita* (holy sites), the island of Ukko on Lake Inarijärvi being the best known of these.

The banks of the Tornionjoki, as well as the mouth of the Kemijoki nearby, developed into busy trading centres during medieval times. Some traces of Viking contacts have been found. The king of Sweden granted the Pirkka people (of Häme) exclusive rights to collect taxes among Lapps in the 13th century, and their centre grew at Tornio. Finns moved further north along the rivers.

Highlights

- Experiencing Finland's best wilderness fell walking under the midnight sun in places like Saariselkä, Lemmenjoki National Park and Kilpisjärvi

- Leading a team of huskies on an extended dog-sledding expedition – expensive but a true Lappish experience

- Taking the opportunity to see the aurora borealis – nature's Arctic light show

- Shopping for handicrafts in the Sami settlement of Inari, and visiting the superb Siida museum

- Winter skiing or snowboarding at some of Finland's best resorts: Levi, Ylläs and Saariselkä

- Dare we suggest it, but finally making it to the Arctic Circle and dropping in on Santa's post office – at any time of year but especially Christmas!

Inari was an important Sami trading centre in the early 1500s, when there were Sami settlements around the vast territory. During the 1600s, Swedes increased their presence throughout northern Finland. In 1670, cult sites and religious objects of the Sami were destroyed by Gabriel Tuderus, who represented the Lutheran Church. Wooden churches were built throughout Lapland, the oldest remaining in Sodankylä and Tervola, south of Rovaniemi.

During the following centuries, more Finns were attracted to the vast province, adopted reindeer-herding and were assimilated into the Sami communities (or vice versa), especially in southern Lapland. In 1800, there were 463 Samis in Inari and only 18 Finns. One hundred years later, there were 800 Samis and 585 Finns. At that time, there were only paths to the northernmost parts of Lapland. The first gravel road to Ivalo was built in 1913, to Inari in 1924 and to Karigasniemi during WWII.

The area of Petsamo, northeast of Inari, was annexed to Finland in 1920 as a result of the Treaty of Tartu and a nickel mine was opened in 1937. Russians attacked the area during the Winter War and the area was evacuated on 4 September 1944. The Soviet Union annexed the mineral-rich area and has kept it ever since. The Scolt Samis from Petsamo were settled in Sevettijärvi, Nellim and Virtaniemi in northeastern Lapland.

The peace agreement of 1944 between Finland and the Soviet Union stated that Germans had to leave Finnish territory immediately, but while retreating to northern Norway the troops of Nazi Germany burned and destroyed all buildings in their path. Apart from a few churches and a few villages, only some isolated houses in Lapland date from the period before WWII.

Lapland has eventually emerged from this devastation as one of the most affluent regions in Finland, benefiting from booming tourism and generous subsidies from the south.

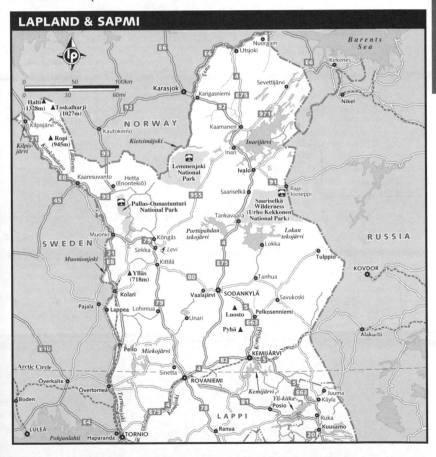

LAPLAND & SAPMI

Rovaniemi

☎ 016 • pop 35,200

Rovaniemi is the capital of and gateway to Lapland. Many travellers make a beeline here from Helsinki, either to say they've visited Lapland or to 'cross' the Arctic Circle. Neither is a major event in its own right, but there's a lot to be said for this latitude in summer – when the midnight sun really does shine – and in winter this is a convenient base for expensive dog- or reindeer-sledding, skiing or snowmobile safaris.

The town itself is modern and relatively uninteresting. After its complete destruction by the Germans in 1944, it was rebuilt from a plan by Alvar Aalto, with the main streets radiating out from Hallituskatu in the shape of reindeer antlers – though this would only be obvious from the air. Until that time, Rovaniemi had been classified as a *kauppala*, or a trading centre. Hidden land mines remained for years following WWII.

Information

Tourist Offices The tourist office shamelessly goes by the name **Santa Claus Tourist Centre** (☎ 346 270; W *www.rovaniemi.fi; Rovakatu 21; open 8am-6pm Mon-Fri, 10am-4pm Sat & Sun June–late Aug, 8am-4pm Mon-Fri rest of the year*), but is an excellent source of information for all of Lapland. **Etiäinen** (☎ 647 820; *open 10am-5pm daily*) at Napapiiri (see the Around Rovaniemi section) is the information centre for the national parks

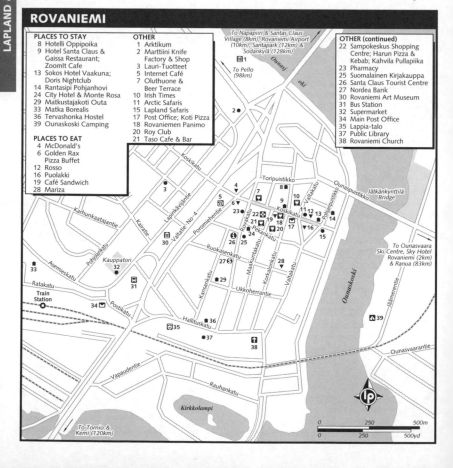

ROVANIEMI

PLACES TO STAY
8 Hotelli Oppipoika
9 Hotel Santa Claus & Gaissa Restaurant; ZoomIt Cafe
13 Sokos Hotel Vaakuna; Doris Nightclub
14 Rantasipi Pohjanhovi
21 City Hotel & Monte Rosa
29 Matkustajakoti Outa
33 Matka Borealis
36 Tervashonka Hostel
39 Ounaskoski Camping

PLACES TO EAT
4 McDonald's
6 Golden Rax Pizza Buffet
12 Rosso
16 Puolakki
19 Café Sandwich
28 Mariza

OTHER
1 Arktikum
2 Marttiini Knife Factory & Shop
3 Lauri-Tuotteet
5 Internet Café
7 Oluthuone & Beer Terrace
10 Irish Times
11 Arctic Safaris
15 Lapland Safaris
17 Post Office; Koti Pizza
18 Rovaniemen Panimo
20 Roy Club
21 Taso Cafe & Bar

OTHER (continued)
22 Sampokeskus Shopping Centre; Harun Pizza & Kebab; Kahvila Pullapiika
23 Pharmacy
25 Suomalainen Kirjakauppa
26 Santa Claus Tourist Centre
27 Nordea Bank
30 Rovaniemi Art Museum
31 Bus Station
32 Supermarket
34 Main Post Office
35 Lappia-talo
37 Public Library
38 Rovaniemi Church

and trekking regions, with information on hiking and fishing in Lapland. The office also sells maps and fishing permits, and books cottages.

Post & Communications The main post office *(Postikatu 1)* is near the train and bus stations. There is a more central **post office** *(Koskikatu 9)*, but most visitors prefer to send their postcards from the busy Santa Claus post office at Napapiiri.

The Aalto–designed **public library** *(Hallituskatu 9; open 11am-8pm Mon-Fri, 10am-4pm Sat)* has several Internet terminals and a newspaper reading room with foreign periodicals. There's a small Internet café in a shop on Poromiehentie (€3 an hour).

Travel Agencies The largest and best established of Rovaniemi's tour operators, **Lapland Safaris** *(☎ 331 1200;* W *www.lapland safaris.com; Koskikatu 1)* and **Arctic Safaris** *(☎ 340 0400;* W *www.arcticsafaris.fi; Koskikatu 6)* has weekly tour programmes for winter and summer, offering everything from river cruises, white-water rafting, fishing and visits to reindeer farms to snowmobiling, sledding and skiing. There are several other tour operators near the main hotels.

Bookshop The **Suomalainen Kirjakauppa** *(Rovakatu 24)* sells English-language paperbacks, and Lapland maps.

Arktikum

With its beautifully designed glass tunnel stretching out to the Ounasjoki river, Arktikum *(☎ 317 840;* W *www.arktikum.fi; Pohjoisranta 4; adult/student/child €10/8.50/5; open 9am-8pm daily June-Aug, 10am-5pm Tues-Sun Sept-May)* is one of Finland's better museums. Exhibition spaces include superb static and interactive displays focusing on Arctic flora and fauna as well as on the Sami and other peoples of Arctic Europe, Asia and North America. Arktikum is far from just photographs and interpretive displays – there are many re-creations of the nomadic camps, canoes, costumes and equipment from several Arctic research expeditions. There's also a multivision theatre and a research library. You should allow yourself at least a couple of hours to get around it all.

Lappia-talo

Rovaniemi's concert hall *(☎ 322 2499; Hallituskatu; open 11am-5pm Tues-Thur, 11am-7pm Fri, 11am-2pm Sat)* is one of several buildings here designed by architect Alvar Aalto (others include the adjacent library and town hall). The hall is used by the Rovaniemi Theatre Company, Lapland Music School and Chamber Orchestra of Lapland, among others. Guided tours (€2) are given from 10am to 2pm Monday to Friday in summer.

Rovaniemi Art Museum

This museum *(☎ 322 2822; Lapinkävijäntie 4; adult/student/child €3.40/1.70/free; open noon-5pm Tues-Sun)* has changing temporary exhibitions of contemporary Finnish art.

Rovaniemi Church

The church *(Kirkkotie 1; open 9am-9pm daily June–late Aug)* was completed in 1950, replacing the one destroyed during WWII. The fresco above the altar depicts a Christ figure emerging from Lappish scenery.

Marttiini Knife Factory

The former factory *(☎ 330 3396; Vartiokatu 32; open 10am-6pm Mon-Fri, 10am-1pm Sat)* of Finland's most famous knife manufacturer is open to visitors. It has a small knife and photo exhibition and shop where you can buy knives cheaper than elsewhere. It's across the road from Arktikum

Ounasvaara Ski Centre

This winter ski centre *(☎ 369 045;* W *www .ounasvaara.net)*, about 3km east of the town centre, has five downhill ski slopes and three ski jumps, plus 123km of cross-country skiing tracks. The longest downhill run is 600m with a vertical drop of 140m. Skiing equipment can be rented at Sky Hotel Rovaniemi, downhill equipment at the Ounasvaara Slalom Centre. In summer, Ounasvaara has a **toboggan run** *(rides €5; open noon-8pm daily mid-June–mid-Aug)* alongside the hotel.

Activities & Organised Tours

If you have the funds for it, Rovaniemi is a terrific base from which to sample 'typically Lappish' activities. There's a greater number of tourists here than elsewhere so tours go out daily during the summer and winter high seasons; the downside is the feeling that you're not quite in Lapland's remote wilderness.

LAPLAND & SÁPMI

Snowmobile and husky- or reindeer-sled **safaris** are popular in winter. Summer tours include **river cruises** (often combined with a visit to a reindeer farm), **white-water rafting** and **fishing** expeditions. Summer tours range from €45 to €115 per person. Unsurprisingly, winter activities are more expensive: snowmobile safaris start at €85 per person and go up to €143, depending on what they're combined with, and there's a hefty supplement if you're only one person riding the snowmobile; snowmobiling combined with snowshoe hiking or a visit to a husky farm is around €95 per person; an ice-fishing trip is around €120 per person; and snowmobiling plus a reindeer-sleigh ride is €143.

For bookings contact one of the travel agencies in town (see the Travel Agencies section earlier) or the tourist office.

Bicycles can be rented from **Arctic Safaris** (*Koskikatu 6*). They cost €18 for 24 hours.

Special Events

Rovaniemi is as busy in winter as it is in summer, so there are festivals here year-round. With the Arctic Circle – and Santa Claus – close by, Christmas is a big time of the year and there are plenty of festive activities in December. The **Northern Lights Festival** in February offers a variety of sports and arts events. In March, Rovaniemi hosts the **Ounasvaara Winter Games**, with skiing and ski-jumping competitions. **Jutajaiset**, a festival in June, showcases folk music, dance and other Lappish traditions.

Places to Stay

Camping In a pleasant spot just across the river from the town centre, **Ounaskoski Camping** (*☎ 345 304; Jäämerentie 1; camping €5*) has tent and van sites only.

Hostels & Guesthouses Services at **Tervashonka Hostel** (*☎ 344 644; Hallituskatu 16; dorm beds €16, singles/doubles €30/36; open year-round*) include a wake-up call to make sure you're out by 10am. It is an 'old-school' hostel but is no worse for that – facilities are not flash by Finnish standards, but it has character. Reception is closed from 10am to 5pm, and closes again at 10pm (ring ahead if you're coming on the night train).

Matka Borealis (*☎/fax 342 0130; Asemieskatu 1; singles/doubles €40/52, €38/50 in winter*), a few minutes' walk from the train station, is a friendly guesthouse offering clean, simple rooms with breakfast included.

Matkustajakoti Outa (*☎ 312 474; Ukkoherrantie 16; singles/doubles €30/40*) is another cheap, no-frills guesthouse with shared bathrooms, but this one is right in the town centre.

Hotels There are a dozen standard business hotels of varying quality in Rovaniemi, but all offer cheap summer and weekend rates, and most include breakfast and sauna in the price.

Hotelli Oppipoika (*☎ 338 8111, 346 969; ⒺQhotel.oppipoika@ramk.fi; Korkalonkatu 33; singles/doubles €73/86, weekends & summer €61/74*) is one of the cheaper hotels but is well equipped with a gym, swimming pool and a highly rated restaurant.

Rantasipi Pohjanhovi (*☎ 33 711, fax 313 997; Pohjanpuistikko 2; singles/doubles €103/121, doubles on weekends €86, doubles in summer €69*) is the oldest hotel in Rovaniemi. It has a legendary restaurant with live music.

Hotel Santa Claus (*☎ 321 321, fax 321 3222; Ⓦ www.hotelsantaclaus.fi; Korkalonkatu 29; singles/doubles €108/130, weekends & summer €83*) is, in spite of the corny name (it had to happen), a very nice, brand new hotel. Unusually large rooms have all the trimmings and some strange '70s touches involving red velour.

City Hotel (*☎ 330 0111, fax 311 304; Ⓦ www.city-hotelli.fi; Pekankatu 9; singles/doubles €78/98, weekends & summer €69/80*) is quite stylish – there's a piano bar in the lobby with chesterfield couches and an American–style restaurant (Monte Rosa) with a summer terrace. Rooms are compact but have style.

Sokos Hotel Vaakuna (*☎ 332 211, fax 332 2199; Koskikatu 4; singles/doubles €106/127, weekends €83, summer €79*) is one of the town's top hotels with elegant rooms, a big breakfast and free sauna.

Sky Hotel Rovaniemi (*☎ 335 3311, fax 318 789; Ⓔ skyhotel@laplandhotels.com; Ounasvaarantie; doubles from €69 in summer, from €126 Jan-May*) is 3km east of the town centre at the top of Ounasvaara Hill. The main reason to stay here is to be on the doorstep of the winter ski centre, although in summer it's a peaceful spot away from the 'bustle' of Rovaniemi, and rooms are quite substantially discounted.

Places to Eat

Rovaniemi has plenty of grillis and hamburger restaurants, including **Harun Pizza & Kebab** in the Sampokeskus shopping centre. This Arctic town is also home to the world's northernmost **McDonald's** – strangely enough a Big Mac tastes the same here as it does in Tasmania.

The partly pedestrianised Koskikatu (between Rovakatu and Pohjanpuistikko) has plenty of inexpensive and mid-range restaurants, including branches of **Rosso** and **Koti Pizza**. **Cafe Sandwich** is a good place for cheap takeaways with sandwiches for around €3, and **ZoomIt** is a big café with a terrace – good for breakfast or lunch. There's a branch of good ol' **Golden Rax Pizza Buffet** on the corner of Poromiehentie.

Kahvila Pullapiika, in the Sampokeskus shopping centre, is a popular meeting place for locals of all ages.

Mariza *(Ruokasenkatu 2; lunch buffet €5.90-6.50; open for lunch Mon-Fri)* is a simple working-class place offering a fabulous lunch buffet of home-cooked Finnish food including hot dishes, soup and salad.

Gaissa Restaurant *(mains €10.50-18.50)* on the 2nd floor of Santa Claus Hotel (above ZoomIt café) serves a well-prepared mix of Lappish and international food including tapas, pasta and curries.

Monte Rosa *(Pekankatu 9; mains €9-12)*, attached to the City Hotel, offers an earthy range of pasta, Tex-Mex (fajitas etc) and American–Finnish dishes, and has a great terrace at the side.

Puolakki *(Valtakatu; mains €15-25)* is arguably Rovaniemi's best restaurant when it comes to traditional Lappish cuisine. It's not cheap and the restaurant itself is unassuming, but the food is delicious and includes reindeer, whitefish, and cloudberry desserts.

Entertainment

Discounting the winter ski resorts, Rovaniemi is the only place north of Oulu with a half-decent nightlife, and along with the partying locals there's always a few curious tourists. In summer it's hard to resist sitting out under the midnight sun in the open beer terrace of **Oluthuone**, set up on the pedestrian part of Koskikatu.

Rovaniemen Panimo *(Koskikatu 11)* is a popular English-style pub with cosy seating, a small terrace and international beers on tap.

Irish Times *(Valtakatu 35)* has a great heated terrace at the back, pool tables downstairs and is a snug place to ensconce yourself in winter.

Taso Cafe & Bar *(Maakuntakatu)* is Rovaniemi's trendiest café, with loungy, lime-green retro furniture, newspapers and magazines, a hip young crowd and DJs on weekend evenings. You can get light snacks here, but it's mainly a place to drink and socialise.

Across the road, the basement **Roy Club** *(Maakuntakatu 24)* takes over some of the Taso crowd after 2am and is usually packed with students.

Roveniemi's major business hotels all have nightclubs and dancing, with a minimum age of 20 to 24 and a cover charge of around €5 on weekends. **Doris Nightclub**, in the Sokos Hotel Vaakuna, is a popular choice, open until 4am most nights. For Finnish-style dancing (tango and *humppa*), try **Rantasipi Pohjanhovi** (see Places to Stay later).

Inside the Sampokeskus shopping centre you'll find a **cinema**, usually offering recent American releases subtitled in Swedish and Finnish.

Shopping

Sami handicrafts made from reindeer skin and horn, or of Arctic birch, are popular souvenirs.

Trekkers may want to buy a *kuksa* (carved birch cup). The traditional Sami costume, which is very colourful, and handmade Sami hats, mittens and shoes are also swift-selling souvenirs.

The widest selection of souvenirs (and decent prices) can be found in shops at the **Napapiiri** (see the Around Rovaniemi section). In Rovaniemi itself, check out **Lauri-Tuottet** *(Pohjolankatu 25)*.

Getting There & Away

Air Rovaniemi is Finland's most northerly major airport, and Finnair has daily flights here from Helsinki, Kemi and Oulu. The stand-by and summer discounted flights can be good value if you want to avoid the long train or bus ride from Helsinki.

Bus Rovaniemi is the main transport hub in Lapland. Frequent express buses go to Kemi (€14.60) and Oulu (€26.70, 3½ hours) to the south; also to Muonio, Hetta (Enontekiö; €35.20, five hours) and Kilpisjärvi (€45.70, eight hours) in the northwest; Kuusamo (€22.90) in the east; and to Sodankylä (€16.80, 1¾ hours), Ivalo (€30.90) and Inari (€36.60) in the north, continuing on to Norway.

Train The train is the best way to travel between Helsinki and Rovaniemi (€69.20, 10 to 12 hours) – it's considerably quicker and cheaper than the bus. There are eight daily trains (via Oulu), including four overnight services. There's one train connection daily to Kemijärvi, further north (1½ hours).

Getting Around

The Rovaniemi airport is 10km north of the town centre. Buses meet each arriving flight (€3.50). Airport buses leave the bus station 50 minutes before flight departures, picking up at several hotels in the centre.

Most major car-rental agencies are represented, and have offices in the centre and at the airport. Try **Hertz** (☎ 313 300; Pohjanpuistikko 2), at Rantasipi Pohjanhovi, or **Budget** (☎ 312 266; Koskikatu 9), beside the post office.

Around Rovaniemi

NAPAPIIRI (THE ARCTIC CIRCLE) & SANTA CLAUS VILLAGE

The Arctic Circle is the southernmost line at which the midnight sun can be seen, at a latitude of roughly 66.5° north. In Finland the Arctic Circle is called **Napapiiri** and it crosses the main Rovaniemi–Sodankylä road about 8km north of Rovaniemi (although, since all celestial bodies affect each other, the Arctic Circle can shift several metres daily). In any case, from here on up the sun never truly sets in midsummer and never rises in midwinter.

Although the Arctic Circle can be crossed by road at several points in Lapland, the official **Arctic Circle marker** is right here, conveniently painted on the roadside – and (surprise, surprise) built right on top of it is the 'official' **Santa Claus Village** (W www.santaclausvillage.info; admission free; open 9am-7pm daily June-Aug & Dec, 10am-5pm daily Sept-May). Rarely do you get a chance to see such unadulterated commercialism in one neat little package. This, if Lapland's claims are true, is the home of Christmas and jolly ol' Saint Nick. The **Santa Claus Main**

Will the Real Santa Claus Please Stand Up?

Finland, and particularly Lapland, has a strong claim to being the home of Santa Claus, popularly known as a roly-poly fellow with a long white beard, clad in a red, fur-trimmed suit, who drives a sled and delivers presents at Christmas time. This isn't the North Pole, but Lapland has the reindeer, the winter climate, the mystique and these days it has Santa's post office. But the historic St Nicholas – the real man behind the Santa myth – wouldn't have known a reindeer from a camel and would have melted in a typical Santa suit, as he lived in temperate present-day Turkey!

The story of the real St Nicholas goes something like this: many centuries ago, a poor peasant, father of three daughters, did not have enough money for their wedding dowries. To ensure that at least two of the daughters would have money enough to attract husbands, the man decided that he would have to sell the youngest daughter into slavery. One sad day the heartsick father announced his decision: the youngest daughter would leave the following morning. The soon-to-be-sainted Nicholas, who may or may not have been a chimney sweep, got word of the terrible situation, crept into the family's house while they were sleeping and magically filled a sock with golden coins. The youngest daughter was saved, all three daughters were joyfully married and the whole family lived happily ever after.

Since then Santa Claus (Santa means saint; Claus is an abbreviation of Nicholas) has been filling socks with presents every Christmas season. In Finland, Uncle Markus, a famous radio announcer since the 1930s, established the Finnish legend that a gift-giving Santa Claus lived in the Korvatunturi Hill, right at the Russian border. Long before that, in pagan times, Finns had believed in an evil male goat spirit that demanded gifts on the shortest day of the year. The two stories, of Santa and the evil goat, eventually blended, which is why the Finnish name for Santa is *Joulupukki*, which literally translates as 'Christmas stud goat'.

Post Office *(FIN-96930 Arctic Circle)* is here and it receives close to a million letters each year from children all over the world. As tacky and trite as this may sound, it's all good fun. You can send a postcard home with an official Santa stamp (you can arrange to have it delivered at Christmas); have a photograph taken with Father Christmas himself (signs warn would-be photographers that Santa is a registered trademark and can only be photographed by his elves!); and for adults, there is a hokey 'Arctic Circle Initiation Ceremony'. Tour groups have great fun crossing the line painted on the asphalt (supposedly marking the circle) in order to be awarded their Arctic Circle certificates.

Even if you're not interested in all the Christmas hype, the village has some of the best souvenir and handicraft **shops** in Lapland, some good cafés and restaurants, a traditional salmon-smoking fire, and Etiäinen, the information centre for national parks and trekking regions (see the Tourist Offices section under Rovaniemi earlier).

Santapark

This Christmas-theme amusement park at Syvasenvaara Mountain *(☎ 333 0000;* Ⓦ *www .santapark.com; adult/child/family €20/15/50; open 10am-8pm daily early Dec–mid-Jan, early June–late Aug & Easter hols, limited hours)* is 2km west of the Rovaniemi airport. Local buses connect the park with the city centre. Additionally, there is a free shuttle service between Santa Claus Village and Santapark, or in winter you can pay a fee to travel by snowmobile or reindeer sleigh between the two attractions. Santapark is built inside a cavern in the mountain and features a Magic Sleigh Ride, a Christmas Carousel, a theatre, a cafeteria and, of course, Santa Claus himself. It's great fun for kids but otherwise give it a miss. Discount ticket packages are available for families.

RANUA WILDLIFE PARK

The town of Ranua, 80km south of Rovaniemi on road No 78, is home to the Ranua Wildlife Park *(☎ 355 1921; adult/student €10/8.50; open 9am-8pm daily June–mid-Aug, shorter hours mid-Aug–May)*, the northernmost of all such parks and a popular (though long) day trip from Rovaniemi. Its 30 mammal and 30 bird species – including brown and polar bears, forest reindeer, owls,

lynx, Arctic fox and wolverines – are native to Finland and Scandinavia and are housed in spacious natural enclosures linked by a 3km circular path. Like any such park or zoo the animals may well be asleep or hiding – time your visit for the morning or evening. Still, this may be your only chance to see *hirvi* – the elusive Finnish moose (other than staring at you from a trophy wall or plastered on the side of the road, of course).

There are daily buses to Ranua from Oulu and Kajaani, and several daily connections from Rovaniemi (€20.60 return, 1¼ hours).

Western Lapland

Lapland is not all bleak wilderness and fell-walking. The southwestern corner of Lapland, which faces the Gulf of Bothnia (Pohjanlahti), is usually referred to as Sea Lapland, and in the south it is relatively urban, industrialised and prosperous. Moving north, the region is dominated by the mighty rivers, Tornionjoki and Muonionjoki, which follow the border from Tornio to Kilpisjärvi. In the remote northwestern 'arm' of Lapland, you'll find Finland's highest mountains, which offer good trekking opportunities and in turn lead to the mountainous regions of Norway and Sweden. In summer, the main reason to venture into this area is for walking, particularly in the Pallas-Ounastunturi National Park and Kilpisjärvi regions, and fishing, kayaking and white-water rafting in the fast-flowing rivers. In winter you'll find some of Finland's most popular downhill ski resorts here – Levi, Ylläs and Olos – along with opportunities for dog-sledding.

This section covers the western route to Norway, from Tornio to Kilpisjärvi (see the Oulu, Kainuu & Koillismaa Regions chapter for details of Kemi and Tornio). Main road No 21 follows the Finnish border with Sweden, and there are six crossings over the Tornionjoki (Torneälv) and Muonionjoki (at Tornio/Haparanda, Aavasaksa/Overtornea, Pello, Kolari, Muonio, Kaaresuvanto/Karesuando). There are no passport or customs formalities and if you're driving along the border you can easily alternate between countries. See the Getting There & Away chapter at the start of the book for more details on border crossings.

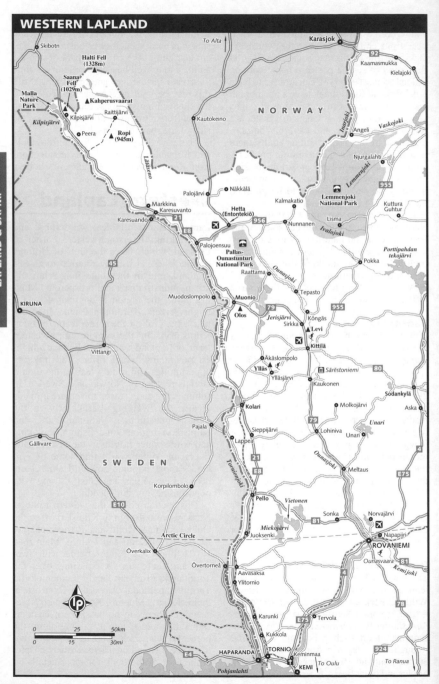

WESTERN LAPLAND

YLLÄS
☎ 016

Ylläs, 35km northeast of Kolari, is the highest fell in Finland to offer downhill skiing. Not surprisingly, it is also one of Finland's most popular skiing centres, particularly among families. There are plenty of events in winter, and a music festival in July. Mountain biking and hiking are increasingly popular summer activities in the Ylläs area, although Ylläs fell itself is the not the prettiest thing to look at in summer – completely denuded of trees as it is.

On either side of the mountain are the villages Äkäslompolo and Ylläsjärvi. Both are typical ski-resort towns filled with top-end hotels and holiday cottages, although Ylläsjärvi is smaller and quieter and it virtually shuts down outside the ski season.

Kellokas Nature Centre (☎ 647 039) is a national parks visitor centre at the foot of the western slopes, about 3km from Äkäslompolo village. It has environmental and geological exhibits on the surrounding area and multimedia displays, as well as maps, information and advice on hiking in the Ylläs-Aakenus Nature Reserve.

For tourist information in Äkäslompolo, contact **Ylläksen Matkailu Oy** (☎ 561 721, fax 561 337) or **Ylläs Holiday Service** (☎ 569 666).

Activities
There's plenty going on in Ylläs virtually year-round, though summer is naturally much quieter. In winter, as well as skiing, you can arrange snowmobiling, sledding and reindeer-herding expeditions.

Skiing & Snowboarding Ylläs sports 37 downhill slopes and 17 lifts, plus special areas for snowboarders. The vertical drop is 463km and the longest run is 3km. Cross-country skiing trails total some 250km. Lift passes cost €26 per day and equipment rental and ski lessons are available. The ski season usually runs from November to May.

Mountain Biking & Hiking In summer Ylläs is popular with mountain-biking enthusiasts. **Ylläs Holiday Service** (☎ 569 666; W www.yllasholiday.com) rents bikes (from €11.80 a day) and has guided bike tours.

There are numerous nature trails and hiking possibilities in the region. The best known are the 3.5km **Varkaankuru** ('Thieves

Gorge') nature trail, and the 12km **Ptarmigan's Round**, both of which start from the Kellokas Nature Centre. For experienced hikers it's possible to walk all the way to Pallas-Ounastunturi National Park.

Places to Stay
There are plenty of empty hotel rooms and cottages around Ylläs during summer but many places close completely – there is no accommodation in Ylläsjärvi during summer. In winter, accommodation is harder to come by, more expensive and some places require a minimum stay of a week or weekend. For accommodation bookings, contact **Ylläs Majoituspalvelut** (☎ 482 000 in Ylläsjärvi • ☎ 0208-692 585 in Äkäslompolo).

Holiday Centre Seita (☎ 569 211, fax 569 360; W www.seitahotelli.fi; 2- to 4-person cottages €52-67 May-Aug), on the main road in Äkäslompolo, is a complex including a hotel, cottages, restaurant, smoke sauna and pool, and is one of the more reasonably priced places. In the winter high season rooms and cottages are let only by the week from €280-560 per person.

Hotel Yllashumina (☎ 569 501; W www.yllashumina.com; Tiurajarventie; apartment doubles from €40-60), also in Äkäslompolo, is a good restaurant-pub with reasonably priced apartments for rent.

Getting There & Away
During the ski season, there is a shuttle service from Kittilä airport to Ylläsjärvi and Äkäslompolo.

The nearest train station is at Kolari and there are connecting buses to Ylläsjärvi and Äkäslompolo.

A few long-distance buses travel via Äkäslompolo each week. For Ylläsjärvi, catch one of the local buses that run Monday to Friday between Kolari and Kittilä.

KITTILÄ
☎ 016 • pop 3000

Although one of the main service centres for northwestern Lapland, Kittilä has little to recommend it to travellers except as a base or jumping-off point for the ski resort of Levi, 20km to the north.

According to legend, Kittilä was named after Kitti, a daughter of the mighty witch Päiviö, who appears in local fairy tales. About the only sights in this one-street village are the old wooden **Kittilä church** *(open Mon-Fri in summer)*, designed by CL Engel and completed in 1831; the **Taidemuseo Einari Junttila** *(☎ 643 687; open Wed-Fri)*, commemorating the work of a mildly renowned local artist; and the Kittilä **open-air museum** *(open Tues-Sun in summer)*, 3km south of the village, featuring the usual jumble of traditional buildings. There's an informal **tourist office** at the Takkaporo souvenir shop on the main road.

The very unusual **Särestöniemi museum** *(adult/student €7/3.50; open daily mid-Feb–mid-Oct)* makes a good day trip from Kittilä. Reidar Särestöniemi, who died in 1981, was the best-known painter from Lapland. Except for the years when he studied painting in Helsinki and in Leningrad (now St Petersburg), he always lived in Särestö. His home has been converted into a museum, where his big, colourful paintings are exhibited, together with some drawings and graphic works. To get there, drive 20km south of Kittilä to Kaukonen village, then proceed 9km east.

Places to Stay & Eat

Kittilä's HI summer youth hostels have closed in recent years, which gives some idea of the town's appeal to budget travellers.

Kittilä Camping *(☎ 642 239; tent sites €9-11, single/double cabins €20/28, large cabins €45-54)*, on the Ounasjoki about 1.5km south of the centre, offers the cheapest accommodation in Kittilä. It's a simple camping ground with a few cabins and cottages.

Gasthaus Kultaisen Ahman Majatalo *(☎ 642 043; Valtatie 42; singles/doubles €40/50 in summer, €50/76 in winter)* is a friendly B&B right in the village centre. No communal buffet breakfast here – it's served in your room when you're ready.

Hotelli Kittilä *(☎ 643 201, fax 643 222; Valtatie 49; singles/doubles €51/59, high season €69/95)*, on the main road at the northern end of the village, is Kittilä's only real hotel. The restaurant serves a good buffet lunch (€5 to €8) and there's dancing and entertainment some evenings.

Getting There & Away

There are daily flights between Helsinki and Kittilä. The airport is 4km north of town.

Four buses a day run between Rovaniemi and Kittilä. All stop at the K petrol station.

SIRKKA & LEVI
☎ 016

Levi is a major skiing centre built around the village of Sirkka (a Lappish village which unsurprisingly no longer retains its Lappish charm). This is one of the most popular ski resorts in Lapland, particularly with the party crowd – while Ylläs is more a family resort, young people come here from Helsinki and other cities purely for the apres ski. There are several nightclubs, some fine restaurants and plenty of accommodation in a fairly compact area. Levi is actually the name of the fell, while Sirkka is the village, but most people simple refer to the whole place as Levi.

The ski season usually runs from November to May. In summer and autumn, trekking and mountain biking are the main outdoor activities.

The efficient **tourist office** *(☎ 639 3300, fax 643 469; ⓦ www.levi.fi; Myllyojantie 2)* is in the centre of the resort. Staff can book accommodation, including cottages, and activities such as snowmobile safaris, dog-sled treks and reindeer rides. Many independent tour operators are based in Sirkka/Levi, making this a good place to join organised tours – from canoeing in summer to dog-sledding in winter – although these activities tend to be priced out of reach of the budget traveller.

Skiing & Snowboarding

Levi ski centre *(☎ 641 246, fax 641 247)* has 45 downhill slopes and 19 lifts (four are free children's lifts, one is a gondola). The vertical drop is approximately 325m, and the longest run is 2500m. There are two half-pipes for snowboarders and several ski runs for children.

Opportunities for cross-country skiing are also good, with trails totalling 230km. There are routes to Aakenustunturi Hill, Särestöniemi and other places. On longer ski treks, you can stay overnight in wilderness huts, which have supplies of firewood.

In the high season (February to early May), lift tickets cost €4/3 per adult/child for a single ride, €13/8 for one hour, €26/16 for one day. Rates are lower in summer (€13/8 for one day) and midwinter (€22/14). Downhill, telemark and cross-country skis, snowboards, sleds and snowshoes are all available for rental. Standard ski rental costs from €17/60 per day/week; snowboards and boots are €30 a day. Lessons are also available at Levi.

Canoeing

The long Ounasjoki is one of the best canoeing routes in Lapland. The river runs from Hetta in the north to Rovaniemi in the south, and passes the small villages of Raattama, Sirkka, Kittilä and Kaukonen. Equipment can be rented at **Pole Star Safaris** (☎ 641 688, 049-391 090, fax 641 687) at the Levin Portti tourist centre. Companies in Kittilä also offer equipment rentals.

Dog-Sledding

There's a **Husky farm** (☎ 040-570 6572; open 10am-6pm daily) at Köngäs, 10km northeast of Sirkka. In summer you can tour the farm (adult/child €3.50/1.80) and meet the dogs. In winter, **Polar Speed Tours** (☎/fax 653 447; W www.levi.fi/polarspeed) organises one- to five-day dog-sledding safaris, with accommodation in wilderness huts.

Places to Stay & Eat

Levi is one of Finland's most popular winter holiday centres and prices are through the roof in the peak season of February to May and in December. Cottages and cabins can usually only be rented by the week at this time. In summer, however, you can get a comfortable cabin sleeping up to five people for as little as €45 per night and hotel prices drop to rates comparable to anywhere else in Finland.

For cottage rentals, head straight for the tourist information office, which can make all bookings.

Levin Matkailumaja (☎ 641 126, fax 641 543; e levin.matkailumaja@levi.fi; cabins per night €42-135) is a pleasant, clean guesthouse consisting of various self-contained bungalows from two to four bedrooms. It has slightly lower rates than regular hotels. Its restaurant serves home-cooked meals.

Hullu Poro (The Crazy Reindeer; ☎ 641 506; singles €60-140, doubles €70-150), a bit off the main Sirkka–Levi road, has apartments and cabins, plus a very popular restaurant with music and dancing. Rooms are more expensive from Thursday to Sunday.

Hotel Levitunturi Spa (☎ 646 301, fax 641 434; W www.hotellilevitunturi.fi; singles/doubles €140/165 in high season, €68/75 May-Sept), opposite the tourist office near the main Sirkka–Levi road, is a big, flashy spa hotel with a pool and Turkish bath. The complex also has restaurants and nightlife.

Nonguests can use the spa facilities for €12 for 1½ hours.

Hotelli Sirkantähti (☎ 640 100, fax 641 494; singles/doubles €145/160 in high season, doubles €66 in summer) is a very good hotel in the centre – all rooms and apartments have private sauna and breakfast is included. There's also a good restaurant.

For a meal or a drink with an outlook, **Ravintola Tuikko** is perched right on top of the fell and has a panoramic view of the surrounding hills and lakes. It's open year-round and can be reached by chairlift or by road.

Getting There & Away

Sirkka and Levi are on road No 79, 170km north of Rovaniemi. Some buses between Muonio and Rovaniemi stop at Sirkka. From the airport at Kittilä (15km to the south) you need to take a taxi.

MUONIO
☎ 016

This small village of Muonio is the last significant stop on road No 21 before continuing on towards Kilpisjärvi and Norway. The wooden **church** in Muonio dates from 1817. When the village was burned during WWII, the church was somehow spared. The local **open-air museum** (admission free; open 10am-5pm Tues-Sat in summer) is a collection of prewar buildings and local artefacts.

Kiela Naturium (☎ 532 280; W www .kielanaturium.fi; open 10am-6pm Mon-Sat mid-Feb–mid-Apr & July-Sept, 10am-5pm Mon-Fri mid-Apr–June & Oct–mid-Feb), opened in 2002. It combines tourist information, a nifty 3D multi-media fells nature display controlled by touch-panel and joystick, an interesting planetarium with an aurora borealis show (adult/child €10/6; every 20 minutes), restaurant and gift shop. Even if you're just passing through, it's worth pausing to look around in here.

South of the centre, the **Harriniva Holiday Centre** (☎ 530 0300, fax 532 750; W www .harriniva.fi) has a vast programme of summer and winter activities. It also rents canoes and kayaks for exploring the Muonionjoki, fishing equipment, mountain bikes, and it organises guided mountain bike or hiking tours. Harriniva has a husky farm with 160 huskies, and a guided tour is €6/3.50 per adult/child. In winter, there are dog-sledding safaris from one hour (€52) to two days

(€390), as well as snowmobile and reindeer safaris. In summer, the centre offers daily guided white-water rafting trips from €22 for a 1½-hour trip.

Lomamaja Pekonen *(☎ 532 237, fax 532 236; Lahenrannantie 10; singles/doubles €26 /40, cottages €27-59; open year-round)* is near the centre of Muonio. It has rooms and a range of cottages sleeping two to four people, as well as canoes and bicycles for rent and guided trips of the Muonionjoki in summer.

If you're taking part in any of the activities, **Harriniva** *(singles/doubles from €65/75, cabins from €17/34)* has hotel rooms, apartments and cabins with seasonal rates

Hotel Olos *(☎ 536 111,* W *www.olos -hotel.com)*, 6km from Muonio, is the centre of the local skiing area and the closest place for nightlife. Also at Olos, **Restaurant Kammari** *(mains €7.50-14.50)* is the best place for pizzas, steaks, hamburgers and kebabs from €2.50.

HETTA (ENONTEKIÖ)
☎ 016

Hetta (previously known and still signposted and labelled on some maps as Enontekiö), is the centre of the municipality of Enontekiö, and a good place to start trekking and exploration of the nearby area. This is the northern end of the popular Pallastunturi Trek (see the following section), which brings many travellers to the village. Connections to Norway

are good, too. Hetta is not a big place, with just a few dozen houses on either side of the road, but travel services are good.

The **Fell Lapland Nature Centre** *(☎ 0205-647 950)* at Peuratie provides information about Pallas-Ounastunturi National Park, and doubles as the **main tourist office** *(☎ 556 211;* W *www.enontekio.fi)*. There are interesting nature displays relating to the park and slide shows (on request) in English, as well as a café.

In the centre of Hetta is **Enontekiö church** *(open daily in summer)*, built in 1952 with the financial help of American churches. The organ was a gift from Germany. The church has an altar mosaic that pictures Christ blessing Lapland and its people.

Places to Stay & Eat
Hetan Lomakyla *(☎ 521 521; single/double cabins from €46/66)* has a very upmarket set of log cabins – the largest, sleeping eight to 10 people, is like a small house with kitchen, sauna and loft. There are various discounts and activities on offer. **Ounasloma** *(☎ 521 055, 049-396 510; tent sites €8, cabins €42-75; open year-round)* is a friendly place with cottages and camping facilities by the river.

Hetan Majatalo *(☎ 554 0400, fax 521 362;* W *www.hetan-majatalo.fi; singles/doubles from €57/76; open year-round)* is a fine guesthouse set back from the main road in the centre. Rooms have TV and bathroom.

The Northern Lights

The northern lights, or aurora borealis, are a vibrant, beautiful sight, and they are visible at most times of year to observers standing at or above the Arctic Circle (latitude 66°), which includes a large portion of Lapland. They're especially striking during the long, dark nights of a Finnish winter.

The aurora appears as curtains of greenish-white light stretching east to west across the sky for thousands of kilometres. At its lower edge, the aurora typically shades to a crimson-red glow. Hues of blue and violet can also be seen. The lights seem to shift and swirl in the night sky – they can almost be said to dance.

The northern lights have a less famous southern counterpart, the aurora australis or southern lights, which encircles the South Pole. Both are oval in shape with a diameter of approximately 2000km.

These auroral storms, however eerie, are quite natural. They're created when energy particles (called photons) from the sun bombard the earth. The photons are deflected towards the north and south poles by the Earth's magnetic field. There they hit the earth's outer atmosphere, 100km to 1000km above ground, causing highly charged electrons to collide with molecules of nitrogen and oxygen. The excess energy from these collisions creates the colourful lights we see in the sky.

The ancients had other explanations for the spectacle: the Greeks described it as 'blood rain'; the Inuit attributed the phenomenon to 'sky dwellers'; and the ancient inhabitants of Lapland believed it was caused by a giant fox swishing its tail above the Arctic tundra.

Hotelli Hetta (☎ 521 361, fax 521 049; W www.hetta-hotel.com; hostel singles/doubles from €49/59 in summer, €67/84 Oct-May, hotel rooms from €64/75), further east towards the visitor centre, has simple 'hostel' rooms, and more expensive hotel rooms, as well as bungalows sleeping up to six people.

Hotel Jussantupa (☎ 521 101; W www .jussantupa.fi) is the town centre and is a bit of a focal point. It has a good restaurant and the most popular bar in town, with dancing on weekends. The hotel has a swimming pool and sauna.

Getting There & Away

Finnair flies to Enontekiö regularly, sometimes via Rovaniemi. The airport is 7km west of Hetta.

Buses to Hetta run daily from Rovaniemi (€35.20, five hours) via Kittilä and Muonio. One bus continues in summer to Kautokeino in Norway. To get to Kilpisjärvi from Hetta, you have to change buses at Palojoensuu.

PALLAS-OUNASTUNTURI NATIONAL PARK

☎ 016

Established in 1938, this is one of the oldest national parks in Finland. It protects the area surrounding Pallastunturi Fell. The main attraction is the excellent 60km trekking route from the village of Hetta to Hotel Pallastunturi, just inside the southern boundary of the park. In winter, Pallastunturi Fell is a small but popular place for both cross-country and downhill skiing. The longest slope is 2km long.

Pallastunturi Nature Centre (☎ 0205-647 930; e pallastunturi@metsa.fi; open daily June–late Sept) at Pallastunturi Fell sells trekking maps, makes reservations for locked huts (€7) and provides information and advice about the region, and its flora and fauna. It has slide presentations in several languages. There is also a **nature centre** in Hetta (see that section earlier).

Trekking Route

The 60km trek from Hetta village to Hotel Pallastunturi (or vice versa) is one of the easiest in the country. It takes three to four days to complete. The route is well marked, with poles every 50m or so, and there are several wilderness huts along the way (see the following Places to Stay section).

The popularity and ease of this trek means that some huts get pretty crowded at peak times – at Hannukuru hut there may be up to 60 people staying at one time!

Day 1 Starting from Hetta village, you must cross a lake to get to the national park. There is a boat-taxi that costs approximately €6. Walk 5km through a forest to Pyhäkero hut, then ascend to the high Pyhäkero, which is part of Ounastunturi Fell. It's 7km to Sioskuru hut.

Day 2 This section of the trail is mostly treeless plateau with good visibility. You might want to take a detour to Tappuri hut for lunch before continuing to Pahakuru hut (10km). If it's full, continue 2km to Hannukuru, the 'capital' of the Pallastunturi Fell area.

Day 3 The first leg is 5km over relatively difficult terrain to a small *laavu* (simple shelter) where you can cook lunch. Another 9km takes you through pleasant mountains to the small hut of Montelli. If it is full, continue 1km on to Nammalankuru hut.

Day 4 The final day takes you through some magnificent high mountains. There is only one place to stop, a simple *laavu* and campfire place 2.5km from Nammalankuru. From here, it's a 10km uphill walk to Hotel Pallastunturi.

Places to Stay

Wilderness Huts For trekkers in the Pallas-Ounastunturi National Park, free accommodation is available in wilderness huts. Following is a list of huts from north to south.

Pyhäkero This hut is 5km from the lake. You cannot sleep here, but there is a gas stove and a toilet. In March and April there's also a café.

Sioskuru Sioskuru is 7km from Pyhäkero hut and accommodates up to 16 people. There are mattresses, a gas stove, a telephone and some dry firewood.

Tappuri This nice hut is 1km off the main path. It accommodates six people, and has a gas stove and good water from a nearby creek.

Pahakuru This hut is 10km from Sioskuru. It sleeps up to 10 people, and has a gas stove and a toilet. You'll need to walk a few hundred metres to get water.

Hannukuru Just 2km from Pahakuru, this hut has room for 16 people, but it is often full. There are mattresses, a gas stove and a telephone here, plus plenty of firewood and a lakeside sauna.

Montelli This intimate little hut on the high fells has a fireplace and sleeps five people.

Nammalankuru Just 1km beyond Montelli hut is this large hut that accommodates 16 people. There is a gas stove, a telephone and fine fell scenery. A café is open in March and April.

Hotels Impressive **Hotel Pallas** (☎ 532 441, fax 532 741; **W** www.pallas-hotel.com; doubles €59-84) is up in the fells, 50m from the national park information centre. The first hotel in Lapland was built on this site in 1938. Rates include a good all-you-can-eat breakfast. Prices are highest during the skiing season.

Getting There & Away
There are daily buses from Muonio to Pallastunturi (to the hotel; €4.50, 45 minutes) and one bus a week direct from Rovaniemi to Pallas (on Saturday morning).

KILPISJÄRVI
☎ 016
The remote village of Kilpisjärvi, the northernmost settlement in the 'arm' of Finland, is on the doorstep of both Norway and Sweden. At 480m above sea level, this tiny border post, wedged between the lake of Kilpisjärvi and the magnificent surrounding fells, is also the highest village in Finland. Unless you're just passing through on your way to Tromsø or Narvik in Norway, the main reason to venture out here is for summer trekking or spring cross-country skiing. There are popular walks to the joint border post of Finland, Norway and Sweden; and to Finland's highest fell, Halti (1328m).

Every Midsummer, the folk of Kilpisjärvi put on a ski race at Saana Fell, where the snow may not melt until mid-July.

Kilpisjärvi consists of two small settlements several kilometres apart – one has a pair of hotels and a supermarket, and the other, closest to the Norwegian border, has the Kilpisjärven Retkeilykeskus (Kilpisjärvi Hiking Centre) and a petrol station.

Information
Siilastupa (☎ 537 741; open daily Apr-Sept), in the Kilpisjärven Retkeilykeskus, is the main information centre and represents the national parks service. This is the place to get advice on routes, buy maps, supplies, fishing permits and book the reservable wilderness huts. **Kilpisjärven Retkeilykeskus** (Kilpisjärvi Hiking Centre; ☎ 537 771) itself is a central meeting place for all trekkers. It's the place to find trekking partners, and hire hiking or skiing equipment, There's also a café here and the closest accommodation to some of the main walking routes.

Trekking
The area around Kilpisjärvi offers fantastic trekking. Routes range from easy day treks to demanding two-week treks into the mountains.

A marked loop route to **Saana Fell** (1029m) starts at Kilpisjärven Retkeilykeskus and takes around eight hours if you walk to the summit, although there's a shorter trail of around five hours.

Another incredibly popular day trek is the 15km route through **Malla Nature Park** to the joint border crossing of Finland, Sweden and Norway. At the border crossing is a free wilderness hut, where you can stay overnight. Alternatively, there's a **boat service** (☎ 537 771; €13; one hour return) at 10am, 2pm and 6pm daily from May to August from Kilpisjärvi to Koltaluokta, only a short distance from the border, allowing you to visit the easy way, or to walk only the return leg.

For experienced trekkers, a one- to two-week trip from Saana Fell to **Halti Fell**, the highest point in Finland (there is still snow in June), is a demanding but rewarding trip. The scenery is magnificent, and there are excellent fishing possibilities and free wilderness huts along the way. At two points you will have to ford rivers. If you are interested in the trek to Halti Fell but are not quite sure of your capabilities, join one of the groups organised by Kilpisjärven Retkeilykeskus – there are a few departures every year.

All trekking routes and wilderness huts around the Kilpisjärvi area are clearly displayed on the 1:100,000 Käsivarsi map (€12). The 1:50,000 Kilpisjärvi topographical sheet (€6) covers a smaller area.

Scenic Flights
There is a heliport at the southern end of the village of Kilpisjärvi. Helicopter sightseeing flights cost around €100 per person with minimum numbers required. Helihikes are also possible.

For information, call **Heliflite** (☎ 532 100; **W** www.heliflite.fi) in Muonio, **Polar Lento Oy** (☎ 537 810) or **Helijet** (☎ 537 743), both in Kilpisjärvi.

Places to Stay & Eat
Kilpisjärven Retkeilykeskus (☎ 537 771, fax 537 702; **e** retkeilykeskus@sunpoint.net; tent

sites €12, singles/doubles €37/50, 4-person cottage €49; open early Aug–late Sept), close to the border, is conveniently close to the trekking routes and is a centre for information. You'll find a range of rooms and cottages here all of them containing a private bathroom. The restaurant dishes up an all-you-can-eat buffet lunch daily in the high season.

Hotel Kilpisjärven (☎ 537 761, fax 537 767; w www.kilpis-hotel.com; singles/doubles €65/75, 3-/4-bed apartments €105/123) is on the main road through Kilpisjärvi, opposite the supermarket. It's comfortable, enough with a restaurant and a range of rooms, but it is several kilometres from the start of the main walks. Rooms with shared facilities at its **Kiruna Hostel** cost €47/61 a single/double.

Peera Hiking Centre (☎/fax 532 659; beds €20-24; open late Feb–late Oct) is an HI-affiliated hostel that, although only 25km from Kilpisjärvi, is a real wilderness place right in the middle of nowhere. It's an extremely cosy and welcoming place where you can spend time walking, fishing and relaxing. There's a kitchen, sauna, laundry, and a café – full board is available by prior arrangement.

Prices at the **supermarket** in Kilpisjärvi are in both euros and Norwegian krona, and there's even a currency-exchange counter here. Although prices are a bit higher here than elsewhere in Finland, they are still cheaper than in Norway.

As well as the **restaurants** at the hotel and Kilpisjärven Retkeilykeskus, there's a cheap **grilli** next door to the supermarket, and **Tuula's Cafe** (☎ 539 229; open year-round), serving yummy Lappish dishes and snacks.

Getting There & Away
There is a daily bus connection between Rovaniemi and Kilpisjärvi (€45.70, eight hours) via Kittilä and Muonio.

The sealed road to Kilpisjärvi is in relatively good condition considering its remote location, though it's warped like a rollercoaster in parts. It's almost 200km from Muonio to Kilpisjärvi and there are service stations at the small settlement of Kaaresuvanto (where there's a border crossing into Sweden) and at the Norwegian border.

Eastern Lapland

Eastern Lapland offers some of Finland's most rewarding and demanding trekking. Here, as in other areas of eastern Finland, proximity to the Russian border gives villages a frontier character. This is the region of the Sami people, the gold rush and the famous Arctic Road, used every summer by thousands of Europeans on their way to Nordkapp, the northernmost point in Europe.

Apart from the sheer wilderness, highlights along here include the Sami community of Inari, with its excellent museum, the amethyst mine near Sodankylä, opportunities to visit reindeer farms, and hiking and boat trips in Lemmenjoki National Park.

KEMIJÄRVI
☎ 016 • pop 10,500
Although a pleasant enough town on the lake of the same name, it's difficult to think of a good reason to stop in Kemijärvi, as it has few attractions or genuine Lappish characteristics. It's the northernmost town in Finland with a train station, and thus something of a gateway to the northeastern part of Lapland.

The **tourist office** (☎ 813 777; Kuumaniemenkatu 2A; open 8am-6pm Mon-Fri, 9.30am-3pm Sat June–mid-Aug, 8am-4pm Mon-Fri) is in the Torikeskus building alongside the kauppatori (market square) and the **public library** (Hietaniemenkatu 3) has free Internet access.

The **local museum** (Kotiseutumuseo; admission €2; open 10am-4.30pm Mon-Fri, 10am-6pm Sat & Sun June–late Aug) features a collection of artefacts and old houses – including a kota (Lappish hut). The **Kemijärvi church**, built in 1951, has a wooden bell tower dating from 1774.

Special Events
The **Kemijärvi Sculpture Week**, a festival of woodcarving, is held late June/early July. It draws artists from many European countries and is an interesting event as all the woodcarvers work outside, in view of the public.

In mid-September, Kemijärvi hosts **Ruska Swing**, a festival of swing dancing and swing music. Participants come from around the world, and there is a special 'Swing Train' from Helsinki.

Places to Stay & Eat

Hietaniemi Camping *(☎ 813 640; tent/van sites €6/17; open Mar–late Sept)* is just 200m west of the town centre on Pöyliöjärvi lakeside. There are no cabins.

Hostel Kemijärvi *(☎ 040-581 2007, 016-813 253, fax 016-813 342; Lohelankatu 1; beds €16-25; open year-round)*, on the lake 300m west of the camping ground, is HI-affiliated, with a kitchen, sauna and boats for rent. The same owners have cottages for rent nearby. Reception opens at 6pm.

Hotel Kemijärvi *(☎ 458 2200, fax 458 2222; Vapaudenkatu 4; singles/doubles €60/65)* is an ageing but reasonably good value hotel situated in the town centre. Rates include breakfast and there's a good restaurant here.

There's a knot of bars and simple restaurants on Jaakonkatu, including **Onnen Paivat** *(mains €7-12)* for pizza and pasta, and **Wanha Kettu**, an old-fashioned Finnish pub with a good terrace.

The best place to dine is the restaurant at **Mestarin Kievari** *(☎ 813 577; Kirkkokatu 9; mains €8-24)* with a menu ranging from pizza and salads to gourmet fish and game dishes.

Getting There & Away

The bus terminal is in the centre of town. There are several buses each weekday to Pyhä (50km), Rovaniemi (85km), Sodankylä (110km), Salla (71km) and Kuusamo (160 km). Bus services are less frequent on weekends.

NORTHEASTERN SAPMI

SODANKYLÄ
☎ 016 • pop 6100

The village of Sodankylä is a busy commercial centre for the expansive surrounding area, which has a population density of just 0.8 people per sq km! Although there's not much to see here, it's a base for visiting the amethyst mine and ski fields at Luosto, and a staging post between Rovaniemi and northern Lapland.

The **tourist office** (☎ 618 168; W www .sodankyla.fi; Jäämerentie 7; open 9am-6pm Mon-Fri) is at the back of the Lapponia handicrafts shop on the main street. Nearby in a small park, the bronze **statue** of The Reindeer and the Lapp celebrates reindeer husbandry, one of Lapland's most important industries. **Andreas Alariesto Art Gallery** (☎ 618 643; adult/child €5/3; open 10am-5pm Mon-Sat, noon-6pm Sun), opposite the statue, displays paintings by the famous Lapp painter Alariesto, who favoured a primitive style. There are many images of Sami life.

The **old wooden church** (open 9am-6pm daily in summer) near the Kitinen riverside is Lapland's oldest – it was built in 1689. It's one of the few buildings in Lapland to survive the massive destruction of WWII.

A couple of kilometres south of the village, the **local museum** (☎ 618 645; adult/child €2/1; open 10am-5pm Mon-Sat, noon-6pm Sun June-Sept) exhibits typical Lappish arts and crafts, tools and such in weathered old buildings.

By now you've probably seen reindeer wandering the roads, but if you want to learn a bit more about these vital livestock, **Mattila's Reindeer Farm** (☎ 633 309; Meltauksentie 975; adult/child €10/5; open 10am-5pm Mon-Fri), at Riipi village 26km southwest of Sodankylä, is a family-run farm where you can meet and feed the reindeer. There are guided tours at 10am, noon, 2pm and 4pm.

Places to Stay & Eat
Camping Sodankylä Nilimella (☎ 612 181; fax 611 503; tent sites €12.60; cabins €34-42; open June–mid-Aug) is across the river from the village. It's a friendly place – if you're travelling alone the owners may let you have a cabin for €17.

Orakoski (☎ 611 965; Jäämerentie 68; tent sites €10), a pleasant riverside camping ground, is about 10km south of Sodankylä. There is a large number of cottages.

Majatalo Kolme Veljestä (☎ 611 216; Ivalontie 1; singles/doubles/triples €35/50/60) is a simple guesthouse about 500m north of the bus station with tidy rooms and a guest lounge and kitchen.

Hotel Sodankylä (☎ 617 121, fax 613 545; Unarintie 15; singles/doubles €82/100, weekends & summer €70/80), across the road from the bus station, is a standard, ageing hotel equipped with saunas and a couple of restaurant-bars.

Seita-Baari (Jäämerentie 62) offers inexpensive home-made food, including Lappish specialities such as poronkäristys (sauteed reindeer).

Cafe Kestuli (mains €7-16) is a lovely little café with soups, quiches, cakes, full meals (including sauteed reindeer), good coffee and a terrace facing the main street.

Getting There & Away
Sodankylä is on the main Rovaniemi–Ivalo road (No 4). There are regular Gold Line and Express buses from Rovaniemi, Ivalo and Kemijärvi. The bus terminal is just off the main road.

PYHÄ-LUOSTO REGION
☎ 016

The area between the fells of Luosto (514m) and Pyhä (540m) forms a popular winter sports centre, with a skiing season extending from February to May. In summer the region is excellent for trekking, particularly in the Pyhätunturi National Park that surrounds Pyhä Fell. Pyhä and Luosto each have resort 'villages' with full services. The Pyhä-Luosto region lies midway between Kemijärvi and Sodankylä.

In Luosto, the travel agency **Pyhä-Luosto Matkailu** (☎ 020-838 4248, fax 624 261; Pyhä-Luostontie 2) has tourist information for the region, and books cottages.

In Pyhä, the **Pyhähippu Reservation Centre** (☎ 882 820, fax 882 853) also offers tourist information and arranges accommodation at 130 cottages and apartments. It has a café-restaurant, showers, sauna and laundry.

For information on Pyhätunturi National Park, as well as about summer activities such as hiking and fishing, drop by the park's **Pyhätunturi Nature Centre** (☎ 882 773, fax 882 824), adjacent to the Pyhä downhill ski centre; follow signs from the main Kemijärvi–Sodankylä road No 5.

Korpikutsu Amethyst Mine

The amethyst mine (☎ 2709 0203; W www
.amethystmine.fi; Lampivaara Fell; adult/child
€11/6; open 11am-5pm daily early June–Sept)
in Luosto is the only working amethyst mine
in Europe. There are guided tours on the
hour, and you get to have a dig around for
your own piece of amethyst. The mine is accessible by forest road from Luosto; follow
the signs.

Pyhätunturi National Park

The 43 sq km park is one of the oldest na-
tional parks in Finland, established in 1938.
The most notable sight is the steep Pyhäkuru
Gorge between the Kultakero and Ukon-
hattu peaks. According to local legend, Lake
Pyhänkasteenlampi (Lake of Holy Baptism),
in the gorge, was where EM Fellman, the
'Apostle of Lapland', forcibly baptised the
Sompio Samis in the 17th century to convert
them to Christianity.

There is a bird-watching tower at the
southeastern corner of the park, about 3km
from the Nature Centre.

Skiing

At Pyhä there are 10 ski runs and seven lifts.
The longest run is 1.8km, with a vertical
drop of 280m. At Luosto, there are seven
runs and four lifts, plus a halfpipe and special slopes for snowboarders. The longest ski
run is 1.5km, with a vertical drop of 230m.

Pyhä has 50km of trails for cross-country
skiers (15km of which are lit), and Luosto
has 95km of trails (25km are lit). You can
rent equipment from the ski centre at either
location.

Trekking

Within Pyhätunturi National Park there are
24km of marked hiking trails, including a
10km loop trail to Pyhäkuru Gorge. Some
16km of trails are open in winter to cross-
country skiers. There is also a 35km trekking
route between Pyhä and Luosto, which
passes through the national park and the protected forest area of Luosto. All trails start at
the Nature Centre.

For an overnight trek, a good map is
highly recommended, such as the 1:40,000
Luosto-Pyhätunturi map, which can be
purchased at the Nature Centre and in local
hotels and resorts. Shorter walks are possible
without a map.

Places to Stay & Eat

There are many designated camping areas
within a short walk from the Pyhätunturi
Nature Centre.

The only hut where you can stay overnight
inside the national park is the Huttuloma
wilderness hut that sleeps six people. On the
Pyhä–Luosto trail, accommodation is possible at Kapusta and Rykimäkuru wilderness
huts.

The hotels in Pyhä and in Luosto are
busiest in the ski season, when rates rise.

Hotelli Pyhätunturi (☎ 856 111, fax 882
740; doubles from €70 in summer) is the best
hotel in Pyhä. There is a good view from the
hotel's restaurant.

Hotelli Ravintola Luostonhovi (☎ 624 421,
fax 624 297; Ellitsantie 6; doubles from €40 in
summer) is a bargain. The restaurant here is
also good value.

Getting There & Away

The easiest connection to the Pyhätunturi
Nature Centre is the morning bus from
Kemijärvi, which operates Monday to Sat-
urday. There are buses between Luosto and
Sodankylä on school days only (ie, Monday
to Friday, from mid-August until the end of
May).

SAARISELKÄ REGION

☎ 016

The Saariselkä region includes villages and
towns surrounding the Saariselkä Wilderness
and Urho Kekkonen National Park (UKK),
the most popular wilderness trekking area in
Lapland, if not all of Finland. These outposts
offer national park information centres, as
well as shops and supermarkets where you
can stock up on trekking supplies.

The Saariselkä region does not have the
greatest downhill skiing, but it is still a
renowned winter resort among Finns.

Saariselkä

Saariselkä village is a winter sports centre
and also a base for trekkers heading into the
Saariselkä Wilderness area – so beware; this
is one of the busiest yuppie resorts in the
whole of Lapland. Still, Saariselkä village is
not a bad place to start hiking – all necessary
trekking supplies are available in local
sports shops and supermarkets, there are
good transport connections to/from town,
and there's plenty of accommodation.

A lot of typically Lappish activities can be organised from Saariselkä including dog- and reindeer-sledding, gold-panning, snowmobiling, fishing, canoeing and mountain biking.

For tourist and accommodation information, contact **Northern Lapland Tourism** (☎ 668 402, fax 668 403; ⓦ www.saariselka.fi; Honkapolku 3).

The Forest Research Institute operates the **Saariselkä Information Cabin** (☎ 668 122), with plenty of free information for trekkers. Saariselkä offers 12 downhill slopes served by six lifts. The longest run is 1300m and the vertical drop is 180m. Cross-country trails in the area total 250km. Cross-country and downhill ski rentals are available in the village.

Each flight arriving at Ivalo airport is met by a shuttle bus to Saariselkä. Northbound buses from Rovaniemi stop on request at Saariselkä, and some buses make a loop through the village.

Places to Stay & Eat Prices in Saariselkä's hotels are highest during the ski season and 'ruska' (late August to mid-September). The **Saariselkän Keskusvaraamo Booking Centre** (☎ 668 400; ⓔ keskusvaraamo@saariselka.fi) can organise most forms of accommodation in the village.

Saariselan Panimo (☎ 6756 500; ⓦ www.saariselanpanimo.fi; singles/doubles from €29/38) is the local village pub with some inexpensive huts for rent at the back. The huts, sleeping six to eight people, have their own kitchen, living room and sauna.

Holiday Club Saariselka (☎ 6828, fax 682 328; ⓦ www.holidayclub.fi; singles/doubles from €100/126) is an enormous spa hotel in the centre of the village. As well as the usual pools and spas, there are plenty of leisure activities on offer here and nonguests can use the spa facilities for €12. The restaurant has a big €14 dinner buffet.

Saariselän Tunturihotelli (☎ 68111, fax 668 771; singles/doubles €95/115) is a fine old hotel with rooms and apartments.

Saariselkä is one of the best places to sample gourmet Lappish food, although high-season prices are notorious. Some of the best restaurants are in the hotels – Tunturihotelli, Holiday Club and Hotel Riekonlinna all have fine restaurants.

Hotelli Teerenpesä (☎ 668 001; Saariseläntie 5; mains €9.50-18.50) is a hotel, pub and restaurant serving a good range of Finnish food. It's popular with locals.

Petronella (☎ 668 930; mains €13.50-28) serves lavish portions of Lappish food and is probably the finest restaurant in Saariselkä.

Kiilopää

Kiilopää, 18km southeast of Saariselkä village, is another major trekking centre for the region. It's probably the best place to start your trek. Marked trails lead from the car park here directly into the wilderness, and you can stay overnight in comfort and dine well at the resort café and restaurant – although if you're on a budget it may pay to bring your own food. The area around Kiilopää is also good for mountain biking.

Hostel Ahopää (☎ 670 0700; dorm beds from €22; open year-round) is a comfortable HI-affiliated hostel with a kitchen, sauna, laundry and café.

Kiilopää Fell Resort (Tunturikeskus Kiilopää; ☎ 667 101, fax 667 121; ⓔ kiilopaa.suomenlatu@co.inet.fi; singles/doubles from €60/70) takes care of all accommodation and services. It rents mountain bikes, rucksacks, sleeping bags, skiing equipment and more. It also sells fishing permits, runs a left-luggage service and dispenses sound advice on trekking. Guided treks are possible. There are also cottages and a café.

Kiilopää is 6km from the main road No 4. The Matti Malm company has several buses that do the one-hour trip between Ivalo and Kiilopää. If you are travelling by bus from Rovaniemi, check whether the bus runs to Kiilopää: some do and some don't.

Tankavaara

Tankavaara, approximately 30km south of Saariselkä, is locally famous as the 'Gold Village', a slightly kitsch reminder of the gold-rush days that once brought hundreds of hopeful diggers to the Saariselkä area. Also here is the useful **Koilliskaira Visitor Centre** (☎ 0205-647 251; ⓔ ukpuisto@metsa.fi; open 9am-6pm daily June-Sept, 9am-4pm Mon-Fri), with plenty of information about activities and trekking in the Urho Kekkonen National Park. It also has nature displays, a theatrette and sells maps. Near the centre are several easy **nature trails**.

The **Kultamuseo** (Gold Prospector Museum; ☎ 626 171; adult/child €7/3.50; open 9am-6pm daily June-Aug, 9am-5pm Sept,

LAPLAND & SAPMI

There's Still Gold in Them Thar Hills

Gold was first discovered in northern Lapland (the only place in Finland where alluvial gold appears) in 1865 and a few years later the rush was on in earnest to find more gold in the Ivalo River.

Given Lapland's isolation, the 500 or so prospectors crowding into Ivalo in those early years was considered a 'gold rush' and, although gold continues to be found, such scenes haven't been repeated. Another rush occurred at Lemmenjoki in 1945 when gold was discovered there. Many of the prospectors were soldiers who had returned from the war. The largest gold nugget found in Lapland was 393g, panned from the Lutto River at Laanila. These days a handful of determined gold prospectors still spend summers out in the wilderness seeking their fortune. If you spend a few hours drinking in a pub in Ivalo or Saariselkä you may run into one, exchanging some gold dust for a pint of beer – one gram of dust buys you about four beers – and exchanging stories with anyone who will listen.

The 'Gold Village' of Tankavaara is another place to get acquainted with Lapland's gold prospecting history, and you can try your hand at panning at the museum.

10am-4pm Mon-Fri) displays tools and other paraphernalia from Lapland's crazy gold-fever years, minerals and gemstones, and extends its scope to gold rushes from around the world. You can try your luck and pan for gold in summer (€3.50/20 per hour/day). Gold-related events and festivals are held in summer, the biggest being the **Goldpanners' Festival** in early August, which includes the Finnish Goldpanning Championships.

Korundi (☎ 626 158, fax 626 261; doubles from €50, cottages €37-50) has doubles and a **café** in summer, and the rustic, timbered restaurant **Wanha Waskoolimies** (Ye Olde Goldpanner; open year-round).

Tankavaara is on the main Rovaniemi–Ivalo road. All northbound buses pass the village, stopping on request.

Savukoski

Savukoski serves as a base for visits to the isolated southeastern part of the Saariselkä Wilderness. The **National Park Visitor Centre** (☎ 841 401; Samperintie 32; open daily) has a wilderness exhibition and slide show. It sells maps and permits.

Joulupukin Muorin Tupa, a shop that sells local handicrafts as well as Christmas paraphernalia, is the 'official workshop' of Santa Claus' wife. According to Finnish legend, Santa Claus' home is in the Korvatunturi Fell, a remote, inaccessible mountain near the Russian border. Savukoski has a **camping ground** with tent sites and cabins.

Tulppio

Tulppio village is just south of the UKK national park boundary, and is a stepping stone to one of the most interesting natural fishing rivers in Finland, the Nuorttijoki (see Fishing, in the Urho Kekkonen National Park section next).

In the early 20th century, the old **steam locomotive** now on display in the centre was transported in pieces from the USA, first by ship to Hanko, then by rail to Rovaniemi, and finally from Rovaniemi to Tulppio by horse sledges over frozen bogs and forests, with temperatures reaching -30°C. It was used by loggers for many decades.

Tulppio was a busy logging station right up until WWI, but little of this legacy remains, as Finnish troops burned down the houses during the Winter War of 1939–40 to prevent the Russians making bases in them.

Tulppio Cottages (☎ 844 101) has spartan but clean rooms. The **café** is a popular beer-drinking bar for locals, but there are also meals available.

A private vehicle is the easiest way to reach Tulppio. Alternatively, you could take a bus to Martti (southeast of Tulppio), then call the Tulppio cottages for a lift.

SAARISELKÄ WILDERNESS & URHO KEKKONEN NATIONAL PARK

The Saariselkä Wilderness – which includes the 255,000-hectare Urho Kekkonen National Park, Sompio Strict Nature Reserve, Nuortti Recreational Fishing Area and also large tracts of protected forestry lands – extends to the Russian border. This is a highly rated trekking area, partly because of the large network of wilderness huts, but also for the unspoilt beauty of the low tunturi hills.

SAARISELKÄ WILDERNESS (URHO KEKKONEN NATIONAL PARK)

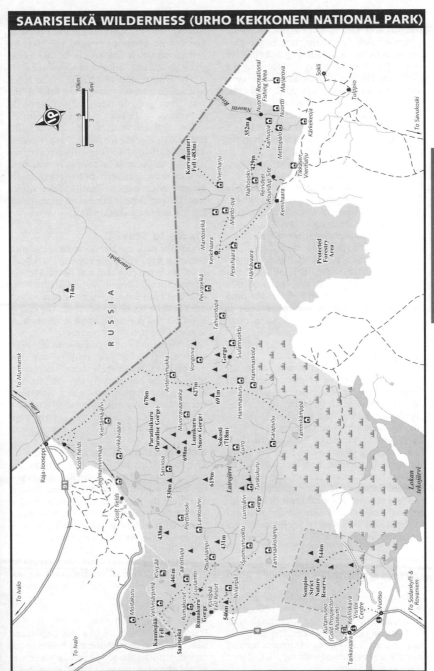

LAPLAND & SAPMI

Orientation & Information

The park is divided into four zones, each with different rules. The basic zone is the area closest to main roads. Camping and fires are only allowed in designated places. In the wilderness zones of Saariselkä (in the west) and Nuortti (southeast, between Tulppio and Kemihaara), camping is allowed everywhere except in certain gorges and on treeless areas. In the Kemi-Sompio wilderness zone (east), camping and fires (using dead wood from the ground) are allowed everywhere.

There are national park visitor centres in Saariselkä, Tankavaara (Koilliskaira) and Savukoski villages. **Kiilopää Fell Resort** in Kiilopää is a good place to pick up valuable practical information on trekking, although it isn't an official information centre. A map and compass are *essential* for the most remote areas of the park. There are three maps available for the area: for short treks around the village of Saariselkä, the 1:50,000 *Sompio-Kiilopää* map will do; the 1:50,000 *Sokosti-Suomujoki* map will take you beyond the lake of Luirojärvi; the entire park is shown on the 1:100,000 *Koilliskaira* map. Each map costs €12.

Things to See

There are several natural attractions within the park boundaries, of which the **Rumakuru Gorge**, near the hut of the same name, is closest to the main road. **Luirojärvi** is the most popular destination for any trek, including a hike up the nearby **Sokosti summit** (718m), the highest in the park. **Paratiisikuru** (Paradise Gorge), a steep descent from the 698m Ukselmapää summit, and the nearby **Lumikuru** (Snow Gorge) are popular day trips between Sarvioja and Muorravaarakka huts.

There are two historical **Scolt fields**, with restored old houses, 2km south of Raja-Jooseppi, and 2km west of Snelmanninmaja hut, respectively.

Trekking

There are a large number of possible walking routes in the Saariselkä area. Use wilderness huts as bases and destinations, and improvise according to your ability: an experienced, fit trekker can cover up to 4km per hour, and up to 25km per day. You will need to carry all food, as wilderness huts in the park are not stocked with supplies. Water in rivers is drinkable.

The four- to six-day loop from the main road to Lake Luirojärvi is the most popular, and can be extended beyond the lake. To reach areas where few have been, take a one-week walk from Kiilopää to Kemihaara.

The most remote route follows old roads and walking routes through the fells all the way from Raja-Jooseppi in the north to Kemihaara or Tulppio in the southeast.

Note that despite its popularity, Saariselkä can be tough going for the less experienced. Trails – particularly in the eastern part of the park – can be faint or almost nonexistent. Winter ski safaris can become especially dangerous during cold spells. Take advice from the park visitor centres on current conditions and route descriptions.

Places to Stay

Within the park are 200 designated camping areas; all free. There are close to 30 wilderness huts in the park that may be used free of charge. Some of these have locked areas with beds and a few cabins within the park, which must both be booked in advance. The charge is €9 per bed per night. Book cabins or beds at any of the park visitor centres.

A few wilderness huts close to the main road are for day use only – you can overnight at one of these in an emergency. More distant huts usually have mattresses, gas or wood-burning stoves and sometimes telephones or saunas. Almost all are near water. The visitor centres can supply maps and details of the huts.

Getting There & Away

The easiest starting points for treks are Saariselkä or Kiilopää. From Savukoski you can catch a post taxi to Kemihaara village, 1km from the park boundary. From Tulppio you'll have to negotiate with locals for a ride closer to the park boundary. (See the relevant earlier sections for more information.)

The Raja–Jooseppi border station is another starting point for a trek, as it takes you directly into the real wilderness. (See the Around Ivalo section later for information.)

IVALO

☎ 016 • pop 3500

Ivalo (Sami: Avvil) may be the undisputed administrative and commercial centre of the region, with all the shops and services you would expect in a small Finnish town, but it makes no pretence at being a tourist destination – there's not even a tourist office.

Ivalo does have a unique subculture though: gold-panners. This is the nearest 'big smoke' for hermits who spend their time panning the Ivalojoki for gold chips. Hotel Kultahippu is one place where any gold found is traded for booze and where incredible tales are told before panners return to their solitary, secretive hunt for the mother lode.

Dog-Sledding

There are several husky breeding farms around Ivalo and in winter, a dog-sledding safari is a superb, though demanding (and expensive), way to experience the Lapland wilderness.

Kamisak (*☎ 667 736, fax 667 836;* e *kami sak@hotmail.com*), run by Eija and Reijo Järvinen, is about 5km south of Ivalo and open year-round. There's a good little café and you can take an informal tour of the husky enclosures and meet the dogs (adult/child €4/2). In winter, from around November to April, they run safaris weekly. These range from a half-day trip with a two-person sled (€100; 10km), full-day safari (€135; 30km) to three- and five-day safaris where participants get their own sleds and are taught how to drive and care for their own team of five to eight dogs. The price includes transportation, equipment, insurance and meals, plus accommodation in wilderness cabins on overnight tours. The Järvinens take solo travellers as well as groups.

Places to Stay

Näverniemen Lomakylä (*☎ 677 601, fax 677 602; tent sites €12, single/double cottages €16/25; open year-round*) is south of Ivalo.

Further south again, close to the airport turn-off, **Kerttuojan Lomamokit** (*☎ 661 619; tent sites €10, cottages €25-55*) is a small place with a kiosk and sauna (€10).

Ukonjärvi Lomakylä (*☎ 667 501, fax 667 516; tent/caravan sites €12/16, cottages €47-75; open May late Sept*), north of Ivalo at the lake of the same name, has fantastic facilities, including boats and a good restaurant and bar.

Hotelli Ivalo (*☎ 688 111, fax 661 905; Ivalontie 34; singles/doubles €63/80*), on the southern approach to the town, is a well-equipped hotel with standard rooms with breakfast and sauna. Bike and canoe hire is available and there's a restaurant and bar.

Hotel Kultahippu (*☎ 661 825, fax 662 510; Petsamontie 1; singles/doubles from €57/70*), the town's main pub, is on the riverside in the north.

Places to Eat & Drink

Lauran grilli (*open to 3am*) is the most popular cheap eatery in Ivalo. It serves kebabs and *poronkäristys* (reindeer stew). **Anjan Pizza** (*Ivalontie 12*), across from the grilli, has the usual pizzas and such.

For a decent Finnish meal the **restaurant** (*lunch buffet €6, meals from €9.50-22*) at Hotel Ivalo is the best bet. It has some interesting dishes such as warm reindeer sandwich (€12) and salmon sandwich (€10).

Hippun Kellari (*open 10pm-4am Fri & Sat*), at Hotel Kultahippu, is the local nightclub where the community gathers for weekly drinking and dancing.

Getting There & Away

There are daily flights from Helsinki to Ivalo, and regular air services from many other Finnish towns. The airport is 12km south of Ivalo; a connecting bus to the centre meets each arriving flight.

Daily buses from Rovaniemi all stop in Ivalo. Car-rental companies with offices at Ivalo Airport (and in town) include Avis, Budget, Hertz and Europcar. Rates are the same as elsewhere in Finland.

The **Raja–Jooseppi border station**, 53km southeast of Ivalo, is a crossing point to Russia for travellers to Murmansk, 250km away. It's also a possible starting point for treks into the Saariselkä Wilderness. A taxi bus travels between Ivalo and the border station, departing from Ivalo early in the afternoon from Monday to Saturday.

INARI

☎ 016 • pop 550

As unprepossessing as it seems at first, the tiny village of Inari (Sami: Anár) is the main Sami community in the region, and a centre for genuine Sami handicrafts – although the galleries and boutique shops have an air of commercialism, this is as good a place as any in Finland to shop for genuine Lappish and Sami handmade textiles, jewellery, silverware and woodwork.

Inari is a good base for exploring far northern Lapland but above all it has some fine attractions of its own. Spend a day or two here visiting the Siida museum, trekking to the Wilderness Church, and taking an afternoon cruise on Lake Inarijärvi.

Information

Inari Info (☎ 661 666, fax 661 777; e inari .info@saariselka.fi; w www.inarilapland.org; open 10am-6pm Mon-Fri year-round), in the centre of the village, has tourist information for all of northern Lapland, as well as Internet access and post office services. It's inexplicably shut on weekends, even in summer, but Siida (see below) can help with most tourist information, particularly information on surrounding national parks.

The **public library** (open 1pm-7pm Mon-Thurs, 10am-3pm Fri), across the road, also has Internet access as well as books and CDs.

Siida – Sami Museum & Northern Lapland Nature Centre

One of the finest conceptual and open-air museums in Finland, **Siida** (☎ 665 212, w www .samimuseum.fi; adult/student & pensioner/ child €7/6/3; open 9am-8pm daily June-Sept, 10am-5pm Tues-Sun Oct-May) should not be missed. Overall, the exhibition successfully brings to life Sami origins, culture, lifestyle and present-day struggles. It also has detailed displays on the Arctic environment, flora, fauna and geological history. Outside is an excellent open-air museum featuring Sami buildings, handicrafts and artefacts.

Pielpajärvi Wilderness Church

The *erämaakirkko* (wilderness church) of Pielpajärvi is accessible from Inari by a marked walking track (7.5km one way) from the parking area at Siida. If you have a vehicle there's another car park 3km north of town, from where it's a 4.5km walk to the church. In winter you'll need snowshoes and a keen attitude to do this. The church area has been an important marketplace for the Sami over the centuries, with the first church erected here in 1646. The present church was built in 1760, and restored in the 1970s.

Sami Church

This church (open daily in summer) was built in 1952 with American financing. The altar painting depicts a wandering Sami family meeting Christ. Inari Sami and Fell Sami are spoken in this church, west of the main street on the road to Lemmenjoki.

Inari Reindeer Farm (Inarin Porofarmi)

Lapland is not short on such ventures, but this reindeer farm (☎ 673 912; Kaksamajärvi), 14km west of Inari on the road to Lemmenjoki, is run by a Sami family and offers a good opportunity to learn a bit about Sami culture and the importance of reindeer husbandry. There are scheduled tours in summer at noon (€10.50), and at other times by arrangement.

Special Events

It doesn't get much more Lappish than **reindeer races** – they're held in Inari, sleds and all, over the last week in May on the lake. It's a local event with festivities, betting and a winner's cup.

Organised Tours

There are **daily cruises** (☎ 663 582) on Lake Inarijärvi from mid-June (as soon as the ice melts from the lake) to late August (adult/ child €12/6). Departures are at 2pm daily, with an additional departure in July at 6pm. Boats leave from the wharf at the Siida car park. The destination is **Ukko Island** (Sami: Äjjih), sacred to the Sami for at least 1000 years. During the brief (20-minute) stop, most people climb to the top of the island, but there are also cave formations at the island's northern end.

Places to Stay & Eat

About 3km from Inari on the road to Lemmenjoki is a small, free **camping ground** with firewood and a pit toilet. **Uruniemi Camping** (☎ 671 331, fax 671 200; tent sites €11, double cottages from €17, for 4 people €34-42; open Mar–late Sept), about 2km south of town, is a well-equipped lakeside camping ground with cottages, café, sauna and boats and bikes for hire.

The nearest **youth hostel** is 24km away near Kaamanen – see that section later.

There are a couple of bungalow villages near the camping ground but closer to town is **Lomakylä Inari** (☎ 671 108, fax 671 480; 2/4-person cottages from €23/67, self-contained cottages with sauna €84-150; open year-round), within easy walking distance of the bus station. It's a well-equipped place with a café and sauna.

Hotel Inari (☎ 671 026; singles/doubles €33.50/38) is the hub of the village and has decent rooms with private bathroom. Rooms are above the bar so it can get noisy on Friday and Saturday nights when everyone in town attends the local disco. The hotel also has a good **restaurant** *(pizzas €4-8, mains €10-13)* with all the Lappish dishes – plenty of reindeer and salmon prepared in a variety of ways. Pizzas include 'sauteed reindeer, peach and onion', and there are inexpensive burgers.

Hotel Inarin Kultahovi *(☎ 671 221, fax 671 250;* [e] *inarin.kultahovi@co.inet.fi; singles/ doubles €62/82)* is tucked away just off the road to Lemmenjoki and is a cosy place popular with tour groups. Rooms are not special for this price but it has a great **restaurant** *(mains €11-24)* with a class à la carte menu of Lappish specialities and a set three-course lunch and dinner menu *(€16)*. It's open all day until 11pm. Appetisers include crepes filled with forest mushrooms *(€5.10)*.

Shopping

Inari is the main centre for *Sami duodji* (Sami handicrafts) and there are several studios and boutique shops in the village. Among the items on sale here are bags, pouches and boots made from reindeer hide, knitted gloves and socks, traditional textiles, shawls and the strikingly colourful Sami hats, bone-handle knives, carved wooden bowls, cups and souvenir handicrafts, jewellery, and CDs and tapes of Sami music.

Sami Duodji Ry *(☎ 671 254; Lehtolantie 1)*, next door to the library, is the main outlet representing the Sami products. It has a good range of Sami books and CDs, as well as beautifully-crafted silverware and clothing.

Samekki *(☎ 617 086; open daily)*, down a small lane behind the library, is the studio of Petteri Laiti – the most famous artisan among Finnish Sami. The silverwork and handicrafts are very highly regarded, hence high prices. You'll often see the artist at work here and you can tour the workshop for a small donation. **Inarin Hopea** sells hand-worked silver items.

Getting There & Away

Heading north on the much-travelled Arctic Road (No 4), Inari is the next stop after Ivalo. At least two daily buses travel between Rovaniemi and Inari, and on to Utsjoki.

LEMMENJOKI NATIONAL PARK

At 2855 sq km, Lemmenjoki (Sami: Leammi) is the largest national park in Finland. Saariselkä is probably more popular with trekkers, but the Lemmenjoki experience is more diverse: slush through desolate wilderness rivers, explore the rough Arctic landscape and bump into lonely gold-panners in the middle of nowhere. The Morgamjoki is the main gold-panning area, and there are several old huts where gold-panners still sleep in summer.

The **Lemmenjoki nature centre** *(☎ 0205-647 793; open 9am-9pm daily June-Sept)* is just before the village of Njurgulahti, about 50km southwest of Inari. It has a small interpretive exhibition, a powerful set of binoculars, and you can purchase maps and fishing permits here. All services are available in the lakeside village.

Sallivaara Reindeer Roundup Site

The roundup site, 70km south of Inari, was built in 1933 (although some huts date back to the 1890s) and used by Sami reindeer herders twice yearly until 1964. Roundups were an important social event for the people of northern Lapland, usually lasting several weeks and involving hundreds of people and animals. The Sallivaara reindeer corrals and cabins were reconstructed in 1997, and it's now possible to stay overnight in one of the Sallivaara huts. Many people come here in spring and summer for the excellent birdwatching on nearby wetlands. To reach the site, park at Repojoki parking area then follow the marked trail, 6km one way. Reindeer roundups are held in this area (although these corrals are no longer in use) – but since the timing is dependent on many factors, to see one requires a great deal of luck or contact with a reindeer herder.

Of the 11 huts now open, it's possible to stay in the Miko Takalo hut; there's another hut with a camping area, as well as an information hut.

Trekking

Almost all trails start from Njurgulahti, including a 4km marked nature trail suitable for families with children. The majority of the trekking routes are within the relatively small area between the rivers Lemmenjoki and Vaskojoki. An 18km loop between Kultala and Ravadasjärvi huts takes you to some of

The Sami of Finland

Sami (Lapps) are the indigenous inhabitants of Lapland and are today spread across four countries from the Kola peninsula in Russia to the southern Norwegian mountains. Around half of the 70,000 Sami population are across the border in Norway, while Finland numbers around 6500, but the two groups maintain close cultural ties. The Sami region is called Sapmi.

According to stone carvings and archaeological evidence, the Sami first migrated to this region soon after the last Ice Age around 10,000 years ago, first settling around the coastal areas of the Atlantic and Arctic Oceans and the Gulf of Bothnia, before moving inland. The Sami originally occupied much of Finland but were pushed north by migrating Finns. They were nomadic people – hunters, fishers and food-gatherers – who migrated with the seasons. They hunted wild reindeer, fished and harvested berries in the summer months, and traded meat, clothing and handicrafts.

Early Traditions & Beliefs

Early Sami society was based on the *siida*, small groups comprising a number of families who controlled particular hunting and fishing areas. Families lived in a *kota*, a traditional dwelling resembling the tepee or wigwam of native North Americans. It could be easily set up as a temporary shelter while following the migrating reindeer herds, and more permanent *kota* were overlaid with turf to insulate the fabric and reindeer pelt covering. A 'winter village' system also developed, where groups would come together to help survive the harsh winter months.

The natural environment was essential to the Sami existence, they worshipped the sun (father), earth (mother) and wind and believed all things in nature had a soul. The stars and constellations provided mythology – the North Star, the brightest in the night sky, was the Pillar of the World. The Sami believed in many gods and their link with the gods was through the shaman, the most important member of the community. By beating a drum, the shaman could go into a trance and communicate with the gods, ask advice or determine their will. The drums featured drawings depicting life, nature and the gods, usually with the sun as the central image. Forced conversion to Christianity in the 17th century spelt the end for the shamans and the traditional drums.

Traditional legends, rules of society and fairytales were handed down through the generations by storytelling. A unique form of storytelling was the *yoik*, a chant in which the singer would use words, or imitate the sounds of animals and nature to describe experiences. The *yoik* is still used by the Sami today, sometimes accompanied by instruments.

Role of the Reindeer

The reindeer has always been central to the existence of the Sami people. They ate the meat, took milk from the cows, used the fur for clothing and bedding, and made fish hooks and harpoons from the bones and antlers. Today most Sami are involved in reindeer husbandry.

Originally the Sami hunted wild reindeer, usually trapping them in pitfalls. Hunting continued until around the 16th century when the Sami began to domesticate entire herds and migrate with them. Towards the end of the 19th century, Finland's reindeer herders were organised into *paliskunta* (co-operatives), of which there are now around 60 in northern Finland. Reindeer wander free around the large natural areas within each *paliskunta*, which is bordered by enormous fences that cross the Lapland wilderness. Each herder is responsible for his stock and identifies them by earmarks – a series of distinctive notches cut into the ear of each animal.

The cycle of the reindeer follows a distinct pattern. Calves are born in May and June. At the end of June the herd is gathered and the calves earmarked. During summer, when not being driven mad by plagues of insects, the reindeer graze on the fells and meadows, growing fat and storing energy reserves for winter. In September, before the rut (mating season), males are herded and separated for slaughter – up to 120,000 reindeer are slaughtered annually. By November the snow has come and the reindeer subsist by foraging for lichen. The animals are herded onto winter grazing grounds and kept together – these days herders use snowmobiles, mobile phones and even helicopters to control their herds, so they no longer need to continually migrate with them.

The Sami of Finland

Sami Clothing & Handicrafts

The Sami have always used the material at their disposal – reindeer furs, antlers and bone, birch burl and wool – to make utensils, carvings, clothing and textiles. The colourful Sami costumes, featuring jackets, pants or skirts embroidered with bright red, blue and yellow patterns, are now mostly used on special occasions and during Sami festivals.

Sami handicrafts (including bags and boots made from reindeer hide, knitted gloves and socks, traditional textiles, shawls, the strikingly colourful Sami hats, jewellery and silverware) are recognised as indigenous art. Genuine Sami handicrafts carry the name *Sami duodji* (see Shopping under Inari for more information).

The Sami Today

Samis have been subjected to humiliation and oppression in the past. They were forcibly converted to (Protestant) Christianity in the 17th century, and their religious traditions were made illegal. This has led to an awkward situation whereby many Sami define themselves not as Sami but rather as ordinary Finns.

They were also heavily taxed by the Swedish state but were not officially recognised as landowners. Today Sami rights are defended and their language is prominently displayed in Sami regions in Finnish Lapland. Finland was the first country to inaugurate a popularly elected Sami parliament in 1972 (Norway followed in 1989 and Sweden in 1993). The universal right to 'Sami territory' (a somewhat blurry definition) is continuously disputed. No 'homeland' or 'reservation' has been created so far, and the parliament does not have power of self-government on issues relating to Sami.

However, the Sami identity is gaining strength in Finland. There is a common Sami flag, Sami National Day is celebrated on 6 February, there is a Sami radio station (101.9FM) in Inari and increased tourism is providing economic benefits through the sale of Sami handicrafts. For more information on Sami culture, visit the excellent Siida Museum in Inari or the Arktikum in Rovaniemi.

Sami Languages

The cultural identity of Finland's Sami population is closely linked to their language, which has undergone a revival in recent years. Sami languages are related to Finnish and other Finno–Ugric languages. There are three Sami (Lapp) languages used in Finland today, although there are under 2000 regular users. Sami is taught in local schools, and legislation grants Samis the right of Sami usage in offices in North Lapland. In Utsjoki Sami speakers constitute almost the majority of the population. You will find another seven Sami languages in Norway, Sweden and Russia.

Fell Sami The most common of Sami languages (also known as Northern Sami or Mountain Sami), Fell Sami, is spoken by Utsjoki and Enontekiö Samis, and tens of thousands of Samis in Norway. Fell Sami is actually considered the standard Sami, and there is plenty of literature, printed in Utsjoki or in Karasjok (Norway).

Written Fell Sami includes several accented letters but does not directly correspond to spoken Sami. In fact, many Samis find written Sami difficult to learn. For example, *giitu* (for 'thanks') is pronounced **gheech**-too, but the strongly aspirated 'h' is not written. Likewise, *dat* is pronounced as tah-ch. You should ask Samis to read these words out loud, to learn the correct pronunciation.

Inari Sami Another language, and although spoken by some people in the region around Lake Inarinjärvi, Inari Sami is rarely written and seems to be heading for extinction.

Scolt Sami The rare Scolt Sami language (Finnish: *kolttasaame*) is spoken by approximately 600 Sami people who live in Sevettijärvi and Nellim villages. Being refugees from the Petsamo region (which was annexed by the Soviet Union), they maintain Russian Orthodox traditions. Scolt Sami contains some Russian loan words.

the most interesting gold-panning areas. As you can do this in two days, many trekkers head over Ladnjoaivi Fell to Vaskojoki hut and back, which extends the trek to four to five days. For any serious trekking, you will need the 1:100,000 *Lemmenjoki* map (€12), available at the Lemmenjoki nature centre.

Organised Tours

In summer, a couple of local boat services cruise the Lemmenjoki valley, from Njurgulahti village to the Kultahamina wilderness hut at Gold Harbour. A 20km marked trail also follows the course of the river – so you can take the boat one way, then hike back. You can also get on or off the boat at other jetties along the route. There are at least two departures a day from mid-June to mid-September (€14/27 one way/return).

Places to Stay

There are two camping and cabin places at the road's end in Njurgulahti, both of which have cafés and operate boat trips on the river. **Ahkun Tupa** *(☎/fax 061-673 435; camping per person €2, 2-/4-person cabins from €21/39)* is a switched-on place with various packages including half and full board. The owner speaks good English and runs river cruises as well as renting canoes (€17/100 per day/ week) and making transport arrangements.

Next door, **Lemmenjoki Travel Service** *(☎ 016-673 430; tent sites €6, rooms per person €10, cottages €20)* has a similar set-up.

Inside the park, nine **wilderness huts** along the most popular trekking routes provide free accommodation (three can be booked in advance for a fee). Several are along the riverboat route.

Heading back towards Inari, on the shores of Menesjarvi, is **Valkeaporo** *(☎/fax 016-673 001; e valkeaporo@pp.ukolo.fi; tent sites per person/family €7/14, 4-/6-person cottages €40/56; open Apr-Oct)*, another good base for river trips on the Lemmenjoki. As well as good facilities and boat and canoe hire, it offers three-hour trips on the river for €22 and all-day gold-panning trips for €37. Both trips require a minimum of six people.

Getting There & Away

There is at least one taxi bus daily between Inari and Njurgulahti village, but timetables may change according to boat schedules; check with the tourist office in Inari. In

summer, the afternoon bus waits in the village until the boat has made the return trip, then drives back to Inari.

KEVO NATURE RESERVE

The 712 sq km Kevo Nature Reserve, northwest of Inari, was established in 1956. Within its boundaries you'll find some of the most breathtaking scenery in Finland (although it's nothing spectacular if you've spent your life in Norway or near the Grand Canyon) along the splendid gorge of the Kevo River (Sami: Geävu), which also has some decent waterfalls.

Rules for visiting the Kevo reserve are stricter than those concerning national parks: hikers cannot hunt, fish or collect plants and berries, and *must* stay on marked trails. The gorge area is off-limits from April to mid-June.

The main trail is 63km long and runs through the canyon, from Lake Ruktajärvi near the Utsjoki–Kaamanen road to the Karigasniemi–Kaamanen road. The trek is rough and takes about four days one way. Use the 1:100,000 *Kevo* topographical sheet.

Places to Stay

You will need a tent if you plan to hike through the canyon, as there is only one wilderness hut within the boundaries of the nature reserve. **Camping** is permitted within the reserve only at a dozen designated sites.

There are three free wilderness huts along a northwestern path that does not descend into the gorge. From south to north, the huts are: **Ruktajärvi**, at the southern end of the gorge route (accommodates eight people and has a telephone and an oven); **Njavgoaivi** (10 people, telephone); and **Kuivi**, inside the park (10 people, oven). It's best to do these as a round-trip trek, from Sulaoja trailhead to Kuivi hut and back.

On the Utsjoki–Kaamanen road, **Kenestupa** *(☎ 678 531)* is an option for those who hike through. It rents cabins and has a sauna, so end your trek here and take advantage of that sauna!

Getting There & Away

The preferred route is to start from the southwest; catch the Karigasniemi-bound bus from Inari and ask the driver to drop you off at the Sulaoja trailhead. From Kenestupa you can catch buses to Inari or Nuorgam.

Those with a car can leave it at Kenestupa, catch the afternoon bus to Kaamanen and change to the Karigasniemi-bound bus.

INARI TO NORWAY
☎ 016

Since Norway stretches across the top of northern Finland, there are three main routes north from Inari into Norway: to the west via Karigasniemi (the most common route to Nordkapp); straight up to Utsjoki; and east to Kirkenes via Sevettijärvi.

Kaamanen

Kaamanen, 25km north of Inari, is little more than the crossing point of the three northern roads. The Kotipuoti shop has postal services and a petrol station. All buses – and most locals for that matter – call at **Kaamasen Kievari**, a busy roadhouse a few kilometres north of the Sevettijärvi turn-off and 5km south of the Karigasniemi crossing. The roadhouse has a café and basic lodging.

Hostel Jokitörmä *(☎ 672 725, fax 672 745; tent sites €12.60, rooms €17.70, single/double cabins €16/25.30; open year-round)*, on the Arctic Hwy about 23km north of Inari, is a great little HI-affiliated hostel, if only it wasn't stuck in the middle of nowhere. It would be better served back in Inari. Still it has cosy two- and four-person rooms, and a separate set of cottages, each with their own kitchen and bathroom facilities, plus there's a sauna.

Karigasniemi

The small village of Karigasniemi (Sami: Gáregasnjárga) is the main crossing point from Finland to Norway along the popular Nordkapp route. It has services such as a bank and a post office. Fell Sami, the language of the local people of Karigasniemi, is a dialect spoken across the border in Norway.

Camping Tenorinne *(☎ 676 113; tent sites €14, 2-/4-person cabins €30/42; open June–mid-Sept)* has rustic log cabins and a pleasant location away from the main road.

Two buses a day travel from Ivalo to Karigasniemi, continuing on to the Norwegian town of Karasjok. A shared taxi travels to Sami villages north of Karigasniemi along the Teno River on Tuesday and Friday.

Utsjoki

The border village of Utsjoki (Sami: Ohcejohka) is not an attractive place, but there's a crossing into Norway here and it's home to a fairly large Sami population. There are two banks, a post office and several shops here.

The tourist office, **Utsjoki Info** *(☎ 686 234, 686 111; open daily June–late Sept)* is jointly run by the municipality and Metsähallitus (the Forest and Park Service). There's a small nature display, maps for sale and information specifically on Kevo Nature Reserve.

Utsjoki Camping *(open in summer)*, at the southern end of the village, is a basic site with cabins and tent sites. There's a kitchen and coin-operated showers.

Utsjoki Aran Hotel *(☎ 677 121, fax 677 126; Luossatie; singles/doubles €55/73, with bath €73/93)*, behind the post office, is the only hotel; as well as hotel rooms there are basic rooms at the side with shared facilities. The **restaurant** here serves full meals, lunch specials, and there's a bar.

There are a couple of fast-food places on the main road, and **Tsarssi**, which promises 'pizza, food, café and music' and is essentially a place where young Samis go.

Nuorgam

Nuorgam (Sami: Njuorggan) is the northernmost village of Finland. Other than the fact that it's the 'John O'Groats of Finland' (but with Norway across the river) its main appeal is the excellent **salmon fishing** in the broad Teno River. Most anglers gather near Boratbokcankoski and Alaköngäs Rapids, 7km southwest of the village centre. The majority of Nuorgam's 200 residents are Sami.

There's not much in the village except a supermarket and **Nuorgamin Lomakeskus** *(☎ 678 312; tent sites €10-16, rooms €25-40, cabins €45-65)*, which has a range of accommodation including camping and log cabins, a café and it also sells fishing permits. It's a good source of local information.

There are **holiday villages** scattered along the narrow road on the Finnish side of the river. They cater mainly to fishing parties and cost from €35 for a basic cabin.

Nuorgam is the northern end of a trekking route from Sevettijärvi (see the Trekking Around Sevettijärvi section later).

A daily bus travels to Nuorgam from Rovaniemi, and there is an additional bus on weekdays. When coming from Norway, it is a 2km walk or hitch from the Norwegian village of Polmak to the border, and another 4km to the village of Nuorgam.

Sevettijärvi

The road east from Kaamanen heads along the shore of Lake Inarijärvi to the village of Sevettijärvi (Scolt Sami: Ce'vetjäu'rr), in the far northeast of Finland. This area is home to a distinctive Lappish group called Scolt Lapps (Kolttalappalaiset); some of the Scolts speak Scoltish, Finnish and Russian. The only reason for travellers to visit is if you're on the way to Kirkenes in Norway, or as a base to trek in the lake-filled, remote corner of Finland to the northeast and northwest.

The Orthodox **tsasouna**, built in 1951, is dedicated to Father Trifon from Petsamo (now part of Russia). The altar has beautiful icons, some of which were brought from the Soviet-occupied monastery of Valamo. **Perinnetalo** *(open Mon-Fri)* is a small museum devoted to Scolt traditions.

Sevettijärven Lomamajat *(☎ 672 215; cabins from €30)* behind the church is a family-run place with two- and four-bed cabins. Amazingly it's not on a lake, but there is a sauna (€3.50).

Nili-Tuvat *(☎ 672 240; tent sites €10, single/double cabins €20/30)*, 3.5km south of Sevettijärvi, is right on the main road but also beside a lake. There are cabins, and a self-contained eight-person cottage with sauna for €70.

Sevetin Baari is the only place that offers meals, snacks and coffee, and is also the local post office. It's open daily until 2am according to signs, but was mysteriously closed when we arrived on a Saturday evening. There is a single **supermarket** in the village.

There is a Gold Line bus connection between Ivalo and Sevettijärvi on weekdays. Although there may be fuel available during the day in Sevettijärvi, don't rely on it – the next nearest services are in the border village of Näätämö, 30km northeast, or Kaamanen, 92km away.

Trekking Around Sevettijärvi

The Sevettijärvi region has more lakes per square kilometre than any other region in Finland. Very few trekkers explore this remote wilderness, yet it is worth the effort it takes to reach it.

Sevettijärvi to Nuorgam This is an established trekking route, and the most popular from Sevettijärvi. You'll need the 1:50,000 trekking maps for the area, available at Karttakeskus in Helsinki.

There are two places to start the trek; the better one is just north of Sevettijärvi, at Saunaranta. You'll see a sign that reads 'Ahvenjärvi 5', and a trekking sign – 12km to Opukasjärvi, 69km to lake Pulmankijärvi. There are six mountain huts along the route; from the final wilderness hut you can walk to Nuorgam along a road, or make a phone call from a local home for a taxi to Nuorgam village.

Sevettijärvi to Kirakkajärvi This is the shortest trekking route in the area, and there are two huts along the way. There is a 1:20,000 trekking map for this route. You can walk the route in two days, or set a more leisurely pace and do it in three. The route takes you across the rocky, hilly region on the other side of the lake of Sevettijärvi. Cross the narrow strait just south of the Siitapirtti. Follow the route northeast, and you'll end up on the other side of Sevettijärvi. At the other end, preferably at the western side of Lake Kirakka, you'll come to a minor road that will take you to the main road to Kirakkajärvi village.

Näätämö to Sevettijärvi This exciting route starts at Näätämö village on the Norwegian border and goes via Jankkila, Routasenkuru, Vätsäri, Tuulijärvi and Sollomisjärvi to Sevettijärvi (or vice versa). There are a few huts along the way, all clearly marked on major trekking maps. First head for Näätämö, right at the border. There is a marked path from there south to Jankkila house (14km). From Jankkila, along the Pakanajoki, there is a path to a large lake, and you have the choice of two routes around the lake. The northern one is easier.

Language

FINNISH

The Finnish language is a distinct national icon that sets Finland apart from its Western European neighbours. Finnish is a Uralic language closely related to Estonian; it has common origins with Samoyed and languages spoken in the Volga basin of Russia. The most widely spoken of the Finno-Ugric languages is Hungarian, but its similarities with Finnish are few. Finnish is not a Scandinavian language, nor is it related to Indo-European languages. There are, however, many words on loan from Baltic, Slavic and Germanic languages, and many words are derived from English. Linguists have also recognised similarities between Finnish and Korean grammar.

Finnish is spoken by some six million people in Finland, Sweden, Norway and Russian Karelia. The country is known as *Suomi*, and the language as *suomi*. Finnish isn't an easy language to learn. There are 15 cases for nouns, and at least 160 conjugations and personal forms for verbs. There are no articles (a, the) and no genders, but the word 'no' also conjugates. Many readers have written to us about their problems with the Finnish language. One particular reader found a clothes store named 'Farkku Piste' (Jeans Point) to be especially amusing.

Fortunately, staff at most tourist offices and hotels are fluent English speakers; bus drivers and staff at guesthouses, hostels and restaurants may not be – though they'll often fetch someone who can help. Finns who speak Finnish to a foreigner usually do so extremely clearly and 'according to the book'. Mistakes made by visitors are kindly tolerated, and even your most bumbling attempts will be warmly appreciated. A final note: in Finnish, ä is pronounced as in 'bat', and ö is pronounced 'er', as in 'her'. These letters are the last two in the Finnish alphabet. Lonely Planet publishes a *Scandinavian phrasebook*, which is a handy pocket-sized introduction to Finnish, Swedish and other languages of the region.

Greetings & Civilities

Hello.	*Hei.*
Goodbye.	*Näkemiin.*
Good morning.	*Huomenta.*
Good evening.	*Iltaa.*
Thank you (very much).	*Kiitos (paljon).*
You're welcome.	*Ole hyvä.*
Yes.	*Kyllä.*
No.	*Ei.*
Maybe.	*Ehkä.*
Excuse me.	*Anteeksi.*
I'm sorry. (forgive me)	*Olen pahoillani (anna anteeksi).*
How are you?	*Mitä kuuluu?*
I'm fine, thanks.	*Kiitos hyvää.*

Essentials

Please write it down.	*Voitko kirjoittaa sen.*
Please show me (on the map).	*Näytä minulle (kartalta).*
I understand.	*Ymmärrän.*
I don't understand.	*En ymmärrä.*
Does anyone speak English?	*Puhuuko kukaan englantia?*
Where are you from?	*Mistä olet kotoisin?*
I'm from ...	*Olen ... -sta*
Age?/How old are you?	*Ikä?/Kuinka vanha olet?*
I'm ... years old.	*Olen ... -vuotias.*

Surname	*Sukunimi*
Given names	*Etunimet*
Date of birth	*Syntymäaika*
Place of birth	*Syntymäpaikka*
Nationality	*Kansallisuus*
Male/Female	*Mies/Nainen*
Passport	*Passi*

Small Talk

What's your name?	*Mikä sinun nimi on?*
My name is ...	*Minun nimeni on ...*
I'm a tourist/ student.	*Olen turisti/ opiskelija.*
Are you married?	*Oletko naimisissa?*
Do you like ...?	*Pidätkö ...?*
I like it very much.	*Pidän siitä paljon.*
I don't like ...	*En pidä ...*
May I?	*Saanko?*
How do you say ... (in Finnish)?	*Miten sanotaan ... (suomeksi)?*

Getting Around

I want to go to ...	*Haluan mennä ...*
How long does the trip take?	*Kauanko matka kestää?*
Do I need to change?	*Täytyykö minun vaihtaa?*
Where does ... leave from?	*Mistä ... lähtee?*
What time does ... leave/arrive?	*Mihin aikaan lähtee/ saapuu ...?*
it	*se*
the boat/ferry	*vene/lautta*
the bus/tram	*bussi/raitiovaunu*
the train	*juna*
the plane	*lentokone*
The train is ...	*Juna on ...*
delayed	*myöhässä*
cancelled	*peruutettu*
left-luggage locker	*säilytyslokero*
one-way	*yhdensuuntainen*
platform	*laituri*
return (ticket)	*menopaluu (lippu)*
station	*asema*
ticket	*lippu*
ticket office	*lipputoimisto*
timetable	*aikataulu*
I'd like to hire a ...	*Haluaisin vuokrata ...*
bicycle	*polkupyörän*
car	*auton*
canoe	*kanootin*
rowing boat	*soutuveneen*
guide	*oppaan*

Directions

How do I get to ...?	*Miten pääsen ...?*
Where is ...?	*Missä on ...?*
What ... is this?	*Mikä ... tämä on?*
street/road	*katu/tie*
street number	*kadunnumero*
district	*kaupunginosa*
town	*kaupunki*
Is it near?	*Onko se lähellä?*
Is it far?	*Onko se kaukana?*
(Go) straight ahead.	*(Kulje) suoraan eteenpäin.*
(Turn) left.	*(Käänny) vasempaan.*
(Turn) right.	*(Käänny) oikeaan.*
at the traffic lights	*liikennevaloissa*

Signs – Finnish

Sisään	Entrance
Ulos	Exit
Avoinna	Open
Suljettu	Closed
Kielletty	Prohibited
WC	Toilets

at the next/second/ third corner	*seuraavassa/toisessa/ kolmannessa risteyksessä*
here/there	*täällä/siellä*
up/down	*ylös/alas*
behind/opposite	*takana/vastapäätä*
north/south	*pohjoinen/etelä*
east/west	*itä/länsi*

Accommodation

I'm looking for ...	*Etsin ...*
the youth hostel	*retkeilymajaa*
the campground	*leirintäaluetta*
a hotel	*hotellia*
a guesthouse	*matkustajakotia*
the manager	*johtajaa*
What's the address?	*Mikä on osoite?*
Do you have a ...?	*Onko teillä ...?*
bed	*sänkyä*
cheap room	*halpaa huonetta*
single room	*yhden hengen huonetta*
double room	*kahden hengen huonetta*
for one night	*yhdeksi yöksi*
for two nights	*kahdeksi yöksi*
How much is it ...?	*Paljonko ...?*
per night	*on yöltä*
per person	*on henkilöltä*
Does it include breakfast/sheets?	*Sisältyykö hintaan aamiainen/lakanat?*
Can I see the room?	*Voinko nähdä huoneen?*
Where is the toilet?	*Missä on vessa?*
I'm/we're leaving now.	*Olen/olemme lähdössä nyt.*
Do you have ...?	*Onko teillä ...?*
a clean sheet	*puhtaat lakanat*
hot water	*kuumaa vettä*

a key	*avain*
a shower	*suihku*
sauna	*sauna*

Around Town

Where is the/a ...?	*Missä on ...?*
airport	*lentoasema*
bank	*pankki*
bus station	*linja-autoasema*
town centre	*keskusta*
embassy	*suurlähetystö*
entrance	*sisäänkäynti*
exit	*uloskäynti*
hospital	*sairaala*
market	*tori*
police	*poliisi*
post office	*posti*
public toilet	*yleinen käymälä*
restaurant	*ravintola*
telephone office	*Tele-toimisto*
tourist office	*matkailutoimisto*

I want to make a telephone call.	*Haluaisin soittaa puhelimella.*

I'd like to change ...	*Haluaisin vaihtaa ...*
some money	*rahaa*
travellers cheques	*matkashekkejä*

Food

I'm hungry/thirsty.	*Minulla on nälkä/jano.*
breakfast	*aamiainen*
lunch	*lounas*
buffet	*seisova pöytä*
dinner	*päivällinen*

café	*kahvila*
food stall	*grilli*
grocery store	*ruokakauppa*
market	*tori*
restaurant	*ravintola*

I'd like some ...	*Haluaisin ...*
I don't eat ...	*En syö ...*

Shopping

I'm looking for ...	*Etsin ...*
the chemist	*kemikaalikauppaa*
clothing	*vaatteita*
souvenirs	*matkamuistoja*

How much is it?	*Mitä se maksaa?*
I'd like to buy it.	*Haluan ostaa sen.*
It's too expensive for me.	*Se on liian kallis minulle.*

Emergencies – Finnish

Help!	*Apua!*
Go away!	*Mene pois!*
Call a doctor!	*Kutsu lääkäri!*
Call the police!	*Kutsu poliisi!*
I'm allergic to ...	*Olen allerginen ...*
penicillin	*penisilliinille*
antibiotics	*antibiooteille*

Can I look at it?	*Voinko katsoa sitä?*
I'm just looking.	*Minä vain katselen.*

Do you have ...?	*Onko ...?*
another colour	*muuta väriä*
another size	*muuta kokoa*

big/bigger	*iso/isompi*
small/smaller	*pieni/pienempi*
more/less	*enemmän/vähemmän*
cheap/cheaper	*halpa/halvempi*

Time & Dates

When?	*Milloin?*
today	*tänään*
tonight	*tänä iltana*
tomorrow	*huomenna*
yesterday	*eilen*
all day	*koko päivän*
every day	*joka päivä*

Monday	*maanantai*
Tuesday	*tiistai*
Wednesday	*keskiviikko*
Thursday	*torstai*
Friday	*perjantai*
Saturday	*lauantai*
Sunday	*sunnuntai*

January	*tammikuu*
February	*helmikuu*
March	*maaliskuu*
April	*huhtikuu*
May	*toukokuu*
June	*kesäkuu*
July	*heinäkuu*
August	*elokuu*
September	*syyskuu*
October	*lokakuu*
November	*marraskuu*
December	*joulukuu*

What time is it?	*Mitä kello on?*
It's ... o'clock	*Kello on ...*

in the morning	*aamulla*
in the evening	*illalla*
1.15	*vartin yli yksi*
1.30	*puoli kaksi*
1.45	*varttia vaille kaksi*

Numbers

½	*puoli*
1	*yksi*
2	*kaksi*
3	*kolme*
4	*neljä*
5	*viisi*
6	*kuusi*
7	*seitsemän*
8	*kahdeksan*
9	*yhdeksän*
10	*kymmenen*
11	*yksitoista*
12	*kaksitoista*
100	*sata*
1000	*tuhat*

one million	*miljoona*

SWEDISH

Swedish is one of the Scandinavian languages belonging to the Indo-European family. It was separated from its original Germanic ancestor some 3000 years ago. *Finlandssvenska*, or 'Finland's Swedish', is very similar to the language spoken in Sweden, but local dialects have many Finnish words, so if you have learned Swedish in Sweden, you'll have some more learning to do! *Kiva*, or 'nice' is probably the most common Finnish word among Swedish speakers. The dialect used in Åland is closest to the Swedish of mainland Sweden. In Helsinki, an archaic, almost awkward form of Swedish is used as one of the two official languages of administration, and many of the city's Swedish speakers use an incomprehensible mix of Swedish and Finnish in conversation. People in farming and fishing communities in the Åland and Turunmaa archipelagos and in the small Swedish communities of the west and south coasts have their own unique dialects.

Greetings & Civilities

Hello.	*Hej.*
Goodbye.	*Hej då.*
Good morning.	*God morgon.*
Good evening.	*God kväll.*

Thank you (very much).	*Tack (så mycket).*
You're welcome.	*För all del.*
Yes.	*Ja.*
No.	*Nej.*
Maybe.	*Kanske.*
Excuse me.	*Ursäkta.*
I'm sorry. (forgive me)	*Förlåt mig.*
How are you?	*Hur mår du?*
I'm fine, thanks.	*Jag mår bra, tack.*

Essentials

Please write it down.	*Var va, skriv ner det.*
Please show me (on the map).	*Var vänlig, visa mig (på kartan).*
I understand.	*Jag förstår.*
I don't understand.	*Jag förstår inte.*
Does anyone speak English?	*Talar någon engelska?*
Where are you from?	*Varifrån är du?*
I'm from ...	*Jag är från ...*
How old are you?	*Hur gammal är du?*
I'm ... years old.	*Jag är ... år gammal.*

Help!	*Hjälp!*
Go away!	*Gå härifrån!*

Small Talk

What's your name?	*Vad heter du?*
My name is ...	*Jag heter ...*
I'm a tourist/ student.	*Jag är en turist/ student.*
Are you married?	*Är du gift?*
Do you like ...?	*Tycker du om ...?*
I like it very much.	*Jag tycker om det mycket.*
I don't like ...	*Jag tycker inte om ...*
May I?	*Får jag?*
How do you say ... (in Swedish)?	*Hur säger man ... (på svenska)?*

Getting Around

I want to walk to ...	*Jag vill gå till ...*
I want to drive to ...	*Jag vill åka till ...*

What time does ... leave/arrive?	*När avgår/anländer ...?*
Where does ... leave from?	*Varifran avgår ...?*
it	*den/det*
the boat/ferry	*båten/färjan*
the bus/tram	*bussen/spårvagnen*

| the train | *tåget* |
| the plane | *flygplanet* |

How long does the trip take?	*Hur länge tar resan?*
Do I need to change?	*Måste jag byta?*
left-luggage locker	*förvaringsboxar*
one-way (ticket)	*enkel (biljett)*
return (ticket)	*retur (biljett)*
platform	*plattform/perrong*
station	*station*
ticket office	*biljettbyrån*
timetable	*tidtabell*

I'd like to hire a ...	*Jag ville hyra en ...*
bicycle	*cykel*
car	*bil*
canoe	*kanot*
guide	*guide*

Directions

How do I get to ...?	*Hur kan jag åka till ..?*
Where is ...?	*Var är ...?*
Is it near/far?	*Är det nära/långt bort.*
What ... is this?	*Vilken ... är detta?*
street/road	*gata/väg*
street number	*gatunummer*
suburb	*stadsdel*
town	*stad*

(Go) straight ahead.	*(Gå) rakt fram.*
(Turn) left.	*(Vänd) till vänster.*
(Turn) right.	*(Vänd) till höger.*
at the traffic lights	*vid trafikljus*
at the next/second/ third corner	*vid nästa/andra/ tredje*

here/there	*här/där*
up/down	*upp/ned*
behind/opposite	*bakom/mitt emot*
north	*norr*
south	*syd*
east	*öst*
west	*väst*
northern/southern	*norra/södra*

Accommodation

I'm looking for ...	*Jag letar efter ...*
the youth hostel	*vandrarhemmet*
the campground	*campingplatsen*
a hotel	*ett hotell*
a guesthouse	*ett resandehem/ gästhem*
the manager	*direktör*

Signs – Swedish

Ingång	**Entrance**
Utgång	**Exit**
Öppet	**Open**
Stängt	**Closed**
Förbjudet	**Prohibited**
WC	**Toilets**

| What's the address? | *Vad är adresset?* |

Do you have a ... available?	*Finns det ...?*
bed	*en säng*
cheap room	*ett billigt rum*
single room	*ett rum for en*
double room	*ett rum for två*

| for one night | *för en natt* |
| for two nights | *för två nätter* |

How much is it ...?	*Vad kostar det ...?*
per night	*per natt*
per person	*per person*

Does it include breakfast/sheets?	*Ingår priset frukost/ lakan?*
Can I see the room?	*Får jag se ett rum?*
It's very dirty/ expensive.	*Det är mycket orent/ dyrt.*
Where is the toilet?	*Var är toaletten?*
I'm/we're leaving now.	*Jag är/vi är på väg nu.*

Do you have ...?	*Har ni ...?*
hot water	*varmt vatten*
a key	*nyckeln*
a shower	*dusch*
sauna	*bastu*

Around Town

Where is the ...?	*Var finns ...?*
town centre	*centrum*
entrance/exit	*ingång/utgång*
hospital	*sjukhuset*
market	*torget*
police	*polis*
post office	*postbyrån*
public toilet	*toaletten*
restaurant	*restaurang*
telephone office	*Tele-byrån*

| I want to make a telephone call. | *Jag ville använda telefon.* |

I'd like to change ... *Jag ville växla lite ...*
   some money   *pengar*
   travellers cheques   *resande-sheckar*

Food

I'm hungry/thirsty. *Jag är hungrig/törstig.*

breakfast	*frukost*
lunch	*lunch*
buffet	*smörgårsbord*
dinner	*middag*
café	*kaffestuga*
food stall	*grill* or *gatukök*
grocery store	*butik*
market	*torg*
restaurant	*restaurang*

I'd like some ... *Jag ville gärna ha lite ...*
I don't eat ... *Jag äter inte ...*

beef	*biff*
beer	*öl*
bread	*bröd*
bread roll	*sämla*
cabbage	*kål*
carrot	*morot*
cheese	*ost*
chicken	*kyckling*
coffee	*kaffe*
drinking water	*drycksvatten*
egg	*ägg*
fish	*fisk*
ham	*skinka*
herring	*sill*
meat	*kött*
milk	*mjölk*
minced meat	*köttfärsk*
mushroom	*svamp*
oats	*havre*
omelette	*omelett*
onion	*lök*
open sandwich	*smörgås*
pea	*ärt*
pepper	*peppar*
pie	*paj*
pork	*svinkött*
porridge	*gröt*
potato	*potatis*
reindeer (meat)	*ren (kött)*
rice	*ris*
rye	*råg*
salad	*salad*
salmon	*lax*
salt	*salt*
sauce	*sås*

sausage	*korv*
soup	*soppa*
steak	*biff*
stew	*låda*
sugar	*socker*
tea	*te*
vegetable	*grönsak*
vegetarian	*vegetarisk*
water	*vatten*

Shopping

How much is it?	*Vad kostar det?*
I'd like to buy it.	*Jag ville gärna köpa den.*
It's too expensive for me.	*Den är för dyr för mig.*
Can I look at it?	*Får jag se den?*
I'm just looking.	*Jag bara tittar.*
big/bigger	*stor/större*
small/smaller	*liten/mindre*
more/less	*mer/färre*
cheap/cheaper	*billig/billigare*

Time & Dates

When?	*När?*
today	*idag*
tonight	*på kvällen*
tomorrow	*i morgon*
day after tomorrow	*övermorgon*
yesterday	*igår*
all day/every day	*hela dagen/varje dag*
Monday	*måndag*
Tuesday	*tisdag*
Wednesday	*onsdag*
Thursday	*torsdag*
Friday	*fridag*
Saturday	*lördag*
Sunday	*söndag*
It's ... o'clock.	*Klockan är ...*
1.15	*kvart över ett*
1.30	*halv två*
1.45	*kvart i två*
in the morning	*morgon bitti*
this morning	*i morse*
in the evening	*på kvällen*

Numbers

½	*halv*
1	*ett* or *en*
2	*två*
3	*tre*
4	*fyra*

5	*fem*		17	*sjutton*
6	*sex*		18	*aderton*
7	*sju*		19	*nitton*
8	*åtta*		20	*tjugo*
9	*nio*		21	*tjugoen*
10	*tio*		30	*trettio*
11	*elva*		40	*fyrtio*
12	*tolv*		50	*femtio*
13	*tretton*		100	*hundra*
14	*fjorton*		1000	*tusen*
15	*femton*			
16	*sexton*		one million	*miljon*

Glossary

You may meet many of the following terms and abbreviations during your travels in Finland. Unless otherwise noted, all entries are Finnish. See also the Language chapter.

aamianen – breakfast
aamu – morning
aapa – open bog
aatto – eve, usually the afternoon/evening before a holiday
Ahvenanmaa – Finnish for Åland (the Swedish, official and locally preferred name)
aikataulu – timetable
aikuinen – adult (plural: *aikuiset*)
aitta – small wooden storage shed in a traditional farmhouse, used for guests
ala- – lower, eg, in place names; see also *yli-*
apotek – pharmacy (Swedish)
apteekki – pharmacy
asema – station, eg *linja-autoasema* (bus station), *rautatieasema* (train station) or *lentoasema* (airport terminal)
avoinna – open, eg, a shop, museum etc

baari – simple restaurant serving light lager and some snacks (also called *kapakka*)
barn – child (Swedish)
bensa – petrol
bibliotek – library (Swedish)
bruk – early ironworks precinct (Swedish)
bussi – bus (informal); 'properly' called *linja-auto*
-by – village (Swedish); as in Godby (in Åland) or Nykarleby (in Pohjanmaa)

eläkeläinen – pensioner, senior (plural: *eläkeläiset*; abbreviation: eläk)
erämaa – wilderness (also called *kaira* or *korpi*)
etelä – south

feresi – traditional Karelian dress for women, formerly worn daily but now worn only on festival days

gamla – old (Swedish)
gatan – street (Swedish)
grilli – stand or kiosk selling burgers, grilled sausages and other greasy snacks

halla – typically a night frost in early summer that often destroys crops or berries

hämärä – twilight
hamn – harbour (Swedish)
hautausmaa – cemetery; see also *kalmisto*
henkilö – person, as in 'per person' (abbreviation: hlö or h)
hilla – highly appreciated orange Arctic cloudberry, which grows on marshlands (also *lakka* or *suomuurain*)
hinta – cost or price
huone – room
hytty – cabin, eg, or a train or ship

ikäraja – age limit, eg in bars and clubs
ilta – evening
iltapäivä – afternoon
istumapaikka – seat, eg, on a train
itä – east; *itään* means 'to the east'
itikkä – mosquito; also called *sääski*

jää – ice
jääkiekko – ice hockey, the unofficial national religion; also informally called *lätkä*
jäätie – ice road; road over a lake in winter
jäkälä – lichen
järvi – lake
joiku – sung lyric poem, also called *yoik* among the *Sami*
jokamiehenoikeus – 'everyman's right', every person's right to wilderness access
joki – river
joulu – Christmas
joulupukki – Santa Claus
juhannus – see *Midsummer*
juna – train

kaamos – twilight time, the period of eerie half-light above the Arctic Circle when the sun doesn't rise above the horizon
kahvila – cafe
kahvio – cafeteria-style cafe, usually more basic than a *kahvila*
kaira – see *erämaa*
kala – fish; *kalastus* means 'fishing'
Kalevala – the national epic of Finland; *Kalevala* is a 19th-century literary creation combining old poetry, runes and folk tales with creation myths and ethical teaching
kalmisto – old graveyard, especially pre-Medieval or Orthodox
kämppä – wilderness hut, cabin
känykkä – usual term for a *matkapuhelin* (mobile phone)

kansallispuisto – national park
kantele – Karelian stringed instrument similar to a zither; its music is hauntingly beautiful
kapakka – see *baari*
karhu – bear
Karjala – Karelia
kartano – manor
kasvis- – vegetarian, eg, *kasvisruoka* (vegetarian food)
katu – street
kauppa – shop
kauppahalli – market hall
kauppatori – market square (usually just referred to as *tori*)
kaupungintalo – city hall
kaupunki – city (plenty of rather small towns have 'city' status in Finland)
kävelyreitti walking track; usually well signposted and marked
kelirikko – season of bad roads after the snow has melted
kelkka – sled or sledge; see also *moottorikelkka*
kello – watch, time (abbreviation: klo)
kelo – dead, standing, barkless tree, usually pine
kesä – summer
keskus – centre (eg, of a town)
kevät – spring (season)
kioski – small stand that sells sweets, newspapers, phonecards, food items and beer
kirjakauppa – bookshop
kirjasto – library
kirkko – church
kirkonkylä – any village that has a church
kiuas – sauna oven
kokko – bonfire, lit during Midsummer festivals
köngäs – rapids, waterfall
korpi – see *erämaa*
koski – rapids
kota – *Sami* hut, resembling a tepee or wigwam (from the Finnish word *koti*)
koti – home
kotimaa – 'home country'
koulu – school
kruunu – crown, krone (Norway's currency)
kuja – lane
kuksa – *Sami* cup, carved from the burl of a birch tree
kunta – commune or municipality, the smallest administrative unit in Finland
kuntopolku – 'fitness path'; jogging track in summer, skiing track in winter

kuusi – spruce
kylä – village
kypylä – spa

lääkäri – doctor
laakso – valley
lääni – province
laavu – *Sami* permanent or temporary open-air shelter, also used by trekkers
lahti – bay
laituri – platform (for buses or trains); wharf or pier
lakka – cloudberry, see also *hilla*
lampi – pond, small lake
länsi – west; *länteen* means 'to the east'
laiva – ship
lappalainen – Finnish or indigenous person from Lapland; this is a contentious term in some parts of the north, and many indigenous people will only refer to themselves as *Sami*
Lappi – Lapland, a province and a popular term, usually applied to the land north of Oulu; it's better understood as roughly the area between Rovaniemi and Sodankylä; north of this is the *Sami* region called *Sapmi* by the *Sami*, which many consider the 'true Lapland'; see also *Sapmi*
lapsi – child (plural: *lapset*; abbreviation: l); *lasten* means 'children's'
lasku – bill; receipt
leirintäalue – camping ground
lentokenttä – airstrip or airport (terminal: *lentoasema*)
liiteri – shelter for firewood
linja-auto – bus (informally called *bussi*)
linna – castle
linnoitus – fortification
lintu – bird
lippu – ticket
lossi – a small ferry for travel across a strait
lounas – lunch
lumi – snow; often in the generic form *lunta*
luontopolku – nature trail
lupa – permit or permission

maa – country, earth, land
maatila – farm
mäki – hill
mänty – pine tree, most common and distinctive of Finnish trees; upper trunk and branches are barkless and almost orange
majoitus – accommodation
makuu – sleep, as in *makuupaikka* (berth on a train or ship), *makuuvaunu* (sleeping car on a train) and *makuupussi* (sleeping bag)

marja – berry
Matkahuolto – national umbrella company managing the long-distance bus system)
matkakoti – guesthouse, inn; also called *matkustajakoti* (traveller home)
matkatoimisto – travel agency
meri – sea
metsä – forest
Midsummer – (or *juhannus*) longest day of the year, celebrated at the end of June, beginning on Friday evening *(juhannusaatto)*. Saturday; Sunday and Monday following are also serious holidays when Finland is basically closed.
mies – man (plural: miehet)
mökki – cottage
moottorikelkka – snowmobile (Finns often call these 'snow scooters' in English)
muikku – vendace, or whitefish, a common lake fish
museo – museum
mustikka – bilberry, resembles a blueberry

nähtävyys – tourist attraction
napapiiri – Arctic Circle
nainen – woman (plural: *naiset*)
niemi – cape
nuoska – wet snow
nuotio – campfire
Norja – Norway

öljy – oil
olut – beer
opas – guide
opastuskeskus – information centre, usually of a national park
opiskelija – (high-school) student; see also *ylioppilas*
Oy – abbreviation for Osakeyhtiö, a joint-stock company; in Swedish it's Ab, short for Aktiebolag

pää – head, end
pääsymaksu – entry fee
päivä – day; *päivittäin* means 'daily'
pakkanen – frost; below-freezing weather
pankki – bank
pelto – cultivated field
peura – deer
pikkujoulu – 'Little Christmas', an informal party arranged by companies or schools leading up to Christmas
pirtti – the living area of a Finnish farmhouse; a word often affixed to a rustic restaurant or tourist attraction

pitkospuu – boardwalk constructed over wetlands or swamps
pitopöytä – major pig-out buffet table
pohjoinen – north; also *pohjois-*
polku – path
polkupyörä – bicycle
polttopuu – firewood
poro – reindeer, a generic term for the common, domesticated variety
poroerotus – reindeer roundup, held annually in designated places in Sapmi
poronhoitoalue – reindeer herding area
poronkusema – a handy Lappish unit of distance: how far a reindeer walks before relieving itself
posti – post office; mail
Praasniekka – also *Prazniek*; Orthodox religious festival that sometimes includes a *ristisaatto* to a lake, where a sermon takes place
pubi – pub serving strong alcohol and very little food
puhelin – telephone; a mobile phone is formally called *matkapuhelin* – see also *känykkä*
puisto – park
pulkka – boat sledge
puro – stream
puu – tree, wood
puukko – Finnish-style sheath knife

raatihuone – town hall; see also *kaupungintalo*
rådhus – town hall (Swedish)
raja – border
ranta – shore
räntä – wet snow (snowing)
rauhoitettu – protected
rautatie – railway
ravintola – restaurant which also serves as a bar (or the other way around...)
reppu – backpack
retkeilymaja – hostel
retki – excursion
revontulet – Northern Lights, literally 'fires of the fox'
ristinsaatto – an annual Orthodox festival to commemorate a regional saint, involving a procession of the cross
roskakori – rubbish bin
rotko – gorge
ruoka – food
ruokalista – menu
runo – poem
Ruotsi – Sweden
rupla – rouble (Russian)

ruska – gorgeous but brief period in autumn (fall) when leaves turn red and yellow

sää – weather
Sami – the term for most Indigenous people in the north of Finland; see also *lappalainen*
saari – island
sääski – mosquito (in Lapland and Sápmi)
sähkö – electricity, eg, *sähköposti* means 'email'
sairaala – hospital
Saksa – Germany
salmi – strait
Sapmi – the area where *Sami* culture and customs are still active; it is a quasi-legal territory covering parts of north Sweden, Norway and Russia as well as the far north of Finland
satama – harbour
savusauna – 'smoke sauna'; these have no chimney but a small outlet for smoke
savuton – nonsmoking
seisopöytä – buffet; see also *pitopöytä*
sieni – mushroom
silta – bridge
sora – gravel
sota – war
sotilasalue – military area
SRM – Suomen Retkeilymajajärjesto, or Youth Hostel Association of Finland
stad – (Swedish) city or town
suihku – shower
sukset – skiis
suljettu – closed
suo – swamp, bog, marsh
suomalainen – Finnish, Finn
Suomi – Finland
susi – wolf

taide – art or skill
taival – track, trail
talo – house or building
talvi – winter
tanssi – dance
tanssilava – dance floor or stage
Tapaninpäivä – Boxing Day
tavarasäilytys – left luggage counter
teltta – tent
tervas – old pine tree stump with a high tar content and a distinctive smell; it burns well, so Finnish trekkers use it to light fires, even in wet weather (also *tervaskanto*)
tie – road
torget – market square (Swedish)
tori – market square; also called **kauppatori**

tsasouna – small chapel or prayer hall used by the Orthodox faith
tukki – log
tulva – flood
tunturi – a northern fell, or large hill, that is treeless on top (as opposed to the less dramatic, tree-covered *vaara*); most of Finland's fells are in the *Sapmi* area, where many are sacred to the *Sami*
tuohi – birch bark
tuomiokirkko – cathedral
tuoppi – beer-glass
tupa – hut
turve – peat

uimahalli – indoor swimming pool
uimaranta – swimming beach
uistin – lure (in fishing)
uitto – log floating
uusi – new

vaara – danger; low, broad hill (typical in Lapland Province and North Karelia)
vaellus – trek (verb *vaeltaa*)
vägen – road (Swedish)
vaivaisukko – a pauper statue outside many of the old wooden churches used as a receptacle for church donations
valaistu latu – illuminated skiing track
valtio – state, or government
vandrarhem – hostel (Swedish)
vanha – old
vappaa – free, available (basic form: *vappa*)
varattu – reserved
vaunu – train carriage or wagon
Venäjä – Russia
vene – boat
vero – tax
vesi – water (generic form: *vettä*)
virasto – state or local government office building
Viro – Estonia
viisumi – visa
vuode – bed
vuori – mountain
vuorokausi – 24 hours (abbreviation: vrk), eg, for rentals
vyöhyke – zone

WC – toilet

ylä- – upper; see also *ala-*
yliopisto – university
ylioppilas – university student
yö – night

Thanks

Many thanks to the travellers who used the last edition and wrote to us with helpful hints, useful advice and interesting anecdotes. Your names follow.

Lynn Ackeroyd, JM Aranaz, Jaco Arthur, Kris Ayre, Michael Baker, Ray Baker, Sylvia Barilkova, Christian Bertell, Keith Blackshear, Carmen Boudreau-Kiviaho, Graham Boyd, Ian Broughton, Steffan Brueckner, Chris Burin, Phil Burton, Christopher Carrier, Michael Cassidy, Scott Caufield, Sener Chatterjee, Elspeth Christie, Abigail Collins, Beat Conrads, Mark Coxon, David Croad, Richard Daly, Nathan Dhillon, Katherine Dixon, Alexander Doric, Emese Dorman, Bruce Doy, Neil Durbin, Kate Eades, Riku Eskelinen, Mario Falzon, Minna Fossi, Ralph Gandy, Rosemary George, Claire Gibbons, Serge Gielkens, Roberto Giugni, Marion Goldwater, Melinda Gottesman, Aja Gubler, Mark Gustafson, David Gyger, Brian Aslak Gylte, Natasha Hadfield, Guy Edward Helander, Lizette Hemmen, Katherine Hess, Brendan Hickey, Tarja Hiltunen, Alan Holder, Carol Holder, Maunu Holma, India Humphrey, Kate Hunter, Darcy Hurford, Ahmet Incesu, Jani Jaderholm, Craig Jeffery, Heike Jewell, Kristine Johnston, Hywel Jones, W Jules, Karles Jutila, Alexandra Kainz, Teemu Kankaanpaa, Karles Karwin, Maria Keshina, Hennie En Knud, Virpi Kopakkala, Eevi Kuokkanen, Satish Kutty, Sebastien Lafond, Anne-Mari Laiho, Anne Laine, Chris Large, Kitty Lee, Naomi Lee, Saku Lehtinen, Karita Lehto, Loretta Lindell, Dennis Livson, Alba Llobet, Torsten Lofhelm, Scott Lundell, Sini Mäkinen, Jonna Makkonen, Maria Martin, Michael & Kathy McClean, Susanne Meyer, Pierre Moermans, Jean Mounter, Tatu Myohanen, Rota Napoleone, Tina Naubert, Petri Nevalainen, Sandra Pagano, Thomas Palkovich, John Patrick, Tuija Paukkunen, Tero Pikala, Rostislav Pilny, Jill Prentice, Samantha Pywell, Quim Quadradas, Noah Rosenberg, Sabrina Scaravetti, Asya Schigol, Robert Schwandt, Steve Sharp, Auli M Skeen, Jaap Smit, Steven Smith, Vic Sofras, Daniele Sommaggio, Niki Steadman, Paul Stewart, Robert Stroethoff, Terence Tam, Satu Teppo, Anke Thoschlaga, Martin Torres, Peter J Towey, Brian Tunnard, Riikka Tuomisto, Alessandro Turato, Martyn van der Heyden, Marcus van Leeuwen, Stefan Vanwildemeersch, Terese Wadden, John Walker, Shirley Walker, Tony Watt, Arjen Werkman, Matthew Whittal, Chris Willows, Jean Willyams, John Wilson, Whui Mei Yeo, Maria Ysebaert

Index

Text

A

Aalto Centre 258
Aalto, Alvar 146, 148, 163,
    199, 210, 258, 291
accommodation 48-51, 50, 57
activities 56-64, see also
    individual entries
air travel
    to/from Finland 65-8
    within Finland 73-4
Åland 229-45, **230**
    travel to/from 231
    travel within 231-2
Alvar Aalto Museum 146
Amos Anderson Art Museum
    88-9
Änäkäinen Fishing Area 175
animals 17-18
architecture 23-4, 146
Arctic Circle 294-5
Arktikum 291
arts 20-6, see also individual
    entries
Askainen 217
Ateneum 87
Aulanko National Park 194-5
aurora borealis 300

B

Bear's Path 58
Bear's Ring 58, 282-5
Bear's Trail 171
Bengtskär 121
bicycle travel 70-1, 79, 167
bird-watching 63, 173
Black & White Horse Puppet
    House 203
boat cruises
    Åland 234-5
    Arctic icebreaker 269
    Jyväskylä 147
    Lake Saimaa 160
    Savonlinna 133
    south coast 125
    Tampere 185
    Turku 208-9
    Uusikaupunki 220
    Vyborg (Russia) 160
boat travel
    to/from Finland 71-2, 160
    within Finland 79-80

books 39
border crossings 68-9
Brändö 243
bus travel
    to/from Finland 69
    within Finland 74-5
business hours 45

C

canoeing 62-3
    Jongunjoki 175-6
    Kitkajoki River 285
    Levi 299
    Oulankajoki River 285-6
    Pankasaari Route 175
    Squirrel Route 141
car travel
    driving licence 32-3
    to/from Finland 70
    within Finland 76-9
castles 29
    Häme Castle 192-3
    Kastelholm 238
    Lumilinna 269
    Olavinlinna Castle 132-3
    Oulunlinna 263
    Turku Castle 207
cathedrals, see churches
children, travel with 44-5
churches 22-3
    Kerimäki Church 139
    Lieksa Church 173
    Oulu Cathedral 263
    Pedersöre Church 255
    Ristinkirkko 199
    St Nicholas Orthodox
        Church 125
    Sami Church 312
    Sankt Göran's Church 234
    Sankt Johannes
        Church 238
    Sankt Lars Church of
        Eckerö 240
    Sankt Mikael Church 237
    Sankta Maria Church 239
    Tampere Cathedral 184
    Temppeliaukio Church 91
    Turku Cathedral 207
cinema 26
climate 16
costs 36
courses 48
credit cards 35-6
cultural considerations 26-7

cycling 70-1, 79, 167
Cygnaeus Gallery 88

D

dance 20, 259
Devil's Nest 201
disabled travellers 44
Dragsfjärd 218
drinks 52-3
driving, see car travel
driving licence 32-3

E

Eckerö 240-1
economy 19
education 20
Ekenäs 113-16, **113**
Ekenäs Archipelago National
    Park 116-17
Ekenäs Museum 114
electricity 40
email access 38
embassies 34
emergencies 45
Enontekiö 300-1
entertainment 53-4
environmental issues 17
Espoo 107

F

Fåboda 255-6
Fagervik Ironworks 112
fauna 17-18
fax services 37-8
festivals 45-8
    Helsinki 92-4
    Iisalmi 155-6
    Ilomantsi 169
    Joensuu 166
    Jyväskylä 147
    Kajaani 274
    Kemijärvi 303
    Kuhmo 277
    Kuopio 152-3
    Lahti 200
    Naantali 216
    Nurmes 179
    Oulu 265
    Pori 225-6
    Rauma 222
    Rovaniemi 292
    Savonlinna 133-4
    Seinäjoki 259

Bold indicates maps.

festivals contd
  Tampere 185
  Turku 209
  Vassa 249
Finnrail pass 75-6
Finström 237
fishing 63
  Änäkäinen 175
  Ruunaa 174
Fiskars 117
flora 17
Föglö 243-4
food 51-2

G
Gallën-Kallela Museum 107
gay travellers 44
geography 15
geology 15-16
Geta 239
Getabergen 239
golf 63-4, 271

H
Hailuoto Island 268
Häme Castle 192-3
Häme region 192-203, **182**
Hämeenlinna 192-6, **194**
Hamina 126-9, **127**
Hamina Fortress 127-8
Hammarland 239-40
Hamnö 244
Hanko 117-20, **118**
Hattuvaara 170-2
Hauensuoli 121
Haukipudas 268
health 40-3
  diarrhoea 42
  HIV/AIDS 42-3
  hypothermia 41-2
  insurance 32
  mosquitoes 43
  water 41
Heinävesi 143
Heinola 202-3
Helsinki 81-104, **84-5**, **93**, **105**
  accommodation 94-6
  attractions 86-92
  entertainment 99-101
  festivals 92-4
  food 96-9
  shopping 101-2
  tourist offices 82-3
  travel to/from 102-4
  travel within 104
Helsinki Card 83
Helsinki City Museum 90
Helsinki Zoo 91
Helvetinjärvi National Park 190
Hetta 300-1

Hiekka Art Museum 183
hiking, *see* trekking
history 10-15
Hollola region 201-2
Hossa 278
Hytermä 138

I
Iisalmi 155-6
littala 196
Ilomantsi 168-70, **168**
Imatra 162-4, **163**
Inari 311-13
Inari Reindeer Farm 312
Inkoo 112
insurance 32
Internet 38-9
Iso-Syöte 286-7
itineraries 30
Ivalo 310-11
Ivalojoki Route 62

J
Jakobstad 253-5, **254**
Jalokivigalleria 269
Jätkänkämpällä Smoke Sauna
  149-51
Joensuu 164-7, **165**
Jokioinen 197
Jomala 237
Juminkeko 276
Juselius Mausoleum 225
Juuka 177
Juuma 286
Juva 140-1
Jyväskylä 145-8, **145**

K
Kaamanen 317
Kainuu region 273-8, **262**
Kajaani 273-5, **273**
Kalajoki 257
Kalela House 190
Kalevala 21
Kalevala Village Theme
  Park 275-6
Kallenautio Roadhouse 190
Karelia 157-80, **158**
Karhunkierros Trek 58, 282-5,
  283
Karhunpolku 58, 171
Karigasniemi 317
Kaskinen 252-3
Kasnäs 219
Kastelholm 238
Kaunissaari 126
Kaustinen 260
Kekkonen, Urho K 14
Kemi 269-70
Kemijärvi 303-4

Kemiö Island 218-19
Kerimäki 138-9
Keuruu 191
Kevo Nature Reserve 316-17
Kiasma Museum of
  Contemporary Art 87
Kiela Naturium 299
Kiilopää 307
Kilpisjärvi 302-3
Kirkkotori 108
Kittilä 297-8
Klobbskat 251
Koillismaa region 279-7, **262**
Kökar 244-5
Kokkola 256-7
Koli National Park 176-7
Kolovesi National
  Park 139-40
Korpikutsu Amethyst
  Mine 306
Korppoo 218
Kotka 123-6, **124**
Köyliö 224
Kristinestad 251-2, **251**
Kuhmo 275-8, **276**
Kukkolankoski Rapids 272-3
Kukouri 126
Kultaranta 215
Kumlinge 242-3
Kuopio 149-55, **150**
Kuortane 260
Kurikka 260
Kustavi 217
Kuusamo 279-81, **279**
Kyrönjoki Routes 62

L
Lahti 198-201, **198-9**
Lakeland 130-56, **131**
Lakeland Trail 62
Lake Pielinen 172-80
Lake Virmajärvi 172
Langinkoski 126
language 31, 319-27
Lapinlahti 155
Lapland 288-318, **289**, **296**
Lappeenranta 157-62, **159**
Lappi 224
Lappia-talo 291
laundry 40
Lebell House 252
Leineperi 228
Lemland 241-2
Lemmenjoki National Park
  313-16
Lenin Museum 183
lesbian travellers 44
Levi 298-9
Lieksa 172-3
Liminganlahti Bird
  Sanctuary 269

Liminka 268-9
Linnamäki Hill 109
Linnanmäki Amusement
  Park 92
Linnansaari National Park 139
Linnoitus 159
Lintula Orthodox Convent 144
Lipponen, Paavo 19
literature 21-3
Louhisaari Manor 217
Loviisa 121-2
Lumilinna 269
Lumparland 242

M

Maakalla Islet 257-8
magazines 39
Mannerheim Museum 89-90
Mänttä 191-2
maps 30-1
Maretarium 124
Mariehamn 232-6, **233**
Marttiini Knife Factory 291
media 39-40
Messilä 201
midnight sun 15
Mikkeli 141
Möhkö 170
money 35-6
  costs 36
  exchange rates 35
  taxes 36-7
  tipping 36
Moomin Valley Museum 183
Moominworld 214
motorcycle travel 70, 76-9
Muonio 299-300
museums 29
  Alvar Aalto Museum 146
  Amos Anderson Art
    Museum 88-9
  Arktikum 291
  Ateneum 87
  Cygnaeus Gallery 88
  Ekenäs Museum 114
  Espoo Car Museum 107
  Gallën-Kallela Museum 107
  Gösta Serlachius Museum of
    Fine Arts 191
  Häme Castle Museums 192-
    3
  Helsinki City Museum 90
  Hiekka Art Museum 183
  Jakobstadsmuseum 254
  Kemi History Museum 269-70
  Kiasma Museum of
    Contemporary Art 87
  Kuopio Art Museum 151

Lahti Historical Museum 199
Lenin Museum 183
Mannerheim Museum 89-
  90
Moomin Valley Museum 183
Museum of Central
  Finland 146
Museum of Finnish
  Architecture 90-1
Naantali Museum 215
Oulu Art Museum 263
Rovaniemi Church 291
Sami Museum 312
Seurasaari Open-Air
  Museum 90
Sibelius House 122
Sibelius Museum 208
Sports Museum of Finland
  91
Suomenlinna Museum 106
Turkansaari Open-Air
  Museum 263-4
music 20-1
Musta & Valkea Ratsu
  Nukketalot 203
Muumimaailma 214
Muurame 148

N

Naantali 213-17, **214**
Naarajoki Trail 62
Napapiiri 294-5
Närpes 253
national parks 18
  Aulanko National Park 194-5
  Ekenäs Archipelago NP 116-17
  Helvetinjärvi NP 190
  Koli NP 176-7
  Kolovesi NP 139-40
  Lemmenjoki NP 313-16
  Linnansaari NP 139
  Oulanka NP 282-5, **283**
  Pallas-Ounastunturi NP 301-2
  Patvinsuo NP 173-4
  Petkeljärvi NP 170
  Puurijärvi-Isosuo NP 225
  Pyhätunturi NP 306
  Urho Kekkonen NP 308-10
Nauvo 218
newspapers 39
northern lights 300
Nousiainen 217
Nuorgam 317
Nurmes 178-80, **178**
Nurmijärvi 175-6
Nykarleby 253

O

Olavinlinna Castle 132-3
Onkiniemi 203

Oravareitti 62
organised tours 80
Orivesi 190
Orrdals Klint 239
Oulanka National Park
  282-5, **283**
Oulu Art Museum 263
Oulu Cathedral 263
Oulunlinna 263
Oulu province 261-73, **262**
Oulu town 261-8, **264**
Ounasvaara Ski Centre 291

P

Paalasmaa Island 177
Paateri 176
painting 24-5
Pallas-Ounastunturi National
  Park 301-2
Paltaniemi 275
Parainen 218
Parppeinvaara 168-9
passport 32
Patvinsuo National Park 173-4
Pedersöre Church 255
Peltohermanni Wine Tower &
  Winery 169
people 19-20, 314
Petäjävesi 149
Petkeljärvi National Park 170
photography 40
Pikku-Syöte 286-7
Pirunpesä 201
Pohja 117
Pohjanmaa 246-60, **247**
politics 18-19
Pori 225-8, **226**
Porvoo 108-11, **109**
Post & Customs House 240
postal services 37
public holidays 45-8, see also
  festivals
Puijo Hill 149
Punkaharju 136-8
Puurijärvi-Isosuo National Park
  225
Pyhä-Luosto 305-6
Pyhäniemi Manor 202
Pyhätunturi National Park 306
Pyynikki Ridge 184

Q

Qwensel House 208

R

radio 39-40
rafting 174
Ranua Wildlife Park 295
Rapolan Linnavuori 196
Raseborg Castle Ruins 116

Bold indicates maps.

Rauhalinna Villa 133
Rauma 221-4, **222**
reindeer 77, 312
religion 27-8
Renko 197
Replot 251
Retretti Art Centre 136
Ristiina 141-2
Ristinkirkko 199
Route 66 190-1
Rovaniemi 290-4, **290**
Ruka 281-2
Runeberg House 109
Ruotsinpyhtää 123
Ruovesi 190
Ruunaa Recreation Area 174-5
Rymättylä 217

S

Sääksmäki 196
Saari Park 197
Saariselkä 306-7
Saariselkä Wilderness 308-10,
   309
safe travel 45, 77
St Nicholas Orthodox Church
   125
Sallivaara Reindeer Roundup
   Site 313
Saltvik 239
Sami Church 312
Sami Museum 312
Sami people 20, 314-15
Sankt Göran's Church 234
Sankt Johannes Church 238
Sankt Lars Church of Eckerö
   240
Sankt Mikael Church 237
Sankta Maria Church 239
Santa Claus 294-5
Santapark 295
Sapmi 288-318
Sapokka Water Park 124
Sara Hildén Art Museum 183
Saramo 180
Särkänniemi Amusement
   Park 184
saunas 152
Savonlinna 130-6, **132**
Savonselkä Circuit 62
Savukoski 308
Säynätsalo 148
Scanrail pass 75
Seal Trail 62
Sederholm House 90
Seinäjoki 258-60, **258**
senior travellers 44
seniors cards 33

Seurasaari Open-Air
   Museum 90
Sevettijärvi 318
shopping 54-5
Sibelius House 122
Sibelius, Jean 20, 193
Sibelius Museum 208
Siikaneva Marshland 190
Sirkka 298-9
Skata 254
skiing 60-1
   Levi 298-9
   Ruka 281
   Ylläs 297
Sodankylä 305
Södra Vallgrund 251
Solf 251
Somero 197
Sonkajärvi 156
spectator sports 54
Sports Museum of Finland 91
Squirrel Route 62
Strömfors ironworks 123
student cards 33
Stundars Handicraft Village
   251
Sulkava 140
Sund 237-8
Suomenlinna 105-7
Susitaival 58, 171
Svartholma Sea Fortress 122

T

Taidemuseo 263
Tallinn (Estonia) 103
Tallipiha Stable Yards 185
Tammela 197
Tampere 181-9, **182**, **186**
   accommodation 187
   attractions 183-5
   entertainment 188-9
   festivals 185
   food 187-8
   shopping 189
   travel to/from 189
   travel within 189-90
Tankavaara 307-8
Tapion Taival 171
Tapios Trail 171
taxes 36
telephone services 37
Temppeliaukio Church 91
Tietomaa Science Centre 263
Tiirismaa 201
time 40
tipping 36
toilets 40
Toriseva 190
Tornio 270-2, **270**
tourist offices 31-2
train travel

to/from Finland 69-70
   within Finland 75-6
travel insurance 32
trekking 56-8
   Bear's Ring 58, 282-5
   Karhunkierros Trek 58,
      282-5, **283**
   Karhunpolku (Bear's Trail) 58,
      171
   Kilpisjärvi 302-3
   Pallas-Ounastunturi National
      Park 301-2
   Pyhätunturi National Park
      306
   Ruunaa Recreation Area
      174-5
   Saariselkä Wilderness 310,
      309
   Sevettijärvi 318
   Sustaival (Wolf's Trail) 171
   Tapios Trail (Tapion Taival)
      171
   UKK Route 278
Tulppio 308
Turkansaari Open-Air Museum
   263-4
Turku 204-13, **205**, **206**
   accommodation 210
   attractions 207-8
   entertainment 212
   festivals 209
   food 210-12
   travel to/from 212-13
   travel within 213
Turunmaa archipelago 217-18
Tuusulan Rantatie 107-8
TV 39-40

U

UKK Route 58, 278
Ulkokalla Islet 257-8
Urho Kekkonen National Park
   308-10, **309**
Utsjoki 317
Uusikaupunki 219-21, **220**

V

Vääksy 202
Vaasa 246-51, **248**
Valamo Orthodox Monastery
   144
Väliväylä Trail 62
Vanha Rauma 223
Vanha Vaasa 250
Vantaa 107
Vapriikki Museum Centre
   183
Vårdö 242
Varissaari 126
Varkaus 142-3

Bold indicates maps.

video 40
Vilkaharju Ridge 140
Viltsafari 240
Virrat 191
Virtain Perinnekylä 191-2
visas 32
Visavuori 196
Vuonislahti 176

walking, see trekking
Wasalandia Amusement
    Park 247
water sports 61-2
white-water rafting 174
wildlife 17-18
winter sports 60-1

Wolf's Trail 58, 171
women travellers 43-4
work 48

Y
Ylämaa 162
Ylläs 297
Yyteri Beach 228

Boxed Text

Alvar Aalto – Architect,
    Designer, Sculptor 146
Canoeing the Squirrel Route 141
Cruising to Russia 160
Cycling the Lake Viinijärvi
    Loop 167
Flying Finns 209
Following the Festivals 46-7
Guide to Finnish Churches, A
    22-3
Helsinki Card 83
Helsinki – Kahvi Drinking
    Capital of Europe 98
Helsinki Walking & Cycling
    Tour 88-9
Interpreting Maps 31
Jean Sibelius 193

Kalevala, The 21
Karelian Treks 171
Kerimäki Church 139
Land of Lakes 136
Little Weekend 53
Midnight at the Green Zone
    Golf Course 271
Midnight Sun & Winter
    Gloom 15
Midsummer Poles 237
Ms Moomin 215
Northern Lights, The 300
Pulp Fiction & Fact 17
Reindeer Roadblocks 77
Sahti – Finnish for Beer 201
Sauna – Smoke & Steam but
    No Sex 152

She Ain't Heavy, She's My
    Wife 156
Summer Cottages 50
Tango 259
Sami of Finland,
    The 315-14
There's Still Gold in Them Thar
    Hills 308
Trekking the UKK 278
Tripping to Tallinn 103
Turku Card 205
Walk Around Vanha Rauma, A
    223
Why Finland? 27
Wilderness Huts 57
Will the Real Santa Claus
    Please Stand Up? 294

MAP LEGEND

CITY ROUTES

Freeway .... Freeway
Highway .... Primary Road
Road .... Secondary Road
Street .... Street
Lane .... Lane
.... On/Off Ramp
.... Unsealed Road
.... One Way Street
.... Pedestrian Street
.... Stepped Street
.... Tunnel
.... Footbridge

REGIONAL ROUTES

.... Tollway, Freeway
.... Primary Road
.... Secondary Road
.... Minor Road

BOUNDARIES

.... International
.... State
.... Disputed
.... Fortified Wall

HYDROGRAPHY

.... River, Creek
.... Canal
.... Lake
.... Flow direction
.... Spring; Rapids
.... Waterfalls

TRANSPORT ROUTES & STATIONS

.... Train
.... Underground Train
.... Metro
.... Tramway
.... Cable Car, Chairlift
.... Ferry
.... Walking Tour
.... Walking Trail
.... Cycling Trail
.... Path

AREA FEATURES

.... Building
.... Park, Gardens
.... Market
.... Sports Ground
.... Beach
.... Cemetery
.... Campus
.... Plaza

POPULATION SYMBOLS

○ **CAPITAL** .... National Capital
◉ **CAPITAL** .... State Capital
● **CITY** .... City
○ Town .... Town
● Village .... Village
.... Urban Area

MAP SYMBOLS

● .... Place to Stay
▼ .... Place to Eat
● .... Point of Interest

✈ .... Airport	⌂ .... Cave	☗ .... Lighthouse	◻ .... Pub or Bar
⊠ .... Archaelogical Site	⊞ ⊡ .... Church	☀ .... Lookout	◪ ..... Shopping Centre
⊖ .... Bank	⊟ .... Cinema	⊥ .... Monument	⚡ .... Ski Field
⊕ .... Border Crossing	⊡ .... Embassy	⊞ .... Museum	◩ .... Swimming Pool
⊟⊡ .. Bus Stop; Terminal	⚓ .... Fountain	⊡ .... National Park	⊟ .... Theatre
⊡ ..... Camping Ground	⊕ .... Hospital	⊡ .... Police Station	⊙ .. Tourist Information
⊡ .... Castle	⊡ .... Internet Cafe	✉ .... Post Office	⊡ .... Zoo

Note: not all symbols displayed above appear in this book

LONELY PLANET OFFICES

Australia
Locked Bag 1, Footscray, Victoria 3011
☎ 03 8379 8000 fax 03 8379 8111
email: talk2us@lonelyplanet.com.au

USA
150 Linden St, Oakland, CA 94607
☎ 510 893 8555 TOLL FREE: 800 275 8555
fax 510 893 8572
email: info@lonelyplanet.com

UK
10a Spring Place, London NW5 3BH
☎ 020 7428 4800 fax 020 7428 4828
email: go@lonelyplanet.co.uk

France
1 rue du Dahomey, 75011 Paris
☎ 01 55 25 33 00 fax 01 55 25 33 01
email: bip@lonelyplanet.fr
www.lonelyplanet.fr

World Wide Web: www.lonelyplanet.com _or_ AOL keyword: lp
Lonely Planet Images: www.lonelyplanetimages.com